Born in the ancient town of Sialkot, in Punjab, Maxu Masood obtained a master's in Pakistan Studies and then worked as a journalist in Islamabad and London. He co-authored *The Khalistan Riddle* with a Canadian social scientist, Dr Peter Stockdale. Set against the background of military operation in the Golden Temple of Amritsar and the subsequent assassination of Prime Minister Indira Gandhi, the book offered valuable insight into the rise of Sikh separatism in India. From 1987 to 1996, Maxu served as Political Assistant to the Australian High Commission in Islamabad. Functionally, the position aimed at watching, from a closer range, the march of current political affairs in the region at a time when the Soviet Union pulled out of Afghanistan and the Taliban took control of Kabul; there was militancy in Kashmir and Pakistan hurried to acquire nuclear capability. While Maxu toyed with the idea of returning back to journalism, his wife, a Molecular Geneticist, aspired to seek environment conducive to her career in scientific teaching and research. With their son, the couple migrated to Australia towards the end of 1996. Arrival and settlement in Sydney turned out to be an amazing voyage from the world defined by the coarseness of religious fervour into that of utter racism concealed beneath elegance of courtesy. Maxu survived the test by serving a spate of low-key unglamorous positions in public and private sectors.

Maxu Masood is contactable at abdusscience@gmail.com

Dedicated to:

Human Quest for Learning, Harmony, Hope and Affection

Maxu Masood

ABDUS SCIENCE

Life in Physics Painted with
Politics and Religion

AUSTIN MACAULEY PUBLISHERS™
LONDON * CAMBRIDGE * NEW YORK * SHARJAH

Copyright © Maxu Masood 2023

The right of Maxu Masood to be identified as author of this work has been asserted by the author in accordance with sections 77 and 78 of the Copyright, Designs and Patents Act 1988.

All rights reserved. No part of this publication may be reproduced, stored in a retrieval system, or transmitted in any form or by any means, electronic, mechanical, photocopying, recording, or otherwise, without the prior permission of the publishers.

Any person who commits any unauthorised act in relation to this publication may be liable to criminal prosecution and civil claims for damages.

A CIP catalogue record for this title is available from the British Library.

ISBN 9781398479661 (Paperback)
ISBN 9781398479678 (ePub e-book)

www.austinmacauley.com

First Published 2023
Austin Macauley Publishers Ltd®
1 Canada Square
Canary Wharf
London
E14 5AA

Table of Contents

Foreword	9
Chapter One: Living in the Age of Bottomless Devotion	27
Chapter Two: In Pursuit of Fading Glory	77
Chapter Three: Career Rebound	128
Chapter Four: House on Fire	186
Chapter Five: On Wings of Ambition	231
Chapter Six: Political Adventure	275
Chapter Seven: My Centre	326
Chapter Eight: Demolition of Sanity	335
Chapter Nine: Excommunication	375
Chapter Ten: Talisman Works	426
Chapter Eleven: Pastime Jumble	444
Bibliography	482
Index	486

Foreword

"And it is unavoidable that if we learn more about a great man's life we shall also hear of occasions on which he has in fact done no better than we, has in fact come near to us as a human being. Nevertheless, I think we may declare the efforts of biography to be legitimate. Our attitude to fathers and teachers is, after all, an ambivalent one since our reverence for them regularly conceals a component of hostile rebellion. That is a psychological fatality; it cannot be altered without forcible suppression of the truth and is bound to extend to our relations with the great men whose life histories we wish to investigate."
(*Sigmund Freud: The Future of an Illusion*)

This is a secular biography of Abdus Salam (1926–1996), the Pakistani scientist who hit headlines worldwide when he shared the 1979 Nobel Prize for Physics. In addition to taking a secular view of his life, the present study prefers to be non-devotional as far as permissible. More than a remarkable success story in Physics, the present account relates largely to his association with military regimes in Pakistan and the cult-like schismatic Ahmadiyah community to which he belonged. He served as Science Adviser to the Government of Pakistan for fifteen years but then resigned from office when his Ahmadiyah community was excommunicated from the pale of Islam by the National Assembly of Pakistan in September 1974. During the course of his association with Pakistan, Abdus Salam made considerable contribution in bringing the professional infrastructure and expertise to a stage where the country headed to achieve nuclear capability. Despite his bitterness over casting out of the Ahmadiyah, he avoided taking bold position in support of non-proliferation.

Abdus Salam was born to a humble family in the land of five rivers, Punjab, at a time when the British colonial hold over the subcontinent raced towards its chaotic collapse. His father, an employee of the Department of Education, claimed lineage to a 12th century Rajput prince who had embraced Islam for its Sufi tradition. Abdus Salam studied in the sunburnt country town of Jhang where electricity and other amenities of modern living had yet to arrive. In actual fact, the place was known more for its arid steppes, tombs, shrines and, at best, the epic love-story *Heer Ranjha*. Early every morning, much before sunrise, Abdus Salam woke up to complete his homework for school under the light of an oil lamp. He topped the Matriculation and Year Twelve lists of examination conducted under the University of Punjab. He then moved to the state capital, Lahore, to enrol for graduate degree programs.

His extraordinary genius, especially in mathematics, enabled him to set extended trails of academic records all the way to completion of Masters in 1946 when the ongoing embargo upon public sector recruitment, since the outbreak of World War II, made it impossible for him to become a top order bureaucrat. Indeed more out of luck and a tad of manipulation, rather than any formal drill for career planning, he made it to Cambridge. At Cambridge, he achieved the rare academic distinction of doing a double Tripos in Mathematics and Physics.

His doctoral work in Theoretical Physics, requiring a three-year statutory term, was completed within a matter of few months winning him an instant Fellowship at the Institute of Advanced Study, University of Princeton. He served academic positions in Lahore and Cambridge before earning the Chair at London's Imperial College. In 1964, he was appointed the founding Director of the International Centre for Theoretical Physics at Trieste, Italy.

By birth, Abdus Salam was a citizen of colonial India but his domicile changed overnight, in August 1947, when political requirements redesigned geographical boundaries in the subcontinent. After taking immense pride for introducing a unified political administration and secular justice in India, the British partitioned the richest segment of their empire on religious grounds; an arbitrarily drawn line of partition unfolded colossal amounts of human misery and mayhem; the colonial masters returned home leaving behind a heavy-duty stock of attrition as a matter of imperial legacy. For its location on the map of bifurcated Punjab, Abdus Salam's hometown Jhang became a part of Islamic Pakistan.

Abdus Salam's life in physics makes a fairly straightforward tale in mathematical genius, academic excellence and hard work. In making it to the top, Abdus Salam had taken the traditionally prescribed route of academic excellence, strategic far sight, planning and enterprise. He was a profoundly ambitious man, if his father dreamed of making a grand civil servant out of him, the son went far beyond achieving an ordinary height in public service. He won the Nobel Prize in Theoretical Physics, the Rolls Royce of Sciences. He relinquished the Chair in Lahore to bag another in London, and then yet another in Italy. He braved through political twists, turns, upheavals and revolutions of his day.

Notwithstanding the inconvenience set in his humble origins, he acted resourcefully and seized opportunities. Like many other great scientists, he trekked to the summit of recognition by prevailing over his cut of tests and tribulations. At 31, he went unseen when the Nobel Prize for Physics was awarded in 1957. Instead of giving in to frustration or dismay, he came to terms with the everyday reality that merit alone did not open all doors in the world. He observed from a close range how maintenance of high-profile and networking of professional contacts benefitted in winning awards and grants. Over the years, after going unobserved for the prize the first time, he was meticulous in making his way to favourable positions and places by a combination of strategic planning and merit.

Although Abdus Salam had spent the best part of his working life in Europe, mostly in England and Italy, he fostered a close relationship with Pakistan. Apparently, he was mindful of the support the newly born poverty-stricken state of Pakistan had provided him by way of scholarship grants and extended sabbaticals. He began popularising science and research in the country, especially in the critical sector of nuclear technology. After 1958, when the first military government in Pakistan adopted him as its Science Adviser, he was able to pursue this mission from a position of influence. He served no less than three martial law administrators in a row and continued to occupy the role even when one of the most brutal military crackdowns of the 20th century was unleashed in the eastern wing of Pakistan prior to the birth of Bangladesh.

His association with Pakistan stood strong when the country set itself upon the course to manufacture nuclear weapons. In view of his substantial contacts with academia and scientists in Europe and the United States, he held a priceless value for Pakistan. He once remarked that the rulers of Pakistan ignored a greater part of his advice. On the balance, however, in the end, his bond with Pakistan turned out to be a two-way arrangement, especially when he succeeded in achieving the International Centre for Theoretical Physics in Trieste, Italy, from the diplomatic pedestal and support provided by Pakistan.[1]

---

[1] After his death, the centre was renamed after him as the Abdus Salam Centre for Theoretical Physics

His love-affair, possibly an infatuation, with Pakistan wavered in 1974. It happened when the Parliament of Pakistan resolved to excommunicate the schismatic Ahmadiyah community to which Abdus Salam and his family devoutly belonged. As such Abdus Salam stood cast out of the Muslim mainstream. Historically, the Ahmadiyah had been founded, about the end of 19th century, as a Muslim brand of evangelical response to the rising tide of Christian missionary movement in India. Over the decades, when the community attempted at redefining some of the core beliefs held by Muslims, its reformist evangelical agenda and cult-like composition were considered an offensive deviation in Islam.

Soon, the majority of top clerics in the Muslim mainstream decreed the Ahmadiyah as a group apart from Islam. For nearly five decades, the Ahmadiyah survived the formal demands of excommunication courtesy the secular-liberal ethos of British colonial rule in India. Once in Pakistan, the fate of the schism was sealed. On his part though, Abdus Salam did not betray any extraordinary signs of being a staunchly religious person, the excommunication skimmed the religious bias out of his personality. He could not come to terms with the verdict of excommunication even when it had been handed down by a duly elected parliament. He resigned from his 15-year-old association as the Science Adviser to the Government of Pakistan.

Somewhat intriguingly, the business of Ahmadiyah excommunication coincided with India's first successful display of nuclear capability in May 1974. Zulfiqar Bhutto (1928–1979), the Prime Minister and up until that point in time an ally of the Ahmadiyah, conscious of the value Abdus Salam held among western scientific circles, wanted him to participate in Pakistan's desire to plan and achieve nuclear parity in the subcontinent. However, in a meeting with Zulfiqar Bhutto, in September 1974, Abdus Salam is understood to have conditioned his support for Pakistan's nuclear pursuit with the retraction of the Ahmadiyah excommunication.

As a politician, Zulfiqar Bhutto avoided to offer him any definite assurance. Abdus Salam distanced himself further; he ended up a suspect, disloyal to the state and ultimately as unforgivable outcast. Although some people saw in him a victim of religious intolerance, yet he was declined full restoration even when he won the Nobel Prize within five years of the excommunication. Some of his detractors went as far as perceiving the very idea of Nobel Prize as some sort of a 'Jewish Conspiracy'.

At the time of winning the prize, Abdus Salam had been out of the pale of Islam for over five years. He went to receive the prize wearing formal Pakistani attire and recited verses from the Koran while speaking at the Nobel Banquet. Given the fact that supreme honours in scientific discovery, especially in fields like Theoretical Physics, were considered a birth right of the Jewish-Christian scholarship churned out by the educational institutions of Europe and the United States, in the wake of Renaissance and Industrial Revolution; he stood prominently apart. His bold choice of turning up in the elegant garb of a Punjabi turban, the long coat *achkan*, the baggy trouser *shalwar* and the conical *khussa* shoes, characteristic of his home district Jhang in Pakistan, made him a celebrity almost instantly. His photographs splashed everywhere; a round of ample applause was evident in Pakistan as well. His name sounded very familiar in the Muslim world.

On his part, for some reason, Abdus Salam believed the prize had secured him a licence to preach science, especially among Muslims. Overlooking the aftermath of his excommunication in Pakistan, he called for an intellectual revolution. His voice was drowned in the shifting balance of power on world stage. In December 1979, that is, within weeks of his winning the Nobel distinction, the Red Army of the former Soviet Union marched into Afghanistan. Pakistan became a frontline state and the base for holy jihad upon godless communists. Hefty chunks of financial and logistical support gushed into Pakistan from countries as diverse as Saudi Arabia and the United States; there was an unleashing of state-sponsored bigotry.

At a time when Abdus Salam anticipated reinventing his role, the world around him crumbled and came tottering down, his mission to popularise science among Muslims was a lost cause. He ended up a lonely man, overtaken by pessimism and disappointment; suffering from a debilitating sickness towards the end of his life.

Much has been written about Abdus Salam in the wake of his prize, especially in Pakistan, India and England; ranging from ordinary media coverage to formal biographies. Presently, any factual data relating to his everyday academic and administrative business has been duly collected, compiled, stacked and catalogued both in England and Italy. His own speeches and writings, dating back to the 1960s, are reachable more or less easily. In this way, there seems to be no shortage of information about his life and times in physics. Nevertheless, with the exception of his biography written by Gordon Fraser (1943–2013), published in 2008, an overwhelming part of popular information about him remains sketchy and generally engaged with his academic excellence and career digression into physics.

Almost invariably, he himself was the sole provider of information, very often in first person. Such was the dependence of his early day profile writers and biographers that story telling about him became a repetitive mix of varying degrees. Over and over again, there was the tale of someone rising from the ashes of southern Punjab to stamp his everlasting mark upon science. His personal and private life was hidden beneath lavish lashings of praise, glorification and superstardom in the world of academia.

When Abdus Salam was discriminated in Pakistan due to his association with the Ahmadiyah community, some zealous profile-writers found an additional cause to nourish the fires of admiration. He made an easy story in the ideological warfare against religious victimisation. Hardly a write-up on him would be considered complete without highly-flavoured expressions of sympathy, he became a standard case in point to ridicule bigotry, a popular cause for human rights campaigners, a martyr in need of devotional narratives. He was accorded the reverence of a saint; it became a fashion to climax his life story in a tragic victimhood. Every now and then, those rich accounts of his huge academic achievement ended upon tragic notes of exile from home. His remarkable assent to the summit of Theoretical Physics would crash-land into the predisposed business of religious chauvinism prevalent in a predominantly illiterate and penniless Pakistan.

Any closer approach to Abdus Salam's life outside physics was concealed by the chorus of esteem. Many delightful aspects and charms attached to his personal and private pastime were overshadowed by the towering figure of a great scientist who dominated the captivating charisma of an everyday man. He fortified the divide himself by exercising strict discretion in sharing information about his life outside physics. At the same time, no visible effort was made by people writing about him to traverse beyond the vastness of his scholarship in physics.

Left on his own, he would make only a passing mention of piety and discipline exercised by his profoundly religious parents and peers. He would recall how the given set of spiritual values contributed towards his personal upbringing. This was where he preferred to stop and, rather amazingly, nobody ever invited him to go any further into his personal life.

For example, he was never questioned as to why he served military regimes in Pakistan. Why was he banded with rulers who did not take the core of his advice in the first place? How did he overlook the plain truth that his own religious bias amounted to isolating him from the mainstream? Did he ever take notice of the cult like overtones of his Ahmadiyah community? What compromises he had to abide by while practicing bigamy in Europe? He held views on a range of Islamic prohibitions and practices but declined to express his opinion publicly, why? He was unsure if people living in some parts of Russia, where temperatures dropped below minus 20°C in winters, could come to terms with a life without alcohol. But he dodged raising the question openly.

Then, while validating the Judaic-Muslim prohibition of pig meat, he would argue that those who consumed pork became 'shameless' like the beast itself. What sort of scale he applied while determining the level of shame among animals? Likewise, even when he held robust opinions about challenges facing Muslims, and a public expression of his views carried weight, there was always the attitude to dodge and find refuge in diplomatic niceties. Possibly it was due to his religious timidity or self-consciousness that he preferred maintaining a correct public image.

With passage of time, rather sorrowfully, the professional challenge in gathering a wide-range of information about Abdus Salam has been compounded by the dwindling number of first and second order sources among family, friends and contemporaries. One of his biographers, Gordon Fraser, has accurately acknowledged the difficulty with potential sources. He was not allowed permission, for example, to access Abdus Salam archives held in reserve at the International Centre for Theoretical Physics in Trieste, Italy. 'No clear reason' for this denial was given to him. Likewise, the biographer was unable to look into the personal diary of Abdus Salam 'which rests with the family'.[1] Rather paradoxically, this was despite the fact that members of Abdus Salam's family reached out to him in every cordial way otherwise.

Abdus Science

Literally, the name *Abdus Salam* has Arabic origin, meaning the Servant of Peace. Abdus Salam's father, Mohammed Hussein, had been only a few days

---

[1] Gordon Fraser: Cosmic Anger, Oxford University Press, 2008, pp. xii-xiii

into his second marriage when he claimed to have received the news about the birth of a son. It happened in the shape of divine revelation during the course of afternoon prayers at the local mosque in Jhang. Along with good tidings about having a son, Mohammed Hussein also gathered Abdus Salam as the name of his promised son. Over the decades, after the birth of Abdus Salam, his father sought an interpretation of the vision. He seemed to have found one when Abdus Salam was awarded the Atoms for Peace medal in 1955.

Although the nature of Abdus Salam's close association with the formative years of weapon-oriented nuclear program in Pakistan remains cloudy in some ways, the explanation of the foretold as advanced by Mohammed Hussein was never revised. By the close of 1980s, when Pakistan stepped closer to achieving nuclear capability, Abdus Salam stood isolated. He might have found solace in the significant meaning of his name as the Servant of Peace.

Abdus Science, the title of this book, is a reverse pun on his name. Even when his role as Servant of Peace was in doubt, he remained a steadfast Servant of Science. It is a down-to-earth journey largely across his life and times outside physics. Woven into contemporary tides of political and religious movements, the narrative of the book is divided into chapters and sections. In order to ensure a smooth chronological flow, the sequence of events and episodes relating to Abdus Salam's life is laced into their historical context. In this way, his life story runs hand in hand with the physical charm and cultural tradition of places where he lived and studied, and around the influential people who called the shots in those days. Also, the study provides a glimpse into the fractured birth and evolution of a nuclear state in Pakistan.

On the whole, the current account endeavours to steal a tender view of Abdus Salam's life apart from his strictly professional engagement as a physicist, and the method adopted for this purpose could be described as non-devotional. What exactly is meant by conducting a non-devotional excursion across the life and times of someone primarily identified with a fundamental discipline of science? Although the self-explanatory description of the term should suffice yet it is necessary to append that the phrase does not in any way imply a licence to being disrespectful, satirical or blasphemous; it is meant to provide a detached, secular and non-judgmental framework. It is important to remember here that devotional mode of writing is essentially religious and has a history dating back to hagiographic accounts of early day Christian saints. Afterwards, around medieval times, this tradition of veneration was not only embraced by Muslim historians, they carried it to hazardous heights of perfection.

Abdus Salam was a scientist, not a saint; it would be deceitful to make him the subject of a hagiographic account. His mark upon physics had been established, the marvellous dignity of his work beamed on its own. No amount of admiration, applaud, slate and scorn will ever add or diminish the glory of his stamp upon the scientific endeavour of 20th century. Do great scientists, making explicit contribution, really need monotonous chorus of acclaim? Praise might be an insult to those who live for science.[1]

One possible example of non-devotional technique comes from an assortment of profiles written by journalist and historian Paul Johnson (1928-).[2] Basically, non-devotional state of mind involves a combination of being inquisitive, exploratory and decently naughty. Abdus Salam's life outside the fort of physics offers a good deal of temptation to get closer to him and take a human view of his personality. Given the series of political judgments made by him, he remains abundantly attractive to the need for a dispassionate, detached and non-devotional inquiry into some sectors of his life.

Optional Hibernation

My interest in writing a biography of Abdus Salam dates back to the 1980s when I struggled to subsist in England. My wife, a university academic in Islamabad, had won the Government of Pakistan grant to study for doctoral program in Molecular Genetics and we travelled to England with our seven-month-old son. It was an England where Margaret Thatcher was reinventing the capitalist order. As an overseas scholar expected to pay fees in full for five years, and this was plainly how poor countries bought education from the rich, my wife qualified to take employment for which she obviously would not find time, whereas I was given a visa that debarred me from seeking any gainful work.

Under the pungency of congealed immigration laws, I confronted stark choices. For the purpose of entry and residence in England, I was granted a grotesque visa package compelling me either to return home without delay or remain jobless for five years at my own cost in order to be with my young family.

---

[1] Virginia Woolf: To the Light House, Vintage Books, London, 2004, p. 22
[2] Paul Johnson: Intellectuals, 1996, Orion Books Ltd, London

Curiously, the law would apply differently if I had been the winner of the scholarship grant and my wife an accompanying spouse. "What is your advice? What do you think is the best course open to me?" I remember asking the officer, clearly embarrassed, at the Home Office establishment in Croydon.[1]

Few months after our arrival in England, I received an offer to work for the London-based franchise of a major Pakistani newspaper. I expressed my inability to taking up the job due to the ugly nature of my British visa. Don't worry, we shall get it fixed for you, the Executive Editor of the newspaper assured me. Ostensibly, the newspaper had a case, an amendment in my visa rested upon grounds of difficulty in finding competent editorial staff with fluency in both Urdu and English languages. This arrangement suited the employer also because it entailed an extended amount of vulnerability in my situation. I submitted my passport, worked for two years, commuting between Brighton and London six days each week; only to find out in the end that an application for a friendlier visa in my favour was never filed by the newspaper in the first place.

My insistence upon sorting the matter out resulted in an abrupt termination of my employment. However, it was during the course of my work at this Pakistani newspaper that a colleague, the late Inam Ashraf, advised me to write about Abdus Salam. Sometimes way back in the 1960s, Inam Ashraf himself had thought about doing the same but Abdus Salam urged him to wait for a while as the coveted prize could be just around the corner. Abdus Salam's obsession with Nobel Prize was boundless, perhaps he considered himself incomplete without the accolade.

By the time the prize arrived, Inam Ashraf had lost enthusiasm. Instead, he produced the first Urdu-language biography of a Pakistani cricket hero, Fazal Mahmood. How could you sell a theoretical physicist of untested locale? I asked Inam Ashraf one day. That exactly is the selling point, his being out of the ordinary, the poverty-stricken exotica. Inam Ashraf delivered the judgement along with cloud of tobacco smoke out of his acutely asthmatic lungs.

On my part, I had known Abdus Salam only from a considerable distance. We heard about him occasionally from our parents, uncles, aunts and teachers. In fact, tales of his legendary grip on mathematics scared most of us. His setting of fresh academic records accompanied by a full-blown obedience to parents, peers and priests tended to terrify rather than inspire the ordinary among us.

---

[1] Imagine the volume of noise and media fury over such discrimination in countries non-compliant towards Thatcherism.

Afterwards, I always wondered how a scientist of his stature reconciled Theoretical Physics and religion.

When Inam Ashraf prompted me to write on Abdus Salam, I had already begun working on a book about the Sikh separatist movement, the struggle for Khalistan, then taking a violent turn in the Indian state of Punjab. In collaboration with a gifted Canadian social scientist, Dr Peter Stockdale, the project was shaping up well. If ever there is the opportunity to write about Abdus Salam, I thought, it should be done in a political medium. Clearly, my knowledge of physics was not likely to take me anywhere near Abdus Salam the physicist. Soon, as Peter and I headed to gain some level of stability with our *Khalistan Riddle* project, there was the temptation to write about Abdus Salam. Then, end of my employment in London saved me lots of time including the hours spent on commuting from and back to Brighton. In this way, the venture to do a biography of Abdus Salam sounded plausible. I started doing the homework about the time when the first draft of *Khalistan Riddle* neared completion.[1]

Early in 1984, I wrote a brief proposal and mailed it to Abdus Salam. His handwritten approval arrived within a matter of days with an invitation to meet him in London. Our first meeting took place at his Putney residence about the end of May 1984. On a tall shelf in the modestly fashioned Drawing Room, I could see books on religion, mysticism, history, politics, poetry and music; adding to my relief there was hardly anything on Theoretical Physics. Somehow we began conversing in Punjabi and I felt even more at ease with the *Jatki* implication of his accent.[2] He had an exceptional glimmer about his looks. I found him direct, forthright, frank and likeable.

At the very outset, I informed him about my intention to write a political rather than purely physics story out of his life. There was hardly the need, with Nobel Prize in his lap, to reaffirm what has already been duly acclaimed and celebrated. He listened to me with amused patience, and then asked me if I had a publisher in mind. None, until we agree upon the market potential of our story, I replied. He accepted it. I asked for a series of spontaneous and extensive interviews with him. Those interviews, I offered, could be scheduled in accordance with his visits to London. He would be welcome to see the list of questions prior to an interview session. There would always be questions within questions. He would be welcome to switch-off the tape-recorder whenever he

---

[1] *The Khalistan Riddle* was published in 1988.
[2] *Jatki* is one of the dialects spoken south of Punjab.

felt the need to go off-the-record. Also, he would be entitled to review the interview transcripts. At the same time, I would take notes in my own way, especially where he went off-the-record. He consented, all agreed upon between us and we started the recording of interviews; the requirement to sign or carry out a formal contract was not considered by either of the sides.

At that time, only one biography, by Abdul Ghani (1982), had appeared on Abdus Salam, and the next by Jagjit Singh (1992) was still on the way. Abdus Salam gave me a signed copy of *Ideals and Realities*, a selection of his speeches and essays.[1] He also gave me a copy of the authorised biography of his father, Mohammed Hussein.[2] He promised to provide me relevant material, depending upon his convenience, in the shape of press clippings, correspondence and other records, including the diary maintained in Trieste, in due course of time.

Between the two of us, we had more than fifteen hours of direct interviews by way of voice recording. On a few occasions, when friends would be visiting him, he asked if they could sit in our company. I always offered him that we could postpone the session if he wished, adding that that there was no problem on my part. Between September and December 1984, I transcribed more than five hundred pages of those interviews for him to comment upon where he felt the need. While responding to most of my questions, he had been natural, extempore and spontaneous; and wealth of refreshing information thus collated constitutes the bedrock of account tendered in this book.

Towards the end of our elaborate exercise of interviews, when we were left only with details relating to family matters, Abdus Salam began having second thoughts over information he had shared with me, especially sections relating to his opinion about intellectual dysfunction among Muslims, the Ahmadiyah and the power politics in Pakistan. He began cutting out large chunks of text from the transcripts of recorded interviews. We had a torrential censor. I felt nervous over dispossession of significantly valuable opinion he held over a range of ideological and political matters. He wanted me to envelop his opinion in my words for such a cover gave him the opportunity to bail-out. I intended to write about him with a good deal of mutually shared exertion, not a sort of authorised biography with the liberty for him to disown arbitrarily or conveniently. Of

---

[1] Published by World Scientific in Singapore (1984) the book includes two introductory articles on Abduls Salam.

[2] This book, edited by Mohammed Hussein's close friend, Mohammed Ismail, was published in Pakistan in 1974.

course we were not doing a book in first person interviews, but there were areas requiring him to own a position one way or another.

For example, there was the increasing need in those days for him to open up with respect to his role in the weapon-oriented nuclear program of Pakistan. Likewise, I believed, people in Pakistan looked forward to getting a comprehensive picture of his Ahmadiyah connection. There was the crucial need for him, from my point view, to go public about the trade-off he had offered Zulfiqar Bhutto, a retraction of the Ahmadiyah excommunication in exchange for Abdus Salam's whole-hearted cooperation in Pakistan's nuclear pursuit. Likewise, I believed a whole lot of his friends and colleagues, especially those residing in the west, desired to know how he practiced bigamy in Europe. Then, in some areas of greater public interest, we could aim at expanding the size of our audience.

Instead, he continued to censor paragraphs one after another making the whole interview session redundant in some instances. Actually, his attitude amounted to an erosion of faith in my propriety in handling the information coming out of him. He insisted that information provided during the course of interviews was for me only, not for public consumption in any sense. Whereas, I rated the information he had shared with me as fairly academic, abstract even insufficient. From my point of view there was hardly anything that could be classified as politically volatile or inflammable in any manner. He was not convinced. Almost two-third of the information stood hushed-up. On the balance, it amounted to washing out a recording of some ten hours, and he was still not sure about the rest.

Hardly much was left in the story as I envisioned it. A good deal of information he had initially shared with me on Pakistan's nuclear history, the Ahmadiyah controversy, intellectual degeneration among Muslims and challenges facing Islam in the modern age; all stood retracted. When I requested him to be spontaneous and natural, he looked for caution and restraint. He went as far as telling me that many statements of political nature had come out of him rather unreservedly. I could see our working ties were in peril.

One day, he asked me to show him the draft of chapters done so far. I replied that we were still in the interview stage which is to be followed by a considerable amount of research in order to evolve contextual framework as well as cross-checking of various accounts with some of his contemporaries. I also underlined the necessity to tap a whole lot of original sources in Pakistan, especially information relating to places and people enriching the formative years of his life. I asked him to complete the interview stage before anything else because, from the point of editorial logistics, there could be information in the final interview actually meant to fit into one of the earlier chapters. Had I been a research fellow under him, he might have shown me the exit outright. I asked for a bit of time and then hurried up to stack a selection of my notes and passed it on to him. He did not seem to enjoy it, and I noted that critical assessment of the draft had been conducted by someone manifestly inclined towards the Ahmadiyah.

By the end of 1984, we confronted a stalemate. At times, I suspected that he was changing positions arbitrarily. For example, he promised to give me access to his diary, personal notes and correspondence, relating to his life outside physics, especially events surrounding the excommunication of the Ahmadiyah in 1974. On the contrary, I was given access only to a hefty bagful of papers, largely in the category of tangential information, all haphazardly lumped together. No doubt the information was valuable from historical viewpoint, but it lacked the political sting.

In fact, I volunteered to organise the crowd of those documents in a chronological order and, at the same time, paste press-clippings in a tidy manner where required. He was pleased with the completed task, still I never had any glimpse of those tremendously valuable and first-hand sources like his diary or the correspondence with the Government of Pakistan.

Writing about aspects of his life outside physics, entering in areas where he was reluctant or just not keen to share information, made it much harder to find authentic information other than reliance on secondary sources and educated conjecturing. In one way or another, the denial of access to his diary and other valuable documents, amounted to ending up with yet another version of imperfection and guesswork. Already, a certain amount of folklore seemed to have crept into some of the Ahmadiyah-sponsored articles about him.

Our last meeting at his Putney residence in London, in December 1984, turned out to be quick to the point. He was unwell and lying on bed. We parted on the fence, agreeing not to proceed any further. Already, there was some speculation in the air that he might return to Pakistan to take up an important assignment under the military government. I concluded that appropriate option before me was to wait for a suitable opening in the future; there was no harm in hibernating upon whatever had been achieved.

Luckily, a certain level of friendly contact survived between us. I remember him calling me in Brighton in December 1985. He intended to seek out with me the merit of his possible return to Pakistan. He could take a better view for himself, I replied. On my part, however, I did not see any major positive change on the way in a part of the world where scientific logic and religious passion continue to overlap massively. I am not sure if he really liked my response.

In April 1986, when my wife completed her doctorate, we went on two weeks of holidays by driving through France, Italy and Switzerland. While in Venice we took a detour to Trieste where it turned out to be a chilly, windy and overcast day. Having lunch with my wife and our son at the institute cafeteria, I saw Abdus Salam seated with his second wife, Professor Louise Johnson (1940–2012) and their son, only a few tables away.[1] His face did not betray any visible signs of the debilitating cerebral palsy that was slithering to overtake him in a matter of few years. He was cosy and warm when I went to see him in his room later in the afternoon. We talked about home. He gave me some of his recent pictures, and then invited me to stay overnight at the institute guest house but we had other plans.

Meanwhile, Pakistan experienced major changes inside out. In August 1987, the Red Army retreated from Afghanistan. One year later, General Ziaul Haq was killed in an unexplained air-crash. Abdus Salam visited Pakistan in May 1989. There was resurgence of hope that a return to democratic order would change the place for the better. I called him at the local Marriot Hotel in Islamabad where he was staying. He asked me to come over. Apparently, he had been placed on hold for an appointment with Prime Minister Benazir Bhutto. We overshot the opportunity to get together due to some bungle up by one of his private minders. In the first week of June 1989, he wrote me from Trieste promising a get-together on his next visit to Pakistan in November 1989. He had fallen sick and his health declined fast. I received the news of his death in Sydney within a few days of our family migration to Australia.

Today, more than three decades after the string of our agitated encounters, I only wish he had been magnanimous with the invigorating treasure of information we shared between us about his life apart from the grand success story in physics. Any suggestion here about his entitlement to privacy needs to

---

[1] Professor Louise Johnson (1940-2012) was an acclaimed Molecular Biologist based in Oxford, England, who might have won the Nobel Prize for her ground-breaking contribution in the area of enzyme crystallography.

be weighed against the somewhat undefined frontiers of celebrity privilege. Can a mutually acceptable deal on universal definition of privacy be struck between celebrities and their fans?

In spite of his captivity in self-restrain, Abdus Salam was a public figure. He seemed to have relished popularity since his mark upon the Punjab University Matriculation Examination way back in the summer of 1940. Over the decades, he possessed an increasingly robust constituency of scholars, students, enthusiasts, fans as well as detractors. As an alien in Europe, the seat of reformation, renaissance and industrial revolution, he was inundated in a crowd of scientists largely from Jewish and Christian religious backgrounds. People wished to know more about him. We know so much about Albert Einstein, from nearly a dozen of women in his life to the strong views he held in religious and political spheres. Does the exposure of those personal choices and publicly stated opinions diminish the giant in any way? It is important to remember that Abdus Salam achieved the status of a giant in the field of Theoretical Physics in which Albert Einstein had excelled in the same period of time.

Also, there is the need to appreciate that a great deal of information he shared with me and was then overtaken by reluctance had been made public in books and essays written about him since 1984 when we agreed to apply breaks on my project. Abdul Hameed's Urdu-language biography of Abdus Salam, published circa 1999, makes a case in the point.

After completing her doctoral degree in Molecular Genetics, in England, my wife returned to Pakistan. She applied for a one-step forward academic position at her university in Islamabad and was invited to appear before the Selection Board. One member of the board asked her to name any three wives of Prophet Mohammed. What had such early Islamic history quiz to do with her area of expertise? She asked. She was advised that it was a statutory requirement in order to establish the religious credentials of a candidate. My wife replied that she had the sufficient knowledge to field such questions but would not do so as a matter of principle. There was a commotion in the room until the Dean Faculty of Natural Sciences prevailed to restore order. My wife won the position in the end but her faith in doing science in Pakistan was shaken to the core. Finding the opportunity, she guided me and our son into the act of migration to Australia. We started all over again. Although, in this way, the drift of events dictating the course of my everyday life hurled me into unchartered territories of migration and re-employment, I did not give up on the dream to write a relaxed and unpretentious account of Abdus Salam's life other than his core occupation with physics.

Note on Formatting of Chapters

Due to the many-sided composition of the narrative on Abdus Salam, especially the need to weave the sequence of his life-story into a fitting context and historical affinity, each of the chapters has been apportioned into sections numbered in italics.

Likewise, excerpts from interviews with Abdus Salam, conducted in 1984, are reported in accordance with the storyline. This methodology, aimed at sharing out the text in accordance with a subject matter, has been pursued throughout the course of current study. At the same time there is the need to appreciate the fact that quotes from Abdus Salam's interviews constitute a translated and edited version of his statements. To the range of questions posed to him, he responded extempore, at leisure in a profuse mix of Punjabi and English languages, jumping from one subject to another of his choice. In spite of the innate nature of professional impediment involved in translation and minor editing, associated with such situations, every possible effort has been made to keep his word as well as intent in order to avoid any misleading impression.

For example, the first chapter *Living in the Age of Bottomless Devotion*, dealing with ancestral legacy and family background of Abdus Salam, and focusing largely upon the life and times of his parents, comprises of discrete sections like the one dealing with a short excursion through Jhang, the remote country town in southern Punjab where the family lived. Then there is a separate section on the schismatic Ahmadiyah community to which the family adhered and the association cast an unavoidable shadow on the political predicament of Abdus Salam.

Statement of Hope

It is hoped that the current account of times, forces and factors shaping the life of Abdus Salam is not the last or the final in any sense whatsoever. It is just one more in the queue encouraging others to participate in writing about him. He was an extraordinary scientist delving into the mind of gods. Surely, the future generations of authors will set upon the clues provided to them by their predecessors and be able to dive deeper and detect unexplored perspectives.

Chapter One
Living in the Age of Bottomless Devotion

When Jhang, a tiny town next to the meeting point of two rivers in southern Punjab, is mentioned as the hometown of Abdus Salam, it becomes obligatory to put up only with forefathers alone as if women simply did not exist. Although such an unkind custom does not make much sense to a citizen of the 21st century, still it may not be fair to release the gender guillotine in haste.

Invariably, ancestral lineage in patriarchal settings tends to reflect a stark neglect of women who gave birth to children along with delivering a whole range of household chores generation after generation without asking for any formal recognition. For this reason, Jhang is deemed to be the place where male members of Abdus Salam's immediate family, along with some others from their Bhatti Rajput ancestry, lived for many generations marrying women locally as well as abroad.

Most places transform with advancing tides of time and economy. But people continue to nurture a rather personal and private memory of the world where they had lived once upon a time, especially in their youth. It could be an expression of melancholy attachment with the bygone. Abdus Salam was born in a small town, Santokdas, some 65 miles southwest of Jhang.[1] Nonetheless, Jhang remained the birth right for him, the place had special place in his memory even when a greater balance of his life was spent in Europe. During his formative years, he had picked up an innocent image of Jhang that always stayed with him. An attempt, therefore, will be made here to relive the place as it must have dwelled and breathed when he resided in the town about one hundred years ago.

---

[1] In Punjab, it was customary for young expecting mothers in those days to be with their parents prior to childbirth. At the time of Abdus Salam's birth, his maternal grandfather served the Department of Land Revenue in Santokdas.

Earlier in the 20th century, Jhang was no more than a microscopic dot on the alluvial plains of Punjab, the land of Five Rivers originating in the Himalayas. One of these rivers, *Jhelum* in the northwest, runs a course of 450 miles to pour itself into the next eastward, that is, *Chenab*, just above Jhang. With *Jhelum* lost into *Chenab*, the pooled flow of the two then heads south to receive the leftover torrents of *Raavi, Beas* and *Sutlej*, near Multan, the city of five thousand years old Sun Temple. Further down in the south, at Punjnad, the merged flow meets the mighty *Indus* to take another five hundred miles of relatively calm journey into the Arabian Sea.

Upon arrival here about the end of 18th century, the British invaders found Jhang a grim station comprising of 'arid steppes scantily inhabited by nomad pastoral tribes'.[1] By name, Jhang means a bush land where any blast of natural bloom depended solely upon seasonal rain and flooding of rivers. If there was no moisture, the panoramic enormity of wilderness tended to maintain its purity.

Travelling through this wilderness, earlier in the 7th century, the Chinese pilgrim Hwen Thsang (602–664), observed the extraction of iron ore from the dark-brown pre-Cambrian boulders of Kirana Hills and a tall Buddhist stupa in Sangla. He also passed through Shorkot, the birth place of famous Sanskrit grammarian Panini, where Kathian tribesmen had given Alexander the Great a hard-hitting battle in the 4th century BC.[2] John Marshall (1876–1958), the British archaeologist, was about to oversee excavation at Harappa, south-west of Jhang, to unearth the remains of a long-gone, over three thousand years old, Indus Valley civilisation.

On the political map, the region surrounding Jhang constituted an arch of Indus Valley sharing borders with three sites of military significance. Down in the southeast on the coast of Sind was the 8th century Muslim state. Up in the northwest was the 10th century route of Muslim invasion connecting Central Asia-Afghanistan axis with Peshawar and Lahore. Adjacent to the two, in the east, was Rajasthan, the abode of ancient Hindu Rajput kingdom, defending the Indian heartland.

Only Sufi saints, accompanying the waves of Muslim invaders from northwest, seemed to have attached value to this vast wilderness of Indus Valley. As a consequence of the Sufi movement, Punjab underwent a tectonic shift in its

---

[1] Gazetteer of the Jhang District 1883-84, p. 40

[2] Har G. Khorana (1922-2011), the winner of 1968 Nobel Prize in Physiology/Medicine, was born in Shorkot.

balance of demography and nearly half of the population in the region was converted to Islam.

About half way through the 15th century, an older settlement of Jhang was founded by a Sial Rajput chief, Mal Khan. Ever since its birth, the history of Jhang had been synonymous with the rise and fall of the Sial fortunes. But the scene changed with the dawn of British colonialism and the chaotic mix of tribal, pastoral and nomadic modes of production gave way to a European brand of feudalism. All the local despots were tamed, and property rights in Punjab were regulated under the Land Alienation Act of 1900. Very soon a reformed class of collaborators flocked around the new rulers. Out of sheer political necessity, the British tolerated the evolution of native nobility, and the two sides gave birth to socioeconomic stability unheard of since the collapse of Mogul Empire. Such was the admiration for British pre-eminence that one officer of the Indian Civil Service, often a Deputy Commissioner, representing the Crown of England, presided over vast tracts of land and large masses of population without resorting naked force.[1]

In the old town of Jhang, built above flood level, the British found some specimens of 'fine and picturesque masonry' and paved tree lined streets. Hindu pilgrims could catch a glimpse of the spire above Lal Nath Temple from far away. A 'howling waste' outside the town was occupied by 'wild races' who flaunted 'doubtful neutrality' during the course of uprising in 1857. Physically, the people of Jhang were described as 'well built, handsome and sturdy' comprising of 'many very fine, stalwart men' free of 'timidity or cringing'. Abdus Salam's Bhatti clan of the Rajput was rated as 'industrious agriculturists, hardly at all in debt, good horse-breeders and very fond of sport'. According to the British, the Bhatti had very little interest in cattle-lifting though they were 'much addicted to carrying off each other's wives'.[2]

Any civic amenities associated with modern civilisation had yet to arrive in Jhang. By the close of 19th century, the town was still devoid of electricity, town water and sewage. Early in the morning, when it was still dark, groups of women went out in the open and respond to the call of nature. Men followed a little afterwards.

---

[1] About two hundred aristocratic families were groomed to play the role of trusted power-brokers, and one thousand officers of the Indian Civil Service controlled the fate of three hundred million people.

[2] Gazetteer of the Jhang District 1883-84, pp. 50-52, 65, 163-164

Muslims made two-third of the population with the rest belonging largely to Hindu and Sikh communities. Invariably, Muslims and Sikhs owned agriculture and Hindus formed the mercantile class including moneylenders and professionals. By and large, communal ties were dictated by the peculiarity of their class character and conflicting economic roles. Then again, the equilibrium of communal harmony was further complicated by the initiative and lead the Hindu community enjoyed in education and employment.

Among Muslims, the majority belonged to the *Sunni* sect of Islam but rather than observing the strictness of Wahabi-Salafi religious code, they preferred to seek inspiration from the teachings of Sufi saints and orders. A big crowd of faithful thronged to attend the festival at Shah Jewna shrine, especially for the concluding session of ceremonies. Pilgrims from far flung villages gathered at the shrine and supplicated for the welfare of sitting saint. To the sheer amazement of a spellbound audience, an oil lamp attached to a pulley fixed in the ceiling of the shrine travelled upward. While the serving saint, seated in a separate chamber, held the other end of the belt and he pulled up the lamp without actually watching it. At any moment, during the course of its ascension, the dying out of light in the lamp was deemed as a bad omen. Whereas, a successful clambering of the flame meant well and it was met with a chorus of relief among the faithful; there would be the cause for celebration. In the event of a grim portent, the saint retired to seclusion and meditated to ward off the impending misfortune; it amounted to reliving the pagan age.

For the *Shia* community among Muslims, the first ten days of Islamic New Year were assigned to mourning in commemoration of the *Karbala* tragedy in the 7th century Iraq when the grandchildren of Prophet Mohammed had lost their battle for Islamic caliphate. On the tenth day, the faithful walked in the town barefoot, singing allegorical chants in chorus and self-bashing their bodies in a powerful thumping rhythm.

Hindus celebrated the fair of Sidh Nath, a reincarnation of Lord Shiva, at an ancient temple on the ridge of Kirana Hills, observable miles away. According to Hindu belief, the Kirana Hills were created by rocks tumbling out of the Himalayas at a time when gods moved the mighty range from its old home in the south to the present location in the north. Somewhat perversely, the religious weight of Kirana Hills survived the making of Islamic Republic in Pakistan. In the 1960s, Pakistan received massive American assistance to construct an airbase base along the range. Some of the mischievous strategists deemed that Hindu pilots of Indian Air Force might think twice before bombing a sacred site. Afterwards, when Pakistan marched towards achieving nuclear parity with India, tunnels were dug beneath Kirana Hills in order to carry out some two dozen Cold Tests for various designs of the atom bomb.[1]

Jhang had its peculiar creed of carefree dervishes, or the *Malang*, who claimed ascetic link with Sufi tradition. Mostly those wandering characters sported long hair, wore colourful long shirts, bangles and necklaces. Some of them held an ebony bowl hanging around their neck; others carried bugles made out of cow horns. They hung about shrines and cemeteries, preparing potions of freshly pounded cannabis, dancing in a circle. Along with the crackling sounds of their bangles and beads, and the accompanying drum beat, they created a vigorous atmosphere in chorus, rhythm, movement and, of course, dust.

An elderly *Malang* in his carefree posture, under the influence of cannabis, often posed extremely intense and philosophical. Staying aloof from communal tension, the majority among those maverick fakirs would be stark illiterate though some in their ranks were genuinely motivated by mysticism. Sultan Bahu (1631–1691), the 17th century saint-poet of Jhang was a *Malang* whose devotion to God equalled self-renunciation.

Many small cultivators lived in tiny hamlets, inhabiting squarish lumps of mud houses and windowless rooms, working with hand-made tools. Those unable to afford a house lived under a moveable thatch, propped upon tree trunks. Families lived together without the slightest notion of need for individual privacy. Water was an asset greater than land. What saved them from dehydration, in the event of delayed rains, was the blindfolded ox walking rounds to propel the Persian Wheel. A creaking chain of wooden buckets rotated on the wheel, dishing water out of the well and splashing it over a hollowed tree trunk serving as the tap.

Men wore *dhoti*, a rectangular piece of cotton wrapped around the lower half of their bodies. In winter, they covered themselves with some heavier fabric to cover the upper half of their bodies. Loosely tailored shirts, turbans and locally stitched *khussa* shoes were reserved only for formal occasions. Any younger person turning up in western outfit was scowled upon as some sort of a shallow copy-cat. Women, on the other hand, enjoyed a certain degree of freedom in the choice of outfit. Going by their age, marital status, and the level of affluence,

---

[1] Feroz Hassan Khan: Eating Grass – The Making of the Pakistani Bomb, Cambridge University Press, India, 2013, p. 185

they wore brightly coloured short blouses and shawls over the unstitched skirt neatly tied about their waist; putting on colourful bangles made of glass or finely carved metal; jewellery awaited festive occasions. Baggy trousers or *shalwars* had yet to come in fashion.

On the average, people in Jhang cooked and ate in handmade earthenware. Invariably, kitchens were set up outdoors with baking to be carried out in a vertically dug clay oven or *tandoor*. Milk constituted the staple diet, even poorer households tended to own a water-buffalo or cow to meet their fundamental dietary requirement. A farmer survived the day with butter milk and *chapatti* bread. Depending upon the amount of stored grain, the *chapatti* was made with barley or wheat flour. During winter, when wheat ran out of stock, the flour was milled from maize and oats. Only rich landowners afforded meat. Jhang was famous for its *piloo* berries and melons.

A good deal of sporting activity in the old Jhang, before the arrival of soccer, cricket, hockey and tennis, was limited largely to wrestling and the sadistic amusement of animal fights. Apart from cock and quail fights, the scale of viciousness and brutality was expressed in the fierce contests between dogs and a restrained bear. Amidst the frenzy of cheering and jeering of spectators, stakes were raised upon favourites. Two ferocious dogs, specially trained for the contest, were unleashed upon an untamed but shackled bear. Every now and then, a bloody bout ended in dead dogs and a miserably mauled bear. Often the dogs belonged to one of the Sial chiefs.

Living in an age of calendars and clocks, people in Jhang quantified a lifetime in terms of childhood, youth, manhood and old age. A man was old when his beard turned greyish, the absence of municipal or parish records made it impossible to figure out the age in years. Women guessed their age by children they had delivered. Likewise, the daily cycle of time was expediently allotted to spells like daybreak, late-morning, mid-day, afternoon, sunset, night, mid-night and late-mid-night. Somewhat ironically, this casual way of time measurement was set against the ancient Indian calendar which offered a marvellously accurate delineation of climatic changes. Then, the distance was measured on a vocal scale. For example, a place could be as far as the sound of a mooing cow or a bleating lamb to reach. Mostly people held a romantic notion of life beyond *Jhelum* and *Chenab*, which they never had the opportunity to cross.

For the most part criminal activity in Jhang revolved around abduction of women and cattle-lifting. Surprisingly the aggrieved party avoided going to police because, under the so-called feudal pride, it amounted to an expression of weakness. Meanwhile the stolen property, women or cattle, shared a common plight. After finding out the location of stolen items through private means, negotiations were conducted by elders who, before anything else, aimed at saving faces. It was very important to avoid an extraction of confession for it amounted to a concession of defeat from someone who might be an ally the day after. During the course of those delicate negotiations, the emphasis was placed upon 'loss of services' rather than a retrieval of the stolen goods. In this way, both women and cattle were identified with services they offered. An emphasis upon surplus rather than the original value, underlining the amount of damage caused to stolen goods, grouped cows and buffalos, horses and donkeys, goats, sheep and women in the same tight spot; all enjoying 'equal rights' providing utilities like milk, transportation, flesh and sex. In the event of failure in achieving any satisfactory settlement, the respectable course of action open before the aggrieved party was to settle the score by staging a greater burglary.

As a matter of fact, this portrayal of everyday life, as drawn above, was not restricted to Jhang alone; the scene covered most of the rural Punjab where vast tracts of land had not been touched by any hint of modernisation. Other than Amritsar, Lahore and Multan, the region could hardly claim much to its metropolitan credit. Nonetheless, the winds of change had begun to blow as the British craved to enhance the state revenue, and for this purpose they had begun lubricating the virgin soil by digging canals, building bridges on rivers, spreading out rail and road networks and providing electricity and telephone connections.

Irrigation facilitated by canals turned 15,000 sq. miles of arid country between *Chenab* and *Jhelum* into cultivable tracts of land. For example, only the *Jhelum* canal from Rasul, near Chaillianwali, irrigated 1,400,000 acres. Three brand new farming towns; Sargodha, Lyallpur (Faisalabad) and Montgomery (Sahiwal) were founded to celebrate the dawn of 20th century.[1]

In Jhang, the small British contingent comprised of civilian officers who, with their families and lavishly hired local staff, lived in a secure enclave called Civil Lines or the Cantonment. Any casual interaction between the ruler and the ruled was rare. Four hundred years of European presence in the subcontinent had failed to produce any citable number of intermarriages. For quite a while, the

---

[1] Some Marxist historians hold the view that colonial government required funds to step up its defence capability by building a chain of military cantonments in order to fight the threat of Russian expansion.

British held the notion that native dignitaries were simply devoid of the intellect required to run modern institutions of finance, economy and politics. Natives did receive some credit, however, for training the 'restive and ill-trained horses' of their masters.[1]

In summer, when Punjab sizzled with temperatures soaring above 45°C, the sprawling, double-brick and high ceilings bungalows in the Civil Lines were cooled with mechanical fans. A rectangular wooden frame and its canvass sheet, hung in the middle of the room, swung back and forth as the string tied to it was pulled and released by a battery of lean-bodied servants sitting in the veranda took turns to do the job like slaves aboard a Roman galleon, or the blind-folded bull doing the rounds at a Persian Wheel. This ceiling fan, prior to the arrival of electricity in rural Punjab, fought heat and humidity, as best as possible, until the spell of dry heat was broken by fierce dust-storms, monsoon rains and setting in of autumn.

Later in the afternoon, those servants sprinkled fresh water, so short in the fields, upon extensive tiled yards. Mosquito nets were stretched out above the rows of beds in the open, under a brilliant starry sky. It was about time for the bosses to end their day, have tea and a cool night.

Abdus Salam remembered the Jhang of his childhood and early youth in a more personal way. 'It was quite a little town with population touching the ten-thousand mark divided largely between Muslim and Hindu communities. On the average, people were poor, qualified individuals like doctors and lawyers belonged to the Hindu community. Members of two communities lived in peaceful accord in separate localities but this division was not very strict'. He began dredging up. 'Among Muslims, the Sial represented a bygone aristocracy running short of money and power, they were occupied in decadent pastimes like breeding animals, birds and dogs, for the purpose of wrestling and sport, and spending their time in pounding cannabis to brew potions. But they continued to own land'. He remembered walking past the spot, where cannabis was pounded, on his way to the local Ahmadiyah mosque next to *Chah Drutta*.[2]

He also remembered a Sial landowner who happened to dig out a pot full of antiquated coins on his land near the city wall. This man sat on his cot for a while then started throwing the coins around towards youth playing in the field.

---

[1] Mortimer Durand: Life of the Rt. Hon. Sir Alfred C Lyall, William Blackwood and sons, Edinburgh and London, 1913, p. 124
[2] Interviews 1984: Folder I, pp. 1-2, 15-16

Everyone, including Abdus Salam, joined the race to pick up a coin. 'I did not have any luck', he added. One thing, he seemed to appreciate about the Sial was their readiness to donate land to build mosques including the one of the Ahmadiyah. 'I have, on a number of occasions, witnessed the arrival of the *Malang*, those carefree people who lived a relaxed lifestyle in accordance with one or another Sufi tradition, it was considered to be a desirable fate for a man. That was the atmosphere we had in those days, an outgoing aristocracy, dog-bear fights, pounding of cannabis, throwing away of money, the *Malang*, and so on'. He remarked.[1]

He reminisced how festivals were convened at saintly shrines, especially the one at the tomb of Shah Jewna. He could visualise the flickering of ascending lamp.

Apart from the Shah Jewna shrine, he remembered the roofless tomb of Heer where a relatively low-profile festival was observed every year. Heer is known all over the subcontinent as the legendary heroin of a romantic folk tale. Although it is hard to keep reality from imagination, Heer, the beautiful daughter of an influential and wealthy Sial chieftain, is trusted to have lived somewhere in the early medieval era. She fell in love with Ranjha, an employee of her father, but was disallowed the match apparently on grounds of tribal arrogance of the Sial. Her own father, Chuchak Khan, is known to have urged his wife to:

Rip apart with a sharp sickle the belly of the spoiled daughter,
Pierce deep into her sparkling beautiful eyes a stinging red-hot needle,
And smash her skull under a solid rod of seasoned wood,
For it is crucial to roast alive a disobedient girl

To which Heer is believed to have responded:

Pity those who slaughter their daughters,
Such a people are bound to perish away,
For they cannot defy the assertion of their innocent victims

According to a relatively popular version of the epic tale, the one attributed to Warris Shah, around 1760, Heer died heartbroken. She was buried in a roofless tomb because, according to the widely held local belief, rain does not fall upon

---

[1] Interviews 1984: Folder I, pp. 19-21

the site. Some people go as far as according her the status of a saint and visit the tomb as pilgrims.

Abdus Salam remembered Heer fondly but avoided giving her the saint status. At the same time, he was not prepared to shunt her out only because of her elopement with Ranjha. He entertained the epic tale as one of the love stories emerging from the banks of *Chenab*, the river of romance. 'I believe Heer as one of our greatest heroines enjoying a prominent place in the cultural history of Jhang. After all, she was one of the daughters of Jhang'.[1] When Abdus Salam won the Nobel Prize and some of his enthusiasts in Pakistan reflected that Jhang, known worldwide due to Heer, had another celebrity, he was quick to correct them by stating that the place will always be known by her name. 'There are over three hundred Nobel Laureates and so many cities associated with their names. But Heer is unique.' He passed the judgment.

In fact, he visited the tomb of Heer afterwards.[2] His younger brother, Abdul Hameed, however, took a conservative view. In his Urdu-language biography of Abdus Salam, published circa 1999, Abdul Hameed has listed half a dozen superstars associated with Jhang and its neighbourhood without making any mention whatsoever of Heer. In all probability, Abdul Hameed shared the righteous view of packing her off as a perilously rebellious female.[3]

II

Abdus Salam's father, Mohammed Hussein, was born on 2 September 1891 to a devoutly religious Muslim household residing in Jhang. It was a time when the British foothold in Punjab had been consolidated and there was a great deal of political stability in the region. Jhang and many other country stations of its kind stood on the verge of economic and social change.

Mohammed Hussein was one of the three children of his parents. His father, Gul Mohammed, belonged to the *Bhatti* clan of the Rajput; and mother, Bhaag Bharee, was a *Mogul* by descent. Going by the literal meaning of two names,

---

[1] Another famous woman in Jhang, though not as well-known as Heer, was Niamat Khatun, the wife of an 18th century Sial chief. She raised a formidable army to check the rising tide of Sikh military power.

[2] Interviews 1984: Folder III, pp. 19, 22-23

[3] Life of Abdus Salam (an Urdu-language biography compiled by his brother Abdul Hameed), Lahore, circa 2000, p. 4

Gul Mohammed meant 'the Flower of Mohammed' and Bhaag Bharee was someone 'Full of Good Fortune and Tidings'. In spite of the acceptability of marrying across racial divide, the children adopted the tribal identity from their paternal line. So even when their mother came from an equally prestigious *Mogul* stock, the children of Gul Mohammed and Bhaag Bharee were bound to be identified as *Bhatti* Rajput.

According to Mohammed Hussein, his forefathers originated in the Rajput royalty; he traced them back precisely to an 11th century Hindu prince by the name of Budhan. Prince Budhan was deeply touched by the egalitarian teachings of a contemporary Muslim saint, Bahawal Haq (1170–1262), and had embraced Islam. Like new converts, the prince had been so carried away by the Sufi wisdom that he relinquished the regal lifestyle and went on to spend the rest of his life in the company of Bahawal Haq. He was given the Muslim name Saad Budhan. After his death, Saad Budhan was buried within the compound of the imposing shrine raised, in Multan, in the memory of Bahawal Haq. In his biographical notes, Mohammed Hussein stated that the offspring of Saad Budhan had been assigned to preach Islam in Jhang country area, where they served as caliphs in the spiritual franchise. Mohammed Hussein testified his father, Gul Mohammed, holding the venerable office. Since the spiritual industry in rural Punjab involved a range of financial endowments, it is possible that some level of income was apportioned to the caliphate handed to the line of Mohammed Hussein's ancestors.

Mohammed Hussein grew up in a deeply religious, scholarly and strictly disciplinarian environment. His parents held allegiance to the *Ahle Hadith* school of Sunni-Salafi mainstream among Muslims. He remembered how one of the ground floor rooms in his parents' home, walking distance from the Lal Nath Temple, was stacked with books, hand-written manuscripts and personal records mostly relating to Islamic theology and medicine. Sadly, this treasure of knowledge was lost to ageing and negligence, taking with it some of the rare genealogical trees of the family. In those days, literacy among Muslims, especially among male members of the family, meant a fairly good amount of proficiency in Persian and Arabic languages. As the language of Koran, Arabic received preference though Persian had its utility in being the official medium of Mogul court and business. As such, Gul Mohammed had a knack of both. Everyday conversation in the family and bazaar was conducted in *Jatki*, a local variation of *Seraiki* dialect of Punjabi spoken in southern districts of Punjab country with an expressive allure of its own.

According to Mohammed Hussein, his father was a general practitioner dispensing herbal medicine. Gul Mohammed offered free treatment to the general body of his impoverished patients and had earned fame in treating people afflicted with tuberculosis. Also, Gul Mohammed abided by a strict code of discipline in his life, he hated wasteful addictions like tobacco. Mohammed Hussein had to change school because his father found boys warming up the *hukkah* of a teacher. On another occasion, when Mohammed Hussein hit upon an unclaimed cap lying next to the school fountain, his father reprimanded him politely advising that even when the item seemed spare it must go back to the spot where it had been left behind by a rightful owner.

Given the cultural inhibition, not much is known about Mohammed Hussein's mother, Bhaag Bharee, though she is remembered as a deeply religious person like her husband. While praying for Mohammed Hussein, his mother entreated God to settle her son in an employment where he earns a salary of more than one hundred rupees every month.[1]

Mohammed Hussein recalled his grandfather, Qadir Bakhsh, staying healthy up to the age of 105. Qadir Bakhsh was a poet who composed mystic verses in Punjabi language. Another of the family peers, Ghulam Mohammed, had served as a gunner in the artillery of Sial chief Ahmed Khan. In 1803, when the Sikh army besieged Jhang, Maharaja Ranjit Singh is believed to have narrowly escaped a shell fired by Ghulam Mohammed.

Again, the available family records do not relate anything about Mohammed Hussein's sister, Jannat; only an occasional mention of her name is deemed sufficient. Literally, the name Jannat means paradise. Like other women in her situation, Jannat does not get a place on the family tree.

Mohammed Hussein's older brother, Ghulam Hussein (1874–1950), turned out to be a trend-setter in the family. He completed education with distinction, picked up a Bachelor's degree at the University of Punjab and found public sector employment at the Department of Education. Due to his considerable seniority in age, Ghulam Hussein had been a father-figure to Mohammed Hussein.

---

[1] Foreign exchange rates by the end of 2018 will keep the figure to little less than one dollar.

Ghulam Hussein is believed to have lived with a maverick streak hidden in his soul. He had been the imam at mosques in Jhang and Lahore. He swung between extremes. At one time he was a fierce opponent of the Ahmadiyah, going as far as writing a book slating the schism. Afterwards, he embraced the Ahmadiyah and became a dedicated member of the party. He would be away from home for months on while his wife and children worried for him. Suddenly one day, to the pleasant surprise of everyone, he would turn up unannounced. He loved going out on prolonged hiking expeditions across Solomon Range to study the medical benefits of wild herbs.

After his retirement from public service in 1932, Ghulam Hussein travelled to the Arabian Peninsula to perform *Hajj*. Nobody heard about him for many months until one day when he returned unannounced and explained the reason behind his prolonged absence. Apparently, during the course of his stay in Arabia, King Abdul Aziz came to know about Ghulam Hussein and his language proficiency and public sector experience in educational administration. As such, the king gave him a project for translation. At the same time the king asked him to submit proposals for improvement of school education in the Arabian Peninsula. While doing the job, Ghulam Hussein is reported to have reminded the king about an oral tradition of Prophet Mohammed. According to this tradition, the advent of Armageddon will be triggered in the lands of Hejaz by a blaze of fire glowing and dazzling all the way to Basra. Ostensibly, it was a prophesy hinting at the presence of oil wells hidden in the region. Some people in the social circle of Mohammed Hussein hold the view that King Abdul Aziz hastened to commission the Saudi Arabian Mining Syndicate to start drilling for oil as a consequence of his conversation with Ghulam Hussein.[1]

As Inspector of Schools, Ghulam Hussein served in many districts in Punjab. Curiously, he used to order the subscription of Ahmadiyah literature for departmental libraries. Then, he was known to indulge in proselytising and preaching of the Ahmadiyah message to school teachers calling upon him in connection with official business. Also, he managed to contract drones of Ahmadiyah youth into employment.[2] It is hard to assimilate how a public servant, accountable to a secular government, could do it all at the cost of public

---

[1] Abdul Hameed (circa 2000): p. 23

[2] Mohammed Hussein (an Urdu-language autobiography edited by Mohammed Ismail), Lahore, 1974, p. 52, 56

exchequer? It is not known how he himself might have justified such a blatant act of partisanship.

Ghulam Hussein was known to brandish a sharp, and at times a weirdly blunt, sense of humour of his own kind. Once he delivered the sermon at Friday congregational in Jhang and was walking home after the service when a Hindu businessman approached him and yelled Mr Hussein you talk a whole lot about Satan, have you ever seen one yourself? Ghulam Hussein signalled this man to follow him. Upon arriving home with him, Ghulam Hussein found a mirror, zoomed it upon the face of this man saying, 'look into it you will see the Satan'.

He was married to Sehba (1885–1960) and the couple had eight children, three girls and five boys. Two of their children, a daughter and a son, died young. After taking retirement from work in 1932, Ghulam Hussein moved to Qadian, the Ahmadiyah headquarter, where he had built a house in order to be able to serve the community. But both Ghulam Hussein and his wife Sehba found themselves on the wrong side of the border, when Punjab was partitioned in 1947. Stranded, the two were obliged to 'migrate' back to their ancestral hometown Jhang that had become a part of Pakistan. In 1949, their daughter, Amtul Hafeez (1924–2007), was married to become Abdus Salam's first wife.

Returning back to Mohammed Hussein, who had completed his education in Jhang and moved to Lahore in order to pursue a Bachelor's degree at one the colleges affiliated with the University of Punjab. He must have been motivated by the brilliant example set by his older brother. He got enrolled for an intermediate level program at the Islamia College, an institution founded in 1892 to promote higher education among Muslims.

Lahore, the capital city of Punjab, some 125 miles east of Jhang, offered an experience world apart to a young man used to living listlessly under parental care and discipline in Jhang. Mohammed Hussein landed in Lahore at the meeting point of two ages. Here, centuries of gifted architecture, dating back to the combined contribution of Mogul Empire and Muslim Sultanate, fused with European gothic styles brought by the British to create a world much bigger than the mere display of imperial palaces, fortifications, mosques and tombs. Lahore mushroomed out of its old city wall and twelve gates, proliferating into new suburbs, markets and avenues. There was the freedom to profess and propagate any faith as conveniently as getting education and employment, social justice and public health under common secular law.

Mohammed Hussein confronted questions and challenges, he lost track of his actual goal, and got himself distracted into an evangelical pastime. He was only 23, gliding into the venerable quest for religious truth. He spent nearly five years in the Punjab metropolis without ever completing his education. He failed to pick a certificate of completion for the year twelve intermediate or an undergraduate Bachelor's degree. He abandoned the religious fraternity of his parents and peers to embrace the Ahmadiyah, a schism breaking out of Muslim mainstream in eastern Punjab just a few years prior to his birth.

Like other clannish cultures, religious conversion amounted to a scandal in Jhang. In 1918, Mohammed Hussein returned home with a double disadvantage. He was an apostate and a dropout who wasted four valuable years of his youth without picking up a college certificate or the university degree. All at once, the impending hardship of unemployment looked him in the eye until his older brother, Ghulam Hussein, rescued him from the financial worry. Ghulam Hussein, then serving as the Inspector of Schools in a neighbouring district, helped his younger brother in finding work. At the High School in Jhang a vacancy appeared for the position of English Language teacher. An influential cousin arranged a letter of recommendation in favour of Mohammed Hussein from the District Judge. After that, Ghulam Hussein ensured the job interview for Mohammed Hussein. With good luck all the way, and despite the fact that Mohammed Hussein's own best mark in education did not go beyond a matriculation certificate of Year Ten, Mohammed Hussein won the position. He was assigned to teach English Language, Mathematics and Science to Year Nine students and General Knowledge to those in Year Ten. After working as High School teacher for a little while, Mohammed Hussein secured a more stable administrative position at the Inspectorate of Schools, Department of Education. His role entailed greater degree of influence and control compared to that of a high school teacher. He served the department for over three decades, in both Jhang and Multan.

In Punjab, the Department of Education, where Mohammed Hussein and his older brother Ghulam Hussein worked, was established in 1854. Initially, the department presided over a limited number of schools to popularise common education. Under the communal segmentation practiced earlier, Hindu children received instruction in Sanskrit and their Muslim counterparts in Persian. Once the experiment of common education succeeded beyond expectations, the door was opened to a unified vernacular system.

Upon receiving the first pay packet, Mohammed Hussein gave the whole amount to his sister and her daughter. Next month, he spent the money on tiling the floor at the local Ahmadiyah mosque. He was three months into service when the department awarded a back-dated pay rise to its employees. Mohammed Hussein worked out that arrears paid to him equalled the sum he had spent on fixing the mosque floor. To him, it was as if God had settled the account with him without any hold-up.[1] In view of circumstances surrounding him, he hoped for better times ahead. But he was not fully out of the woods yet; the blemish of conversion was set to haunt him for some time to come.

Soon as some level of stability was achieved in employment, it was time to get married and start the family. Mohammed Hussein was betrothed to the daughter of a maternal uncle, Ghulam Isa, who did not approve of the Ahmadiyah belief. In fact, other close relatives and acquaintances also viewed the Ahmadiyah as a divisive schism and heresy. Ghulam Isa became furious when Mohammed Hussein declined to offer the obligatory set of daily prayers behind his future father-in-law. Almost immediately, the wedding engagement was terminated and then the local clerics from Sunni mainstream proclaimed a *fatwa* declaring Mohammed Hussein a heretic and fit for social boycott, even punishment by death. Mohammed Hussein was damned to isolation because the Ahmadiyah did not have any sizeable presence in Jhang. Only the secular common law of the British saved him. On hot Friday afternoons, when Ghulam Hussein would be in Jhang, the two brothers walked to the twin town of Mighyana for the congregational service with few other members of the Ahmadiyah fraternity.[2]

In April 1922, Mohammed Hussein was married to Saeeda who passed away two years later while giving birth to a daughter who was named Masooda.[3] Mohammed Hussein became a single parent; he struggled to survive in the role.

Three years after the death of his wife, in May 1925, Mohammed Hussein got married again, now with Hajira (1903–1977). Hajira's father, Nabi Bakhsh (1868–1942), was among the founding members of the Ahmadiyah. Both Mohammed Hussein and Hajira had a loving and dedicated married life spanned over 40 years; the two had eight children, seven boys and a girl.

---

[1] Mohammed Hussein (1974): p. 29. Also in Abdul Hameed (circa 2000): pp. 10-11
[2] *Al Nahl* (Fall 1997): P. 26
[3] Abdul Ghani: Abdus Salam - A Nobel Laureate from a Muslim Country - A Biographical Sketch, Ma'aref (Printers) Limited, Karachi, 1982, p. 3

By instinct and temperament, Mohammed Hussein was more of a conformist, abiding by work and family routine besides observing his religious beliefs in letter and spirit. He lived in the old family house located in a relatively deprived quarter of the town. It was a two-storey house in which the ground floor was allotted to storage of old books, hand-written manuscripts and pharmacopeia; all dumped in a bleakly ventilated space. Mohammed Hussein, Hajira and their children lived in two-rooms on the upper floor. One room was occupied by Mohammed Hussein, the second by an increasing number of children, all squeezed together, with Hajira shuttling between the two the family lived happily and in contentment. Few years later, Mohammed Hussein managed to build a second house in a moderately better locality but the family did not move there for quite a while. Mohammed Hussein's older brother, Ghulam Hussein had retired from work and awaited completion of his own house in Qadian. Mohammed Hussein had given the new house to his brother.

'Our house was situated almost on the fringe, away from the main populated areas of the town next to barley and melon fields. My father built another house later on which in those days, when I was a child, looked quite far but was just a five-minute walk away. So we had two houses, old and new. The old house was very small, it comprised of two storeys. The lower storey so dark that nobody lived there, it was made up of mud bricks with no windows except for the doors. In my day, it used to be full of books and old manuscripts. A part of it was occupied by a hand-pump for water. We used to live in two rooms upstairs. When I say we, it means a big family including my father, my mother and three of my brothers and two sisters. We used to live essentially in one room; my father occupied the other where I slept sometimes. His room also had lots of old books and manuscripts which are unfortunately lost. Those manuscripts were handwritten. I say we were left with one room essentially because I don't remember if a part of the dark downstairs was ever used by us. In the old house, it was very cramped.

'For quite sometimes after the completion of the new house we did not move in it because it was occupied by my uncle, who became my father-in-law later on. He was the elder brother of my father and had retired by that time so he was given the house until he shifted over to Qadian. My father's adoration of his older brother was evident. For example, as children we used to feel envious when, in Multan, my father would send a crate of mangoes to our uncle before he got some for us.

'Three of my brothers were born in the new house and we lived there until my father won a promotion at work with transfer to Multan as in charge of the Divisional Inspector's office of education. By virtue of his work, both in Jhang and Multan, a good number of teachers visited our house. As I was going through the process of intermediate examinations, my father postponed moving the family over to Multan. He bore all the privations of living alone for my sake. I feel grateful for his decision. I still remember the day my examinations were over, the family moved from Jhang to Multan the same day. In those days, people used to travel from Jhang to Multan by train by changing at Shorkot or Khanewal and the journey used to take about six or seven hours. While alone in Multan, my father used to visit us in Jhang every week or fortnight.

'The old house was situated in a poorer locality, so the life was different in the new house. The upper storey of the old house does not exist anymore; it had to be brought down due to concerns for safety. This storey does not exist anymore. My father, in his last days, supervised the demolition of the upper storey. I also helped when I visited him from London. The lower level of the house, once occupied by my grandfather, is what has been left of this house'. Abdus Salam recounted the tale of his two family-homes in Jhang.[1]

It is worthwhile to note here that the Government of Pakistan had acquired Abdus Salam's old family house in Jhang to convert the site into a national monument. Somewhat ironically, Abdus Salam was neither born in this house and nor does the upper level where he lived with his parents and siblings exist anymore for it had been demolished. In fact, one of Abdus Salam's younger brothers had questioned the state acquisition of the house without any compensation whatsoever to the family'.[2]

III

In April 1959, Mohammed Hussein and his wife Hajira travelled to England to spend time with their son. By that time Mohammed Hussein had retired from work and Abdus Salam was well settled into the prestigious position he had won at the Imperial College and also bought a house of his own in Putney. Abdus Salam had fallen for Putney not only because the suburb was close to work, just

---

[1] Interviews 1984, Folder I: pp. 4-6, 9-11, 17 [Also see Folder II: p. 26
[2] Interviews 1984, Folder I: p. 3

across the river, but also due to its proximity to the Ahmadiyah mosque. He wanted to make the access easy for his parents when they visited him. As expected, his parents benefitted from the neighbourhood, going to mosque every now and then. Mohammed Hussein and Hajira spent a couple of years in England and returned to Pakistan after performing the out of season Islamic pilgrimage of *Umrah* in Saudi Arabia by the end of 1962.

Somewhere during the London visit of his parents, Abdus Salam had requested Mohammed Hussein to write down some sort of an autobiographical journal for the benefit of younger generations in the family. Mohammed Hussein granted the request by writing down an assortment of family related information along with the tale of his lifelong association with the Ahmadiyah. Above all, he shared anecdotes of his spiritual encounters like, for example, on occasions in his life, when he received divine guidance through visions and dreams. He heard voices and would be foretold about things to come. He believed that his conversion to the Ahmadiyah and the birth of Abdus Salam had been sanctified.

Within a few years after returning from England, in April 1969, Mohammed Hussein passed away. Abdus Salam decided to publish the memoirs left behind by his father. One of Mohammed Hussein's friends, Mohammed Ismail, an erstwhile journalist who used to work as a newspaper editor in Jhang, was commissioned to do the job. Abdus Salam also participated in the editorial process and, in this way, an authorised biography of Mohammed Hussein shaped up for publication in 1974.

Written in Urdu-language under the title 'Autobiography of Mohammed Hussein' the book provides a bona fide view into the range of cultural and religious values ordering the lives of Mohammed Hussein, his parents, peers and children. At the same time, the book sheds light upon various influences regulating Abdus Salam's own personality. Essentially, the bulk of profiles, anecdotes, memories and experiences reported in the book hold a strongly pro-Ahmadiyah sectarian tilt thus defining its core audience, accordingly. Often, the narrative sounds like a sermon promoting the Ahmadiyah brand of personal piety. In other words, the book tends to cut out considerable chunks of its audience among Muslim fans of Abdus Salam. Particularly, the recurring theme around Mohammed Hussein's devotion to the Ahmadiyah seems to mirror stringent hallmarks of an enthusiastic devotee. For a secular-liberal reader, the book provides a remarkable insight into the act of religious conversion and a wilful plunge into organised religion and evangelical penchant.

Typically, Mohammed Hussein belonged to the generation of people who, earlier in the 20th century, lived in a forward-looking secular, liberal and multicultural world and yet they yearned the past. What makes them behave in this manner? What compels them to keep looking backward? How could future be searched in the past? Questions of this kind hold tremendous value. Here we see the need to find satisfactory answers in the interest of diversity, openness, secular tolerance, democratic order and institutional accountability.

Mohammed Hussein's biography is a plain reflection of his profoundly religious opinion on a whole range of subjects; from the status to be accorded to women to the belief that the Ahmadiyah constituted the most genuine and authentic face of Islam. His judgment holds tremendous value towards building up a context around political choices made by Abdus Salam. Also, a detached case study of Mohammed Hussain's boundless devotion to the Ahmadiyah religious cause, set against the communal predicament facing Muslims of the subcontinent, provides many valuable clues into a deeper understanding of the age in which he lived.

Mirroring an utter neglect of women, in the world in which he lived, Mohammed Hussein's biography offers only a nominal mention of female players in the family. This absence of women from the mainstream of biographical scene is so striking that females simply do not make it to the family tree tracing the ancestry of Mohammed Hussein and his children back to ten generations living over eight centuries. Rather adamantly, the disregard is repeated by discounting the names of women in a more current family tree in the Urdu-language biography of Abdus Salam written by his brother, Abdul Hameed.[1] As if, despite giving birth to generation after generation of children, on the average up to half a dozen to every husband of a lifetime, women just simply did not exist. In the event of an occasional mention, females are not given full name; they are referred to by the common surname of *Begum*. Sadly, those missed out may just not be there anymore in anyone's memory among younger members and generations of the family, especially those young ones abroad who Abdus Salam intended to be the audience of his father's inspirational life story.

Mohammed Hussein was a staunch advocate of *purdah*, seclusion and confinement of women within well-defined boundaries, insisting that women were better off under Islam. In support of his position, he quoted examples from

---

[1] Abdul Hameed (circa 2000): page number not listed, please refer to the page next to the one with introductory note.

ancient Greece, medieval Russia, and 19th century England, where women were condemned to seclusion in the interest of a one-way sexual morality. He defended polygamy. He held the view that Europe, where the balance between male and female population turned disproportionate after World War I, could have been saved from inundation into the deluge of sexual permissiveness only if the outstanding women were consumed in polygamy.[1]

Young people, Mohammed Hussein pressed, should be despatched into wedlock at sixteen so that they are saved from the cascades of obscenity, pornography and gossips.[2] He suspected that the current craze to pile up capital and occupy posh residences was a clear sign of the approaching apocalypse.

As expected, he abhorred alcohol, gambling, racing and free mixing of sexes. For him, even lighter pastimes like cinema, playing cards and chess, kite-flying, and female children playing with dolls; all amounted to an evil wastage of time. He despised those bloody contests between specially trained animals otherwise so popular in his home town. Tobacco was another of his absolute taboos. He worried that modern societies were deeply steeped into those 'sins'. He believed that it was not possible to steer clear of moral accidents without very special blessing of God. Alcohol, in his list of prohibitions, was the mother of every shape and form of licentiousness.

At work, he interacted with teachers who visited him in connection with departmental business. Some of them sought transfers to reunite with families; others simply sniffed the possibility of shortcuts to favours beyond their entitlement and merit. Often, those fishing for undue favours attempted at offering bribe. Some of the teachers would come loaded with gifts, presents and souvenirs. Mohammed Hussein had issued strict advice to his children never to accept any gift whatsoever from any of those teachers. Sometimes, considering that Abdus Salam was a child, they would try to give him something, may be a rupee coin. Because his father had directed the children to steer clear of enticement, Abdus Salam would bluntly refuse to accept whatever was offered to him or just throw it away. He ended up tossing away money one his uncles once gave him, and affair caused a bit of stir within the family and Mohammed Hussein was obliged to redefine his piece of advice.[3]

---

[1] Mohammed Hussein (1974): pp. 123-124, 128
[2] Mohammed Hussein (1974): p. 113
[3] Interviews 1984: Folder II, pp. 4-5

Historically, this attitude of buying favour through enticement was not confined to Jhang, Punjab or the subcontinent alone; it was a worldwide expression of offering tribute to the powerful and influential. In the modern day west, where so much of pride is attached to ethical probity and performance, the exchange of favours is superbly camouflaged under the guise of networking. With a great deal of sophistication today, networking is lubricated with flower bouquets, chocolates and wines.

In his financial predicament, Mohammed Hussein juggled between the demands of a large family and meagre income. Battling with inducement was not easy in his situation. Nonetheless, he managed to stand firm and polite in declining offers made to him every now and then. While caring about the education and welfare of his children, he managed to stay down to earth. Luckily, he lived in an age of relatively plain lifestyles, at a time when the majority of ordinary citizens did not fall in tax brackets, they were free from everyday liabilities like mortgages and hefty costs of water, gas, electricity, council rates, condo-strata contributions, vehicle registry tokens, pink and green slips; and what not. On the contrary, public education up to year ten was almost free, and any costs involved at college and university levels were manageable. Today, living in the 21st century, the challenge confronting Mohammed Hussein and his children would have been tougher.

He lists many examples of his lifelong battle with and victory over temptation. For example, he longed to purchase a cow but did not have enough money to go for one of a quality breed. One day a headmaster of school arrived to present him with one. Mohammed Hussein declined the offer with thanks but in his heart he realised the vulnerability of financial squeeze besieging him. Grant me strength, my Lord! He remembered supplicating with his face turned towards the sky. Only a few days later he fell ill, ran high temperature and had to see Doctor Sham Das, the local General Practitioner. After check-up and prescription, the doctor asked Mohammed Hussein for a small favour. He was being transferred to another station at a short notice and hardly had time to sell his premier pair of cows, the doctor stated, adding that he would be ready to give the two at the price of one. He asked Mohammed Hussein to sound the neighbourhood and check if someone might be interested. Mohammed Hussein offered the doctor to buy one and proposed donating the other to local Cow

House run by the Hindu community. An agreeable deal was struck almost instantly.[1]

One winter morning, Mohammed Hussein went to attend the recitation of hymns at the local Hindu temple. He wore a blanket to fight the chill; still one of the school teachers in the assembly recognised him. When the recital ended and the audience began dispersing, this man greeted Mohammed Hussein and then offered him a barrel of pure butter oil as gift. Mohammed Hussein apologised stating that he was bound by a deal with the Almighty for the supply of such provisions. 'Who would look after me if I breach an enduring accord?' He asked the somewhat embarrassed school teacher.[2]

On another occasion, a school teacher arrived at his office and disregarded all norms of decency by offering hard cash to Mohammed Hussein straightaway. Almost instantly, Mohammed Hussein made up his mind to handle the situation somewhat differently. He feigned a readiness to accept the money provided the two of them were not caught while doing the transaction. Looking around, the teacher whispered that all was well and nobody looked at them. Are you sure? Mohammed Hussein asked him. Yes, I am, the teacher replied. Not even God is watching us? Are you sure? Mohammed Hussein shot back.[3]

At some point in time, the colonial government announced plans for subdivision and development of land near Jhang. A considerable chunk of real estate was offered to public servants and Mohammed Hussein stood fairly good chances of buying a 50-acres block at control rate provided he agreed to live locally. He weighed his options and worked out that the existing educational facility available to his children constituted a better investment and much bigger asset. He declined the offer.[4]

Mohammed Hussein reminisced about his meeting with a group of school teachers who had gathered to attend the Shah Jewna festival in Jhang. Somehow their conversation turned towards professional challenges, pressures of modern life and the financial plight of school teachers serving distant country locations. Mohammed Hussein took the queue and narrated to them his own life story. He recounted the challenge of meeting the average needs of a large household with small salary. He told his audience that contentment held the secret; it was the

---

[1] Mohammed Hussein (1974): p. 68
[2] Mohammed Hussein (1974): p. 70
[3] Mohammed Hussein (1974): p. 250
[4] Mohammed Hussein (1974): p. 75

power to resist temptation and live within means that saved him. Can any one of you cite an instance where I had accepted any undue favour? He asked them. After a brief spell of silence, one teacher recollected how Mohammed Hussein had returned, with thanks, the bunch of grapes this teacher had once offered him as a gift. Walk straight with dignity and you surely win the grace of God. He advised them.[1]

He guarded the ethical bar relentlessly. In his Annual Confidential Reports of the Education Department, Mohammed Hussein always won laurels for his superior work ethics. Sterling, in those reports, was the term used to describe his character as an officer.[2]

Every now and then, beneath its calling for the Ahmadiyah brand of religious piety, Mohammed Hussein's biography offers many warm-hearted examples of his compassionate personality. He would reach out to his family, circle of friends and colleagues. While at work, he did not discriminate on grounds of race, religion or class.

He exercised tremendous patience with his children, would address each of them with respect, never hit or slap a child. Often, he gave them worldly advice like, for example, upon the need to take utmost care while picking up friends in life. He urged his children to keep their utility items, books and stationery in tidy order. 'Find a place for everything and keep everything in its place'. He used to say.[3]

IV

It is time to get acquainted with the schismatic Ahmadiyah sect that Mohammed Hussein joined when he was 23 and then remained a staunchly steadfast member of the party the rest of his life. Essentially an introduction to the Ahmadiyah here is meant to provide a contextual appreciation of the religious faith to which Mohammed and his family adhered. At the same time, a comprehension of the troubled ties this sect has traditionally persevered with Muslim mainstream will assist the reader to take an informed view of several

---

[1] Mohammed Hussein (1974): p. 71
[2] Abdul Hameed (circa 2000): p. 12
[3] Abdul Hameed (circa 2000): pp. 12-13

decisions Abdus Salam made during the course of his over two decades of political association with Pakistan.

As a brain-child of Muslim preacher, Ghulam Ahmed (1835–1908), the Ahmadiyah was founded about the end of 19th century. A brief study of his legacy, in the following paragraphs of this section, will desist from passing any judgment on the theological merit of the product he offered. At the same time, this short portrayal will stay away from getting sucked into studies proposing that a considerable part of the package proposed by Ghulam Ahmed was suitably amended by his heirs. As making any broadly agreeable statement on matters religious is nearly unachievable, an effort has been made here to confine the description to the needs of Abdus Salam's biography as best as possible.

Ghulam Ahmed, a scion of the demoralised Mogul aristocracy, lived in Qadian, a small village in East Punjab. His ancestors owned a considerable estate but over time, after the decline and collapse of Mogul Empire, a good part of the clan ownership was lost to Sikh warlords who invaded Qadian in 1818. Ghulam Ahmed's father, Ghulam Murtaza, managed to strike a peace agreement with the Sikh leadership; he hoped to have his estate, about the size of 85 villages, restored in this way. He expressed a readiness to join the Sikh army. Only five villages had been returned to the family when the Sikh commander, Maharaja Ranjeet Singh (1780–1839), died and Punjab plunged into political vacuum soon to be filled in by a relatively long-term presence of the British. Ghulam Murtaza is understood to have made last minute bid at changing sides by supporting the British in the armed uprising of 1857, but he was outwitted by other embarrassingly more loyal and resourceful chieftains. Subsequently, He landed himself into a painfully protracted and expensive process of litigation with the British government. Often, the young Ghulam Ahmed was directed by his father to appear for court hearings at Dalhousie and Lahore. Over the years, Ghulam Ahmed witnessed his father degenerating into infirmity and bitterness. His father passed away in 1876. Then 37, Ghulam Ahmed suffered from a series of ailments; he also faced bankruptcy. Severe anxiety overtook him and his pious bent of mind pushed him deeper into religion. In what might have been a severe psychotic episode, he began hearing voices and divine messages of comfort and self-assurance. This hearing of voices continued the rest of his life as he considered it divine revelation.

Historically, he lived at a juncture in history when Muslims of India suffered from a severe psychological stress at national level, the British Empire had established its hold all over the subcontinent, the Salafi-Wahabi armed resistance in the northwest headed towards its suicidal conclusion, the political skill and military might of the British was a reality; and there was no comfort in sight. As if adversity was in short supply, Christian missions had arrived in India and they posed an added threat. Earlier in the 11th century, in the wake of Muslim invasion from Afghanistan and Central Asia, Punjab was known to have experienced mass conversion in favour of Islam. Now, it could go other way round.

Having received schooling in Arabic Language and Elementary Logic, Ghulam Ahmed developed a taste for catechism and theological reading. He went through the Koran and volumes of Islamic tradition, studied religious philosophy and comparative religion. At the age of 16 he is reported to have familiarised himself with the Bible and the Vedas. In 1864, he moved to the neighbouring town of Sialkot and briefly worked for the government. His stint in Sialkot enabled him to witness the ongoing Christian missionary activity from a fairly closer range. Occasionally, he availed the opportunity to debate with some of those missionaries and was deeply impressed by their eagerness to preach and proselytise. He was impressed by the disciplined manner in which they conducted their evangelical business. Why not defend Islam in the same way, he felt, with reason and rationale. He could see the advantage print media had come to offer. On a relatively broader scale, the contest with Christian missionaries was a compulsion arising out of the need to survive. Apart from Muslims, the resistance to Christian preaching was already evident among Hindu and Sikh communities where reformist *Arya Samaj* and *Akali* movements had begun picking up momentum.

He returned to Qadian and made a debut on the public scene by launching his treatise, the *Braheen-i-Ahmadiyah*, in four volumes, advocating the superiority of Islamic creed over contemporary religious thought. He argued 'very much like a medieval logician in love with his syllogisms' challenging 'to prove dialectically that no other religion could compare with Islam'.[1]

By this time, Punjab had become fairly well accustomed to printing press and the technology was in vogue all over government departments, educational institutions, publishing companies, local and national newspapers, journals, banks and private businesses. Then, print media served as an efficient weapon in the religious warfare triggered by Christian missions. As a prolific writer,

---

[1] Freeland Abbot: Islam and Pakistan, Cornell University Press, Ithaca, New York, 1968, p. 148

Ghulam Ahmed authored books, pamphlets and fliers; mostly in the contemporary thick of fiercely polemical Urdu-language, a glutinous amalgamation of words borrowed predominantly from Arabic, Persian and Sanskrit.

After securing a small niche of followers, Ghulam Ahmed felt increasingly confident. He began proposing doctrinal reform in some of the age-old beliefs held among Muslim mainstream. He took a rather bold position on matters otherwise believed to have been settled long ago. For example, he redefined the concept of finality in Islamic prophethood. Traditionally, the overwhelming majority among Muslims held the view that the purpose of prophethood, as a vehicle of divine revelation, had achieved finality with the advent Islamic era. They believed that Koran embodied the completion of divine law and, as such, Prophet Mohammed, in his role as the final bearer of God's word, precluded the scope or need for any additional prophet-hood. This venerable concept had been very highly valued among Muslims for it furnished them with the pride of ideological superiority, cultural integrity and distinction.

Ghulam Ahmed defined finality as the 'seal of completion' rather than the termination of divine revelation. Actually, in doing so, he justified his own claim as a regular recipient of divine revelation. He advocated that prophethood was permissible in Islam as long as new prophets did not change the Koranic law.

Next, he offered a novel explanation relating to the crucifixion and resurrection of Jesus Christ. As an expression of passion in religious syncretism, the majority among Muslims trusted that Jesus Christ had been saved from the Cross and escorted to Heaven in order to return to earth and conclusively exterminate the evil. Precisely how, why and when such an elaborately quixotic fancy had made it to the reservoir of Muslim memory is not very hard to sort out. Often in the past, especially during the course of testing times, the oppressed and humiliated masses of people have yearned for the coming out of restorers, redeemers, mightier champions, the Mahdi and the Messiah to 'fill the world with equity and justice' and destroy the satanic partnership of Gog-Magog. In the past, when Muslim hold on Spain was reduced to Grenada, the faithful 'felt grievously the need for such a restorer and Mahdi'. They rested their hopes, as in other similar conditions, upon oral traditions attributed to the Prophet.[1] This age-old human desire to seek out redemption under the guidance of promised

---

[1] Shorter Encyclopaedia of Islam; edited on behalf of the Royal Netherlands Academy by A. A. R. Gibb and J. H. Kramers, Leiden, 1953, pp. 312-313

Messiahs and Mahdis seemed to have conveniently made it to Muslim psyche from its Biblical precursor.

At a time when Mogul and Safavid Empires had fallen in India and Iran, the Ottoman Empire tottered in Turkey; the stressed outpost-Mogul Muslim mind ached for a redeemer. It was expected that at an appointed time in the 14th *Hijra*, coinciding with 19th century of Christian era, Jesus Christ would descend upon the eastern minaret of the cathedral mosque in Damascus, Syria. An alliance between Jesus and Mahdi, the Muslim liberator scheduled to appear about the same time, would save the world from imminent obliteration at the hand of evil forces.

According to Ghulam Ahmed, Jesus Christ had been saved from crucifixion, nursed to health by some of his disciples enabling him to migrate all the way from Palestine to Kashmir where he lived up to a ripe age of 120 years.[1]

Here, Ghulam Ahmed seemed to appreciate the plain fact that a return of Jesus Christ to deliver the followers of Islam from their tribulations at the end of days did not make much sense, it amounted to vindicating only the Christian faith. Possibly, he intended to clear the deck to establish his own claim. In doing so, he made a two-in-one offer, that is, by promoting a Messiah-Mahdi union and, accordingly, claimed himself to be both. He considered himself, as a Muslim, to be better qualified to deliver than Jesus Christ who owned an exclusive pre-Islamic law of his own. Howsoever convoluted this theological complexity may sound, he went through the daunting drill in order to work out the logic tying up his various claims by redefining, all the way, settled doctrines relating to the crucifixion of Jesus Christ to the finality of Islamic prophethood. Some scholars hold the view that a part of his claims, especially those relating to derivative prophethood, were not as lucid as interpreted by some of his over-zealous successors afterwards. Often, his son, Bashiruddin Ahmed, is held responsible for going too far in glorifying the father.[2]

Finally, Ghulam Ahmad redefined the concept of Islamic holy war, *jihad*. He abrogated the militant part of it. In the age of scientific discovery and technological advancement, he stated, pen was the chief weapon of *jihad*. He

---

[1] This view of Ghulam Ahmed coincided with the publication of comparable research conducted by the 19th century Russian scholar Alexander Notowitch (Holger Kersten 1996).

[2] Yohanan Friedmann: Prophecy Continuous - Aspects of the Ahmadi Religious Thought and Its Medieval Background, Oxford University Press, 1989, pp. 151-162

abolished the concept of holy war with weapons.[1] This elegant preference of scholarship over military warfare did not impress the majority among Muslims, especially those who abhorred British colonial rule and trusted *jihad* as one of the five pillars of Islamic faith and identity. Ghulam Ahmed seemed honestly convinced about the invincibility of the British in a foreseeable future. He appreciated the government neutrality in religion, especially the freedom the British had granted to profess and propagate.

Here, as a matter of historical fact, Ghulam Ahmed was not alone in proposing peace with the British. One of his contemporary, the towering educationist, Syed Ahmed (1817–1898), had been equally vocal in advocating the compromise. But then Syed Ahmed was careful not to go as far as proposing an entire package of doctrinal reform in Islam.

A greater part of Ghulam Ahmed's final years was spent in debating with Christian missionaries, Hindu reformists and the orthodox leadership among fellow Muslims. Some of those debates prolonged beyond the staying power of his audience, and turned into vile bitterness. He was in the habit of delivering curses upon those who challenged him. Every now and then, he prophesied death and destruction of one or another of his opponents. In the summer of 1893, his debating encounter with a Christian missionary is reported to have gone on uninterrupted for twelve days. He provoked his opponent to seek 'divine wrath' in order to determine the victor. It seems the Church Missionary Society was aware of Ghulam Ahmed's vulnerability and heretic ranking among Muslims. 'Though he has made a great stir, his actual followers are extremely few' observed the Society report, adding 'we told him that while the children of darkness might curse each other, we followed the Prince of Peace, and we were commanded to bless and curse not'.[2] Ostensibly, the acceptance of challenge put up by Ghulam Ahmed was declined on grounds of its pagan merit.

While locked in a vociferous campaign in defence of Islam, Ghulam Ahmed isolated himself from the main block of Muslim clergy. He was judged as the architect of a dangerous deviation in Islam. In the end, he made enemies all over the place; among Hindus as well as Christians. At times, his penchant for calling

---

[1] It was not a new idea, medieval Europe had already debated the supremacy of pen over sword

[2] Spencer Lavan: The Ahmadiyah Movement - A History and Perspective, Delhi, 1974, p. 31-32

names and invoking divine wrath upon opponents landed him in legal difficulties.[1]

Ghulam Ahmed launched the Ahmadiyah on 12 January 1889, the day his son, Bashiruddin Ahmed (1989–1965) was born. He claimed the birth of his son had been foretold. On 23 March 1889, he began taking the formal oath of allegiance from his followers. Initially, the response to his call came only from districts neighbouring Qadian. Five years on, the numerical strength of the formally enrolled members of his party stood just around 300. Less than a hundred people attended the annual gathering, convened in Qadian, in the winter of 1891. By 1901, the number of the Ahmadiyah faithful was recorded just above one thousand. In 1905, the party organ, *Al-Hakam*, originally launched 1897, achieved a print order of 900.[2]

Those joining the ranks mostly came from peasantry and junior ranks of public service, only few of them held professional background. Mohammed Hussein joined the Ahmadiyah twenty-five years after its formation, and by that time the numerical strength of the faithful might have doubled, even tripled; the figure can be safely placed anywhere on the lower side of five-thousand mark. On the average, the majority of the followers were 'individuals who preferred to accept the authoritarian leadership and charismatic programme of the Promised Messiah' while some others simply sought commitment 'to a new Islamic outlook'.[3]

A general survey, conducted across personal accounts and memoirs of the faithful, published in the party organ *Al-Fazal,* reveals that an overwhelming majority of the founding members were driven to join the Ahmadiyah, just like Mohammed Hussein, after receiving signals in their dreams. Someone with a secular disposition will find it hard to understand the digging out of religious truth by way of dreams and hearing of voices. But such an experience could be attributed either to a state of 'heightened imagination' as depicted by Russian writer Anton Chekov (1860–1904) in his famous tale The Black Monk or it remains a subject for psychologists to explore.

---

[1] Yohanann Friedman (1989): P. 10
[2] Spencer Lavan (1974): p. 44
[3] Spencer Lavan (1974): p. 47

V

From 1914 to 1925, Mohammed Hussein's life was a testing time of hardship, suffering and anxiety. He had been away from home for many years and returned with the stigma of religious conversion instead of being decorated with better education. He got married, fathered a daughter at the cost of his wife. He was an untrained single-parent facing religious persecution, struggling to hold on to the freshly found employment and in need of skills to demonstrate his worth.

Worrying about the health and welfare of his new-born daughter, he begged God to grant him a spouse 'who could give birth to an illustrious son of unique intellectual capabilities'. He desired to have a son 'in whom he could invest and work on to develop a great man to nullify his own image of failure in life'.[1] He was 36 when a match, within the Ahmadiyah fraternity, shaped up for him. On 12 May 1925, he got married to Hajira. He began settling down into a regular routine around family and work, well on the way to survive religious persecution. His newly found religious fraternity, work and wife gave him the hope that he might be on the threshold of change for better times ahead, a way out of protracted tribulation.

One way of taking a positive view of his stint in Lahore was the benefit of being able to build up lifelong friendships with of some prominent members of the Ahmadiyah. He became acquainted with Zafarullah Khan (1893–1985), the young lawyer who had returned from London, after being called to the bar at Lincoln's Inn, and was well on the course to making an elaborately stretched-out high-profile career in public life.

Hajira (1903–1977) was the younger daughter of Nabi Bakhsh (1867–1942), serving as land records officer in the Department of Revenue. Nabi Bakhsh was a *Hafiz*, that is, he memorised the Koran by heart. He was venerated as a companion of Ghulam Ahmed, the founder of the Ahmadiyah. Hajira had three brothers and six sisters. One of her brothers, Fazalur Rahman, made history in Ahmadiyah chronicles by pioneering the party's missionary activity in Africa.

After the celebration of her wedding in Jhang, Hajira departed to spend, as was customary in those days, the next forty days with her parents who lived in

---

[1] Abdul Ghani: Abdus Salam - A Nobel Laureate from a Muslim Country - A Biographical Sketch, Karachi, 1982, p. 3

Santokh Das, south of Jhang. Within a few days of her departure, Mohammed Hussein had a psychic experience he would rejoice the rest of his life. It happened on 3 June 1925 when he was in the midst of early evening prayer service at the mosque. He recited the Koranic verse *'And those who say, Our Lord, grant us of our wives and children the delight of our eyes, and make us a model for the righteous'*.[1] Precisely at that moment he saw an angel appearing on the scene and handing over to him a male child by the name of Abdus Salam.

Mohammed Hussein was overjoyed by the vision and took it as an answer to his prayer and supplication. He was hardly into the third week of his wedding with Hajira and there was this vision with an exhilarating piece of news. Only the mention of a son cheered him up as he had been longing to have one. He began reading deeper into the encounter. As a loyal citizen of the British raj, Mohammed Hussein attached significance to having the prophecy on 3 June 1925, the birthday of King of England, an auspicious occasion celebrated all over the empire; surely it meant something much bigger.[2] An answer to his supplication had finally arrived; he could place the whole episode in perspective. His wife being the daughter of a saintly person meant the couple would be granted with a very special male offspring. Although this tradition of prophecies about male heirs could be traced all the way back to Biblical era, Mohammed Hussein lived in a state of mind that he believed it to be a turning point in his life. He felt extraordinarily privileged for being foretold about the birth as well as name of his son, Abdus Salam.

First thing, next morning, Mohammed Hussein wrote Hajira a detailed letter about his vision. Later in the day, he went to see his friend Nasir Ali, a member of the Ahmadiyah comradeship in Jhang. Ignoring the June heat, Mohammed Hussein cycled all the way about three miles. 'I have come to share a piece of news with you', he told his baffled friend how, in the midst of prayer, an angel had appeared on the scene and handed over to him a male child named Abdus Salam. He requested Nasir Ali to bear witness when time came for it. In his memorial essay on Mohammed Hussein, published in the party organ on 2 May 1969, Nasir Ali validated the story.[3]

On 29 January 1926, Hajira gave birth to a male child in Santokdas. Mohammed Hussein wrote a letter to the Ahmadiyah leader requesting, out of

---

[1] The Koran 25:75

[2] Mohammed Hussein (1974): p. 47

[3] Mohammed Hussein (1974): p. 258

sheer devotion, a name for the child. He also described how the birth of the newborn had been foretold. When God Himself has named the child, how can we change it? The leader of the Ahmadiyah replied rather expertly.

Although Mohammed Hussein had the prophecy, he did not seem to know much about the destiny of his promised son beyond a wishful anticipation. For nearly two decades, from 1926 to 1945, the best he could dream about was a career for Abdus Salam in the coveted Indian Civil Service. On other occasions, Mohammed Hussein wished Abdus Salam to achieve success and fame just as he had witnessed in the rise of Zafarullah Khan who, starting as a young lawyer in Lahore became a Member of Viceroy's Council within a matter of two decades.

Mohammed Hussein's desire to find a more accurate validation of his vision persisted with the evolution of Abdus Salam's professional career. Years later, when Abdus Salam won the chair at London's Imperial College (1957) and was elected Fellow of the Royal Society (1959), Mohammed Hussein revisited the regal connection of his vision.[1] On other occasions, he tended to go by professional triumphs of his son. When Abdus Salam was decorated with the Atoms for Peace award (1968) for his committee work at the United Nations, Mohammed Hussein focussed upon the literal meaning of his son's name, *the Servant of Peace*.

Occasionally, a considerable amount of folklore surrounded the class of Abdus Salam's doctoral work at Cambridge. In his biography, Mohammed Hussein relates how research done by Abdus Salam turned out to be beyond the grasp of his supervisors in England and it had to be despatched to Albert Einstein, then unwinding in Princeton, and so on.[2] It remains a mystery though as to how and why Abdus Salam, the sponsor of Mohammed Hussein autobiography, and otherwise so firm about picking up frailties of reporting, overlooked the need to correct or comment upon those passages in his father's biography.

In all probability, it is the ambiguity attached to visions and prophecies that makes the experience worthwhile from a religious point of view. Sadly, Mohammed Hussein did not live long enough to witness the formal recognition of his son's epoch-making contribution to the annals of 20th century science. By the time, Abdus Salam won the Nobel Prize; he stood marginalised in Pakistan for being perceived as an opponent of the country's drive to gain nuclear parity

---

[1] Mohammed Hussein (1974): p. 47
[2] Mohammed Hussein (1974): p. 45-46

with India. Suddenly then, some of his enthusiasts woke up to the meaning and significance of name the *Servant of Peace*. Even when Abdus Salam yearned to win the prize, especially after coming so close to sharing it in 1957, none of the interpretations relating to his father's vision ever hinted in the direction of Nobel accolade accorded to him in October 1979.

No matter what those interpretations, relating to his father's vision of June 1925, aimed at, Abdus Salam loved his name. 'My father always attached a special significance to my name Abdus Salam'. He recalled, adding that after winning the Nobel Prize, when he went to Morocco someone applied the local tradition of nomenclature and felt only Abdus Salam was not enough. He was named as Ahmed Abdus Salam. 'I said it is a good name and I felt proud of the addition but as I don't want a change because of the vision of my father, you may call me Abu Ahmed Abdus Salam which is correct'. When he visited Dubai, the prefix Mohammed was attached to his name. In Kuwait, keeping in line with the last name of his father, he became Abdus Salam Hussein. It was all under the influence of manner in which people were named in Arab countries. 'Now on my Arabic pad in Trieste, I have inscribed it as Mohammed Abdus Salam; how can one refuse the name Mohammed'. He stated.[1]

Between 1926 and 1939, Mohammed Hussein and Hajira had seven more children, one daughter and six sons, all after the birth of Abdus Salam. In this way, Mohammed Hussein had nine children with his two wives. He loved all of his children without ever compromising on the unimpeachable uniqueness of promise associated with Abdus Salam. Did Mohammed Hussein work as hard on any other of his children as he did in the case of Abdus Salam? Anyone reading the biography of Mohammed Hussein would know the answer to this question but Abdus Salam had more to say. First of all, he agreed that the vision of his father carried a great amount of weight. 'I think the reason is I was the first child. I was the only child for a long time. My younger brother was born about five-year latter. Also, when my brothers started going to school, our father had been transferred to Multan where atmosphere was very different from Jhang'.[2] Abdus Salam speculated fully ignoring the fact that his half-sister Masooda, born in 1922 by the first wife of Mohammed Hussein, was the first child. Similarly, he overlooked his real sister, Hameeda, born about a year after him in 1927. Optimistically, one can only guess that he was not in the same state of mind

---

[1] Interviews 1984: Folder II, pp. 13-14
[2] Interviews 1984: Folder II, pp. 17-18

under which family trees were sketched out in those days, with an utter disregard of female ancestors, siblings and children. Abdus Salam was asked if his father ever talked, in the family or with children when they grew up, about the psychological misery he went through for five years from 1920 to 1925.

'No, he never told us about it, nothing more than what he mentions in his memoirs. He must have felt the tragedy very strongly. We never heard much about it from him'. Abdus Salam replied.[1]

In fact, Abdus Salam's first biographer, Abdul Ghani, had the privilege of taking this matter up with Mohammed Hussein. It was way back in 1964, many years before the biography Abdul Ghani wrote in the wake of Abdul Salam's Nobel Prize. Mohammed Hussein is reported to have opened up about the trauma he suffered in the death of his first wife, Saeeda. This personal tragedy overtook him against the backdrop of his failure in picking up any certificate or degree in Lahore. Accordingly, Mohammed Hussein confided about taking a deeper plunge into religion and profuse supplication before God. Abdul Ghani points toward a state of mind in which Mohammed Hussein 'solicited soul searching and fervent prayers' begging God to 'supplement his impoverished life with another spouse' and 'an illustrious son of unique intellectual capabilities' so that 'his own image of failure in life' is rectified.[2]

This observation about the combined effect of Mohammed Hussein's failure to complete education in Lahore, death of his wife and religious persecution in Jhang, back in 1922; all paving the way for him to dream about pulling off the miracle of change and correction tends to fit into psychological logic. When Abdus Salam was invited to comment upon it, he avoided to either accept or reject outright the construction of Abdul Ghani. Abdus Salam agreed that his father's inability to obtain either a certificate for the intermediate level or a Bachelor's degree in Lahore was bound to affect him in some way. 'He may have felt sorry, it is possible, but again, we never heard much about it from him. I don't know what the situation was for him, and he never discussed it with us in detail'. Abdus Salam stated with a conjecture that the major conflict he believed his father had in Lahore was 'perhaps the controversy relating to the Ahmadiyah'.[3]

---

[1] Interviews 1984: Folder II, pp. 13, 26
[2] Abdul Ghani (1982): p. 3
[3] Interviews 1984, Folder II, pp. 24-26

Abdus Salam was requested to comment on his father's exacting keenness over a career in the coveted Indian Civil Service. He believed it made sense because public service was one of the best and most treasured options available in those days.

VI

Life, people say, changed for them forever the moment they embraced their first-born child. It is hard to guess how much of Mohammed Hussein's life changed when he carried his first-born child, Masooda, in 1922. Most certainly his life did translate into an endless revolution the day he first took Abdus Salam in his arms. He had the reason and faith to take parental responsibility. His attention to detail in monitoring and keeping a track of Abdus Salam's education, from the very outset onward, offers parents and educational planners a most remarkable case study in success.

Like Isaac Newton (1643–1726), who was born prematurely to give the nurses attending his mother a dread that the new-born might not live at all,[1] Abdus Salam started with a scrawny physique and encountered health issues but he managed to stumble through despite a lack of paediatric care in Jhang. Mohammed Hussein saw the link between physical fitness and healthy mind; he began giving his little son massages with butter and steam baths.[2] No matter what the logic behind this recipe, it worked and Abdus Salam gained weight, even picked up a prize, his first ever, at a local contest of child health. Baby Abdus Salam turned out to be the toddler in the pink; he measured well and had the right weight. He was chubby enough to catch the attention of judges from the local health department. As often is the case with chubby children, he turned lean and light over the next few years permitting the gymnastic team at his school to allot him the top slot in their pyramid displays.[3]

Still, Abdus Salam's childhood was not silky all the way; he had his share of a few mishaps. First, he hit upon a container of poison pellets meant to ward off mice, took the find as some sort of minty toffee and swallowed a few. He was

---

[1] Louis Trenchard More: Isaac Newton: A Biography, Dover Publications Inc., New York., 1962, p. 4
[2] Mohammed Hussein (1974): pp. 36 and 250
[3] Interviews 1984: Folder I, p. 29-31

rushed to the doctor for stomach wash.[1] Then, he gave his mother a real scare by delaying speech; she panicked and feared her son might be dumb. It turned out to be only a false alarm. Next, while he was grappling to find something at the top of a tall shelf in the house, a sharp geometrical instrument fell upon his face striking his right eye. Luckily, the accident did not cause any big damage other than a minor hole in the eye, his vision was saved. 'I still have a puncture in this eye', he remembered in 1984. On another occasion, he got his hand caught in the bicycle chain, had a cut and dazed off for a while.[2]

Breaking the age-old family tradition, Abdus Salam was not admitted to a mosque school. Instead, the foundation stone of his education was laid by a woman. His mother familiarised him with Arabic alphabet so that he could start reading and reciting the Koran. Once fluent, he moved on to reading and writing in Urdu, the lingua franca taking its alphabet and script from Arabic as well as Persian languages.

Seeing that Abdus Salam had picked up pace in reading, Mohammed Hussein arranged a steady supply of story books to lure his son into the enchanting world of written word. Very soon the little boy devoured so much that he felt bored with formula themes and demanded change and variety. In a matter of few months, he exhausted the stock of story books and journals available at the local District Board library. In 1936, Mohammed Hussein received from one of his friends a set of collected works in Urdu literature, including an anthology compiled by Allama Tajwar Najibabadi (1890–1951) along with classical elegies written by eminent poets like Mir Babar Ali Anees (1803–1874) and Mirza Salamat Ali Dabir (1803–1875). Abdus Salam went through most of those and refined his literary taste at a much early stage in life.

He was admitted first to the Khiva Gate Primary School and then, at the age of six, moved to the Municipal Board Middle School where the headmaster enrolled him straight into Year Four. Both his father and uncle had studied in this school. Situated in the old quarter of the town, those schools dated back to the previous century. On his way to school every morning, Abdus Salam walked behind a group of Hindu boys who memorised multiplication tables by repeating the numbers in a loud chorus. Mohammed Hussein was pleasantly amazed to discover one day that his son memorised the tables up to forty within a matter of few days.

---

[1] Abdul Hameed (circa 2000): p. 26
[2] Interviews 1984: Folder I, pp. 27-28

Wishing his son to learn beyond school curriculum, Mohammed Hussein would take Abdus Salam on bicycle rides into the world around Jhang where the magic of industrial age engineering had already pulled out quite a few miracles. Both father and son would picnic around bridges, flour mills, cotton ginning factories, railway engines, automobiles and other products of electrical and mechanical technology. It was the rural Punjab, placed between two world wars, falling in love with new farming techniques. With those cycling excursions, Mohammed Hussein aimed at giving the little boy a taste of the experimental side in life. Abdus Salam remembered the day when he had accompanied his father to see waterworks and the power generation plant recently constructed at Trimmu, at the point where the two rivers *Jhelum* and *Chenab* merged above Jhang. Abdus Salam set upon preparing a clay model of the barrage first thing after they returned home.

Occasionally, Abdus Salam contributed to the children's page of a local newspaper, *Urooj*, or the Rise. In this way, Abdus Salam made it to print media when he was about eight or nine.[1]

'On the way back home from one of those trips, I remember, we stayed for an evening meal at the construction contractor's place. There, for the first time, I had potato chips, fried in front of us in the open. It was a totally new experience for me'. Abdus Salam reminisced afterwards.[2]

Every evening, Mohammed Hussein asked his son about the day at school. He would impress upon Abdus Salam for the need to prepare his lessons a day in advance. He wanted his son to wield the advantage of having prior idea of what would unfold in the classroom the following day. Control over things makes life much easier, he taught his son. Abdus Salam was encouraged to be in bed early in order for him to feel fresh next morning. Please wake me up at four, he would ask his mother before going to bed. His older sister Masooda woke him up and fixed the kerosene lamp for him. Many localities in Jhang had yet to enter the age of electricity and other amenities of modern civilisation. Early in the morning, during summer, Abdus Salam sat in front of the window to inhale occasional whiffs of cooler breeze. He believed it was an ideal time to study with none distraction other than a distant fading out noise of barking dogs, laughing hyenas and howling jackals. For a change, sometimes, Abdus Salam went out to

---

[1] Mohammed Hussein (1974): p. 342
[2] Interviews 1984: Folder II: p. 29

read a book under the street lamp. When his classmates discovered about it, they gave him the nickname *kada*, a nocturnal moth attracted to light.[1]

Soon after starting school, Abdus Salam settled into a watertight discipline that helped him the rest of his life. First he attended the pre-dawn prayer service and then went through a reading session, had his breakfast and got ready for school. In the beginning he walked to school, afterwards his father bought him a bicycle. He returned home later in the afternoon, took a brief break before doing the homework, played around, had dinner and went to bed. With minor readjustments, this regime stayed more or less unchanged in the following years and decades of his life.

'We did not have electricity, not even when we shifted to our new house. I think we did not have electric supply the whole stretch of my stay in Jhang. I used to get up at three in the morning sometimes. My parents woke me up then my sister would fix the hurricane lamp for me. Being very dear to my father, the whole family looked after me quite well. After my father, I was the most important person in the family'. Abdus Salam remembered.[2]

One day this routine was disrupted by the death of Baba Bakha, an elderly member of the family. Abdus Salam remembered Baba Bakha, an uncle who enthralled children with his endless stock of folktales and melodious songs. Baba Bakha did not have any children of his own yet he was an adept charmer to the young ones. On the morning of Baba Bakha's death, Abdus Salam got ready for school. His mother politely explained the need for him to stay home on that day for it was an occasion to mourn the departure of a grand old man.[3]

By the time he sat for Year Five examination, Abdus Salam was well on the way to winning positions, prizes and awards. Some of his earlier achievements included medals in calligraphy and map-drawing. At the age of 12 he began qualifying for scholarship grants thus sharing the cost of education with his parents.

His main competitors at school came from the Hindu community. He remembered two of his school mates, Bodhraj and Amir Chand. Like Mohammed Hussein, the father of Bodhraj, Ram Piyara, who owned a chickpea salad stall outside the school, kept asking teachers, again and again, to provide necessary guidance and support to his son so that the boy studied well and

---

[1] Zakaria Virk: *Ramooz-i-Fitrat*, Kingston (Canada), 1996, p. 196
[2] Interviews 1984: Folder I: pp. 6, 14
[3] Mohammed Hussein (1974): p. 49

became a big officer. It was an attitude driven by the belief that education changed family fortunes. Both Abdus Salam and Bodhraj were friends and sometimes the two played together. Abdus Salam did not forget the older sister of Bodhraj who avoided physical contact with anyone outside the Hindu community; it amounted to a brush with impurity. As a result, she took it incumbent upon her to perform the act of ablution by bathing even when the Muslim playmate of her brother would accidently run into her. While playing around, it was not possible sometimes for the wildly running boys to observe her oddly conservative peculiarity. In the end the poor girl became so obsessed with water that she contracted hydrophobia and died young. Bodhraj, a couple of years later, moved to a private school funded by the local Hindu business. Somehow the change did not help him and, about 1940, he too died after a brief illness.[1]

Amir Chand continued to compete with Abdus Salam as the two were together in the college. His family moved to Delhi when rioting and communal violence erupted in the wake of partition in Punjab. Fearing for life, nearly all the Hindu and Sikh residents of Jhang were obliged to run away from what had been home for generations. On a visit to India, Abdus Salam rediscovered him after forty years. At that time, Amir Chand was serving a senior position at the Geological Survey Department of India. Abdus Salam was amazed to see how the ageing members of those Hindu and Sikh families preserved the memory of Jhang they had left behind. They had a formal Jhang fraternity in New Delhi, holding regular functions, sharing a newsletter from time to time.[2]

Abdus Salam was invited to portray the building of his school. 'It still exists, a very old building, perhaps from early British days. It was renovated only recently. Now raised to the High School standard it used to be Middle School at that time'. He replied, and then paused before topping up the memory of his school with a more recent episode relating to the Government of Pakistan. Upon winning the Nobel Prize, Abdus Salam was invited to visit home by General Ziaul Haq (1924–1988), the military ruler of Pakistan. Abdus Salam replied that he surely would and then requested the General to consider celebrating the occasion by allocating a grant of ten million rupees[3] in order to fund scholarship grants to talented students for research in science and technology. Abdus Salam

---

[1] Interviews 1984: Folder II: p. 16 [Also see Folder I: p. 14]
[2] Interviews 1984: Folder II: p. 16
[3] About $60,000 in June 2020

expressed a readiness to put his 'prize money into the fund'. Apparently, the General supported the idea and confirmed it in a cable to Abdus Salam. Later, when the two met in Islamabad, their first ever meeting, and Abdus Salam raised the subject of scholarship grants, the General advised that the 'Governor of Punjab will follow it up with you on your visit to Lahore'.

Once in Lahore, the Governor of Punjab, General Sawar Khan (1924-), asked Abdus Salam how much was he donating to the proposed fund? Abdus Salam quoted his share of the prize amounting to just over half a million rupees. In his speech at the state banquet, held in the honour of Abdus Salam, the Governor announced that that the government would match the figure the Professor had indicated to donate. 'I was shocked and felt extremely unhappy. I felt the government should keep its money and I will keep mine'. Abdus Salam remembered.[1] After that, when the Government of Pakistan asked him about the amount of money committed by the Governor of Punjab, Abdus Salam proposed the sum to be donated to the refurbishment of facilities, especially science laboratories, at his old school in Jhang. 'They acted on the advice and that was how the school got renovated'.[2]

Like other school buildings dating back to the final decades of 19th century, the one where Abdus Salam studied in Jhang had many classrooms and corridors though the teaching aides were limited to chalkboards, students sat on scuffing jute rugs; laboratories had only few spirit lamps, test tubes and thermometers.[3]

Abdus Salam held a very high opinion of his school teachers, he remembered each one of them by name and fondly, including the Attendance Officer Sher Afzal who wrote poetry in Punjabi. He reminisced about his mathematics teacher Maulvi Abdul Latif who once gave him a *paisa* as reward for solving a problem promptly. Given the meagre income of school teachers, it was the 'maximum he could afford', Abdus Salam recalled. He remembered the eyes of his loveable teacher getting moist with emotion. Another of the teachers was so delighted to read an essay Abdus Salam had written that he wished to give the promising pupil a gold coin *ashrafi* in reward.[4]

---

[1] With his prize money Abduls Salam set up a small foundation to award scholarship grants as far as possible.
[2] Interviews 1984: Folder I: pp. 22-25
[3] Interviews 1984: Folder I: pp. 25
[4] Interviews 1984: Folder I: p. 30-31

In his early school days, he used to be very particular in getting to the correct meaning of terms. One of the teachers one day expressed his doubt whether a certain word of Urdu language originated from Arabic or Persian. Abdus Salam remembered how restless he felt until lunch break when he ran home to check the Persian language dictionary. Upon failing to find the word, he rushed back to school and informed the teacher about his research asking if the ruling out of Persian meant the correct answer was Arabic? He was in such a state of excitement that his teacher, about to drink water from the glass he was holding, calmed him down. 'Son, could you give me a moment, let me have some water first', the teacher said.

Did Abdus Salam get any special level of treatment from teachers due to his father's position at the local education office? He felt it might be true only partly but, in the end, his own performance made the difference. 'Bright students always get more attention. Since my father worked at the local Inspectorate of Schools, his word carried a great deal of weight. They listened to him more carefully than they might have to other parents. My father encouraged teachers to discuss academic matters with me and suggest new material to read. As a result of this, at quite an early stage, I had gone through a vast amount of books'. He replied.[1]

Did Abdus Salam participate in sports? Not exactly, in fact his daily routine had cut him out of the sporting age group. Many boys in his age group and neighbourhood were duty bound to help out their fathers involved in various small trades like tailoring, welding, brew-baking, fuel-gathering, straw-making, weaving, pottery and so on, in the town. Casting bronze in those days was a prominent trade making great noise during the night when hot metal was beaten rhythmically by men who slept in daytime after taking opium. 'Play, in those days used to be just running in the nearby streets. We had a football team comprising of older boys. I used to join them'. He recalled.

'Since I was good at school, number of my class-fellows would come to our house in succession, they would copy the homework already completed by me and then we played together. I still meet some of them'. He stated. Then, shortage of time was another factor. Already, his father had begun preparing him to sit for the coveted Indian Civil Service examination. 'He made available for me the

---

[1] Interviews 1984: Folder I: pp. 12-13, 32

Indian Civil Service examination papers while I was still in middle level at that time'.[1] Abdus Salam recollected.

VII

When asked to reminisce about his parents, Abdus Salam was delighted to share the stock of memories.

'Although we were poor but my father was a highly regarded man in Jhang society. In that society, he was presumably much better off than many others. The whole society was extraordinarily poor, the Hindus being comparatively comfortable were still quite poor'. Abdus Salam replied adding that deference towards his father was mainly due to the piety and charitable contribution of the family in the past, especially services their elders had rendered in saintly guidance and public health.

'My father was very fond of keeping cows. He believed that buffalo milk coarsened the brain so one must have a supply of fresh cow milk. He considered the buffalo as a stupid animal which transmits all its coarse qualities in its milk. He thought of buffalo as extremely obstinate. I think the modern dietary theory would support his ideas. It is now established that a few molecules of certain kind in your diet can affect you greatly in a particular way. Such are the grounds on which pig meat has also been prohibited in Islam. Pig consumption would lead to shamelessness and un-cleanliness which are traits of pigs. I would believe that the milk of cow and buffalo may carry molecules of distinct types thus affecting the instincts of regular consumers in a different manner. I don't know much about it but from modern work on diets I tend to support my father's keenness towards cow milk which we always had in surplus.

'In the dark downstairs, we had a cow which, during the day, would be sent out to the fields with a cowherd. Every morning around five, my mother would milk the cow, and then churn the milk to make butter and *lassi* (butter-milk). A whole neighbourhood would line up for a share of the *lassi* which my mother dispensed as a kind of charity'.[2]

---

[1] Interviews 1984: Folder I: pp. 7-9, 27

[2] Interviews 1984: Folder I: pp. 6-9

Abdus Salam recalled that his father was well built, a very strong man who, in his youth, used to chop wooden logs for use at home, play football and hockey as these were his favourite sporting indulgence. 'He was much stronger than me. He was handsome and had great presence. Unlike him, I dress casually, while he always made sure to dress up formally before going out and was very particular about the stiffness of his freshly starched turban. My mother too was very particular about his clothing'. Mohammed Hussein, according to Abdus Salam, had simple eating habits. He was very hospitable and would lovingly dish out the choicest morsels to his children.[1]

His father used to organise the night watch in order to check break-ins and robberies in the locality though it was hard to stop crime. Early in the morning people woke up to find a big hole in the wall somewhere. 'Then trackers were summoned and investigations started'. It was interesting to observe, Abdus Salam recollected with a tinge of amusement, how the majority of bandits ended up at the rail tracks, walked on wooden sleepers ensuring not to leave any footprints behind. Otherwise, an excellent tracker could 'study the footprints' and provide a 'perfect description' of the offender.[2]

Was the overcrowded small house, where the sizeable family lived in two rooms and struggled to survive with limited income, ever set off feelings of discomfort and acrimonious argument between his parents?

No, never, he replied. Even when the family was large and had to meet ends, his father was the 'kind of tribal leader'. Being older in age compared to his wife, Hajira, who was eleven years younger, Mohammed Hussein symbolised authority. Like other women in her situation, Hajira was at ease with a second-in-command role, calling the shots on domestic front. Abdus Salam reminisced about those *parathas* and delicious curries his mother was adept at making. Personally, Abdus Salam preferred *chapatti* over rice that was set aside for special festive occasions. Not highly educated herself, Hajira expected her children to be the best. She told her children bedtime stories. Abdus Salam remembered her as 'an extremely affectionate mother, smiling always. She recited the Koran regularly in her beautiful voice. Her father had memorised the Holy Book by heart'.

Hajira's brother, Fazalur Rahman, had served as the Ahmadiyah missionary in West Africa. Abdus Salam held tremendous affection for his maternal uncle

---

[1] Interviews 1984: Folder II: p. 30, 34
[2] Interviews 1984: Folder II: p. 18

and thought of him as someone who mirrored the life of sacrifice. Fazalur Rahman was away, preaching somewhere in Africa, when his parents died. He sent a memorial note to be engraved on their tombstones. 'I was out serving the way of Prophet Mohammed and could not be with you when you died', Fazal Rahman wrote. Fazalur Rahman also wrote a book on the life of Prophet Mohammed. According to Abdus Salam this book, published by Oxford University Press, was incorporated in the syllabus at some level in Nigeria. 'I once met the former president of Nigeria, Shehu Shagari (1925–2018), and he remembered my uncle'.[1]

When did religion claim the life of Abdus Salam? Realistically there was hardly the need to place a timeframe because he seemed to have grown up practicing religion. In the first place, he had his upbringing in an intensely religious environment. His education commenced with reading of the Koran, and regular visits to the local Ahmadiyah mosque that he looked after a lot. 'I took great pleasure in cleaning the mosque'. At the age of 12 he was invited to lead the prayers, especially when nobody else with requisite learning happened to be in attendance and those present in the mosque agreed to go along with him.[2]

Occasionally, Abdus Salam attended public debating or *Munazira* between the Ahmadiyah preachers and their opponents. Once in a while, there would be contest with Hindu priests especially when a pundit offended Muslims. On such instances, the Ahmadiyah hastened to grasp the initiative as the defenders of Islam. Abdus Salam seemed to agree that public debating of religious beliefs did not change any heart. In fact, very often the viciousness of jargon exchanged between the two sides added to communal tension and bitterness. In order to demonstrate its neutrality and secular preference, on such occasions, the colonial government stood apart and intervened only when sectarian hostilities turned into a law and order situation. Abdus Salam did not seem to relish when those debating bouts were weighed against the more or less equally exciting sport of animal fights sponsored by the Sial. But he agreed about the futility of such debating as it did not conclude in clear victory or defeat of the participants. Only once, he recalled, in the midst of a debate, a potter by the name of Jiwan Khan, sitting in the audience got up in a state of frenzy, raised his arms, and announced his conversion to the Ahmadiyah.[3]

---

[1] Interviews 1984: Folder I: p. 33-34
[2] Interviews 1984: Folder II: pp. 9-10
[3] Interviews 1984: Folder II: pp. 8-9

Abdus Salam gave a fond account of his trips to the Ahmadiyah headquarter in Qadian to participate in the three-day annual congregation, or *jalsa*, convened during the Christmas holiday break. 'It used to be a great event in our lives. First of all there was the excitement of its concurrence with the end of the year, then the journey to Qadian with a spate of bus changes at Lyallpur, Lahore, Amritsar and Batala. Finally the short train trip to Qadian. All of this used to be very eventful with the Sikh drivers of those buses racing with each other, of course a very dangerous sport with our lives. In Qadian we put up either at the house of my maternal grandfather or with our uncle who by then had settled in the town'. At one of those annual congregations the leader of the community announced numerous of scholarship grants for gifted students. To the delight of his father, Abdus Salam won each one of those, one after another, all the way to post-graduate level.[1]

While reciting the Koran in his youth, did Abdus Salam ever think that it was a foreign tongue after all?

'No, because it was so much recited around. At the very outset we were taught to read and recite the Koran, when we were still very young. I went through the translation while at school. In fact, my mother always recited the Koran with translation. It was so much repeated in that way in our house that it became a part of our life very early. I was more or less regular in prayers since my childhood but reciting the Koran and offering prayers became an important and meaningful component of my life rather late, after the death of my father. During his lifetime one might be doing it as discharging a responsibility laid out by him but after his death it became my personal responsibility. Now I read the Koran to understand it. This year I have already finished it twice'. Abdus Salam replied.[2]

What was Abdus Salam's childhood image or picture of God? 'Now it is very difficult to describe and I suppose it is sometimes a personal experience. I would consider this type of anthropomorphism quite blasphemous'. Abdus Salam replied. He stood the ground even when urged to search for a picture of God as a blend of beauty, love, compassion and grandeur; with someone handsome, imposing and caring, like the image of Baba Ahmad Bakhsh Bakha in his family. He seemed to come around his childhood image of Baba Bakha

---

[1] Interviews 1984: Folder I: pp. 36-38
[2] Interviews 1984: Folder I: pp. 38-39

resembling an imaginative picture of God but then withdrew hastily adding rather firmly that 'I still shun the thought as being blasphemous'.[1]

Keeping the flow of discussion, Abdus Salam was asked if he had ever doubted, wavered and questioned religion. Had he ever landed himself into an argument with his father? Never, he shot back and then went on to mention something that had been on his mind. 'I was perturbed recently when someone asked me about amputation as the punishment for stealing. Do people enforcing the sentence recite *bismillah* before doing the job? I was questioned. I certainly became very keen to find an answer. Well, you see, these phases last a short while. I would not like to describe it where religion is so deeply engraved. One may feel agitated, only to come back'.[2] He maintained stating that there was no point in debating religion with his father who held absolute faith in God. 'My father's reliance on God was perfect but he was not mystical in the strict sense of the term'.[3] Religious belief, Abdus Salam felt, signified such an integral part of his father that any attempt at characterising him for the secular audience did not sound logical.

Did Abdus Salam ever feel angry or rebellious towards his father?

Not in a mundane way exactly, he replied, because at the end of the day it was affection on the part of his father that prevailed. Actually, Abdus Salam acknowledged being grateful for the push he received from his father. Still, there were few occasions when he felt things could have been taken at ease. For example, he recalled, there was his failure to score First in the Middle level examination in Punjab. Abdus Salam recalled how his father went through the tribulation and trial of procuring the home scripts of the boy who stood first. Abdus Salam was, sometimes bothered by the multiplicity and traffic of teachers offering him all sorts of advice. 'But you must not forget that all of this happened up until matriculation after which I was independent and on my own, from Lahore onwards'.

His father's hypothesis about the herbal merits of *Neem* tree[4] was certainly a cause of agony for Abdus Salam. Mohammed Hussein believed that *Neem* extract, despite its pungently bitter taste, enshrined in its nature a great deal of health benefits. As such, Abdus Salam was expected to drink the potion

---

[1] Interviews 1984: Folder I: pp. 40-41
[2] Interviews 1984: Folder I: pp. 41-42
[3] Interviews 1984: Folder II: pp. 20, 35
[4] Azadirachta indica, the Indian lilac of the mahogany family Meliaceae

whenever his father prepared it. 'Several times in my youth, I had to drink it despite great protest. Another item where our taste met head-on was his idea of mixing milk and cleared butter *ghee*. My father loved it and I would simply throw it up. He considered it as the secret of one's strength. This used to be one of my pet loathing and his love'.[1]

Only on one occasion in his life Abdus Salam did react sharply towards his father, and this was when the matriculation result was received in Jhang and more or less everyone in the town applauded the top position Abdus Salam had secured and he aspired to visit his teachers with trays of confectionery. He wanted to call upon his teachers somewhat ceremoniously. Mohammed Hussein expressed readiness to accompany his son but did not have enough money to buy confectionery. 'I was very angry with my father and declined to accompany him. I remember we both went to Mighyana, the satellite town next to Jhang, to the owner of a stationery shop, Gulab Singh. My father borrowed two rupees from him. I am sure my father must have felt quite miserable over this borrowing'. Armed with trays of locally prepared sweet stuff, the two of them called on the teachers. It was once in a lifetime act of rebellion on the part of Abdus Salam 'when my poor father didn't have enough money' to buy what was integral to the occasion. He recalled.[2]

VIII

Mohammed Hussein died on 7 April 1969. He had a history of heart condition which was complicated by diabetes. He was buried in Rabwah, a small town on the right bank of river *Chenab,* near Jhang. After the Partition of Punjab in 1947, as a result of which Qadian became a part of India, the majority of the Ahmadiyah made the move to Pakistan and founded a new headquarter near Kirana Hills. About one thousand acres of land was leased for this purpose and the estate named as Rabwah, literally meaning an elevated location. Mohammed Hussein had purchased a grave-site in the deified cemetery in Rabwah.

He left behind a will urging his children and grandchildren to live their lives in adherence with the monotheist tradition. This will makes a part of his biography. Instead of making any mention of assets, as is often believed to be

---

[1] Interviews 1984: Folder II: p. 19
[2] Interviews 1984: Folder II: p. 33-34

the purpose of wills, Mohammed Hussein directed his offspring to always stand loyal to the Ahmadiyah leadership and that they must never expect any reward in return for their services to the holy cause. He reasserted his belief that the only party capable of telling the good from evil was the Ahmadiyah, the party of the Lord.[1]

His wife, Hajira, survived him by eight years. She died in London in October 1977. Her remains were flown to Pakistan for burial next to the grave site of her husband. Like Mohammed Hussein, she too had bequeathed a considerable part of her property to purchase the site in advance. She was a tireless house manager who woke up for prayers well before the daybreak and then worked whole day to run the house smoothly. Even when her parents were understood to be more affluent compared to Mohammed Hussein's family, she lived in contentment. Somewhat precariously placed between her rigidly scrupulous husband and the genuine demands of growing up children, she kept her pleasing poise; always staying polite and loving, never losing temper.[2]

Although both Mohammed Hussein and Hajira did not live long enough to share the delight of Nobel Prize their son Abdus Salam won in 1979 but the two were satisfied to witness all of their children settling well in employment and having their families. Somewhat fatefully, however, the countryside Jhang, where Mohammed Hussein and Hajira had spent a good part of their lives, submitted itself to a shockingly bleak decline. First of all, the town lost its religious and cultural diversity at the time of the Partition in 1947. Nearly all of its Hindu and Sikh residents were obliged to quit what had been home to them and their ancestors for many generations in the past, the void created by their exodus was filled in by Muslim migrants who had been uprooted with matching viciousness elsewhere.

Equally far-reaching was the remodelling of the ruling class. If the British, under colonial plan for plunder at the top, had managed to maintain a considerable semblance of good governance, their successors in Pakistan did not have any experience or clue to running an independent country. Jhang, like the rest of Pakistan, inherited rulers who were used to playing the second fiddle at best; inclined to strike backdoor deals in order to seek favours. Finding themselves at the helm of affairs overnight, calling the shots, they went on a stealing spree straightaway without any need or fear of accountability. Pakistan

---

[1] Mohammed Hussein (1974): pp. 227-228
[2] Interviews 1984: Folder I: p. 33-34

plunged itself into the dark ditch of economic, political, social and civic corruption.

By the close of 20th century, Jhang shared its misery with the rest of Pakistan. As such, the laid-back country station of Mohammed Hussein, Hajira, their children and contemporaries, Jhang, lost it natural poise and virgin beauty. It did not take long for Jhang to become a lump of civic chaos, political hypocrisy, financial embezzlement, intellectual degeneration, departmental corruption and religious bigotry.

On the landscape known for the serenity and innocence of its wilderness, Jhang housed pollution of every possible category; from dust, noise, filth, industrial waste, rubbish, grime, and stench to ugly plastic containers serving as rooftop water tanks, and plastic shopping bags caught into dying branches of acacia trees. An uneven colourless asymmetrical housing along with tube-wells and electricity generators replaced the scenic skyline adorned with Persian Wheels and whistling flour mills. Overloaded clunkers had driven ox-driven wooden carts to extinction. Those colourful *cholis* and *dhotis* of the bygone era were shunted out by shalwars, long *kurtas,* even jackets and jeans; and the town centre was overtaken by a chaotic mix of horse-driven *tonga* taxis, over-loaded and outdated automobiles, bicycles, shabbily turbaned pedestrians, aimless youth; vendors, untidy small businesses, unclean food-vendors, unemployed labour, unfenced livestock, stray canine, abandoned feline and burqa-clad women. Occasionally, there would be funeral processions solemnly marching in the direction of a cemetery.

Above all, the explosion of population had annihilated a whole heap of wildlife, flora and fauna. All those jackals and hyenas, howling and laughing under moonlit nights, had been replaced by an under-development of human crowding and settlement.

Chapter Two
In Pursuit of Fading Glory

Punjab was annexed by the British, almost two hundred years after their military victories in Bengal. As such, the fractional westernisation accompanying colonial onslaught was gradual, and provinces in northeast and central India took a certain degree of lead in adopting British methods in government, economy, business and education. Punjab figured out the benefits of universal education when universities and colleges in Calcutta, Lucknow and Bombay were already bragging about their gains in education and employment. Punjab was perceived to be timidly caught in the feudal age. But the expanse did not take very long to realise the value attached to education. More than a pathway to higher scholarship, education offered the short and quick route to better employment.

On the average, a small town like Jhang had a high school and an intermediate college, whereas higher education degree programs were available in few bigger cities like Lahore, Amritsar and Multan. Besides, annual examinations from year ten matriculation or school leaving certificate upwards were conducted by the University of Punjab. Students aspiring to study undergraduate degree programs in medicine, engineering, commerce, accounting, law and public service were required to complete year ten matriculation at the local high school and then pass year twelve examination at an intermediate college with good grades before applying for admission in medical, engineering, commerce and other university colleges in Lahore.

Seeking admission in medicine and engineering was tougher due to competition. A couple of colleges at the University of Punjab offered degree programs in pharmacy and chemical engineering but it was hard to find employment in those areas due to a subdued growth of related industries in Punjab. Somewhat ironically, students failing to follow the standard route to meaningful employment often ended up doing a Master's degree program in one or another discipline of natural and social sciences and oriental languages in order to find jobs in college teaching at best.

Girls did not receive much encouragement to go beyond high schools because they were not supposed to make a working career and be on their own. Approaching puberty, they were bound to stay home, get married, mother children and manage domestic business of a household be it Hindu, Muslim, Sikh or else. Even when some of them made it to postgraduate levels, purely by dint of merit, their fate in the role of a housewife was sealed.

Among boys, those aiming to study law had to complete the Bachelor's program at a degree college before being able to apply for admission in the Law College in Lahore. Finally, there were those who, like Abdus Salam, wished to sit for the coveted Indian Civil Service examination; aimed at making it to the Government College in Lahore to study for an undergraduate degree program with a combination of subjects and English Literature. One of the sure ways to make it to the college was to pass the year ten matriculation examination at the prestigious public sector Central Model School in Lahore.

Just when Abdus Salam passed the year eight Middle Level Examination, his father took him to Lahore in order to explore the possibility of the boy's admission in Central Model School. Only brilliant boys dreamed of securing a place at this highly selective school. Once at the Central Model School, a good student would be only two years away from getting into the Government College across the road. While Mohammed Hussein pleaded the case for his son's admission, the Headmaster looked at the modestly dressed Abdus Salam wearing the fez, a traditional headgear that was fast running out of fashion due to the demise of Ottoman Empire. Although the boy seemed to qualify for admission on academic merit, the Headmaster told Mohammed Hussein, the school would rather decline admission. What for? Asked Mohammed Hussein. Well, the Headmaster replied, the boy came from a country town, wore the fez, displayed provincial manners; all put together made him an easy target of bullying by the extrovert youth of Lahore hence a headache for the school administration.

Such peevish conduct of the Headmaster did not keep Abdus Salam from breaking academic records, in order to set his own, and make it to the Government College in time. Munir Khan, a college-mate of Abdus Salam and making it to lead the Atomic Energy Commission of Pakistan at a crucial time three decades later, felt amused to imagine the amount of regret the Headmaster of Central Model School must have lived with the rest of his life.[1]

Actually, this little known story corroborates with Mohammed Hussein's dream to make a bureaucrat out of his son. It shows how, from the very outset, Mohammed Hussein had begun working out necessary calculations towards Abdus Salam's career in public service. In exploring the possibility of admission at Central Model School, Mohammed Hussein was actually charting out Abdus Salam's route to the Government College, just next door, across the road, in Lahore. Given the shape of social ladder in those days, Mohammed Hussein was not wrong. He appreciated the fact that a well-earned Bachelor's degree amounted to equally improved career options. In colonial India, higher education did not mean an elevated level of scholarship and research in natural and social sciences. As such, Abdus Salam had just passed the year eight examination, when his father brought him a set of civil service examination question papers to start practicing.

In this order of education and employment, a tremendous amount of excitement was associated with the publication of year ten result-sheet, issued annually by the University of Punjab, it equalled no less than a grand sporting event. Every year examination for year ten was conducted about the end of spring, and results made public in summer.

Abdus Salam remembered the sizzling hot day in the summer of 1940 when the result of his year ten examination was received in Jhang. Sitting in his father's office, in the government block of buildings in Mighyana, he waited for the man who had gone to the rail station to pick up a copy of the gazette notification. Before even that man returned from the railway station, telegrams of congratulations began landing on Mohammed Hussein's desk.

When the gazette copy arrived, Mohammed Hussein started searching the roll number 14888 in the list of successful candidates until someone reminded him that he might find this roll number on the front page; and there was it. Abdus Salam had secured 765 out of a total of 850 marks; he stood first in the 1940 Matriculation Examination of the University of Punjab. Besides, he had smashed all the previous records by setting one of his own. *Praise be to the Lord of Universes*, his father whispered the Koranic verse. Soon as the euphoria settled

---

[1] In due course of time, Munir Khan came to preside over Pakistan's success in achieving nuclear parity with India. He mentioned the Central Model School episode in his contribution to Trieste Tribute (1997).

down, Abdus Salam was permitted to go home to break the news upon his mother.

One day before the declaration of university gazette of matriculation results, Abdus Salam happened to have gone for haircut to the local barber. He was handed over to an apprentice who came fairly close to turning the boy into a skinhead. Getting ready for press pictures, Abdus Salam felt obliged to cover his head with a turban. For a 14-year-old student to make it to the top from the middle of nowhere like Jhang sounded unbelievable. Soon the management of a leading high school in Lahore despatched its contingent of teachers to visit the godforsaken place and learn few lessons about the miracle. Upon arriving in Jhang, those teachers met Abdus Salam and took his photographs.[1]

Never the rest of his life could Abdus Salam forget the manner in which the Hindu businessmen in the bazaar gave him the reception as he cycled home. Usually, on hot summer afternoons, it would be time of siesta. Since the news of his result had made it to the bazaar before him, the shop owners waited for him, standing in his honour as he passed through the street. Even though the town did not fare anywhere on the scale of economic advancement, the love of scholarship displayed by its residents was unforgettable. Abdus Salam was a local celebrity, a household name to parents who, like Mohammed Hussein, desired their children to achieve the top in education. This was how Abdus Salam staged his first appearance before the small intelligentsia of Punjab. Hardly anyone could foretell that he had set the standard and pace for his future achievements in the world beyond Jhang.

At the same time, he stood vindicated before his father who had gone crazy a couple of years ago when Abdus Salam was unable to lead the year eight result list in Punjab. Mohammed Hussein could see the diligence of his son, yet he would take a short while before any let up in his relentless monitoring.

At the age of 14, Abdus Salam was admitted to the Intermediate College in Jhang. Founded in 1926, this institution was exactly as old in age as Abdus Salam himself. Soon after his admission, Abdus Salam volunteered to organise the college library and its catalogue of search. He knew it would enable him to spend more time in the company of books. Due to his involvement with library work, he happened to miss the physical training session and, under college rules, was served with a notice of penalty. He went straight to the principal and requested remission. 'Sir, I have never defaulted in attendance but it was just not possible

---

[1] Abdul Hameed (circa 2000): pp. 31-32

for me to leave the library work halfway'. He pleaded before the Principal, a Sikh gentleman, who was so overwhelmed with Abdus Salam's case that he summoned an urgent assembly of students to announce the remission.[1]

His hours spent in the library, enabled Abdus Salam to write two research papers, both published in prestigious literary journals when he was only 15. His first paper dealt with determining a closest possible date when the famous Indian poet, Asadullah Khan (1797–1869), seemed to have switched his *nom de poete* from Asad to Ghalib.

Born in Agra, the city of the Taj Mahal, Asadullah Khan descended from the Turkish nobility hanging upon the decadent Mogul court in Delhi. He took pride in his ancestry but lived in challenging times of personal and political misfortunes. His father had died early and he went under the care of an uncle who also did not live very long. His brother went insane and was murdered. One of his very dear nephews died young. Above all, the Mogul court, to which he was attached for allowance, disintegrated. He started writing poems at 11 and his first collection of Urdu verses was published in 1816. In a bid to secure income, he got sucked, like the father of Ghulam Ahmed, into protracted litigation with the British. He faced bankruptcy and was sentenced to six months of jail on charges of running a gambling den. In a bid to bail himself out, he wrote a eulogy in praise of Queen Victoria. Instead of any hope of reward, he annoyed the English bureaucracy by sending his work directly to the monarch. Even a favourable description of the massacre of English officers and their families in Delhi, in 1857, did not help him much. He is known to have depicted the killing as:

Spring, wallow in your own blood, like a stricken bird;
Age, plunge in blackness, like a night without moon;
Sun, beat your head until your face is bruised and black;
Moon; make yourself the scar upon the age's heart.[2]

Regardless of the personal tragedies and incorrect political choices, Asadullah Khan was endowed with a profoundly original power of expression. He reigned supreme in the literary consciousness of northern India as the universality of both his poetry and prose is appreciated by a broad range of

---

[1] Mohammed Hussein (1974): p. 42
[2] Ghalib - The Poet and His Age; edited by Ralph Russell, London, 1972, p. 19

people in South Asia where rich and poor, religious and godless, mediocre and intellectual, all adore him. He is held in high esteem by Hindu, Muslim, Buddhist, Jain, Sikh, Christian, liberal and communist, believers and non-believers all over the subcontinent.

Asadullah Khan had a fine taste for Indian mangoes and Portuguese wines. His sense of humour was limitless. He was once reproached by a priest who believed alcohol took people away from God. Asadullah Khan is reported to have rebuked the priest by stating that who cared about almighty so long as the supply of good wine was ensured? On another occasion, someone asked him if he was a Muslim? Only by half because 'I don't eat pork, just drink alcohol', he is reported to have responded.

At some point in his glorious literary career, Asadullah Khan had switched his *takhalus*, that is, *nom de poete* from Asad to Ghalib, but it was not known exactly as to when he made the change. Out of mere curiosity, Abdus Salam pondered over the possibility of exploring the nearest possible date of the switch-over. He ran through the rare Bhopal copy of the poet's earlier works and sifted out dates where they were available. He reached fairly close to place a reasonable timeframe on the switch over. Based upon his findings, he wrote a paper that was first published in the college magazine. Afterwards, he sent a copy of it to the *Adabi Dunya,* a journal of literary standing. The article was accepted for publication almost instantly. In fact, the editor wrote back a letter of acknowledgment and appreciation.

Abdus Salam remembered that he had been lucky to find the *Bhopali Nuskha* of Asadullah Khan's collection at the college library in Jhang. 'Even Government College Lahore did not have this *Nuskha*, it was a non-conventional *Nuskha* in a sense that it contained number of those works which at one stage were deleted by Ghalib. 'I don't remember in detail but I was very much interested in his switching over of *takhalus*'. He recalled.[1]

How did Abdus Salam, in the first place, fall in love with the verses of Asadullah Khan?

One of his teachers often encouraged him to speak about Mohammed Iqbal (1877–1938), a famous Muslim poet and thinker who is usually credited with articulating the need for a separate homeland of Muslims in India ahead of Mohammed Ai Jinnah (1876–1948), the father of Pakistan. Abdus Salam stated

---

[1] Interviews 1984: Folder III, pp. 3-4

that a good knowledge of Mohammed Iqbal made it easy for him to step closer to Asadullah Khan.

When asked which of the two poets he liked more, he avoided to respond directly by taking refuge into the story of his Government College Lahore teacher, Ish Kumar, who loved Mohammed Iqbal as 'the greatest poet of mankind' but then moved on to discover a much bigger world in Asadullah Khan. 'As a young man, one tends to go for Iqbal. His language and Islamic themes are very attractive but when you come to life and its experiences as a whole Ghalib has a lot to offer'. Applying his diplomatic code, Abdus Salam distanced himself from the lousy manner in which the much broader premise of Mohammed Iqbal was limited only to the pan-Islamic requirements of an insecure state in Pakistan. Instead, he expressed agreement with Professor Ish Kumar.[1]

'My research article regarding Ghalib was first published in *Chenab*, the college magazine in Jhang. Afterwards, I sent it to *Adabi Dunya* or the Literary World, a standard journal, where it was accepted with gratitude'. Abdus Salam stated adding that if he saw those writings today, he would not feel like making any changes.[2]

Greatly encouraged, Abdus Salam wrote his next paper on the contemporary trends in detective fiction being produced in Urdu language. He picked up detective fiction from a private library in the town. In those days, people could hire books and, although some parents rejected the whole idea fearing that fiction bred unbridled distraction among the youth, Mohammed Hussein had no qualms about it. Abdus Salam was free to make the choice. In fact, he had begun reading detective stories when he was nine. He remembered the marketing gimmick of publishers when every now and then a story ended with the promise of follow-up in next publication. Abdus Salam must have made a double-century of those hair-raising tales in crime and espionage before contemplating to venture on his second research paper. He set out to classify the most popularly repeated themes and characters. He recollected how some of those detective novels ended inside an imaginary spaceship made up of bluish glass sheets and lifting off smoothly

---

[1] Interviews 1984: Folder III, pp, 5-6
[2] Interviews 1984: Folder III, pp. 7, 10

toward the sky from a mysterious location in Delhi. Inside the spaceship would be the chief villain saved for the next round of story.[1]

His research article dealt with tracing the evolution of detective fiction in Urdu publishing business. Like the one on Asadullah Khan, it was well received. In spite of the fact that mature readers did not take spy stories much seriously, they found the analysis educating.

Abdus Salam was not sure how well the quality and standards of detective fiction in Urdu were maintained afterwards. 'These days, I have seen a tendency of very lengthy novels with a dominant sexual theme; whereas, many in our days were quite original'. He recalled adding that he had read about two hundred spy stories before writing his essay.[2]

While studying for year twelve, he edited the college magazine, *Chenab*, a bilingual publication in English and Urdu languages, of the Intermediate College in Jhang. At the same time, he worked for the Translation Society of the College entrusted to render into Urdu quite a few elaborate passages from books and journals available only in English. He remembered attempting to convert Oscar Wilde's Salome into a vernacular poem.[3]

About when Abdus Salam headed to sit for year twelve examination, his father was transferred to Multan. Mohammed Hussein, as narrated in the previous chapter, deferred moving the whole family. Instead, he went to Multan alone to save Abdus Salam from any disruption. Hajira and children followed him the day examination ended.

As a part of the matriculation and intermediate levels of curriculum, Abdus Salam had studied, and passed with distinction, a range of subjects including Mathematics, General Science, Physics, Chemistry, General Studies, English, Arabic and Persian languages.

While going to Multan, to spend the term break before next stage of his studies at Government College in Lahore, Abdus Salam was not aware that the journey amounted to a kind of permanent farewell to Jhang. He would, of course, continue visiting the town every now and then but never to settle or live there

---

[1] Detective stories about *Neeli Chatri* (Blue Spaceship) were first written by a retired police officer, Zafar Umar, who had made a name for his leading role in arresting the bandit *Sultana Dakoo*. [QAH 1999, pp. 182, 185]

[2] Interviews 1984: Folder III, p. 9-10

[3] Presidential Address at the annual convocation of Government Intermediate College, Jhang, in 1971-72

permanently. Jhang would stay in his memory as the town associated with his childhood and early youth, not a place where he would come to settle or consider spending retirement. From Multan, he would travel to Lahore, complete the Bachelors, and also do a Masters, without being able to secure a position in the public service as dreamed by his father. An indefinite embargo on public sector recruitment, due to the outbreak of World War II, would take him elsewhere, in unchartered territories in the world of scholarship.

Upon receiving the result of his year twelve examination, Abdus Salam went to pay a farewell call on the Principal. He received a glittering reference letter, jam-packed with adjectives and superlatives, from the Principal. Abdus Salam had been introduced as a 'thoroughly straightforward and unassuming' student armed with the rare capability of effectively combining 'brilliance of mind and dogged perseverance in pursuit of a definite aim'.

On his part, Abdus Salam considered himself lucky in having a whole lot of able and affectionate teachers from all sections of the society. 'It remains a reality, however, that the bedrock of my academic career was laid here, in this college. Any credit to my later day achievement is due to this institution and my teachers in Jhang'. He acknowledged at the annual convocation ceremony of the college in 1972 by remembering the names of his teachers from Hindu, Sikh and Muslim communities.

Before the arrival of monsoon rains in 1942, Mohammed Hussein and his family reunited in Multan, they left Jhang the day Abdus Salam sat for the last paper of his intermediate examination.

II

One hundred miles southeast of Jhang, where the combined flow of *Chenab* and *Jhelum* received the waters of *Ravi* and *Sutlej*, Multan was the last big station south of Punjab. Towards south, Multan was flanked by the vast expanse of *Cholistan* and *Thar* deserts; and up in northwest, the preferred route of invaders from Afghanistan and Central Asia deflected east in the direction of Lahore and Delhi. In this way, Multan was appreciably saved from repetitive aggression.

Among those affording the logistics of a military expedition to Multan was Alexander the Great. He marched down from northwest in the 4th century BC and encountered a tough resistance put up by the local *Malli* warriors. He was so grievously wounded that his infuriated generals ordered a general massacre of citizens in Multan.[1] Some twelve hundred years later, earlier in the 8th century, a youthful Arab commander, Mohammed Bin Qasim, won the uniqueness of marching into Multan from southwest. He was stunned upon finding a huge trove of gold concealed in a chamber underneath the idol of Sun Temple. Ever since the invasion of Mohammed Bin Qasim, Multan remained slackly attached to Muslim caliphate of Baghdad. In the second millennium on Gregorian calendar, Multan endured a spate of masters from Turkish sultans to Moguls, Mongols, Afghans, Sikhs and finally the British.

Immersed in distant deposits of mythology, superstition and folklore; the origin of Multan was dated back to time immemorial. Like other ancient places in the world, the birth of Multan was attributed to a highly venerated Hindu site of worship, the five-thousand-year-old Sun Temple. It was believed that a tyrant ruler had ordered the execution of his pious son who was held in high esteem by the people. Like the great Mesopotamian patriarch, Abraham of Biblical era, the execution of the prince was to be carried out by roasting him alive in a furnace. But the pyre flames cooled down by the intervention of Vishnu, the God of Fury in the Hindu trinity; and the innocent prince was saved. In a show of gratitude toward the Council of Gods, the Sun Temple was raised upon the site. Pilgrims from far away stations, loaded with offering and tribute, began visiting the temple. Over time, a bustling a city, the precursor to Multan, emerged around the holy site. At one stage, during the course of its veneration, the pinnacle of temple spire is believed to have reached well above three hundred feet. Among the flocks of pilgrims were members of royalty from powerful Hindu principalities in Rajasthan as well as rich businessmen.

HwenThsang, the 7th century Chinese explorer, who had travelled near Jhang, visited the temple and was fascinated by its exquisite edifice in the heart of a city humming in trade and commerce.

Abul Hassan Al-Masudi (896–956), the 10th century Muslim historian who is remembered as the Herodotus of Arabs, also came here and described Multan as a frontier province dividing the kingdom of the faithful from that of the infidel. In his treatise, *The Meadows of Gold*, he narrated how men and women from all parts of India converged upon Multan to perform a pilgrimage at the Sun Temple. Obviously, the Muslim rulers of the city did not object to the practice for they had financial and political stakes in the flourishing business of the temple. A

---

[1] Syed Mohammed Latif: The Early History of Multan, Calcutta, 1891 (reprinted in Lahore 1965), pp. 29-30

greater flow of tourists meant more income for local businesses and the expansion of imports via Arabian Sea.

On a visit to Multan, Abu Rehan Al-Beruni (973–1048), the Iranian scholar, is reported to have found the image of Prophet Job idolised in the temple. Mohammed Al-Idrisi (1100–1165), the Arab Geographer, recorded that no idol in India was more revered than those in the Sun Temple of Multan.[1]

Mohammed Qasim Ferishta (1560–1620), the Muslim historian of Iranian origin who served as chronicler to the rulers of Deccan, held a different view. He believed that Multan had been founded by a great-grand son of Noah settling here in the aftermath of the Great Deluge.[2]

Imbued with an ancient tradition of Hindu mysticism, Multan endowed a fertile substrate to the various Sufi orders of Islam flourishing here in the medieval age. This experiment in religious cross-breeding and syncretism proved vulnerable to political intrigue and religious bigotry, it was not trouble-free for monasteries, mosques, tombs and temples to live in a state of everlasting harmony and peace.

Khawaja Moinuddin Chishti (1141–1236), a highly revered Muslim saint, arrived in Multan in 1188. He lived in boarding house of the Sun Temple for five years to study and gain proficiency in Sanskrit. He ended up making a monastery in Ajmer; deep inside Rajasthan, an access the proud Rajput warriors denied the majority Muslim military invaders.

Bahawal Haq (1170–1262), the spiritual guide of Abdus Salam's ancestors, followed Khawaja Moinuddin Chishti and settled down in Multan to be venerated as the patron saint of the city. It is believed that the trustees of the Sun Temple had offered Bahawal Haq a considerable chunk of estate for the foundation of his Suharwardy monastery.[3] He had following all over the Indus Valley and was equally revered among rich and poor, landed aristocracy and peasantry, village and town, farm and bazaar, in north as well as south. *Dum Bahawal Haq* chanted the boatmen in Arabian Sea believing that the soul of their saint would save them from merciless tides. Some of his followers went as far as the Strait of Malacca. He offered them business incentives to combine preaching and livelihood.[4] An imposing octagonal mausoleum was built upon his grave.

---

[1] Syed Mohammed Latif (1965): p. 40
[2] Syed Mohammed Latif (1965): p. 12
[3] The Frontier Post, Peshawar, 20 January 1993, p. 12
[4] The Frontier Post, Peshawar, 18 July 1995, p. 6

Visible miles away, the glazed dome of his shrine thumped the hearts of barefoot pilgrims marching towards it from distant villages in Sind.

An equally glorious tomb was raised upon the grave of his successor and grandson, Sheikh Rukunuddin (1251–1335). Its slanting walls, double octagon dome and turrets; and the varying glaze of its azure, blue and red tiles, at different times of the day, left a memorable image upon pilgrims. Due to its glory and elegance, the tomb picked up the popular name *Rukun-i-A'alam* or the Pillar of the Universe.

Multan had its more than fair share of saints originating from southwest and central Asia rather than the birthplace of Islam, Arabian Peninsula. Shah Yousuf Gardez (1058–1136) was fabled to have entered the city riding upon a lion and holding an enormous serpent as the whip.

Then there was Shamsuddin Tabrezi (1165–1276) who was believed to have traversed across the swollen waves of Indus by hovering upon a magical prayer-mat. According to the oral tradition, Bahawal Haq greeted the newcomer with a tumbler full of milk to politely convey the message that Multan was already saturated with saints. Shamsuddin Tabrezi returned the glass with a flower floating on the surface of milk to signify that there was always room at the top.

But then, the Sun Temple and Muslim Sufi saints were not the only features of Multan. Outside the old city was a pond where ablution ceremonies were performed twice a year, only on the night of half moon. Pilgrims flocked to this pond from distant places to purify them from the lifelong load of their sins.

More than a dozen grave-sites of *Nine-Yarders* offered another relic in the old city. Some people believed that buried inside those extraordinary crypts were Muslim warriors who embraced martyrdom in jihad against the infidel Hindus. According to another explanation those were the tombs of superhuman heroes who sacrificed their lives while resisting the British. But the most exciting rationale attributed the enormousness of those graves to the size of people dwelling upon the earth during the Great Deluge and the age of dinosaurs. Remarkably, both Hindus and Muslims revered the mythical characters by lighting lamps on sites of their choice every Friday evening.

In a way, the mystical and spiritual tradition of Multan was best summed up in the folktale relating to Budhu, an employee at a toll checkpoint who, somewhere in the past, had been assigned the job of calling out figures off the weigh-station. One day, while calling out *Kul Unhi Hai*, meaning the weight is nineteen in all, he experienced a sudden fit of spiritual elation. What he had just called out also meant *All is Him, the Almighty!*. A fakir passing by started repeating the phrase. Budhu resigned from work instantly and rushed into woods across the river. Within a matter of few days his fame was established as someone in an advanced stage of mystical seclusion. Reminiscent of Lord Buddha, the last glimpse of Budhu people had was while he rested under a banyan tree. His whereabouts were not known afterwards. Never missing the opportunity to revere a fakir, the people of Multan raised a shrine upon the site where Budhu was last seen for pilgrims to flock and commemorate. Keeping with Hindu preferences, meat was disallowed at the shrine.

For its climate, Multan was the land of extremes; here a record low in rainfall was outdone by devastating floods bringing fresh layers of rich silt over millions of cultivated acres. Once in a while, the torrent forced rivers to change their course, giving birth, once again, to the evolution of deities. According to Hindu tradition, the bend in *Ravi* was straightened out by Lord Ram in order to keep a watch and ensure privacy while his beloved Sita bathed for ritual ablution. Disinclined to appreciate the charm of such a romantic account, Muslims attributed the alteration in the course of Ravi to a miracle performed by Shah Yousuf Gardez.

Besides its mystical and spiritual tradition, temples, tombs, saints and the persecuting weather; Multan was famous all over the subcontinent for its mangoes, oranges, pomegranates, mulberries, melons, guavas, dates, falsa berries, jaman and some unique varieties of cotton. Also, for its glazed pottery, lacquered woodwork, hand-knotted carpets and lampshades made of camel-hide. Sometimes Multan appeared to test the patience of its citizens and visitors by the abundance of beggars and dust pollution. 'I loved Multan, besides other things, for its fruits. We had orchards of *jaman*, *falsa* and pomegranate near our house. Now I do not hear much about *jaman* or *falsa*. Mangoes were, of course, an identification mark of Multan'. Abdus Salam remembered. One big disadvantage of Multan in his day, he added, was the stagnant water causing malarial epidemic every now and then. He hoped the problem had been fixed. 'Where we lived was known for its dust storms, sometimes the dust would be reddish in colour'. He remarked hoping, once again, that irrigation projects must have settled the dust down.[1]

---

[1] Interviews 1984: Folder III, p. 37 [*Jaman* is also known as Java Plum, and *Falsa* is Grewia Asiatica]

Abdus Salam had about eight weeks to explore Multan where the proverbial heat wave persisted without any let up in sight. While living in Jhang he had only a romantic notion of everyday life in a big city. In 1942, Multan represented a charming architectural mix of ancient, medieval and modern ages. Up until the close of 17th century the city was walled with four gates to the world outside. A great deal of civic modernisation arrived with the British who demolished many sections of the city wall to clear out any pockets of resistance. Two extra gates were added to facilitate a more efficient flow of increased traffic. Then there was the steady march towards European standards of municipal hygiene, sanitation and drainage. Multan received its first clock tower and cantonment town. Soon the district housing the Fort, Sun Temple and Bahawul Haq shrine was uncluttered.

From Damdama Point in the Fort, a tourist took the spectacular view decorated with countless number of minarets, domes, towers, spires, mosques, temples, tombs, gurudwaras and churches in the vast city where life zigzagged in streets, narrow lanes and alleys. Everywhere out there was history and tales in mysticism, spirituality, warfare, gallantry, political intrigue, business, love and hate.

For Abdus Salam it was like falling in love with Multan at the first sight. Unlike Jhang, where everyone knew everyone else and every street and lane sounded familiar, Multan was full of strangers, unknown faces and places to be known and explored.

He walked endlessly and was fascinated by the archaic grandeur of Multan. In many ways, he would discover it soon, the old walled cities in Multan and Lahore were alike, a loveable maze of narrow, brick-paved, semi dark, undulating, twisting and bending network of streets; a mysterious labyrinth of medieval superstition. He went to see the 18th century *Eidgah* Mosque where two British officers taking refuge for safety, during the siege of 1848, had been mercilessly killed. 'Within this dome', recorded the inscription on the wall, 'on 19 April 1848, two British officers, Patrick Vans Agnew of Bengal Civil Service and Lieutenant William Anderson of First Bombay Fusiliers, were cruelly murdered'. Once the city was taken, a summary court was convened at the site and the mosque was returned to Muslims on a precondition to retain the memorial plaque.[1] At the same time, a fifty feet tall obelisk was installed in the Fort to remember the two officers. Ironically, the two were on a peace mission

---

[1] Syed Mohammed Latif (1965): p. 67

seeking the surrender of Dewan Mulraj, the last Governor of 19th century Sikh state in Punjab. 'Your slave desires only protection for his own life, and the honour of his women', the Dewan had pleaded before Major General Whish of the British army. 'You are an ocean of mercy, what more need be said. I would never have done what I have, nevertheless, I confess myself an offender in every way. You are a sea of compassion; if you forgive me, I am fortunate; if you do not, I meet my fate with contentment'. He begged. Responding to this pathetic plea, General Whish curtly stated that 'I have neither authority to give your life, nor to take, except in open war. The Governor General only can do this; and as to your women, the British Government wars with men, not with women. I will protect your women and children to the best of my ability'.[1]

Not far from this monument was the tomb of the last Afghan Governor, Nawab Muzaffar Khan Sadozai who, with his eight sons, had died valiantly in resisting the Sikh army in 1818.

In the cantonment district, occupied mostly by the British army officers and their families, Abdus Salam discovered a bookshop selling Penguin paperbacks at an affordable price. With one of his Hindu friends, he frequented the place regularly. Occasionally, the two raced to buy new arrivals. It was a time of war and the Department of Defence encouraged people to join the army. In fact, a small reward in cash was given to those who convinced others to draft. Abdus Salam coaxed a friend to join the ranks. Somewhat amused by such dicey persuasion, his friend responded that by joining the army he would have to wear a uniform, salute and take orders. What would you do with the small amount of reward? His friend asked him. Honestly, replied Abdus Salam, he might buy a couple of paperbacks. But this love of fiction did not last very long. In a matter of few years, with his mind taking a deeper plunge into Theoretical Physics and time running short for leisure, Abdus Salam settled upon the easy and non-pretentious Pelham Grenville Wodehouse (1881–1975) popularly known as P G Wodehouse.

Between reading books and exploring the city, Abdus Salam occasionally went for fresh water fishing at a stream passing by their house.[2]

Later, after his move to the Government College hostel in Lahore, when Abdus Salam would be in Multan during summer holidays, he found

---

[1] Major Herbert B Edwardes: A Year on the Punjab Frontier in 1848-49, vol. II, reprinted in Lahore (1964), p. 566-67
[2] *Khalid*, Rabwah, December 1997, p. 52

employment as a tutor. He coached the two sons of a local landlord, Omar Ali, who was a member of the Ahmadiyah community. Not only there was enough money for paperbacks, he accompanied the two boys to Simla, the summer capital of the British, all paid by Omar Ali. Apart from being able to buy paperbacks, Abdus Salam earned a cool break from the roasting heat of Multan.

Abdus Salam remembered how the sizzling summer of Multan, when temperatures soared above 45 degrees on centigrade scale, dehydrated the human body with thirst. Fasting during the month of *Ramazan*, his father would sit in a tub of water in the afternoon to survive the remaining part of the day. At the same time, there was the excitement to flock around kiosks selling iced drinks, deserts and bowls of *faluda*. Prepared with chilled wheat noodles, syrup, ice-cream, soaked basil seeds and flavourings; *faluda* was one of the hit recipes to fight the heat. Multan offered culinary delights for every occasion and season. In winter, *faluda* was replaced with the variety of *halva*, a caked pudding of semolina, butter, sugar, nuts and herbs.

Multan was a busy market of silk, cotton, indigo, perfumery, spices, glazed pottery, tiles and art-work. Although the city had its own tradition of arts and crafts, the fine art of painting pottery was known to have been introduced here by the Chinese wife of Tamerlane. Markets in *Chowk Bazaar* and *Hussain Agahi*, the hub of commercial hustle and bustle, were drenched with customers from all over the subcontinent.

A substantial segment of Muslims in Multan belonged to the Shia community and, as such, the celebration of *Muharram* was an important feature of religious culture. On the 10th day of Muharram, the members of Shia community walked barefoot, self-chastising; the procession of mourners was accompanied by exquisitely made multi-storey *Ta'azia* floats, signifying the passion of condolence. In tinsel craft, those floats depicted the spires and domes of the most revered Shia shrines in Iraq.

Holding on to his fond reminiscence of Multan, Abdus Salam hated to evoke the memory of Hindu-Muslim communal animosity though it was not within his power to fix the centuries old problem.

In all probability, both Hindus and Muslims had begun suspecting each other the day the young Arab general, Mohammed Bin Qasim, found troves of gold amassed in secret chambers of the Sun Temple. Instead of questioning the stocking of gold in a place of worship, Hindus preferred to perceive the invader as more of a robber. Next, there was 10th century Muslim Governor of Multan who, acting under the influence of Qaramatian radicals, destroyed the Sun Temple, massacred the assembly of Hindu priests and then, in his madness, went as far as closing down the mosque originally built by Mohammed Bin Qasim. Ironically, the mosque was restored by the Afghan war lord, Mahmood of Ghazni, who did not care much about the temple. Hindus rebuilt the temple with its shining dome, lofty columns and colourfully decorated walls. Sooner than later, the adorable idol of Sun God, with its gold crown and hands firmly resting upon knees, returned to its pulpit under a tastefully gilded interior of the dome.

Then there was Aurangzeb Alamgeer (1618–1707), the last of Greater Moguls, who proclaimed jihad upon idolatry. Some historians maintain that thousands of Hindus were executed in Multan alone. According to Hindu tradition, one of the goddesses in an ancient temple was so grieved by the cruelty of the king that she drowned herself to death in a nearby well.[1]

Next, in 1881, when Hindus planned to raise the height of temple spire above the dome of Bahawal Haq shrine, the design provoked fierce rioting and violence between the two communities. Army troops had to be rushed in to restore peace.

In 1942, it was Abdus Salam's turn to have a taste of the tension he had so far been saved from in his hometown Jhang. Early one morning, soon after his arrival in Multan, he thought of visiting the Sun Temple. A couple of his friends accompanied him. They had known the place from a distance and never had the opportunity to go inside the temple. They were not aware of the fact that non-Hindu pilgrims were not supposed to proceed beyond a certain point in the temple, it amounted to sacrilege. Abdus Salam and his friends stranded into the forbidden sanctum of the temple when a Hindu priest checked their advance. He asked them if they were Muslim and then signalled them to follow him. Typical of the mob instinct, it did not take long before Hindu pilgrims present in the compound sniffed the aliens, and the atmosphere geared into an inflammable tension. Any unintentional message off the body language could be misunderstood. For many years, Abdus Salam could vividly relive those tense moments charged with the bleakness of mob mania. He appreciated how the priest escorting them did not wish any clash inside the holy sanctum and just hastened the intruders in the direction of outer courtyard.

Suddenly, they heard the chant *'Dum Bahawal Haq'* emerging from somewhere far away. Then they saw the line of Muslim pilgrims climbing up the cliff. Those pilgrims must have begun their barefoot sojourn several days ago; in

---

[1] Syed Mohammed Latif (1965): pp. 57-58

a remote part of Sind, and now, upon the sight of the dome above Bahawal Haq shrine, they were overcome with delight. Holding hands and attired in their colourful long shirts and baggy trousers, they danced and sang in ecstasy. In a matter of minutes, the mood of the mob closing upon three boys changed; they were permitted to leave, unhurt. 'Hindu Muslim tension was on the rise, one could clearly see a spectre of riots ahead'. Abdus Salam recalled. When Mohammed Hussein came to know about this close brush his son had at the Sun Temple, he hastened to dispatch Abdus Salam to a Nepalese instructor for lessons in *shamsheer zani* or archery, just in case! This was Abdus Salam's taste of extremes in Multan. He had just completed the First Aid training course at Saint John Ambulance Association, and now he was directed to learn archery.[1]

Mohammed Hussein aimed at making sure that Abdus Salam did not get distracted. During college vacations, when Abdus Salam visited Multan, his father used to book a room for him in one of the high school hostels to ensure calm and peace for study. In this way, even when it was holiday time, Abdus Salam continued to abide by his schedule and study eight hours in a row every day.

In spite of living abroad for decades on, Abdus Salam saved the images of Multan he had picked up in his younger days. Multan changed much after the making of Pakistan. In the wake of a two-way mass exodus imposed by the partition of Punjab in 1947, Multan lost its multi-cultural face. Over the decades, there had been an unchecked race for urbanisation bursting the city at seams. With modernisation of farming methods and introduction of fertilisers, Multan witnessed a multiplication of output but the affluence was expressed in traffic jams caused by robust models of four-wheel drive jeeps. Instead of domes, minarets and spires; the city skyline was inundated with television antenna, electricity and telecommunication cables, metallic poles, concrete structures, air-conditioners, slums and shanties and layers of dust, smoke, industrial pollution and haze. An almost complete expulsion of non-Muslims brought the flow of worshipers at the Sun Temple to an abrupt halt.

In 1972, in the wake of Pakistan's military humiliation and the emergence of Bangladesh, the President of remaining Pakistan chose Multan to announce his intention about going nuclear.

In December 1992, when frenzied mobs of Hindu bigots demolished the medieval Babri Mosque in India, an equally rabid mob of Muslim zealots in

---

[1] Interviews 1984: Folder III, p. 39

Multan paid back by levelling to the ground whatever was left of the Sun Temple. Instead of making the future, both India and Pakistan attempted at re-writing the past.

III

Holidaying in Multan ended with the publication of 1942 year twelve intermediate examination result by the University of Punjab. Once again, Abdus Salam topped the list by securing 555 out of a total of 600 marks. His majors included Mathematics, Physics and Chemistry besides language studies in English and Arabic. Among the messages of congratulation he received was also a letter from Afzal Hussein, the Vice Chancellor of Punjab University.

With his grades in year twelve examination, Abdus Salam could have gone straight into studying medicine or engineering, even law; he might as well had stayed on with the family in Multan by getting enrolled into an undergraduate degree program at the local branch of university college. In fact, studying medicine at the King Edward Medical College, established in the 1860s, was considered an enormous professional advantage. A career in medical practice amounted to achieving an affluent lifestyle along with the personal satisfaction of serving the humanity. But making a career in medicine was never an option for Abdus Salam, he was destined to study at Lahore's Government College, an institution considered to be the academic mill manufacturing civil servants. His father, who called the shots on behalf of the son, had a fixation with the civil service.

Previously known as the Imperial Civil Service, under the East India Company, the agency had been rebranded as the Indian Civil Service to take direct control of affairs after the armed uprising of 1857. As a matter of rule, the senior positions in the service went to an exclusive club of white British officers, and the lower clerical positions were dished out to natives. On the average, from 1858 to 1947, about one thousand officers of the Indian Civil Service ruled a population of 300 million in 250 districts of the subcontinent.

Over the decades, as the criteria and process of recruitment was reformed, natives were granted entry into the higher echelons of service though with a good deal of reluctance. Due to competition in qualifying for the service, very few among natives succeeded in getting the commission every year. By the end of 19th century, only seven of 928 officers in the Indian Civil Service belonged to native races because the profession was supposed to symbolise 'the mind and intent of the Government.'[1] With time, however, the proportion of native officers picked up momentum and in 1947, when the British left India, the service comprised of 322 native officers as compared to 688 white British. There is hardly the need here to mention the brazen disparity of salary structure and benefits accorded to the ruler and the ruled. Examination for recruitment in civil service was convened in August every year, and the age limit for applicants was set from 21 to 24. During the probation period of two years, the trainee officers studied in Cambridge, Oxford, London and Dublin. In the old days, the capability to ride horses was also a pre-requisite.

In India, natives qualified to sit for the entry examination if they met the age limit and held Bachelor's degree from one of the few local universities. During the course of their probation at the assigned institution, the trainees studied law and other subjects related to India. On the basis of their performance, the graduates were assigned to different government departments ranging from district administration and police to financial and diplomatic services.

With eyes fixed upon civil service as the professional destination of his son, Mohammed Hussein made a short list of about half-a-dozen names, from the Ahmadiyah caliph to the Inspector of Schools in Multan.[2] He intended to seek their advice about career-related options before Abdus Salam. At the same time, the purpose before Mohammed Hussein, apart from requesting for guidance, was to establish communication with spheres of influence, just in case. Although Mohammed Hussein preferred to be portrayed as a devoutly religious man dwelling in the power of supplication, he did not cut himself from the everyday mundane reality of social networking. During his half-a-decade of sojourn in Lahore, when he fell for religious conversion rather than completing education, he seemed to have learned a lot about the real world surrounding the successful people. Also, there is the indication that, in view Abdus Salam's academic potential, his Ahmadiyah fraternity had great hopes attached to the launching of his career in the public service. After the success of Zafarullah Khan on public scene, the idea constituted an important requirement in the consolidation of Ahmadiyah political clout.[3]

---

[1] Sir Richard Temple: India in the 1880, London, 1881 (Second Edition), p. 43
[2] Abdul Hameed (circa 2000): p. 37
[3] Ram Prakash Bambah: Trieste Tribute to Abdus Salam, edited by Hamende A.M, 1997, p. 49

Mohammed Hussein's letter to Zafarullah Khan received an efficient response. Zafarullah Khan wrote back with somewhat of a worldly advice urging Abdus Salam to consider tapping every possible source of knowledge like travelling and tourism as dependence on books alone was not sufficient. This was a suggestion underscoring the need to learn about practical side of life, a world beyond academic idealism. Typically, before closing his letter, Zafarullah Khan wished Abdus Salam all the best in life 'in service of Islam and the Ahmadiyah'.

Likewise, Mohammed Hussein's letter to Afzal Hussein, the Vice Chancellor of Punjab University, received worthy attention. Afzal Hussein marked the mail to Abdul Majid, a member of the Indian Civil Service. In August 1942, Abdul Majid contacted Mohammed Hussein and canvassed in favour of Mathematics and English Literature as subjects of choice for Abdus Salam. Citing his own example, he stated the fact that a good mathematician always made the big difference in the aggregate, especially while sitting for Indian Civil Service examination. Abdul Majid had scored 95% marks in Mathematics alone, he did not buy the popular trend of falling for History and Oriental Languages. Any good student, he remarked, could cover these areas independently.

As stated earlier, the Government College in Lahore seemed to constitute a kingpin in the scheme of things before Mohammed Hussein. Why? Simply because the institution was considered to be the training ground for civil service recruitments. Not only students from all over the northwest of India arrived here to learn and pick up degrees, they were expected to gain fluency in English language and be able to live and think as best as possible like their colonial rulers. Even though the college did not resemble Harrow and Eton schools of England, it was meant to deliver a matching product in support of imperial bureaucracy. Inaugurated on the New Year Day in 1864, the college flaunted its pride for showing youth the way to lucrative employment in both public and private sectors. There was the widely held belief that admission in the college equalled a license to enter government.

Anyone visiting Lahore, by crossing *Ravi* in the west, faced the imposing minarets of the *Badshahi* or King's Mosque next to the Fort, both completed in the 17th century. Turning right in front of the mosque towards The Mall, the visitor would pass by the splendid red stone towers and gothic archways of the college built upon an elevated mound on the left. Up over the manicured lawns, sloping towards the Lower Mall, the main court of the college faced the river while its well-kept rose gardens divided administration blocks and teaching departments. Almost adjacent to the college was the Senate Hall of Punjab University, and only walking distance away were university colleges of law, oriental languages, pharmacy and chemical engineering. In this way, the prime location of the college made it easily accessible to the medieval and the recent boroughs of the city; even the colourful red-light district was not far away.

Despite its affiliation with Punjab University, the Government College enjoyed a presence much larger than other educational institutions offering degree programs. Occasionally, the college posed itself to be autonomous in relation to the university to which it was accountable for academic policies, procedures, syllabi and examination assessments. In Lahore, enrolment in degree programs was assigned on the basis of a communal quota system, with nearly 80 percent of seats were more or less equally divided between Muslim and Hindu students; the policy was aimed at achieving a sort of 'positive discrimination' to check the otherwise unstoppable march on merit of the scholarship-loving Hindu community. In a way, the quota system also mirrored the communal demography of Punjab, especially in order to secure education and employment opportunities in favour of religious communities other than the highly competitive Hindus. An overwhelming majority of students hailed from urban middle class. Those from the rich feudal families went to the Atchison Chiefs College near the Governor House. Due to sociological conditions of the time, fewer girls made it to higher education.

Historically, Lahore had started off as a settlement on the left bank of river *Ravi*. Originating in the Himalayas and then arriving upon the Punjab plain after a course of approximately 450 miles, the river marked the western border of old Lahore. Unlike Multan, Lahore lacked any glorious feature in the class of Sun Temple in its ancient history. Prior to the waves of Muslim invasions from northwest, the town had been ruled by Rajput kings belonging to Solanki, Bhatti and Chauhan houses. Located on the invasion highway, from Peshawar to Delhi, Lahore gained extraordinary strategic significance. Invaders from Afghanistan, Iran and Central Asia destroyed and remade Lahore. Armies led by Chengis Khan, Tamerlane, Zaheeruddin Babur and Ahmad Shah Abdali trampled Lahore and massacred its residents. Medieval strategists held the popular view that once Lahore was taken; Delhi would be a piece of cake. No wonder the greater Moguls camped here to keep a vigil on their empire stretching from Afghanistan and Kashmir to Indian Ocean. Akbar the Great had spent the best part of his reign here. Both Jehangir and his queen Noor Jahan were buried in Lahore. Shah Jahan, the creator of Taj Mahal, was born here and he gave the city Shalimar Gardens. His son, Aurangzeb Alamgeer built the Badshahi Mosque. Lahore's Muslims rulers gave the city fortifications, palaces, mosques and imposing tombs; marked by a striking lack of any meaningful intellectual tradition or prestigious educational institutions.

After the collapse of Mogul Empire in the 18th century, the city went under a wavering interlude of Sikh confederacy. Any sites of Mogul memory were targeted with a policy of revenge and insult. In the 19th century, when the British annexed Punjab their foremost objective was to raise revenues in order to fortify defence along the north-western borders; they feared Russia. As such, an infrastructural modernisation and reform ensued at an unprecedented scale. Lahore, being the seat of government in Punjab, benefitted most by undergoing a thorough whitewash of European influence and discipline.

Abdus Salam arrived in a Lahore that was more advanced than the one of his father's day. Twenty years appeared to have made a big difference as the old city, hidden behind its thirteen gates, had been humbled by the progressive march of suburbs sprawling outside the crumbling city wall.

Life around Government College, during the course of working week, was hectic and noisy. Walking south on the Lower Mall between the college and the Central Model School there was the complex of District Courts whining with chambers of judges and lawyers, stationary shops and tea stalls; all humming with clerks and clients, typists and touts, hand-cuffed offenders and police officers, witnesses and vendors. Next, there was the Government Secretariat where the *Latt Sahib*, or the British Governor, worked with his lean team of aides. Further south, between university grounds and the riverside, towards the road to Multan, lived the affluent Hindu community in their exclusive suburb of *Krishan Nagar*, or the Home of Lord Krishna.

Walking south on the Lower Mall, one would turn left on The Mall or *Thandi Sarak* lined with trees, spacious service lanes and wide footpath on both sides, it was the central business district in Lahore. Strolling up The Mall was a fashion among the cultured citizens of Lahore, a delightful experience round the year, be it a warm summer morning or the chilling winter evening when mist settled upon apartments. Starting from its western end, the thoroughfare was decorated with impressive buildings. First on the left was the entrance of Punjab University Senate Hall guarded by the statue of Alfred Woolner (1878–1936), who had served the institution first as its Professor of Sanskrit and then as the Vice Chancellor.[1]

Zamzama, an eye-catching specimen of 18th century artillery, cast in Lahore in 1757, the year of British victory in the battle of Plassey in Bengal, was installed on a platform in front of the Museum. With its 250 millimetre bore barrel, resting upon two huge wheels, the gun was known to have been used in many encounters. *Zamzama* had been allotted its prime parking slot on the Mall in 1870, much before its introduction to the English-speaking world by Kim, a fictional character of Rudyard Kipling. Like many other pompous imperialists in his racist frame of mind, Rudyard Kipling believed that the British colonial rule had been a blessing for India and its second-class humanity. His father served as the Principal of the Arts College and he himself had briefly worked at *Civil and Military Gazette* in Lahore. Rudyard Kipling's rather paternalistic view of the British colonial hold over India was turned upside down within a matter of few years.

Leaving *Zamzama* and the Museum behind, walking further eastward, one passed by the impressive buildings of Town Hall, College of Arts, General Post Office, Punjab High Court and Punjab Assembly. From Museum upwards, The Mall was lined with a few statues including those of a couple of natives like Ganga Ram (1851–1927), the commanding philanthropist; and Lajpat Roy (1865–1928), the political activist who had succumbed to injuries received from police bashing while he led an anti-British rally. Then there was the elegant and meaningful statue of John Lawrence (1811–1879) who served as Governor of Punjab before his promotion as Viceroy of India. Holding the sword in one hand and pen in the other, he faced the sandstone turrets of Punjab High Court while the inscription on his figure in bronze stated 'I serve you with pen and sword'. Typically, it was a reflection of the time-tested carrot and stick policy of invaders in Punjab. A few minutes of walk away from the statue of John Lawrence, was Charring Cross where the statue of Queen Victoria stood in shining white marble. Curiously though, the queen appeared to face the Freemasons Lodge and Lahore Zoo, with her back on the imposing columns and domes of Punjab Assembly Hall. Her statue was installed in 1902, a year after her death.

Further up, The Mall got lost into the predominantly European district, curving along the Government House, built out of deep red slabs of a 17th century

---

[1] Professor Woolner is buried in Lahore; his wife is known to have bequeathed a greater part of the family estate to Punjab University.

Mogul tomb, facing the lush green Lawrence Gardens housing the Montgomery Hall and its starch white columns. Endless rows of trees, rose-beds, lawns and a cricket ground defined the class of Lawrence Gardens. One block of the hall, next to the Race Course, housed the exclusive Gymkhana Club, where natives and dogs, whatever their pedigree, were not permitted to enter up until the final years of the British raj.

Beneath the rising levels of communal tension, class barriers, gender and age split; the people of Lahore tended to share fun, puttering, punting, betting, cockfights, quail fights, dogfights, wrestling, flying and crisscrossing kites, marbles, spinning tops, *guli-danda*, cricket, hockey, soccer, theatre and cinema; they worshiped and hated politicians, clergymen and film stars.

People of Lahore had the most versatile palate. Depending on their religious and culinary preferences they could gobble, gulp, swallow and devour anything from Kashmiri bread loaves, chapattis, curried trotters and tripe, deep fried pancake prathas, pakoras, samosas, chickpea mesh, pilaf, kebabs, and fried fish fresh from *Ravi*. Almost always, the main courses were followed by chilled glasses of yogurt *lassi*, sweetened or salted according to taste. Healthy items like salad were often in short supply, instead hot chutney and pickle lubricated assimilation. On the average, cuisine in Lahore was influenced more by Peshawar, Kashmir and Delhi.

Syed Ali Hajveri (1009–1072), the patron saint of Lahore, came from Afghanistan. Upon arrival in Lahore, he camped outside *Bhatti* Gate. When someone urged him to rename the gate, he declined on grounds that tampering with precedence and antiquity was not a good idea.[1] Apart from Syed Ali Hajveri, Lahore was also known for saints like Mian Mir, Madhu Lal Hussein, Bawa Shah Jamal and Hakikat Rai.

Lahore's old city, inside the wall, comprised of narrow streets and lanes, paved with outdated bricks, turning into steps where sloping was deemed unsafe. Daily life in the labyrinth of such bygone architecture and town planning seemed to reflect an ageless contentment with dwindled space. Woven in the jumble of ancient dwellings, reluctantly resting upon rotting bricks and cancer-eaten adhesive, arches and wooden balconies, were bazaars for every kind of merchandise and craft. Any foreigner used to living in the age of electricity and telephone cables, town water and sewer drainage would be mystified to imagine

---

[1] Daily Jang, Rawalpindi, Friday Magazine, 18-24 August 1989, p. 9

the skeleton, if any, of those services. Often, newcomers lost their sense of direction within moments after entering the city through one of the gates.[1]

When Abdus Salam arrived to study in Lahore, the Government College offered Bachelors, Honours and Master's Degree programs in various disciplines ranging from history, politics, economics, philosophy, psychology, mathematics, physics, chemistry and biology. There were advanced study courses in languages and literature of English, Arabic, Persian, Sanskrit and Punjabi. Many of the faculty members had topped up their qualifications at universities in Cambridge, Oxford, London, Edinburgh and Paris.

Lahore in the 1940s was a fairly fashionable place where educated middle class chased lifestyles closer to European examples of the day rather than the conservative majority living in smaller town and villages of India. A whole lot of brilliant students landed here seeking qualifications in a variety of disciplines in both social and natural sciences as well as, if they wished, to excel in sporting activities of their choice.

IV

While seeking enrolment for the Bachelor's degree program at Government College Abdus Salam picked up a combination of subjects just as Abdul Majid had proposed. He was aware that candidates sitting for civil service examination could take mathematics worth 800 marks. Mathematics, Abdus Salam felt confident, would give him the lead over other candidates. Ironically, he did not go anywhere near Physics. In view of his impressive academic record, he was enrolled straightaway. According to the picture his father had in mind, Abdus Salam was set to complete the undergraduate Bachelors Level and then sit for the Indian Civil Service examination within a couple of years.

Abdus Salam was allotted a room in the New Hostel that had recently been added to the old Quadrangle. Every year, the college offered about 350 occupancies in 172 cubicles and 52 dormitories of the two blocks; facilities for recreation and convenience were shared. In view of the Hindu prohibition of meat, the kitchen operated with discretion for Hindu and Muslim boarders though the weekly menu was set by committees. A limited number of servants

---

[1] Lahore: A Sentimental Journey, written by Pran Nevile (1922-2018), is recommended for further reading.

employed by the college were shared among students. Because a dormitory was shared among five or more boarders from various social backgrounds, there was no privacy and everyone kept an eye on everyone else and learned to accept each other in their smells, noises, gestures, tastes, good and poor habits.

In order to accommodate the scions of rich houses, the college also offered a limited number of double-room suites, popularly known as A-Sets. Abdus Salam remembered how his neighbour, Aziz Ahmad, who came from the princely state of Bhopal, lived in his A-Set accommodation in the company of a servant. On their own, those boys from wealthy families were well mannered but their presence injected the class bar as a result of which some other students pretended to be exclusive. At college canteen, for example, the show off was expressed by an outpouring display of hospitality, with some of the boys ordering elaborate menus, often beyond their means. Others tended to climb up the class ladder by hiring a full tonga-taxi instead of sharing the journey to save the money hard earned by their parents.

Approaching 17, it was Abdus Salam's first experience to be on his own, living far from the constant watch of Mohammed Hussein. He did encounter a bit of culinary bump in switching from the home-made curries of his mother over to hostel cuisine. But it did not take him long to adapt with frequently served dishes like *Aloo Gosht* or the curried mutton-potato.[1] Mohammed Hussein cared for his son as best as could be possible by striking a deal with Baba Saida, the chief Gardner at college. From time to time, Baba Saida provided additional food items meeting Abdus Salam's taste.[2]

He was quick in demarcating his routine between study and a bit of leisure. After classrooms and libraries, he studied in his room. He is known to have asked a hostel employee to lock his room from outside to dampen any interruption for long hours. Because internal locks had not come in fashion so any of his neighbours, classmates and friends would see the padlock hanging upon the bolt and then just leave without bothering to knock. Living in a world of his own for a greater part of the day, he lost touch with reality sometimes.

At times, Abdus Salam worked up to 14 hours in a single stretch.[3] Other boarders in the New Hostel thought of him as a 'lean, tallish, handsome young man from Jhang who sported a fine moustache and was rarely seen abroad'. All

---

[1] The Friday Times, Lahore, 27 June-3 July 1996.
[2] *Khalid* (December 1997): p. 191
[3] Mohammed Hussein (1974): pp. 41-42

sorts of stories circulated about his indefatigable ease with numbers, calculations, equations, diagrams and graphs. In his room, he was rumoured to be rolling in the rustle of rough sheets, full of mathematical equations and formulae.[1] But then the pressure of academic challenges did not appear to pose much of a strain upon Abdus Salam. Over the years, he had been so well at ease with disciplined learning, especially Mathematics, that he could perform far better and faster than his contemporaries. His intellectual edge enabled him to manage with time comfortably.[2]

He found intellectual atmosphere in Government College quite superior and inspiring. 'We had very highly qualified teachers, a number of them graduating at Cambridge and Oxford. In Mathematics, we had Sri Chowla who moved on to become a professor in Kansas. He was one of the most encouraging of all the people. I did my first research problem in Mathematics with his blessings. He would come to the class, give us a problem and explain its higher ramifications. When I found a better solution of the problem compared to the one previously proposed by Ramanujan, I was so excited I went straight to the residence of Professor Chowla, who lived on campus, and woke him up deep in the night. Our professors were very good and competition very strong'. He remembered. Relax, go get some rest and then write the paper, Professor Chowla had told him. Abdus Salam's simpler course in one of the complex equations of Srinivasa Ramanujan (1887–1920), the great Indian mathematician, made the basis of his first ever research paper in Mathematics. His paper was accepted for publication in the *Mathematics Student*, a reputed science journal of India.

For the benefit of students less inclined towards physically demanding outdoor sports like cricket, hockey, soccer and swimming; there was the Common Room offering pastimes ranging from chess, carom, and table-tennis to games of cards. Given his disinclination towards outdoors, Abdus Salam acquired a taste for chess. He was coached by Khushia, the Common Room attendant, who came from Nepal.

Occasionally, Abdus Salam broke out of his strict discipline to have a round or so with Khushia who commanded the reputation of being invincible. 'He would not prompt anyone to challenge him. Instead, he sat quietly in a corner and obliged only when invited by someone'. Abdus Salam recalled afterwards, adding that it made news when someone checkmated Khushia. One Sikh

---

[1] *Al-Nahl*, a publication of Ahmadiyah community in the USA, Fall 1997, p. 149
[2] Ram Prakash Bambah - Trieste Tribute (1997): p. 48

classmate of Abdus Salam, who was adept at making some of the deadliest moves with unassuming pawns, had humbled Khushia on a few occasions. Abdus Salam could have excelled in chess but he received a stern warning from his father. In fact, someone had turned him in by conveying his new found taste for chess. Look, it is impossible to make up for the lost time, Mohammed Hussein had argued with his son. Almost instantly, Abdus Salam distanced himself from his brief indulgence in chess. He could see the size of addiction in a group of his classmates who spent night after night in playing the Bridge. He did not mind the reprimand. 'I don't think my father was being harsh, even when the vigilance made me unhappy it was only for a couple of days'.[1]

Instead, he joined the Rowing Club and occasionally went out to paddle in the river. This was perhaps the only outdoor taste he acquired in Lahore. He appreciated the value of breaking the monotony of academic routine for it was like getting recharged. 'I was very fortunate in utilising my time'. He acknowledged afterwards.[2]

On other occasions he would just walk around the college, especially to bookshops. One day, Abdus Salam and his friend Waheed Qureshi (1925–2009), walked in the Anarkali Bazaar. Few minutes of walking distance from the college, the bazaar had ascended upon the tomb of Anarkali, a beautiful courtesan at the Mogul court, who was buried alive for falling in love with prince Saleem, the romantic son of Akbar the Great. For their spending spree of finest perfumery, makeup creams, lotions, garments, footwear, household items and general goods, imported from all over the world; rich housewives made it a point to visit the bazaar at the first available opportunity.

Waheed Qureshi was studying for a degree program in Persian Language and Literature at the Government College; he aspired to become a linguist and historian. When the two friends entered the bazaar from college end, Abdus Salam offered to play a little game of memory by calling out the names of businesses on one side of the street without looking up at their billboards. He asked Waheed Qureshi to act as the examiner. Amused, Waheed Qureshi consented but then he was amazed when Abdus Salam called out names in exact order from one end of the bazaar to the other. Waheed Qureshi gave his friend full marks. In all probability, it was an exercise on the part of Abdus Salam; he wanted to check if his power of retention was still as strong as the primary school

---

[1] Interviews 1984: Folder II: p. 35

[2] Interviews 1984: Folder III, pp. 41, 48

days in Jhang where he had committed to memory the Multiplication Tables up to forty by merely walking behind the chanting group of accounting school students.

Many of the faculty members at the college hailed from affluent and educated families and had been at Cambridge or Oxford. Occasionally, enthused by the latent desire to be like their rulers, some of them mimicked British traditions, at times donning the Cambridge-Oxford rivalry in Lahore. It would not be far off the mark to describe Government College as an island closer to Britain than anywhere else in Punjab. Since the college had opened its doors to female students, few girls making it to degree programs attracted a great deal of attention from their male classmates.

Did Abdus Salam encounter any difficulty in coming to terms with a predominantly metropolitan order and faster pace of life in Lahore? Apparently, not in any big way because from the very outset, the discipline around study and schoolwork had prepared him to be on his own. For the sake of goals to score at different stages in his life, he was used to being solitary and autonomous. Moving from Jhang to Multan and then Lahore did not matter much in terms of social adjustment. In fact, he thought only The Mall gave Lahore an edge over Multan. In this way, Lahore to him was just a bigger version of Multan. After seeing places of architectural charm in Lahore, which did not take very long, he settled down to his old pastime of visiting bookshops near the college.

How much of Lahore did Abdus Salam actually wish to see? Lots of trendy restaurants, coffee shops, cinema houses, nightclubs and bars were on The Mall. But his personal temperament coupled with limited financial resources kept him from indulgence. In the beginning, he found very little to do outside the college other than visiting bookshops or sometimes just walking around to see places of historical and architectural significance. Although a teenager, his personal discipline and control was immaculate.

With income from scholarship grants on top of what Mohammed Hussein afforded to send him, Abdus Salam kept the tidiness of his budget by managing to stay on the safe side of one hundred rupees a month bar. 'I was one of the un-prosperous students, basically from a very poor family. Although my father went out to make every sacrifice in desire and preference, I was not able to afford the way other boys used to live and spend'. He recalled. But then a freedom from pretentiousness made life much easier for him. He understood how his college-mates from relatively affluent background ordered fruit, confectionary and drinks to entertain guests in their rooms, he could see how boarders occupying A-sets, coming from strikingly rich families, lived lavishly. At the same time, he was amused to observe the class consciousness among the insecure. There were occasions when some of the boys tended to overplay the class act. For example, the small journey from rail station to the college. Some of the boys owned cars, many of them could afford the horse-driven tonga taxi by full. Others, like Abdus Salam, were obliged to share the one-way fare. 'Entering the hostel would be an important event in the sense that so far you have managed the baggage yourself but now you suddenly tend to become a *sahib* by shouting at one of the hostel employees to take charge of your paraphernalia. This was the sort of *riyakari* sanctimonious pretension by not doing your work with dignity struck me as a worst part of the hostel life. After carrying your stuff all the way from your house in Multan to the rail station and finally to hostel where you suddenly try to act like a *sahib*. I always hated this hypocrisy. Other than that I did not find it difficult to adjust with life in the hostel'. He stated.[1]

One example of this steadfastness was evident in his attitude towards cinema. He had arrived in Lahore at a time when cinema was in fashion. Alexander Korda's Elephant Boy, based on a story written by Rudyard Kipling, had been released. Many of Abdus Salam's close friends talked about Clark Gable, Spencer Tracy, Robert Taylor, Bob Hope, Humphry Bogart, Gregory Peck, Lawrence Olivier, Vivien Leigh, Rita Hayworth, Marlene Dietrich, Greta Garbo, Heddy Lamarr et al.

But watching movies was prohibited by the Ahmadiyah; the party considered the pastime as one the modern gateways to licentiousness, especially the manner in which women in films were shown enticingly dressed, freely mixing with men, singing, dancing, even romancing brazenly. How could promiscuousness so enormous sit with the stringency of Islamic limitations on cross-gender socialisation? Was it possible for the Ahmadiyah or any other group, matching them in self-imposition of obsessive wishful barriers, to stop the march of technology? Still, Abdus Salam, on his part, accepted the Ahmadiyah prohibition. He kept himself from cinema in letter and spirit even when it was hard to snub close friends who every now and then tempted him to come along. One of his friends praised the Ahmadiyah caution but argued that restraint needed to take a softer view of good movies worth watching. One day, Abdus Salam gave in and agreed to watch a movie with his friends, Shaukat Awan and

---

[1] Interviews 1984: Folder III, pp. 25-27

Aftab Ahmed. At that time, Abdus Salam was the President of the Hostel Union and Shaukat Awan was the Hostel Prefect. But once in the cinema hall, Abdus Salam shut his eyes throughout the show. 'I heard the film but did not see it'. He recalled but did not recollect how the situation evolved.[1]

A few years later, circa 1955, the three of them happened to meet in Karachi and Shaukat Awan insisted they watch a Punjabi movie. By then, Abdus Salam had developed taste for a selected class of movies, he agreed but it was the first occasion for him to watch a Punjabi movie. 'It was so ridiculous, I and Aftab laughed so much about the story, plot, theme and presentation of the film that Shaukat got very angry'. Abdus Salam remembered how he and Aftab Ahmed united to tell Shaukat Awan that if this was what films were about, they have not missed anything. 'Of course, in Cambridge, I saw classic English films. I was a member of the Film Society. He added.[2]

In 1944, Abdus Salam passed the Bachelors by obtaining 451 out of 500 marks, making it to the top in aggregate as well as each of the subjects in the program. He kept his pace of breaking the old and setting new records. He qualified for five different scholarship grants, simultaneously. Under the rules, he could avail only one of those grants. In view of his extraordinary performance, Punjab University amended the statute book by granting him permission to avail two.

Although he had succeeded in setting a new record, Abdus Salam did not sound very pleased with his assessment in Urdu Language paper. He had been given 30 marks out of a total of 50 in the paper for Urdu Language. He had scored 121 marks out of total of 150 in English Language paper and full marks in Mathematics. 'Our Urdu papers were usually marked in Aligarh. We always suspected those examiners'. Effectively, he was referring to the paternal attitudes of Aligarh examiners who, rather possessively, owned Urdu Language as their mother tongue in which people from other provinces were not supposed to excel or be equal. Abdus Salam was sure to have gone further up in the ladder of aggregate if the Aligarh bias towards students from Punjab was not in the interplay.[3]

With Bachelor's degree completed in flying colours, Abdus Salam was all set to sit for civil service examination. But he was held back by a moratorium

---

[1] Interviews 1984: Folder III, p. 46

[2] Interviews 1984: Folder III, p. 46-48

[3] Interviews 1984: Folder III, pp. 7-8

upon all public sector recruitments due to World War II. Entering into its fifth year, the war had channelled government attention almost exclusively into defence and military effort. At the same time, the popular demand for self-rule in India had picked up an irreversible momentum and there was no easy way to guess the shape of future after the end of war. Thick clouds of uncertainty hung upon the political horizon everywhere. As war lingered, so did the scepticism over the very future of British rule in India.

What was he going to do if public service recruitment did not resume soon? He was only 18, had time on his side to meet the age limit for a while but living in limbo did not make sense, especially at a time when political fate of the subcontinent hung in balance. Someone in the family advised him to consider doing a degree in Law to enter public life like Zafarullah Khan. Abdus Salam sounded unsure, he felt the requisite mobility to stand out in politics was not in his makeup. He believed it was not possible for him to respond sharply in all sorts of situations.

He felt slightly panicked and mailed an application for the position of an engineering apprentice at North-Western Railways. He received invitation for the job interview, got short-listed and was asked to go for medical examination. Not knowing what future had in store for him, he failed to pass through the medical test due to an eye condition that involved the risk of colour blindness.[1]

Some of his teachers at the college impressed upon him to get enrolled for a Masters in English Literature. Personally, he was inclined towards doing a Masters in Mathematics, and considered migrating to the University of Calcutta where, keeping with the tradition of Srinivasa Ramanujan, the Faculty in the Department of Mathematics was known to be more progressive than anywhere else in India. He thought of enrolment in the doctoral program in Calcutta. It was an unsettling time in his life. After weighing his options, and logistics available to the family, he enrolled for Master's Degree program in Mathematics at the Government College.

V

Quite fairly, the Government College boasted about its highly educated teaching staff. Professor Gurudat Sondhi (1890–1966), the native gentleman to

---

[1] Interviews 1984: Folder IV, p. 38

become the Principal at Government College, was the son of a rich barrister; he had studied at Trinity College in Cambridge. Against the largely old-fashioned social scene of Punjab, where open mixing of genders was stalled, frowned upon and almost forbidden; the college constituted an opportunity to intermingle, come closer and be able to speak and understand each other. Professor Sondhi encouraged sporting activities across gender barriers and, while occupying The Lodge, that is, the principal's house on campus, he was often seen around with his wife and two beautiful daughters. His older daughter, Urmila Sondhi, enrolled in English Literature degree program at the college, was a popular member of the community with her share of fans.

Urmila Sondhi was a year senior to Abdus Salam and, like him, among the top students and a record-holder in English Literature. A year later, Abdus Salam broke her record by setting his own. He was reported to have had a crush on her[1] though it seems hard to square such indulgence into the cultural reticence of his makeup. He did not confess his fancy of Urmila but some of his contemporaries hold there was something for sure. He may have been an innocent victim of her attraction in a setting in which she was the sociable city girl teasing his conservative shyness. But the social profile of Urmila Sondhi steadied when she fell for her English Literature teacher, Sirajuddin Ahmed, who was already married to Razia, a painter of considerable standing in her own right. According to college grapevine, when the news of her husband's fancy reached Razia, she allowed Sirajuddin to obey his heart. Soon afterwards, Razia moved to Oxford in England and Sirajuddin got married to Urmila Sondhi, both living happily the rest of their lives. Razia and Sirajuddin Ahmed remained good friends.

This proposition of Abdus Salam's crush on Urmila Sondhi holds only a theoretical significance and loses a great deal of its spicy taste after she got married with Sirajuddin Ahmed. What seemed to have lived much longer than the reported crush was the tension between two scholarly men, Abdus Salam and Sirajuddin Ahmed. Somehow, Abdus Salam held a murky record in the good books of Sirajuddin Ahmed. On his part, Abdus Salam tended to trace the friction to his better performance in English Literature examination especially when he smashed the record set earlier by Urmila Sondhi. 'I have no reason to believe it but perhaps my pre-eminence in beating Urmila's record in English Literature

---

[1] Gordon Fraser (2008): p. 58 (the author does not cite any source but there is the indication that the information came from one of Abduls Salam's contemporaries like Ram Prakash Bambah)

was not quite welcomed'. He tended to estimate much later. But there again, the spinning of academic competition into personal rivalries has never been a rare phenomenon, it must have been the case in Lahore's Government College of the 1940s as anywhere else. Today, the need to conduct an exhaustive search into the whole Abdus Salam-Urmila Sondhi-Sirajuddin Ahmed affair would hardly make much sense but, as will be seen in the next chapter of the current study, the baggage of bitter taste lived on for a quite a while.

Aftab Ahmed, who studied at Government College in the 1940s, holds the view that Sirajuddin Ahmed wanted Abdus Salam to do the Masters in English Literature but the proposition did not materialise because Abdus Salam had his heart in Mathematics.[1]

When Abdus Salam was questioned about his romantic fantasies of the past, he avoided a direct answer by making a rather academic remark. 'In our social structure, you know very well', he said, 'we do not come across the opposite sex. We had three or four girls in whole of the Government College Lahore. There were none in Jhang. How do you expect anybody to develop anything?'[2]

Still, it is important to remember that even when he came from the country outback and his family adhered to religious conformism of the Ahmadiyah, Abdus Salam was not a recluse in the strict sense of the term. After leaving Jhang, liberated from the puritan gaze of his parents, Abdus Salam must have undergone a great deal of emotional transformation. His intellectual progress and superiority of scholarship was bound to open upon him the window to an enlightened view of the world abroad. Living in Lahore, in the 1940s, an outright rejection of the social soul of Government College did not make much sense. If Lahore represented an enlightened microcosm out of the laid-back Punjab, Government College was a refined portrait of the city that had been home to Abdus Salam for the past four years. He lived and breathed in the company of his fellow students and their scholarly teachers. While studying the best part of the day, he was still not removed from social preferences, religious affiliation, political disposition, views, tastes, professional rivalries, likes and dislikes of people making the society around him.

A political animal began waking up in his personality. Apart from his academic exploits it was the friendly disposition that made him popular among students. In times of need he would reach to help friends as best as possible. For

---

[1] Aftab Ahmed: Personal Profiles (Urdu), Islamabad, 2005, p. 7
[2] Interviews 1984: Folder III, p. 45

example, when his college-mate Prem Luthar had appendicitis, he spent two sleepless days nursing the patient just like a family member.[1] His popularity spanned across the rising tides of communal divide. In the academic year 1945-46, he won the rare distinction of serving three offices simultaneously. He was the Editor of college magazine Ravi, the president of New Hostel residents association and the president of the students union. Winning all those offices in an electorate deeply divided along communal lines was not an ordinary achievement. He succeeded due to a good deal of respect he commanded among Hindu, Muslim, Sikh, Christian, urban, rural, rich and poor students.

Coincidentally, it was during his tenure as the president of the New Hostel union that college authorities decided to abolish A-Sets. About then, college administration approved plans for the overdue renovation of the Quadrangle, and there was the need to temporarily accommodate some of the Quadrangle borders in New Hostel. Speaking at the annual dinner of the union, Abdus Salam referred to the abolition of A-Sets as an achievement in equality, and the hospitality offered at New Hostel to displaced boarders as an act of fraternity. He concluded by calling for unity as national freedom from colonial yoke was not very far away. Years on, he did not forget the standing ovation given to him for making such a fine speech. Abdus Salam felt pleasantly amazed himself. 'I came to discover my capability to express myself'. He recalled in 1984.[2]

One of his teachers from the Department of English Literature, Inder Varma, walked up all the way to rostrum to congratulate and pat Abdus Salam on the back. 'It was the best speech we had from a student after a long time, let me have a copy of it'. Inder Mohan is reported to have asked Abdus Salam.[3] In a way here, Abdus Salam was caught in the crossfire between Inder Varma and Sirajuddin Ahmed. A few years earlier, Inder Varma had fallen in love with the young painter, Razia, who married Sirajuddin Ahmed. In a bid to settle the old score in some way, Inder Varma would not let any opportunity pass unutilised. By patting Abdus Salam for the annual dinner speech, he intended to tell his student to keep it up and go for Urmila Sondhi. Of course, those gestures constituted a small subsidiary of the professional dictates defining the college. Regardless of personal preferences, Sirajuddin Ahmed appointed Abdus Salam as the Editor of college magazine *Ravi* as a matter of professional choice. At the

---

[1] Ram Prakash Bambah - Trieste Tribute (1997), P. 48

[2] Interviews 1984: Folder III, P. 29

[3] Interviews 1984: Folder III, p. 30

same time, Sirajuddin Ahmed was among those faculty members who, up until recently, had canvassed Abdus Salam to do Masters in English Literature instead of Mathematics.

Those students and their teachers, making the cream of multicultural intelligentsia in Lahore, hailing from Muslim, Hindu, Sikh and other religious communities, walking across college corridors, strolling up and down its lawns, caught in academic pursuit, falling in love and building lifelong bonds of friendship; all continued to live in hope, they had no idea what the future held in store for them or how the chain reaction of political dynamite will blow up on their faces within a matter of few months. However, keeping in line with the proud tradition of Government College, a number of Abdus Salam's friends and contemporaries in the college made it to the top in India and Pakistan. For example, in Pakistan alone, Altaf Gauhar became the information secretary to Field Marshal Ayub Khan, Ehsan Malik served as Major General in the army and later as Political Adviser to President Ziaul Haq, Masood Mahmood served as the security chief of Zulfiqar Bhutto, Aftab Khan and Shaukat Awan worked as Pakistan's ambassadors in Rome and Cairo, respectively; and the list went on.

Only a couple of years prior to Abdus Salam's admission to the college, the All India Muslim League party had resolved to achieve a separate homeland for Muslims of India. As the war bolted towards its costly conclusion, so did the fickle fate of British colonial hold over India. His enrolment for Masters in Mathematics coincided with the end of war. Still, the schedule for resumption of public service recruitment was not in sight. In fact, the British were under tremendous pressure to proclaim a timetable for the independence of India. Not merely an offensive graffiti, the end of the raj was written on the wall. Two world wars in three decades had broken the financial back of Britain as the champion of capitalist order. Although the movement for freedom had picked an irrevocable thrust, it was still not clear as to how and exactly when the British would pack up. Some conservatives like Winston Churchill among them hoped to defer the cut-off date by another two decades.

Britain owed a sum of £4200 million to the United States in war supplies, and another £1400 million to India in debt. Then internal arrears to the tune of £26000 million were due to the rebuilding program. In 1945, the export trade of Britain had shrunk by 29% of its 1939 mark. As such, the imminent bailout revolved around 'selling' a part of the empire. No harm was seen in a transfer of power, that is, handing the charge of world domination over to the United States.

Such a transaction amounted to replacement of sterling with dollar at a time when the Americans looked forward to inheriting strategic commercial advantages in the Middle East, South Asia and the Indian Ocean.[1] It was about time to transfer the supremacy to the United States, also the need to overhaul and sophisticate the very mechanism of colonial hold. An advanced regime of colonialism, to manoeuvre hegemony through remote financial control, had to be evolved.

Lahore, in 1946, experienced an unprecedented popularity of the demand for Pakistan as an independent Muslim homeland in South Asia. Every now and then, mass rallies were staged to promote the Pakistan idea. No matter what communal equilibrium separate electorates and communal quotas in employment and education had achieved was flushed down the drain and Punjab headed for anarchy. With patchy presence of Muslims, dispersed all over the subcontinent, hardly anyone had much of a clue about the shape of an exclusively Muslim homeland. For example, what will happen to the sizeable non-Muslim communities in Punjab or eastern Bengal? How will those communities survive and feel secure in the Islamic state of Pakistan? What was the point in smashing the multicultural face of India if those non-Muslims could live amicably in Pakistan? How will a state created in the name of religion stay tolerant? Before someone attempted at finding satisfactory answers to such questions, the All India Muslim League party, demanding Pakistan, turned the table on its opponents. When elections to the Punjab Legislative Council were convened in December 1945, the party won by a landslide, the Unionists were routed to absolute redundancy.

In the political environment thick with readymade power-sharing schemes for a free India, the unity of Punjab was at stake. Evan Jenkins (1896–1985), the last British Governor, made the strong remark that 'no one community can rule Punjab with its present boundaries except by conquest'. He lamented that the unity of Punjab was not impossible 'provided we think as Punjabis'.[2] But then, with the British intentions to quit already made public, nobody was prepared to take him seriously. In fact, some of his colleagues in the colonial setup schemed to create an Islamic state in the northwest with strong strategic justification for

---

[1] Paul Simpson: Imperial Mendicancy and Resource Diplomacy (thesis submitted to the University of New South Wales, Sydney, Australia, in partial fulfilment of an Honours Degree in Arts, November 1974)

[2] Select Documents on Partition of Punjab, Edited by Dr Kirpal Singh, Delhi, 1991, pp. 19, 21.

the idea. Olaf Caroe (1892–1981), the last British Governor in Peshawar, who had served as the foreign secretary of colonial India, is known to have held the view that that an Islamic state in the northwest of the subcontinent would be more trustworthy in ensuring the safety of oil fields in the Middle East and Arabian Peninsula. There was the deep suspicion about the nationalistic colours of the All India National Congress hence the party could not be trusted with western strategic needs. In a way, the thinking reflected the erstwhile British fixation with the so-called expansionist designs of Russia.[1]

In June 1946, Mohammed Ali Jinnah, the Muslim leader often accused of nurturing secessionist tendencies to tear apart the holy motherland, played his master stroke.

On behalf of his party, he announced the acceptance of the Cabinet Mission Plan promoted by Field Marshal Archibald Wavell (1883–1950), the second-last British Viceroy of India. This plan manifested the last-minute hope for India to live as a confederation of Hindu and Muslim majority states. Mysteriously, the plan was rejected by the All India National Congress, the champion India's integrity day in and day out. By a Caesarean section of Punjab, Pakistan was well on the way.

While waiting for the war to end, and enrolled in the Masters of Mathematics degree program, Abdus Salam did not have the need to be knowledgeable about political storm gathering over the subcontinent. Still, he did not shut his eyes upon political realities unfolding in Lahore. In the final year of his Masters, he contested the election for student union leadership and campaigned hand in hand with Muslim, Hindu and Sikh students. Some of his Muslim classmates privately advised him to avoid cross-communal socialisation still he won the election, the last of united shows in Government College. Soon, his mettle of leadership was put on test.

In view of the political unrest and time lost in the ensuing chaos, some student unions in Lahore demanded to defer the annual examination. A joint delegation of students, including Abdus Salam, called upon Madan Singh, the Registrar of Punjab University, to press for the demand. Madan Singh, according to Abdus Salam, was a very decent man of excellent literary taste but he did not take a firm position in defence of the University Calendar. Instead, the Registrar betrayed signs of weakness by creating an impression that the matter could be

---

[1] Olaf Caroe: Wells of Power, Macmillan, London, 1951

placed before the University Syndicate for a sympathetic view.[1] Always out in search of cheap popularity, the All India Muslim League party supported the demand for postponement of annual examinations. Subsequently, the examinations were postponed.

Afterwards, even when it was painfully futile to find a back-dated explanation, Abdus Salam felt guilty beyond doubt. He repented for riding the crest of popularity wave. 'I feel sorry about the course of events. I wish to have publicly dissociated myself from the whole business of demanding the postponement. In fact, I should have condemned publicly the high-handedness of my erstwhile colleagues in the union'. He wished to correct the past. Possibly, the reason behind Abdus Salam's post-dated remorse was the scale of party-political meddling in educational institutions of Pakistan. He deemed the political meddling of 1946 amounted to setting an irreversible trend. He acknowledged that dimensions of political conflict were somewhat unique in 1946. But the fact that Abdus Salam did not oppose the demand for putting off examinations made him guilty about the whole affair. Even when he did not play much of a role in the course of events, there was reason for him to feel implicated. He considered the postponement of examinations under political pressure 'a bad omen for times yet to come. I still remember when politicians jumped in to take sides with us. I regretted and thought this was a beginning of the end. Our demands were to be settled between us and the university administration. Politicians were never a party to it. We never had this politics of Right and Left in our times, that is, the crucial 1940s. For our times, we lived in the worst of political crisis with so much at stake'.[2]

In spite falling to the wrong side of temptation, Abdus Salam did share a good deal of the emotional frenzy with Muslims of Lahore. He was a member of the student delegation calling on Mohammed Ali Jinnah when, in 1946, the Great Leader visited Lahore.[3]

After sitting for the final examination, Abdus Salam went to spend summer vacations with his parents in Multan. He had no idea as to what future held for him. When the result came, he passed the Masters in Mathematics by securing 573 out of 600 marks, another first, once again in flying colours. Where from

---

[1] In an isolated act of communal violence, a few weeks later, Madan Singh, was hacked to death.

[2] Interviews 1984: Folder III, p. 32-35

[3] Interviews 1984: Folder IV, pp. 52-53

here? Abdus Salam faced this question when there was only the vague expectation that an examination for the Indian Civil Service could be called sometimes in 1947. As long as Abdus Salam continued to meet the selection criteria, he stood fairly good chances of making it to a coveted position.

Once again, Mohammed Hussein approached Afzal Hussein, the Vice Chancellor of Punjab University, for advice. By this time, Afzal Hussein seemed to have been quite well aware of Mohammed Hussein's fascination with Indian Civil Service. He offered Mohammed Hussein a piece of advice that changed the course of Abdus Salam's life.

With his natural gift in Mathematics and time on his side, Afzal Hussein advised, Abdus Salam could afford to wait for the resumption of civil service recruitment. In the meantime, however, Abdus Salam should consider studying Mathematics at the University of Cambridge by seeking enrolment in Tripos Part II. Even when the majority of Indian students preferred pursuing a doctoral program after Masters, he held the view that Tripos presented Abdus Salam a more trustworthy route to the frontiers of knowledge.

Afzal Hussein was the half-brother of Fazal Hussein (1877–1936), the founder of the Unionist Party who had served as the Chief Minister of Punjab in the 1920s before being a Minister in the cabinet of British Viceroy from 1930 to 1935. Afzal Hussein had graduated from the University of Cambridge where he aspired to become a scientist and pursue research in Botany but then for some reason adopted a career in public service. His advice carried weight, and Abdus Salam took it by sending, in March 1946, an application for admission to Cambridge University.

Apparently, he did not seem to have much idea how the cost of his studying in Cambridge will be met. He must have been fed up with the lengthening delay in civil service recruitment. Mohammed Hussein in the meantime had not given up on his dream to discover a grand public servant in the promised son. At the time of Abdus Salam's journey to Cambridge, the balance of ethnicity in the coveted Indian Civil Service had begun tilting in favour of the native. So why was Abdus Salam permitted to leave home when the embargo on public sector recruitment might have ended? Any suitable answer to this question could be found in the post-dated postulation over accidents driving Abdus Salam in the direction Physics.

VI

A substantial window of opportunity opened up for Abdus Salam when, after the end of war in 1945, the Government of Punjab announced half-a-dozen scholarship grants for postgraduate studies abroad. Money that had originally been raised in Punjab as part of the war effort was not fully expended. Almost 40% of militia in the royal army, in recent decades, had been recruited from Punjab alone, mostly from Muslim and Sikh farming communities. Those Punjabi soldiers were known to have fought valiantly alongside the British. Khizer Hayat Tiwana (1900–1975), the Chief Minister belonging to the cross-communal Unionist Party, had defended and promoted war as an ideological compulsion against fascism. It was with the available surplus of war fund that the Government of Punjab founded a Peasant Welfare Scheme. Among other items of public interest, six scholarship grants were created under the scheme. Keeping with the spirit of communal quota, three of those grants were to benefit Muslim candidates and the rest to those from non-Muslim communities.

With his meritorious academic record, Abdus Salam could easily pick up one provided his father qualified as a small farmer or peasant. Apparently, Mohammed Hussein was none of the two. According to the government definition, a small farmer was someone who paid twenty-five rupees or less in land tax. One possible way for Mohammed Hussein to meet the test was if his older brother, Ghulam Hussein, who owned a block of agricultural land near Qadian, helped him out.[1] Mohammed Hussein travelled to Qadian, informed his brother about the scholarship scheme, especially about the clause relating to the ownership of agricultural land. Surely, Abdus Salam met the selection criteria if Ghulam Hussein transferred some of his agricultural land over to Mohammed Hussein enabling the latter to satisfy the definition of a small farmer.

Ghulam Hussein, an erstwhile educationist and the future father-in-law of Abdus Salam, appreciated the value of an overseas scholarship grant; he expressed his readiness to oblige.[2] In other words, no harm was seen in finding a convenient filler to meet the statutory requirement.

In spite of Abdus Salam's strength on merit, it was just not possible for his parents to afford the cost of sending him abroad for study. As for the question of land ownership, it did not matter much in the closely knit kinship of an extended family structure. In another few years, Abdus Salam was bound to marry Amtul

---

[1] Mohammed Hussein (1974): p.44. Also see Abdul Hameed (circa 2000): p. 46]
[2] *Al-Nahl* (Fall 1997): p. 61-62

Hafeez, the youngest daughter of Ghulam Hussein. It was not a big deal for Ghulam Hussein to transfer the ownership of his land to Mohammed Hussein. Once done, Mohammed Hussein qualified as a farmer. Before the end of 1945, Abdus Salam had made up his mind to study in Cambridge. He began preparing sets of necessary documentation to apply for the grant, admission in Cambridge as well for a passport to travel abroad. In those days, good character certificate was one of the requirements to qualify for a travel passport.

Professor Eric Dickenson (1892–1951), the Principal of the Government College, wrote a strong letter of reference for Abdus Salam. 'The distinctions he won at the Government College besides those in the field of study have been as rare as they have been well deserved. He was not merely an academician, pure and simple. He was very popular with the student community. He commended their trust and confidence, and there was no important office in the college that he did not hold'. Stated the Principal adding that 'very few candidates in recent years so eminently qualified to benefit from the advantages a scholarship abroad confers'. In a separate hand-written note, introducing Abdus Salam to the Secretary Education, Government of Punjab, the Principal remarked 'I should be very grateful if you would lend him your good offices as he is certainly one of our most successful and brilliant products'.[1]

Early in September 1946, Abdus Salam received the news of his selection on Muslim quota of grants. Afzal Hussein headed the Selection Committee and he did not see the need to invite Abdus Salam for an interview.[2] At that time, Abdus Salam, was in Multan. In order to get the grant formally released, he was required to submit the confirmation of his admission abroad. Always a step forward, he had already mailed his application for admission in Cambridge though there was no assurance of getting a place in the forthcoming term. One of his teachers, Abdul Hameed, who himself had been to Cambridge earlier in the 1930s, advised him to queue up on standby, just in case someone dropped out at the last minute. Abdul Hameed had such an eye for detail that he urged Abdus Salam to send a reply-paid self-addressed envelope with the application.

Abdus Salam's application for admission at Cambridge was supported by a hefty bunch of persuasive reference letters by his college professors, including those of the Principal and the Head of Mathematics Department. He received the

---

[1] Eric Dickenson, Principal, Government College Lahore: 1May 1946
[2] Abdul Hameed (circa 2000): p. 46

confirmation of his admission almost back-to-back with the award of scholarship grant.

Also, in the first week of September 1946, he received an urgent message from the India Office in London stating that an unexpected vacancy had surfaced at St John's College in Cambridge. It amounted to brightening up his chances of enrolment in the Winter Term beginning in October 1946. He was exhorted to cable back with his intent of acceptance. At the same time, he was asked to send by 'return air mail' the original copy of his Master's degree and a certificate, duly signed by the Registrar, of attendance of at least three years at the University of Punjab.

To his amusement afterwards, he discovered that the process of admission at St John's College, Cambridge, might have been delayed due to a mix up of names. Another applicant by the name of Abdus Salam, from the University of Hyderabad, had applied for enrolment in a research program, whereas, the Abdus Salam from the University of Punjab sought admission in Mathematics Tripos II. Luckily, the error was caught and fixed in time.[1]

While going through those bureaucratic procedures, Abdus Salam waited for a formal communication, from the Government of Punjab, offering him the scholarship grant. He boarded the first train to Lahore to personally explore if the final list of awards under the Peasant Welfare Scheme had been approved, and if so then what was holding up the release of letters. Upon arriving at the Department of Education, he discovered that a good part of the Punjab Government Secretariat was still camping in the cool of Simla, the Summer Capital of the government, in the Himalayas. Next day he was in Simla, climbing up and down through layers of mist loaded with pine fragrance. He had some familiarity with Simla. Earlier in the afternoon, sweating and breathing heavily, in search of Punjab government huts, he had the feeling as if someone was chasing him. He could see a shadow over his shoulder, and then someone caught up from behind and introduced himself as an employee at the Department of Education. 'Look, I must congratulate you for winning the scholarship. We have mail for you. Had I not sighted you by chance, the official mail would be out later today taking a bit longer in reaching you'. He signalled the pleasantly amazed Abdus Salam to follow him.

A few moments later, Abdus Salam found himself in the company of Ghulam Khaliq, an officer at the Department of Education who used to teach History in

---

[1] Abdul Hameed (circa 2000): p. 47

Government College. Ghulam Khaliq happened to be another of Abdus Salam's admirers. Abdus Salam was handed over his copy of the award notification, dated 6 September 1946.

Ghulam Khaliq had graduated from Cambridge and he was delighted to find out that Abdus Salam had already secured a place at St John's College. Almost instantly, he began preparing Abdus Salam for life in England. Hot homemade pickle, Ghulam Khaliq alerted Abdus Salam, was necessary to spice up the bland English food. Likewise, he added, there will be need for almond oil in order to maintain intestinal lubrication, just in case.

After this piece of personal advice, Ghulam Khaliq gave Abdus Salam a letter of recommendation to arrange for an earliest possible passage to England. He urged Abdus Salam to proceed straight to Delhi to book a berth on the first available vessel leaving Bombay. It was a time of huge rush due to the heading home of British families; getting a berth in time could turn out more difficult than getting a grant on merit. Good luck and all the very best! Ghulam Khaliq got up to shake hands with Abdus Salam.

It marked the beginning of a warm friendship between the two of them though Abdus Salam did not know how Ghulam Khaliq will continue reaching out to him in the future.

Next morning, Abdus Salam arrived in Delhi feeling glad for having enough money in his pocket to travel around in order to save time. In Delhi, it was a Saturday, the half working day prior to weekend. He was on time at the ticketing office where an enraged clerk snubbed him. How dare you expect a last-minute booking when the multitude of British officers is going home? No, it won't do, the clerk ruled rather bluntly.

Crestfallen, Abdus Salam walked out. Once again, he had the notion that someone closed upon him from behind. On this occasion, it was Mubarak Ali, a junior clerk at the Booking Office. After introducing himself, Mubarak Ali said that his boss, who had just told Abdus Salam to get lost, was an Anglo-Indian Christian, devastated by the British withdrawal. You know, Mubarak Ali postulated, we have people more loyal to the Crown than the King himself.

This outwardly racist expression of eccentricity was not far-fetched. In nearly four centuries of British settlement in India, the numerical strength of the so-called Anglo-Indian community, born out of restricted conjugation between two sides, was estimated at 150,000. Ironically, the Anglo-Indian community met an equally disobliging treatment from both European as well as native sections of the society. On the brink of geographical partition, India stood fragmented socially. Mubarak Ali gave Abdus Salam the booking slip. Go straight to Bombay, he said, get into the queue and try your luck on standby. Mubarak Ali offered Abdus Salam a glimmer of hope.

Thankfully Abdus Salam shook hands with Mubarak Ali and then rushed towards the Post Office. He sent a cable to his father, boarded the first available train service in the direction of Multan. After changing connections, he arrived in Multan, the city silenced by curfew in the wake of communal rioting. It was just after midnight. In the pitch dark of platform, he found his father, holding a lantern and waiting for him. Mohammed Hussein had to obtain special permission from the Deputy Commissioner to get through curfew pickets and be at the rail station on time.

I have come to say farewell. Abdus Salam informed his father and then explained, as the two walked home, the nature of urgency to queue up for a berth. Stopping every now and then for identification before the patrolling police, Abdus Salam felt the hasty succession of events overtaking him during the last one week was about to conclude fruitfully. 'There is simply no time left. I have to make it to Bombay to take the chance on berth. I shall have to leave instantly, otherwise I will not be able to catch the ship'. He pleaded with his father.[1]

Looking back, decades later, with a mix of melancholy and amusement, Abdus Salam used to narrate his hectic journeys in September 1946, especially when suddenly he discovered that he had only a couple of days to spend with the family and friends before rushing to catch the ship from Bombay.

Time went fast in packing and meeting relatives and friends. He wanted some money to purchase few items for the journey overseas but did not have enough money, neither did his father. In the spirit of the day when the result of Year Ten Matriculation was announced six years ago, Mohammed Hussein managed to borrow nine hundred rupees from a friend.[2]

Abdus Salam bought a steel chest and dumped all of his mathematics books in it without having the slightest notion about their nearly total redundancy in Cambridge.[3] He crowded the trunk with a jar full of homemade turnip pickle and a bottle of almond oil as advised by Ghulam Khaliq.

---

[1] Interviews 1984: Folder IV, p. 14

[2] Abdul Hameed (circa 2000): p. 49

[3] Interviews 1984: Folder IV, pp. 6, 14

Multan was still under curfew, and he was scheduled to take the night service to Lahore from where connections were available for Bombay. Mohammed Hussein had arranged a curfew pass for his son.

When the moment arrived to say farewell to the family, Mohammed Hussein declined to accompany his son to the railway station. Instead, in exchange of those few more minutes of company, he preferred to rather stay back and pray for the safe journey and success of his son.

Mohammed Hussein reminded his son about the oral tradition attributed to Prophet Mohammed according to which a father's supplication for his son was like the prayer of a traveller for those who had been left behind; it was granted most likely.

'I entrust thee in the custody of Lord, my son' was all the overwhelmed Mohammed Hussein could say. It was an unfamiliar mix of sadness and hope for Abdus Salam. He was leaving his family behind but heading with excitement into the unknown territory of future. On his first journey overseas, Abdus Salam left home. He would be on his last train journey in the united India.

Bombay, like Multan, was under curfew; as if there had been a grotesquely abnormal agreement between Muslims and Hindus to slaughter each other anytime, everywhere, anywhere. Enraged mobs settled the age-old accounts across villages, towns, cities, districts, provinces and regions; all over the subcontinent. In Bombay, passengers intending to travel overseas were advised to stay in their hotels and boarding houses within the vicinity of Victoria Terminus, the central rail station.

Abdus Salam was lucky yet again, he found a berth aboard F.O. Franconia, an enormous vessel that was sailing home with English families and Italian Prisoners of War. He found just enough time to buy a Macintosh and a hat.

An era appeared to close upon him; given his own financial resources, he could have imagined studying abroad only in a fit of wild dreams.

VII

Into midnight before his departure next morning, Abdus Salam had just fallen asleep when someone began banging the door. He was staying in a hotel and did not know anyone in Bombay. Who on earth might have come to see him at that sunken hour in the night? He thought before reluctantly opening the door. Hands up! You are under arrest! One of the two army officers who crashed in shouted, their pistols pointing at Abdus Salam. Apparently, they had information that a deserter of the Royal Navy was holed up in the room. Abdus Salam showed the officers his identity and travel documents. Once convinced, the two apologised and left the room; one of them wished him success at Cambridge.

After the heavy noise of thumping boots faded away, Abdus Salam attempted to sleep. Suddenly, he woke up again. Those military officers were not very wrong. He was a deserter, after all. He was deserting the Indian Civil Service just when the schedule of recruitment in the coveted cadres was about to be announced. What he did not realise then was the crucial reality of his departure from the shores of united India.

Not only the war had saved him from pursuing a career in public service, it had financed his education abroad. All of a sudden, there was yet another dimension added to interpretation of his father's vision. Abdus Salam, *the Servant of Peace*, was going to benefit from funds collected for war.

Afterwards, when his career in physics was well established, he used to reflect about the sudden turn of events in 1946. In an attempt to highlight the absence of science in poor countries, he would state that his journey into the world of physics was triggered by 'a series of accidents'. It became a style for him to state that he was an accidental physicist. Why did he harp upon the oblique term of 'accidents' is not clear. He might as well, with his religious bent of mind, explain the tale of his professional life in terms of 'miracles'. Such analogy fitted more naturally into his father's vision of June 1925. Whatever the choice in terminology, he found a way out of his father's obsession with public service.

Abdus Salam's first encounter with the colossal sea, previously known to him only in geography books, was pleasantly smooth. He was lucky to have been saved from sea-sickness. Every afternoon, he strolled or read a book on the upper deck. At times, he would quietly recite verses of Mohammed Iqbal and felt carried away by their philosophical command.

More than anything else, the small group of students travelling with him felt more impressed by his ability to steer clear of sea-sickness. How he came neat and clean out of the monstrous tides of Arabian Sea, was a mystery to them more than his brilliant academic record. On his part, Abdus Salam, attributed the serenity of his guts to the prayers of those he had left behind in Multan.

Within a couple of days, Abdus Salam struck a sociable troika with Saeed Minai and Fazal Rahman, the two students who were wonder struck by the wealth of his degrees and certificates, especially by the reference letter Zafarullah Khan had written for him. Saeed Minai ended up serving senior positions in the State Bank of Pakistan and the World Bank. Fazal Rahman (1919–1988) became a professor at the University of Chicago and authored important works on Islam.

Leaving Bombay and Aden behind, after sailing across the restless Arabian Sea and a peripheral fringe of the comparatively calmer Indian Ocean, the ship dropped anchor at the port of Naples where Italian Prisoners of War were disembarked. Abdus Salam had lived a bit too long under the romantic notion that best fruit in the world came only from Multan, he did not believe his eyes when he saw the size of grapes on sale at the port of Naples. This was his first glimpse of Europe, the second continent entering his life. From Gibraltar, the impressive rock on which a Muslim commander had valiantly burnt his boats and invaded a part of Spain twelve hundred years ago, the ship navigated towards Liverpool Docks.

England was not into winter yet while Abdus Salam shivered, he found the overcast sky, strong wind, intermittent drizzle and chill in the air; all so unlike Punjab. He found himself in a crowd of unfamiliar faces, men and as well as women. He desperately missed the heat and humidity of Multan, Lahore and Bombay. Suddenly, his eyes were fixed on the familiar face of Zafarullah Khan who had come to receive a family member. Abdus Salam had only seen the high-profile Ahmadiyah from a distance in Qadian. He stepped forward, introduced himself and, to his pleasant surprise, found that Zafarullah Khan already knew him as the brilliant son of Mohammed Hussein.

Abdus Salam looked for a porter to assist him with his metallic trunk. Observing the misery on Abdus Salam's face, Zafarullah Khan shrugged off his broad shoulders the cosy raincoat and offered it to Abdus Salam. Forget about porters, Zafarullah Khan observed and lifted the steel chest, full of antiquated mathematics books and turnip pickle, all the way from Multan, from one end signalling Abdus Salam to hold the latch on the other side and they started walking towards the rail station.

Are you heading for London? Shall we travel together? Zafarullah Khan asked.

For next three hours, Abdus Salam relished the enthralling conservationist in Zafarullah Khan who, acting as an adept tour guide, instructed his fellow travellers with information regarding places and sites the train passed by. This was the starting point of another lasting friendship for Abdus Salam. Amazed at the sight of cow herds, grazing on rolling slopes of English countryside, Abdus Salam was spellbound. He wondered whether the miserable lean beasts back home were worth Hindu-Muslim communal rioting.

Once in London, Abdus Salam spent his first night in England at the Ahmadiyah Mission House in Putney, south of river Thames. He did not know that one day, within a matter of few years; he would own a house walking distance from the mosque. Instead, lying in bed, before falling asleep, once again he thought fondly of his elders, parents and siblings; of sacrifices and efforts they had made in educating him.

Next morning he reported at the India Office to receive information about the breakup of his scholarship grant. A sum of twenty-five hundred rupees was allocated to cover his travel expenses to and back from England. He was entitled to four hundred rupees a month in living costs. His scholarship grant was tenable for a period of three years and he was permitted to take up any other approved courses of study in addition to the Tripos in Mathematics. On the average, the figure of scholarship money sounded much modest in pound sterling than its value in rupees.

Later in the day, he went to Liverpool Street Rail Station and boarded the train to Cambridge. He would always remember the date, it was 10 October 1946, and the winter term had just begun. He hired a taxi, drove through Hills Road, Regent Street, St Andrew Street, High Street and finally making it to St John's Street. There he was, as the travelling spree and thrill overtaking him five weeks ago ended in front of the Bursar's office. For a few moments, he was speechless, suffering from a complete loss of words. 'My voice failed me. This was a moment of emotion. After all those days and nights of journeying and voyaging, I was there, in Cambridge'. He vividly remembered his descent upon the college. A porter greeted him with a built-in smile and pointed towards the trolley to move the luggage. What a stir and sensation the arrival, at the New Hostel in

Government College, in a taxi cab might have caused. He felt amused by the thought.[1]

Quietly, he loaded the trolley and pushed it towards a three-room suite allotted to him in the New Court. He was rather pleasantly surprised to find the previous occupant still in the suite. May I stay another night? He asked. Abdus Salam had none objection whatsoever. Keeping his word, the gentleman left early next morning.

About the end of January 1947, Abdus Salam wrote a letter to Abdul Khaliq pleading that his scholarship grant was just not enough to meet his expenditure at Cambridge. Within a month, he received the encouraging reply. Abdul Khaliq had promised to take the matter up with the Government of Punjab. 'You must not, however, feel depressed or impatient. Try to get along'. Abdul Khaliq had remarked.

---

[1] Interviews 1984: Folder IV, P. 22

Chapter Three
Career Rebound

At the very outset of his life in Cambridge, Abdus Salam was dismayed to find out that the stocky trunk full of mathematics books he had so painstakingly packed and transported all the way from Multan did not carry much value. He could see the difference in content as well as style of teaching compared to the old-fashioned approach of his teachers in Lahore who laid a greater emphasis on pure mathematics. He had studied an elaborate course of Dynamics for two years from a text book written somewhere in the 1880's. He recalled how secretive one of his teachers had been about the key to problems. In Cambridge, he found Analytical Dynamics by Edmund Whittaker (1873–1956) listing soluble problems at the very start of a chapter.[1] 'This was practically a condensation in one chapter all we had been doing over two years. Professor Servi Chowla was one of the few people inclined towards research. His father also had been a professor at Government College. Then we had Professor Omar Hayat who taught us complex variable theory, an area with few untied knots. He knew his area but lacked interest in research.' Abdus Salam reminisced about the change he observed in Cambridge.

One of Abdus Salam's great Indian predecessors at Cambridge, Srinivasa Ramanujan (1887–1920), attributed his mathematical genius to a direct communication with gods. Abdus Salam had landed in Mathematics as a matter of his own choice essentially to command lead in civil service examination. For years, Literature tempted him but he remained faithful to Mathematics. He was educated in a culture steeped in literary tradition. 'In my career you will see a slant in favour of Mathematics right from the beginning. Because our whole

---

[1] Edmund Whitaker (1873-1956) had been a Fellow at the Trinity College, Cambridge. He is known for his contribution to applied mathematics, theory of special functions and mathematical physics.

culture is literary, it was never easy to escape. I don't think I would become a great literary figure. My contribution to literature had been limited to a couple of research papers. All my life I have composed one *ghazal* (ode), perhaps'.[1]

In Cambridge, he found himself more advanced than the majority of his classmates. He covered two years of work in one to finish the Tripos II in Mathematics. He was established as a Wrangler, a recognition granted to sturdy mathematicians. What impressed him most was the air of intellectual freedom and flexibility going side by side with the solemnity of undergraduate classrooms. Every student would come well prepared, armed with whole paraphernalia of writing and drawing aides; pens and pencils of different gauges and colours, rulers and protectors. They prepared neat and tidy notes as if it was an exercise in calligraphy. Most of his classmates had come directly from school; they were younger in age but full of self-confidence, proud of sharing their citizenship with men like Sir Isaac Newton. He remarked later.[2]

This air of intellectual freedom and solemnity Abdus Salam encountered in Cambridge was not won overnight. As one of the greatest institutions of learning, Cambridge University, was a federation of colleges founded upon endowments from both crown and church, had its history spanned over seven centuries. Some of those colleges, like Trinity and St John's, occupied nearly half of the old university campus.

In the beginning, learning at Cambridge was restricted solely to canonical and scholastic knowledge but the policy changed as Europe passed through the furnace of renaissance and reformation. As the stranglehold of Catholic Church relaxed, Cambridge had place for classics, mathematics and physics. Over time, the university survived many challenges by becoming one of the richest educational institutions in the world with its endowments reaching nearly six billion pounds by the beginning of 21st century. With over two dozen colleges, well over one hundred teaching departments and faculties, over one hundred libraries and a central research library holding well above five million volumes; the university justified its status in the world of learning. At a time when higher education was not purely a cost accounting business, and rich were not free to purchase places with money alone and the brilliant among students staked their scholarly claims on merit, the University of Cambridge was one the few most sought-after places in the world.

---

[1] Interviews 1984: Folder IV, pp. 2, 6
[2] The Pakistan Times, Islamabad, 7 May 1990, p.4

Founded earlier in the 16th century, Abdus Salam's St John's College grew up into four courts. In medieval times, the sculptured towers and the statue of St John the Evangelist, at the entrance of college hall, were rated as models of fine architecture in Cambridge. Opening upon St John's Street, with Trinity College towards north, St John's College stretched out across river Cam. In old times, the uninhabited side of the river, beyond walks and gardens, was termed as the wilderness. Some of the elms lining those walks were originally planted as early as 1685, when Sir Isaac Newton studied at the Trinity College. Connecting the two rear courts of the college, the covered bridge over Cam was named after the Bridge of Sighs in Venice.

Cambridge was a whole new world, nowhere near what Abdus Salam had so far experienced in Jhang, Multan and Lahore. England, the home of British Colonial Empire, encompassed a geographical and cultural mix poles apart from Punjab. While leaving home for Cambridge, Abdus Salam had been alerted about the trial ahead, especially about the ferocity of weather and insipidity of food. Any imagination relating to those words of warning was lost in the excitement of journey abroad, and now he confronted the reality. Early signs of winter, within a couple of months of his arrival, unnerved him. Addicted to the mild and pleasantly bright winters of Punjab, where heat and humidity rather than chill tested one's patience, the ferocity of English weather shook the balance of his personal biology. He felt devastated by the persistence of a deeply overcast sky unleashing wet and cold winds most of the time; heating the three-room suite allotted to him posed a major challenge. It was the post-war England where several basic amenities were rationed; residents were entitled to three buckets of coal from an outlying bunker. He did not mind transporting his share but found it hard to consume the quota so economically as to survive the whole week. He bungled up the equation between supply and glow of coal, and quite naturally so for someone hardened in the climatic furnace of Punjab. In a way, this botched experiment in heating the apartment was a sign of things to come. He gave up and instead began spending longer hours in the library that was a complete world in its own right.

Abdus Salam's next major dilemma was the peculiarity of English food served in the dining hall of the college where menus were made, once again, under the post-war restraint. He had succeeded in finding a way out of the heating problem by spending more time in the library, whereas the matter with food seemed hermetically sealed. Sometimes he wondered if people outside the subcontinent really had any taste buds. He might have attempted at preparing few simpler dishes himself but his disaster with tending the fire killed the desire in the bud. He was obliged to live with the house menu revolving around steamed potatoes and precisely cut portions of boiled fish. He would be in a greater mess when fish was replaced with equally miniature portions of dubious meat. Was it *halal*? How could it be? Was it pig? In that case the very question about *halal* turned redundant. Why do they have to eat such ugly animals? He wondered in frustration.

His learned uncle, Fazal Rahman, the Ahmadiyah missionary in West Africa, constantly bombarded him with the need to abide by the Islamic code of prohibitions; an almost naked reference to pork, alcohol and women. As for beef, mutton and poultry, even though permissible, the question relating to their being *halal* continued to haunt him. Like the Jewish code for kosher, *halal* meat among Muslims was required to meet a certain criteria. For example, there was the need to make sure that the permissible beast had been slaughtered in the name of God, the Creator, and been bled comprehensively. Abdus Salam led himself into a state of voluntary starvation, if not fasting day in and day out, struggling to accept the fact that curries and *chapattis* were history, at least for the time being.

He needed to be reminded about the testimony of Thomas Lever, Master of St John's College somewhere in medieval era when students were served with a 'penny-sized portion of beef' and that too after broth had been extracted out of the meat. Also, in those days, students were advised to 'run up and down half an hour to get heat on their feet' before slipping into bed.[1] Had Abdus Salam read Sigmund Freud's *Totem and Taboo*, he might have been better off, at least philosophically. What could one do when life ate life in order to sustain life? 'Intent determined conduct' was an Islamic principle he could rely upon to allow flexibility of judgment. But he did not appear to gather enough courage.

In those days, Cambridge had only one Indian restaurant *Taj Mahal* specialising in South Indian dishes, mostly vegetarian and often quite expensive. Given the logistics of his daily routine and financial affordability, he could eat out once in a while. One day, he managed to pick up a small portion of Kosher mutton from the nearby Jewish food business and convinced the college cook to have it roasted for him once a week. He did not forget the evening when his cherished share was cross-served over the table to someone sitting on the

---

[1] Rashdall's Medieval Universities (Edited by Powick, F.M. and Emden, A.B.), Volume II, Oxford, 1936, p. 414

wheelchair. Rubbing salt to the injury, Abdus Salam was served with a portion of straightforwardly steamed fish and potatoes. Such was the price for believing.[1] On a subsequent visit to London, he took the matter of *halal* up with some of his religious peers in the Ahmadiyah Mosque. Apparently this was one of the crucial questions Muslim expatriates confronted. Zafarullah Khan advised Abdus Salam to invoke the name of Lord the Creator before laying hands on the permissible categories of meat. This was an ideal solution, providing Abdus Salam with sufficient ground to stand upon. He could quietly recite the mandatory verse 'In the name of Allah, the Great' and then go for a dish of meat as long as it was not pork.

On the balance, however, the scholarly delights of Cambridge outweighed those momentary surges of personal temptation. Of course, the leap forwards from Lahore to Cambridge posed physical and cultural challenges; Abdus Salam was overwhelmed by the quality of academic tradition in the small university town. Everything in Cambridge seemed to be regulated and geared to encourage knowledge and learning. With his upbringing under the watchful parental discipline, Abdus Salam was rather pleasantly amazed to observe that, during the course of a term, students were not permitted to stay out beyond midnight; penalties applied otherwise. Likewise, failing to pass the Bachelors in first attempt meant total disaster as there was no place for supplementary or replacement examination. Apart from the quality of scholarship cascading out of its colleges, classrooms, halls, laboratories, libraries and residential courts; the architectural magic of towers, spires, domes, arches, chapels, bridges, patterns of brickwork, sculptures, courts, lawns and rose gardens, streets, lanes, alleys, paved walk-ways, canals and the river; all added up to the uniqueness of Cambridge.

Situated on the river bank, the college library, where Abdus Salam often found cosy refuge, was housed in the Third Court built during the reign of King Charles II (1630–1685). For a long time the place had been famous for holding a rare copy of Cranmer's Bible printed on vellum earlier in the 16th century. Abdus Salam was spell bound to encounter the wealth of knowledge, ranging from mathematics, sciences, law and medicine to classics, art and divinity; available mostly in original form. Apart from translated works, the library housed a rare collection of oriental manuscripts. For the first time in his life, he came across works on nearly every aspect of Indian life, from religion and

---

[1] Interviews 1984: Folder IV, pp. 24-27

sociology to history and politics. He was able to read Max Muller's compilation of Vedic scripts and James Todd's history of Rajput tribes. Then, like the Internet today, he could top up his everyday political knowledge by reading regular updates off Keesing's Archives on world affairs.

Apart from filling-in for his social loneliness, those times lived in the library liberated him from the onerous responsibility of heating the apartment. From a 'non-social' point of view, he used to remember the time as the few happiest years of his life when it was possible for him to absorb large figures of knowledge over and above the core areas of study. Apart from Mathematics and Physics, he digested into his system comparative religion, ideological movements, history and politics.

He was a regular customer at Heffers and Bowes & Bowes, the two popular bookshops in Cambridge, keeping himself well informed about fresh arrivals in Mathematics and Physics. He was so regular that even a slight change in the order of title display alerted him. Over the years, upon discovering that text books did not keep pace with recent research, he developed a preference for scientific journals. He remembered how a bookshop had declined to refund him money, against one of his recent purchases, on grounds that the item would be deemed as 'second-hand'.[1]

Socialisation was another trial in that post-war complexion of campus life. Many students belonged to senior age groups and they lived with their families. On the other extreme were those Abdus Salam viewed as high school children. As such, he did not fit well into either of the two. With his level of education and familiarity with English language, Abdus Salam did not encounter much of a difficulty in communicating with people; both his accent and faintly husky voice were tuned to the mainstream without imitation or faking. Still, he found it even more demanding to attend to other favourite pastimes like dancing and drinking.

Other than few foreign students living in university towns like Cambridge and Oxford, the sighting of a non-Caucasian face was relatively rare in the England of 1940s. Even the size of seasonal tourists was limited due to war and costly air travel. Of course, the imminent need for factory workers and labour was set to change the urban demographic scene in the near future. As such, therefore, English people who had not been overseas themselves looked towards an occasional Asian in their midst with friendly curiosity. In fact, it was fashionable among the educated to ask a student from overseas to tea or a garden

---

[1] Gordon Fraser (2008): p. 93

party. Abdus Salam remembered receiving invitations to visit people acquainted to him in the town. He valued the invitation for it enabled him to benefit from the world across social barriers and racial division and an opportunity to open up. He comprehended a deeper side of such hospitality when his classmate Christie invited him to be the family guest during Christmas break of 1946. Abdus Salam accepted the invitation and stayed with the family. He enjoyed the experience, especially the discovery that warmth, compassion and cordiality was not a birth right of Punjab alone.

He remembered Christie's great knack for western classical music. 'He used to educate me about the history and philosophy of classical music'. Abdus Salam recalled while reminiscing over his early weeks in Cambridge. It was delightful to know that unlike Punjab, where the fine art of musical composition was monopolised by few families, travelling down from one generation to the next in the shape of memory, the tradition had been different in Europe due to the transcription and preservation of the art in the shape of writing in symbols and signs.

Christie made an attempt at giving Abdus Salam a few lessons in piano. 'I did try to read through a few essential elements to acquire an appreciation of western classical music. But this was too vast an ocean'. He reminisced.[1]

For the purpose of outdoor sporting activity, Abdus Salam returned to his Government College choice of rowing. But the silver-grey currents of Cam demanded a set of skills and responses much different compared to the thick brown mud of *Ravi* back in Lahore.

Within a few months of settling down in Cambridge, Abdus Salam got rid of his self-styled shyness towards cinema. He joined the Film Society and began acquiring taste for English as well as sub-titled French movies. But, like his fleeting affair with fiction, the pastime did not take him far. For quite a while though he remembered watching the original version of American classic *Gone with the Wind*. He had just walked out of the cinema hall to read the newspaper headline at a stall that the prophet of non-violence, Mohandas Gandhi, had been assassinated by an extremist Hindu. 'Cinema today', he remarked rather sarcastically, 'has turned itself into an absurdly inexcusable repetition of undressing women'.[2] Later, when the imam of Ahmadiyah Mosque in London, invited him to watch a film on the *Hajj*, the annual Muslim pilgrimage to Mecca,

---

[1] Interviews 1984: Folder IV, pp. 54-55
[2] Interviews 1984: Folder III, p. 50

Abdus Salam declined on grounds that he would rather go for the ritual than watching it on the screen.

Along with his largely academic and few social engagements, Abdus Salam maintained a close contact with Muslim students stationed in Cambridge. Soon after the making of Pakistan, he was elected as the founder-President of Pakistan Society or the *Majlis*, in Cambridge. Some Muslim students found in him the *Imam* to lead Friday afternoon congregation. He remembered one of his regular *muqtadees*, in the congregation, was Princess Dina Bint Abdul Hameed (1929–2019), soon to be the Queen of Jordan from 1955–1957, who was then studying for a Degree in English Literature at Girton College in Cambridge. She belonged to the royal Hashemite house of the Middle East and held the title of Sharifa.[1]

II

In June 1947, that is, within ten months of his arrival in Cambridge, and still battling with double persecution of English weather and food, Abdus Salam passed with distinction the Preliminary Examination in Mathematics. In the early days of term break, he happened to be staying at 63 Melrose Road southwest of London when the news arrived from his Tutor, James Wordie. 'The total places you high in the list and the College has decided to elect you to a Foundation Scholarship to the titular value of £60'. James Wordie stated in his letter dated 19 June 1947. Any rise, howsoever little, made good news. On top of his Peasant Welfare grant, Abdus Salam was getting merit allowance from the Ahmadiyah Jubilee Fund. Although the total did not make him wealthy by any standard but, like his self-training in Lahore, he budgeted discreetly and did not take long in achieving a stability of everyday expenditure in Cambridge. In fact, soon he began saving money to support the family back in Pakistan.[2]

During the summer break, Abdus Salam visited Europe where war had ended only recently, leaving behind some dreadfully ravaged sites. It was Abdus Salam's first experience of witnessing the horrors of war. He had only read about what wars do to places and people. In Germany, he saw people living on ruins,

---

[1] After her marriage with King Hussein Bin Talal (1935-1999) ended in 1957, Dina re-married in 1970. Her second husband was a Palestinian guerrilla fighter who held high profile in Palestinian Liberation Organization (PLO) and was captured by Israel. Dina's influence is known to have won him, along with another 8000 prisoners, freedom.

[2] Gordon Fraser (2008): pp. 75-76

without shelter and food, in a country devoid of economy, currency and government of their own. Witnessing the devastation, misery and demoralisation plunged him into sadness. He found rations were so meagre that his own stint of self-imposed starvation in Cambridge amounted to a luxury in comparison. This part of his tour had been sponsored by a pro-west segment of the International Union of Students. In the midst of deprivation and tragedy, he witnessed a unique aspect of German character, the everlasting passion for scholarship. He was camping, with other delegates, in a park outside Munich when someone mentioned that a German gentleman had been looking for him. Who on earth could this person be? He kept guessing until a lean, emaciated, shrivelled, war-eaten middle-aged man turned up to see him.

'I am compiling a small German-Punjabi dictionary'. He told the spell-bound Abdus Salam.

While serving his term as a prisoner of war in one of the allied camps, this man happened to befriend a couple of Punjabi guards. He had made up his mind, during the course of his efforts to communicate with them, to compile one day a German-Punjabi dictionary for popular if not purely professional purpose. He briefed Abdus Salam about the progress he had made so far on what seemed to be an unbecoming project by all standards of common sense. It was essential for him, in the interest of his mission, he added, to keep a track of any Punjabis in the vicinity. He looked for assistance whichever way, shape and quantity it came. Abdus Salam was visibly impressed by the small collection of his books.

How much of eccentricity one could afford? Abdus Salam thought. At a time in history when this man's country was perhaps the most unequal on earth, he intended to do a German-Punjabi dictionary. 'Unfortunately I could not offer much help; it was equally hard for me to build upon the collection of few classical romantic tales gathered by this man. I have no idea how far did he go in his vocation that sounded like a wild pursuit. But he made a remarkable story in love of knowledge'.[1]

Other than the war-ravished Germany, he travelled in France, Switzerland and Holland; putting up as a lodger in Ahmadiyah mission houses wherever it was possible. He remembered how his peer in the Ahmadiyah community, Zafarullah Khan, had advised him to tap travelling as a rich source of knowledge. Now was the time to act on the advice. He visited museums, art galleries, universities, libraries and laboratories; picking up an authentic feel of places

---

[1] Presidential address: Annual Convocation 1971-72, Government College, Jhang.

previously known to him only through books. He felt as if a part of Europe was being reborn.

'I was surprised to find a very large number of Muslims in Paris'. Abdus Salam scribbled on a sheet. 'I was told that they numbered seventy thousand. Almost all belonged to French dominions in Africa, mostly they were Algerians. Very few of them were of pure Arab stock.' He found those Muslims speaking a dialect of their own, a mixture of Berber and Arabic. They were mostly small-scale traders, from fruit-sellers and street vendors to rug-merchants, even black-marketers and those engaged in the underworld of currency exchange. 'On this account', he felt, 'the French people and government take a very pessimistic view of Muslims in general'. He was rather amused to note that the average lot of citizens in France was quite nervous about increasing unrest in Tunisia and Morocco, especially after the escape of political activist Abdul Karim. Everyone seemed to guess about Abdul Karim's future course of action.[1] Certainly, political activities of people like Abdul Karim, freedom-fighters in their part of the world, invoked fear and suspicion among those who had committed monstrous crimes against humanity. Those were the days, in fact, when the direct face of colonialism had begun rolling back and great philosophers like Jean-Paul Sartre (1905–1980) and Frantz Omar Fanon (1925–1961) demanded justice.

While in Paris, Abdus Salam visited the grand mosque constructed, on a considerable block of land donated by the French Government, and with financial support of Arab rulers. He was impressed by its exquisite architecture and the elegance of Koranic verses inscribed in *Kufic* calligraphy on its walls. He found the main prayer hall was colourfully carpeted with precious rugs donated by the kings of Egypt, Syria and Palestine. He was rather saddened to note that, in spite of its enormous charm, the mosque remained largely unattended; and very often only the imam and his deputy filled in the mandatory quorum required for each of the five daily congregations. 'I sincerely trust', Abdus Salam wrote, overwhelmed, that God 'will soon rise a generation of vigorous Muslims' to break the silence in mosque with cries of Allah-o-Akbar. He may have intended to send his travelogue for publication somewhere because a pointer, in the draft, suggests the possible position for mosque picture.

---

[1] Abdul Karim Al-Khattabi (1882-1963) was a Moroccan freedom fighter and reformer of Berber origin who made it to the cover of Time magazine on 17 August 1925. He died in Cairo while in self-exile.

He was rather puzzled to observe the stringency of animal welfare legislation in Switzerland where Muslims did not enjoy much of a presence and yet slaughtering of animals in Islamic way amounted to cruelty. As a result, he noted, even the Jewish people were obliged to import kosher meat from abroad.

In Holland, Abdus Salam found a considerable number of Muslims of Indonesian origin who intermarried locally and were permanently domiciled in the country. 'No stigma is applied to them on the basis of colour or creed, as far as I could see'. He noted with appreciation for the Dutch way of family life. With the knowledge of colonial atrocities in Java and Dutch East Indies fresh in his mind, he was pleasantly surprised to observe the social scene in Holland. 'The Dutch are a people apart; their family tradition is so strong with them that it governs all their conduct'. He found it wonderfully reassuring to move about in streets in the company of an achkan-sherwani wearing Ahmadiyah missionary inspiring a sensation of wonderment rather than resentment among the town people. He observed that it was not just 'stare and finish' business. Often people in streets called each other out to examine the exotic garment. Smiling politely, even those in their balconies, expressed keen interest in the two aliens in their midst. He felt reassured to notice that nobody expressed hostility towards his foreign features.

He was even more delighted to discover that few affluent Dutch families had converted to Islam at their own free will. He made personal calls on two such people, one of them a woman, and felt amazed to see that 'they were entirely devoted to Islam'. Before leaving Holland, he visited Leiden University and was deeply impressed by its rich stocks of oriental scholarship, especially on Sufi doctrines.

By the time he returned to England, the political chaos in India had begun taking its toll.

In many districts, especially in Bengal, Bihar and Punjab; communal rioting and mutual slaughtering had begun. More than fighting the fire, therefore, the foremost aim before the colonial government was a quick and safe evacuation of men, women and children whose ancestors had 'civilised' the immense colony; it was time to rush back home. While handing the charge over to the last Viceroy, his predecessor referred to 'Operation Madhouse' which included details for evacuation of civilians and soldiers from Bengal to Punjab, from the first province of their occupation to that of the last.

Lord Louis Mountbatten (1900–1979), the last Viceroy, suffered from a deep-rooted condition of narcissism. His fondness of superficiality was boundless. On his first day in office, he began work by signing of the Black Warrant, that is, the approval of death penalty handed down to an offender. He announced the schedule for Independence of India without caring to consult anyone, even his bosses in London. India was to be divided on the basis of religion, as if this was the only logical conclusion to a century of secular governance. Never tired of boasting about the much-touted non-interference in the religion of its subjects, the British Empire caved in to uphold the cause of the faithful by chopping Muslim majority provinces of Bengal and Punjab.

In a display of partisan political wit, the Labour Government in England picked up a London-based lawyer, Cyril Radcliffe (1899–1977), holding only the most egotistical knowledge of India, to define borders of the new Muslim homeland in Punjab and Bengal. His foremost qualification for the onerous responsibility was his singular lack of education about the shared physical features of lands in question. Looks like, he hated the assignment from the day he actually arrived on the scene to perform the duty entrusted upon him. His rather sinister sense of judgment over the partition line pulled up a mass exodus of population henceforth unprecedented in human history. For serving the nearly vanished empire in this way, he was awarded with life peerage in the House of Lords, while millions had been made homeless in the subcontinent. Once in Lahore and thoroughly suffocated by heat, monsoon humidity and the ground realities; he opted to trust a butcher's axe upon the surgical scalpel actually required to do the job [1]

Like the proverbial monkey assigned the tedious task of dispensing cake between warring parties and ending up by serving all to itself, those drawing the line of demarcation hurried to neglect the physical and economic features, rivers, canals, hydroelectric works, embankments, social integrity of settlements, villages and even private residences. In a cunning move, the Muslim majority district of Gurudaspur, in Punjab, was handed over to the Indian side thus blocking Pakistan's contiguity into the Himalayan valley of Kashmir dominated by Muslim majority. In spite of all the pump and show of hurry and haste, triggered by the blue-eyed Louis Mountbatten, the international boundaries of

---

[1] Larry Collins and Dominique Lapierre., Freedom at Midnight, New York, 1975, p. 224

India and Pakistan were announced three days after the independence of two countries.

In this way, the act of Partition was carried out in a shamelessly arbitrary and disgustingly heartless manner, clearing the way for the bigoted to carry out suitable communal cleansing. For the ordinary lot of citizens, counting the blessings of raj day in and day out for three generations, the reward of loyalty descended in the shape of a human tragedy costumed in anarchy, massacre, mayhem, rape and ransack. Over ten million refugees were left on each side of the callously drawn-out line lifting floodgates upon the greatest show of human exodus ever witnessed in the history of civilisation. According to safer estimates, around 300,000 people were massacred in cross-migration, as they had been caught in rioting while attempting to flee for safety of their lives.

Fury was let loose in cities, towns, villages, wards, bazaars, mosques, temples and gurudwaras. Trapped in the blazing flames of religious revenge, furious mobs of Sikhs and Muslims settled scores upon each other. In the holy city of Amritsar, a troupe of abducted and raped Muslim women was forced to march naked on city streets.[1] When the 10-Down train service from Lahore rolled into Amritsar station, it carried only the butchered bodies of Sikh and Hindu men, women and children evicted from their homes in western Punjab. 'We are faced not with an ordinary exhibition of political or communal violence, but with a struggle between communities for the power which we are shortly to abandon', observed the last Governor of united Punjab.[2]

For decades since World War I, when the notion for self-rule leading to independence of India shaped up and gained momentum, Abdus Salam's Ahmadiyah party did not see the British quitting India in a foreseeable future. There was panic when the hour arrived.

Abdus Salam's family was partitioned with Punjab. His parents and siblings lived in Multan, waking up with Pakistani citizenship one morning in August 1947. Whereas, his uncle Ghulam Hussein, aunt Sehba and their children, including Abdus Salam's future wife, Amtul Hafeez, all living in Qadian, found themselves stranded in a hostile India. They were obliged to leave what had been fondly adopted as home only a few years ago and make it to safety across the unguarded border in one of convoys risking massacre.

---

[1] John Connel: Auchinleck, Cassel, London, 1959, p. 906
[2] Hodson, H.V., The Great Divide, Oxford University Press, Oxford (U.K.), 1985, p. 341

Stationed in England, over six thousand miles away from home, people like Abdus Salam welcomed the blood-soaked dawn of independence with a weird mix of suspicion, uncertainty, bitterness, hope, confidence and vision. But they were shaken to the core, worrying about their extended families back home.

Abdus Salam's sources of information ranged between regular news bulletins of the British Broadcasting Company (BBC) World Service and various rumour mills of panicked expatriates who received all sorts of news in dramatized mail from family and friends back home. He went through an emotional tumult and considered rushing back home. It was a pre-digital age when a great deal of personal information travelled in the shape of hard copy taking time to reach the destination via air and sea routes. Often, airmail took about a week and the bulk of ordinary correspondence and parcels took up to four weeks by sea. Making telephone calls was both tedious and expansive. Only the affluent had home connections and there again it was not possible to dial overseas directly and calls were made through local and international exchange systems.

'At that time, I felt there was no point in carrying on studying and that I must return home. I used to correspond with Bashir Ahmed, a friend of mine who lived in Lahore. What nonsense are you talking about? What difference will your presence make in the carnage that is unfolding here? He wrote back in response to my temptation to pack and return'. Abdus Salam remembered how forcefully his friend had urged him to better stay in Cambridge to complete what he had gone to achieve.[1]

No doubt, the bluntly sincere piece of advice tendered by Bashir Ahmed proved its value but living, back in 1947, was a test of its own kind. A whole generation of people in the subcontinent, passing through the trauma first hand, had been maimed to live in pain the rest of their lives. If Abdus Salam could draw any self-seeking consolation it would come from the fact that both Multan, where his parents and siblings were stationed, as well as the family hometown Jhang, had been allocated to the new state of Pakistan. In other words, they happened to be on the right side of the callously drawn international border and liberated from taking the risk of migration with one or another largely defenceless convoy. At the same time, they had been saved from opting out between India and Pakistan, their citizenship of Pakistan came seamlessly.

---

[1] Interviews 1984: Folder IV, pp. 40-41 [Basheer Ahmed joined the Foreign Service and served as Pakistan's ambassador in Brazil.]

With whole of Punjab turning into a colossal river of fire, blood and extermination, it was not possible to live without worry. Like other expatriates and students from India, he feared all sorts of news anytime. Incidentally, the Partition of Punjab intersected with the Islamic fasting month of *Ramazan*. Abdus Salam moved to the Ahmadiyah mosque in London and retired into the act of *Eitkaf*, a ten-day discretionary seclusion observed by the devout. Over and above fasting, during the course of *Eitkaf*, the faithful stay in an isolated chamber in the mosque offering both obligatory and optional prayers services and reciting the Koran; they leave the hollow only for washroom calls within the mosque; simple food is served upon them at the commencement and breaking of daily fasting. For Abdus Salam, it was his first public display of a deeper plunge into religion. Was it an isolated act of temporary refuge in response to the ugly turn of events back home in Punjab? Was it an expression of search for cultural identity? How deeply religious he was at that point in his life? Possibly, the answer lies in the mix of stimuli and his upbringing.[1]

III

Effectively, to Abdus Salam, the packing up of British colonial empire from India meant a little more than independence and creation of Pakistan. With raj rolled back, the goalpost that had eluded him for nearly ten years was dismantled for good. He had been liberated from what had so far been the singular aim of his life, that is, to win a place in the coveted Indian Civil Service. Now he was required to change around and retune his working career in Pakistan, the promised homeland of Muslims in the subcontinent, brought into being out of a frenzied Caesarean section, struggling to survive the shooting pains accompanying its birth. Sooner than later, the new state was likely to utilise the potential of educated and talented young men like Abdus Salam.

On his part, at a purely personal level, Abdus Salam felt he might be running out of time. Even though, he was young and well educated, the course of his life did not happen to follow the standard routine. In the first place, his father had taken time in starting work and family. At 56 in 1947, Mohammed Hussein neared superannuation and none of his children was employed or married to settle down and have family lives of their own. Had there been no war or the end

---

[1] Interviews 1984: Folder IV, p. 51

of British raj, Abdus Salam might have been a gainful civil servant in 1944, established and well on the course of sharing the burden of family leadership with his ageing father. Five of his younger brothers were still studying, with two sisters yet to be married. Apart from contributing financially, he was supposed to mentor his brothers, offer them advice in the course of their studies and career planning. Customarily, the older children, especially the male, were trusted to share the load efficiently and in time. He was betrothed to his cousin, Amtul Hafeez, and it was time for the two of them to get married. Amtul Hafeez was two years senior to him in age. If there had been no war, and the schedule of civil service recruitment was not disrupted, Abdus Salam would have won a lucrative position, got married to Amtul Hafeez with the two of them settled into a family.

After spending nearly five years in hope and suspense, the waiting game ended in a naught. Not only the war had blown up the prospects of public civil service recruitment, those playing the role of employers were gone. Abdus Salam was back to square one. Like the self-righteous leadership of his Ahmadiyah community, he was among those who had not imagined the departure of the British and coming of Pakistan at a pace as it turned out to be in the end. While making it to Cambridge, rather hurriedly, by winning the scholarship grant under Peasant Welfare Scheme when his father barely qualified as a farmer, Abdus Salam did not seem to set his eye upon a clear aim. In all probability, he just marked time for the political uncertainty to clear up in the subcontinent. But the strategy did not seem to work. He was enrolled to do Mathematics Tripos II, and disciplined to work up to sixteen hours a day, and yet driven by a lack of logic toward career planning.

Back in the infant state of Pakistan, his father continued to dream about the civil service vocation. Mohammed Hussein wanted his son to join public service in Pakistan where government was in the early stages of its evolution and bureaucracy constituted only a shadow of its predecessor. Abdus Salam revered the spirit of his father's wish but he appeared to have developed some degree of an aversion towards making a career in civil service. If true, his state of mind could be justified on the amount of time he had spent caught on tenterhooks. Also, Cambridge had enabled him to take an alternate view of events and objectives in life. Heading to appear for Mathematics Tripos II examination, and suffering from emotional strain caused by uncertainty, he started toying with the idea of converting his course of studies into a Tripos in Mechanical Sciences.

Apparently, the aim was to fast track his employment in engineering. He consulted his father who viewed the proposition as nothing short of a crashed dream. Mohammed Hussein was deeply perturbed. In actual fact, the fixation Mohammed Hussein had in relation to a civil service career for Abdus Salam entailed more than merely a dream of success story associated with imperial glitter. Serving the government in a position of power and influence was not just good income and job security; it amounted to a display of enhanced social status and valuable contacts in the corridors of power. He wrote a letter to Afzal Husain, urging the peer to intervene.

'Your father is disappointed'. Afzal Husain wrote to Abdus Salam, circa 24 August 1947, that is, within a couple of weeks of the making of Pakistan.[1] Afzal Husain was referring to the end of Indian Civil Service dream of Mohammed Hussein. But then the scientist sitting inside Afzal Husain could weigh up the value attached to a Cambridge Tripos in Mathematics. He disagreed with Abdus Salam's contention to study Mechanical Sciences. 'I have no doubt that you are making the best use of your time. I am afraid I will not advise you to take this course. You should take the Mathematics Tripos and obtain a First Class and a good position. On your return you will find many opportunities of your continuing in Mathematics as a teacher and a research worker'. Afzal Hussain concluded.

With his personal keenness on Mathematics, Abdus Salam took the advice and gave up on Mechanical Sciences though he was still not clear about the choice of a career that awaited him in the near future. It is worthwhile to mention here that the story of Abdus Salam's life at that time comprised of events he used to dish out as 'accidents'. He was on the course to an unplanned journey in the direction of Theoretical Physics. Here the majority of his biographies and profiles, therefore, closely match in citation of his first-person accounts. None of the contemporary writers felt the need to cross-check his version. Even though an exercise of the sort was not meant to cast any doubt about the authenticity of the version of events he himself offered; the effort might have opened up the possibility of more valuable clues into the scene of that period of his life.

In June 1948, that is, within less than two years of his residence at St John's College, Abdus Salam passed the Mathematics Tripos II examination, and he was 'admitted to the Degree of Bachelor of Arts' at the University of Cambridge

---

[1] Mailed from Lahore, this letter of Afzal Husain is undated though 24 August 1947 seems to be the closest to make out of postal office stamp on the aerogram.

'at a full congregation holden in the Senate House on 22 June 1948'. During the course of his Mathematics examinations, he won prestigious awards like the Wright's Prize and the Smith Prize.

Historically, in view of the ground-breaking accomplishments the university had made in the fields of mathematics and physics, Tripos examination was a sort of national event. In old days, the examination constituted written tests in sixteen papers covering over 200 questions and students faced the trial for days on. Finally, after the examination, a formal order of merit was published and results were read out from the balcony of the Senate Hall. Those achieving top positions were accorded the special recognition as Wranglers. Girls, howsoever brilliant and sharp, were not permitted to sit for the examination and this practice continued up until the closing decades of the 19th century. According to Cambridge folklore, a female student by the name of Charlotte Angas (1858–1931) was awarded special permission to sit for the Tripos examination. She was believed to have made it to the eighth position on the order of merit; still her name was not read out. She missed out public recognition just as generations of women had on Abdus Salam's ancestry tree. In Cambridge, however, in due course of time, the rigidity of Tripos examination was streamlined.

Abdus Salam's triumph in completing the course within two years made it to some of the English-language newspapers back home in Pakistan where prominent dailies like *Pakistan Times*, *Civil and Military Gazette* and *Dawn* carried stories of his success introducing him as 'a gifted scholar of mathematics' interested in 'aesthetics, sociology and Physics'.[1]

Had Abdus Salam been born somewhere in England and graduated through local high school stream, he might have completed Tripos in 1946 and saved two years.[2] Still, having completed the Mathematics Tripos II ahead of the stipulated timeframe, he had one year of his scholarship grant at his disposal. He had two options. One, pack up from Cambridge, return home, find work, get married and settle down as second-in-command to share the burden of family welfare with his parents. Two, stay on in Cambridge, continue studying Mathematics or try his luck with Physics. During the course of his Mathematics Tripos II, he had attended lectures of Paul Dirac purely out of intellectual curiosity. Those lectures

---

[1] Apparently released by a news agency known by the name of Star, the story appeared in the Karachi-based daily newspaper *Dawn* on 15 July 1948; and the Lahore-based daily newspapers the *Pakistan Times* and *Civil & Military Gazette* the day after.
[2] Abdul Ghani (1982): p. 15

were a part of the Quantum Mechanics and Relativity course in Physics Tripos III. Abdus Salam's own familiarity with Physics was nominal and dated back to an Intermediate level course, way back in Year 12, when their class teacher himself was not sure about the distinction between stress and strain. But if Physics could be Quantum Mechanics and Relativity, as taught by Paul Dirac, then Abdus Salam's dearth of knowledge in high school text book Physics did not really matter. He could spend the remaining balance of his scholarship grant in studying Physics.

Mathematics came to him naturally. He had studied and flourished in the subject with loyal consistency all the way from Year Eight in Jhang to doing the Tripos in Cambridge. Now he felt fascinated by the shared territory between Mathematics and Theoretical Physics.

It was an age dominated by names like Albert Einstein (1879–1955), Max Born (1882–1970), Niels Bohr (1885–1962), Wolfgang Pauli (1900–1958) and Werner Heisenberg (1901–1975). Some of them visited Cambridge where Abdus Salam enjoyed the privilege to attend their lectures. He was amazed by their conversation about complex numerical formulae, equations, dimensions and algorithms; all in the mathematical tongue of gods who created universes and forces of nature. For their contribution towards the understanding of atomic structure, especially in the development of quantum electrodynamics, Paul Dirac and Wolfgang Pauli inspired a whole generation of younger physicists. Abdus Salam was enticed to a degree where the early signs of his imminent love affair with Theoretical Physics were evident.

Paul Dirac (1902–1984), the Lucasian Professor of Mathematics in Cambridge, had shared the 1933 Nobel Prize in Physics with Erwin Schrodinger (1887–1961). He was the son of a Swiss immigrant and had made it to St John's College, like Abdus Salam, on the basis of his strength in Mathematics. Known for his prediction about the existence of antiparticles, he could speak English, German, French and Russian languages and was still a man of few words. It is said that he intended to decline the Nobel Prize on grounds of his aversion to publicity. He caved in only when Earnest Rutherford alerted him that declining the accolade might bring greater publicity. Paul Dirac's view of religion and politics brought him fairly close to contemporary Marxist opinion. He was Abdus Salam's lifelong hero, a physicist bigger than Albert Einstein.

Why some mathematicians were inspired to do physics? One possible answer to this question was provided by the Polish mathematician Mark Kac (1914–

1985). Finding something in Mathematics, according to Mark Kac, amounted to accepting a well-known fact; whereas, discoveries in Physics led to a feeling of real achievement. 'If doing mathematics or science is looked upon as a game then one might say that in mathematics you compete against yourself or other mathematicians; in physics your adversary is nature and the stakes are higher'. Mark Kac observed.[1]

Actually, the transition from Mathematics to Theoretical Physics did not constitute a dramatic deal; good mathematicians flourished in intersecting areas of scientific knowledge and it was hard to imagine if physicists, chemists and molecular geneticists were not first-class mathematicians in the first place. Almost every leading physicist in the 20th century, the dawn of nuclear age, had been an outstanding mathematician. Abdus Salam was aware that the source of his strength rested with Mathematics, the repository of Physics.

For Abdus Salam, an inclination to study Theoretical Physics constituted only one part of the puzzle facing him. If he decided to make a life in Theoretical Physics, he would require an extension of his scholarship grant to do doctoral research. He was not sure how poverty-stricken Pakistan or his family would afford such extravagance. How would he gather sufficient courage to break the news of giving up on civil service upon his father? He was 22, on the threshold of making a vital decision, all by himself, to change the course of his life. Unlike buying a house or a car where one hoped to fix things even if something went wrong with the transaction or the acquisition, he confronted the dilemma of Indian youth falling in love and getting married over and above parental preferences. Hesitant in arriving at a decision, Abdus Salam sought advice from two of his teachers, Fred Hoyle and James Wordie (1889–1962).

Fred Hoyle (1915–2001), passing Mathematics Tripos III with distinction, had been a research student under Paul Dirac. When Abdus Salam asked the question as to what he should do in the final year of his scholarship grant? Fred Hoyle returned the question as what would *you* like to do? Abdus Salam replied that he wished to study Theoretical Physics though his background in the subject was limited. 'I can aim at a first-class result in Mathematics, but surely not so in Physics, especially on the experimental side'. Abdus Salam stated. Fred Hoyle was blunt and honest; he cautioned Abdus Salam that science was another name for experimentation.[2] His advice for Abdus Salam to do one year of advanced

---

[1] Mark Kac: Enigmas of Science, University of California Press, 1987, pp. xxiii-xxiv
[2] Abdul Ghani (1982): p. 18

course in Physics and learn the subject for this was the best way to look professional physicists in the eye.[1] 'You must, even if it kills you, take this last year for experimental physics. Are you with me?' He is reported to have told Abdus Salam.[2]

James Wordie (1889–1962), listened to Abdus Salam and then asked, just as Fred Hoyle had done earlier, the same question. What would *you* like to do? Abdus Salam opened his heart by confessing to the dilemma of his loyalty split between Mathematics and Physics. 'Oh, you must do physics in that case.' James Wordie, the celebrated explorer of the Arctic, passed an instant judgment. But then in the same breath he warned Abdus Salam that two leading physicists of the time, George Thomson (1892–1975) and Neville Mott (1905–1996), had failed to do so within one year.

At this point, the Ahmadiyah caliph advised him to benefit from the scholarship grant comprehensively because quitting half-way amounted to cowardice. Coming from someone wielding the status of a divinity and acting under the guidance of God, it was suggestion both Abdus Salam and his father would take as equalling a decree. Abdus Salam made up his mind in favour of Theoretical Physics. He wrote to his father, accordingly, conveying the decision to study Physics despite a 'poor knowledge' of the subject. He begged his father to pray for him.[3]

Although, in a way, this declaration of Abdus Salam to study Physics amounted to death sentence on pursuit of a career in civil service, Mohammed Hussein wished his son the very best.

On the balance, in terms of available logistics, the decision to study Physics was not a rash judgment. Given the options available to him, Abdus Salam felt safe. If the love affair with Physics failed, he could wind up at Cambridge, return to Pakistan and sit for the civil service examination. He met the age criteria and stood fairly strong chances of making it to one of the top cadres in the government.

It was time to take a break from the hectic rush of events demanding tough choices. In the summer break of 1948, he was invited to attend the Second International Youth Congress at Munich. Once again, he availed the opportunity to travel and refreshed his knowledge of grand reconstruction in Europe.

---

[1] Jagjit Singh (1992): p. 11
[2] The Illustrated Weekly of India, 1 February 1981, p. 11
[3] Mohammed Hussein (1974): p. 45

After the summer vacations and his enrolment in Physics Tripos II, Abdus Salam was dispatched to the Cavendish Laboratory for experimental work. Since the intellectual revolution, triggered in Europe by Galileo Galilee (1564–1642), Mathematics presented the route to understanding laws of nature, especially in the spheres of gravity, magnetism, light and motion. In 1873, when James Maxwell published his monumental work on Electricity and Magnetism, the experimental work had picked up momentum. Around this time, William Cavendish, the Seventh Duke of Devonshire, founded in Cambridge a laboratory that was named after him, and James Maxwell was appointed as the First Cavendish Professor of Physics. In old days, the Cavendish Laboratory was located on Free School Lane, in the heart of the town, and it was just another name for the Department of Physics in Cambridge. Over time, the institution had well over two dozen Nobel Prize winners to its credit.

Incidentally, Abdus Salam's draft into Physics coincided with X-ray crystallography of cellular structure and the view of poetic double-helix of Deoxyribonucleic Acid (DNA) at the Cavendish Laboratory. Placed against such an outstanding breakthrough, Abdus Salam was expected to sit for the final examination in six papers of theory and one of experiment within a matter of six months. He acknowledged his lack of fresh knowledge in physics but had no idea how the trial of hands-on experimentation was going to unnerve him in the coming days. He could see the roots of his disability with experimental work. Having come from Jhang, where the age of electricity dawned after the taming of nuclear energy in Europe and the United States, he had none experience whatsoever in laboratory work.

He was assigned to compute wavelength variation in two sodium spectral lines. It took him a week to get familiarised with the equipment, and once three readings were available, he rushed to show the result to Denys Wilkinson (1922–2016), the nuclear physicist who then worked as a Demonstrator in the laboratory. In later years, Denys Wilkinson served many scientific and academic positions including the one as the Vice-Chancellor at the University of Sussex for 11 years from 1976–1987. He dismissed Abdus Salam, almost summarily, as a third-class student.[1] Three readings? Denys Wilkinson shot back were just not worth grading the result of an experiment.[2] Evidently, it was a bad omen for someone who looked forward to finishing the Physics Tripos II within a matter

---

[1] The Illustrated Weekly of India, 1 February 1981, p. 11
[2] Jagjit Singh (1992): p. 12

of few months. Abdus Salam found laboratory work daunting where nothing seemed to favour him.

In 1949, Abdus Salam sat for the final examination. On the day of practical tests, which were supposed to continue for nearly eight hours, he arrived in the laboratory with his lunchbox full of chicken sandwiches. Half way through, he was horrified to discover the ineptness of his method. Not enough time had been left to repeat the experiment. Although he was quite confident about getting a good result in the six papers of theory, yet panic overtook him. Somewhat frightened, he almost gave up hope for passing the examination. 'My practical examination has not gone well at all and I might not get through on this occasion'. He wrote to his father, begging for prayers to achieve a miracle.[1]

He had the miracle of getting away with a first-class result, standing vindicated before the cautious counselling of Samuel Devons and James Wordie. But his supervisor at the Cavendish Laboratory, Denys Wilkinson, attributed the feat, rather diplomatically, to error people make in judging others. On his part, Abdus Salam wanted to resolve the mystery. He went to double-check the result. What was the secret behind his good grades? It turned out that due to the bulk of his strong performance in six papers of theory, the examiners did not feel the need to bother about results of laboratory work. 'It was all by the Grace of God and due to my father's prayers'. Abdus Salam used to say afterwards.[2]

Messages of congratulation arrived from his teachers. 'By getting six firsts in Physics the College has done exceptionally well, and I am grateful to you for your share in this magnificent result'. Kenneth Budden (1915–2005), the physicist acknowledged for his work in ionosphere and long radio waves, wrote in his handwritten message.

'I should like to take this opportunity of congratulating you on your high place in Physics in making a so-called Double First with Mathematics'. James Wordie wrote.

Denys Wilkinson took time in offering an explanation of his judgment. 'I prize, as one of my major contributions to our understanding of the physical world, the fact that when in charge of the experimental physics teaching laboratory I persuaded Abdus Salam that his talents must lie in theoretical rather

---

[1] Mohammed Hussein (1974): p. 45
[2] Abdul Hameed (circa 2000): p. 59

than in experimental physics'. He stated later, as a sort of improvement upon his earlier observation.[1]

Fred Hoyle is reported to have canvassed Abdus Salam to stay on for research with a scholarship grant forthcoming from St John's. Abdus Salam sought the opinion of his close friends, Ram Prakash Bambah and Nitya Anand, a carryover of camaraderie dating back to Lahore's Government College.

What should I do? He asked referring to the offer of scholarship grant. 'On the other hand, my father is not getting younger, my brothers are growing up, they need my emotional support, and they will need my financial support also. Its time I went and earned something for my family, and here they're asking me to stay on for research. I have my obligation to my community. I should be useful to them if I join the higher Civil Service'.

His friends counselled him to go for research and forget about civil service. 'Pakistan has many people who would make good administrators, may be better than you, but it's hardly likely that there'd be somebody who would be able to make the type of contribution to science that you may be able to make'. Ram Prakash Bambah advocated.

A couple of days later, Abdus Salam turned up with bags packed and stated. 'I will go back to Pakistan. If I can manage something which allows me to help my family and also pay my way here, I'll come back and retrieve these trunks. Otherwise, you may ship them back to me'. He announced.[2]

Although, in order to get his son the scholarship grant under the Peasant Welfare Fund, Mohammed Hussein had qualified as only a pretend farmer, Abdus Salam utilised the money to the best of its spirit. In less than three years of his stay in Cambridge, he had to his credit the double Tripos in Mathematics and Physics. All he required now was an extension in his scholarship grant in order to do a doctorate in Theoretical Physics. But how might this happen? How was he going to finance further study? This was a big question as the united Punjab, where Peasant Welfare Scheme had been created, did not exist anymore. Pakistan was a newly born state struggling to survive beyond its mystifying birth.

IV

---

[1] Denys Wilkinson 1995: Blood, Birds and the Old Road (www.annualreviews.org/aronline)

[2] Ram Prakash Bambah - Trieste Tribute (1997): pp. 47-53

At the time of its birth, Pakistan comprised of the far less developed northern hinterland of the Indian subcontinent. Apart from facing the chaos and bloodbath accompanying its creation, the new state was in dire need of educated cadres in both public and private sectors of economy. Lacking a continuity of political tradition, democratic culture and accountability; the leadership in Pakistan had none experience whatsoever in the running of an independent state. In fact, when the demand for a separate Muslim homeland was first canvassed in the 1940s, many economic experts attached very little hope for the proposal to work without Indian cooperation and patronage. There was a widely held belief that only friendly ties with India, that is, the heartland of South Asian economic activity, could promise stability in Pakistan. Nobody seemed convinced that a geographical region producing cotton, jute and hides could generate revenue sufficient to run an independent country and viable economy. Almost all of the main business centres and ports were located in what had become India. If the western Pakistan produced 40 percent of the raw cotton, nearly all the mills processing the fibre operated in India. As a result of the Partition, India inherited 380 cotton mills compared with only 14 in Pakistan. Likewise, the eastern wing of Pakistan provided 75 percent of raw jute without having a single mill to process the so-called golden fibre. Such a distorted economic geography was further complicated by communal demography, the majority of Muslims populated the hinterland, and Hindus controlled the commercial activity of heartland by virtue of their better education in business and accounting. Amidst communal rioting, the majority of banks had closed down in districts assigned to the new country, shrinking their presence from 487 branches steeply down to 69. Pakistan comprised of 23 percent of the geographical mass of the subcontinent with less than 10 percent of share in industrial infrastructure.

One of the founding fathers of Pakistan remembered how temporary tin-shed dwellings were hastily raised in Karachi to provide for office accommodation to public servants struggling to meet shortages in 'even the most ordinary stationery supplies like pens and pins'. Five superannuated officers of the erstwhile Indian Civil Service were summoned from England to serve as secretaries to the Government of Pakistan. One British firm, Thomas De La Rue, had been commissioned to set up the security press in Karachi to print currency notes and other legal documents.[1]

What manner of support Abdus Salam expected to get from a place where survival of the state was foremost national priority, where both public and private sectors had yet to evolve. From the colonial subcontinent, Pakistan had inherited only two universities and barely two dozen colleges in the higher education sector. Back in 1949, fewer jobs and scholarship grants were advertised in the limited number and circulation of national newspapers. His parents just could not finance his ambition to continue studying abroad for another three years. Given the circumstances, his only hope was Afzal Husain who presided over the Central Public Service Commission, in Karachi, a statutory organisation entrusted with recruitment of government employees. Back in June 1942, serving as Vice Chancellor of Punjab University, Afzal Husain had sent Abdus Salam a message of congratulation upon achieving the First in Year Twelve Intermediate Examination. 'I am glad to see your result and congratulate you on your very creditable achievement in standing first. I shall watch your future academic career with great interest and I hope you will continue to win fresh laurels'. Afzal Husain had written.

Abdus Salam had already mailed his Mathematics Tripos II result to Afzal Husain hoping the influential peer to respond with some clue.

Afzal Husain (1889–1970) belonged to an influential household in Punjab, his older brother Fazal Husain (1877–1936), was the founder of cross-communal Punjab Unionist Party, had held high-profile public offices under the colonial government. Afzal Husain had studied at Christ College in Cambridge and passed Natural Sciences Tripos I and II under the famous British Zoologist Stanley Gardiner (1872–1946). He returned home in Punjab to start his professional career as an Entomologist but then ended up serving senior administrative positions. He had served as Vice Chancellor of Punjab University on two different occasions, from 1938 to 1944 and then again from 1954 to 1958. He also served as the Chairman of Central Public Service Commission in Pakistan from 1948 to 1952 holding other senior positions in between. Originally, the commission was established in 1926, the year of Abdus Salam's birth, with a view to bring transparency into public service recruitments.

---

[1] Chaudhry Mohammed Ali: The Emergence of Pakistan, Columbia University Press, New York & London, 1967, pp. 336-351

Always geared up to lend a hand to promising students, Afzal Husain stepped forward without the slightest hesitation. He took the matter of Abdus Salam's predicament up with his former colleagues Ghulam Khaliq, Mohammed Sharif and Bilal Hashmi at the Department of Education in Lahore. Incidentally, those three officers had in the past been members of the Government College faculty and were rather fondly familiar with Abdus Salam's academic performance.

In a letter, dated 1 January 1949, Afzal Husain assured Abdus Salam about the possibility of an extension in scholarship grant as well as professional opportunities, in Lahore, in both Mathematics and Nuclear Physics. 'You must let me know in greater details about the monetary side. There should be no difficulty in getting you a further extension of the same or some other scholarship. You need not worry about it, but steps must be taken at once so that the scheme matures well in advance. Now let me have details of your program as settled in consultation with your teachers, and if it is supported with a letter from your teacher, indicating the period for which you should remain at Cambridge and so on, I will move in the matter'. Afzal Husain added that the Government College could soon be inviting expressions of interest for the position of a Professor in Mathematics and that Abdus Salam stood fairly bright chances of fitting into the emerging order of things.

'Even as Professor of Mathematics at the Government College, you could do research in Nuclear Physics. Pakistan is also thinking of setting up National Laboratories, but it will take time. You need money and men. We are short of both at present. One must be prepared to start low and then build up'. He remarked adding that Pakistan was proud and duty-bound 'to render every assistance' to people like Abdus Salam. 'Do not hesitate to write to me', he concluded.[1]

By electing to do doctoral research in Theoretical Physics for three years, Abdus Salam had, in fact, raised questions more than providing answers. Other than rushing into a job and start supporting his family, he needed money to stay on in Cambridge. Where was the money going to come from? Now he had the concrete assurance, relating to both an extension of scholarship grant and academic employment, from someone as influential as Afzal Husain. In this way, the year 1949 emerges as a crucial time in the life story of Abdus Salam when the foundation of his career in Theoretical Physics was laid by one of his erstwhile promoters. Afzal Husain's letter amounted to a New Year gift for

---

[1] Afzal Hussain to Abdus Salam: 1 Jan 1949

Abdus Salam. Apart from the reassurance to get an extension in his scholarship grant, Abdus Salam looked forward to taking up the chair of Mathematics in Lahore.

At the same time, he applied for allocation of a doctoral project at Cambridge. About the end of April 1949, he was advised to report at the Cavendish Laboratory to discuss his research project with Otto Frisch (1904–1979) and another physicist Edward Shire (1910–1992).

If everything went by plan, he hoped to visit Pakistan with a double Tripos from Cambridge. Once home, he could spend time with family besides personally following up with his applications for the extension of scholarship grant as well as employment in Lahore.

Soon, as alerted by Afzal Husain, Punjab University invited applications for ten positions of professors in various disciplines of natural sciences. 'Applicants, who must have high qualifications and research and teaching experience, will be required to lecture, to promote and guide research, to coordinate higher teaching in their respective subjects in Lahore, and to stimulate their teaching in affiliated colleges. Knowledge of English is essential'. Expounded the job advertisement appearing in the *Times of London* Education Supplement, and applicants were advised to send their expressions of interest to the High Commissioner of Pakistan, in London, by 25 May 1949.

Abdus Salam set himself upon organising sets of necessary documentation to draft his expressions of interest seeking extension in scholarship grant as well as for a teaching position in Lahore. His teachers at Cambridge gave him persuasively worded letters of recommendation.

Francis White (1893–1969), the Fellow at St John's College, acknowledged Abdus Salam's 'outstanding performance' in Cambridge. 'As lecturer and Director of Studies in Mathematics in St John's College, I have been in close touch with Mr Salam for the whole period of his residence here. He is undoubtedly a man of distinction, attractive personality and of vigorous enthusiasm for his work. I can confidently recommend him as likely by teaching and research, to prove a most excellent Professor of Mathematics'. He wrote on 12 April 1949.

James Wordie (1889–1962), the Senior Tutor at St John's College, certified that Abdus Salam had been a member of the college since October 1946. 'I have no hesitation in recommending Mr Salam as suitable in every way for the post for which he is presently applying'. He wrote on 27 April 1949.

Leslie Howarth (1911–2001), the University Lecturer and a Fellow at St John's College, was another of Abdus Salam's teachers supporting him in the strongest possible terms. He rated Abdus Salam as 'a first-class mathematician I have always believed him to be' he described the applicant as 'hardworking, of pleasant personality' with 'clear exposition' required to make 'an excellent University teacher when he returns, as I understand he intends, to his native country'. Leslie Howarth stated in his letter, dated 14 May 1949.

Otto Frisch, one of the pioneers in nuclear fission and a member of the *British Mission* heading the Critical Assembly Group in Manhattan Project, supported Abdus Salam coherently. 'We are extremely pleased with the First-Class result obtained by Abdus Salam, of St John's College, Cambridge, in Part II of the Natural Sciences Tripos this year. As a consequence of this result, and our acquaintances with him during his time in Cambridge, we feel that his proposed future work in scientific research in Pakistan would be very much helped if he could have at least two years training and practical experience in research in the Cavendish Laboratory. This is practically true, as I understand that his research work will be in the field of nuclear physics, which I believe is only just being started in Pakistan. This is a field in which experience with the techniques and apparatus already developed is of very great importance. Our own best people pursue a course of research of this nature if they are to undertake research as their life's work. We would very much like to see this young man given an opportunity to undertake the course of advanced study, which we feel should benefit him so much, and we would be most pleased if your government could arrange to finance him. I am certain that any money devoted in this way would be of the greatest value to the future of research work in Pakistan'. He wrote in his letter, dated 18 June 1949.

Everything seemed to fall in place. Abdus Salam cabled his Physics result in the Natural Sciences Tripos II over to both Afzal Hussain and Ghulam Khaliq in Karachi and Lahore, respectively. Making copies of documents was a somewhat tedious task in those days, it was accomplished by inserting carbon films in between paper sheets, all fed into manual type machines. Nobody in those days had imagined the dawn of an era full of multi-purpose computers, photocopying, scanning, printing and faxing, email attachments, telephone messaging; all in colour. He made two separate portfolios of the result along with letters of recommendation to deliver by hand in next few days.

On 29 May 1949, Abdus Salam informed the High Commission of Pakistan in London about his program to return home. He intended to leave by the end of June 1949 and, as such, requested for the release of £70 as return fare seeking permission to travel by air which in those days was termed as 'the overland route'. He looked forward to the family reunion after about three years. It was going to be his first visit to Pakistan. He hoped the combination of double Tripos with firsts in Mathematics and Physics was very likely to win him a job in Lahore along with an extension of scholarship grant. But just when he was ready to leave Cambridge, a letter arrived from Ghulam Khaliq advising him that the Government of West Punjab had extended the term of his scholarship grant for another one year and that he could stay on in Cambridge up until September 1950. 'In case you are not in a position to take your Ph.D. degree by September 1950, attempt will be made to extend your scholarship for another year or so to enable you to complete your course'. Ghulam Khaliq wrote in his letter, dated 14 June 1949, clouded with bureaucratic jargon.

His scholarship grant had been extended without granting him any break to be able to visit home and spend time with his family because the terms of original award covered just one return fare to England. 'Therefore, if you intend to continue your research work from October 1949, your trip to Pakistan for the summer months this year will have to be undertaken by you at your own cost'. As the extension had presupposed continuity of the ongoing grant, travelling home amounted to a violation of the contract. 'I have, however, a strong suspicion that you may not be able to find money to return to England in September this year to resume your studies there, so that once you come back at this stage you may be coming back for good'. Ghulam Khaliq raised the alarm. 'This will cause a certain amount of disappointment to those who feel that by doing research work after your Physics Tripos at Cambridge you will improve your qualifications considerably and will thereby be of greater use to your country'. Ghulam Khaliq concluded.

While Abdus Salam did not have time to retract and alter his travel itinerary at the last minute, he boarded the flight to Karachi. His hopes were discoloured and he was not sure as to what the fate actually held in store for him.

V

Abdus Salam arrived in Pakistan in the last week of June 1949; he landed in Karachi to take the train to Multan, where his father still worked at the Department of Education. He had hardly enough time to spend in Karachi. Yet he considered it necessary to call upon his benefactor, Afzal Husain, as a gesture in courtesy. Pakistan, in the end, was a society dictated by tribal and feudal ethos. Howsoever strong one might be on merit, the social and political clouting was inescapable; unless people stood up and demanded to be counted by way of one social connection or another, there was always the likelihood of getting trampled under the stampede of stooges. Having witnessed the value of professional networking, fraternities and clubs in the west, he understood it all very well, at the age of 23.

Karachi, the burgeoning port on the Arabian Sea, sizzled with a fierce mix of heat and humidity. For three years he had struggled to come to terms with overcast sky, chill, rain, snow and blizzards of England; now it was a test on the other extreme where the midsummer of Cambridge was replaced with soaring temperature and an airless oppression of humidity. At the same time, he felt good to be in Karachi, the capital city of his independent homeland. He had not been to Karachi before and was amazed to observe the difference the Pakistani capital city presented compared to London and other metropolitan centres of Europe. There was hardly the need for a fiscal dissertation to measure the gap between the developed and the backward, the damage and disability inflicted by colonialism expressed itself so strikingly. If he was amused to observe camel carts and their colourfully dressed indigenous drivers, the spectacle of refugee camps, colonies and shanty towns pained him.

He went straight to Lakham House to see Afzal Husain without a formal appointment. Afzal Husain had just returned from a business meeting, in Dhaka, in the eastern wing of Pakistan, but he was able to go through his mail including the portfolio of Physics Tripos II result and letters of reference mailed by Abdus Salam. When an office assistant announced the arrival of a visitor from England, Afzal Husain was delighted to receive the guest.

After the usual exchange of cultural pleasantries, and few casual remarks about the striking difference of weather between Cambridge and Karachi, Afzal Husain picked up Abdus Salam's portfolio from the in-tray. Splendid! Splendid!! He exclaimed.

Afzal Husain was aware of the fixation Mohammed Hussein had for Abdus Salam to become a civil servant. 'If you are still interested, the doorway to the Civil Service of Pakistan is open. But once a bureaucrat, you may have to forget about physics and research. So where exactly do you stand today?' Afzal Hussain is reported to have asked. He then cited his own example of the unfulfilled desire to continue research in Entomology.

Only if he could get an extension in the scholarship grant and find some manner of employment anchorage to placate his father; higher studies and research in Theoretical Physics would be his only goal. Abdus Salam pleaded straightforwardly.[1]

Afzal Hussain expressed his readiness to be the advocate of Abdus Salam. He was aware that Pakistan needed leaders in science and technology as much as experts in administration, business and finance. Above all, he wielded enormous amount of influence among senior bureaucrats in Pakistan. 'He helped me to get the scholarship grant extended for another three years'. Abdus Salam acknowledged.[2]

Reassured, Abdus Salam referred to the bureaucratic caution raised by Ghulam Khaliq in relation to rules covering the return fare. It was not easy for him to change his travel plans at the very last minute, he explained. Afzal Husain believed that fixing this little hitch with return fare would not be a big deal provided the scholarship grant was extended. He advised Abdus Salam to call on Abdul Latif, the Deputy Secretary at the Ministry of Industries and Education, before leaving for Multan. Incidentally, Abdul Latif had been a lecturer at Government College and, like other members of the erstwhile faculty; he was fondly familiar with Abdus Salam. He acted almost instantly by urging the concerned officer, Bilal Hashmi, to settle the payment of fare favourably.[3]

After making a few social calls on some of his friends in Karachi, Abdus Salam headed for the rail station to board the northbound service to Multan. His parents and siblings awaited him in Multan any day though they did not have exact knowledge of the service he was likely to catch from Karachi. On land route, the over twelve-hour tiring journey between Karachi and Multan was accomplished on old-fashioned carriages pulled by archaic coal-powered steam engines swivelling over nine hundred miles of single track laid across the lower

---

[1] Interviews 1984: Folder IV, pp. 39, 43
[2] Interviews 1984: Folder IV, p. 45
[3] Abdul Latif to Bilal Hashmi: 27 June 1949

tracts of Indus Valley. Only a service or two each day linked Karachi with Lahore and Peshawar covering Multan in between. As Mohammed Hussain had only an approximate idea about his son's travel plans, he asked Abdus Salam's younger brother, Abdul Hameed, to go to the railway station and check out the service arriving from Karachi. Abdul Hameed was rather pleasantly surprised to find his brother disembarking from the afternoon train from Karachi. By the time the two of them made it home, Mohammed Hussain had already returned from work. This was how, decades prior to the age of mobile telephones and text messages, in a world where an overwhelming majority of ordinary households did not have the luxury of ordinary landline telephone connections, people returned home from faraway lands by cabling their tentative travel schedule.

It was a long-awaited, exhilarating and noisy family reunion. At the peak of sizzling summer, the fruit markets in Multan were flooded with syrupy, fragrant and cool outburst of mangoes, rock melon, watermelon and falsa berries. Abdus Salam's memories of college holidays spent with his parents were revived. During the course of following weeks, he shuttled between Multan, Lahore and Jhang; catching up with extended family and friends besides keeping a track of progress in relation to his scholarship grant and employment. He made up on those meat and vegetarian curries his mother was so adept at cooking. He was somewhat shocked to observe the cultural transformation overtaking the place. As partition had deprived the western districts of Punjab, especially places like Multan and Lahore, of their multicultural ways of life. He missed the marked absence of elegantly bound turbans of Sikh men and the enchantingly wrapped colourful *saris* of Hindu women. Walking through the corridors, classrooms and foyers of the Government College in Lahore, he reminisced about his old teachers and mates; those familiar faces and their affectionate smiles were nowhere to be seen, never to return.

Once through with unwinding, Abdus Salam briefed his father about the meeting he had in Karachi with Afzal Husain and the new horizon opening up before him. He hinted at the possibility of securing both an extension in the scholarship grant along with prestigious employment in Lahore before returning to Cambridge for doctoral study. Apparently, Mohammad Hussein had already come around to accepting the fact that the dream of finding his son a career in the coveted Indian Civil Service was drowned in the wake of war and partition. He gave Abdus Salam his blessings and a whole-hearted support to go for Physics.

Afzal Hussain was true to his promise. He corresponded with Bilal Hashmi, the Director of Public Instruction in Lahore, advocating the case of Abdus Salam. By achieving three first class results in Mathematics and Physics in a row within three years, Afzal Husain wrote, Abdus Salam had proved himself to be 'a man of extraordinary merit'. Getting to the top while doing the Tripos in Physics at Cambridge, without ever having any formal background in the subject, was a testimony to Abdus Salam's 'first class intellect and capacity for intensive work'. He added.

'I have seen him and discussed his future with him. I have seen his teachers' testimonials and other letters. Whatever you can do for him will not be enough, because it is not every day that you can get a young man of Abdus Salam's intellect and character. He could without effort get into the Pakistan Administrative Service through an open competition. He is, however, not interested in this. He wants to pursue his research. Whatever facilities you can provide for him will be well deserved'. Afzal Husain wrote while building up the case of extension in Abdus Salam's scholarship grant.

Afzal Husain went as far as pressing that Abdus Salam fell 'outside all rules and regulations' governing the ordinary lot of scholarship. 'I will, without the slightest hesitation, recommend that Abdus Salam be given scholarship for the period his teachers at Cambridge recommend, and besides he should be given special grant for visiting Nuclear Physics institutes on the Continent and in USA. He should be assured that his training would not suffer for want of funds. I will go further. If it were necessary for him to support his family, and begin to earn I would be prepared to give some allowance to his people. Looking at it from the point of view of Abdus Salam's family, this young man should start earning. If he is prepared to delay his wage earning for the sake of research, the community should make it easier for him to do so. Looked at from this point of view Abdus Salam is sacrificing his own interest, and deserves help. I feel this because I suffered in the same manner. I obtained my appointment in 1917, and also won scholarship for research. I delayed my departure for two years and lost in seniority, and almost six people went over me and blocked my path. But placed in the same situation today I will not hesitate to follow the course I did then. I am certain Abdus Salam can get a job today and start earning. If he is prepared to sacrifice his own interests and his family's interests for the sake of research, he should be given the fullest assistance. In case you are not able to get Abdus Salam scholarship for the full period of three years, I am sure it would be possible to collect sufficient funds for the purpose from some other source'. Afzal Hussein went on.

In his letter, gaining tremendous historical value over time, Afzal Hussain also reminded Bilal Hashmi that the current head of the provincial administration in Lahore, Francis Mudie (1890–1976), the Governor of Punjab, had himself studied Mathematics at St John's College in Cambridge. 'He knows what a First Class from Cambridge means. I am sure His Excellency will accept my views'.

Before closing his letter, Afzal Hussain also referred to the bureaucratic hitch relating to Abdus Salam's travel grant. 'There is a small matter of £150 or so for passage. If you are able to grant a scholarship I am sure you will be able to manage this small amount also. Do let me have a line to tell me that you are able to manage all this. We should be proud of Abdus Salam. He has brought much credit to Pakistan'.[1]

It is important to note here how, in his correspondence, Afzal Husain pressed for the need to finance Abdus Salam's visits to Nuclear Physics establishments in Europe and the United States. Although Pakistan's formal journey to attain nuclear capability had yet to commence, the manner of Afzal Husain's advocacy of Abdus Salam's case entails a considerable amount of value for astute historians of nuclear proliferation in South Asia.

Afzal Husain's sponsorship worked the miracle in every possible manner. Soon Abdus Salam received the advice to pay a courtesy call upon Francis Mudie, the Governor of Punjab.

Once again, Abdus Salam's flare in public relations came into action. He sent an urgent message to Mohammad Hussein, in Multan, asking for the St John's necktie to be pulled out of his travel bag and dispatched to Lahore as early as possible. He was aware of the fact the Governor had been a student at St John's College in Cambridge. A few days later, when he arrived at the Governor House, Francis Mudie was delighted to receive a college-mate who happened to be an academic superstar as well. Abdus Salam moved another step closer to getting the study grant extended. As the Governor was due to relinquish his gubernatorial position in a few days, the signing of the approval in favour of Abdus Salam was, in all probability, one of Francis Mudie's final acts of administration in Lahore.

Within few weeks, the outstanding business began sorting itself out at a pace much quicker than expected. On 4 August 1949, Abdus Salam filed his

---

[1] Afzal Hussain to Professor Bilal Hashmi: 27 June 1949

expression of interest for the position of Professor in Mathematics, and he got the job before the end of September 1949. Graded as Class I officer of the Provincial Education Service, he was offered a basic salary of Rupees 300 per month along with recommendation for a group of advance increments. He was invited to assume duty, straightaway, in order to qualify for study leave abroad. 'It was arranged that the professorship would be given to me from immediate effect with an unheard salary of 630 rupees per month. But I was supposed to join this post in 1951, when the salary would commence, after returning from the U.K. I was given two years of leave of absence before even reporting for duty'. Abdus Salam recalled.[1]

On the same day, the Government of Punjab extended the tenure of his scholarship grant enabling him to continue studying in Cambridge for another two years. He was entitled to a provisional sum of £600 per year subject to revision 'in the light of advice from the High Commissioner of Pakistan in London'.

Also, the outstanding business of return fare was satisfactorily sorted out and he was permitted to spend a sum of £200 towards the extra visit home. Typical of bureaucratic peculiarity, the government did not seem to have any problem with his travelling back to England by air, but he was supposed to 'return by sea after the completion of his course'. Possibly, the best part of the whole package was the study leave to complete his doctoral research.

Should he report on duty instantly to ensure seniority of service? Abdus Salam asked Afzal Husain for advice. 'I have no doubt that they could offer you an appointment today and permit you to join after the completion of the course of your training at Cambridge'. Afzal Hussain responded on 23 August 1949. 'I am, however, doubtful if you could count on your seniority from the date of this offer. The seniority usually depends on the date of taking over [and] one has to take chances in all these matters. My advice to you would be to accept the stipend, complete your studies at Cambridge and not worry about the rest'.[2]

By providing Abdus Salam an extended scholarship grant as well as employment security at a time when he needed the two most, Pakistan enabled him to launch his career in Physics. He would never forget this gesture of magnanimity on the part of a poverty stricken two-year old state. Although any direct evidence is not available, one of Abdus Salam's close friends, Ram

---

[1] Interviews 1984: Folder IV, p. 45
[2] Abdul Ghani (1982): p.119

Prakash Bambah, has alluded to the likelihood of Zafarullah Khan's political clout playing a role in sorting matters out for Abdus Salam.[1]

Along with employment, study grant and work leave; Pakistan also gave him a bride. In August 1949, he got married to his first cousin, Amtul Hafeez (1924–2007), the daughter of Abdus Salam's uncle, Ghulam Hussein. Not only Ghulam Hussein had been a father figure to Mohammed Hussein, he had transferred a part of his property to his younger brother thus paving the way for Abdus Salam to qualify for scholarship grant under the Peasant Welfare Scheme in 1946.

Ghulam Hussain approached 75 while Mohammed Hussain was close to retirement from work. Both Abdus Salam and Amtul Hafeez had been engaged already. Now, in the emerging set of events, Abdus Salam might not find the opportunity to return from Cambridge for another three years. It was about time to go ahead with the wedding. In yet another display of utter devotion, the family travelled all the way from Multan and Jhang to Quetta, in Baluchistan, where the Ahmadiyah caliph was camping in those days to escape the blistering heat of Punjab. While performing the Islamic ritual of *Nikah*, the caliph blessed the couple with Koranic prayers and then remarked that all fathers dream the best out of their sons; Abdus Salam, he added, happened to be among sons who realised the dreams of their fathers.

Perhaps the only minor variation in this arranged marriage of first cousins was Amtul Hafeez's seniority to Abdus Salam by a couple of years in age. Customarily, brides in the subcontinent were expected to be relatively younger. But then the age difference did not matter much in the relationship into which Abdus Salam and Amtul Hafeez were destined to settle. Amtul Hafeez was fated to be the housewife, with a clear-cut role and well-defined position description.

Abdus Salam and Amtul Hafeez started their married life when Pakistan celebrated its second anniversary of Independence. Hardly much of dramatic change was expected to overtake their lives. Regardless of a love affair before or after the formal marriage ceremony, the strength of matrimonial fulfilment was evident in the fact that the two belonged to the same indivisible family fraternity.

With varying degrees of seclusion, Amtul Hafeez remained a housewife; even when she moved to England a few years later, there was hardly much for her in terms of sharing the life of Abdus Salam outside their house. Had she been a scientist, her occupation as a full-time housewife might have been some kind of an enigma at best. In her role as a full-time housewife, she enjoyed freedom

---

[1] Trieste Tribute (1997): pp. 47-53

in a different way. She was present among her children, relatives, circle of friends and the activities of the local fraternity of Ahmadiyah women.

About six weeks after his wedding, Abdus Salam left Multan to board the London-bound flight from Karachi. He was ready to commence his doctoral research in Cambridge.

Although, very often, the credit for the birth of Abdus Salam's life in Theoretical Physics is assigned to a variety of accidents, events and people; from a suitable reinterpretation of his father's June 1925 vision to the abundance of scientific scholarship in Cambridge, the truth could be rather easily traced back to the singular contribution made by Paul Dirac and Afzal Husain. First, Abdus Salam was inspired to test his mathematical genius into the realm of Theoretical Physics by Paul Dirac; and then a whole package of financial logistics for him to leap forward was fixed by Afzal Husain.

VI

About six weeks after getting married, Abdus Salam returned to England alone. His newlywed wife, Amtul Hafeez, was obliged to stay behind in Pakistan because the scholarship grant was not sufficient for the couple to subsist in Cambridge. In those days, Pakistani brides were not accustomed to employment along with their husbands and pay off the house mortgages faster. At the same time, Cambridge was not much of a job market like London and other commercial centres in England. Actually, leaving Amtul Hafeez behind in Pakistan was also indicative of the fact that her husband did not envisage staying abroad beyond the academic requirement.

To the delight of Abdus Salam's Punjabi friends, his coming back to Cambridge liberated them from the responsibility of freighting over to Pakistan those boxes he had left behind in a state of uncertainty. He had returned well equipped with an extended scholarship grant along with an academic position secured back in Lahore. In a way, Ram Prakash Bambah had been mathematical about the emerging necessity of nuclear scientists rather than generalists in Pakistan.

As mentioned earlier, Abdus Salam had received the advice to discuss his project for doctoral research with Otto Frisch and Edward Shire at the Cavendish Laboratory, and a formal meeting for this purpose was scheduled in April 1949. Apparently, during the course of that meeting, he was assigned to do the experimental work. How on earth, in full view of his recent debacle at the Cavendish Laboratory, he accepted such a proposition remains unexplained.

His supervisor, Samuel Devons (1914–2006), was a nuclear physicist deeply steeped in Laboratory culture. By winning a scholarship grant at the age of 16, Sam Devons, the son of a Jewish minister of Lithuanian origin, had just completed his doctorate when the World War II started. During the war, he served as a scientific officer with Royal Air Force and then moved on to do intelligence work aimed at interrogating scientists associated with the Nazi regime.

At Cavendish Laboratory, the work allocated to Abdus Salam on this occasion dealt with deuteron-tritium scattering. It was an experiment involving the firing of hydrogen atoms upon deuterons in order to measure the dimensions of resulting collision. In his later days, he would remember the project as fairly straightforward for those gifted with experimental inclination. As Abdus Salam struggled to set up the equipment and make it work only to revisit his own lack of aptitude in experiment, Samuel Devons must have watched the tortured research student with a mix amusement and compassion.

On his part, Abdus Salam remembered the time spent in Cavendish Laboratory as the 'agonising months' of his professional life. He pleaded guilty of failing to accumulate experimental data. His deficiency in handling the 'recalcitrant equipment' frozen into the age of Ernest Rutherford accompanied by a 'sad lack of the sublime quality' called patience terminated the tryst. He admitted frankly.[1]

'It was not a question of hard work. I was simply not cut out for it. There are people who sniff a lock and it opens. In my case, the cultural aptitude too made a factor. We, in Jhang, lived in what was nearly a pre-Bronze age. Even our buttons were made of wood. I came from a civilisation altogether devoid of laboratories'. He postulated. 'We, in Jhang, had never witnessed a workshop processing metallic products of any kind. Even the buttons in our garments were made of timber. The whole civilisation was so primitive. As a result, the very apparatus at Cavendish was simply alien to me'. He remembered citing the cultural gap within the family. His son, Ahmad Salam, born and brought up in England, seemed to possess a somewhat inborn knowledge of automobiles than he could ever imagine claiming for himself.[2]

---

[1] Ideals and Realities (1984): p. 325
[2] Interviews 1984: IV, pp. 58-59

He felt 'miserable' and let down at the Cavendish Laboratory, shouting upon some of his close circle of friends who had encouraged him to make a career in scientific research rather than public service in Pakistan. According to Ram Prakash Bambah, he would offload his disappointment by using 'very strong Punjabi expressions'.[1] Abdus Salam attributed his return to experiment to an upside-down tradition at the Department of Physics in Cambridge, under which those graduating admirably were expected to do experimental rather than theoretical work. He recalled how the presence of a towering figure like Paul Dirac, working next door in the Department of Mathematics and turning up for tea at the Cavendish Laboratory almost daily, had none effect whatsoever to a worthwhile recognition of theoretical work. Even when Quantum Theory was taught in the Mathematics Department, it did not matter much to the Physics course.

'If only I had pursued that experiment, I would have become famous'. Abdus Salam used to exchange joke with his erstwhile supervisor Samuel Devons. If there was any consolation for him, it was in the fact that he was not alone in lacking a taste of experiment. To name a few, Werner Heisenberg, Homi Bhabha and Robert Oppenheimer among contemporary theoretical physicists fell in the same category.

Around December 1950, Abdus Salam took the matter up with Samuel Devons; he aimed at exploring the possibility of switching over to theoretical side. Any persistent failure in experimental work might cloud his very future in Physics. Also, there was the fact that countdown upon the extended term of his scholarship grant had already begun. Personally, Samuel Devons did not have any problem with the proposition. He was a seasoned man who could see the predicament confronting Abdus Salam.

'Well, by all means, but we'll have to find a supervisor for you. We shall back you up with a solid reference'. Samuel Devons gave Abdus Salam the green signal to start looking around for a slot in the theory group. Easing the disturbed soul out in the direction of theory was a realistic option.

Abdus Salam requested an appointment with Nicholas Kemmer (1911–1998), the Stokes Lecturer heading the Theoretical Physics group at Cambridge in those days.

Born in St Petersburg, Russia, to a Lutheran father and Russian Orthodox mother, Nicholas Kemmer had been baptized as a Roman Catholic for the sake

---

[1] Trieste Tribute (1997): pp. 47-53

of religious compromise. His father, a businessman, purchased rolling stocks on behalf of the Tsarist regime and, at the same time, worked for a British subsidiary of the United States-based Westinghouse Corporation. Nicholas Kemmer was only five when his parents left Russia, back-to-back with the onset of Communist Revolution. His family moved first to England and then to Germany; where he graduated at the University of Gottingen in 1932. He enjoyed the rare privilege of having studied Physics under three great teachers of his time. He had been a student of Max Born, Werner Heisenberg and Wolfgang Pauli. A year later, as the Nazi power ascended, he went to Switzerland to do his doctorate in Theoretical Physics. He was on a fellowship at London's Imperial College when the war began compelling him to participate in British effort behind the Manhattan Project. After the war, he won a Fellowship at Trinity College in Cambridge.

Early in the spring of 1950, when Abdus Salam sought enrolment in the theory group under Nicholas Kemmer, the history of physics had already advanced from its classical era well into major atomic discoveries. Initially, Nicholas Kemmer resisted the idea to take one more student for he already had eight on board to supervise. At the same time, he was not sure if his area of expertise in quantum electrodynamics had enough fresh ideas to work upon. He held the view that a good deal of theoretical work in the field of Quantum Electrodynamics had already been completed by Sin-Itiro Tomanaga (1906–1979), Julian Schwinger (1918–1994), Richard Feynman (1918–1988) and Freeman Dyson (1923–2020). Not many stones were believed to have been left unturned in the subatomic meson theories.

'You must accept one more student for this one has done better in his finals, both in physics and mathematics, than anyone we sent you before'. Some of his colleagues at the Cavendish Laboratory pleaded with Nicholas Kemmer. Who was this student, by the way? Nicholas Kemmer questioned out of curiosity. An Asian, a Pakistani, he was advised.[1]

In recent years, a number of theoretical physicists like Hendrik Kramers (1894–1952), Werner Heisenberg, Wolfgang Pauli and Robert Oppenheimer had strived to dig out the mathematics of field equations in particle interaction. Nicholas Kemmer himself had tabulated the first set of meson theories. Abdus Salam had already been reading Walter Heitler (1904–1981), the German scientist who married Physics and Chemistry. In Birmingham, Professor Rudolf

---

[1]Jagjit Singh (1992): pp. 13-14

Pierels (1907–1995) presided over a sizeable department of Theoretical Physics. Nicholas Kemmer had the possibility in mind to deflect Abdus Salam in the direction Birmingham. But Abdus Salam did not wish to give up on Cambridge.

Do you mind if I work with you only peripherally? Abdus Salam almost begged Nicholas Kemmer. It turned out to be a melting point. Nicholas Kemmer signalled Abdus Salam to call on Paul Matthews (1919–1987), who was busy tidying up the remaining of meson theories. Born to missionary parents, serving a remote town in the Madras Presidency of colonial India, Paul Matthews arrived to study in Cambridge in 1938 but the outbreak of war disrupted his degree program. For over two years he served as a volunteer in China, organising distribution of medical supplies from a base camp in Burma. He completed his degree soon after the war.

While going to see Paul Matthews, considered to be one of the ablest students among the theory group, Abdus Salam did not have the slightest notion that he was walking into a lifelong friendship. When the two met, in the spring of 1950, Paul Matthews had already been through with the *viva voce* examination in defence of his work for the doctoral thesis. He intended to avail a brief interlude of holidays before starting the fellowship at the Institute of Advances Studies in University of Princeton. He urged Abdus Salam to get out of Walter Heitler and start reading the more recent contribution made by the younger lot of theoretical physicists like Richard Feynman, Julian Schwinger and Freeman Dyson. He then handed the unresolved segment of his renormalisation project over to Abdus Salam. It is all yours as long as I am on holidays; Paul Matthews is reported to have made the offer. 'If you solve it by September, it is yours; if you don't, I'll take it back'. Abdus Salam accepted the deal, just as he had accepted the challenge to do the Physics Tripos in one year.

Before leaving on vacation, however, Paul Matthews explained the holdup and advised About Salam to read Freeman Dyson's paper on 'overlapping infinities' before they could proceed any further.

According to one of Abdus Salam's biographers, the encounter between Abdus Salam and Paul Matthews stored good luck in favour of the former.[1] Undoubtedly, among the lot of people facilitating Abdus Salam's dawn in Physics, Paul Mathews stands fairly close to Afzal Husain and Paul Dirac. 'You see, he had the whole framework ready, and he bequeathed it to me. I was very lucky because I did not have to go through the motions to set the problem out. I

---

[1] Gordon Fraser (2008): p. 94

had the problem ready-made. I had also a time limit, which was conducive to concentration of mind'. Abdus Salam acknowledged.[1]

According to one of their contemporaries, both Abdus Salam and Paul Matthews 'were very different in temperament' yet they would brilliantly complement each other in professional output. It was a combination of the 'never failing enthusiasm and prolific if occasionally wild inventiveness' of Abdus Salam and the 'incisive clarity of thought and comprehensive understanding' of Paul Matthews that constituted the bedrock of 'an extremely productive collaboration'.[2]

After taking charge from Paul Matthews, the first step Abdus Salam took was to make a telephone call to Birmingham. He arranged a swift appointment with Freeman Dyson who was about to leave for the United States in a day or so. Freeman Dyson, the rising star on the horizon of Theoretical Physics, had studied Mathematics in Cambridge. He had been a Fellow at Trinity College before migrating, in 1947, to the United States. He used to spend a part of the year in Birmingham.

For years, Abdus Salam would not forget the spell of excitement under which he had embarked upon the journey to Midlands for it amounted to having an audience with a young idol in the world of Physics. Like a school boy from Jhang, who expected the teacher to know all the right answers, he considered Freeman Dyson a sort of demigod. He arrived in Birmingham later in the evening, put up for the night with Richard Dalitz and his wife Valda. Up until recently, Richard Dalitz (1925–2006) had been in Cambridge as a student of Nicholas Kemmer.

How was the obscurity in overlapping infinities tackled? Abdus Salam asked Freeman Dyson the next morning. Reportedly, Freeman Dyson did not have a convincing answer beyond a conjecture. Somewhat crestfallen, Abdus Salam did not believe the explanation offered by someone he trusted knew all. 'When I heard these words it was like the earth slipping from under my feet. Dyson was like a demigod to me and I had expected him to know all the answers.

---

[1] Crease & Mann Transcripts: Part II, 27 May 1984, p. 8

[2] Thomas Kibble's memorial essay on Paul Matthews: Biographical Memoirs of Fellows of Royal Society, Vo. 34 (December 1988), pp. 555-580. The Royal Society, London.

Nevertheless, he gave a highly illuminating exposition of the subject and that put me on the right track'.[1]

Amused to read the signs of setback on the face of his visitor, Freeman Dyson asked Abdus Salam if the two of them could save time by travelling together to London from where he was supposed to rush to Southampton to catch the boat for the United States. It might be an opportunity to talk more about the widening scope of Particle Physics. Still recovering from the initial shock, Abdus Salam agreed. On the way, as the two of them opened up with each other, Abdus Salam sketched the big picture and expectations attached to meson theory in those days. But the most important lesson for him to remember the rest of his life was that scientists do not hold an absolute sway or prophetic finality in knowledge.

Upon returning to Cambridge, Abdus Salam briefed Nicholas Kemmer about his encounter and train ride with Freeman Dyson. While the project began rolling, Abdus Salam maintained a regular correspondence with Freeman Dyson, seeking second opinion when required over finer details of the problem. At times, Abdus Salam remembered, Freeman Dyson would respond to his queries 'with a beautiful solution.' On his part, Nicholas Kemmer felt satisfied that Abdus Salam had found a *de facto* supervisor in Freeman Dyson. Abdus Salam worked at St John's, whereas Nicholas Kemmer was based in Trinity, yet the two met regularly.

Over the years, Nicholas Kemmer had drifted away from his direct contribution to research, and he was not working on anything of his own in particular. As Senior Lecturer, most of his time was consumed in teaching and supervising students. What's the news? Is there anything in the mail? He would ask Abdus Salam from time to time in order to make sure that Freeman Dyson was still counselling Abdus Salam from the other end. 'He expected us to produce a result every hour. This was very encouraging. He lived through us, in a way, and it was such a good thing to have a supervisor with whom you were not competing'. Abdus Salam reminisced about those early days of his research career.[2]

It did not take Abdus Salam long in finding the mathematical route to Freeman Dyson's conjecture about overlapping infinities. He solved the puzzle well ahead of the deadline agreed between him and Paul Matthews. As such, the speed with which he worked the way out triggered a mix of awe, surprise and

---

[1] The Illustrated Weekly of India, 1 February 1981, p. 11
[2] Crease & Mann Transcripts, Part III, 27 May 1984, p. 8

amazement; even disbelief. But once accepted, his answer to the problem brought him fame, almost instantly, among colleagues in Particle Physics. His contribution amounted to a 'vital cleaning operation' in ridding modern physics of an absurdity. 'In the previous theory, there was nothing to stop an electron from having an infinite mass and an electric charge. With great insight, physicists Julian Schwinger, Richard Feynman and Freeman Dyson had indicated how the difficulty could be overcome, but the complete mathematical proof was lacking'. This proof had been supplied by Abdus Salam.[1]

In his memorial essay on Abdus Salam, written nearly half a century down the bridges of time, Freeman Dyson recounted it all. 'I met him first in England when he was twenty-four; a student recently arrived from the turmoil of newly independent Pakistan. I was then supposed to be a leading expert on the theory of quantum electrodynamics. I quickly found out that Salam knew as much about that subject as I did. He asked me for a topic for his research. I gave him the topic of overlapping divergences, a highly technical problem that had defeated me for two years. He solved it in a few months'.[2]

Before the end of summer in 1950, that is, within few months of getting the two-year extension in his scholarship grant, Abdus Salam had sufficient data for the doctoral thesis. Under Cambridge calendar, however, he could not be awarded the doctoral degree before three years. For what was described as the 'most outstanding pre-doctoral contribution to Physics' the University of Cambridge awarded him the prestigious Smith's Prize.[3] With professional recognition, time and the stock of scholarship grant on his side, he was geared up to learn more. He could move about and socialise with the top minds in the world of Theoretical Physics.

In a letter of recommendation to Robert Oppenheimer, the Director of the Institute of Advanced Study at Princeton, Freeman Dyson introduced Abdus Salam as 'an Asian' yet 'exceptionally brilliant young man.[4] But then a much stronger note of praise came from Nicholas Kemmer who, until recently, was not sure if he should take aboard another student, an Asian, a Pakistani.

---

[1] Ideals and Realities (1984): p. 14

[2] Freeman Dyson: Abdus Salam 29 January 1926 - 21 November 1996, Proceedings of the American

[3] Earlier in 1854, this prize was awarded to James Clark Maxwell.

[4] Abdul Ghani (1982): p. 22

'Abdus Salam has been my research student since the beginning of the year'. Nicholas Kemmer wrote to Robert Oppenheimer early in November 1950. 'His development has been the most remarkable I have ever seen. In the few months I have known him, he has changed from a beginner to a leading expert in the important and extraordinarily difficult field of quantum theory. The work he is doing is connected closely to the recent pioneering developments due to Tomanaga, Schwinger, Feynman and Dyson; whose work is yet only understood by very few people, Salam being one of them. The papers he is about to publish will, I am confident, be recognised as of first-rate importance and quality. I know that Professor Dyson (now at Princeton) has a similarly high opinion of him. It is thus not only in Salam's interest, but also in the interest of International Science that all facilities for Salam to continue his studies in close contact with other leading experts should be given to him'.[1]

Robert Oppenheimer responded on the very day he received the mail by inviting Abdus Salam at the Institute of Advanced Study. 'We were delighted to have your good letter'. He wrote back to Nicholas Kemmer. 'I am sending you two application forms for your records, one for Salam and one for yourself. In neither case will it be necessary to provide references, since what you have already written of Salam, together with what we know of him from Dyson and Matthews, is sufficient. If you wish, you may tell Salam that when we have his forms, we shall admit him to membership in the second term of this year, which incidentally begins about February 1st. I should think that a grant of $1,500 for that time would be enough, since I believe that he can pay his travel from his Pakistan grant. We would be grateful to you for telling us if this is not adequate'.

Nicholas Kemmer passed the news on to Abdus Salam. Receiving an instantaneous invitation from the Institute of Advanced Study, where leading physicists gathered from all over the world to share most recent developments in the discipline, was an exceptional event in the life of someone who had started research only three months ago.

Robert Oppenheimer extended a formal invitation to Abdus Salam. 'With the concurrence of the faculty in physics, I am pleased formally to offer you a membership in the School of Mathematics of the Institute for Advanced Study for the second term of this academic year. Our spring term begins on January 29th and ends on April 28th; but you are welcome to come as soon as you wish and to stay as long as long as you wish. We can make available to you a grant

---

[1] Nicholas Kemmer: 2 November 1950

in-aid of $1,500 to take care of your expenses during your sojourn in Princeton. We do not plan to report this grant as taxable income to the Bureau of Internal Revenue in the United States. We all look forward with great pleasure to having you with us for a visit'. He wrote on 15 November 1950.

Being an employee of the Government of Pakistan, Abdus Salam lodged a formal request at the Pakistani High Commission in London for permission to avail the opportunity. He asked for approval to spend eight months in the United States in order to divide his time between the Institute of Advanced Study in Princeton and at Cornell University in Ithaca. His desire to visit Ithaca was motivated by Freeman Dyson's presence in Cornell University.

When the news of fellowship arrived in Pakistan, Afzal Hussain sent Abdus Salam a note of congratulation. 'I offer you my most sincere congratulations on the wonderful success you are achieving. We are all so proud of you and we pray for your further successes'. Afzal Hussain wrote on 23 November 1950. He wished Abdus Salam a fellowship of the British Royal Society, even a Nobel Prize. 'There is no reason why you should not be all this and more'. He added affectionately.

On 29 November 1950, Abdus Salam was granted the No Objection Certificate (NOC) by the Government of Pakistan. He was cleared for 'attachment to the Institute of Advanced Study' up until the end of September 1951 provided the change of station did not cost the government any extra funds.[1]

---

[1] Memo Number 26111/A of the Director of Public Instruction, Lahore, dated 29 November 1950.

VII

Earlier in the 20th century, Louis Bamberger (1855–1944), an American tycoon of German-Jewish origin and philanthropic disposition created a multi-million-dollar endowment to establish the Institute of Advanced Study in Princeton to benefit abstract scholarship. Abraham Flexner (1866–1959), the founding Director of the institute, was conscious of the fact that large sums of money alone could not purchase prestige to a centre of learning. He banked upon the exodus of Jewish scholars and intellectuals from Europe to the United States. His calculated gamble seemed to have worked the miracle of bringing fame to the institute when he succeeded in winning Albert Einstein over to join the institute. In 1933, after Albert Einstein migrated to Princeton, the popular media promoted the institute as a sort of shrine for scientists all over the world. In 1947, the institute won another medal of popularity by employing Robert Oppenheimer, the father of the first atomic bomb, as its Director.

Robert Oppenheimer (1904–1967) was born to affluent and tasteful Jewish parents. His father, a wealthy textile importer had migrated from Germany to the United States somewhere in the 1880s. His mother, a graduate of Harvard University, painted. In Germany, Robert Oppenheimer had studied Theoretical Physics under Max Born and then served various research and teaching positions in Harvard and California. When the United States military high command decided to assume control of the Manhattan Project, he was appointed as the director-in-charge to coordinate the technocratic effort by bringing together a team of physicists and engineers. After Hiroshima and Nagasaki, Robert Oppenheimer became famous and powerful but he developed differences with the administration, especially over ongoing plans to utilise nuclear energy in defence sector alone. Physically lean, and a chain-smoker, Robert Oppenheimer had an element of loneliness about his personality. In his youth he had sided with radical causes like collecting funds in support of the republican movement in Spain. He was viewed to be 'dangerously' close to some of the leading communist leaders of his time. As a result, his loyalty came to be questioned in the United States. His personality appeared to be a mix of contradictions, he lived in affluence and fell in love with radical causes, hated experimental work but supervised the production of first nuclear bomb.

For his first trip to the United States, Abdus Salam had a postcard image of New York skyline, the Statue of Liberty and Manhattan skyscrapers. His faithful impression of the west was confined predominantly to an everyday even-tempered lifestyle of Cambridge besides few quick trips abroad. As a student, he had come to England at the meeting point of two ages, a time when the old medieval curriculum comprising of Latin, Greek, Logic, Metaphysics and Mathematics had begun giving way to a redefinition of inter-discipline overlapping, while education was not an exclusive privilege of the aristocracy and upper classes; wars and revolutions mellowed political culture in Europe. Once on the east coast of the United States, he encountered a hectic spate of connections among boats, trains and buses; and, above all, the crowds of people in an unforeseen state of hurry. He went through a series of climatic and cultural shocks, simultaneously.

Eleanor Leary, the efficient Housing Bursar at the institute, had booked him a room on campus, in accordance with his readiness to share common facilities of the apartment with Faqir Chand Aulakh who taught Physics at a college in New Delhi and happened to be visiting the institute for the same term.

At the institute, Abdus Salam went straight to meet Paul Matthews who, in order to fulfil the technical requirement, was going to be his supervisor at the institute.[1] It was about tea time, Paul Matthews told Abdus Salam, an opportunity to get introduced with other staff members. 'We have been waiting for you'. Robert Oppenheimer welcomed Abdus Salam who felt a bit embarrassed. Such an earnest reception put Abdus Salam on the defensive. He was viewed as 'the man from afar who could make unwanted infinities disappear'.[2]

Abdus Salam found himself in a predicament resembling Albert Einstein who had become famous for his work in the special theory of relativity in 1905 while still a Patent Officer in Bern, Switzerland. Gaining prominence within few weeks of work in Theoretical Physics did not mean he had settled into a durable career in research. He used to regret being caught off the cuff in his very first meeting with Robert Oppenheimer. He remembered the significance Robert Oppenheimer then attached to the work done by Ning Hu (1916–1998), a prominent theoretical physicist of Chinese origin. 'We want to know your views about this piece of work'. Robert Oppenheimer is reported to have asked. 'This work is worthless; there are lots of ghosts in it'. Abdus Salam shot back. Although he was familiar with the work done by Ning Hu, there was always the need for restraint or diplomacy his much-experienced host might have expected.

---

[1] Gordon Fraser (2008): p. 97
[2] Gordon Fraser (2008): p. 99

Robert Oppenheimer remained silent; he might have taken the comment as an expert opinion and ignored its outward abrasiveness.

Some senior physicists, whose years of professional experience easily surpassed Abdus Salam's age, were treating him as a mature man. All of this was happening in the midst of a personal dilemma. He still lacked a formal post-graduate degree in Physics, and except for few months of research, his entire knowledge of the discipline was limited to a personal effort at best. 'It was not a favourable interaction', he used to say afterwards. Early fame had begun taking its toll. Abdus Salam suffered a repression from within; he avoided raising simple questions, fearing it might reveal his ignorance.[1]

'I had behaved like a cad, even though he had treated me as a senior, mature man, whose opinion needed to be taken. I mean, he was a wonderful man, but he just walked away. He didn't say anything'. Abdus Salam remembered the episode with Robert Oppenheimer.

A few days later, Abdus Salam placed a piece of his renormalisation work in the Director's mail only to realise afterwards that he had forgotten to attach the set of diagrams. By the time he returned with diagrams, Robert Oppenheimer had already gone through the paper, and as an outstanding physicist himself he could appreciate the quality of work. In fact, he made some favourable remarks about the work.

'But, I suppose, you cannot grasp it without these diagrams'. Abdus Salam charged, handing the set of graphics over to Robert Oppenheimer. Once again, he had failed in keeping himself from pouring his mind out. On this occasion, however, he did observe the colour changing on the face of Robert Oppenheimer. But then all his polite host could say was that results spoke for themselves, one hardly felt the need for diagrams.[2]

Looking back into those bygone years, Abdus Salam would be horrified to recollect how some of the leading physicists treated him as an expert theorist. 'I knew nothing of Physics except what I had done myself. The results for me of this enforced seniority were disastrous. I was afraid to ask questions and betray my ignorance of areas on which I had not researched. In learning you have to ask questions which are sometimes exceedingly foolish, if you don't know the

---

[1] Robert Crease and Charles Mann (1986): p. 235.
[2] Abdul Hameed (circa 2000): p. 68

subject'. He recalled in 1984. His 'real education in broad areas of physics' was yet to begin.[1]

In the following days at the institute, Abdus Salam worked in collaboration with Paul Matthews, and the two succeeded in finding 'a general proof applicable to all renormalizable theories'.[2] There was hardly the time, therefore, to visit Cornell University in Ithaca.

Albert Einstein, the media star who had become synonymous with science for his contribution in theories of relativity, lived on 112 Mercer Street in Princeton. He was 72 and used to briefly show up to work in his room at the institute. People waited outside his residence to be able to walk in his company as he headed for the institute. This practice was repeated when he returned home after a while. In Princeton, he was more of a saint to those who revered him. Mothers brought their children to him with a view to secure an inspirational moment upon the memory of young ones.

'He used to come to the Institute but would not join parties, seminars and lectures. One had to look for an occasion to meet him'. Abdus Salam recalled how he and the Indian physicist, Faqir Chand Aulakh, briefly encountered with Albert Einstein. 'We stood and waited outside his house which was on the other side of the ground. Then we walked with him. He accompanied us and then stood outside his office talking with us, for about half an hour, on Quantum Theory. His ideas were very heterodox, not the conventional ones. He was one of the inventors of this theory but he never accepted the statistical aspects of it. He was always inclined towards a non-dice playing God. This gradually turned him out of the quantum laws and he took an opposite position finally. As a result he was cut off from the rest of scientific establishment. As soon as he saw some younger people, he would speak about his ideas. That's what he did to us. We were just only politely listening, enjoying the sensation of talking with him rather than an agreement'.[3] One day, Albert Einstein looked at Abdus Salam and asked him about his area of research. Abdus Salam politely responded that he worked in renormalisation. Albert Einstein is reported to have remarked that this was not his piece of cake.[4]

---

[1] Crease & Man Transcripts, III, dated 27 May 1984, p. 10
[2] Kibble, T.W.B., Biographical Memoirs of Fellows of the Royal Society, Vol. 34 (Dec 1988), pp. 555-580
[3] Interviews 1984: Folder VI, pp. 1-3
[4] Abdul Hameed (circa 2000): p. 68

While still in Princeton, Abdus Salam took a break from work and travelled along the East Coast of the United States in the company of Zafarullah Khan.[1] In those days, Zafarullah Khan served as the Foreign Minister of Pakistan and visited New York, every now and then, hunting a United Nations sponsored resolution of the Kashmir dispute. How much of the holidaying Abdus Salam enjoyed in the company of man more than thirty years senior to him in age remains an open question. Living by himself all along those five years, since 1946, away from the watchful eyes of his parents and Ahmadiyah peers, Abdus Salam appeared to have abided by sort of self-imposed celibacy and did not have a girlfriend. Zafarullah Khan had been a household name and an ideal in the social environment surrounding Abdus Salam's childhood and upbringing. Although the first formal encounter between the two happened somewhat recently in Liverpool, England, Abdus Salam held the peer high. 'He loved the weekend outing. As a marvellous conversationalist, he was always accurate about dates, times and places of his reminiscences. His lifestyle offered us an example to live in the west. It has always been a pleasure and scintillating experience to have his tremendous company'. Abdus Salam stated. He cited the 'graciousness' of Zafarullah Khan in accepting the invitation to have breakfast every Sunday at Abdus Salam's residence near Ahmadiyah Mission, in London, where the peer lived a part of the year after his retirement from active public life.

Six months of spell in Princeton turned out to be one of Abdus Salam's longest stay on the American soil. His first impression of the capitalist superpower was one of an overtly competitive environment where, despite the heat and humidity of New York region, 'everyone raced with everyone else'.

About the end of spring in 1951, Abdus Salam received a telegram from Cambridge; he had been elected a Fellow at St John's College. He received messages of congratulation from his teachers and well-wishers including David Schoenberg, Afzal Husain, James Wordie, Mohammad Sharif and Nicholas Kemmer. 'I hope this will give you an opportunity of a larger stay in Cambridge, you will now have no excuse for not talking to the Kapitza Club'. David Schoenberg wrote to him.[2] 'God willing, you will bring credit and fame to Pakistan'. Mohammad Sharif prophesied.

---

[1] Gordon, Fraser (2008): p. 100

[2] Named after famous Russian scientist Pytor Kapitza (1894-1984), the winner of 1978 Nobel Prize in Physics.

Afzal Hussain also wrote a message of congratulation to Mohammad Hussain stating that people like Abdus Salam did not belong to any particular community or country. 'Their place is among the most brilliant in the world and, therefore, they belong to the entire humanity'. He judged. In all probability, Afzal Hussain wanted to make sure that Abdus Salam did not land himself in a drab inhibiting his intellectual growth. In his letter to Mohammed Hussain, he went as far as proposing that the Government of Pakistan should support Abdus Salam in every possible manner to stay where he could to work to his best.[1]

When the Princeton fellowship concluded Abdus Salam might have stayed on in Cambridge to write his doctoral thesis. Entitled to a further extension in his scholarship grant, he might have explored the possibility of doing another research project. Instead, he asked the University of Cambridge to permit him a submission of his dissertation from Lahore. In fact, his *de facto* mentor, Freeman Dyson, pressed him to stay on either in Europe or the United States and ensure keeping up the momentum of intellectual productivity. It was the best advice at the time, and Abdus Salam fully realised the value of this view. A withdrawal from the forefront of research in Europe and the United States, only for the sake of a predominantly under-graduate teaching position in the largely feudal backyard of South Asia amounted to self-harm outright. Basically, the choice before him was fairly simple. Could he afford to defer Physics for a while? But he felt morally obliged to return to serve those who had paid for his education.

'If he should decide to stay in England or America, a brilliant research career awaited him'. Freeman Dyson wrote in his memorial essay on Abdus Salam. 'He was at the height of his intellectual powers, an outstanding talent in the rising generation of physicists. But his conscience would not allow him to stay. He felt a compelling duty to go home and do whatever he could to help his people. Pakistan, in spite of its poverty, had paid the expenses for his living and studying in England. Now it was his turn to repay his debt to Pakistan. He discussed his dilemma with me. I advised him strongly to come to America, to plunge into research for five years first, and then help his people afterwards. He thanked me for my advice and told me he was going home. Physics could wait, but his people could not'.[2]

---

[1] Abdul Hameed (circa 2000): pp. 72-73

[2] Freeman Dyson: Abdus Salam (29 January 1926 - 21 November 1996), Proceedings of the American Philosophical Society. Vol. 143, No. 2 (June 1999), pp. 347-350

On the way back home, Abdus Salam paused in England to wind up at Cambridge. He received a message from the Master of St John's. An oath-taking ceremony of his fellowship at the college had been scheduled in the Combination Room. 'I will meet you there a few minutes earlier and explain the procedure'. The Reverend John Boys Smith (1901–1991), wrote to Abdus Salam in a calligraphically hand-written note. He took the oath on 1 July 1951. 'I, Abdus Salam, elected Scholar of the College of St John the Evangelist, do solemnly promise that I will submit myself cheerfully to the discipline of the College, and obey its orders, according to the Statutes. So far as in me lies, I will endeavour, by diligence and innocence of life, to promote the peace, honour and well-being of the College, as a place of education, religion and learning'. He read out. Once a Fellow, he was entitled to live on campus, get a room to work, have free dinners and, finally; a free funeral, just in case. He served as a Fellow at St John's up until 1956.

About the end of summer in 1951, Abdus Salam left England for Pakistan. Before leaving Cambridge, he requested his research supervisor, Nicholas Kemmer, for a reference letter. 'It should be other way around, you should be testifying for me'. Nicholas Kemmer is reported to have commented lightly. In his formal report on Abdus Salam's performance, Nicholas Kemmer placed a warm-hearted confession on the official records. 'I feel that I must preface my report on Mr Abdus Salam's thesis by an explanation of my personal position in relation to this remarkable young man and his work. In January last year, I became his research supervisor after he had spent one term under the supervision of an experimental physicist. I was quite reluctant to take him as I already had more research students than ideas for problems, but I was pressed to accept him. I anticipated that he would not give me much trouble for the first year as he had no previous knowledge of the field of research I was interested in and would, like other such men I had encountered, necessarily spend that time studying other people's work. However, things developed very differently, within six weeks or so he had solved a problem which the best of my students had failed to solve, and within another month I was asking him for clarification of details in the latest publications'. Nicholas Kemmer wrote, concluding his report with a fond remark that he considered himself as Abdus Salam's student rather than a teacher. 'I do not think I have been taken in judging him so highly'. He added.[1]

---

[1] Abdul Hameed (circa 2000): p. 69-70

Under the terms of his scholarship grant, Abdus Salam was entitled to parcel the bulk of his baggage and belongings; it enabled him to save money on freighting hefty items like books and journals. Travelling light, he decided to avail the opportunity by taking a brief stop in Switzerland where Freeman Dyson happened to be visiting Zurich. Actually, he aspired to discuss his work in scalar electrodynamics with Wolfgang Pauli, then serving as Professor of Theoretical Physics at the Eidgenössiche Technical University in Zurich. He thought of asking Freeman Dyson for a formal introduction with Wolfgang Pauli. Why did Abdus Salam wish to call upon Wolfgang Pauli? Possibly, Abdus Salam had marked the giant out as an authentic guide to chat about the emerging scenario of subatomic particles.

Freeman Dyson arranged the introduction but he seemed to have overlooked the need to alert Abdus Salam about the temperamental tides of Wolfgang Pauli.

VIII

'Professor Pauli, could you please be as kind as to look at this paper and let me know what you think of it?' Abdus Salam is reported to have addressed Wolfgang Pauli upon his first one to one encounter with the giant.[1]

'I have to be careful not to use my eyes too much. I will not read your paper'. Wolfgang Pauli snapped back, he was known the world over for his heartless spontaneity, unique eccentricity, and hatred of ceremonious formalities. Caught unprepared, Abdus Salam blurted out an expression of thanks and quietly walked out of the room.

Among the constellation of superstars, shaping the course of scientific discovery in the earlier decades of the 20th century, Wolfgang Pauli (1900–1958) was born with an academic hallow. His father served as Professor of Colloid Chemistry at the University of Vienna. He had famous physicist Ernest Mach (1837–1916) as his godfather; another great physicist, Arnold Somerfield (1868–1951) taught him at the University of Munich. Wolfgang Pauli completed his doctoral degree at 21. Four years later, he contributed his 'exclusion principle' to Physics and Chemistry. He postulated the presence of neutrino as the particle devoid of mass or charge. Both of his discoveries qualified for colossal

---

[1] Freeman Dyson (1999): pp. 347-350

recognition in their own separate right though he was awarded the Nobel Prize for just one. He had been nominated for the prize by Albert Einstein.

By temperament, Wolfgang Pauli used to take time in publishing his ideas. Instead, he preferred writing detailed letters to his colleagues and close friends like Werner Heisenberg and Niels Bohr. When it came to claiming the credit, he was more of a stoic. A whole heap of folklore surrounded him. For example, his mere presence in the vicinity of an experimental setup was rumoured to cause the breakdown of the equipment, and the episode came to be fondly remembered as 'Pauli Effect'. He was known to have an obsession with perfection, earning him the title as the Chief justice of Physics. Out of his eccentricity and fierce wit, he is remembered to judge substandard work as not 'even wrong'. Paul Ehrenfest (1880–1933) was a leading physicist, he admired the contribution made by Wolfgang Pauli but had never met him. When the opportunity came, Paul Ehrenfest could not keep himself from saying 'I suppose your papers are more likeable'. Wolfgang Pauli shot back that he liked Paul Ehrenfest more than his work.

In a sad reflection upon the social pressures of their time, Wolfgang Pauli and his parents had abandoned Judaism for the sake of a brief embrace with Roman Catholic faith. Over time, he acquired a good deal of sarcasm towards religion. When Paul Dirac asserted God was only a figment of human creation, Wolfgang Pauli supported the idea. 'I do not recognise any religious myth,' he remarked, adding 'God does not exist but Paul Dirac is his prophet'.

After the end of his first marriage in a divorce, Wolfgang Pauli is reported to have made the caustic remark about his success in academia and failure with women. In 1931, he suffered a nervous breakdown and went to see Carl Jung (1875–1961), the well-known psychiatrist who lived near Zurich. Carl Jung is understood to have analysed and documented more than 400 of Wolfgang Pauli's 'deeply archetypal' dreams and the interaction was published under the title of *Atom and Archetype*.

With such a peculiar personality, the treatment Wolfgang Pauli meted out to Abdus Salam was not worth making news. Still, Freeman Dyson sent a note of apology to Abdus Salam. On his part, Abdus Salam rated the terse encounter as a squandered opportunity to discuss things exciting.[1] But then it did not last long for Abdus Salam and Wolfgang Pauli to become friends and interact professionally and on a more or less regular basis. Much senior in age, Wolfgang

---

[1] Freeman Dyson (1999): pp. 347-350

Pauli came around to regard Abdus Salam as a young physicist who could not be undervalued.

During the first two years of his life in Physics, that is, between 1949 and 1951, Abdus Salam had succeeded in building up a number of lifelong professional contacts and connections. But he was not far off the mark in making the confession about his naivety in Princeton. He did perform admirably in Physics, still there was a whole lot to learn about the conduct and niceties of professional business in the west. While being referred to as an Asian and a Pakistani on more than one occasion, he overlooked the need to draw distinction between wit and political correctness; whereas, it was all the more important to nip the evil in the bud at a time when many of the top scientists lived in a closed world of their own in those days.

Three decades on, after sharing the Physics Nobel Prize of 1979, Abdus Salam recounted tales of his take-off and formative years in Physics. He seemed to have piled up an animated stock of stories, to be repeated over and over again, all in first person, with endless amount of relish. Unfortunately, none among the first row of his biographers appeared to have considered the historical call to expand upon what passed down as largely a one-sided version while the majority of his contemporaries, both in and out of Physics, phased out untapped. Not that he made up suitable versions; it is just that a good deal of his own life story stands diminished; deficient of alternate vistas. At the same time, those references to his Asian and Pakistani origin went unchecked.

In the third week of September 1951, Abdus Salam reported on duty as Professor of Mathematics at the Government College in Lahore. According to the notification issued by the Government of Punjab, he had availed himself of 'one year, eleven months and eleven days instead of two years extraordinary leave ex-Pakistan'.[1] One copy of the gazette notification was forwarded to the Accountant General of Punjab to start processing Abdus Salam's monthly salary. Recognising his performance abroad, the government gave him seven annual increments in advance.[2]

Why exactly did he return to Pakistan? In the well-known academic wilderness of Lahore, how exactly did he intend to fit with his doctorate in Theoretical Physics? If public service was the aim, why did he go to Cambridge, in the first place? His family had never been into farming so what sense did the

---

[1] Government Notification Number 26420-Z, dated 27 September 1951
[2] Abdul Hameed (circa 2000): p. 75

rush and fury make in claiming the Peasant Welfare scholarship grant under a made-up claim? With his 1946 first class Masters from the University of Punjab, he might have been a Professor of Mathematics supporting his family. There will always be the temptation to raise and attempt at addressing questions of this kind.

Chapter Four
House on Fire

In September 1951, Abdus Salam returned to Pakistan and reported for duty at Government College in Lahore. Within a month of his homecoming, the first prime minister of Pakistan, Liaquat Ali (1895–1951), was gunned down at a public rally in the cantonment city of Rawalpindi. Said Akbar, the assassin sitting in the front row of prime minister's audience, hailed from Afghanistan and had been in service of British intelligence. More recently, he had been a participant of *jihad* in Kashmir.[1]

In this way, the logic behind the need to create a Muslim majority state towards the northwest of Indian subcontinent, as advocated by Olaf Caroe in his *Wells of Power* thesis, began casting the die of ideological template for future of Pakistan.

Up until the dying days of British raj in India, the idea of Pakistan as an independent sovereign homeland for Muslims was only a vague proposition, picking up momentum primarily out of communal mistrust rather than a protracted history of desire for secession. In March 1940, the All India Muslim League party, headed by Mohammed Ali Jinnah, demanded only regional autonomy for Muslim majority provinces, not an independent state. Being the largest religious minority, Muslims enjoyed the best bargaining position in a united India; they were ideally placed to dictate electoral results in dozens of marginal constituencies by holding the key to power for quite a while.

Mohammed Ali Jinnah (1876–1948), emerging as the chief exponent of demand for Pakistan, had studied law in England and was widely respected for his legal acumen. Although his opponents accused him of conducting political business with a rigidly legalistic frame of mind, he stood up to some of the highly

---

[1] Said Akbar was shot and killed at the spot by a police officer under order. As a result, the inquiry conducted into the assassination of Liaquat Ali remains inconclusive.

egotistic and pampered personalities of his time.[1] He is remembered to have played his master stroke in June 1946, barely weeks before the capitulation to Pakistan demand, by accepting the Cabinet Mission Pan for a confederation rather than an outright partition of India. By that time, in the aftermath of World War II, the spanking reality of communist military power called for building up strategic security posts and alliances. As such, the partition of India giving way to the creation of an Islamic Pakistan, flanking communist giants like the Soviet Union and China, seemed to settle suitably into the upcoming capitalist world order.

Even if the signs of such engineering or machination were not evident in the 1940s, the subsequent course of events demonstrated the quality of services Pakistan rendered to the capitalist block. It is not a deep historical mystery anymore as to why the British set aside their secular-liberal preferences and partitioned India on religious grounds in order to create Pakistan for Muslims. Pakistan was meant to serve the west more than Muslims; the enormity of economic, social and security challenges facing the new state coerced its future into a secure bondage. A cursory view of the range of congenital disabilities associated with the birth of Pakistan should self-explain the lumbering down of hope from the very outset.

In spite of his secular-liberal disposition, the otherwise sharp lawyer in Mohammed Ali Jinnah was unsure about the role of religion in a modern state. In his policy statement to the Constituent Assembly of Pakistan, made on 11 August 1948, he declared that 'Hindus would cease to be Hindus and Muslims would cease to be Muslims, not in the religious sense, because that is the personal faith of each individual, but in the political sense as citizens of the State'.[2] Few months later, he advocated that the Islamic *Shariah* law would guide the constitution making effort in the country.[3] With its predominantly Muslim population, there was hardly the necessity in Pakistan for reaffirmation of religious identity. Such shielding might have made sense in the undivided India, in a framework of communal power politics, to bargain upon and secure the rights of a religious minority.

---

[1] Jaswant Singh, the author of Jinnah: India-Partition-Independence (2009) and a prominent member of India's right-wing Hindu fundamentalist Bhartiya Janta Party, seemed to support this viewpoint.

[2] Constituent Assembly of Pakistan: Debates, Vol. 1, No.2 (Aug 11, 1947), p. 20

[3] Dawn, Karachi, 26 January 1948

Those inheriting the mantle of political responsibility from the British were starkly incapable of governing an independent country, they had been trained to play the second fiddle to invaders and colonisers. At the same time, many of them had lost their electoral constituencies due to partition, they had no future in a democratically elected government.

Within weeks of its birth, Pakistan was inundated with over ten million refugees, those dislodged from Muslim minority districts. Nearly four million Hindus and Sikhs living in western districts had been exchanged with a much greater number of Muslim influx from the opposite direction in Punjab alone. Some 6,000,000 acres of land was estimated to have been abandoned by the relatively affluent members of Hindu and Sikh communities. Hence the frenzy to grab the vacated agricultural tracts, businesses and homes. Of the 1,345,000 acres of land abandoned in Sind, nearly 800,000 was snatched by local landlords.[1] Then, Muslim refugees hailing from Bihar and Uttar Pradesh provinces of India outwitted government functionaries with disproportionately inflated claims regarding their abandoned properties. In this way, the very childhood of Pakistan was disfigured with widespread corruption and disregard of law. People aimed at becoming rich and fortunate overnight in what was viewed as the 'promised land'.

At the same time, the tone of ties between India and Pakistan was set by nasty disputes over settlement of public sector assets the British had accumulated over the decades. Those assets included ordinance factories and logistics, communications and transport, financial infrastructure, buildings, office equipment, even stationery. Dozens of committees were established to accomplish the apportionment within a matter of few weeks of what had been achieved in well over a hundred years. As a result of the bickering, the two sides ended up digging deeper into their firmly held positions of animosity and suspicion.

Amidst the air thick with apprehension and acrimony, a decisive blow to the prospects of accord was dealt by India's victory in winning over the accession of former princely states in Kashmir, Hyderabad and Junagadh. Pakistan side was 'humiliated and outraged' by the 'force and legal sophistry' of its Indian

---

[1] Ayesha Jalal: The State of Marshal Rule - The origins of Pakistan's political economy and defence, Cambridge University Press, Cambridge, England, 1990, pp. 79-80, 87

counterparts.[1] Regardless of an agreement over the criteria for accession, it was hard for Pakistan to forfeit the catchments of Kashmir, the lifeline of agriculture and hydroelectric power generation in the Indus valley. Kashmir amounted to lifting of the curtain on a long and sad tale in mistrust, conflict and war; even nuclear proliferation.

Pakistan had a population nearing 75 million divided between nationalities, ethnicities and religious minorities. Above all, the geography of Pakistan was blown apart by one thousand miles of alien territory. About ninety percent of people in the country were illiterate and they lived in poverty, bondage and social repression. This gigantic mass of largely uninformed, displaced, fragmented and traumatised electorate was represented by 79 indirectly elected members in the Constituent Assembly. Apart from the fact that each member appeared to represent a million people, it was hard to tell who represented which constituency. As such, there was no method to hold those elected members to accountability.

Religion, validating the partition of India, was wedded to the politics of convenience. With chaotic spontaneity, Pakistan found in Islam a readymade panacea to fix every problem; all the way from settlement of refugees, allotment of evacuee property, discord among nationalities, widespread corruption and political adventurism to outbreak of hostilities with India. An atrocious blend of Islamic fraternity and spirit of jihad was supposed to galvanise the dawn of relief all over the place; the birth and evolution of state in Pakistan offered a unique case in studying the rare fusion of religion and politics in modern age.

Once the moral bankruptcy of Muslim League leadership was evident, the mainstream Sunni clerics decided to make their move. They urged the government to set up a permanent Ministry of Ecclesiastical Affairs to be headed by one the leading clergymen. Traditionally, social roles assigned to Muslim clerics had been limited to the management religious ceremonies associated with birth, marriage and death. Hardly anyone had ever expected from them a leadership in national affairs of political significance. In fact, the ruling elite held the opinion that clerics were incapable of running the day-to-day affairs of a modern state, economy and government business. But when politicians began playing the religious game, the clerics lost patience; they were not prepared to follow those who had deserted the mosque-based instruction and fallen for

---

[1] Keith Callard: Pakistan - A Political Study, George Allen & Unwin Ltd., London, 1958, p. 16

heathen syllabi of western curriculum. Just as politicians suspected the ability of clerics in running a modern state, the mullahs lacked faith in the very competence of politicians in implementing *Shariah*. In the end, the patience and tact with which the clerics played their cards in the unfolding drama proved remarkable. Hardly anyone among the leadership of ruling Muslim League party appeared to have cared to calculate the cost of multiplying religion with populism.

When clerics sought a proof of sincerity, the political elite nosedived into the trap. Early in March 1949, the government headed by Liaquat Ali moved the so-called Objectives Resolution in the Constituent Assembly. It was an impressively worded statement of intent providing clerics the guarantee that Pakistan would be anything but explicitly secular. On 12 March 1949, the resolution was adopted without any meaningful debate in the house. All Muslim members favoured whereas non-Muslim members opposed it.

If the intention behind the adoption of Objectives Resolution was to deposit the modern concept of political sovereignty in God alone, the authors of the statement might have received inspiration from some of the advanced capitalist countries like, for example, the United States of America where strong suggestions of Christian spirituality did matter over and above the formal separation of church and state. Still, the principle of relegating final authority to God did not sound sincere in a situation where the fate of predominantly illiterate citizenry rested in the hands of feudal lords who hated democratic accountability.

Due to their inexperience in presiding over a sovereign state, those running the government desired to blend their highly subjective notions of Islamic values with western enlightenment. Born Muslim but educated in British secular institutions, they perceived Islam and parliamentary democracy as complimentary to one another. In all likelihood, they suffered from a psychological condition and hallucinated about the merger of old-fashioned Islamic values and 20th century politics.[1] This state of duality, in public affairs, turned religion into 'a matter of political tactics rather than one of principle'.[2] Yet, some politicians nurtured the wishful thinking that differences among various schools of Islamic jurisprudence were bound to defuse the pressure pumped in by the clerics. Also, there was the wishful thinking about clergy falling victim to its own burden of antiquity. If, by getting the Objectives

---

[1] Keith Callard (1958): p. 201
[2] Leonard Binder: Religion and Politics in Pakistan, University of California Press, Berkeley and Los Angeles, USA, 1961, p. 237

Resolution hastily pass through the Constituent Assembly, Liaquat Ali hoped to gain some breathing space in order to clean up the fallout of partition, he did not live long enough to witness the consequences of his quick fix. Two years later, he was assassinated by a *mujahid*, one of the lot the prime minister of Pakistan went out to win over by populist appeasement rather than education. Sadly, Liaquat Ali was the first but not the last among Pakistani leaders meeting the fate of violent removal from political scene.

II

Fortunately, weather did not try out Abdus Salam's patience because September in Punjab was a time of the year when summer gave way to autumn and the sun burnt plains seeped into cooler nights and crisp bright mornings. Free from the unkind liaison of heat and humidity, and away from industrial pollution imminent to engulf the city in the near future, Lahore looked out for months of its mild winter and a spring blushing with blossom.

But fine-tuning with change of weather did not compare with the unbridgeable cultural gulf between Cambridge and Lahore. Over the years, Abdus Salam had become accustomed to Cambridge, a university town steeped in centuries old tradition of scholarship. Lahore, on the other extreme, had been a military garrison where foreign invaders from northwest took respite before bagging Delhi. If Cambridge had Isaac Newton, Maxwell Clark, Ernest Rutherford and Paul Dirac, to name a few, to its credit; Lahore was identified with army generals and commanders. Cambridge had libraries and laboratories as opposed to fortifications and tombs of Lahore. One enriched by five centuries of scholarship and the other indebted to its millennium old role as the relief camp of invaders. Cambridge, over the centuries, had grown above its ecclesiastical beginnings; whereas, Lahore wrestled to grasp the gift of freedom. Cambridge was benefitted by enlightenment and industrial advance in Europe; Lahore had been disabled by centuries of despotism and colonial yoke, condemned to mediocre craftsmanship instead of scientific scholarship. Perhaps the closest Lahore came to science was when Faqir Azizuddin, an advisor of Maharaja

Ranjeet Singh, set up an observatory of astronomical research. But then, like the ancient Greeks, the exercise ended up blending physics with theology.[1]

Lahore in 1951 was not the place to dream about saving a career in Theoretical Physics. Here, other than Abdus Salam, the familiarity with Paul Dirac's famous equation was restricted to just one other man, that is to say, Professor Mohammed Rafi, an experimental physicist who had been a student of Ernest Rutherford in Cambridge. In fact, Freeman Dyson had already warned Abdus Salam about the predicament awaiting him in Lahore. Primarily, Abdus Salam had returned home under the moral weight of an obligation to be with his people, it was a personal decision with a cost. In all honesty, the dream to do world class physics in Lahore was nothing more than a fantasy. Such an ambitious dream could just not be realised by juggling to utilise vacations in Cambridge; the truth must have been well known to him. He was still young and could afford marking time until there was a better opening.

Lahore personified an altogether new social scene in the wake of exodus *en block* by its Hindu and Sikh residents. City streets and neighbourhoods stood deprived of their millennium old multicultural tradition and vibrant diversity. But the Government College, in spite of the communal carnage and bloodbath in Punjab, continued to prepare its graduates for public and private sector employment, as if time was frozen in a Spartan age. There was no change other than a revised enrolment policy under which the college offered 75 percent of its seats on academic merit, 20 per cent to those faring exceptionally well in sports, with the remaining few seats going to the wards of the alumni. Some sort of merit replacing communal quotas sounded progressive.

While starting his professional career, as Professor of Mathematics in Government College, Abdus Salam tended to take a lighter view of the tradition prided by the institution. This was despite the fact that he himself had spent six years of his youth in a row while waiting in vain for recruitment into the Indian Civil Service.

After formally reporting on duty in the administration block, Abdus Salam went to pay the customary courtesy call upon the College Principal, Sirajuddin Ahmad, the dashing Lecturer of English Literature only a few years earlier who had won the heart of Urmila Sondhi. Giving in to a brief spell of nostalgia, the

---

[1] Gulshan Lall Chopra: The Punjab as a sovereign state (1799-1839), Hoshiarpur (India), 2nd Edition, 1960, p. 110

two talked about old times, common friends and contemporaries, and those belonging to the Hindu and Sikh communities they might never see again.

Sirajuddin Ahmed (c1910–1986) had obtained his Masters in English Literature from the University of Punjab, joined Government College as a Lecturer and then proceeded to the University of Oxford, in England, for further studies. He was known to be an ardent lover of literature, fine arts, painting, music, rose gardens and sports. His close friends and associates considered him a hedonist more than a devout believer. Many generations of his students, the majority of them making it to senior ranks of public service, remembered the profound involvement with which he would teach William Shakespeare (1564–1616). Like any other principal in a college, Sirajuddin Ahmed enjoyed tremendous amount of respect and authority. He might have acknowledged the impending need in Pakistan for leaders in science but it was beyond his beat to bring about any radical change in Government College, nicknamed as the so-called 'Harvard of Lahore'. As Principal of the college, Sirajuddin Ahmed had a whole lot of administrative and financial business to conduct, he looked straight without falling to the temptation of radical ideas aimed at churning out scientists more than public servants. What an educational institution like Government College should produce was a matter of policy to be shaped up at the Department of Education, not the Principal of a college. There was no urgency at the Department of Education to enhance investment in post-graduate education and research in natural sciences as long as Pakistan did not have employment opportunities in this sector.

In an impersonal way, Sirajuddin Ahmed alluded to the 'proud traditions' of the college by grooming its graduates to snatch the best jobs; he urged Abdus Salam to wake up to the difference between Cambridge and Lahore and just forget about research.[1] Abdus Salam did not agree with such an antiquated perception of the college. He felt there was the need to shake off a bit of the historical rut relating to college prestige as the recruitment agency of public service. Scientific research, howsoever residual, he argued, could not be isolated from postgraduate programs, especially in Natural Sciences. He did not seem to please the principal. At the very outset of their working ties, in this way, the two fell apart. Abdus Salam found himself caught into a series of skirmishes with Sirajuddin Ahmed.

---

[1] Jagjit Singh (1992): p. 26

As a matter of administrative practice, Sirajuddin Ahmed invited Abdus Salam to join the mainstream of college culture by becoming either a hostel warden or chairman of the committee for financial management or take over as the manager of football team. Contrary to the popular observation made by most of Abdus Salam's biographers, there was nothing abnormal or sarcastic about the offer made by the Principal. An invitation to take up an administrative assignment over and above the teaching load was a matter of routine in local colleges. Although he did not have much of a taste for outdoor sports, Abdus Salam opted to become the manager of football team. He would watch the boys play in university grounds, made sure that they were well fed and did not suffer from a great deal of stress about their house examinations. He ended up forging a friendly relationship with many of them. On this account, therefore, he struck peace with the Principal.

While starting work at the Government College, Abdus Salam had hoped that one day soon he would get a university position and then gradually evolve a research group of his own. But there was no easy escaping from the tangles of fate. Out of nowhere, the government announced a departmental restructure and marking of clear boundaries between the University of Punjab and Government College.

For nearly seventy years, the two institutions had been interwoven like joined twins in a manner that it was often hard to tell the college from the university. In fact, the college was inaugurated in 1864, that is, some eighteen years before the establishment of Punjab University in 1882. In the beginning the college was affiliated with the University of Calcutta but after 1882 it had been a part of Punjab University; both sharing students, courses, classrooms, libraries, laboratories, teaching and administrative staff, and a whole lot of other facilities. Under an interim setup, the university was chartered to devise syllabi, set academic standards, conduct examinations and award degrees to students enrolled at affiliated colleges. In Lahore, the University had about half a dozen colleges offering professional degree programs in medicine, engineering, law, business and commerce, fine arts and oriental languages. Ordinarily, colleges located in far flung districts, enjoyed considerable autonomy in everyday administrative and operational matters whereas, for staffing and budgetary allocations, they reported to the Directorate of Public Instruction.

In this multi-tiered set up, the Government College in Lahore enjoyed an exceptional status. Mainly due to its seniority in age, the college had been running a few degree programs of its own, leading to duplication in some areas. For example, both the college and the university offered degree programs in European and Oriental languages, Economics, History, Political Science, Philosophy, Psychology, Geography, Mathematics, Physics, Chemistry, Botany and Zoology. Curiously, some of the college professors headed teaching departments in the university. It was really hard to tell one from the other, and the gravity of situation was further complicated by the fact that both were housed in the same education district, next to one another.

Somewhat excusably, the government plan of action to separate the college from the university turned into a fierce war of attrition. There was round after round of departmental wrestling over what belonged to whom and claims and counter-claims on libraries, laboratories, classrooms, furniture, equipment, stationery and staff. In Sirajuddin Ahmed, Government College found an ideal crusader to defend its hitherto unmarked boundaries. He worked passionately to salvage the original college that over the decades had been lost in the university. He abhorred the very notion of conceding the college identity to a franchise of Public Instruction. Abdus Salam, in this battle, was caught unprepared, he found himself in the midst of a crossfire. For quite a while in the beginning he failed to appreciate what the whole fuss was about. He believed, rather wishfully, in the execution of separation scheme with the precision of an executive writ. One day, the Principal summoned him to explain the amount of time he had been spending with university students. Stop it, the principal told him.

On a weekly basis, Abdus Salam had allocated six hours for undergraduate students directly enrolled at the college; the rest of his time went to postgraduate students at the university. In future, the Principal directed him, the best part of his time would go to the needs of college students. Why should we mind the enemy business? Sirajuddin Ahmed asked him.

In principle, the Principal was correct. He had the payroll in mind. But Abdus Salam did not wish to be in a situation where his postgraduate students were disadvantaged. Why should the students suffer or be made to pay for something that was not of their making? He asked Sirajuddin Ahmed. In ordinary circumstances, six hours sounded sufficient for the undergraduate; and if it was not for the bargaining tactics, the teacher in Sirajuddin Ahmed might have ignored the balance in Abdus Salam's work load. But he was in the midst of an all-out open war with the university.

Abdus Salam could see that the Department of Mathematics at the University of Punjab was outdated, shallow and weak. He aspired to build up the department for scientific research. At times, during the college-university separation process, he felt the separation might be a blessing in disguise paving way for the establishment of a relatively autonomous School of Mathematical Physics. His fate was not tied for ever with undergraduate students. He was not prepared to abandon his postgraduate students but a stand on this account amounted to direct clash with Sirajuddin Ahmed. He found himself confronting the Principal, once again. It was 'quite an embarrassing situation', he remembered later. Sirajuddin Ahmed was correct in taking the position that as an employee of the college he had been spending 'more time on research with university students'. Abdus Salam confessed.[1]

After settling down into a steady routine with work, Abdus Salam desired his wife, Amtul Hafeez, and their daughter, Aziza, to join him in Lahore. Since their wedding two years ago, soon after which Abdus Salam had returned to Cambridge, Amtul Hafeez lived like a nomad, spending time with her parents in Jhang and in-laws in Multan. Soon after starting work at Government College, Abdus Salam worked out a paying guest arrangement with one of his colleagues, the Deputy Principal and Professor of Philosophy, Mohammed Aslam, who lived on campus.[2] Mohammed Aslam had graduated from Cambridge and, like Abdus Salam, he belonged to the Ahmadiyah community. It was an interim setup and Abdus Salam was supposed to move out soon after finding a suitable accommodation for his family. Meanwhile, he travelled to Multan every second weekend, embarking upon a train journey with the round trip costing him nearly fifteen hours. He hunted to rent a house preferably close to the college because not many people owned private transport in those days. Buying a house in Lahore was out of question for him as he just did not have enough money for this purpose. It was not possible to go for a mortgage because Pakistan did not have the industry. In fact, the very idea of mortgage was viewed with distaste due to the Islamic veto to interest.

Finding rental accommodation posed a tough proposition because the real estate business in Lahore was far from the shape and size of a post-Internet age. There was no place whatsoever where people could go to check the lists of properties available for sale or leasing. Hardly any advertising of the sort was

---

[1] Interviews 1984: Folder IV, pp. 30 and 41
[2] Jagjit Singh (1992): p. 27

carried out in the classified sections of daily newspapers. Lahore, and for that matter other cities in Pakistan, faced a severe shortage of housing due to the massive influx of refugees. At the same time, refugees were viewed as potential squatters; it was not easy to evict a refugee tenant. Already many people had occupied spacious lots of the evacuee property and they awaited formal orders of allotment. Actually, an estate agent in those days often turned out to be a part-time employee at one of the local municipalities operating without business license and contact details. Because telephone lines were limited to the privileged few, this so-called estate agent functioned from home, catering only for a well-defined personal network in the community. In the aftermath of partition, when nearly every city and town had been over-crowded with alien faces, it was not easy to carry out identity checks. There were tales of bungling, cheating, fraud, false claims, fake documentation, extortion, crime, desperation, and what not. In Lahore alone, refugee aliens constituted 43 percent of the population. If Abdus Salam did not strike luck in finding a house to rent, his let-down was obvious.

Above all, he went through a long-drawn-out period of distress and frustration at a time when a house within the college precinct could have been made available to him. Of the half-a-dozen staff residences on campus, the best in size and location, popularly known as The Lodge, had been set aside for the Principal; the remaining were allotted to teachers in order of their merit. As a professor at the college, Abdus Salam met the criteria for allotment and he could have easily made it to one on campus, walking distance from work. But it was possible only if Sirajuddin Ahmed made the move to The Lodge that had been lying vacant since the departure of former Principal, Professor Gurudat Sondhi. For reasons better known to him, Sirajuddin Ahmed delayed the move under one pretext after another. If Sirajuddin Ahmed moved into The Lodge, to which he was entitled as the Principal, a vacancy would be available for another staff member. Unfortunately, Sirajuddin Ahmed did not seem to be in any hurry to oblige; effectively, he was holding two residences. Hence there was no quick fix to the problem faced by Abdus Salam.

While he was waiting for the vacancy on campus, one of Abdus Salam's friends urged him to try his luck for the allotment of a house as a refugee. After all, he was an adult citizen, who did not own property anywhere in the subcontinent when Pakistan was established, he stood fairly good chances in meeting the criteria. But then it was possible only if he wielded influence and political clout in the public sector bureaucracy. This was a different world where his academic superstardom did not count much. Already, by the end of 1951, the number of available evacuee properties had shrunk drastically; his chances of success were slim at best. Still, in spite of the obvious odds, he did file an application and went to see Fida Hassan, the Commissioner of Lahore, who sounded sympathetic and that was all.[1] On the contrary, there was more bitterness when, afterwards, Abdus Salam got sucked into an argument with one of the allotment officers. Why on earth should a plain mundane requirement of finding a house to live take so much of time and effort? Abdus Salam remembered asking the officer. Why can't you teach like a missionary and forget about the house? Shot back the bureaucrat. 'I suppose public servants are required to set the precedence in missionary work'. Abdus Salam counter-attacked.[2] Another officer went even further in testing Abdus Salam's patience by indicating his readiness to grant the application provided the act was returned favourably.

What do you mean? Abdus Salam asked.

Get my son admitted into Government College. This officer proposed as a matter of fact but then lost interest soon as Abdus Salam began explaining the enrolment criteria and procedural requirements of admission at the college. 'Your son should not have any problem in getting a place provided he qualifies'. Abdus Salam stated.

As a last resort, he sought an interview appointment with the Minister, Abdul Hameed Dasti, a feudal lord who owned vast tracts of agricultural land south of Multan. In view of his circumstances, Abdus Salam pleaded, it was getting exceedingly hard for him to concentrate on work. He explained that he was at a breaking point, running out of patience and could be obliged to quit. At this point the Minister ran out of patience and terminated the interview by telling Abdus Salam to exercise the choice.[3] On that day Abdus Salam lost hope to get a house allotted from the quota for refugees. Already, he had lost count of his calls made upon public servants, now disillusionment started taking the shine off his love affair with Lahore.

Nearly sixteen months passed in the search for a place to move his wife and their daughter. Often he thought of Cambridge, where the only requirement to get a house was to be sure about the date or week to move in, and then bursars

---

[1] Interviews 1984: Folder IV, p. 8
[2] The Herald, Karachi, August 1984, p. 115
[3] Abdul Hameed (circa 2000): p 77

and estate agents took care of the rest. He had never imagined putting in so much of his time and effort in such a rudimentary requirement like accommodation. Practically, he lived single in Lahore, visiting his family in Multan. On Saturday afternoon, once in a fortnight, after finishing work at college, Abdus Salam boarded the train to Multan, some 350 kilometres southeast of Lahore. If trains were on time, which often was not the case due to frequent crosses and manual signalling on the single track, he would arrive at his parents' home somewhere around midnight. On the average, it took him no less than seven hours plus on trains rolled by an obsolete late 19th century steam engine technology. He afforded only the economy class, which meant hassling and pushing the way through to find a place to sit. Even when a traveller was lucky enough to secure sufficient space and stretch upon hard wooden benches, the marathon journey to Multan would be marked with noise, dust and stink in the largely neglected carriages. Because economy class cars were not air-conditioned, or well insulated, a passenger travelling long distance melted to putrefaction in the summer heat or froze to numbness in winter. After reaching Multan, he had barely one day to be in the company of his family, embarking upon return journey to Lahore on Sunday night in order to be at the college next morning.

According to Abdus Salam, the saddest part of the whole story was that all along those months of struggle for accommodation, a house lay vacant in the college as Sirajuddin Ahmed delayed moving into The Lodge for one reason or another, from small-time repairs to fumigation and painting, and so on. At one point, Abdus Salam made the offer to move into The Lodge in whatever dilapidated shape the building stood but the idea was turned down by the Principal.

Finally Sirajuddin Ahmed caved in. He did make the move to The Lodge and there was a house available for allotment to Abdus Salam. Still, finding an accommodation was his first experience of disenchantment with Lahore. Such was the bitterness that for years on he would just not wish to think or talk about it. Instead of hanging on to two residences for almost two years without much of a convincing reason, Sirajuddin Ahmed could have moved to The Lodge in time and created a vacancy for the next candidate aspiring to live on campus. Abdus Salam felt very strongly about the delaying tactics of the Principal.

What kept Sirajuddin Ahmed from accommodating a colleague? He was asked. 'I don't know, there may have been a legitimate reason about the dilapidated state Principal's house. But the fact remains that I was the one who suffered. I don't think he cared much'. Abdus Salam remembered those days as 'one of the worst period' of his life when he felt totally unsettled. He found himself caught in a completely 'non-productive struggle'.[1]

III

In his working career, 1952 was the first year when Abdus Salam came face to face with the depressing picture of everyday life in Lahore. Starting as Professor of Mathematics at 25 he could go a long way and become the college principal or university vice-chancellor one day not in a too distant future but an achievement of this kind would be administrative more than a pursuit in research. Doing scientific research depended upon availability of resources but the postcolonial economy of a predominantly feudal and insecure Pakistan was far from affording it.

Then, as the eldest son, he had already been late in taking the charge from his father who was crossing 60 and contemplated taking retirement from service. Nearly all of Mohammed Hussein's children had entered adulthood and the family sought financial stability. Abdus Salam's two sisters had been married and were settled in their own families in Multan. But his six younger brothers, aged between 13 and 21, were still on the way to completing their studies. Abdus Sami, who turned 21 in March 1952, was about to start a career in the Punjab Irrigation Department. Apart from offering financial support to his brothers so that they completed their education, Abdus Salam was expected to counsel and guide them until they start employment, got married and settled to found their own families.

Caught in the mix, Abdus Salam tasted 1952 as the first reality saturated year of his life. His tense ties with college Principal dampened any hopes of professional growth. But then there was something to cheer up, he began receiving job offers. There was one from Damascus inviting him to deliver a series of lectures, it must have been triggered by his brief visit to the University of Damascus on the way back from spending summer vacations at Cambridge. Then, there was another for a chair at the University of Peshawar, some 500 kilometres northwest of Lahore, on the border with Afghanistan. He had been invited to set up a School of Mathematics plus the offer entailed better salary

---

[1]Interviews 1984: Folder IV, p. 7

along with free housing. Next offer, rather surprisingly, came from the Chairman of India's Atomic Energy Commission, Homi Bhabha, who was also the founding Director of Tata Institute of Fundamental Research in Bombay. In June 1952, Homi Bhabha offered Abdus Salam the position of Readership in Theoretical Physics, assuring that the incumbent would 'enjoy the same independent status as the Professors.'

Above all, during the course of his brief summer visit to Cambridge, he had been made a verbal offer for the position of Senior Lecturer at St John's College.

Whatever its merit, the offer from India was unworkable due to the nature of suspicion between India and Pakistan. Unless Homi Bhabha had lost touch with sanity, he was not expected to make such an offer in the first place and there again with the size of offer matching, somewhat frivolously, Abdus Salam's current income in Lahore. Given the state of fierce hostility between India and Pakistan, Abdus Salam was not expected to jump at the proposition. Instead, he adopted a diplomatic stance because of the influence Homi Bhabha wielded among the top echelons of physicists in the west.

As for the offer from Peshawar, he felt it was desirable but the northwest of Pakistan required literacy before higher education or a school of mathematics. It was difficult then, as it remains today, to foresee any revolution in a part of the world where educating women equalled sin. He took a while to think it out before sending his note of apology.

In September 1952, Abdus Salam faced a departmental inquiry asking him to hand in information about his current and future employment plans. It is not clear, in the absence of access to college records, if this inquiry was a part of some government survey related to the institutional split between the University of Punjab and Government College or the stipulation was aimed at Abdus Salam alone. Abdus Salam responded to questions raised in the inquiry designated as The HCM Inquiry.[1] Whatever the purpose, the exercise amounted to a blatant disregard of individual privacy.

In his response, Abdus Salam acknowledged filing an application for the honorary position of a professor at the University of Punjab with explanation that his application had been forwarded through the proper channel, that is, the college Principal. He denied applying anywhere else but cited those unsolicited offers from Damascus, Peshawar and Cambridge. Then he went on to explain

---

[1] In local bureaucratic jargon, the initials HCM appear to stand for Honourable Chief Minister.

that his Fellowship of St John's College was more of an honour that could be held outside Cambridge. He concluded with a strong observation on his part. 'I have felt dissatisfied with lack of opportunity to build up a first-rate research school here and to serve my country and nation as much as I can'. He stated before signing off as was the custom in those days. 'I remain, Sir, your most obedient servant'.

Rather astonishingly, however, he did not mention the job offer that had been made to him by Homi Bhabha in India. In all probability, the discretion was meant to steer him clear of any greater trouble with the bureaucracy in Lahore.

Any hopes of some accord between Abdus Salam and Sirajuddin Ahmed were blown further apart by a chain of events triggered about the end of 1952. Abdus Salam travelled to India to participate in a short course at the Tata Institute of Fundamental Research in Bombay. From Bombay, he proceeded to attend the 40th annual session of Indian Science Congress in Lucknow. He might have gone straight to Lucknow, attended the congress and returned home within a couple of weeks but the temptation to visit Bombay turned out to be much stronger.

It was in November 1952 when he received an invitation from Homi Bhabha, to visit Bombay where Wolfgang Pauli was scheduled to lecture and conduct a seminar on Theoretical Physics. Abdus Salam and Homi Bhabha had known each other since their first meeting back in Cambridge. Given the sensitivity of political ties between India and Pakistan, it would not be difficult to ignore the invitation from Homi Bhabha but Abdus Salam was carried away by possibility of an intellectual encounter with Wolfgang Pauli. In spite of the snub received last year, he had not given up on the chief justice of physics. His mind was almost instantly made up to cross the border, without even calculating the amount of time involved and the leave he required to cover the two events, that is, about four weeks in Bombay followed by another two in Lucknow. Whereas, under the statutes, he did not have sufficient leave in the balance.

Homi Bhabha (1909–1966) was born to wealthy parents closely related to the famous Indian tycoon Dorabji Tata. After receiving early education in Bombay, he went to study for a Mechanical Engineering degree program in Cambridge. Instead, inspired by Paul Dirac, he decided to make a career in Theoretical Physics. His pioneering work, in determining the cross-section of electrons scattering positrons, won him fame. During his stay in England, he befriended Jawaharlal Nehru at a time when both suffered from socialist idealism. He joined the Tata Institute of Fundamental Research as its founding

Director in 1945. In August 1947, Jawaharlal Nehru appointed him the chairman of India's atomic research committee. Apart from theoretical physics, Homi Bhabha was known for his keenness on painting, poetry, piano recitals, classical dancing and gardening. He was among the rare breed of scientists who lived free of financial insecurity. On 24 January 1966, he died in an air crash over Mont Blanc in Switzerland. At the time of his death, Homi Bhabha was believed to have come fairly close to graduating India into the exclusive nuclear club. A section of his enthusiasts in India hold the view that the air crash killing him had been mastered by the Central Intelligence Agency (CIA) of the United States to dampen India's nuclear ambition.

In his letter dated 12 November 1952, Homi Bhabha had offered Abdus Salam travel and lodging costs for 'no less than 15 days' of stay at the institute. While he weighed his options, Abdus Salam received a telegram from Wolfgang Pauli urging him to reach Bombay. Then another telegram came from Homi Bhabha asking Abdus Salam for support in providing company to Wolfgang Pauli who felt 'very lonely, as there was no one able to talk with him'. Educational institutions in Lahore, in those days, went on a short winter break soon after the end of term in-house examinations toward the end of December to reopen in the second week of January. Abdus Salam thought he could make it to India by a little bit of stretching out with dates on both ends; at the same time it was not a big deal to make an arrangement with a colleague to conduct the examination in his place. Professor Muhammad Aslam, happened to be acting as the Principal, did not have any issues with Abdus Salam's request for a slightly extended leave.

It did not take long for Abdus Salam to pick up the visa at Indian Consulate in Lahore where an erstwhile staff member of Government College happened to be the chief. Abdus Salam made it to Bombay with connections at New Delhi and Nagpur, and then went straight from airport to the institute, located in those days next to Apollo Pier and Gateway to India monument. He found Wolfgang Pauli lodged in the only air-conditioned room of the institute, a very special gesture of hospitality on the part of Homi Bhabha.

For years to come, Abdus Salam remembered the cordial reception he received from Wolfgang Pauli who sat on a sofa facing the door. Instead of exchanging any words of greeting, as the two came face to face for the first time after their aborted meeting in Switzerland more than a year ago, Wolfgang Pauli gazed at the visitor and then declared that renormalisation pathway worked out by Julian Schwinger was wrong. 'I can prove it.' He kicked off as if the two had left their discussion at that point only last evening. Abdus Salam loved this side of Wolfgang Pauli. On this occasion, however, he had come somewhat prepared to face the unexpected. 'I am dead tired. Can we take it up later?' He asked politely and went to his room.[1] Over the next few days, the two had great time together. Homi Bhabha had all arrangements in place to take his guests over to science organisations and laboratories in Madras and Calcutta.

One day, in Lucknow, Wolfgang Pauli asked Abdus Salam for a quick proof of the relativistic invariance of Freeman Dyson's S-Matrix in renormalisation. Later, it amused Abdus Salam to discover that the oracle required the information for his lecture before the largely mixed gathering of Indian Science Congress. As such, the dosage of entertainment followed when Wolfgang Pauli left the stage and asked Abdus Salam to face the barrage of questions. But then due to a sudden fit of indisposition, Wolfgang Pauli was obliged to cut short his visit to return home. Even when Wolfgang Pauli had developed a fondness for Abdus Salam, he could never come to terms with the religious component of his younger friend's personality. For example, an over-citation of Julian Schwinger or Freeman Dyson by Abdus Salam would trigger Wolfgang Pauli to twist the Islamic profession of faith by another turn. He horrified Abdus Salam by amending his earlier pun about God and Paul Dirac to the effect that there was no god but Schwinger and Salam was his prophet.[2]

While in Bombay, Homi Bhabha repeated his eagerness to employ Abdus Salam at the institute. Come over, it is a far more exciting place, he is reported to have said. 'I am not ready to leave my country'. Abdus Salam remembered telling his host.[3]

At the Indian Science Congress, Abdus Salam opened his lecture with remarks that he intended to deal mainly with ideas and concepts by trying to use the minimum of Mathematics which was 'the most eloquent language man has invented for the expression of the most abstract of ideas, if only one can learn it'. He then dealt with the history of human effort in studying the composition of atom, the nature and behaviour of subatomic particles and the manner in which

---

[1] Interviews 1984: Folder IV, pp. 34-35
[2] Crease & Mann Transcripts: 23 Feb 1984, p. 18. (Originally, as reported by Werner Heisenberg in his Physics and Beyond, published by HarperCollins in 1971, Wolfgang Pauli had aimed the pun at Paul Dirac).
[3] Interviews 1984: Folder IV, p. 36

they were charged to interact with one another. Starting from the early day Greek perception to those revolutionary advances made in the 20th century, when every now and then there was the feeling that all necessary answers had been provided for, he referred to the 'even bigger surprises' facing scientists. 'It seems we shall have to revise the metaphysical foundations of physics. We had to revise these metaphysical foundations when the principle of relativity was propounded. We had to give up the simultaneity of events. We had to revise them again at the advent of quantum theories. The continuity of energy had to be given up. We may now have to give up the concept of continuity of time. Perhaps the structure of space and time is granular. Physics needs a Messiah once again'. He concluded.

Upon returning to Lahore, in the second week of January 1953, he faced a departmental inquiry for breaching the leave rules. Sirajuddin Ahmed charge-sheeted Abdus Salam for travelling abroad without getting a formal ex-Pakistan leave as required under the statutes. Abdus Salam laboured to defend his visit to India on grounds of the need for enhancement of scientific research. He cited his collaboration with Wolfgang Pauli 'on a problem in Field Dynamics'. He begged for approval of leave arrangement as agreed with the acting Principal. Agreeing partially, the Department of Education granted him duty leave only for the Indian Science Congress segment of his journey. As for Abdus Salam's attendance of research workshop in Bombay, Sirajuddin Ahmed declined to budge. As such, the tension between the two sides dragged for months on, adding to the embarrassment of those not wishing to take sides.

Perhaps, Sirajuddin Ahmed suspected traces of insubordination in Abdus Salam. In the 1952 Annual Confidential Report on staff performance, the Principal recorded that Abdus Salam might have been an excellent physicist but not an appropriate choice for teaching at Government College. As a part of service account, the report constituted an unavoidable scale for salary increments, higher placements and promotions; a career-minded employee dreaded adverse entries. At this stage, the Education Secretary to the Government of Punjab, Muhammad Sharif, moved in decisively to impose a cease-fire. He asked the principal to grant Abdus Salam a leave without pay for the disputed gap and close the departmental inquiry once and for all. Abdus Salam did not have much of a choice, he accepted this incontestable act of arbitration with 'great displeasure'. He would never forget the episode as yet another 'mean and useless exercise in wastage of time'.[1] For a long time, he remembered his life in Lahore, all those administrative battles and inquiries, in utter distaste.

Often, Abdus Salam's biographers and profile writers tend to pass here a rather hasty judgment by labelling Sirajuddin Ahmed as some kind of a vindictive man. Then, rather conveniently, the history of ties between the two men is traced back to the decade when Abdus Salam was known to have nurtured an innocent crush on Urmila Sondhi, his English Literature course-mate about to get married with Sirajuddin Ahmed. It seems worthwhile to dig out a detached view remembering, in the first place, the fact that Abdus Salam himself avoided making much mention, other than an odd indirect reference, of the lingering mistrust between him and Sirajuddin Ahmed.[2] Whereas, Sirajuddin Ahmed is just not known to have ever gone public relating to any personal aspect of his ties with Abdus Salam. In all fairness, in the end, Sirajuddin Ahmed emerges as someone conducting the official business in purely professional manner. He could be termed as cold, brutally honest and blunt. Asking Abdus Salam to take a responsibility over and above the teaching load was not sarcastic, it constituted a standard practice in everyday administration.

Next, Sirajuddin Ahmed, did appear to hold back a residential vacancy yet his attitude did not betray any signs of personal vindictiveness; there might have been a spate of genuine reasons keeping him from moving into The Lodge. At best, the whole affair remained an unexplained mystery, especially in the absence of any independent account. Likewise, the protracted bitterness over settlement of ex-Pakistan leave in favour of Abdus Salam remains clouded under the stringency of existing statutes more than much to do with Sirajuddin Ahmed.

Basically, Abdus Salam did not have much of a choice. He had returned home to get into stable employment and start supporting his family, and Lahore welcomed him for this purpose, not for a research career in Theoretical Physics. He was victim of his own personal choice. On the other hand, Sirajuddin Ahmed was coldly honest in stating that the college under him was anything but a research station. In fact, in the end, those battles with the Principal, on one account or another, strengthened Abdus Salam's case to pack up and leave when the appropriate moment arrived. Given the fact that returning to Pakistan was Abdus Salam's own decision, the dramatization to portray him as the victim does

---

[1] Interviews 1984: Folder IV, pp. 37-38
[2] Jagjit Singh (1992): p. 27

not make much sense. He was bound to remain under-utilised in a college in Lahore.

In the midst of commotion arrived a piece of good news. Sirajuddin Ahmad moved into The Lodge and a residence on campus, situated next to the University Post Office, in the street leading to Lower Mall, fell vacant for allotment to Abdus Salam. No more of those strenuous train journeys to Multan, and no need of house hunting; Abdus Salam had plenty of time to spend with his students. His family moved from Multan to Lahore. He had a place where his parents could come and stay with him. Such was the comfort of a family environment that his hopes of survival in Pakistan were rekindled all over again.

Keeping in line with the family tradition, he purchased a cow to milk the beast by himself every day for Amtul Hafeez to do the rest, that is, fermenting and churning the surplus to split out butter. A household from Jhang was transplanted in the heart of Education District in Lahore. Abdus Salam started at the college early so that he had more time for postgraduate students at the university. Later in the afternoon, he walked to university grounds near *Chauburjee*, the 17th century gateway to Mogul gardens, on Multan Road. As football team manager, he watched the boys practice for annual tournament. Instead of pretending to whistle and scream like a traditional coach, he just sat there to make sure they played without squabbling.

In the annual progress report for the Department of Mathematics, for the academic year 1952–53, he recorded that 279 students were enrolled in Year 12 Intermediate level classes. Another 108 in Undergraduate, 15 in Honours and 19 in Master's degree programs. On the average, the size of each section at Intermediate level reached 70. Clearly, the disproportionate balance in student-teacher ratio was evident. Abdus Salam and his colleagues in the Mathematics Department introduced a system under which every week one period was allocated to the assessment of homework given to students. Obviously, there was the dire need for more teachers to achieve a reasonable balance in the student-teacher ratio. His report also made a mention of research activities citing publications he had contributed mostly to international journals. Besides these publications, he had presented two papers on Cosmology at the Pakistan Science Conference convened in Lahore in February 1953. He had lectured at the Punjab University Mathematical Society on topics like 'History of Mathematics' and 'Group Theory'. He also made a brief mention of his research activities abroad, and concluded the report with information that nearly 100 new titles had been added to upgrade the college library.

He advocated the proposal to create a Research School in Mathematics and Mathematical Sciences in order to offer advanced courses and promote research opportunities. For this purpose, he wrote both to the Secretary of the Education Department and the Director of Public Instruction. He asked for employment of at least two full-time research fellows and the need to encourage student enrolment in doctoral programs.

Even though the prevailing state of affairs was not promising, he did not give up. His basic salary was fixed at 630 rupees per month and the University of Punjab appointed him as an Honorary Head of its Mathematics Department, only a ceremonial role without any financial benefits. As the Convener of university Board of Control for Mathematics, he began overhauling the courses for the Master's Degree program and went on to introduce new subjects like Theory of Matrices, Group Theory and Quantum Mechanics. For the first time in the history of a South Asian university, courses for Applied Mathematics were brought at par with those in Pure Mathematics; all due to his effort.

In a separate report, he pressed for the need to build-up the tempo of teaching schedules. He had observed that a string of local, national, religious and cultural holidays punctuated teaching terms every now and then. Actually, it was not easy to standardise term times because both Gregorian (solar) and the Islamic (lunar) calendars were followed in Pakistan. Without fearing the wrath of orthodox among his colleagues, he proposed to evolve a system under which holidays could be avoided during the term. He worked out that students enrolled in degree programs were required to hit an attendance of about 104 weeks, and the target was not easily achievable due to the fact that nearly half of the time got flushed out in vacationing and holidays. He suspected that an 'attitude of casualness' among students could be traced back to a disruption of term tempo by religious, political and sporting events. He appreciated the need to accommodate major Islamic festivals and events but there were occasions where holidaying should be discouraged. It was not possible to build nations 'by stopping work on national days, they are built rather by working harder.' He remarked.

During the summer vacations of 1952, Abdus Salam managed to travel to Cambridge by purchasing the air ticket at concession rate. Technically, he was still a student at the University of Cambridge. He had been granted permission by St John's College to utilise his Fellowship during the summer break. Although he had to meet a good part of the travel expenses from his own pocket, a component of the grant was provided by the Directorate of Public Instruction in Lahore. This was his way of meeting ends as best as possible. His salary bills of June and July 1952 were forwarded to his Cambridge address, and a government notification permitted him to be treated on duty during the break.

On his way back from Cambridge, Abdus Salam briefly stopped at Damascus where he had been invited to speak at the Syrian Engineers Club. He talked about recent discoveries in nuclear physics. Two leading newspapers of Syria seemed to have taken great pride in the fact that 'a scientist of the east' was capable of dealing with 'momentous subject like the atom.'

In view of being able to visit Cambridge in the summer of 1952, Abdus Salam cherished the idea of dividing his time between Pakistan and abroad. He considered it was the only way for him to survive as a physicist. He knew how to procure travel grants and fellowships. In October 1952, he wrote to the United States Education Foundation (USEF) seeking travel grant for the following summer. He received a positive response from the Karachi-based Executive Officer of the foundation.

In the third week of November 1952, Abdus Salam received a letter from the University of Cambridge, advising him that the Board of Research, meeting on 11 November 1952, had approved his name for the award of doctoral degree. Also enclosed in the mail was an approved copy of his dissertation.

Theoretically, Abdus Salam was not left with much of a reason to squabble about his circumstances in Pakistan; the new-born poverty-stricken country had given him scholarship grant, a college chair with study leave. He had the house on campus and was able to spend summer vacations in Cambridge. His doctoral degree had been awarded. But then something much bigger had begun unfolding in Pakistan to change the course of his life all over again.

IV

It was the eruption of anti-Ahmadiyah sentiment, in Pakistan, spinning into a mass agitation countrywide that seemed to have sealed the fate of Abdus Salam's career in Lahore. Public rallies and protest demonstrations were organised to press for a formal excommunication of the Ahmadiyah from the pale of Islam. A grand alliance of leading Sunni clerics demanded curtailment of Ahmadiyah presence in key positions of civil service and public life. There was the call to sack Zafarullah Khan as the foreign minister of Pakistan. Soon the agitators began resorting to violent tactics. Early in March 1953, when civilian authorities lost control, Lahore was placed under the first martial law of Pakistan. Some of the senior bureaucrats, used to performing their duties, up until recently, in an impersonal secular policy environment, were appalled to witness the behaviour of ruling party politicians. After the military takeover and restoration of peace, the government appointed a panel of Lahore High Court judges to investigate into circumstances leading to the fiasco in the shape of a martial law. According to the report submitted by the panel of judges, the fire of sectarian hatred was master-minded by Mumtaz Daultana (1916–1995), the Chief Minister of Punjab, who aimed at a power showdown with some of his rivals in the federal government.

From a practical viewpoint, the inquiry report holds tremendous value for its survey of mechanics overarching power-politics, populism and religion; especially in settings where ambitious and yet vulnerable minorities appealed to political adventurists. In the first place, Pakistan, after the violent removal of Liaquat Ali from political scene, had put on show a peculiar act of succession. Through an extra-ordinary reshuffle in government, the Governor General, Khawaja Nazimuddin, demoted himself to become the prime minister while his finance minister, Ghulam Mohammad got promoted as the Governor General. In fact, those used to playing the second-fiddle with the British had yet to work out a system for political pecking order. Hence a guiltless game of musical chairs was played in which the boss and the underling swapped jobs without the slightest qualms of indignity.

Khawaja Nazimuddin (1894–1964), an ethnic Kashmiri, was born to the bygone royal family of Bengal. Having received early education at Dunstable Grammar School in Bedfordshire, England, he studied at Trinity College in Cambridge and returned home to make a career in public life. Knighted in 1934, he was an old styled gentleman of mild manners who took time in making decisions. Pakistan, on the other hand, was in urgent need of dynamic leadership to fix the range of ailments accompanying its premature birth, from settling disputes with India to achieving a constitutional consensus over power-sharing among regional stake-holders. In the absence of any quick and easy answer, everyone resorted to Islam as the universal panacea fixing every economic, political, internal and external challenge. Hardly anyone, in the given rush of events, had ever pondered about the benefits of European experience in keeping state from religion. In fact, an exclusive reliance on religion was congenital to the state created in the name of God. Even Zafarullah Khan, a senior member of the government with rich experience of serving senior public offices under the impersonal colonial raj, failed to exercise discretion. Instead of raising the alarm about perils of coupling politics and religion, he boarded the bandwagon. 'Those who seek to draw a distinction between the sphere of religion and sphere of politics as being mutually exclusive put too narrow a construction upon the functions of religion. To them religion signifies, at its highest, purely individual spiritual communion with the Creator, and normally only the performance of certain formal and ceremonial acts of what they call worship. This is not the Islamic conception of religion'. He is known to have articulated. [1]

In other words, the outbreak of anti-Ahmadiyah sentiment seemed rather appropriately occasioned. But why was the focus sharpened upon the Ahmadiyah alone? After all, the by and large monolithic Pakistan had quite a few other religious minorities to agitate against, raise alarm and divert national attention if that was the provisional fix.

Upon the map of religious denomination, 85% of the country's population professed Islamic faith, with well over 80% of those constituting the Sunni mainstream along with a sizeable 12% of those belonging to Shia sect.

Unlike the tombs and shrines in the countryside, where spirituality clouded conformity, a good deal of religious activity in urban areas was conducted through mosques and *madrassa* seminaries largely sponsored by formally trained theologians claiming their entitlement to leadership on scholarly merit more than any hereditary privilege. Also, the location and size of a mosque or seminary gauged the extent of their influence. For example, Wahabi clerics based in the few big cities like Karachi, Dhaka, Lahore and Peshawar were often more highly regarded than their counterparts in smaller towns. Due to wrangling, in the past, over management of grants and endowments associated with mosques and seminaries, the colonial authorities had introduced a system of public trusteeship. This arrangement continued to work even after the creation of Pakistan.

Hindus constituted about the 15 per cent of the population in the erstwhile eastern wing of Pakistan. By virtue of their superiority in education and professional skills they enjoyed an easier sway in public and private sector

---

[1] Quoted in 'Pakistan Transition from Military to Civilian Rule' written by Golam W Choudhury, Scorpion Publishing Ltd., Essex (England),1988, p. 81

employment. This otherwise well-earned competence of Hindus worried the insecure among Sunnis. Every now and then a whispering campaign, conducted by self-proclaimed champions of national security, created an impression that Hindus could not be loyal to Pakistan.

Christians made only about one per cent of the population and they faced a dismal predicament rooted in the previous century conversion of low-caste Hindus. Although embracing Christianity had offered them the hope to escape social stigma attached to birth, the curse of hardship had lived on. There was a strong chain of English-medium educational institutions presided over by various Christian missionary organisations benefitting the Muslim middle class more than the average lot of Christians relegated to urban fringe. Whereas, a socially exiled Christian minority was set to become increasingly vulnerable in the coming days; the bulk of Muslim clerics despised English-medium education as a menace to Islamic tradition and cultural values.

Notable among religious minority groups, holding a disproportionately higher profile in public life, were the *Ismaili* and the *Bohra*. Historically, the origins of *Ismaili* and *Bohra* could be traced back to the Shia sect of Islam. When Pakistan was created, some of the *Ismaili* and *Bohra* businessmen migrated to Karachi and pioneered banking and industry in the new country.

Then there were much smaller religious communities like, for example, the *Zikrees* in the coastal areas of Baluchistan, *Kafirs* in Chitral, and Buddhists in a tribal belt bordering Assam in the erstwhile eastern wing of Pakistan.

Numerically, the Ahmadiyah did not pose any meaningful threat to the majority Sunni population, yet their educational competitiveness and networking was perceived to propel them into public and private sector employment faster than those in the mainstream. Then the community feigned itself to be the most genuine face of Islam. By and large, the mainstream clerics resolutely denied the Islamic credentials of the Ahmadiyah and the sect was dumped as a schismatic deviations undermining the doctrinal purity of Islam.

Mohammed Iqbal, the Muslim poet-thinker advocating the creation of a separate homeland for Muslims in the subcontinent, viewed the Ahmadiyah 'as a serious danger to the solidarity of Islam'. In the earlier years of his life, Mohammed Iqbal appeared to have maintained a relatively softer view of the Ahmadiyah set of beliefs but then he did not take long in discarding the concept of 'shadow prophethood' claimed by Ghulam Ahmed. Such doctrinal deviation, he believed, was a breach 'since the integrity of Muslim society is secured by the idea of the Finality of Prophethood alone'. His articulation gained widespread approval of the Muslim mainstream paving the way for formal demand toward the excommunication of the Ahmadiyah from the pale of Islam. Accepting the fact that 'the British policy of non-interference with religious groups was inevitable' Mohammed Iqbal felt that casting the Ahmadiyah aside 'would be perfectly consistent' with the isolationist preference of the community itself.[1]

Growing up under the secular-liberal policy of the British, who tended to steer clear of religious and cultural beliefs of the colonised as long as social peace was not threatened, the Ahmadiyah became addicted to a forged sense of security. Never any thought was given among them to imagine a life beyond the British rule, especially about the vulnerability of a noisy schism under Muslim majority rule. On the contrary, the community continued to maintain a disproportionately high public profile with its gaudy claims upon the ownership of Islam. On the one hand, there was the exclusiveness stretched as far as living like a cult and not intermingle with Muslims at any level or cost, at the same time a relentless claim was laid upon excessively higher presence in public service and armed forces quotas assigned to Muslims. In 1914, Bashiruddin Ahmed, the son of Ghulam Ahmed, had made it to the Ahmadiyah caliphate at the cost of a major defection and desertion by many founding members of the party. He had come fairly close to losing the battle for succession. Living under a shadow of insecurity, he ended up imposing upon his faction of the party a uniquely stringent writ of holiness by blending the Muslim concept of caliphate with Roman Catholic papal authority. For example, a caliph was male, divinely guided hence infallible, entitled to hold office for life, and so on. He went on promoting the legacy of his father as he perceived it or as it suited him.

In spite of the assertion that caliph was divinely guided, which amounted to confusing caliphate with prophethood, Bashiruddin Ahmed decided, in 1947, to opt for the Muslim majority Pakistan over and above a multicultural India where his party might have lived safely cushioned among other religious minorities. Next, instead of pausing for a while to calculate the repercussions of a fundamental change in ground realities, he went on making a spree of indiscreet, even provocative, statements every now and then. For example, he went public in expressing his desire to convert the entire population of Baluchistan over to the Ahmadiyah faith. Disregarding the core of political establishment, he called for adoption of Bengali as the national language in East Pakistan. Then, he urged

---

[1]Spencer Lavan (1974): p. 173

the Government of Pakistan to claim territorial rights on the Maldives islands to ensure a safer naval link between the two wings of Pakistan. He raised alarm over Pakistan's increasing reliance on the United States. He went as far as proposing a rail-link connecting Pakistan, Iran, Iraq and Syria.

Even when this jumble of his recipes made pragmatic sense, the exercise amounted to meddling in politics without a popular constituency. He did not seem to realise that his very license to speak on behalf of Muslim mainstream of Pakistan was questionable. Had he played safe and created a few friendly pockets to achieve some level of reconciliation with his adversaries before being so loud, the outcome might have been favourable or at least put the Ahmadiyah on alert. His reckless championship of Islamic causes and the bid to set up a political clout in the newly born country had a price. His opponents went on the offensive.

On the evening of 11 August 1948, a young army doctor Major Mahmud Ahmad, was lynched to death in Quetta, in Baluchistan, by an enraged mob of anti-Ahmadiyah fanatics. Major Mahmud Ahmad, a member of the local Ahmadiyah community, was 'literally stoned and stabbed to death, his entire gut having come out'. Afterwards, the post-mortem report indicated that he had upon his body 'as many as twenty-six injuries caused by blunt and sharp-edged weapons'.

What shocked the authorities was the fact that not a single witness turned up to identify the murderers, and the case had to be filed among the non-traceable homicides. Very few people in Pakistan realised the fact that this atrocity was committed precisely on the first anniversary of a policy speech Mohammad Ali Jinnah, the Father of Pakistan, had made before the Constituent Assembly promising to keep religion out of politics. At the time Major Mahmood Ahmad was murdered in Quetta, Mohammed Ali Jinnah lay on his deathbed, about 75 miles away, at the hill station in Ziarat.[1]

Any likelihood of accommodation generated by the sympathy wave out of Quetta lynching was washed away within a matter of days. On 11 September 1948, Mohammed Ali Jinnah passed away and Zafarullah Khan baffled the world by putting up an utterly offensive show of his religious rigidity. He turned up at Exhibition Ground in Karachi, where the state funeral service was in progress in honour of the departed leader, only to stage an abstention. Brazenly, he sat apart. It remains a deep mystery as to why Zafarullah Khan, the chief diplomat of Pakistan, had to demonstrate his refrain so wide openly. Even if it

---

[1] Report of the Court of Inquiry (1954): pp.13-15

was the decades old Ahmadiyah boycott of intermarrying and sharing rituals with Muslim mainstream that had held him back, the funeral service for someone in the class of Mohammed Ali Jinnah was not the occasion to bring the sanction out so loudly. After all it was one of those occasions when people tended to be compassionate and gracious. He might have easily got away with a bit of tactful discretion instead of outraging a nation in mourning. A reporter from the Reuter news agency walked up to Zafarullah Khan and asked for an explanation of his peculiarity. Responding rather cheekily, Zafarullah Khan remarked that he might be considered as the Muslim foreign minister of a non-Muslim government or the vice versa.

Evidently, Zafarullah Khan handled the situation with typical stiffness of a deeply religious psyche that turns people into a piece of stone. If it was not possible for him to participate in the congregation headed by a cleric who had judged the Ahmadiyah as heretic apostates liable to death, and so on, Zafarullah Khan might have stayed back home. Perhaps, he did not wish to be viewed as a hypocrite, but then nobody in the mainstream appreciated the doctrinal nicety behind the show he staged so mercilessly. His boycott of the funeral service of someone no less than the father of the nation amounted to an act of haunting haughtiness. By performing the unique show, he became the father of religious animosity and hatred, it cost his professional image in the country a great deal of penalty and misgiving. First, the intricate legal service he had rendered before the Boundary Commission, in defence of Pakistan in 1947, was questioned. He was held responsible for the prejudicial partition of Punjab that denied Pakistan territorial benefit including a strategic passage to Kashmir. Then, despite being an economical foreign minister, at a time when Pakistan lacked much of resources, his contribution was tainted.

Zafarullah Khan's involvement with advocacy of Pakistani position on Kashmir obliged him to spend months at a stretch in New York where he was required to win over influential friends in the capitalist world beside championing, in between, various Muslims causes in the Middle East and North Africa. Pakistan's Kashmir case before the United Nations Security Council rested largely upon the military balance in battlefield where a hastily imported uprising had begun waning. Zafarullah Khan put up a good defence of his country but it did not take him long to sense that the influential members of the Security Council, especially the United States and the Soviet Union, looked towards Britain to tidy up its unfinished agenda in the subcontinent. In March

1948, he sent a cipher telegram to Liaquat Ali Khan suggesting that any favourable resolution of the dispute was hidden in a military rather than an internationally brokered diplomatic course of action.[1]

By 1952, however, it was clear that Kashmir dispute had been stored in the deep freezer of United Nations' good-intentioned resolutions. As for Zafarullah Khan's advocacy of Muslim causes, whereby he resented the partition of Palestine, pressed for decolonisation in the Middle East and Africa, urged at striking better deals for the Sudan, Algiers, Morocco and Tunisia; his job was complicated by Muslim countries like, for example Egypt, where Pakistan's pan-Islamic push was perceived as divisive rather than a unifying force.

Occasionally, Zafarullah Khan acted as the prime minister. Although it was a standard practice in his role as senior minister in the government but then it would be a reason sufficient to ruffle the feathers of his detractors. After leaving the ministerial position in 1954, he represented Pakistan at the United Nations presiding over the General Assembly for two years. In 1964, he joined the International Court of Justice and served as its president for three years. After a rich run of public life, by holding one high-profile office after another, he retired to divide the remaining years of his life in London and Lahore. In Pakistan, no matter what the legacy of his public life holds in its otherwise worthwhile stock, he was to be remembered for the public display of tactlessness in defence of his manmade faith. His decline to participate in the funeral service of Mohammed Ali Jinnah amounted to a perfect proof of the schismatic character attributed to the Ahmadiyah.

V

In Pakistan, the opening torrent of fire upon the Ahmadiyah was fired at a public rally of the *Ahrar* party convened in Jhelum as early as May 1949, that is, within months of the murder of Major Mahmood Ahmad in Quetta and the funeral service of Mohammed Ali Jinnah in Karachi.

Founded in December 1929, the *Ahrar* comprised of firebrand activists and orators branching out of the erstwhile *Khilafat Movement* (1919–1924) for preservation of Muslim caliphate in Ottoman Empire. Once the caliphate was sorted out by the Turkish leadership under Mustafa Kemal Ataturk (1881–1938),

---

[1] Zafarullah Khan (1971): pp. 555, 566-567

the *Khilafat Movement* in India became clueless. Yet the agitated, nationalistic, anti-imperialistic and anti-establishment enthusiasm compelled the *Ahrar* to seek some cathartic venue. It did not take the party long to find a readymade soft underbelly in the Ahmadiyah, an ideal jumble of heresy inimical to the Muslim spirit of jihad that had been rather loudly espousing the blessings of British raj. On their own, the *Ahrar* set themselves upon achieving the irrevocable mission of safeguarding Islam from deviations such as the Ahmadiyah, the enemy from within. To the *Ahrar*, the sycophancy of the Ahmadiyah was beyond doubt. Right from the teachings of Ghulam Ahmed to the celebration in Qadian of the British military occupation of Baghdad in World War I and the Ahmadiyah insensitivity toward merciless massacre in Amritsar.

Earlier, in the 1930s, Bashiruddin Ahmed had attempted at exploiting the plight of Muslim majority suffering under a Hindu maharaja in Kashmir. It was an ambitious undertaking to champion the cause of an oppressed community but he was effectively checkmated by the *Ahrar* who questioned his very credentials as a Muslim. After that the *Ahrar* went on the offensive by staging, in October 1934, a landmark public rally in Qadian. Even the British officials, who had been soft on the Ahmadiyah, were spellbound to witness the turn up at the rally. As many as 300 Muslim clergymen, some of them not in full agreement with the *Ahrar* and yet united in confronting the Ahmadiyah, arrived to attend the rally.[1] More than a mere show of strength staged by the *Ahrar*, the event amounted to public undressing of the Ahmadiyah isolation. It was from this popular platform that the demand for the excommunication of the Ahmadiyah had been formally tabled for the first time.[2]

Now, in Pakistan, where ground had already been cultivated by the ineptitude of ruling party and the Ahmadiyah, in their own different ways, the time was ripe for the *Ahrar* to harvest the crop. After repeating the demand for the excommunication of the Ahmadiyah, the party offered electoral support to the ruling Muslim League party in Punjab. Soon, as favourable signals were received, the agitators resorted to a binge of thanksgiving rallies to send out the message that anti-Ahmadiyah campaign had been sponsored by the government. Over next few months, the Ahmadiyah loyalty with Pakistan was questioned by relating to Zafarullah Khan's sell-out and incompetence, from his fruitless

---

[1] Spencer Lavan (1974): p. 166
[2] Spencer Lavan (1974): p. 167

performance before the Boundary Commission in getting a larger Punjab to the washout of Pakistan's Kashmir case at the United Nations.

In order to ensure clerical support, the *Ahrar* resorted to populist tricks like targeting women who did not observe the Islamic code of *purdah*. Liaquat Ali's wife Ra'ana, a Hindu converted to Islam, was cited as an example. At the same time, guns were turned upon high-profile communists like Mohammad Iftikharuddin. Mumtaz Daultana, the ambitious and powerful Chief Minister of Punjab, did not take long to fall for the temptation, he had a good deal of score to settle with some of his rivals in the federal government.

As the agitation picked up momentum, and other political organisations started joining in for fear of isolation, the *Ahrar* broadened their list of demands. Apart from asking for the excommunication of the Ahmadiyah, they called for sacking of Zafarullah Khan and forfeiture of the Ahmadiyah estate in Rabwah. In addition, there was the demand for cleansing of public sector bureaucracy by removal, especially from all key positions, of officers belonging to the Ahmadiyah community. According to intelligence abstracts, a total of 390 public rallies were convened in Punjab between 1951 and 1953, and quite a few of those were presided over by leaders of the ruling Muslim League party.

In May 1952, the agitation took another vicious turn when Zafarullah Khan addressed an Ahmadiyah conference in Karachi. He did so despite the disapproval of the prime minister, Khawaja Nazimuddin, who desired his foreign minister to steer clear of sectarian warfare. Zafarullah Khan seemed to have acted in line with the precedence set in Punjab where government officials attended the *Ahrar*-sponsored rallies. He was principled enough, however, to have offered his resignation to the prime minister. In his speech at the Ahmadiyah rally, he postulated that Islam without the Ahmadiyah 'would be like a dried-up tree having no demonstrable superiority over other religions'.[1] His opponents were incensed even further. Within a matter of few days, all the prominent religious parties adopted the *Ahrar* program declaring support for the list of demands. Once again, it was an amazing reminder of the unity of purpose the *Ahrar* had successfully staged in October 1934.

At that time, the leading clerics struggled to achieve an Islamic constitution for Pakistan. Suddenly, they found themselves on the centre-stage of national politics. Their favourite agenda demanded the state to be run by Muslim males with 'sound mind, not being totally blind, deaf or dumb; being wise and

---

[1] Report of the Court of Inquiry (1954): p. 75

sagacious, having mental poise and composure, and not being captive of a foreign government'.[1] Rather amusingly, any mention of the nationality or citizenship of the candidate for leadership was disregarded. Any 'most pious person' qualified to become the Head of the State.[2] Next, the clerics demanded the government to take full responsibility for the propagation of Islam and the missionary activity, both inside Pakistan and abroad.[3] Finally, there was the call to legalise the offering of five daily prayers in mosques 'for all Muslims with defaulters to be punished'.[4]

Effectively, the clerical formula for 'purification' of society and politics was bound to expel women and non-Muslims minorities from the national mainstream of life once and for all. It may be worthwhile to note here that all of this actually happened in Pakistan nearly half a century before the rise of the Taliban Movement in Afghanistan or the emergence of Islamic State Caliphate in Iraq and Syria.

It was time for the clerics to take every possible advantage from the political opportunism of the ruling Muslim League party. Possibly, inspiration was drawn from an ancient Punjabi fable in which a sovereign granted one of his loyal servants to ask for the fulfilment of his three wishes. Upon getting the two fulfilled, the clever servant would ask for another three, and there was no end to his demands. This was exactly what the clerics did, they would make few gains and then retreated to wait for the next opportune moment.

On 27 July 1952, the Council of the Punjab Muslim League party adopted a resolution demanding the classification of the Ahmadiyah 'as a non-Muslim minority'. At a three-day rally in Rawalpindi, in November 1952, the Ahrar leadership declared that the extermination of the Ahmadiyah was a religious obligation of Muslims. When the agitation curved into civic turmoil, its chief architect, Mumtaz Daultana, proposed a constitutional solution of the problem at national level. Speaking at a public rally, on 30 August 1952, he stated that the Ahmadiyah were 'separate from us in every department of life' as they 'have confined their personal, political and social activities to their own class'. He went

---

[1] Leonard Binder (1961): p. 162
[2] Sir Michael Drayton, the Chief Drafting Office of the Constituent Assembly of Pakistan, is believed to have underlined the need for nationality clause.
[3] Leonard Binder (1961): p. 127
[4] Keith Callard (1958): p. 93

as far as accusing public servants of Ahmadiyah background for taking sides with their own kind in the allotment of evacuee property.[1]

At a public rally in Sargodha, the *Ahrar* passed death sentence upon the Ahmadiyah on charges of altering the Koran. They accused Zafarullah Khan for causing bitterness between Pakistan and Afghanistan. Overnight, the sectarian tension in Sargodha shot up to a frightening level. Dr Hafiz Masood Ahmad (1922–1996), a General Practioneer and the Secretary of the local Ahmadiyah organisation, cabled the government to check provocation before it was too late. He warned that the lives and properties of the Ahmadiyah were under grave threat and the government was required to make a determined move.[2]

When authorities attempted to keep agitators from using mosques for political ends, a leading cleric in Sargodha challenged the government to shut down mosques. In Gujranwala, the faithful were urged to treat the Ahmadiyah as untouchables unfit to share common public facilities like water supplies and burial grounds with the mainstream. At food outlets, it was deemed that the Ahmadiyah should be served in marked utensils. In October 1952, the Deputy Inspector General of Police Intelligence reported that many women and children belonging to the Ahmadiyah community had been granted permanent settlement permits by the High Commission of India as they intended to return to Qadian.

In January 1953, a national alliance of prominent clerics took charge of the agitation. An ultimatum was served upon the government to either meet the package of *Ahrar* demands or face 'direct action'. As if jihad had been proclaimed upon the infidel, thousands of volunteers offered to participate in the holy war against the Ahmadiyah. In Punjab alone, where the initial target for recruitment was set at 50,000, the intelligence reports indicated that more than 55,000 volunteers had already been enrolled.

At this point, a prominent member of the *Ahrar* approached the prime minister, Khawaja Nazimuddin, and explained upon him the unceremonious and profuse manner in which the Ahmadiyah copy-catted Islamic titles, honours and phraseology traditionally credited to the family and companions of prophet Mohammed. Shocked he must have been, the prime minister 'expressed sympathy with the demands' but declined to concede.[3]

---

[1] Report of the Court of Inquiry (1954): pp. 97-98
[2] Report of the Court of Inquiry (1954): pp. 46-47
[3] Report of the Court of Inquiry (1954): p. 133

Most notably irked in this hideous interplay of constitutional, political and sectarian warfare were the top bureaucrats who despised street agitation and lawlessness. To them, the hurricane of hatred and fanaticism, fathered by politicians, was much bigger than the writ of civilian authorities, hence the need to invite the armed forces.

Anwar Ali, the Deputy Inspector General of Police, commented that if Pakistan intended to be democratic and progressive state then 'sectarian activities must be put down with firmness'. Otherwise, he feared, the country might be ending up as a medieval and reactionary place.[1]

Waking up to the harsh reality knocking its doors, the government was obliged to make the move. On 27 February 1953, it was decided to arrest all the prominent leaders of the *Ahrar*. Three newspapers were banned from publication. All district commissioners were directed to signal situation reports on a daily basis. In a top priority coded telegram, the federal government made it clear that it had no intention to oblige the agitators because the Ahmadiyah 'or indeed any section of the people' could not be coerced into 'becoming a minority community'.[2] Likewise, the employment of public servants could not be terminated on grounds of their religious belief.

Retaliating over the spate of arrests, the clerics forced a general strike upon Lahore. Unruly mobs went on rampage by clashing with police and courting arrests. On 2 March 1953, the army high command was briefed about the law-and-order situation. Early next morning, troops were camped in the Lawrence Gardens. On 4 March 1953, the Direction Action Committee of the clerics occupied the 16th century Wazir Khan Mosque. It was a strategic move to keep the police at bay in an old impregnable quarter of the walled city where narrow streets and alleys impeded the movement of armoured vehicles.

Meanwhile, wild rumours began making the rounds; there were tales of police brutality. Someone claimed that more than one thousand people had been butchered by police in Sargodha and Jhang districts. A message broadcast from Wazir Khan Mosque suggested that all public servants had gone on strike to express solidarity with the holy cause. Above all, rumours relating to the desecration of Koran raised the pitch of psychological combat.

Rioters began attacking the Ahmadiyah residences and businesses, stabbing their victims to death or causing severe injuries. One of the dead bodies was

---

[1] Report of the Court of Inquiry (1954): p. 44
[2] Report of the Court of Inquiry (1954): p. 147

burnt on a pile of destroyed property. Unruly mobs clashed with military patrol. Students walked out of classrooms and took to the streets. Leaflets went into circulation urging the police to participate in jihad instead of firing bullets upon the faithful. Two police officers were kidnapped and removed to the Wazir Khan Mosque. One Deputy Superintendent of Police, caught in the mob was instantly hacked to death with all sorts of sharp and blunt weapons. 'He had as many as fifty-two injuries on his person'.[1] Curfew was clamped on Lahore as the 'city was literally in a state of tumult and throughout the night weird and dreadful noises could be heard over long distances'.[2] When the Chief Secretary wanted an official statement to be drafted, he made the awful discovery that his clerical staff had gone on strike and there was no one around to take dictation from the boss.

Some of the labour unions joined the movement. Rail link with Rawalpindi was snapped. Power supply to the Governor House was disconnected, and telephone lines with Karachi were silenced. A nervous Home Secretary had to use the Military Trunk Line to apprise federal authorities of the situation obtaining in Lahore. Anarchy reached a stage where the so-called silent majority of people got fed up with the government, the *Ahrar* and the Ahmadiyah. Without caring much about the constitutional merit of demands, or the description of Ahmadiyah schism, people simply wanted a quick way out of the mess. It would not matter much if a resolution of the crisis amounted to committing grave injustice to a section of the populace; everyone viewed the Ahmadiyah as a dead liability.

In Karachi, the federal government went into a crisis session. About mid-day, during the course of lunch-break, the Defence Secretary, Major General Iskander Mirza, called the General Officer Commanding, General Azam Khan, in Lahore on secure line and asked for a military assessment of the situation. General Azam Khan replied that the city was in a bad shape but army could restore peace at a short notice. One General ordered the other to march in and do what was required.[3] Lahore went under a limited martial law and the agitation fizzled out within a matter of few hours. In a quick succession, the political calling of Khawaja Nazimuddin and Mumtaz Daultana ended for good; the meteoric rise of the *Ahrar* met the fate of a meteor. Topping the list of new

---

[1] Report of the Court of Inquiry (1954): p. 156
[2] Report of the Court of Inquiry (1954): p. 157
[3] Zafarullah Khan (1971): pp. 599-600

players were the clerics and the generals, both waiting in the wings for the next round.

VI

As for Abdus Salam, his fate was sealed and the dye cast for him to quit Lahore. He found an opening and left the country, living the rest of his life torn between Physics, Pakistan and, above all, the Ahmadiyah. For a while, he held the wishful belief that clerics had been dealt with a fatal blow by the army. On a couple of occasions, during the course of the anti-Ahmadiyah campaign, Abdus Salam and his parents had some close encounters with infuriated agitators.

In January 1950, the *Ahrar* convened a two-day rally in Multan where Mohammed Hussein presided over the local Ahmadiyah chapter. How fairly did he juggle between the detached role of a public servant and the demands of his religious pursuit remains an ethical mystery. In a bid to counteract the *Ahrar*, he organised a rally of the Ahmadiyah but had to call it off half way through when a group of agitators turned up at the scene and the Duty Magistrate feared rioting. Police filed a case against the trouble makers and Mohammed Hussein was summoned to present evidence at the local court. When questioned about the Ahmadiyah perception of Muslim mainstream, Mohammed Hussein stated that he did not have any issue whatsoever with their Islamic credentials.[1] This random signal of peace was overlooked in the heat of the campaign in Multan where, up until then, six people had died in a mob attack on a police station. So even if Mohammed Hussein made the statement in a court of law, as the president of local Ahmadiyah chapter, it did not really matter much. In order to tone down the tension, the Ahmadiyah caliph was required to come out in the open himself, give up on some of his self-styled arrogance and exclusiveness, and start searching for common ground to at least neutralise the bitterness of the mean show Zafarullah Khan had put up in Karachi.

Personally, Mohammed Hussein ended up terminating his public service career for the sake of the Ahmadiyah. He was transferred from the desk he occupied in Multan, the *Ahrar* pressed for his removal. He felt obliged to apply for an early retirement.[2]

---

[1] Mohammed Hussein (1974): pp. 32-33
[2] Mohammed Hussein (1974): pp. 33-34

Abdus Salam was in Cambridge, making the most of his 1952 summer vacations in research. By the time he returned home, rioting began taking an uglier turn. Worried about the safety of his family, he had asked his parents to move to Lahore. As law-and-order situation worsened in Lahore, he could feel the heat of hostility in body language and gestures, looks and taunts of people especially crowds outside the college walls. It was not safe to continue pretending as if nothing had happened. By the end of February 1953, when angry mobs took to the streets and looked for trouble and dark clouds of fear and insecurity polluted the crisp air and bright mornings of spring, a rally of students, supporting the Ahrar, marched toward Government College. Then there was the rumour that Abdus Salam had been killed in the ensuing violence. When security situation deteriorated further, employees of the college known for their membership of the Ahmadiyah community were advised to keep their heads low and move to safer places. At one stage, the football team, Abdus Salam had so reluctantly given in to look after, volunteered to set up a neighbourhood watch on his residence.

Both Abdus Salam and his Ahmadiyah comrade Mohammed Aslam, the Deputy Principal, considered moving out of the college temporarily. Where to go? Asking friends for asylum at a time when tempers ran high amounted to an embarrassing proposition in itself. At that point, the family of an old acquaintance, Abdul Hameed, who had counselled Abdus Salam to apply for admission in Cambridge in 1946, stepped forward. Abdul Hameed had passed away in 1950 but his sons did not hesitate for a moment in expressing their readiness to play the courageous hosts to Abdus Salam and Mohammed Aslam. Early one morning in the first week of March 1953, Abdus Salam remembered, the advice came to members of the Ahmadiyah community to leave the college premises as no assurance could be given for their safety. 'It might have been out of those false alarms but the air in Lahore was so dense with rumours that we felt ourselves hostages in that situation'. Abdus Salam recollected somewhat reluctantly as he did not wish to revisit those unpleasant memories.

Nearly a dozen of adults and children managed to pack themselves into the loyal Hillman car of Mohammed Aslam. Driving across Anarkali, on Upper Mall and Queens Road, they passed by deserted localities, burnt properties and charred vehicles; making it to Warris Road house of the late Abdus Hameed. Abdus Salam recalled how the busy shopping centre of Anarkali 'presented a rare scene of silence' and other than the smoke rising out of burnt properties 'the bazaar betrayed no signs of movement, whatsoever.' This relatively large contingent of unexpected guests met a generous reception at Warris Road. Men in the house volunteered to sleep on the floor due to shortage of bedding logistics.

Over the years, the memory of anti-Ahmadiyah agitation made Abdus Salam sad and sorry. He felt bitter especially over the manner in which 'the mullahs inciting the youth just disappeared and went underground' in the wake of military action. He would be rather amused to mention the clumsiness of a prominent cleric, Abdus Sattar Niazi (1915–2001), who disregarded his publicly acclaimed desire to embrace martyrdom, shaved off his handsome beard and was caught in the guise of a burqa-clad woman attempting to escape from the Wazir Khan Mosque.[1]

As the sectarian strife of Pakistan hit headlines worldwide, Abdus Salam's friends in England felt deeply worried about his welfare and safety. Rudolf Peierls (1907–1995), the Professor of Mathematical Physics at the University of Birmingham, who was originally from Germany and could feel the pinch of persecution, offered Abdus Salam a Fellowship. Writing back, Abdus Salam thanked for the proposition and then added that the anti-Ahmadiyah sentiment alone did not provide him a compelling reason to leave home.[2] Looking back with a bit of retrospection, it seems the anti-Ahmadiyah rioting might have been the very reason keeping Abdus Salam in Pakistan; he was not prepared to desert his parents and siblings so soon after what they all had been through for months on. Unsuspectingly, however, he began giving into temptation when a chain of events was set in motion in Cambridge. One of the greatest physicists of the 20th century, Max Born (1882–1970), then serving as Tait Professor of Natural Philosophy at Edinburgh University decided to call it day and take retirement. Abdus Salam's former supervisor, Nicholas Kemmer was invited to fill in the vacancy which translated into the availability of a position in Cambridge.

About this time, Abdus Salam had applied for Professor of Mathematics position in Punjab University and requested Nicholas Kemmer to be his referee. In his reply to Abdus Salam, on 25 March 1953, Nicholas Kemmer promised to oblige. 'You certainly ought to get that chair, but at the same time I don't want you to resign yourself to staying there'. He wrote adding that an opportunity was on the way in Cambridge. He then went on to explain the imminent possibility

---

[1] Interviews 1984: Folder V, pp. 9-22
[2] Interviews 1984: Folder VI, pp.11-14

of a Lectureship falling vacant due to the movement of Phillip Hall (1904–1982)[1] in the Sadleirian Chair.[2]

'If subjects are considered we have no claim, but I am on the Appointments Committee and I have definitely set it across that you are an overwhelmingly strong candidate, if you are a candidate'. Nicholas Kemmer added. He asked Abdus Salam to apply for Lectureship hinting that two other staff members, that is, Raymond Lyttleton (1911–1995)[3] and Frank Smithies (1912–2002)[4], sounded supportive. 'So, if you are ready, please apply at once, the Committee knows I am drawing your attention to the vacancy. The closing date will be April 30th. Things are much more favourable than last year. In your application, state definitely that you would not consider an Assistant Lectureship. For your information, I have not heard a word from Edinburgh. If I were to go there I imagine your appointment would be a walkover. I really hope very much that you will give the business a try'. Nicholas Kemmer concluded.

In June 1953, upon receiving a formal confirmation of his selection as the Tait Professor of Natural Philosophy in Edinburgh, Nicholas Kemmer wrote again. 'Now, I hope this will interest you in strict confidence, I think that as far as the Faculty of Mathematics is concerned you could succeed me in Cambridge without lifting a finger. The ground has been prepared well'. In order to 'ginger-up' and gain favourable attention of the selection committee so that the college part of the job might as well be secured, Nicholas Kemmer had been 'dropping remarks that Trinity might consider electing' Abdus Salam. 'However, as I haven't the means to attract you to Edinburgh, I am very keen indeed to see you back at Cambridge and, when we meet, I shall try very hard to persuade you to consider coming back, even though the college part of the job might have to wait'. He pressed with the firmness of an older brother.

Finally, Nicholas Kemmer was vindicated in his persistence to rope Abdus Salam in for the Lectureship at Cambridge. In the summer of 1953, Abdus Salam was in Cambridge when he received the offer to serve as Stokes Lecturer for a three-year term. Later, he used to relish the memory of the event as it happened

---

[1] Philip Hall was the Reader at the Faculty of Mathematics in Cambridge in 1949.
[2] Sadleirian Chair of professorship in pure mathematics was created at Cambridge in 1701.
[3] Stokes Lecturer/Reader in Theoretical Astronomy at the University of Cambridge in the 1950s
[4] Lecturer at the University of Cambridge in the 1950s

before even the formal filing of an application by him.[1] He was urged to make up his mind and accept or decline the offer by 30 September 1953.

Nicholas Kemmer did not stop at securing the invitation for Abdus Salam. He went as far as canvassing the significance of the position with Abdus Salam's employer in Lahore. 'Lectureships at Cambridge are offered only partly to secure good teachers; we set much greater store on appointing leaders in their fields of research'. He wrote to the Government of Pakistan stating that his colleagues were unanimous in holding the view that Abdus Salam was the best choice 'before anyone else in the world'. Nicholas Kemmer hoped, almost prophetically, that given the stimulus of 'close contacts with workers in allied fields' Abdus Salam could take advantage of his 'scientific productivity' when it was at its best and become a focus of international attention in the near future. He cautioned the Government of Pakistan that if Abdus Salam were to stay on in Lahore, isolated and inevitably burdened with very elementary teaching, he better forget about frontline physics. 'Even the best young scientists in a field such as ours could not be expected to thrive without concentrating on advanced work and constant stimulus from others of similar intellect and interests'. He stated adding that by supporting Abdus Salam the Government of Pakistan 'will be acting in the interests of international science, of one of your greatest citizens and of your country'.

By this time, Abdus Salam had become increasingly clear about the choice between Pakistan and Physics. He did not wish to miss the physics boat but his relatively short service record did not qualify him to avail an extended sabbatical or long service leave. He was worried as to what might happen after completing his three-year contract at Cambridge? He could find another job in Pakistan but then a disruption in the continuity of service meant loss of seniority. He asked his father for an opinion. Mohammed Hussein was well versed with administrative procedures and practices in the Department of Education. He advised to explore a safer option like, for example, secondment or some sort of secondment. Abdus Salam asked Mohammed Sharif, the Secretary Education, for advice. Mohammed Sharif looked at the offer from Cambridge as well as the supporting letter from Nicholas Kemmer; he granted Abdus Salam the permission to go ahead under a secondment. An invitation to teach Mathematics in Cambridge was not an ordinary thing, Mohammad Sharif observed, it brought tremendous honour to Pakistan. At the same time, Mohammed Sharif believed

---

[1] Interviews 1984: Folder VI, pp. 14-15, 36-41

Abdus Salam's presence in Cambridge served as a valuable contact for Pakistan. Finally, the Education Secretary, considered the availing of offer made to Abdus Salam presented, at the same time, a decent way out to peace with Sirajuddin Ahmed.[1]

Deep in his heart, Abdus Salam was aware of his inability to any meaningful research in Lahore. He had returned home under an ethical as much as personal obligation to give the place a go. He was not rich enough like Robert Oppenheimer and Homi Bhabha to afford physics at his own cost in any case.

Three years spent in Lahore had been wasted in frivolous warfare. What terrified Abdus Salam most was the absence of funds for education and research, libraries and journals. His personal copy of *Physical Review* was the only window for him to get a glimpse of new discoveries. He found his students were not prepared to break out of their deeply examination-oriented psyche. Writing a first-class paper, coming so easily in Cambridge, required struggle in Lahore. Rolling between Field Theory and Superconductivity, taking an occasional plunge into Cosmology, he had become somewhat unsure about his own destination. After reading through the works of Hermann Bondi, he went to deliver a lecture at the Pakistan Science Conference of 1953, only to have the afterthought that it was 'more of a review of the current developments in the subject'. He feared losing originality. His 'creative fecundity' was 'decaying with disuse'.[2] He suffered from lack of purpose and excitement, could not talk to anyone.

On 30 September 1953, that is, the last day to accept or decline the offer, Abdus Salam cabled Cambridge that he would be pleased to take up the job provided permission was granted to him to start early in January 1954. Cambridge did not have any problem with the reporting date.

Once again, Pakistan came to his rescue. Ordinarily, seniority in service was counted from the date of confirmation in job after successful completion of probation period. In his case, he was scheduled to be confirmed on 18 September 1952 but a bureaucratic fix established his confirmation with effect from 28 September 1949, that is, the day he had first reported on duty prior to travelling abroad for doctoral study program. Mohammed Sharif made sure that no hurdles were created in the approval of his leave on this occasion.

---

[1] Interviews 1984: Folder V, pp.36-41
[2] Jagjit Singh (1992): p. 27

On 30 October 1953, Abdus Salam wrote to the Reverend John Boys Smith, the Senior Bursar at St John's College, asking for the residential allotment. Within two weeks, he received the advice that 35 Bridge Street, Cambridge, had been set aside for him. On this occasion, Abdus Salam travelled to England by sea in the company of his wife Amtul Hafeez and their daughter Aziza. While leaving Pakistan, he did not realise that his move out of the country was permanent. As events unfolded in the following years and decades, numerous journeys had been made home every now and then, but a permanent come back remained a dream.

Leaving Pakistan, one his biographers remarked, was equal to physical parting with one's natural environment, social habitat, siblings and the extended circle of family and friends.[1] But had he stayed on, kept his head in the sand, made some unscrupulous compromises; the day was never too far for him to end up as the vice chancellor of an intellectually debauched university, a secretary of education department, even a government minister in one of the military governments. He could have been anyone, but a great physicist. By bailing himself out in time, he saved physicist if not the political animal residing inside his personality. For many years, he hoped to return home one day and quell any regrets over leaving the land of his birth; that day did not come.

He would not entertain the proposition that his exit had much to do with the rising tide of anti-Ahmadiyah sentiment. He claimed that it had none effect, whatsoever, upon him. He felt that all the right-thinking people in Pakistan did not approve bigotry. Also, he felt reassured by the swiftness of military action. 'Certainly this had no bearing on the issue of my leaving Pakistan. Not for once did this influence me in any way'. He insisted.

Likewise, he acquitted Sirajuddin Ahmed from causing any offence. In fact, he went as far as conceding that Sirajuddin Ahmed, as the Principal of Government College, was justified in defending the college territory. 'I have never kept any grudge towards anyone all my life. Instead of carrying it along, I express my displeasure instantly. I must have been very angry then, but not anymore. It is beyond my nature to keep a grudge. Whenever in Lahore afterwards, I would always visit Sirajuddin Ahmed at his residence and found him very affectionate. Our conflict, or whatever it was, turned out to be a blessing in disguise'. He remarked.[2]

---

[1] Jagjit Singh (1992): p. 29
[2] Interviews 1984: Folder V, pp. 40-42

Unsurprisingly, Abdus Salam did not wish to memorise much about his teaching career at the Government College. 'I never sat in the Common Room. Being bitten by the research bug my whole attitude was different'. He stated as if the college was an entity apart from him.

He regretted, however, for not attending the lectures of contemporary scholars like Ghulam Mustafa Tabassum, the Professor of Persian Literature. 'I wanted to but never found the courage because of being a senior professor myself. I wish I had been to his classes. He made literature come alive. Apart from this, the college remained foreign to me. Now that I look back, even if Sirajuddin Ahmed had not been a factor, and although I tried my hardest, it was still not my place. I left at the end of 1953 but had become a foreigner already'. He reminisced without any hint of nostalgia.[1]

---

[1] Interviews 1984: Folder V, p. 43

Chapter Five
On Wings of Ambition

Addicted to staying at the top, an important lesson Abdus Salam learnt in Lahore was that merit alone did not open every door of accomplishment; there was always the need to back the talent up with vigilance, discretion, strategic planning, and an influential network of favourable decision-makers. Lahore sharpened his skills as a street fighter and he was much better off in dealing with the real world of everyday life. He could see that merit alone had not been sufficient in getting t him safely through those twenty-seven months of his life in fighting mundane battles one after another in Lahore.

He responded to the invitation arranged by Nicholas Kemmer and returned to England. He was lucky to reclaim the disrupted career in Physics with considerable ethical vindication to his credit. His sharp appreciation of the ideal as well as mundane strata of professional occupation provides an exceedingly valuable model to generations of talented youth; he leaves behind an underlined message that a meaningful trajectory of professional ambition should not rest upon the advantage of merit alone. A closer observation of his professional journey in the guild of high-profile physicists in addition to profitable interaction among those wielding influence reveals how watchful he had been in hitting upon one gainful niche after another.

Early in 1954, the foremost task before Abdus Salam was to catch-up with discoveries made in Physics and cover-up the gap created by his self-selected distraction in Lahore. He was familiar with the set of initial trials in England, from climatic acclimatisation to social accommodation, and did not have to build up resilience on that account all over again. Actually, on this occasion, he was better placed because his wife, Amtul Hafeez, accompanied him to care for the domestic front. He was free to spend the best part of his day working at the college, surrounded by colleagues and students. He was able to do research along with teaching a fine lot of students. No place other than Cambridge could have been better for him at such crucial juncture when he aimed at levelling his losses in Theoretical Physics. 'During the years of my absence, the very subject of elementary particles had acquired a new status. New discoveries had been made about strange particles and I knew nothing about them. My foremost preoccupation, therefore, was to fill the gap as early as possible'. He remembered.[1]

When Abdus Salam reported at Cambridge, he was asked to teach Quantum Mechanics because Paul Dirac had gone on to avail a sabbatical leave at the Institute of Advanced Study in Princeton. Although it was an honour to 'deputise for the quantum master' yet Abdus Salam aimed at originality instead of descending to the level of a 'common denominator'.[2] He took up the challenge well, and if teaching advanced Mathematics served as a gauge to popularity, the size of his audience in graduate level courses like electricity and magnetism won him the day.[3] Not a bad show at all for someone who had been rusting for over two years.

Earlier on, the task of supervising students was shared between Nicholas Kemmer and James Hamilton (1918–2000). After Nicholas Kemmer went to Scotland, the onus of responsibility to look after an entire set of students fell upon Abdus Salam who felt lucky to have some of the best students around him. He met students head on checking out difficulties they wished him to sort out for them; the approach saved a good amount of time on both ends.[4] Like before, the inkling was that theoretical effort in Physics could be reaching a saturation point and, as such, there was the desire to brim over and dig up mysteries in adjoining areas of natural sciences. One of Abdus Salam's students Walter Gilbert (b1932) did the same and moved from Physics to Genetics and won the Nobel Prize for Chemistry in 1980.

For three years from 1954 to 1956, Abdus Salam worked at a steady pace focussing upon the singular desire to gain excellence in Theoretical Physics. Layers of lethargy gathered in Lahore wore off swiftly. During this time, Abdus Salam published ten papers, mainly in 'quantized fields' and 'generalised dispersion relations'. While working on parity violation, in 1956, he had a fairly close brush with the Nobel Prize awarded in 1957. Just as Fred Hoyle had urged him to do, he was able to look physicists in the eye. He reclaimed recognition

---

[1] Interviews 1984: Folder VI, pp. 22-23
[2] Gordon Fraser (2008): p. 114
[3] Jagjit Singh (1992): p. 30
[4] Gordon Fraser (2008): p. 114

despite his teaching load that involved searching and reading recent literature to prepare for lectures and tutorials, setting up tests and assignments, finalising results and evaluation reports, sitting on academic committees, interviewing students, doing and publishing his own research, and so on. Most of the work sounded ordinary and time consuming but it was a part of the game preparing him for more lucrative rounds of employment.

For the first time in his working life, he enjoyed a certain degree of financial freedom. His position as Stokes Lecturer earned him something close to £1000.00 per year; the package included £450.00 for lectureship, £300.00 as the Fellow at St John's College, and £200.00 in allowance.[1] On top of that he received a secondment allowance of 180.00 rupees per month from his employer in Lahore.[2] He had sufficient money to live comfortably in Cambridge and, at the same time, continue supporting his parents and siblings in Pakistan. One day soon he could buy a house.

His elevated status as a Fellow qualified him to privileges such as entitlement to college accommodation and High Table dinning. Since old times, the tradition of High Table dinners had prevailed at university colleges in Cambridge, Oxford, Dublin and Durham. In essence the custom was aimed at encouraging scholarly interaction among the Fellows and students. With students occupying the main space in the hall, the Fellows were seated around a slightly raised High Table. As the Fellows were permitted to invite guests from different walks of life, Abdus Salam utilised his turn by asking Zafarullah Khan, then serving as a judge at the International Court of Justice, as a guest. On another occasion, he had his brother Abdul Hameed (1933–2005) over to a High Table dinner. 'In my college, we had about 70 Fellows in different subject areas. We had specially invited guests every now and then, and it used to be my enormous privilege to share the table and converse with people who commanded recognition in one or another field of specialisation'. He remembered fondly.[3]

More than anything else, and for all that the medieval university town offered in the shape of its libraries, bookshops and scholarly ambience; Abdus Salam was indebted to Cambridge for enabling him a life mainly focussed on Physics.[4]

---

[1] Jagjit Singh (1992): p. 30
[2] The Government of Punjab, Lahore, Notification No. 6075/2, dated 16 February 1954 (as quoted by Ghani, p. 32)
[3] Interviews 1984: Folder VI, pp. 28-29
[4] Interviews 1984: Folder VI, p. 25

He did not take long in making up for losses incurred in Lahore and regain control over the direction and pace of his life. At the same time, instead of waiting leisurely for the next big opportunity to turn up on its own, he was attentive to possibilities in the making.

In October 1954, Abdus Salam received the invitation to attend the High Energy Physics Conference scheduled to be held at Rochester, in the United States, from 31 January to 2 February 1955. It was the fifth annual gathering of famous physicists from all over the world.

Originally, the idea for the conference was masterminded by Robert Marshak (1916–1992), the professor of physics at the University of Rochester. He came from a humble family background in the Bronx borough of New York and, like Abdus Salam, had made his way into Theoretical Physics by virtue of some favourable accidents. As a member of the migrant Jewish community he had fought anti-Semitism prevalent in some sections of society in the United States. In the beginning, only physicists based in the United States attended the Rochester Conference but gradually the scope of its membership was broadened. Over the following years, the conference began holding its sessions at other places without changing the title associated with Rochester. Holding international conferences before the dawn of digital revolution was a cumbersome task. Still, the convention served the purpose of bringing distinguished scientists together face-to-face under one roof and provide them with the opportunity to 'conduct an audit of discoveries made in physics in the given timeframe'. An invitation to participate in Rochester Conference amounted to professional recognition at the highest possible level. Abdus Salam remembered the earlier rounds of Rochester Conference as an opportunity to meet great physicists he had known only through their research publications.

When the invitation arrived, Abdus Salam found himself on the defensive because the schedule of the conference clashed with term dates in Cambridge. Leaving the town during the course of term was unimaginable. With the bitter taste of Lahore, where a charge-sheet had been served upon him and his salary deducted for leaving the college during the term break, there was the need to tread with caution. He requested the Old Schools General Board of the Faculties for leave of absence to be able to attend the conference. 'From the point of view of our research group here and its activities it is very desirable that I should accept the invitation'. He wrote to the Secretary General of the Board on 13 October 1954. 'I hope to be able to suggest arrangements for my lectures to be given in my place'. He pleaded adding that his colleagues Fred Hoyle and Ernest Lapwood (1910–1984) had expressed their readiness to fill in for him during the leave. He was granted leave for up to ten days to attend the conference. He also received the assurance that there shall be no deduction from his stipend 'on account of this dispensation'. He felt himself to be utterly lucky that despite the rigid convention about leave during the term, Cambridge had been more accommodating. 'Cambridge sounded to me so conservative in this respect. Nobody imagined leaving the campus during those 24 weeks of teaching, and no one bothered you for the rest of 28 weeks. Fred Hoyle was very kind to stand in my place for two lectures'. He recalled later.[1]

Attending the conference turned out to be an 'unnerving experience' as Abdus Salam could not keep himself from comparing the striking difference of work ethics between Europe and the United States. He felt appalled to observe how Europe lagged behind the United States, and wondered what future held for British schools of fundamental physics. 'I have seen for a week, a set of energetic enthusiastic physicists talk physics, dream physics and teach physics to each other'. He wrote to Neville Mott (1905–1996), the Cavendish Professor of Physics, and pressed for liaison between theoretical and experimental centres of research in Britain. 'There must be the easiest possible travel arrangement between Cambridge, Birmingham, Manchester, Harwell, Bristol, Liverpool and Glasgow. Physics is one, our problems are one and if the Americans can spend one term at one university and the next at another, I do not see why we cannot do so'. He rebuked the discriminatory treatment meted out to theoreticians. 'People at my age and level must be freed from the excessive teaching and supervising load'. He concluded by slating the practice under which wages were paid to academics in proportion to the supervisory work they would be prepared to take leaving them with hardly enough time to do research; whereas those preferring research ran short of income.

Rochester gave him a rich taste of international meetings. 'The main challenge to physics remains more or less unchanged, that is, to understand the structure of matter and unification of forces. In 1955, the particular issues were related with particles and symmetry. But theories of those times have now become a very small part of the much bigger perspective, classical fractions of the ongoing developments. So much has changed'. He observed afterwards.[2]

---

[1] Interviews 1984: Folder VI, pp. 39-40

[2] Interviews 1984: Folder VI, pp. 30-50

In February 1955, Abdus Salam received the invitation to attend an international conference on quantum electrodynamics and the theory of elementary particles called by the Academy of Sciences in the former Soviet Union. Lev Landau (1908–1968), who won the Nobel Prize in 1962 for his work on liquid helium, was going to chair the conference scheduled for seven days between 31 March and 6 April 1955. Appreciating the political and military significance attached to high energy physics in the wake of atom bomb, Abdus Salam wanted to attend the conference. It was a great opportunity to have a glimpse into what had been happening in Russia. One day soon Pakistan was required to achieve and develop nuclear knowhow. But he could not make up his mind to visit Moscow as conveniently as had been the case with Rochester; the Cold War raged between communist and capitalist blocks of power. In view of security considerations, he could not accept outright the invitation from Moscow; the air was thick with deep suspicion and maliciousness. Any curtailment on his freedom to move around in the west could inhibit him to play a role in the acquisition of nuclear technology by Pakistan especially when he felt the need to visit places like Brookhaven Laboratories in the United States in the near future. In a world in which the fate of people like Julius and Ethel Rosenberg was determined by ideological preferences, he did not wish to find himself in the midst of crossfire, on the wrong side of the fence.

He began consulting some of his well-placed colleagues only to discover that their opinion was divided. Before anyone else, he went to the Master of St John's College, James Wordie, who in turn sought the opinion of his counterpart, Edgar Adrian (1889–1977) at the Trinity College. In a brief note, dated 4 February 1955, Edgar Adrian responded to James Wordie by hinting that a visit to the Soviet Union of Abdus Salam amounted to landing in trouble with the Americans. 'I think you might find that after a visit to Russia it would take you longer than before to get a visa for the United States of America. I understand that the application would have to go to Washington and could not be settled at the Embassy in London. But clearly the extra delay would be reduced to a minimum for you and it may well be that your application would always take longer than mine, for instance, since they are always rather more careful about atomic physicists'. James Wordie wrote to Abdus Salam on 25 February 1955.

Similar advice came from John Cockcroft, the chief of Atomic Energy Establishment in Britain. 'You probably know that if you go this might prevent you from obtaining a visa to the United States in future…I will ask the Foreign

Office informally if they have any views on your acceptance of the invitation'. John Cockcroft wrote to Abdus Salam on 7 March 1955.

Gunnar Källén (1926–1968), the Swedish physicist who died young in a tragic air crash, suspected the conference in Moscow could be 'some kind of communistic propaganda show'.

At the Cavendish Laboratory, on the other hand, the invitation from Moscow was viewed as an advantageous opportunity in establishing contact with Russian science. Abdus Salam was considered as an 'admirably qualified' physicist who could 'understand the work' being carried out in the Soviet Union. But Abdus Salam's former teacher Denys Wilkinson raised the alarm that it was an area where opinions could change 'in any instant' and 'trip the balance' unfavourably. Denys Wilkinson was the first foreigner to have been granted permission to work at Brookhaven Laboratories in the United States.

Richard Feynman also received invitation but he remained unsure until the last minute and finally gave up on the idea to go for the conference. In a brief note, dated 14 March 1955, he informed Abdus Salam about his inability to make it to Moscow.

Freeman Dyson put up a good battle with the Department of Justice in the United States. He aimed at getting an assurance that his chances of re-entry into the United States would not be compromised. He held the view that those managing to 'get to this conference will not regret' their decision. But then after a meeting at the Immigration Service in Washington, Freeman Dyson surrendered. He had been advised that his re-entry into the United States could not be guaranteed under the law.

Abdus Salam received the best piece of advice from Professor Rudolf Peierls, who believed that an acceptance of the Moscow invitation was not enough to jeopardise the prospects of a visit to Brookhaven. Above all, Rudolf Peierls comforted Abdus Salam that Brookhaven was not the only place to learn high energy physics. 'If you should have any trouble with Brookhaven I do not regard this as the only Laboratory where one can bring oneself up to date on high energy physics, because the results are widely known. There are people in many other places who work on such problems and know all the experimental material and the fact that you happen to be close to the machines actually doing the work is of rather minor importance. I always think it is stimulating to be near an experimental group, both because one has therefore to consider their problems in planning experiments and also because one has a group of people close by who read the experimental papers and can discuss them intelligently, but all these factors apply to more permanent residents than to a visit of a few months'. He wrote to Abdus Salam on 22 February 1955.

More than the opening or closing of doors in Moscow or Brookhaven, the gentleman philosopher in Rudolf Peierls was actually worried about the mechanics and capacity of prejudice. He spoke out of his own experience in Germany and warned about latent bigotry. He knew what happened when 'perfectly reasonable people' gave in for the sake of appeasement. 'I am watching this now in the question of the colour bar which is becoming acute in the Birmingham area and where one always hears of people who profess to be unbiased but who nevertheless oppose the employment, say of West Indians, because of the probable reaction of people who are prejudiced. Exactly the same thing happened in the beginning of the Nazi regime in Germany (though I am not of course implying that the situation either in America or here has otherwise any similarity) and this explains in part why I feel so strongly on the principle'. He stated by offering Abdus Salam help in every possible manner to visit Brookhaven laboratories. 'On the question of organising a Brookhaven invitation for next summer, I understand that Goudsmit and Collins are in charge of independent sections of the Laboratory and one should approach either of them. Since Collins' section includes the cosmotron work and also since you have met him, at least casually at Rochester, it would be best to write to him. Now this could either be done by your writing to him, but in that case it might help if I also wrote saying that I know about your approach and giving him a little background. Alternatively, if you prefer, I could write to him in the first place, but I am not sure that this would be the right idea because it somewhat conveys the impression of your being a rather junior sort of person who has to be sponsored'. He assured advising Abdus Salam to accept the invitation from Moscow.

Because Pakistan had already joined the western jihad against the godless Soviet Union, Abdus Salam approached the Pakistan High Commission in London for guidance. On 16 February 1955, he received the advice in a letter marked 'confidential' that a visit to Moscow alone did not prejudice the chances of getting Abdus Salam a visa to the United States in the future. But it all sounded merely bureaucratic. Abdus Salam could not make up his mind to visit Moscow after Richard Feynman and Freeman Dyson had given up. Few years later, in

1959, he did travel to Soviet Union to participate in a meeting held in Kiev.[1] By then, he was in a much stronger position to face the music if there would be any.

Whatever the merit of political and security considerations, the exercise Abdus Salam went through illustrated the shape of barriers and bias posed by wave after wave of religious and ideological bigotry, all over the place, from an underdeveloped Pakistan to the industrially advanced west. Even though he preferred neutrality in purely scientific matters, the rigorous exercise of caution and reluctance prepared him well for the days ahead.

Life in Cambridge delighted Abdus Salam but it was a different story for Amtul Hafeez. She did not mind the role of a full-time housewife, but Cambridge sounded like an exile of some sort especially with her husband spending long hours at work. Other than the monotonous routine of everyday household chores revolving around cooking, cleaning, washing and childcare; a Punjabi housewife in her situation did not know what else to do. Then, before leaving Pakistan, she had only a distant notion of European winter. Once in Cambridge, she found herself in the midst of piercing chill, rain, sleet, snow, and shorter days under a darkly overcast sky; the sun when it showed up was nothing more than a lifeless cold plate of bronze. If Abdus Salam's foremost occupation was to catch up with new discoveries in Physics, Amtul Hafeez confronted the challenge of getting used to an inclement weather. When would this miserable, wet and biting chill come to an end? This was one of the earliest questions Punjabi housewives raised soon after their arrival in the post-war England. Out of his own experience, back in 1946, Abdus Salam did not have much consolation to offer. He just dashed off to work. With her memory of a sparkling blue sky and mild winters of Jhang, Multan and Lahore, she looked forward to returning home soon after the completion of her husband's contract with Cambridge. Had someone convinced her that a permanent return to Punjab was off the shelf, and wet cold greyish England was home forever, she might have succumbed to some breathless seizure of panic. Asifa, the second daughter of Abdus Salam and Amtul Hafeez, was born in November 1954 effectively translating into more work for the traditional housewife.

In view of the scarcity regarding family related information, it is hard to speculate how much of a role Amtul Hafeez played in her husband's social engagements. On her part, in those early days in England, Amtul Hafeez was not much at ease in a mixed company. Then, earlier in the 1950s, Cambridge offered

---

[1] Gordon Fraser (2008): p. 206

Punjabi women, bound by linguistic and cultural inhibitions, hardly much of opportunity to socialise around or consider finding some kind of lighter employment.

About then, Abdus Salam's younger brother, Abdul Hameed, arrived in Cambridge to study for a degree in Natural Sciences. After a while he moved to Peterborough, not very far from Cambridge, to do a graduate apprenticeship with an engineering conglomerate. Not a record-roller like his older brother, yet Abdul Hameed seemed to be doing pretty well with hands-on applied business. On weekends, he would turn up at Cambridge to spend time with the family of his brother.

A daily routine of starting early and finishing late did not hand in Abdus Salam much time to spend with family. But then after picking up a stable momentum at work, he would find time to do things together. Cambridge had a whole lot to offer in the shape of its manicured lawns, flower gardens, riverside walks and a host of local tradition. On a weekend sometimes, when weather permitted, he would take the family to punting over the Cam, one of his favourite pastimes in Cambridge. Amtul Hafeez and children sat on the front, Abdus Salam stood on the rear end and, armed with the pole, struggled to keep the boat in smooth motion. When he lost control or the pole slipped out of his grip, the punt was paddled back to the river bank.[1]

His brother, Abdul Hameed would remember for a long time the pilaf party the two of them had when Amtul Hafeez had been on a visit to Pakistan. Abdus Salam announced one day that he was going to cook *pilaf* for dinner.[2] Abdul Hameed felt a bit alarmed because he had not seen his brother much around in the kitchen. Do you know how we do it? He asked Abdus Salam.

What's so special about it? Abdus Salam shot back with the confidence of an experienced chef but then ended up cooking an unpalatable morass of every masala he could lay his hands on in the kitchen. Abdul Hameed remembered the product as anything but the fragrant mouth-watering *pilaf*. Abdus Salam did not take very long to surrender, and signalled his brother to dine out at the local Taj Mahal restaurant.[3]

---

[1] *Al-Nahl* - Fall 1997: pp. 50-54

[2] A rice and mutton dish prepared on ceremonial occasions, it is popular from North Africa to Southeast Asia.

[3] Abdul Hameed (circa 2000): p. 95

II

Four fundamental forces of nature, according to physicists, are: gravity, electromagnetism, strong nuclear and weak nuclear. These forces are evident everywhere, from subatomic particles all the way to universal domains. Functionally, from a layman's point of view, gravity described inter and intra regulation among terrestrial and celestial objects; electromagnetism illustrated relationship between charged atomic particles; strong nuclear force was the attraction between protons and neutrons keeping the unity of nucleus; and weak nuclear force determined particle decay. Gravity became the source of fame for Isaac Newton (1643–1727) though some aspects of his work in the area were improved upon by Albert Einstein (1879–1955). A great deal of credit for insight into electromagnetism went to Michael Faraday (1791–1867), James Maxwell (1831–1879) and Heinrich Hertz (1857–1894). In particle physics, the floodgate of discoveries relating to strong and weak nuclear forces was lifted in the closing years of 19th century with ground-breaking contribution made by Wilhelm Rontgen (1845–1923), Henry Becquerel (1852–1908) and Joseph Thomson (1856–1940).

On this ordinary chronology of human effort to understand nature, Abdus Salam started his professional journey as a mathematician and then made it into particle/nuclear physics. Due to his extraordinary proficiency in Mathematics, the language of gods, it did not take him long to arrive at the forefront of Quantum Mechanics studying the characteristics and behaviour of subatomic particles by way of highly advanced and complex mathematical formulae and equations.

Any deeper delving into the subject will be avoided here because the present biography of Abdus Salam aims to focus more upon his life outside Physics.

Eugene Wigner (1902–1995), the mathematician-turned-physicist born to Hungarian parents of Jewish background, is known for popularising Quantum Mechanics with mathematical formulations more explicable compared to his German contemporary Hermann Weyl (1885–1955). For his extensive contribution to Theoretical Physics, Eugene Wigner won the 1963 Nobel Prize in Physics. He had studied and worked in Budapest and Berlin before migrating to the United States where a job was offered to him in Princeton with salary reportedly many times more than his income in Germany. In 1939, he signed the correspondence along with Albert Einstein and Leo Szilard (1898–1964) to alert the American President, Franklin Roosevelt (1882–1945), about German progress in the direction of making the atom bomb. One of Eugene Wigner's sisters, Margit, was married to Paul Dirac, Abdus Salam's erstwhile peer in Cambridge. For quite a while, in the light of mathematical evidence worked out by Eugene Wigner, it was assumed that parity conservation principle applied on weak interactions just as it did in the case of strong interactions.

In September 1956, Abdus Salam attended the International Congress of Physics at the University of Washington in Seattle. He was among the 'limited group' of physicists receiving 'special invitations' for the event. At the congress, he heard the Chinese-born American physicists Chen Ning Yang (1922-) and Tsung-Dao Lee (1926-) raising doubts about the left-right symmetry in weak interactions. It was a dramatically novel idea shaking the ground under time-honoured parity principle somewhat blindly applied since the work Eugene Wigner had done on strong interactions. While flying back to England aboard a comfortless flight of the United States Military Air Transport Service, Abdus Salam pondered over it. Then, all of a sudden, he found a possible clue in the question Professor Rudolf Peierls, had asked him during the course of his doctoral examination. If the photon mass was zero, why did the same apply to neutrino? Rudolf Peierls had asked. Abdus Salam remembered how uneasy he felt because it was a question the answer to which nobody knew at the time. As 'the role of massless neutrino' flashed into his mind he was tempted to take the plunge into what sounded like 'a romantic exaggeration'.[1]

Back in Cambridge next day, he started making calculations and then travelled to Birmingham to seek the opinion of Rudolf Peierls before formally drafting the paper. Rudolf Peierls listened but declined to accept the explanation Abdus Salam presented. In fact, the peer went as far as telling his excited visitor that such an idea was not worth touching 'with a pair of tongs'.[2] Unperturbed, Abdus Salam wrote the paper, made a copy and while in Geneva handed it to Felix Villars (1921–2002), a fellow physicist who was going to see Wolfgang Pauli in Zurich the day after. Abdus Salam asked Felix Villars to pass the copy on to Wolfgang Pauli. Like Rudolf Peierls in Birmingham, Wolfgang Pauli rejected outright Abdus Salam's contention that left-right symmetry could be sacrificed in neutrino interactions. In fact, the 'revered and feared' and 'universally acknowledged Chief Justice of Physics', responded by advising

---

[1] Gordon Fraser (2008): p. 133
[2] Abdul Ghani (1982): p. 42

Abdus Salam to better do something useful.[1] Staying on the beat, Abdus Salam submitted his paper to the *Physical Review,* a more sought-after journal among mainstream physicists. But then he had cold feet and withdrew it. Instead, he mailed the paper to *Il Nuovo Cimento*, a relatively obscure Italian journal where it was published in January 1957.

Whereas, Chen Ning Yang and Tsung-Dao Lee, the two American physicists working on the problem longer than Abdus Salam had no reason to succumb to reluctance. Their joint paper 'Parity non-conservation and a two-component theory of the neutrino' was published in the *Physical Review* in March 1957; and, ironically, the publication carried an acknowledgment of similar work done by Abdus Salam. Chen Ning Yang and Tsung-Dao Lee had recommended experimentation to verify the truth behind parity conservation. Upon reading their paper Rudolf Peierls supported the idea.

Soon the experimental evidence arrived, and it amounted to handing down death sentence upon parity conservation. In other words, the very foundation exploded under what thus far had been a profoundly admired theoretical scheme in understanding the behaviour of elementary particles. This led to media furore, all leading newspapers and magazines in the United States reported the breakthrough. For example, *The New York Times* carried a four-page report on the work of Chen Ning Yang and Tsung-Dao Lee. Within a matter of few months, Chen Ning Yang and Tsung-Dao Lee were awarded the 1957 Nobel Prize for Physics. Chien-Shiung Wu, who provided the experimental evidence, and was fondly named as the 'First Lady of Physics' for her precision, had been completely overlooked by the Nobel Committee. Despite being 'the first to realise that parity violation could be tied to the existence of a neutrino' and putting together the theoretical explanation for it, Abdus Salam's precedence seemed to have been drowned under the obscurity of *Il Nuovo Cimento*.[2]

Misgiving about missing the prize is not something that happens rarely. What amazed scientists was the speed with which the prize was awarded in 1957. Rarely in physics had great discoveries been acclaimed as swiftly as the Nobel Prize of 1957. It had taken Max Born 28, Albert Einstein 16 and Subramanyam Chandrasekhar 53 years to win the prize. Two Dutch scientists, George Eugene Uhlenbeck and Samuel Abraham Goudsmit, the pioneers in finding the particle

---

[1] Gordon Fraser (2008): pp. 124, 131

[2] Robert Crease and Charles Mann (1986): p. 236

spin, were somehow ignored all the way.[1] Abdus Salam's friend and colleague in Cambridge, Fred Hoyle, was among those who deserved but never received one. Frederick Reines (1918–1998) received the prize only two years before his death for the work he had completed over 40 years ago.

On 1 November 1957, *The Times of London* questioned as to why Abdus Salam and Lev Landau were missed out despite giving similar results'. Muhammad Ikramullah, the Pakistani High Commissioner in London expressed his readiness to trigger diplomatic fuss over the veracity of Nobel Prize Committee and the 'injustice' but then Abdus Salam preferred peace.

In a letter to fellow physicist Victor Weisskopf (1908–2002), Wolfgang Pauli acknowledged receiving the manuscript of Abdus Salam's paper about eight weeks ahead of the formal publication of the one by Chen Ning Yang and Tsung-Dao Lee. Did anyone in the United States know about the work done by Abdus Salam? He asked. 'It is good that I did not make a bet. It would have resulted in a heavy loss of money (which I cannot afford). I did make a fool of myself, however (which I think I can afford to do)—incidentally, only in letters or orally and not in anything that was printed. But the others now have the right to laugh at me'. He went on lightly. On 19 January 1957, in his letter to Chien-Shiung Wu, the experimental physicist who had played a decisive role in confirming the theoretical scheme proposed by Chen Ning Yang and Tsung-Dao, he confessed being doubtful about the whole affair. He remarked that Abdus Salam's proposal had 'a certain beauty in itself' in relation to the 'description of the neutrino with a two-component spin only'.[2] Finally, he went public in offering the apology to Abdus Salam. He admitted discouraging Abdus Salam from publishing what held a vital value.[3]

Then there was the speculation that had Abdus Salam, after returning to Cambridge in 1954, cultivated stronger links with experimental physicists, he might have been better off rather than ignored. It sounded like an oblique reference to Abdus Salam's keenness on mathematical aesthetics overlooking the range of 'actual possibilities'.[4]

---

[1] *The Khaleej Times*, 23 August 1995, p. 4
[2] Abdul Ghani (1982): pp. 123-125
[3] The News, Islamabad, 29 January 1996, p. 6
[4] Jagjit Singh (1992): p. 54

According to Abdul Hameed, the benefit of United States citizenship might have won his brother greater publicity making him less likely to be overlooked.[1] Although the proposition sounded farfetched but made a certain amount of sense in view of Abdus Salam's relatively slender profile in the world of science in those days. At the Rochester Conference Banquet, only few months prior to the announcement of prizes for 1957, the influential physicist Victor Weisskopf referred to the recent breakthrough in parity violation and attributed the success to the international spirit of modern physics. He listed Lev Landau, Chen Ning Yang and Tsung-Dao Lee, missing out any mention of Abdus Salam, for developing the two-component theory. This was rather blatantly curious in view of the correspondence Wolfgang Pauli recently had with Victor Weisskopf. Abdus Salam did not take it silently. 'Your remark on internationalism would have been reinforced if you had mentioned my work also'. He walked to Victor Weisskopf and reminded him of the slip, intentional or otherwise.[2]

What exactly happened then is history today but to miss the Nobel Prize at 31 was not an ordinary setback for Abdus Salam. On his part, he made only a veiled mention of the episode in his Inaugural Lecture at Imperial College London on 14 May 1958. He did not touch the subject for years on. As a result, people seem to forget how close he came to getting the prize in 1957.

'It was a very well-deserved prize. Frank Yang and Tsung-Dao Lee had made a revolutionary suggestion to test the truth behind parity violation, and they won the recognition. The only thing that surprised many people was the speed with which the prize was announced. Although Alfred Nobel would have liked such efficiency but the recognition within months of a discovery had never happened before. What else do you want me to say?' He observed in 1984.[3]

He kept none grudge whatsoever against Wolfgang Pauli. In fact, after sharing the prize in 1979, he became magnanimous. 'The very fact that Wolfgang Pauli was interested in those topics meant he had the flexibility. Many other equally great physicists had simply given up the desire. If you are interested, you make remarks, right as well as wrong. Albert Einstein and Paul Dirac had returned into their shells, refusing to address questions the majority of younger scientists raised. With age they were hard bound in their old ideas and notions. They seemed to have lost the ability to question. Wolfgang Pauli had

---

[1] Abdul Hameed (circa 2000): p. 93
[2] Transcript of Interviews with Crease and Mann: February-March 1984, p. 34
[3] Interviews 1984: Folder VII, pp. 59-60

marvellous ideas. Even when he did not work on a new set of ideas, he listened and expressed his opinion. This was his style of enriching physics. Consider Paul Dirac, who stopped at 45, and went on doing, I should not say so, little things. It is better to be wrong than to fall out of the mainstream altogether. A pride over achievements has the built-in tendency to displace your focus of attention and people tend to develop a fear of being proved wrong. The world at large may still consider you a great man, but so far as problems of today are concerned the people in your subject area might take a different view. So much has changed in my own life time, since the Rochester Conference of 1955. At that time we considered strange particles as the whole problem and thought if this was solved there would be nothing more to do. Today, in 1984, not only have those issues disappeared from the scene but they are now a classical fraction of the current development. This is what makes science exciting'. He remarked.[1]

Rushing to seek the opinion of two peers was reminiscent of an old peculiarity from the past. Upon finding the meaning of a term, as a school boy in Jhang, Abdus Salam had almost ambushed his Arabic Language teacher. Such was the state of his excitement that his teacher reminded him to calm down. Moments after finding a different route to one of Ramanujan equations in Lahore's Government College, he had gate-crashed into the residence of his Mathematics professor at midnight. This state of innocent elation, he worked out in due course of time, did not payback in every moment of discovery. He began coming to terms with the fact that a full-blown reliance on merit alone could be deceitful. It did not take him long to appreciate the advantage Chen Ning Yang and Tsung-Dao Lee had commanded by staying in constant touch with the team of experimentalists under Chien-Shiung Wu.

Then, lapses in the memory of well-known scientists like Victor Weisskopf illustrated the eternal need to be on the guard and be counted instead going unnoticed. It was one of the vital lessons Abdus Salam had picked up in missing the prize. In future, he had to make sure that his contribution did not go unobserved.

---

[1] Interviews 1984: Folder VI, p. 44

III

Loyalty, Abdus Salam once remarked, constituted an important component of his life.[1] He was not far off the mark for there have been quite a few occasions in his life when the trait was duly demonstrated yielding outcomes both favourable and otherwise.

One such occasion was when he bypassed the offer of fellowship from Trinity College. It is not clear though when, how and in what shape the offer came but he was believed to have received one. As one of the oldest and most prestigious colleges in Cambridge, Trinity also profited from the charismatic glow created around it by Isaac Newton, his Principia and, of course, the famous apple tree. Standing side by side since medieval times, both Trinity and St John's had given England an enormous assortment of great scientists, philosophers, poets, writers, artists, clergymen and politicians. In this race and rivalry of scholarship to produce great minds, Trinity commanded a distinct lead over its neighbour. Especially, the list of Nobel Laureates in various disciplines of Natural Sciences at Trinity was three times bigger than that of St John's.

One of Abdus Salam's friends, Peter Lazette, a radio journalist in those days, promoted Trinity. Abdus Salam was not sure if he was prepared to cross the line. His friend asked him to cite a single good reason. You see, the lawns and rose-beds are better in St John's! Abdus Salam is reported to have shot back.[2]

His biographer, Abdul Ghani, a physicist himself, embellishes it as one of the rare occasion when someone preferred St John's over Trinity.[3] Speaking technically, Abdus Salam was a Research Fellow at St John's whereas Trinity offered him the position of Staff Fellowship. 'The Master of St John's was my old tutor and he indicated to accord me the same status. In those days, Staff Fellows supervised the college staff and in return received a special sum of money. I turned down the offer from Trinity'. Abdus Salam stated. 'I don't know if it was the first time that someone had refused the offer from Trinity, but certainly a very rare thing to happen. Although colleges do not matter much for physics which is a university affair, yet they pride the social life. Those lawns and rose-beds were most certainly an important element in the making up of my

---

[1] Interviews 1984: Folder VI, p. 33

[2] Ideals and Realities (1984): p.13

[3] Abdul Ghani (1982): p. 34

decision. I walked there and had the best of my thoughts. If not a Fellow at St John's, I would be chased out as a foreigner. Only college fellows were permitted to walk on those lawns, at least in my day. I feared a loss of the majestic privilege. It took me a long time to make the decision. Perhaps, I did not wish to be disloyal'. He recollected.[1]

Even when loyalty constituted a vital element of his personality, he understood its worth as a two-way affair. Over the years, with the taste of time spent in Lahore still fresh in his memory, he could not afford to be platonic all out. Time was fast approaching, he could see, to test the strength of his devotion and dependence on Cambridge.

An audit of options available to him by the close of 1955 was plain and straightforward. His contract for Stokes Lectureship was due for renewal by the end of December 1956. He stood fairly good prospects of getting an extension but the question was how long someone in his class and situation could continue hanging on to lectureship contracts? Would the Government of Pakistan be equally responsive in stretching his secondment? In spite of everything, his substantive position of a chair in Lahore was permanent. It amounted to financial stability. On the domestic front, as such, he was expected to share the burden of educating his siblings until they could be on their own. His own family was young; he had yet to buy a house. A lectureship in Cambridge would run out of its provisional value one day not far away. But then going back to Lahore would most likely compromise his career in Physics. Three years of professional effort at Cambridge had brought him back upon the centre-stage of Theoretical Physics but the essentials of long-term financial security stood more or less unchanged. Cambridge or elsewhere, his future in Physics depended upon securing a position that made it possible for him to focus upon research, build up a team of his own and achieve a certain degree of logistical liberty.

So, there were questions within questions. Still, he found himself much better placed. Albert Einstein had published three classic papers on Brownian motion but it took him nearly ten years to complete his journey from the Swiss Patent Office to Kaiser Wilhelm Institute in Berlin. Abdus Salam was luckier to have been saved from serving a purely non-academic position at any point in the formative stage of his career. While teaching at Cambridge, he was strategically stationed to seek a higher position somewhere in England.

---

[1] Interviews 1984: Folder VI, pp. 30-34

About the end of autumn in 1955, the position of a Readership in Theoretical Physics fell vacant at the University of Liverpool in northern England. It happened so when the incumbent, Kenneth Le Couteur (1920–2011), accepted the position of Foundation Professor of Theoretical Physics at the Australian National University in Canberra. In a matter of days, Abdus Salam received encouraging signals. Although Liverpool was far away, the pressure to find a permanent position compelled him to pursue the opportunity. In November 1955, he received a letter from Herbert Fröhlich, the Professor of Theoretical Physics in Liverpool University, confirming the availability of job. 'We are now looking for someone who is interested in meson theory and Nuclear Physics and who would like to have some contact with the experimental work going on here. I wonder whether you are interested'. Herbert Fröhlich asked him. Looks like universities in England, in those days, were packed with scholars and scientists of Jewish origin. Herbert Fröhlich (1905–1991) had studied physics at Munich University and had to leave Germany due to racial discrimination unleashed by the Nazi regime.

Seeking an opinion, Abdus Salam approached Nicholas Kemmer who responded on 1 December 1955 and sounded cautious rather than cheerful and underlined the need to check out few items before arriving at a decision. From Nicholas Kemmer's point of view, it was necessary to make sure that sufficient funds were available for fellowships and that the Reader in Liverpool had a role in the future planning. Also, there was the need to ensure that a good level of cooperation existed with experimental physicists. Ideally, he advised Abdus Salam to visit Liverpool and 'talk things thoroughly over' with Herbert Fröhlich. Because Abdus Salam was keen to have his parents over from Pakistan, Nicholas Kemmer commented that Liverpool did not match the diversity of London yet the place had much to offer than getting stranded in some other farther location. At this point in his letter, Nicholas Kemmer hinted that the Imperial College in London was scheduled for expansion and Patrick Blackett, who headed the Department of Physics in the college, might consider offering Abdus Salam a Readership. Apparently, Patrick Blackett had asked Nicholas Kemmer if Abdus Salam might be interested. 'I did not answer this question with a direct no, but pointed out the special financial commitments that you would have. I have not heard from him since, and except for the fact that the Imperial College job still seems to be unfilled, I am not aware of any vacancies in London'. Nicholas Kemmer informed Abdus Salam. 'One more point perhaps—since I do feel that it ought not to be very long before you get a full chair, accepting Liverpool might mean two moves within a short time and that of course is always a problem, particularly as in my experience at least, one always seems to lose in buying and re-selling a house'. He concluded in a tone matching, once again, that of a caring older brother.

It is hard to guess how much of future Abdus Salam could read in his situation back in 1955, but he seemed quite clear on three counts. One, if he wanted to do Physics, the mistake of a return to Lahore must be avoided. Two, the Stokes Lectureship at Cambridge was not an end in itself; he had to leap forward sooner than later. Three, London more than Lahore or Liverpool suited best for the kind of career and lifestyle he aspired to achieve. By then, he received another offer from the University of Rochester in New York though it was for a Visiting Professorship. With a permanent job in Lahore, offers received from Liverpool and Rochester, and one year to go in the renewable contract with Cambridge, he stood firm. Like an adept player of chess, he was set to make smart moves.

On 27 January 1956, Herbert Skinner (1900–1960), the Lyon-Jones Professor of Physics in Liverpool University, offered Abdus Salam the Readership in Liverpool with an annual salary of £1850. Herbert Skinner chaired the Nuclear Physics Research Laboratory. After studying Physics in Cambridge, he had been a leader of the physics division at Harwell, the home of British nuclear energy research establishment. During World War II he was a member of the British team working on development of radar system. He sounded very keen to bring Abdus Salam over to Liverpool. In a follow-up to the offer of Readership, Abdus Salam received further information to the effect that the Senate of Liverpool University had granted approval to fill in the vacancy and the position would not be advertised. 'This was specially arranged so that an offer could be made to you, so there is no doubt at all that if you want it you can have the post at a salary of £1850'. Herbert Skinner wrote hoping that Abdus Salam's appointment would make a big difference. 'I am sure our experimental staff as well as the theoretical staff would be very happy if you could see your way to accepting the appointment'. He remarked.

By then, however, Abdus Salam received an unexpected visitor in Cambridge. This visitor was Patrick Blackett, the Head of Physics Department in London's Imperial College. Over twenty-five-year senior in age and saturated with worldly experience, Patrick Blackett (1897–1974) had worked at the

Cavendish Laboratory under Ernest Rutherford, winning the 1948 Nobel Prize for his work in atomic transmutation. He had championed the cause of operational research in Britain during World War II.

Ideologically, Patrick Blackett was fairly close to being a militant socialist. He enjoyed friendship with Homi Bhabha, the Chairman of India's Atomic Energy Commission, and had been a frequent visitor to India as the guest of Prime Minister Jawaharlal Nehru. He was known also for his readiness to advocate and provide political asylum to Jewish scholars who had been uprooted in Europe, in the wake of Nazi tide.[1]

Although Abdus Salam was fond of implanting a bit commotion into the memory of his first one on one encounter with Patrick Blackett, back in the Spring of 1956, as an episode bursting out of the blue, there is indication that their meeting was already in the making. While headhunting academics for expansion of Physics Department in Imperial College, Patrick Blackett had already checked out with Nicholas Kemmer if Abdus Salam might be interested in a Readership. As for the Chair in Mathematics, it was first offered to Brian Flowers (1924–2010) who declined to accept creating space for Abdus Salam though inadvertently. On a subsequent visit to Cambridge, Patrick Blackett went to seek staffing advice from an old friend, Hans Bethe. Known to one another for nearly two decades, as the two shared interest in cosmic radiation, Hans Bethe nodded that the man Patrick Blackett was looking for worked next door. Patrick Blackett took the advice in letter and spirit, he went to see Abdus Salam and found him drowned in a stack of notes in the Reading Room. He tapped Abdus Salam on the shoulder, stretched out his hand and introduced himself. Abdus Salam warmly shook the hand of the unexpected visitor he had known only from a distance. Can we go for coffee? Patrick Blackett asked. Sure, Abdus Salam replied and the two stepped down three flights of stairs to walk towards the kiosk.

With two solid references supporting Abdus Salam, one from Nicholas Kemmer and the other from Hans Bethe, it did not take Patrick Blackett long in arriving at a decision. As soon as the two sat across the table, he offered Abdus Salam the Chair of Mathematics at Imperial College. 'Of course, you will have to go through the formalities of selection procedure', Patrick Blackett stated.

---

[1] Originally, the campaign for this purpose was launched by scholars like George Trevelyan (1876-1962), Joseph Thomson (1856-1940), Ernest Rutherford (1871-1937) and William Beveridge (1879-1963). [Refer to David Cannadine's biography of G M Trevelyan, Penguin Group, 1992]

Abdus Salam was overwhelmed in advance when Patrick Blackett told him about the imminent creation of an independent Department of Theoretical Physics in Imperial College.

Later, Abdus Salam used to revisit the episode of his encounter with Patrick Blackett as one of the favourite moments of his life. 'He ordered coffee and then asked if I would accept a Chair at the Imperial College. I was taken aback and asked where? In the Department of Mathematics at the Imperial College, he replied. This was the Chair once held by Alfred Whitehead. I could only stammer out an affirmative. That was my first meeting with him though I knew about him and his work. He was a very tall and handsome man, very highly respected in the British circles of science and technology, afterwards a president of the Royal Society. His question sounded very strange to me'. Abdus Salam remembered his surprise visitor who then went on to explain the administrative hierarchy in Imperial College by comparing the system with Cambridge.

On top of earning the offer of a Chair in London, Abdus Salam prided the role played in its finalisation by Hans Bethe (1906–2005), the star-gazing nuclear physicist known for his breakthrough in the understanding of stellar energy. What a sparkling sky, Hans Bethe's wife is reported to have said as she stood next to her husband facing Mexican desert. 'You know, my darling, you are standing next to someone in this world who knows as to *why* stars sparkle'. Hans Bethe is reported to have replied; it was the evening he had completed his work for which the Nobel Prize was awarded to him some three decades later.

Effectively, the appeal of Readership in Liverpool should have ended there and then, just as abruptly as the offer of a Chair in London had fallen in his lap. But Abdus Salam preferred to wait for a formal confirmation from Imperial College. As such, the process of negotiation with Liverpool continued uninterrupted. On a visit to London, Herbert Skinner invited Abdus Salam over for dinner at the Athenaeum Club, a magnificent venue to dine. Since its foundation more than a century ago when Michael Faraday served as its first secretary, the club membership prided upon names like James Maxwell, John Ruskin, Charles Dickens, Thomas Hardy, Herbert Spencer, Alfred Tennyson, Benjamin Disraeli and Rudyard Kipling. In more recent times, the club had made it to a section of the political fiction produced by Charles Snow (1905–1980) and themes woven around the Soviet espionage of British nuclear program. As for Abdus Salam, he did not wish to slam the door on Liverpool apparently for two reasons. One, he felt vulnerable until the chair in London was secured. Two,

Liverpool held enormous value in the framework of his ambition to play a role in bringing nuclear knowhow to Pakistan in the near future. He was not secretive at all. In fact, he appeared to have shared the information of upcoming chair in London with Herbert Skinner. All at once, throughout the course of negotiations with the University of Liverpool, he kept Mohammad Ikramullah, the Pakistani High Commissioner in London, in the information loop.

In the process, there were occasions when he came fairly close to testing the patience of his prospective employers in Liverpool by asking them for terms under which he could spend up to four months of a year in Pakistan. He went as far as exploring the possibility of getting a family fare from Pakistan. 'If you had been resident in Pakistan at the time of your Cambridge appointment, the University would have been willing to pay. But the difficulty is that you are in fact resident in England and the appointment looks like subscribing to a holiday. If it was in the terms of your appointment at Cambridge that they would pay for sending you and your family back to Pakistan at the end of your contract, this might possibly alter the way in which the University would look at the matter, though I certainly cannot guarantee that. The University will pay your removal expenses up to a sum of £50'. A nearly stressed-out Herbert Skinner wrote to Abdus Salam on 3 March 1956.

On 20 March 1956, the Registrar of the University of Liverpool, Stanley Dumbell, formally invited Abdus Salam 'to accept appointment' as Reader in Theoretical Physics at the Faculty of Science as from 1 April 1956. While waiting for a formal follow-up from London, Abdus Salam considered visiting Liverpool. He asked Herbert Skinner if Liverpool University could upgrade its offer. 'These matters are subject to a definite formal routine—they have to be passed through the Senate, and of course there is some possibility of opposition. The difficulty is that, in theory, a professor is supposed in British Universities to be the head of a department, and we already have a professor of Theoretical Physics. But things are beginning to change'. He explained the situation to Abdus Salam in his letter dated 27 June 1956 promising to 'put into action the same mechanism' for Abdus Salam. But he was not in a position to make any definite commitment in terms of timeframe. 'I am afraid this is as far as I can go. I have so far been successful with most of my proposals, but in an organisation such as a university, it is impossible to make a definite promise beforehand'. Unaware of the Ahmadiyah preference for introversion, Herbert Skinner tempted

Abdus Salam to consider Liverpool on a religious scale as well. He reckoned Abdus Salam's family 'would be happier in Liverpool than in London'.

On 25 April 1956, Abdus Salam received a brief note from Patrick Blackett stating that Reginald Linstead, the Rector of the Imperial College, was about to invite him for an interview 'to talk over matters'. This signalled the formal commencement of selection procedure in London. Abdus Salam received the invitation; he went to meet the Rector who then directed the University of London to convene the job interview against the vacant Chair of Applied Mathematics at the Imperial College. James Henderson, the Registrar of the University of London, confirmed the interview date the next day. 'Reasonable travelling expenses (including 3rd class railway fare) may be claimed. The decision of the Board of Advisors cannot be made known on the day of the meeting and you will be free after your interview'. The Registrar advised Abdus Salam.

After being shortlisted as the only candidate, Abdus Salam was predestined to win the Chair. He appeared before an interview panel comprising of four members, that is, the Vice-Chancellor and the Academic Registrar representing the University of London; with professors George Temple and Patrick Blackett as subject experts. Professor George Temple (1901–1992), who occupied the Sedleian Chair of Natural Philosophy at the University of Oxford, invited the candidate to comment upon the 'Fundamental Theory' of Arthur Eddington. Abdus Salam expected to face this question in some shape because he was aware of George Temple's keenness on the subject. He did not wish to embroil himself by appearing to take a position, one way or another. It had not been possible for him to read through 'the works of Sir Arthur with the detachment of a dispassionate mind'. He replied. George Temple was visibly amused with the diplomatic deflection. Although Abdus Salam escaped the momentary trial of raising doubts about the Fundamental Theory, he still had good reasons to admire Arthur Eddington.

Earlier in the 20th century, the Royal Society of Britain had granted Arthur Eddington (1882–1944) a sum of £10,000 to observe the solar eclipse of May 1919. His photographic measurements on the deflection of light, recorded in the island of Principe near Africa, confirmed the Theory of General Relativity (1915) securing Albert Einstein instant fame worldwide. In 1920, Arthur Eddington pioneered the idea that stellar energy resulted from a nuclear fusion of hydrogen and helium. But then he evolved a unification model in his

Fundamental Theory that many of his younger contemporaries believed was more of a mystical rather than a scientific exercise.

By the end of summer 1956, Abdus Salam received the job offer from Imperial College. He was invited to start in October the same year. Reginald Linstead, the Rector, sent him a note of welcome. Geoffrey Lowry, the Secretary to the College Administration advised him about his entitlement. 'There is a small fund here for such emergencies, and the maximum grant that can be authorised to assist a new Professor for removal and for travelling expenses of himself and members of his family is £250. The Rector has agreed that the maximum grant of up to £250 should supply in your case'. Abdus Salam expressed the desire to assume charge of the position with the beginning of 1957. His request was granted by the Imperial College.

Turning 31 in another few months, Abdus Salam was set to occupy the Chair once owned by the eminent British philosopher and mathematician Alfred North Whitehead (1861–1947). Had his contribution towards parity violation been taken into account, he might have come with a Nobel Prize. 'In about three years' time we hope to have a new Physics Building and then be able to allocate in it a number of rooms for members of the Mathematics and Physics staffs who would like to use them'. His sponsor, Patrick Blackett, assured him.

According to his biographer, Abdul Ghani, the success of Abdus Salam in making it to the Mathematics Chair in the British capital betrayed hopes of intellectual revival among Muslims who had lost the initiative 'in the face of the revolutionary progress of the Christian world'.[1] Historically, the only citizen of the subcontinent who held a Chair in England before Abdus Salam was Servepalli Radhakrishnan (1888–1975), the Professor of Eastern Religions and Ethics at the University of Oxford. In 1962, Servepalli Radhakrishnan became the President of India.

Brian Flowers, who had declined to accept the position before it was offered to Abdus Salam, went on to serve as Rector of Imperial College from 1973 to 1985. After winning the Nobel Prize, when Abdus Salam arrived to deliver a talk at the college, Brian Flower is reported to have lightly remarked that he had turned down the job offer in 1956 'to the lasting benefit of the College'.[2]

Before starting work at the Imperial College, Abdus Salam consulted his peers in Pakistan. He received the advice to go ahead for his appointment as a

---

[1] Abdul Ghani (1982): p. 36
[2] Gordon Fraser (2008): p. 139

professor in London amounted to enhancement of Pakistan's national prestige abroad. He reported for duty in the first week of January 1957 and resigned from his substantive position in Lahore. In London, he was going to earn three folds more than his annual income in Cambridge. All new professors were expected to deliver an Inaugural Lecture at the Imperial College in order to introduce themselves and their work. Usually, a lecture lasted for one hour and ranged between six to eight thousand words. Often, in those days, the function started with late afternoon tea followed by the lecture after which guests dined together. Abdus Salam's Inaugural Lecture was scheduled to take place on 14 May 1957. Reginald Linstead ((1902–1966), the Rector, guided Abdus Salam with useful hints about the complexion of the audience.

While preparing for his inaugural lecture titled as Elementary Particles, Abdus Salam felt the need for a bit of celebration. Fitting the occasion, he wished to be formally dressed. He had heard that the founder of Pakistan, Mohammed Ali Jinnah, used to have his clothing tailored in London's Mayfair district at a prestigious establishment on Seville Row, near Regent Street. He signalled his brother, Abdul Hameed, to accompany him and the two walked into Gieves & Hawkes, a tailoring business known for its services to the aristocracy. An elderly salesman received them with a question mark on his face. Have you been here before? Do you have a reference letter from any of our esteemed clients? He asked. Somewhat embarrassed about the prerequisite, Abdus Salam pulled back. 'Well, in that case, I am sorry, sir, we cannot offer you much assistance', came the verdict from the salesman. But then, just as the two brothers walked out, the salesman enquired Abdus Salam about the nature of his work. 'Oh, I teach at the Imperial College'. Abdus Salam introduced himself unpretentiously.

'Well, in that case', as if the salesman underwent an instant metamorphosis, 'it would be our honour, sir, to serve a university academic'. He invited Abdus Salam to select the fabric of his choice. For years, Abdul Hameed remembered how the measurements were taken there and then for the dress to be ready in time. He believed the sudden change of mind on the part of Gieves & Hawkes reflected the European regard for scholarship.

On the day of his lecture for which posters had already been displayed around the college, Abdus Salam stood before an audience comprising of the Imperial College Governing Board, honorary fellows, professors emeriti, serving academics, members of the boards of study for physics and mathematics, chief scientific liaison officers from the embassies of India and Pakistan, selected media representatives, and Abdus Salam's own guests from universities and research institutions in Cambridge, Birmingham, Manchester and Harwell.

Professor Patrick Blackett, Dean of the Royal College of Science, presided the meeting. Before introducing the speaker, he reminded the audience that they were actually sitting in the very building where, in the 1920s, famous Indian astrophysicist Professor Meghanad Saha (1893–1956) had collaborated with Professor Ralph Fowler (1889–1944) to study ionisation in stellar atmosphere thus opening up a whole new branch of Physics. Then he turned his attention towards Abdus Salam. 'I want just to say, how extremely honoured we are here at Imperial College to have as a professor a citizen of the great subcontinent' and 'we hope he will be with us for a very long time and distinguish himself, as I know he will, and bring glory to his colleagues'. Patrick Blackett decanted lavish praise by recounting Abdus Salam's 'meteoric academic career' in the final days of colonial Punjab when the choice before him was whether to study English Literature or Mathematics. 'Luckily for Physics and Imperial College, he chose the latter'.

When Abdus Salam started speaking, he remembered the piece of advice Rector had offered him about the absorption capacity of a general audience before him. He summed up the contribution of modern age physicists, hastened to recapitulate more recent developments, then rephrased the Orwellian jargon by referring to the current classification of nuclear interactions as 'all particles are elementary, but some are more elementary than others'. He pictured challenges confronting his own generation of physicists by citing recent events relating to parity violation in weak interactions. In his concluding remarks he acknowledged being a part of the generation of scientists entrusted with the fascinating challenge of finding answers to the finer mysteries of nature. 'The u-meson may seem out of place to-day. When we discover its real nature, we shall marvel how neatly it fits into the Great Scheme, how integral a part it is of something deeper, more profound, and more transcending.

'This faith in the inner harmony of nature has paid dividends in the past. I am confident it will continue to do so in the future.' He ended by quoting a verse from the Koran:

Thou seest not in the creation
Of the All-merciful any imperfection
Return thy gaze; seest thou any fissure?

Then return thy gaze again, and again,
And thy gaze comes back to thee, dazzled, aweary[1]

Displaying one's religious makeup out in the open was out of fashion in those days, especially in a London carried away by secular-socialist anti-war movements. Possibly, Abdus Salam aimed at touching upon a chord of cultural identity. Twenty-two years later, he recited the same verse in his speech at the Nobel Banquet in Sweden.

Somewhat appallingly, in view of the quality of his work, none gesture whatsoever was made to save him for something worthwhile in Cambridge. Perhaps the closest a couple of his colleagues came in convincing him to stay on in Cambridge was by way of arrogant sarcasm. To people in Cambridge, Imperial College equalled the workplace of a blacksmith where crude business of machine tools took precedence over sophisticated instruments of surgery. Neville Mott (1905–1996), the Cavendish Professor Physics, offered Abdus Salam to join the editorial team of *Philosophical Magazine* and not leave Cambridge. It sounded honourable but the exercise amounted to less money for more of the same work.

Apart from Stokes Lectureship, Cambridge had decorated him with prestigious prizes like Hopkins and Adams but the offer a chair did not turn up. This reticence remains a mystery. Once, after winning the Nobel Prize, he was invited to comment on his chances of promotion in Cambridge. He took the remissive fatherly position and made only a hypothetical statement that positions in Cambridge depended upon work and vacancies. He did not rule out the possibility of becoming a professor at Cambridge one day, especially in view of his work in parity. But then, he remarked, it was all 'very speculative' way back in the 1950s.[2]

Later, one of Abdus Salam's contemporaries in Cambridge, Fred Hoyle, commented that an offer of professorship, even a delayed one, might have worked. 'I always hoped that one day Abdus Salam would return to Cambridge and I think that an offer of a Chair in Theoretical Physics would indeed have brought him back'. Fred Hoyle recalled. No such offer was ever made. On a couple of occasions though, the Faculty of Mathematics opted to fill in vacancies with people having expertise in Quantum Mechanics rather than Theoretical

---

[1] Arberry, A. J., The Koran Interpreted, L XVII (2-4)
[2] Interviews 1984: Folder VI, p. 104

Physics. 'This I did not believe myself and it was one of the reasons why from the mid-1960s my relations with the faculty fell to zero point'. Fred Hoyle stated.[1]

Years of Abdus Salam's close association with Cambridge ended in December 1956. He took time in conquering the withdrawal symptoms. In spite of making the move to London, he retained the house in Cambridge for many months.

'The great beauty of Cambridge and its intellectual atmosphere made the main reason behind my reluctance. I knew London as a very different place, a city where it was hard to find a decent bookshop. Even after migrating there, I kept visiting Cambridge and Oxford only to explore bookshops. He reminisced later by accepting the fact that a saturation point of his career had already been achieved in Cambridge where a great deal of his energies and time got consumed into supervising undergraduate students. 'This was what made me leave Cambridge when I was offered a chair at Imperial College. I did not have great desire to leave a delightful place like Cambridge, an institution geared to scholarship. It has got all facilities to do research with its marvellous community. I was so attached that I kept my house there for six months after my departure, it just remained empty but I didn't leave it. Then of course I had to give it up, it was stupid keep paying the rent for the college flat. My Cambridge life is full of rich memories. This small town offered all facilities of learning'.[2]

Perhaps his only sour memory of Cambridge was the failure in picking up the Driving License in the first round. He paid for his inability in reversing satisfactorily.

Moving to London ushered an era of great gains in both his personal and professional spheres of life. He was familiar with only a part of the city but had not come to live there as such on a permanent call. His wife, Amtul Hafeez, was in Pakistan when he began working at the Imperial College. In December 1956, she had given birth to their third and youngest daughter, Bushra. Initially, Abdus Salam made a temporary arrangement to share accommodation with his brother, Abdul Hameed, who rented a flat on Old Brompton Road not far from the Imperial College. Living near the college enabled him to spend more time at work and be able to build up an efficient routine from the very outset.

---

[1] Abdul Hameed (circa 2000): pp. 55-56
[2] Interviews 1984: Folder VI, pp. 23-24 and 67-68

IV

Within one year of his move to London, Abdus Salam was elected to the fellowship of Royal Society. At the time of his election to the society, established in 1633, he was 33 and one of the youngest to have been honoured with membership. Overjoyed, his father believed it was time to revisit the vision foretelling Abdus Salam's arrival on the birthday of the King of England. In this way, he found another connection underlining his vision; to him the prophecy made a greater sense in the context of his son's academic gains at Imperial College and Royal Society.[1]

London, one of the most adored and sought after places in the world, the capital city of England, the home of Hyde Park, Buckingham Palace, Westminster Abbey, Westminster House, Monument to the Great Fire, St Paul's Cathedral and over two dozen bridges connecting the banks of River Thames. With an eventful history spread out upon two millennia, and despite the end of raj, the place continued to be a major hub of financial drama on capitalist centre stage. This imperial seat of British Empire, from where the fate of three generations of Abdus Salam's forefathers had been dictated, opened its arms to embrace him as one its proud residents. In 1957, When Abdus Salam made London his home, the less than a hundred population figure of the original Roman settlement upon river Thames had geometrically multiplied to approach the nine million mark of a vastly bustling modern metropolis.

Life in London manifested another striking change in Abdus Salam's social environment. From the tranquillity of medieval university town and its colleges in Cambridge, he found himself in the midst of corporate business, from a classical environment of fundamental sciences to the forefront of technological advancement. London represented a high-tech and high-speed life of finance, business, politics, diplomacy and defence, all overlapping upon one another. His journey from Jhang to Multan, Lahore and Cambridge had brought him into a world of buses, underground trains, supermarkets, shopping malls, cars, clubs, night life, tourists, show biz, fashion, celebrities, politicians, diplomats, high-rise architecture, traffic jams, evening newspapers, crime, television, cinema, air-travel, traffic lights, neon signs, and what not. Lifestyles in London ranged between cut-throat competition to being trampled over by the clever and the

---

[1] Mohammed Hussein (1974): p. 47

cheeky. He was going to see how the boy from rural outback of Punjab would fare in London, the most substantial of all stations in his life. Winning the Chair at 31, something the majority of university academics took twenty years to gain was a challenge in itself. On the plus side, he was starting where others concluded.

After settling down to a steady routine at work, there was the need for him to consider buying a house. As far as one could see into the future, he was going to be a more or less permanent resident of London from now onwards. He ended up finding a house on Campion Road in Putney, a suburb next to Wimbledon in the south-western borough of Wandsworth. Putney attracted him not because the suburb was closer to Imperial College, across the river, or that it had been the home of great English statesman Oliver Cromwell (1599–1658), historian Edward Gibbon (1737–1794) and the post-war prime minister Clement Atlee (1883–1967); his choice was based upon the easier access the suburb offered to Ahmadiyah mosque in Southfields. He looked forward to having his parents over soon.

Mohammed Hussein and Hajira arrived in England in April 1959. About then, Abdul Rashid, one of the younger siblings of Abdus Salam, migrated to England. His arrival made life much easier for the family in many ways. He fitted himself smoothly into the role of a dependable resource person everyone could count upon in everyday contingencies. He would drive or pick up his brother to and from Heathrow airport at a much shorter notice, and quite enthusiastically. Abdus Salam's parents lived in London for nearly three years. By then, Amtul Hafeez had become well accustomed to life in England. Adept at looking after the home front, she was doubly bonded to her in-laws. London, unlike Cambridge, offered her a good deal of opportunity to socialise. She had begun taking active part in the Ahmadiyah women organisation, *Lajnalma'ullah* or the *Housekeepers of Lord*.

Occasionally, Abdus Salam felt worried that his father might be bored sitting home all the time. One day, he had an appointment with Queen's husband Prince Phillip (1921–2021), the Duke of Edinburgh. He asked his father to come along and meet the prince. But then he found a more regular solution by asking the Imam of the Ahmadiyah Mosque to create voluntary work for his father. It did not take very long for the Imam to oblige.

Often, Mohammed Hussein took the bus to Ahmadiyah mosque where the faithful revered him for the astonishing example he had set in bringing up a son like Abdus Salam. He coached the children of the first-generation of expatriates by nourishing their need for the Ahmadiyah brand of spirituality. This pastime of Mohammed Hussein liberated Abdus Salam from the worry that his ageing father might feel lonely or stranded. It did not take Mohammed Hussein long to acknowledge the fact that his son had bought the house in Putney due to its convenient access to the Ahmadiyah mosque. While writing down his memoirs, he recounted an episode from the early history of Islam. According to the tradition, a devotee had requested Prophet Mohammed to bless his newly built dwelling. Upon arriving at the site, the Prophet pointed at a window and asked the host what purpose it would serve? Ventilation and light, of course, replied the disciple. Correct, remarked the Prophet, adding that the window also enabled him to receive the call for prayer, the *azan* and that it should be heeded as a source of lifelong blessing upon the house. Drawing the parallel, Mohammed Hussein observed that Abdus Salam's choice to live conveniently near the Ahmadiyah mosque, for the sake his parents, was a source of lifelong blessing to a caring son.[1]

Some 64 years later, in November 2020, the English Heritage, an institution minding hundreds of historical sites, installed its Blue Plaque on the street face of this house Abdus Salam had bought soon after accepting the Chair in Imperial College. This superbly engraved blue ceramic plaque, acknowledged the residence as a place where Abdus Salam had lived between 1957 and 1996. His achievements listed on the plaque defined him as a Physicist, Nobel Laureate and a 'champion of science in developing countries'.[2]

This house on 8 Campion Road comprised of average features in a Putney home, that is, four rooms with common areas and a lawn on the rear. Soon the traffic of guests picked up momentum; relatives and friends from Pakistan, both London-bound and those who were in transit en route to destinations across the Atlantic, paused to spend time with the family. Then there was a steady stream of Abdus Salam's colleagues and students. He invited them every now and then over masala curries prepared by Amtul Hafeez. 'My father', Abdus Salam's eldest daughter Aziza Rahman remembered, 'loved to invite people to our house which he called as the best restaurant in the city'. It was his fitting tribute to the cooking expertise of Amtul Hafeez.

---

[1] Mohammed Hussein (1974): p. 49-50
[2] Putney Newsletter: 4 December 2020 (online edition)

Once in London, Abdus Salam got exceedingly busier. His much-adored lifestyle of Cambridge was history. Before the end of his first decade in London, he took different roles upon himself and juggled to strike a balance. From 1958 onwards, he found himself exceedingly involved in the development of scientific and educational infra-structure in Pakistan. Later, in 1964, he became the founding Director of the United Nations sponsored International Centre for Theoretical Physics in Trieste, Italy. As such, his full-time work at Imperial College was scaled down to a visiting professorship.

He considered himself very lucky to own a house, southwest of river Thames, for its quicker approach to Heathrow airport. While buying the house, he had not truly foreseen the size of travelling his professional life was about to demand. 'Between 1958 and 1968, when Ayub Khan was still very strong; much of my time and thinking were spent in service of Pakistan. Frequent trips to Pakistan had become an important feature of my routine. Then, Trieste was added to the itinerary in 1964. All this would have been simply impossible had I lived on in Cambridge'.[1] He recalled.

His later day roles demanded a nomadic life-style. There would be occasions, he remembered, when his lectures were scheduled in four or five countries within one week. Drifting away from the family, farther on the map of professional rather than a personal world, he became an extremely preoccupied father to his children. He realised it, and felt the pinch. Aziza Rahman remembered how travelling took her father all over the world. He attempted to relieve himself of the anxiety, especially the concern about the education of his children, by giving them heaps of assignments from workbooks. He would direct them to dispense with the allocated work by the time of his next visit home. He would keep a watch on their grades and academic progress reports. 'Do your best and leave the rest to Allah'. He would tell them just as his father had told him. Aziza Rahman recalled.

One day, he showed one of his daughters a novel way to solve the mathematics problem she had brought as homework from school. Next day, the girl received a reprimand from her mathematics teacher. 'Either you fail in the examination or listen to your father'.

He did not approve of television and believed it amounted to an outright squandering of valuable time. As a result, the family did not own a television set. 'Of course, as children, we used to complain about this, but now I am truly

---

[1] Interviews 1984: Folder VI, pp. 61-68

thankful to him because in the end we benefited as we spent more time reading'. Aziza Rahman reminisced. She remembered the day when, to the utter surprise of children, he invited them to watch *Lawrence of Arabia* in a cinema hall. There was such an excitement but they had been only half way through when he declared the film was bloody well too long and it would be better to leave it there and return home. 'Terribly disappointed, we begged him to let us see the rest'. He gave in but went out of the cinema hall himself to wait for them in the car. After the film, the children found him doing theoretical physics on sheets of paper balanced on the steering wheel. Upon returning home, he asked them to write an essay on Colonel Thomas Lawrence (1888–1936) to appreciate how his life and times had inspired the film makers.[1]

On his way to the college on Sunday mornings, sometimes he took children with him and then would leave them at the Natural History Museum in Kensington. On other occasions, when the girls stayed behind his son, Ahmad Salam, accompanied him to the college. He would leave the little boy under the care of one or another of his doctoral students. Ahmad Salam remembered those childhood visits to Imperial College as an indicator on the part of his father to culture in him an interest in mathematics and physics. 'I do not know who was more nervous in those situations', Ahmad Salam recalled later picturing the plight of his reluctant carers.[2] In due course of time, when Ahmad Salam matured to take the responsibility of driving his father around, he realised the value of company the two had shared. Over time, it became harder to expand the delight of being together 'in the space of a few short hours' especially when his father happened to be 'on a fleeting trip to London'.

Coming to terms with the sorrow of a childhood and youth without full-time father around must have been tough for the children. 'I remember clearly, at the age of six or so, moving my bedding into his room just so that I could be with him on one night when he was in London. I now realise that when he would ask me to come and drop him at Imperial College, or come to the airport to see him off, this was his way of trying to find time to be with me. These car journeys became extremely important for him to catch-up and give me a few ideas and some guidance, and though I did not realise it, it taught me some very valuable lessons. More often than not, it would be for him an important opportunity to give me an explanation on how something worked, such as a car engine, or

---

[1] *Al-Nahl* (Fall 1997): pp. 50-54
[2] *Al-Nahl* (Fall 1997): p. 55

human heart, or how to solve simultaneous equations, or to give some story of a famous Rajput warrior or prince. These were extremely important moments for both of us'.[1]

Abdus Salam wanted his children to be on their own. He declined Ahmad Salam a loan to buy car on grounds that his son needed to appreciate the effort required to achieve an ambition.[2] On other occasions, he encouraged his children to visit places of historical, archaeological and cultural significance. Whenever the family could avail the opportunity to picnic in Richmond Park, an extensive nature reserve west of London, he would switch off the car engine to demonstrate and explain how gearing regulated the relationship between mass and motion. His children were required to relate to the physics lesson in their next trip to Richmond Park as they watched him in excitement to see 'if he remembered to apply the brakes'. No wonder he had failed his first Driving Test in Cambridge.[3]

Time management made the day for Abdus Salam since his childhood when he tended to take a rather obese table-clock from home to the playground. Time and tide waited for none, was not just a proverb to him. He worked tirelessly. 'Even when at home, he would spend hours engrossed in hard toil in his room, coming out only on meal times'. According to Aziza Rahman, wastage of time would be an intolerable sin for him. Unless he was travelling, Abdus Salam worked without distinction between weekdays and weekends. He went to bed by nine in the evening to wake up very early in the 'silent hours' of the night to resume his work which amounted to reading, writing, thinking, calculating and planning. Despite his own stoicism towards health or money matters, he alerted his children to the need for 'early to bed and early to rise' in order to be 'healthy, wealthy and wise'.

He found the climate in Europe unacceptably cold and preferred to heat up his room even when other members of the family found the weather generally pleasant. He aimed at creating a distinctively unique ambience in his room. In her memorial essay about her father, a rare touch upon some personal and family aspects of Abdus Salam, his daughter Aziza Rahman dredged up her memories in 1997. 'My father had created his own very personal atmosphere tinged with

---

[1] Trieste Tribute (1997): p. 128
[2] *Al Nahl* (Fall 1997): p. 56
[3] When it was possible for him to afford, Abdus Salam bought a Mercedes Benz car, a status symbol among affluent Pakistanis.

an air of mystery in his room'. He had incense sticks strategically lit around him 'sending spirals of heavily perfumed smoke in all directions'.

While working he hated noise, especially the screeching of vehicles speeding on Campion Road. For that reason, the windows were sound-proofed and double glazed with impenetrable velvety drapes. 'From an early age, we all knew not to raise our voices or run around inside ... even the phone was taken off the hook if it rang once too often'. He loved though to have an audio-cassette of Koranic recitation switched on in the background.

His lengthy sessions of sturdiness with work were punctuated with 'brief catnaps' and an endless supply of sweet and hot tea. Before going to bed, Amtul Hafeez and the girls made sure to top up his thermos of tea and the snacks on the side table. As for his keenness on swirls of incensed smoke and sweet hot tea, the peculiarity amused his children because they were strangers to the shrines and roadside kiosks of rural Punjab. More than taming the European weather, the 'mystery-laden' atmosphere of his room reflected perhaps the desire to relive Jhang in London.

Three years after joining the Imperial College as Professor of Mathematics, Abdus Salam moved to the Department of Physics as a part of the college expansion plan discussed between him and Patrick Blackett. 'I founded this Department at Imperial College, and the first man I brought here was Paul Mathews, who was Reader in Birmingham'. He recalled later.[1] Apart from sharing a mutual interest in research, both Abdus Salam and Paul Matthews started promoting an international image of the newly established department. They would invite 'distinguished speakers' and looked after their guests as best as possible as an exercise in public relations. At times, the two went as far as picking up their guests up from the airport and 'arranging entertainment in London to suit their individual tastes.[2]

After serving the Imperial College for nearly forty years, by holding the Chair for Mathematics and Theoretical Physics for eight years in a row between 1957 and 1964, Abdus Salam changed his role to that of a visiting professor for 29 years from 1964 to 1993; and finally as a Senior Fellow when his health began failing him. He hit the half century of his research publications and supervised over two dozen doctoral students in the earlier years of his service to the college.[3]

---

[1] Interviews 1984: Folder VI, pp. 66-67

[2] Gordon Fraser (2008): p. 139

[3] Abdul Ghani (1982): p. 39

Making London home on the threshold of the 1960s also amounted to political education and enrichment of Abdus Salam's world view. He was able to take a fairly close view of the world beyond the exclusive sphere of Theoretical Physics. It was a world full of crafty politicians, adventurous military generals, story-telling bum-licking bureaucrats, egotistic media moguls, obese north, underfed south, greedy capitalists and agitated masses. There was a spate of political assassinations. High and powerful like John Kennedy and his brother Robert Kennedy, the Civil Rights leader Martin Luther King, African freedom fighter Patrice Lumumba and the Argentinean Marxist revolutionary Che Guevara were slaughtered rather heartlessly. None of this sounded very promising as the decade unfolded. Still, on the positive side, a peaceful way out was found out of the Cuban Missile Crisis, youth demanded end of war in Vietnam, women asked for equality of citizenship and Beatles popularised music. In a bid to liberate communist ideology from Stalinist hold, the New Left emerged on the scene with an alternate crew of ideologues, thinkers and writers like Jean Paul Sartre, Bertrand Russell and Kingsley Martin. Man landed on the moon. In other words, one had the choice to take refuge in the dialectical jargon of Charles Dickens to portray the scene as a time of optimism and hope, and a time of despair and desolation.

Among the group of people around him, Abdus Salam observed Patrick Blackett who was known for his sympathy with socialist causes and the Labour Party of Britain. Then there was the ideologue Charles Snow (1905–1980) who had studied Physics at Cambridge and worked for the government before making it to public life and the House of Lords. Abdus Salam appreciated how some of those people he knew brushed with politics and yet steered clear of picking up any radical tags. His brief taste of politics, as a student leader in Government College Lahore, during the turbulent year prior to partition of Punjab, began stirring him up. Already, he had been dreaming about playing a role in the upcoming science and education sector of Pakistan, a largely risk-free podium. Of course, he would not compromise his deep association with orthodoxy. Still, the bedrock of financial stability coupled with sharpened political awareness provided him the courage to think left-ward. After all, he lived in a world of stark disparity, abundance in the west and dearth in the east troubled him.

At a peace rally in London, one day in 1962, Abdus Salam met the young physicist, Louise Johnson, and is reported to have fallen almost instantly in love with her. Her response changed the orthodox pattern of his personal life forever.

One of his biographers has remarked that it was like 'an emotional lightning strike' the like of which Abdus Salam had not known 'since seeing the inaccessible' Urmila Sondhi in Lahore some two decades ago.[1]

Louise Johnson (1940–2012) was born to affluent parents in Worcester, West Midlands of England, where her father, George Edmund Johnson (1904–1992), traded wool. Earlier, he had served the Royal Air Force. Her mother, Elizabeth King (1914–1992) had been a student at the University College in London. Between 1952 and 1959, Louise Johnson received education at Wimbledon High School for Girls and then, like her mother, joined the University College London to study Physics. She was one of the four female students in a class of 40. After studying theoretical physics she worked at Harwell atomic energy establishment and then made the lateral move into Biophysics to obtain a doctorate in 1962. She was enrolled as the youngest member of the team pioneering crystallography of an enzyme with a chain of 129 amino acids. In 1967, she travelled to the United States and worked at the University of Yale. Upon returning home she was employed by the University of Oxford. In 1990, she won promotion to the David Phillips Chair of Protein Crystallography. She occupied the position up until her retirement from the university. In recognition of her contribution to science, she was elected Fellow of the Royal Society and was made Dame of the British Empire.

As one of the pioneers of biochemical crystallography, a process leading to better understanding of complex protein structures, Louise Johnson was one of those female scientists of her day who won tremendous recognition in their own right. It may not be far off the mark to imagine that standing solid in the given field of research, she might have ended up with a Nobel Prize in her own right.

In 1968, Louise Johnson and Abduls Salam got married at a 'religious ceremony' during the course of which Paul Matthews, then a Professor in Imperial College, played the role of an 'unlikely witness'. Apparently, the purpose of this ceremony was to abide by 'the edicts of a religion that expressly forbids fornication'. Five years later, a second wedding ceremony, the *Nikah*, was held and the Islamic requirement of two witnesses got fulfilled.[2] According to one of their contemporaries, apart from being happy together Louise Johnson and Abduls Salam 'perfectly matched intellectually'.[3] Over the years, the couple

---

[1] Gordon Fraser (2008): p. 229

[2] Gordon Fraser (2008): pp. 230, 232

[3] Tom Blundell, Structure 20, 7 November 2012, pp. 1197-1798 (online)

had two children, a son Umar Salam born in 1974 and a daughter Saeeda Hajira in 1982. Imagine the trial the two must have been through to make the match worthwhile, especially on the part of Louise Johnson who happened to be an outsider, an intruder into the time-tested closed family structure to which Abduls Salam belonged.

Even when Abduls Salam preferred privacy, his public profile made him a person of interest and the inherent conflict by avoiding to open up gave way to greater curiosity. It was not easy to slam the door upon gossip and guesswork. As such, therefore, quite a few questions remained untapped. For example, did Louise Johnson convert to the Ahmadiyah schism of Islam ahead of the wedding ceremony? Why the two ceremonies were held five years apart? How did the children, with their upbringing in England, come to terms with cultural corollaries involved? How the two wives managed to accommodate one another on family occasions and festivals? How the bigamous association was synchronised with the legal, secular, social and common law environment of Europe?

Any presumption of peace in between sounds highly mythical. Actually, the time taken in bringing about the accord speaks for itself. Abduls Salam and Louise Johnson first met in 1962, got married in 1968 after which it took the two of them another five years to perform the *Nikah* ceremony.

Before anyone else, therefore, the pickle of falling in love all over again was a tall test for Abduls Salam himself. Back in 1946, it was Ghulam Hussein, the father of Amtul Hafeez, who had surrendered his land ownership to enable Abduls Salam to qualify for scholarship grant under the Peasant Welfare Fund. How could Abduls Salam, under the shadow of loyalty, pay back the debt by marrying another woman? Ordinarily, in rural Punjab, an event of this category was unlikely to go away without triggering a trail of emotional explosions and muscular fireworks.

As a full-time housewife, Amtul Hafeez (1924–2007) had arrived in England in 1954 when she was 30 and without any social exposure beyond closed family network. She was neither expected to nor educated and trained sufficiently to work hand in hand with her husband. Instead, she depended upon her husband. Did her life story then portray the standard tragic tale of a female victim? In all probability, the popular scale of victimhood does not seem to make sense in her case. Over the years, Amtul Hafeez gave Abduls Salam four children. She cared for the home front without ever bothering her husband to worry about anything.

Her position description covered the range of duties from child bearing and rearing to shopping, cooking, washing, cleaning and the list went on. She braved it all single-handedly, from Cambridge to London, from the birth of her children to their education and wedding. In London, she began taking the added responsibility by of volunteering for the Ahmadiyah women group, by holding local offices of the party and top leadership roles. In her example, Amtul Hafeez seemed to have pre-empted the risk of victimhood. Abduls Salam was conscious of her contribution.

'He knew that while he focused on his work, we were in the best possible hands of someone who would not only take care of our physical necessities, but also our moral and spiritual needs; he could leave it to someone uniquely qualified and able to do a first-class job of bringing the four of us up: our mother'. Ahmad Salam remembered his mother. Harking back to the jargon that behind every great man there was a woman, Ahmad Salam acknowledged the debt owed to his mother. 'My father always recognised that without her incredible ability to raise four children, run the house, which in itself was no mean feat in those days, take care of all the problems a man would normally do, all in addition to pursuing her own career as National President of the Ahmedi Muslim Ladies Association, he could never have had the time to pursue his goals and make them realities. She gave him the freedom and support he needed, and was able to take away much of the drudgery'.[1]

Somehow, in the end, a way out of the shaken pride was found, and the credit for it goes to the whole family. With her academic life secure in Oxford, Louise Johnson had nothing to trample over in the London world of Amtul Hafeez. With Louise Johnson based in Oxford, another station was added into the hectic life of Abduls Salam. When he travelled to Stockholm to receive the Nobel Prize, his two wives and their children accompanied him.

V

Pakistan, Abdus Salam left behind in 1953, struggled to strike a national consensus on power sharing formula to satisfy interest groups vying for power and control.

---

[1] Trieste Tribute (1997): pp. 128-129

Although the Westminster model of parliamentary democratic system sounded familiar to the majority of politicians, there was the deep suspicion that in direct elections held under universal adult franchise Bengalis from the eastern wing of Pakistan would always be in majority. This was not acceptable to feudal lords, tribal chiefs and military generals in western provinces of Pakistan. In the absence of agreement to formulate a constitution, the state business was conducted under the Government of India Act of 1935 with minor amendments. Addicted to taking orders from colonial bosses, the ruling party lacked confidence and courage to make bold decisions. Over and over again, the vision of a modern, democratic and tolerant society was compromised with the desire to find quick answers and easy repair in religion.

First of all, the task of preparing the constitution, along with occasional legislation, was assigned to an impulsively designed Constituent Assembly. Originally, the members of this assembly were drawn from state legislatures elected, in 1946, for a different role, that is, to implement the colonial agenda. It was a single chamber house, comprising 76 members who represented about 15% of eligible voters in their respective constituencies. Ideally, fresh elections on the basis of adult franchise should have been called in Pakistan but the exercise was avoided, on one excuse after another, for fear of facing the unknown verdict delivered by the largely illiterate electorate. As a result, those 76 members of the Constituent Assembly represented nearly eighty million people and that too without the responsibility of being held accountable to clearly defined constituencies. In its legislative role, the assembly passed 44 acts in seven years. For some reason, the legislation did not require a seal of approval from the Governor General, and once passed and signed by the President of the Constituent Assembly the act was published as the law. During the life of the assembly, its maximum attendance was recorded at 57. Effectively, it meant that only 30 members could do whatever they wished. About the end of 1954, the Governor General, Ghulam Mohammed (1895-1956), sacked the Constituent Assembly as well as the federal government headed by Khawaja Nazimuddin. When the action of the Governor General was challenged in the Federal Court of Pakistan, Justice Alvin Cornelius (1903–1991), defined the ditched assembly as 'a body created by supra-legal powers to discharge supra-legal function'.

Against this background, the very need for democracy was questioned. One influential member of the federal government maintained that if they are given the choice the 'overwhelmingly illiterate' people of Pakistan were 'bound to act foolishly'. He advocated for the need to introduce 'controlled democracy'. Pakistan, it was argued, did not resemble British colonies such as Australia, Canada or New Zealand. Democracy in Pakistan was equated with the dictatorship of the illiterate. In those early days, the size of the 'well-defined group of men' ruling Pakistan was restricted to 'about twenty individuals' who 'made all important political and governmental decisions at every level'. It was incredible to witness how so few played with the lives of so many.[1]

Consequently, the political arena of Pakistan was characterised with short living governments in which regional interest groups, senior bureaucrats, military generals, feudal lords, businessmen and religious clerics struck suitable deals with each other.

For example, when both clerics and politicians called for allocation of separate electorates to non-Muslim citizens, it was argued that the uniqueness of Muslim identity could not be compromised by granting equality of citizenship to those who happened to be outside the pale of Islam. In actual fact, cutting Hindus out was a trick to neutralise the threat of Bengali majority. Then there was a growing preference for 'secret diplomacy' over debating in the parliament or open discussion. Instead of preparing their briefs to face the house committees, or political opponents for that matter, they reverted to the medieval pastime of court intrigues, backstabbing, shady deals, horse-trading, patronage and even persecution. As such within few years of its independence from the British, the country suffered seven changes in government; not one of those through democratically convened election. One president, four governors-general, seven prime ministers and numerous federal and provincial ministers were arbitrarily disposed of without any recourse to standard parliamentary procedures or the need to face the electorate. In the absence of democratic accountability and viable party-political culture there was temptation for other players to take the turf. It did not take long for an alliance of the armed forces recruited mostly from northwest and the civilian bureaucracy comprising largely of migrants from India, to shape up opening the door wide open for military adventurism.

At the same time, it is important to remember at this point that the militarisation of the state was eased and greased by geostrategic dictates of the Cold War between communist and capitalist spheres of power. Pakistan shared borders with India, Afghanistan, Iran, the former Soviet Union, the Peoples Republic of China, and the oil shipping Persian Gulf and the Arabian peninsula.

---

[1] Keith Callard (1958): pp. 25-26

Even when India commanded the definite lead in her physical depth, diversity and business potential; the geopolitical value of Pakistan was evident in its very location. Then, the country had arrived on the world scene at a time when the power vacuum caused by the shrinkage of British Colonial Empire was being hurriedly filled in by the United States. There was the urgency to protect oil fields, supply routes, waterways and friendly regimes in the Persian Gulf, Iran, Iraq and Saudi Arabia. If the strategic map outlined by Olaf Caroe, in his *Wells of Power*, made sense then time had arrived for Pakistan to deliver goods.

Sir Olaf Caroe (1892–1981) was a policy expert who held senior public offices in British India. His extraordinary ability to articulate over strategic matters was highly valued. He had coined the term *Wells of Power* to highlight the value of those oil fields in the world economy.[1] India, he believed, had been pushed to the fringe, and 'Pakistan on the other hand lies well within the grouping of south-western Asia'. He urged the United States to step in and bolster the new state of Pakistan. His opinion regarding the military value of Pakistan was vindicated when Jawaharlal Nehru, the prime minister of India, began championing the cause of non-alignment. Against Russian 'shadows lengthening from the north' Pakistan became a more convenient station in defence of West Asia and the Middle East.[2]

Stakes were raised at the Directorate of Military Intelligence in Rawalpindi, where Brigadier Shahid Hamid (1910–1993) prepared frightening dossiers about the sharp surge of Soviet-sponsored communist influence in Pakistan. Shahid Hamid, the maternal uncle of famous writer Salman Rushdie, had a military career spanning over three decades; he retired as Major General in 1964. Apparently, his purpose behind gathering such 'intelligence' was to gain the attention of British and American diplomats; and the ploy really worked.

Already, at a conference of United States' ambassadors in Ceylon (Sri Lanka), early in the spring of 1951, Pakistan had received strong preference over India and envoys posted in the Middle Eastern countries argued that the defence of Iran-Iraq sector was not possible without Pakistani assistance. There was a conclusive resolve to build up Pakistan army as a matter of urgency.[3]

---

[1] Olaf Caroe: Wells of Power, Macmillan & Co., London, 1951
[2] The Making of US Foreign Policy for South Asia, Economic and Political Weekly, 25 February 2006, pp. 703-708.
[3] Ayesha Jalal (1990): p. 125-126

A number of bilateral and multilateral agreements were signed to facilitate economic and military partnership with the United States. In May 1954, a mutual defence assistance agreement cleared the way for Americans to set up their presence at the military General Headquarter in Rawalpindi. Next, Pakistan joined defence pacts like the Southeast Asian Treaty Organisation (SEATO) and the Central Treaty Organisation (CENTO). Americans were permitted to setup an exclusive military base near Peshawar. Pakistan, in the words of General Ayub Khan, became 'America's most allied ally in Asia'.[1]

An impending showdown with the Soviet Union, within a matter of few years, secured lucrative employment opportunities for both generals and clerics. From 1948 onwards, Pakistan began spending nearly 70% of its income on defence; and because its under-developed economy could not afford an oversized war machine, loans poured in from the United States. Soon the bulk of annual budgeting went on defence spending and debt-servicing. Primarily the justification for this fiscal imbalance was sought in the security mess left behind by the British, that is, the Indian threat; whereas, in actual fact, it was the cost of wars Pakistan incurred as the champion of capitalist causes.

More than being a dependent economy, Pakistan characterised a bondage in which income was generated by unmanageable loans in order for the postcolonial state to finance alien military adventures like jihad against 'godless communist bastards' and then service the never-ending debt to avoid blacklisting by big powers.

---

[1] Mohammed Ayub Khan (President of Pakistan): Friends Not Masters (A Political Autobiography), Oxford University Press, London, 1967, p. 130

Chapter Six
Political Adventure

On 27 April 1954, the Foreign Minister of Pakistan, Zafarullah Khan, stated that his country 'did not have a policy on atom bomb'.[1] At a time when drawing distinction between peaceful and violent values of nuclear energy was more of an academic exercise, this statement of ambiguity did not matter much but it gained tremendous value in due course of time. Hiding behind the haziness of its position on non-proliferation for over three decades, Pakistan went nuclear and gained parity with India.

Abdus Salam had begun aspiring to play a leading role in the nuclear excursion of Pakistan at a much earlier date. At the time of its creation, Pakistan comprised of a part of the world where scholarship, if any, was restricted to a small class of people, mostly clergymen and poets patronised by rulers. Virtually, in this way, the body of scholarship had been confined to the well-defined domains of theology and literature. Of course, some manner of accounting was in fashion to keep a track of state revenues, but then the expertise for this purpose rested almost exclusively with Hindu knowledge of book-keeping.

Pakistan's intellectual heritage, therefore, did not have much to boast about outside Islamic theology and largely devotional poetry and literature. Bearing children in the class of Abdus Salam posed an irony to the intellectually barren land of Pakistan. On the sanguine side, however, the challenge to learn science and technology had to be taken up head on as a matter of historical compulsion.

Once again, the determination for Pakistan to confront odds came from India. Back in the mid-1950s, the state of scientific and technological infrastructure in Pakistan was no match to India where the nuclear energy commission, headed by Homi Bhabha, operated directly under the Prime Minister, Jawaharlal Nehru.

---

[1] Ashok Kapur: Pakistan's Nuclear Development, Croom Helm, New York, 1987, p. 34

India aimed at achieving self-reliance in nuclear capability for both civilian and military purposes. A good deal of infrastructural support was available in the shape of qualified scientists, engineers and laboratories. In fact, a recognition of the need to evolve viable nuclear programme, between Jawaharlal Nehru and Homi Bhabha, could be traced back to pre-independence days. Nuclear Physics had gained a weirdly quixotic significance in August 1945 after the American atomic hit on Japan. On one hand, the progress achieved in reactor technology promised power generation; on the other end, there was the temptation to produce weapons of mass destruction. In December 1953, President Dwight Eisenhower of the United States offered the world nuclear education under his 'Atoms for Peace' initiative. India qualified to benefit from the opportunity more than any other place in the world.

Within few months of the presidential address, the United States Atomic Energy Act was amended to export nuclear technology to many countries including India, Pakistan, Argentine and Brazil. Foreign scientists were welcomed to receive training at the School of Nuclear Science and Engineering in Argonne, outside Chicago. Volumes of nuclear records were declassified to assist friendly countries. An international conference for peaceful uses of atomic energy was called in Geneva. Pakistan expressed its readiness to participate in the conference with Abdus Salam as a part of the Pakistani delegation. Mohammed Mir, a sociable Pakistani diplomat, working in New York under Zafarullah Khan, secured Abdus Salam one of the slots allocated to science secretaries of the conference. Abdus Salam remembered Mohammed Mir, who later served as the President of United Nations Economic and Social Council in 1957, as a 'very handsome and polished diplomat'.[1]

Personally, on his part, Abdus Salam, took the assignment very seriously. He spent a good deal of his time in New York to participate in briefing sessions. He urged his Pakistani colleagues to prepare 'a draft plan for development of nuclear power in Pakistan'. Once in Geneva, he arranged for the delegation to meet John Cockcroft, the Director of Britain's Atomic Energy Research Establishment, in order to explore the venues of mutual cooperation in peaceful utilisation of nuclear energy.

Inaugurated in August 1955, on the 10th anniversary of atomic strike on Japan, the so-called Atoms for Peace Conference went on for 12 days. One of its sessions was presided over by Homi Bhabha, the father of India's nuclear

---

[1] Interviews 1984: Folder VI, p.26

program. Nearly 1400 delegates from 73 countries and an equally large number of observers attended the conference.

To many of the younger participants, especially those from the under-developed countries like Pakistan, it was a sensational experience to witness the Swimming Pool Research Reactor. Abdus Salam's effort paid off when the projection over energy requirements and the need for nuclear power in Pakistan was discussed in one session. His performance earned him instant popularity among the small community of Pakistani scientists. Some of those scientists urged the government to start setting up infrastructure for introduction of nuclear technology in Pakistan and bring Abdus Salam back home.[1]

Much to the chagrin of Pakistan, India topped the list of countries profiting from the American initiative by receiving $93 million in Atoms for Peace loans and grants. Evidently, it was in line with western security interests in Asia, and of course a response to the aggressive socialisation of Homi Bhabha. Pakistan was overlooked possibly because of its weak infrastructure and dearth of duly qualified scientists. In other words, the field was open for Abdus Salam to plough, he could be the Homi Bhabha of Pakistan though it was easier said than done.[2]

Nothing apart from Theoretical Physics was common between Abdus Salam and Homi Bhabha. There again, Abdus Salam had begun his career at a time when Homi Bhabha was out of active research. Homi Bhabha, the scion of an affluent Parsi business house, brandished connection with those in power; he benefitted from India's international image, political stability, constitutionality, secularism, skilled manpower, economic infrastructure and trade potential. Whereas the humble Abdus Salam was derided by Pakistan's political instability, social under-development, religious fanaticism and nearly total economic dependence on foreign assistance. Unlike Homi Bhabha, who carried tremendous weight among decision-makers in India; Abdus Salam was obliged to work his way across patronage and paternalism of largely feudal Pakistan. In 1955, when India wanted to procure a 40-megawatt nuclear reactor from Canada, it was delivered without any safeguards, whatsoever. Homi Bhabha placed India on the highway of electronic age within five years of the independence. Abdus Salam was obliged to plead the case of education and research before anything

---

[1] The Nucleus: A Quarterly Scientific Journal of Pakistan Atomic Energy Commission (1996), p. 1
[2] Interviews 1984: Folder VI, pp. 21-28

else and that too in an environment choked with disregard toward the need for scientific inquiry.

What prompted Abdus Salam to revisit Pakistan at a time when possibilities in Physics had begun opening up before him in England? Why should he get distracted instead of staying focussed? How could he risk the momentum he had picked up in Physics within a year of coming so close to professional jeopardy in Lahore? Was he not aware of his vulnerability as a member of Ahmadiyah? In spite of all such questions, he took the plunge in Pakistan tearing his time out of Physics for nearly twenty years. Instead of treading cautiously, he got himself embroiled in a business of political variety. It is essential, therefore, to look rather carefully into his state of affairs in relation to Pakistan. So far this crucial aspect of his life seems to have been hidden beneath the blanket of preferential reporting and good faith. His admirers hold the opinion that he aspired to payback and serve Pakistan. They believe he received an unfair rebuke due to his Ahmadiyah connection. Abdus Salam's business with Pakistan, spanned over two decades, it requires a dispassionate audit; it is an area of exploration for the current chapter.

In actual fact, Abdus Salam's involvement with Pakistan was a peculiar mix of gratitude, ambition and political clouting. With temperamental overtures from time to time, it was an ad-hoc arrangement suiting both sides. If Pakistan benefitted from Abdus Salam, so did Abdus Salam from Pakistan. Had the Ahmadiyah factor not intruded the way it did, the bargain might have lived longer.

Soon after attending the Atoms for Peace conference in 1955, Abdus Salam visited home and expressed the hope that Pakistan might have a reactor soon.[1] He met the Prime Minister, Chaudhri Mohamed Ali. In a way the two knew each other as Chaudhri Mohamed Ali's son, Javaid Akhtar, had been tutored by Abdus Salam. Chaudhri Muhammad Ali (1905–1980) had studied Chemistry at the University of Punjab, made a career in public service and gained expertise in financial management. After the making of Pakistan, he served super-bureaucratic positions and strived hard to build up the government structure in the new country. He valued the significance of science in modern world and agreed with Abdus Salam that in order to take advantage of the United States offer of cooperation in nuclear know-how, Pakistan would be required to build up infrastructure and skilled manpower. Abdus Salam was delighted to observe

---

[1] Abdul Hameed (circa 2000): pp. 89-90

how well the Prime Minister understood him in prioritising matters scientific. Ever since leaving Lahore in December 1953, this meeting with the Prime Minister was Abdus Salam's first highest level of contact in the government.

Apparently, the Prime Minister signalled Abdus Salam to step forward and play a leading role in the birth of nuclear energy program in Pakistan.

In a note of thanks, handwritten on the letterhead of Karachi's North Western Hotel and dated 24 September 1955, Abdus Salam thanked the Prime Minister for meeting him. 'May I, before leaving, say how deeply I am stirred by the confidence and the trust you so kindly placed in me, and in my ability to shoulder the responsibility for a Nuclear Enterprise in Pakistan'. He stated and then added 'Allow me to express my sincerest gratitude for it. I pray and hope I should prove worthy of your expectations'.

A great deal of fog concealing the early history of Abdus Salam's ties with Pakistan may disappear once state records, if ever they were maintained, stand declassified.

II

His performance at the Atoms for Peace Conference brought Abdus Salam to political spotlight, especially the few in Pakistan who attached value to nuclear energy and appreciated his utility. As a young physicist of international standing he was ideally suited to fit into the upcoming nuclear establishment. In fact, it was another venue of employment he aimed at tapping. With more than a year still to go in his Stokes Lectureship in Cambridge and encouraging signals springing from Liverpool and London, he did not have to get stressed out about employment. If ever he was compelled to return home, a suitable and purposeful job in the emerging set up of nuclear technology in Pakistan was most likely to save him from another stint in Government College. Somewhat pensively and rather wishfully, his best shot could be a flexible presence both in Pakistan and abroad. It would be no ordinary feat to be able to serve Pakistan and, at the same time, continue doing the frontline physics. How might this be possible? There was no easy answer to this question. In the first place, an employment package of this kind was not in fashion either in Pakistan or elsewhere. Secondly, getting work at a nuclear establishment usually entailed a greater degree of security grading and travel restrictions.

After meeting the Prime Minister of Pakistan, Abdus Salam returned to England, he felt confident about getting a major role in the nuclear set up shaping up in Karachi. He began being wishful that his perception of flexible employment might be agreeable especially when the need to travel abroad for research led to professional enrichment. He expected a call from Karachi anytime soon, and hoped receiving the offer of a job as Director Research. His state of ecstasy wore off just as fast as it had overtaken him. Soon he found himself caught in the bureaucratic inertia. Pakistan took a while in starting the nuclear journey. To start with, a public sector company was established to procure and dispose radioactive materials in accordance with international standards of safety. This company was placed under the supervision of a high-powered committee assigned to watch over the selection and training of personnel, creation of research groups, conduct business with international stakeholders, pursue installation of reactors; all aimed at benefitting agriculture, health and industry. It did not take long for the committee to be upgraded as the Atomic Energy Commission of Pakistan.

Pakistan in those days was not advanced enough to boast about any sizeable community of scientists. In fact, the main purpose of higher education was focussed upon producing generalists rather than scientists. All employment pathways led to graduation in medicine, engineering, law, commerce and public service. Only those dropping out of the rush for lucrative positions defaulted into teaching natural sciences. Not much thought appeared to have been given to adoption of science and research as a career in itself. By default more than a personal choice, therefore, the majority of those holding degrees in mathematics, physics, chemistry and biological sciences found themselves facing an impasse by becoming teachers at best due to lack of other options. In fact, the weak industrial base did not have much to offer for absorption of science graduates. Those, if any, aspiring to become scientists were on their own. According to one estimation, Pakistan in the 1950s had just one science teacher in a population unit of one hundred thousand, the total number of qualified physicists in the country was recorded at sixty.[1] Just one undersized High Tension Nuclear Research Laboratory operated in Lahore.

Nazir Ahmad (1898–1973), an experimental physicist who had been a student of Ernest Rutherford in Cambridge, was appointed as the head of atomic energy establishment in Pakistan. He had not been active in frontline research

---

[1] Ideals and Realities (1984): p. 82

for nearly three decades and had turned into more of a bureaucrat overseeing the tariff commission for cotton exports. In the absence of any kinship of scientists, the vital linkages between technology and economy were non-existent. As a result, opinion expressed by people in the class of Nazir Ahmad could be trusted only if they expressed themselves as public servants, not as scientists. He established contact with Abdus Salam and the two started exchanging letters. Nazir Ahmad expressed his keenness to get Abdus Salam back to Pakistan but he sounded non-committal and relying largely upon bureaucratic jargons. 'I quite appreciate that time is the essence of the matter, and I also appreciate your anxiety; but wish to assure you that on our part we are trying to do the best we can under the circumstances'. He wrote to Abdus Salam in January 1956.

On his part, against a background of having been bitten in Lahore a couple of years earlier, Abdus Salam tended to raise pertinent questions about the emerging shape of organisational set up. How long would it take for the proposed research institutes to be in place and start training people? What level of budgetary freedom would be granted to scientists? He pressed for the need to move faster in order for Pakistan to secure a role in the upcoming International Atomic Energy Agency under the United Nations. He seemed to have worked out that Pakistan could launch its nuclear power generation program with a sum of up to six million pounds. But any such effort, in view of the poor state of science base in the country, had to be preceded with facilities for research and training. He argued that self-sustaining teams of scientists and premium quality of research benefitted more than costly equipment. It was never too far to create such teams provided the operational control rested with scientists rather than public servants.

As Abdus Salam was travelling to the United States to attend the Sixth Rochester Conference in April 1956, when he considered visiting Oak Ridge. In view of the assignment he was expecting in Pakistan, a short training course at the National Laboratories could be worthwhile in topping his knowledge pertaining to experimental and practical aspects of nuclear technology especially reactors. He sounded the possibility with Nazir Ahmad who appreciated the professional value of such a visit but sounded somewhat pessimistic in getting the necessary sanction in time due to lengthy departmental procedures and the stringency involving foreign exchange. 'I shall be glad if you will kindly let me know as soon as possible what will be the approximate total expenditure involved in your visit to Oak Ridge during Easter and how much it will be in pound sterling and how much in dollars. I should also like to have a little more detailed programme of your visit to America and the purpose of this visit. All this information will be required to get necessary sanctions'. Nazir Ahmad advised Abdus Salam on 21 January 1956. Abdus Salam provided the required information by working out a figure around $240 for travel and lodging. But he was unable to travel due to delay in getting the approval in time.

Invariably, the response from Karachi was muted advising him to wait until 'certain clarifications' were made and 'certain obstacles' were overcome. It did not take Abdus Salam long to find the clue to holdup. He received a hand-written note from Mohammed Mir, the Pakistani diplomat based in United Nations headquarter in New York, who happened to have met Nazir Ahmad over lunch about the end of October 1955. 'He did not seem any more enthusiastic than he has been about the training of students or the ordering of a reactor'. Mohammed Mir stated. 'I am not aware if our government has made any progress in selecting and placing scientists for nuclear research either in England or in the USA'. This detachment was more pronounced when Nazir Ahmed invited Abdus Salam to set out his terms and conditions to work for the atomic energy establishment. 'This enquiry', he hastened to add, 'is without any commitment on the part of the Government'.

With offers of employment picking up momentum in Liverpool and London, Abdus Salam sounded pragmatic. 'I place the greatest emphasis on our research Establishment resembling a university rather than a Government Department'. He wrote back to Riaz Ahmad, an engineer attached to Radio Pakistan who had been charged with running the administrative business under Nazir Ahmad.

As Abdus Salam expected to direct the 'scientific side' of the nuclear energy programme, he believed the terms of his employment could be settled in line with current practices in Pakistan and other countries. 'The salary could presumably be determined by considering the salaries paid to directors of similar enterprises in other countries and the salaries of other positions in our own committee. I feel it would be invidious of me to name a figure'. He added and then underlined the indispensable necessity to travel abroad and maintain regular contact with mainstream of research and nuclear installations. He cited the example of Cambridge University where a fund of £250.00 per annum had been allocated to him to travel to Birmingham; and the fact that this was in addition to two sponsored visits to the United States. He proposed to raise a sum of at least £1500 a year enabling him to do the same in the event of his stationing in

Pakistan. At this point in the letter, he mentioned the two job offers coming his way, one from Liverpool and the other from London. Between February and March 1956, Abdus Salam advised Riaz Ahmed that a Chair in England had a salary ranging between £2000–2500 per annum. He remarked the job offer from Liverpool involved 'attractive possibilities' for him to work with a unique flux machine in the world.

How on earth was he expecting the package of his wished-for employment to be matched in Pakistan, a country starting with *per capita* income of 15 cents a day, remains a mystery. Other than a remote quirk of national susceptibility, he was not under any compulsion to return home and give in to cold-blooded bureaucrats. As soon as the offer of Chair in Imperial College London matured, he was ready to take it. During the course of his job interview, Abdus Salam had mentioned about the 'tentative offer of an appointment, possibly as Director of the Pakistan Nuclear Institute'. Upon hearing this, one of the members of Selection Board, the Vice Chancellor of London University is reported to have 'voiced the concern' towards 'making a stable appointment' by selecting Abdus Salam for the Chair for Mathematics. After his selection, Abdus Salam reminded Mohammed Ikramullah, the High Commissioner of Pakistan, that he had accepted the Chair for a term of five years with a provision to retain 'an association' with the Atomic Energy Commission of Pakistan 'returning to it during vacation as adviser'. In his handwritten note, Abdus Salam also recalled that he had accepted employment in London 'only after discussions with' the Prime Minister, the Atomic Energy Commission and the High Commissioner himself.

'Your Excellency is aware how strongly I feel that my rightful role lies in the development of my country, in Physical Sciences, in Research and in Atomic Energy. I do not wish to remain a mere spectator, in voluntary exile. As it is, I already have the feeling of an outsider. If I am to return to the Commission, I must feel part of it' in order to play a role 'in shaping its work and pattern; a role which I consider belongs to me by right'. Once again, at this point, he returned to his emphasis upon the flexibility of employment in Pakistan enabling him to travel abroad to stay abreast with current discoveries in research and technology. Abdus Salam requested the High Commissioner to arrange his appointment with the Prime Minister, Chaudhri Mohamed Ali, who was due to visit London within few days. 'I would feel very grateful if I could see him and receive his blessings' for a future course of action.

Any details of the meeting between Abdus Salam and Chaudhri Mohamed Ali held only an academic value because of another political shake up back home. Due to an in-house betrayal, in September 1956, Chaudhri Mohammed Ali was obliged to resign from office. Yet there is sufficient evidence that Abdus Salam abided by the state protocol. He accepted the offer of Chair in London with the consent of Prime Minister Chaudhri Mohamed Ali and High Commissioner Mohammed Ikramullah; and resigned from his substantive position at Government College. 'I am glad that you have accepted the Chair at the Imperial College of Science & Technology, London, in accordance with the advice given to you by the Prime Minister and the High Commissioner. I have no doubt that you will make a great name in your new assignment. I shall continue to seek your advice on our programme of educational development'. Abdus Salam's former boss in Lahore, Mohammed Sharif, then serving as Secretary Education to the Government of West Pakistan, wrote to him on 15 September 1956.

As for his repeated assertion regarding the freedom to travel in the interest of professional enrichment, Abdus Salam stood vindicated beyond doubt. By the end of 1956, he received offers of part-time fellowship at the European Organisation for Nuclear Research (CERN) in Switzerland and Summer School teaching in Grenoble University in France.

III

After the adoption of Constitution, general elections were called in Pakistan but then Iskander Mirza, the retired army general who had been sworn-in as the President, expressed his distrust in the process. He believed that an overwhelmingly uneducated, ill-informed and illiterate electorate of the country could not be trusted with making any sound judgment. He suspected that public mood and opinion could be carried away under the influence of radical element like socialist and nationalist parties. He abrogated the constitution and proclaimed martial law. His own fate was sealed within a matter of days when General Ayub Khan, the Commander-in-Chief of the army, took the charger. Iskander Mirza was despatched to England on a long-service leave.

Used to living under various shades of autocracy, the people of Pakistan did not mind the dawn of military rule; they were not expected to take any stand for democracy, something totally unknown to them. In fact, there was a sigh of relief in cities and towns. People observed the striking difference between civilian and army outfits. Much younger and physically fit army troops, briskly jumping out of their armoured vehicles, presented a somewhat promising sight as opposed to the rather boring, obese, lethargic, sly and corrupt spectacle of police personnel. Without firing a single shot, the lightening visits, melancholy detachment and disciplined body language of army troops emitted efficiency and purpose. Overnight, the quality of municipal services seemed to get better and the change sounded like an expression of good governance. In the first decade of its independence, the promised land of Pakistan had failed to address the challenges posed by poverty, social ignorance, regional disparities, and hostility with neighbouring countries. Not long ago, the intelligentsia had witnessed the speed and efficiency of military troops in saving Lahore from the fit of religious lunacy. If military coup served any purpose, it was entitled to be given a chance.

An ordinary citizen of Pakistan was not qualified enough to weigh the shifting balance of power in the neighbourhood. In Iran, next door, Prime Minister Mohammed Mossadeq (1882–1967), who nationalised oil exports, had been overthrown. President Jamal Nasser, in Egypt, assumed control of the Suez Canal. A socialist revolution brought down the pro-western monarchy in Iraq; the king and his prime minister were assassinated and their bodies dragged on the streets; angry mobs gutted the British Embassy. An 'alarming' wave of nationalist sentiment picked up momentum in the Middle East. Pakistan, a loyal ally of the capitalist block, sitting on the 'arc of danger', was required to tidy up its deck in defence of oilfields and their supply routes.[1]

Ayub Khan (1907–1974), had been the commander-in-chief for eight years and ideally placed to oversee the upbringing of military state in Pakistan. He was a descendant of the *Tareen* tribe rooted in Afghanistan. His father, Mir Dad Khan, had served the British army in Hodson Horse, a unit named after William Hodson (1821–1858), the founder of a mercenary force raised to quell the Indian armed uprising. Mir Dad Khan desired his son to memorise the Koran by heart and become a *Hafiz* before receiving formal education and seek employment in the Indian Civil Service. At the age of four, the little boy was despatched to the local mosque where for some reason he slapped the revered cleric on the face bringing an instant end to the first part of his father's dream. Ayub Khan ended up joining the army by making it to the officers' corps, he received military training in the Sandhurst royal academy in England. While at the academy, he

---

[1] Olaf Caroe (1951): p. 165

discovered the disadvantage of being a citizen of the colonised country. 'In those days, anyone coming from a subject race was regarded as an inferior human being and this I found terribly galling. The tragedy of belonging to a subject race depressed us more poignantly in the free air of England'. He recalled afterwards in his political autobiography *Friends Not Masters* published in 1967. 'I discovered that the trust so solemnly reposed in me meant that while the rifles of other cadets were inspected every day, mine was exempted from inspection. I had no command over anybody. I was an honorary Corporal and not allowed to command any British cadets'. He remarked.[1]

When his son was about to graduate from Sandhurst, Mir Dad Khan fell fatally sick and passed away. But, in a bid to save his son from emotional distraction, he wrote down a few letters in advance and then arranged the delivery of mail at regular intervals. As a result, Ayub Khan came to know of his father's death three months later, just when he looked forward to returning home. Sailing back from England, he pondered over the loss. 'At night I stood on the deck and it seemed that someone had magically arranged an illumination of the ocean. In the calm of the night and amidst the colours of the sea the thought of my father's death weighed heavily on me'.[2] On 10 April 1929, Ayub Khan started his career in the British Army and began climbing up at a steady pace. In September 1950, he was promoted to replace General Douglas Gracey (1894–1964) as the Commander-in-Chief of Pakistan Army. His promotion into the top slot was necessitated by the ardour of General Douglas Gracey to take orders directly from Field Marshal Claude Auchinleck (1884–1981) and Louis Mountbatten (1900–1979) rather than his immediate boss Mohammed Ali Jinnah. 'After nearly two hundred years, a Muslim army in the sub-continent would have a Muslim Commander-in-Chief'. This was how Ayub Khan remembered his elevation into the top job. He took command at a time of logistical paucity when each soldier was permitted only five rounds of practice ammunition in one whole year. Under him, the Pakistan army became a fine fighting machine in South Asia. His job became delightful when the capitalist camp, headed by the United States, began financing Pakistan and the state evolved a political economy complementing the peculiarities of its creation.

After the making of Pakistan, dozens of vacancies at the top end of business fell vacant in Karachi due to the exodus *en block* of non-Muslim merchants and

---

[1] Mohammad Ayub Khan (1967): p. 10
[2] Mohammad Ayub Khan (1967): p. 11

financiers. As the new country offered enormous opportunity, the void was conveniently filled in by Muslim business houses from Kathiawar, Calcutta, Bombay, even East Africa and Iran. Those businessmen went straight into accumulation of mercantile capital before turning their attention to industry. Karachi, the only viable port, became the hub of commercial activity offering all sorts of entrepreneurial adventures.

Hurriedly ballooned profits were pumped into setting up industries in textile and sugar; all without much of regulatory intervention by the government. Many industries were set up by the government only to be passed on to privately owned companies on soft terms of loan. Sociologists, as much as economists, were startled to witness the proliferation of profits, concentration of wealth and control restricted to a few business houses emerging from Memon, Bohra, Khoja, Ismaili, Marvari, Isphahani, Saigol and Sheikh ethnic communities. Karachi became identified with names like Adamjee, Dawood, Valika, Colony, Crescent, Fancy, Bawany, Habib, Saigol, Hoti, Nishat, Karim, Hyesons, and a few more. Nearly 50% of all the private sector assets were owned by business houses numbering around two dozen; they owned two-third of the industrial assets and 87% of banking and insurance finance in the country. Fourteen business houses controlled more than half of the textile industry, another five enjoyed 85% of ownership in jute business; and four had monopoly over sugar and edible oil sectors. Similarly, 80% of assets in private commercial banking belonged to nine families. Thirteen business groups held direct representation at the Board of Directors in commercial banking sector. Mercantile capital was converted into industrial assets without any expansion of ownership at the base.

A bureaucratic-military alliance shaped up to protect the blossoming of economy in whatever shape it might take; the state encouraged growth and expansion of capital. In some instances, investment into industry was recovered within one year.[1] This pyramid of industrial power and financial control was characterised by a total lack of accountability, checks and balances. In the absence of duly earned revenue, the tilt in fiscal balance was met with heavy reliance on massive doses of foreign assistance; an ugly trap within the system. It did not take long to be overtaken by swelling deficits and, finally, becoming a permanent hostage to defence spending and debt-servicing. There was never enough money for projects in social infrastructure, health, education and human resource development. In 1955, the Chief Economist of the State Planning Board

---

[1] Hassan Gardezi and Jamil Rashid (1983): pp. 228-269

issued a warning that per capita income in the country had tripped below the mark recorded at the time of partition.

Just as British colonial rulers had ventured to build up communications and waterways in the 19th century Punjab in order to jack up funds for military defences against Czarist Russia, the stranglehold of fiscal balance in Pakistan turned out to be a stable bondage in servitude of capitalist block. With loans advanced by the capitalist block, Pakistan was bound to purchase military hardware from western countries to fight their wars, that is, jihad against godless communists; and then service the compounding debt at its own cost. Ayub Khan, in this way, came to preside over a frontline state envisaged in the *Wells of Power* scheme outlined by Olaf Caroe.

Outwardly, Abdus Salam did not appear to have much of a clue about his place in this political scenario emerging in Pakistan. His performance at the Atoms for Peace Conference had won him the admiration in a section of the intelligentsia and then he was over and done, especially after the removal of Chaudhri Mohamed Ali from the power scene. Even the Atomic Energy Commission did not show much keenness in seeking him out. Some of his friends in Pakistan advised him to be pragmatic. His old friend, Mohammed Aslam, the Professor of Philosophy in Lahore, urged him to halt hoping that someone in Karachi would ever agree on flexible terms of employment such as the permission to spending part of the year abroad. He wanted Abdus Salam to give up on the idea of converting people in the Government of Pakistan in favour of science and research. Like a scholarly elder, Mohammed Aslam stated that Abdus Salam's 'professional advancement' was an achievement in itself 'in the interest of Pakistan'. He updated Abdus Salam about recent staff movements in Lahore. 'Who presides over the Directorate of Public Instruction in Punjab and who turns up as the Principal at Government College should not bother you anymore'. Mohammed Aslam wrote in February 1956. 'I shall, therefore, ask your father to pack up the bags and get ready for a journey to Europe'. He concluded as a matter of fact.

Still, Abdus Salam did not give up on Pakistan. He gathered essential data about the British Swimming Pool Reactor and passed it on to the Atomic Energy Commission of Pakistan. In May 1956, Nazir Ahmad acknowledged by expressing a readiness to follow the matter up with John Cockcroft (1897–1967), the Director of the Atomic Energy Research Establishment at Harwell, England.

At one time, hardly anyone outside the limited circle of family and few friends knew Abdus Salam in Pakistan. His academic high-profile and the headlines he had made in the Punjab University matriculation award way back in 1938 became history. He had been just about washed out of the memory of the emaciated intelligentsia in Pakistan until the substantive breaking of news about him, in August 1957, by one of the leading newspapers. His second debut on the public scene was prompted in the summer of 1957 when Mohammad Iftikharuddin (1907–1962), the owner of a newspaper chain in Pakistan, visited London. During the course of a private errand, in the summer of 1957, Mohammed Iftikharuddin met Abdus Salam and found it hard to believe that the Chair of Mathematics in Imperial College was held by someone from Pakistan. Understandably, the scepticism could be traced back to the mindset of colonial subjugation and the widespread erosion of self-confidence among the conquered. Pakistan did not rank high in the world order of academic eminence. Enslaved races were awfully distrustful of their own level of scholarship and intellectual tradition. Is this really true? Mohammad Iftikharuddin, who himself had studied at Oxford, repeated the question over and over again.[1]

Upon returning home, Muhammad Iftikharuddin directed his Lahore-based English-language daily newspaper *The Pakistan Times* to run a special feature report on Abdus Salam. Consequently, a detailed story titled *A Pakistani Physicist Makes His Outstanding Contribution*, appeared in the newspaper on 20 August 1957. Abdus Salam in this manner was introduced all over again to a much wider audience in Pakistan. 'Very few people outside the small circle of the world's outstanding physicists happen to know the contribution a Pakistani scientist has made to theoretical physics early this year. Fewer still know his achievement in his own country'. Went on the report referring to Abdus Salam as the 'youngest professor' ever employed in Imperial College London. 'He is the first and the only person from any Commonwealth country to occupy this position and the first Asian to be appointed to the Chair of a Science faculty in any university in Britain'. After a rather indulging barrage of superlatives, the writer of the report summarised Abdus Salam's area of specialisation. Here, against a background of the media fury in the United States, the newspaper did not sound much pleased about the manner in which Abdus Salam's contribution towards symmetry violation had been overlooked. In a reminder of Abdus Salam's under-utilisation in Lahore recently, the newspaper seemed to justify

---

[1] Abdul Ghani (1982): p. 38

London as the station for 'full play of his talents, ability, attainments and an inexhaustible zest for work'.

According to one of the early biographers of Abdus Salam, the publication of this feature report in *The Pakistan Times*, amounted to his rediscovery in Pakistan. Within a matter of weeks, Punjab University conferred upon him the Honorary Doctorate of Science.[1]

Abdus Salam made it to the prestigious list of state awards in Pakistan. On 23 March 1958, the Republic Day of Pakistan, Abdus Salam was decorated with the Presidential Award comprising of a medal and 20,000 rupees in cash. His name for this purpose had been proposed by Chaudhri Mohamed Ali.[2]

In 1958, Abdus Salam participated in the second round of Peace Conference convened in Geneva under the United Nations sponsorship. Once again, he acted as one of the science secretaries. On this occasion, however, Sigvard Eklund, a physicist from Sweden, presided over the conference. With such an early exposure to international platforms, placements and interactions, Pakistan enabled him to evolve useful ideas and valuable friendships ahead of time. His diplomatic and political skills began sharpening up. He aspired to bank upon the United Nations to benefit the 'scholarship of developing countries'. His ambition to achieve an international centre for Theoretical Physics, he recalled later, could be traced back to those early encounters with the United Nations.[3]

IV

Although transition from the predominantly academic serenity of Cambridge to the corporate frenzy of London proved testing, Abdus Salam did not take long in picking up pace with varied demands of his work in Imperial College. Unlike Cambridge, his role in London entailed more than teaching, research and supervision of postgraduate students. By the end of 1957, approaching 32, he achieved a great deal of professional autonomy. His flight from Jhang to London, taking twenty eventful years, was a radiant example in talent, toil and the ability to act in time. On top of his academic excellence, he had been fortunate in attracting the attention of peers as diverse as Afzal Hussein, Bashiruddin Ahmed,

---

[1] Abdul Ghani (1982): p. 65
[2] Abdul Hameed (circa 2000): p. 94
[3] Interviews 1984: Folder VI, pp. 26-27

Zafarullah Khan, Paul Dirac, Nicholas Kemmer, Freeman Dyson, Robert Oppenheimer, Patrick Blackett and Chaudhri Mohamed Ali to mention a few. He would always love to top up a list of this kind with the unforgettable contribution made by his parents and teachers who laid the foundation for him to build upon and take off in the world of scholarship. He was perfectly positioned to stride ahead. With a greater part of his life allocated to Physics, he stood on the threshold of securing a place on the international stage.

General Ayub Khan had known Abdus Salam from a distance only through a couple of good news stories. It was at a state dinner, following the annual science conference in Karachi in 1959, when the two of them formally shook hands for the first time. General Ayub Khan was invited as the President of Pakistan, he arrived in the company of Britain's Prince Phillip, the Duke of Edinburgh (1921–2021), who happened to be visiting the country. At the very outset, Abdus Salam observed the difference between the General and the Prince. Ayub Khan betrayed a taut shyness associated with his effort to fit into the number of roles he had imposed upon himself. Whereas, the Prince looked pleasantly relaxed with a mix of regal detachment. Abdus Salam remembered that Ayub Khan dressed in full military uniform decorated with medals and stars. 'He stood next to the Duke of Edinburgh in the Line of Reception. For the office he had come to hold as the President of Pakistan, I remember, Ayub Khan appeared very stiff at that time. We only exchanged courtesies'. Abdus Salam recalled.[1]

Mohammad Shoaib (1907–1976), the old school financial disciplinarian who served the Finance and Economic Affairs Minister of General Ayub Khan, approached Abdus Salam after the banquet. He asked Abdus Salam to advise the government in relation to purchase of a suitable nuclear reactor. Abdus Salam was conscious of the fact that the United States had offered Pakistan a light-water reactor, whereas Nazir Ahmad, the Chairman of the Atomic Energy Commission, wanted to go for a CP5 Reactor functioning on heavy water. Apparently, the commission did not have much luck in rallying political and financial backing of the government and the deal had been put on hold.[2]

At the very outset, Mohammad Shoaib made it clear that he was speaking on behalf of the President. He then dropped a few hints about changes imminent in the atomic energy establishment as Nazir Ahmed intended to take

---

[1] Interviews : Folder VI, P. 54
[2] Ashok Kapur (1987): pp. 38, 42

superannuation. Without mincing his words, Mohammad Shoaib told Abdus Salam that military was there to stay for the foreseeable future; at best the regime could redress itself into some fashion of civilian attire. He alerted Abdus Salam that the President would be inviting him for a follow-up discussion in the near future.

In a formal meeting, following the science conference, Ayub Khan offered Abdus Salam the membership of two public sector commissions the military regime had set up for development of science and education. Abdus Salam was also invited to become a part-time member of the Atomic Energy Commission.[1] Once again, this meeting was attended by Mohammad Shoaib, the Minister for Finance and Economic Affairs; an expression of bureaucratic decorum. Those membership offers were made prior to an exchange of views over the imminent acquisition of nuclear reactor. Abdus Salam accepted offers made by Ayub Khan. He seemed to have hit an instant fondness for the candid and unpretentious disposition of Ayub Khan.

When Ayub Khan came to address the inaugural session of Pakistan Science Commission, convened in August 1959, he expressed his delight to find Abdus Salam among his audience. 'I must say how happy I am to see Professor Abdus Salam in our midst. His attainments in the field of science at such a young age are a source of pride and inspiration for us and I am sure his association with the commission will help to impart weight and prestige to the recommendations of the commission'. Remarked the President.

While visiting home to participate in the Eleventh Annual Session of All Pakistan Science Conference, in December 1959, Abdus Salam delivered a lecture at the Dow Medical College in Karachi. He talked about recent discoveries in his area of expertise and lightly referred to neutrino as a sort of 'devil' among the henceforth known galaxy of particles. A middle-aged man sitting in the front row of the audience was visibly motivated in picking up the professional jargon. After the lecture, Abdus Salam found the opportunity to meet up with this man who introduced himself as Ishrat Usmani, the Director General of the Pakistan Geological Survey department.

Ishrat Usmani (1917–1992), had graduated with distinction from the University of Bombay in 1936. He then proceeded to England to study Physics under the supervision of George Thompson (1892–1975). After completing doctorate at 23, he returned home only to start a career in the public service, that

---

[1] Abdul Hameed (circa 2000): p. 111

is, the exact opposite of choices made by Abdus Salam. When the partition arrived in 1947, Ishrat Usmani opted for a placement in Pakistan and migrated to Karachi where, due to shortage of skilled manpower, quick promotions awaited him. After serving government departments of Industries and Commerce, he had recently been transferred to head the Geological Survey Division.

On a train journey to Multan, a few days later, Abdus Salam ran into Ishrat Usmani once again. Travelling from Karachi to Multan, in those days, as hinted earlier, was no less than a marathon expedition taking more than twenty hours on five hundred miles of single track, with trains stopping every now and then on signal crossings more than rail stations. Even when the ageing carriages were considerably uncomfortable and the journey arduous, Abdus Salam had to visit Multan to be with his family. Preparing himself for another round of the ordeal, he was pleasantly surprised to find company in Ishrat Usmani; the two could talk Physics. Likewise, Ishrat Usmani had been looking forward to another meeting with Abdus Salam after their brief encounter at the Dow Medical College. As the Peshawar-bound train whistled across the lower Indus valley, Abdus Salam and Ishrat Usmani talked about Imperial College and the recent discoveries relating to subatomic particles; the two fondly reminisced about the fabulous George Thompson. Abdus Salam was delighted to note that despite deserting Physics for the sake of a career in public service, the razor-sharp intellectual wit of Ishrat Usmani had survived the numbness of bureaucratic life-style. At one stage, during the course of their journey together, Ishrat Usmani invited Abdus Salam to join him over the packed meal he was carrying in a Tiffin all the way from home in Karachi. Abdus Salam accepted the invitation, and they kept talking. Seeded in the encounter was an enduring alliance and the foundation of a friendship that would survive many tests over three decades.

Upon the retirement of Nazir Ahmad, when Ayub Khan asked Abdus Salam to propose someone to head the Atomic Energy Commission, the name of Ishrat Usmani shot out without hesitation or reluctance; there was an almost instant agreement over the candidate. In due course of time, Ishrat Usmani expressed his readiness to take up the challenge on one condition. He asked for freedom to exercise his professional discretion. 'Ishrat Usmani was purely my choice. I judged the tremendous initiative he commanded. From his appointment onwards, we both worked together to build the Pakistan Atomic Energy Commission'.

Abdus Salam recalled later. His choice of Ishrat Usmani rested on the belief that the commission would be run by scientists rather than the bureaucrats.[1]

For Abdus Salam, it was the starting point of a deeper political involvement with Pakistan, an arrangement spanning over fifteen years and three martial law regimes in a row. Even though the benefit of hindsight makes it harder to mark out the shape and nature of this association, largely ceremonial and amorphous, Abdus Salam did not seem to waver when Ayub Khan got sucked into a futile war with India and Yahya Khan ordered a merciless military operation in East Pakistan. He clung on even after Zulfiqar Bhutto declared to go nuclear; his loyalty with Pakistan stood stubbornly resolute. Why and how did he come to terms with such a drawn-out relationship with military? It is not easy to dig out any quick answers, he lived in a world where favourable military coups served a purpose and were not detested.

What, in the first place, motivated Abdus Salam to take a plunge into Pakistan at a time when he had secured a Chair and bought a house in London? Did the political indulgence in Pakistan not entail a risk of deviation from Physics? He might have, in his fancy to retain link with home, acted on impulse but the time proved it was not a bad investment. Over the years, however, Abdus Salam's association with Pakistan benefitted both sides. In fact, his fondness of Pakistan needs to be audited at two different levels. Emotionally, the country constituted a birth right of his family and ancestors. At the same time, he felt obliged to payback and participate in national progress. After all, the poverty-stricken land had financed his education and training abroad at a time when there was no way he could have been able to afford it by himself.

On the practical side, his association with Pakistan had three tiers. First of all, there was his hardcore business-like professional involvement with the Atomic Energy Commission. Next, he reached out to advise the government in building up the policy framework for educational and scientific development. Holding the membership of education and science commissions, founded by the military government, he advocated for expansion of resource allocation. Finally, there was the freedom he enjoyed in forwarding proposals in the interest of national security and defence by approaching the President directly.

Although Abdus Salam had begun offering Pakistan advice relating to acquisition of nuclear technology in 1955, he was popularly branded as the Chief Scientific Adviser to the President of Pakistan only after the military coup in

---

[1] Interviews 1984: Folder VI, p. 57

1958 staged by Ayub Khan. He had been in contact with the former Prime Minister, Chaudhri Mohamed Ali, and the Chairman of Atomic Energy Commission, Nazir Ahmad. In recognition of his services to the country, he was awarded the Star of Pakistan medal, in 1959, by the military government. By moving closer to the military regime, Abdus Salam acquired the reputation that his advice was heard at the top. At once, he was elected to lead the Pakistan Association for Advancement of Sciences. What is often overlooked in this regard is the fact that he had begun serving the regime without any formal administrative, statutory or financial and logistical bearing. He did not sign any contract covering the scope, nature or terms of services provided by him. No office space, equipment or staff establishment was ever provided to him.

His advisory role was largely ceremonial, the title bestowed upon him lacked the bureaucratic support and departmental accountability in the framework of a position description. Effectively, he was neither an employee nor a consultant. Not even a cost centre had ever been allocated to cover the range of duties he appeared to have voluntarily taken upon himself. He was, as mentioned above, entitled to travel expenses and accommodation only while visiting the country for a meeting of the Atomic Energy Commission. 'No such thing as salary or allowances at any stage. It was purely an honorary arrangement, which started in 1958, when I began advising the President in my personal capacity'. He stated. In fact, an effort was often made to schedule his various engagements in one block in order to benefit from his presence in the country. In this way, the annual meetings of the Atomic Energy Commission were programmed accordingly.[1] But then the lack of structure and control surrounding his role, raised bureaucratic questioning. Some of the top bureaucrats desired to regulate the relationship in view of security-related sensitivities involved in the sharing of classified information and Abdus Salam's access to the President.

In the Spring of 1961, an in-house memorandum was submitted to the President seeking his permission to formalise Abdus Salam's appointment through a notification in the state gazette. Qudratullah Shahab (1917–1986), the Principal Secretary to the President, drafted the memorandum. He stressed upon 'the urgent necessity of establishing international liaison at the highest level' with the appointment of Abdus Salam as 'Chief Scientific Adviser to the President, with the status of a Minister without Cabinet rank'. As such, the submission pressed for the need to route policy matters 'concerned with

---

[1] Interviews 1984: VI, P. 82

programming and planning of scientific research in Pakistan' through the Chief Scientific Adviser instead of directly approaching the President. Abdus Salam happened to be visiting Pakistan when he was asked to meet General Ayub Khan in Lahore. He was aware of the proposal and felt uncomfortable fearing the loss of freedom by turning himself into bureaucratic stereotype. But then he yielded under the pressure exerted by Qudratullah Shahab.

'I was asked to come and stay at the Government House. I just could not sleep that night. There was this feeling of being knotted into a bureaucratic structure. I felt bad about ending up as a tool in the government machinery. Early in the morning, I asked Shahab to cancel the whole thing. I would continue to advise the Government with delight, like before; anywhere, anytime. But the assigning of a gazette nomenclature to my services amounted to a loss of freedom to me. I felt like losing virginity without enjoyment. Shahab was a wise man. He said the government required to notify the appointment in order to make sure that the advice I offered was taken and paid due attention. All governments made such arrangements, he added. He silenced me, and then the President signed the orders later that morning. Now, in the end, as I look back, the appointment had both positive as well negative aspects. For example, people outside the government system thought of me as a very important functionary whose voice they believed was heard. Whereas, the well informed within the government cared the least for they knew my position carried no weight. There were occasions when I registered protest directly with the President, and it worked'. Abdus Salam recollected the day he was formally appointed as the Chief Scientific Adviser to the Government of Pakistan.

His attitude remains a matter of speculation. Why did he take something that had made him apprehensive? Apparently, at that time, he was under no compulsion of giving in to an insipid procedural requirement. He could have extricated himself rather politely on grounds of his workload in London. One possible explanation comes from his abhorrence of blatant authority and control he had experienced at Government College in Lahore. Consequently, he preferred flexible arrangement with opportunities budding in Pakistan. Serving the country in some workable capacity was excellent of course but he felt safe on his own flexible terms. He was inclined to get along with Ayub Khan without a clear-cut job description, departmental accountability, chain of command, state protocol and so on. His preference for an unchained liaison, supported by the stability of a Chair and lifestyle in London, appeared to suit both sides. As such, the presidential notification of his appointment as Chief Scientific Adviser did not really matter much in the end.

Doing physics most of the time, Abdus Salam required a bit of political education. In one of his earlier encounters with Ayub Khan, he proposed the nomination of former prime minister, Chaudhri Mohamed Ali, as the Chairman of the Pakistan Science Commission. Ayub Khan did not have any problem with Chaudhri Mohamed Ali. In fact, the President seemed to like the idea but he advised Abdus Salam to first check the proposal out with Chaudhri Mohammed Ali. When Abdus Salam had the opportunity to do so he found Chaudhri Mohamed Ali was not pleased with the imposition of martial law, abrogation of the Constitution and termination of democratic process. He declined the proposition for it amounted to playing the second fiddle with military. In fact, Chaudhri Mohamed Ali warned Abdus Salam, rather sarcastically, to be watchful of the Punjabi preference to side with the winning party. Abdus Salam felt embarrassed for failing to do the homework before going to Ayub Khan directly. He should have gone to Chaudhri Mohamed Ali first. 'It was my idea. I knew Chaudhri Mohamed Ali very well. He was a very fine man. And then, of course, all those people knew me as a scientist. His son, Javaid Akhtar, was my student in Government College; a very bright boy, indeed. I had met Chaudhri Mohamed Ali on several occasions. After relinquishing charge as the prime minister, whenever he visited London, I saw him regularly. But when I talked with him about the Science Commission, he was very reluctant to get back into some sort of government business. Basically, he was an intellectual'. Abdus Salam remembered the episode.[1]

V

Popularising science was a bleak business in Pakistan, a country in which national literacy rate had yet to score its incidence in double-digit, where feudal lords felt threatened by education and the mainstream religious leadership confused social enlightenment with unpardonable apostasy. But after securing the political clout and making it to the invitation lists of few science and education groups, Abdus Salam found the forum and audience to deliver his

---

[1] Interviews 1984: Folder VI, pp. 83, 90-92

recipe for demolition of poverty and ignorance. An economic revolution to gain affluence, he postulated, was achievable by getting hold of scientific scholarship.

In January 1961, he arrived in Dhaka to read a paper at the annual science conference. Taking the stage, he gave his audience a bit of surprise. 'I would have liked to speak about the scientific field I have been privileged to work on, about the elementary particles of physics, those ultimate constituents of which all matter and all energy in the Universe is composed. I would have liked with you to explain the frontiers of our knowledge and our ignorance, to tell you of some of the concepts the physicist has created to comprehend God's design. I would have liked to show you that with all his pragmatism, the modern physicist possesses at once the attributes of a mystic as well as the sensitivity of an artist. I would have liked to convey to you some of the wonder, some of the fascination, as well as some of the heart-breaks of the physicists' craft. But I shall not do this.' He declared.

Instead, he focussed his attention on widespread poverty prevalent in Pakistan and pressed for the need to change. 'We, in Pakistan are very poor. This poverty we share with the majority of the human race, with some one thousand million people in about a hundred countries'. He cited figures to illustrate the stark disparity of income between the rich and the poor inhabiting the planet. 'The facts of our poverty are obvious enough and I am not going to mince words about it. You can go out in the streets and see it all around you. We live with a crushing poverty of the sort which Europe or America have not seen since the day when Dickens wrote'. He stated by citing examples of places where the tide of poverty had been turned by technological revolution. 'You just cannot believe the plenty—the plenty not for the few but for everyone. Every time I am privileged to visit that great country, I have to remind myself afresh that it is indeed possible to produce so much for so many'. He referred to the United States of America. 'I do not say all this in any spirit of envy. This prosperity is due to an organisation of society where scientific knowledge is fully exploited to increase national productivity. This prosperity is a portent of hope; hope that possibly within our lifetime, using the same methods, we in Pakistan may also achieve the same'.

He then went on to advocate that change was possible with 'scientific mastery of natural law'. He declared there was no 'physical reason' to tolerate the 'existence of hunger and want' anymore. 'I have great hopes that all this is going to change'. He appeared to prophesise, drenched with the optimism of a left-wing politician, anticipating 1961 as the year of watershed.[1]

This talk in Dhaka marked the birth of his mission to popularise science as a political campaign. He would continue harping upon the core of his argument, that is, alleviation of poverty by scientific means, for years on to a general audience in developing countries, especially Muslim. In doing so, he must have been motivated by some of his senior colleagues like, for example, Patrick Blackett, in London, known for their left-wing leaning. Over the years, he polished and sharpened up his oratorical performance with a blend of inspiring accounts from history. At times, he would relive the relatively close standards of living in medieval age when monuments of stunning beauty like Taj Mahal and St Paul's Cathedral were built. Europe began taking the lead, he used to argue, due to the monumental works of scholars like Isaac Newton (1643–1727).

Having lived in England for more than ten years and been able to travel to Europe and the United States on many occasions, Abdus Salam could just not close his eyes upon the torrential affluence in the west. Somehow he could not stay away from comparing the western comfort and wealth with naked destitution of Pakistan. While making his case about economic disparity, he alluded to the medieval Muslim physician, Al-Asuli, who is known to have compiled a pharmacopeia dealing with the diseases of the rich and the poor, separately. In a way, he sounded like a hard-hitting Marxist; to him the apparently unbridgeable gap and economic inconsistency between the poor and rich did not make sense. Although he would not say it loudly but his message was clear and straight to the point. There was wealth, affluence, abundance, surplus and privilege on one side; and poverty, depravity, shortage and scarcity on the other end. He lived in a world one part of which was home to the overpaid, overfed, oversexed, pampered, obese and neurotic; and the other half occupied by the underpaid, malnourished, bullied, tormented, oppressed, desperate, miserable and self-destructive. 'Fifty per cent of people in my country of Pakistan earn and live on eight cents a day. Seventy-five per cent live on less than fourteen-cents. This fourteen-cents includes the two daily meals, clothing, shelter, and any education'. He worked out.

'To us, the unresolved conflicts of the East and the West appear as distant wearing conflicts, inevitable luxuries of a state of physical well-being. For us, the nuclear problem is tragic only in that it leads to a criminal waste of earth's

---

[1] Ideals and Realities (1984): pp. 71-84

resources. Year after year I have seen the cotton crop from my village in Pakistan fetch less and less money; year after year the imported fertiliser has cost more. My economist friends tell me the terms of trade are against us. In 1957–1958 the underdeveloped world received a total of $2.4 billion in aid and lost $2 billion in import capacity (through paying more for the manufactured goods it buys and getting less for what it sells), thus washing away nearly all the sums received in aid'.[1] He stated by focussing his attention on global discrimination, inequity and preferential trade regime.

Over the years, the theme of addressing poverty and ignorance with education and science evolved as an idealistic patent of Abdus Salam. Even though any change for the better remained a dream unrealised, he brought together, in the process, a sizeable constituency of his admirers and devotees. Younger scientists looked towards him for inspiration, guidance and patronage. Armed with facts and figures, he continued battling against global inequality. In Pakistan, his title as Chief Science Adviser to the President licensed him to articulate with a whiff of authority. Abroad, representing Pakistan on international forums like the United Nations, he was privileged with an extent of diplomatic entitlement; a clout that paved the way for him to campaign and accomplish the International Centre for Theoretical Physics in Italy.

According to his biographer, Abdul Ghani, the strong position Abdus Salam began taking on poverty and dispossession cost him falling out of step with the conservative ruling elite and their 'established order' in Pakistan.[2]

Breaking apart from the centralised configuration of colonial era, Pakistan faced a dire shortage of qualified manpower to support the birth and budding of its industrial base. At the time of partition in 1947, Pakistan had inherited from united India only five diminutive research stations in hydraulics, irrigation, jute production and fruit preservation. Only two universities catered for higher education through a scanty network of affiliated colleges offering degrees in social rather than natural sciences. Very few among the small community of university teachers were actually involved in scientific research at postgraduate level. With the country's population mass crossing the hundred million mark, the total number of research scientists was estimated to be somewhere in the range of 300, and the majority among those were employed at the Pakistan Council for Scientific and Industrial Research (PCSIR), an organisation created in 1953. A

---

[1] Ideals and Realities (1984): p. 4
[2] Abdul Ghani (1982): pp. 70-71

force of at least 3000 qualified engineers was required to meet the bare minimum goals set in the public sector. Likewise, the grim state of health sector was evident in rural areas where just one doctor was available to more than 25000 people.

Even when Abdus Salam's ambition to popularise science in a predominantly feudal society sounded like an idealistic mission, there was no escaping from the growing demand for qualified manpower in public and private sectors. He cited the examples of Russia and China, the two communist giants bordering Pakistan, in picking up pace in achieving 'economic transition to prosperity'. He hoped the miracle could be pulled out in Pakistan 'without the corresponding cost in human suffering'.[1] Clearly, his optimism was overblown and against the nature of military state in Pakistan. Despite his praiseworthy homework in digging out the roots of global disparity and injustice, he overlooked the plain fact that militarisation of state in Pakistan had been predestined to wage jihad against communism. Somehow his political imagination evaded to take note of the fiscal noose tightening on the economy of Pakistan. As stated before, Pakistan sought high-priced loans from the capitalistic world only to purchase their somewhat outdated military hardware and then fight alien wars. Any move in the direction of egalitarian cost centres like health, education and social development required capital investment. Where would the money come from when the bulk of it was being sucked into militarisation of the state and servicing of loans destined to be spent on alien causes?

In the beginning, Ayub Khan appreciated the need to popularise education and science, but he tended to behave like a consumer fascinated with the end product alone. Lacking the requisite patience, he aimed at taking the shortest route by way of technical and vocational colleges. 'His concept of modernisation was modest and centred on inculcating respect for manual skills and the introduction of more vocational, technical and scientific subjects into the curriculum, together with more rigorous teaching and examination standards. His preference was implicitly for an elite orientation in higher education, with a gradual expansion of public primary education at the base'.[2] On this account, Abdus Salam held his reservation and pressed for the need to build up

---

[1] Ideals and Realities ((1984): p. 84

[2] Dawn E. Jones and Rodney W. Jones; Education Policy Development in Pakistan: Quest for a National Program. [Essay contributed to 'Contemporary

educational base first of all. Going for vocational training, he believed, made sense only after the apprentices had been through a certain level of conceptual drill in literacy and numerical skills. He was proved correct, rather sadly, during the war with India in 1965 when Pakistani soldiers drove their tanks into enemy territory only to get bogged down in the midst of sugarcane fields. They had been unable to carry out the simple calculation about fuel consumption and just 'could not compute how much petrol was needed to bring them back if need arose'.[1]

According to Abdus Salam, the President would listen with interest, often looking almost convinced but then the scene changed as soon as he went to his secretaries of finance and planning, and this effectively brought an end to the whole affair. For quite a while Abdus Salam did not seem to have much of a clue. While passionately pressing for an allocation of at least one percent of the Gross National Product in favour of scientific endeavour and research, he did not take into account the influence of powerful foreign players. Pakistan just could not escape the cost it was incurring on defence and debt servicing. Actually, in this way, his battle was lost before its commencement.

Asking the government to fund programs in scientific research was just one aspect of the struggle Abdus Salam had taken upon himself. He asked for statutory autonomy of research organisations by advocating that only scientists were qualified to run professional institutions where the rules of procedural game were not required to comply with those usually applicable in the governing of public sector departments. Such organisations were bound to flourish around 'tribal leaders of science, creative men, often highly individualistic, who respect only merit and not seniority in service'. This he wrote to the President of Pakistan, in March 1961, making a copy of his letter apparently on the Imperial College letterhead of Patrick Blackett. Often, he seemed to overlook the fact that all statutory bodies were inherently bound to end up as jealously guarded bureaucratic islands within the bigger ocean of officialdom seeking a smooth flow of annual grants.

Some of the top bureaucrats surrounding Ayub Khan were not prepared to confide in Abdus Salam, they would be wary of his part-time association with Pakistan. Serving a permanent position in London, they argued, divided him between England and Pakistan; it was not possible to hold him accountable with sensitive and classified information. Few others, who would not dare stepping

---

[1] Interviews 1984: Folder VI, p. 96

forward due to secular preferences of the government in those days, went as far as splitting his dedication among England, Pakistan and the Ahmadiyah schism.

In actual fact, it was in the nature of Abdus Salam's wobbly attachment with the Government of Pakistan from where a great deal of ambiguity emitted about his role. Because he was an adviser without any clear-cut administrative and operational portfolio, his advice was welcome but then nobody in the government could discern its utility in the absence of follow-up channels and chain of command. If he was at ease with the sluggishness of a ceremonial title, there would be hardly any reason for those in the government to get worked up. Those bureaucrats, he suspected of playing foul with him, were supposed only to wait for his return to London within a matter of days.

As for the bureaucratic inkling about his divided loyalties, Abdus Salam did not feel the need to provide any certification or proof. On a number of occasions, however, he appeared to be driven most certainly by his personal devotion to Ayub Khan more than anything else. Later, he viewed the liaison with military regime as an idealistic glint shooting out of his 'years of innocence and hope'.[1] But then he had extraordinary knack of salesmanship for Pakistan. At his invitation, John Cockcroft, the chief of British nuclear establishment, visited Pakistan in January 1961. In those days, the Atomic Energy Commission of Pakistan had just begun setting up its nuclear research laboratories in West Wharf district of Karachi. Abdus Salam desired to send across the message that young Pakistani scientists were in no way lesser than their kind elsewhere in the world. He noticed that someone had wiped the meson theory equations off the wall screen in a lecture room. Without waiting he jumped forward to write those equations on the board and involved a group of younger physicists in discussion. About then, John Cockcroft walked into the room. 'So you have already set up a research group here'. He is reported to have remarked upon finding Abdus Salam in the midst of a tutorial scene.[2]

In January 1962, Abdus Salam urged Nazir Ahmad, Secretary to the Ministry of Defence, to allocate a sum of five million rupees for the creation of Defence Science Organisation. 'As you are fully aware, modern warfare is as much a test of technological and scientific competence of a nation as of the courage and skill of its soldiers'. He reminded Nazir Ahmad that Pakistan lacked in a trained corpse of scientists in the Defence sector.

---

[1] Jagjit Singh (1992): p. 32
[2] Abdul Ghani (1982): p. 67

Next, in May 1962, he urged Agha Shahi at the Ministry of Foreign Affairs to invite Paul Johnson for a visit to Pakistan. In those days, Paul Johnson (b1928) worked as leader-writer and deputy editor at the London-based *New Statesman*. Mindful of India's popularity among the left-wing intellectuals in England, Abdus Salam considered making inroads for Pakistan. 'Paul Johnson is a very influential left-wing writer', he informed Agha Shahi. 'Can you arrange to have him invited to Pakistan by an organisation like Association of Science Workers or International Affairs Club? We have to give these men a correct appraisal of the country'. He urged knowing well that an Association of Science Workers or an International Affairs Club did not exist in Pakistan and might have to be created on paper to build up the case for invitation.

Few weeks later, he went on to advise Agha Shahi that Maneklal Thacker, the Secretary to the Ministry of Science and Research in India, was scheduled to visit Karachi early in June 1962 and should be well looked after. Maneklal Thacker (1904–1998) held a high-profile in the science establishment of India and had been decorated with the Padma Bhushan award. 'Kindly do make some fuss about him. He is a friend of Pakistan'. In his hand-written note, Abdus Salam urged Agha Shahi to do the job 'as a matter of personal favour'.[1]

One of the glaring examples of Abdus Salam's devotion to Ayub Khan was evident in September 1962 when the President visited England to participate in the Commonwealth Heads of Government summit conference. Abdus Salam arranged to invite Bertrand Russell (1872–1970), Kingsley Martin (1897–1969) and few other prominent scholars at Claridge's Hotel in London where Ayub Khan was putting up.[2] Promoting a military ruler was not an easy task at a time when popular opposition to war in Vietnam and proliferation of nuclear weapons was picking up pace. 'I wanted to have a good image of the President. We invited about forty intellectuals at a reception at Claridge's Hotel. It was a very different experience for our President, the experience of being in the company of philosophers and sages'. He remembered the occasion.[3]

---

[1] From 1969 to 1974, Maneklal Thacker headed the Indian Freemasonry. He held the Most Worshipful office of the Grand Master of the Grand Lodge of India for two consecutive terms.
[2] 'When I die, take me to Claridge's rather than heaven' is a remark attributed to famous American actor Spencer Tracy (1900-1967).
[3] Interviews 1985: Folder VI, pp. 97-102

Bertrand Russell, reaching 90, was frail but alert and prepared to meet anyone to gain support for his Peace Foundation. Apparently, Abdus Salam had known Bertrand Russell from Cambridge, since the latter was employed as a Lecturer at Trinity College and occupied rooms once associated with Isaac Newton. Abdus Salam remembered the meeting between Bertrand Russell and Ayub Khan as the peak point of the reception at Claridge's. While receiving the distinguished guest, Ayub Khan was escorted by Abdus Salam, Foreign Minister Zulfiqar Bhutto and Education Minister Abdul Mustafa.

Mr President, how do you square this with Islam? Bertrand Russell asked when Ayub Khan poured a glass of whisky for the sage. 'I take it as a medicine for my heart condition'. Ayub Khan responded with a gentle smile, and the ageing philosopher accepted the drink. Ayub Khan began talking about the sourness of India-Pakistan ties. 'One day, I am sure, the Indians would realise the cost of holding on to Kashmir', Ayub Khan remarked somewhat eloquently. Bertrand Russell listened with patience and then, with a twinkle in his eye, returned the logic. 'I hope, Mr President, the cost of holding on to the conflict is already well known to Pakistan'. Abdus Salam recalled Bertrand Russell telling Ayub Khan.[1]

Before leaving the reception, Bertrand Russell invited Abdus Salam to come over to Knightsbridge for tea someday. Abdul Mustafa, the Minister for Education, overheard the conversation. He prevailed upon Abdus Salam to join in and the two went to meet Bertrand Russell a few days later. Abdus Salam was astonished to observe Abdul Mustafa, a proclaimed agnostic, arguing in favour of God. It was too late for him to get back into the trap, Bertrand Russell remarked politely. He asked Abdus Salam to name a humanist believer of God. After thinking for a while, Abdus Salam came up with the name of Mohandas Gandhi. 'But he was a cruel man who had deprived his wife the pleasures of matrimonial relationship by adopting her as a mother', Bertrand Russell shot back.

There was an occasion when Abdus Salam got carried away and stumbled upon a half-baked possibility to benefit Pakistan. It happened during the course of his visit, earlier in 1961, to the United States to participate in the Massachusetts Institute of Technology centenary celebrations. He was accompanied by Patrick Blackett. While speaking on the occasion, Patrick Blackett is known to have remarked that acquisition of technology did not pose

---

[1] Interviews 1985: Folder VI, pp. 97-102

a problem anymore because everything was on sale in the open market. Abdus Salam disputed the view on grounds that a certain level of scientific proficiency was prerequisite to benefit from technological advancement. He cited the problem of water-logging and salinity in his homeland where nobody knew how to fix the problem. He went on to explain how the network of canals, dug by the British planners in the 19th century, had resulted into the scourge of water-logging and salinity eating up vast tracts of agricultural lands east of the Indus valley.

Only seventy years ago, he recalled, the British feat of engineering had converted some 23 million acres of arid land into a fertile granary of the subcontinent. But then all human innovations, he stated, have a mortal life span and there is a price for the insatiable desire to profit from natural habitat.

Pakistan, an economy essentially based on agriculture, lost almost one-fifth of its cultivable land in Punjab and Sind to water-logging and salinity precisely about the time when the British withdrew from India. He informed his audience.

Sitting there was Jerome Wiesner (1915–1994), a Professor at the Massachusetts Institute of Technology who had been appointed as Chairman of the Science Advisory Committee of President John Kennedy. After the session concluded, Jerome Wiesner approached Abdus Salam and proposed that the two of them travel together to Washington and explore what needed to be done to help Pakistan. In July 1961, when Ayub Khan visited the United States, the issue of water logging and salinity was discussed at the presidential level and a formal offer of assistance was made to Pakistan. Abdus Salam was asked to stay back in Washington and follow up with the proposal. As a result of his consultation with experts in the area, it was decided to launch the pilot project for installation of electrical pumps in selected agricultural tracts of Punjab. One of the founding fathers of campaign raising alarm over global warming, Roger Revelle (1909–1991), a scientist with career in defence production, was appointed to supervise the experiment.

After conducting research in a part of the affected areas, the team of American experts recommended vertical rather than a horizontal drainage of excessive water table underneath the soil surface. Pakistan could not afford the recipe and as such the whole effort turned out to be an exercise in futility. Because Abdus Salam had been closely involved in the effort, his contribution, along with that of Jerome Wiesner, was duly recognised in the presidential correspondence between John Kennedy and Ayub Khan.

At a very early stage of its journey in the world of science, Pakistan took the lead in South Asia by launching a small satellite rocket of its own. It was made possible by the initiative snatched by Abdus Salam. At a state dinner in Washington hosted in the honour of Ayub Khan, in July 1961, Abdus Salam found himself seated next to James Webb (1906–1992), the Administrator of the National Aeronautics and Space Administration, who was known for his ability to win colossal sums of budgetary allocations in favour of space programs. At the very outset of their encounter, Abdus Salam liked James Webb for his candid disposition. 'Why don't you visit our Wallops Island Station? We shall see what needs to be done to get your country into the space age'. Abdus Salam heard him making the proposition. It was an extraordinarily tempting offer, out of the blue, apparently. He thought for a moment and then picked up the 'rocket idea' as a versatile weapon in popularising science and technology in Pakistan. There was also the opportunity to lure the powerful military establishment into the venture.

'At that time the space activity at Wallops Island consisted of sounding rockets to trace wind movements in the upper atmosphere. I said we were not interested just in sounding rockets. We would like to know how to manufacture and launch such rockets. It was all very new in those days'. He recalled his encounter with James Webb.[1]

In an age preceding digital revolution, the focus of United States space research was restricted to radio transmission at relatively lower altitudes and rockets fired from Wallops Island Station used to monitor weather patterns and traces of nuclear radiation. Against a background of the suspicion that communists were busy making weapons of mass destruction, any information on radiation measurement could prove vital. In a way, therefore, the offer made by James Webb sounded more than a purely platonic overture.

After the state visit concluded and Ayub Khan returned home, Abdus Salam went to see the Wallops Island Station. We can launch a small rocket of our own, he thought confidently, provided the mechanical blueprints were made available to us. He travelled to Pakistan and convinced Ayub Khan to launch a space programme. As soon as Ayub Khan agreed, necessary arrangements were lined up. Abdus Salam and Ishrat Usmani were entrusted to co-chair the space research committee constituted for this purpose. Four employees of the Atomic Energy Commission and a Regional Director of the Department of Meteorology were

---

[1] Interviews 1984: Folder VI, pp. 70-81

selected for training in the United States. As a gesture of goodwill, the Americans gifted Pakistan a set of four rockets free of cost.

However, unlike the openness exercised in Revelle Mission, the business about space research was shrouded under thick layers of secrecy. On 29 September 1961, the Government of Pakistan issued a 'top secret' memorandum, signed by Mumtaz Mirza, the Secretary to the Ministry of Finance. An exclusive bank account was opened in foreign exchange to facilitate the procurement of necessary equipment and services related to space project. Abdus Salam was granted permission to 'incur expenditure out of the foreign exchange allotment' through Aziz Ahmad, the Pakistani ambassador in Washington. Ishrat Usmani was appointed as the accounting officer and funds were to be drawn on the basis of 'as and when required'.

Originally, the expectation was to fire a couple of rockets about the end of summer in 1962. Afterwards, the schedule was tightened to coincide the firing of rockets with Ayub Khan's plan to lift martial law and promulgate new constitution. Working at a feverish pace, Abdus Salam travelled from London to Washington and Karachi; meeting one timeline after another. One of his handwritten worksheets illustrates how, over a period of 123 days from July 1961 onward, he juggled among overlapping priorities. He appeared to have ended up giving 40% of his time to physics, 40% to assignments in Pakistan; and the rest, including weekends and any holidays, was left for family, home and rest.

In Washington, he invited a select group of Pakistani students for lunch at a cafe near the Embassy of Pakistan. 'I have promised with President Ayub Khan to launch a rocket from our soil in nine months from now. We want this time to beat India in space'. He told them. 'You will do three months of training here in the United States. We shall then get into business in our country. Only necessary equipment is to be purchased here, the assembling will be carried out at the rocket launching site in Karachi. You will be required to construct the range and all the rest that is necessary in rocket firing systems. We do not expect any American expert to help you at the site; you will have to do it all entirely by yourself'. He told his somewhat spellbound audience urging them to work out a mutual division of labour, select roles and responsibilities. Tariq Mustafa was nominated as Technical Leader of the team. 'Remember, we have to hit the target in nine months and countdown for it begins today'. Abdus Salam emphasised.[1]

---

[1] Interviews 1984: Folder VI, pp. 70-81

A relatively forlorn site of Sonmiani in Baluchistan was selected as the range for rocket firing. An American expert, monitoring the project, raised objection on grounds that this place was too close to a densely populated area. He was prevailed upon with assurance that any 'heavier launchings in the future' would most certainly be carried out by moving the pad to a barren site 'several hundred miles up the coast'. After studying the blueprint of launching pad, Ishrat Usmani felt reassured that there would be no difficulty in getting the structure ready within the tight timeframe.[1]

Against reports that Egypt might gain rocket technology from the Soviet Union, Abdus Salam found a reason to firm up Ayub Khan. He visited the Ordnance Factories in Wah, next to Rawalpindi cantonment, to explore if the motor and propellant for a smaller rocket could be fabricated locally. Once the locally made rockets were fired successfully, the Space Committee could get authorisation to develop a missile guidance systems. He then wrote to Ayub Khan, asking for permission to enlarge the size of his rocket firing team by recruiting 'about eight young physicists and electronics engineers on a more or less permanent basis'. In his letter to the President, he cited the example of an ongoing cooperation between India and the Federal Republic of Germany. Next, he pressed Ayub Khan to grant permission for the training of some 40 young scientists to tap possibilities in the field of aeronautical engineering.

In order to make sure that his proposal was not lost in the bureaucratic clog, he took Qudratullah Shahab, the Principal Secretary to the President, into confidence. 'I am enclosing a letter for the chief which deals with the matters we discussed together. The aeronautical studies are really a matter of life and death for the nation. If we get the green signal we can build this side up. The present total budget of the Space Committee is about 110,000 rupees. I would like this committee to be treated as an *Advanced Projects Organisation* to remain directly under the President to carry through things'. He pressed his case by adding 'I cannot tell you how deeply I feel we must not let the usual procedures halt progress. Please use all your force and (silent) eloquence'. He stated in the handwritten cover note, dated 11 November 1961, addressed to Qudratullah Shahab.

Almost everything went by plan until one day someone at the Ministry of Foreign Affairs woke up to the suspicion that the Peoples Republic of China, the

---

[1] Apparently, Pakistan army continues to test its missiles and rockets in Sonmiani Range

second most powerful communist country sharing a strategic segment of international border with Pakistan might frown upon the rocket program especially when such devices were used to gauge levels of nuclear radiation. Nobody in Pakistan wanted to create any disorder at a time when Ayub Khan himself supervised the process of improving ties with the Peoples Republic of China. Only a few days ahead of the date fixed for rocket firing, the Ministry of Foreign Affairs directed Ishrat Usmani to freeze the programme instantly. Ishrat Usmani begged the Ministry of Foreign Affairs to get clearance for the firing of one rocket the least. At the same, he despatched an urgent message to Abdus Salam. Upon receiving the message, Abdus Salam boarded the first available flight to Karachi.

Ishrat Usmani received Abdus Salam at the airport. 'Our only hope', the bureaucrat in Ishrat Usmani stated, 'rests with a direct intervention by the President'. Abdus Salam took the connecting flight to Rawalpindi and from the old Chaklala airport he went straight to the President House. He arrived at the President House just minutes before a historical session of the federal cabinet. Ayub Khan was about to promulgate his presidential constitution. Pakistan, in this way, Abdus Salam must have calculated, was well on the dot to have a new constitution and a debut into the space age.

'You can imagine all those flight connections and the fact that approaching the President out of the blue was not an easy task. When I reached there, the cabinet meeting had not yet started. I saw the President climbing down the stairs from his suite in the Presidency. He was on the way to the Cabinet Room, and his ministers and secretaries were respectfully lined up in the foyer'. Abdus Salam recalled the episode in an interview in 1984.

Ah! Professor! What are you doing here? Ayub Khan is reported to have exclaimed upon sighting Abdus Salam among his ministers and secretaries.

Sir, I have just come all the way from London and this is my story. 'In few sentences I then recounted how with his blessing we had planned to fire the rockets within a given timeframe. Now, when every minute detail was in order and only a button had to be pushed, we have been advised to hold back. Sir, I said, the driving force for us was the desire to take a lead upon India and enter space ahead of our rivals'. He remembered his brief speech, delivered in an emotionally charged voice. Ayub Khan must have been greatly amused by this thrilling performance of his thought-provoking science adviser. He proclaimed that the Professor needed to fire the rockets and Agha Shahi should face the consequences! Abdus Salam rushed back to board the closest flight to Karachi.

'That same evening, we made the first shots. I remember the whole scene. Perhaps none of us was familiar with the magnitude of explosion when the rocket blew out of the pad. It was a unique experience. We had entered space as a result of the effort put in by our own young scientists. There and then, Usmani and I prostrated into the thanksgiving *Sijdah* posture. Pakistan Enters Space Age was how the newspaper headlines screamed next morning. The whole country was taken by an enjoyable surprise. Very few people in the country were aware of the operation up until that day'. He remembered.

By launching those rockets successfully, Pakistan had become the third country in Asia and the Middle East, and the tenth in the world, to score such victory in display of technological know-how. By firing the first rocket in the subcontinent, Pakistan had indeed taken the lead over India. In June 1962, therefore, Ayub Khan was credited not only for giving Pakistan a constitution, but also for taking the country into space age. Abdus Salam used to relate to the early history of Pakistan's journey into space age as a tale in national pride. There was no denying the fact that Pakistan's achievement in space programme, with of course the American encouragement to do so, opened the door for development of missiles locally.[1]

'Incidentally, the rocket we fired was the only modern radar we had in the 1965 war with India. We gave it to Pakistan Navy for they had none other. This was the only effective radar in Karachi. It had been loaned to us by the Americans because we did not have enough money to pay. In fact, they protested over its use in the war'. Abdus Salam recalled the excitement he had experienced in 1962 with his friend and colleague, Ishrat Usmani.[2]

Historically, after its inaugural demonstration, the Space and Upper Atmosphere Research Committee was a prelude to the acquisition of modern missile firing technology, especially in the development of ballistic missile program.[3]

---

[1] Abdul Ghani (1982): p. 67

[2] Interviews 1984: Folder VI, pp. 70-81

[3] Feroz Hassan Khan (2013): p. 236

VI

As noted above, at the time of its birth, little over ten years ago, Pakistan was a state without sufficient stationery to run the federal government secretariat, facing dire shortage of rudimentary ordnance for the army. Hardly much had changed on the economic front when Abdus Salam and Ishrat Usmani set upon raising the foundation to gain expertise in nuclear technology. With their imaginative contribution and relentless determination, the dynamic duo did not waste time in bringing the country, at a pace faster than their own expectations, to a stage of irreversible aptitude. Soon as there was the need, Pakistan took a detour and gate-crashed into the exclusive nuclear club. By all conceivable standards it was like climbing uphill without the benefits of healthy lungs and body muscles. Despite financial restraints and bureaucratic resistance, the two men pulled the miracle out within a matter of few years. Abdus Salam stood vindicated in discovering Ishrat Usmani to preside over the Atomic Energy Commission.

Nazir Ahmad, the previous Chairman of the Atomic Energy Commission, happened to have been a victim of political instability; he served at a time of in-house coups with governments falling in a quick succession. He is known to have left the commission in a state of disappointment.[1]

Ishrat Usmani, on the other hand, took charge under a military junta that had come to stay. Sponsored by the capitalist west, Ayub Khan was perceived as an omen of stability to trounce the communist threat. In other words, the political fortunes of Abdus Salam and Ishrat Usmani were protected by a powerful clout of international players. As a physicist with rich experience in public sector bureaucracy, Ishrat Usmani represented an ideal combination to lead the Atomic Energy Commission. He did not waste time in bringing the organisation up to the professional level of a fine scientific institution. A meticulous package of policies and procedures was put in place to safeguard the administrative and operational autonomy of the commission as a statutory organisation under the federal government. Before long, the commission began setting up essential laboratories and regional centres under its jurisdiction. Tirelessly, Ishrat Usmani dealt with everyday challenges in policy, administration, operations and finance. He initiated, planned and monitored projects, withstanding pressures of

---

[1] Feroz Khan (2013): p. 30

increasing costs and diminishing resources. He fought fierce battles to win grants in order to meet budgetary constraints.

Together with Abdus Salam, holding a prestigious high-profile academic position in London, Ishrat Usmani succeeded in raising the professional image of the commission to a level where networking among international stakeholders was made possible to the best advantage of Pakistan. In a matter of less than five years, the effort jointly put in by the duo bore fruit. Pakistan gained sufficient confidence to condition its support for the United Nations sponsored non-proliferation treaty to boldly demand nuclear equality in South Asia. Pakistan would be ready to sign the treaty only if India did the same.

As a Member of the Atomic Energy Commission for 16 years (1958–74), Abdus Salam was closely involved with the foundation and shaping-up of nuclear establishment in Pakistan. He made it a practice to spend three weeks in a row in the first half and another three in the second half of the year in Pakistan. He worked in close collaboration with Ishrat Usmani and the fact that the two could converse in the language of physics with professional ease, their interaction proved highly economical and productive. In the given order of state protocol, Abdus Salam could approach the President almost directly. Whereas, the chain of command for Ishrat Usmani obliged him to route official communication through the federal minister in-charge for nuclear energy. He could not imagine short-circuiting the ranks above him.

But then despite the dissimilarity of station, Abdus Salam and Ishrat Usmani complemented each other as natural allies. While Ishrat Usmani manoeuvred the everyday reality, Abdus Salam harmonised the effort at presidential and international levels. Their working relationship reflected an inter-dependence into which the two of them were rather pleasantly locked for nearly twelve years.

Pakistan's excursion into atomic age started with the typical assertion to tap alternate sources of energy. Ishrat Usmani based his case upon the remoteness and obsolete nature of Pakistan's hydroelectric sources. He argued that 'rapid advances in nuclear technology' held tremendous promise to addressing under-development. His submission about the feasibility of nuclear energy was routed through the National Planning Commission, an organisation he suspected as 'one of the most hollow establishments' comprising of members unfamiliar with nuclear business. 'I have accordingly moved Sterling Cole to send a high-powered mission to Pakistan sometimes in December to review the report. I hope you will agree with this strategy'. He corresponded with Abdus Salam in October 1961.

William Sterling Cole (1904–87) was a Republican Congressman in the United States House of Representatives. He had served as the first Director General of the International Atomic Energy Agency (1957–1961). Typically, Pakistan was required to involve international consultants and some of the leading American firms to justify the case for technical and economic assistance in the area of nuclear technology. 'If I had not handled it, the consultants would have swallowed us alive and completely destroyed our case'. Ishrat Usmani added and then asked Abdus Salam to read through and comment upon the accompanying report. 'I don't think you have any idea of the amount of work which I and my young colleagues have put in to get the report in the shape in which it appears in its final form. It is now up to the Government to act. If you, in your capacity as Chief Scientific Adviser to the President, can strongly recommend the launching of the nuclear power programme, I am sure it will go a long way to help us to pilot it through the Cabinet'. He urged.

Ishrat Usmani sounded quite hopeful that a couple of ministers in the federal government, such as Zulfiqar Bhutto, would favour the cause of nuclear technology. He was not wrong as Zulfiqar Bhutto, the Federal Minister for Fuel, Power and Natural Resources, strongly advocated the case prepared by the Atomic Energy Commission. In his introductory letter to the President, written toward the end of November 1961, Zulfiqar Bhutto termed the proposal for nuclear power 'to be not only philosophically sound but economically good'. He urged the President to grant approval for the nuclear programme 'without loss of time' or getting entangled into the 'webs of bureaucracy'. Zulfiqar Bhutto proposed that 'the task of negotiating the terms' of foreign assistance should be entrusted to the Chairman of the Atomic Energy Commission. He remarked that the value of setting up nuclear power stations in the country was 'too obvious to be emphasised' and well above ordinary economic considerations. 'I am sure the country will be grateful to you for this momentous decision which will truly symbolise its entry into Atomic age'. He commended the President in advance.

Given the conservative outlook of public sector leadership in those days, the approval to pursue nuclear energy as an alternate source of power generation was a major breakthrough in itself. Once the government signalled to go ahead, the next big challenge was to assemble an appropriately skilled workforce. Abdus Salam remembered his relatively recent experience in Lahore, the Punjab metropolis, where only one person had some level of familiarity with Dirac's Equation. In one of his reports, Mohammed Sharif, the Federal Secretary for Education and Scientific Research, the man known to have enforced peace between Abdus Salam and Sirajuddin Ahmed only a few years ago, found that the poverty of science education was illustrated in the absence of laboratories, equipment or qualified science teachers. In this way, the dream to go after nuclear energy required a start from the scratch; and such an undertaking amounted to some kind of compromise among the departments of education, finance and planning.

Securing budgetary allocations from the departments of finance and planning was so hard that success in dragging out less than a dozen annual grants for doctoral programs abroad was rated as an enormous victory of Abdus Salam.[1] At best, the whole exercise guaranteed a frivolously meagre size of eighteen highly qualifies scientists in three years. There was no way the tiny community of physicists could satisfy the demands of an upcoming nuclear industry. Somehow, in the end, the miracle happened as the joint effort put in by Ishrat Usmani and Abdus Salam began bearing fruit. Over 300 science graduates were selected for higher education and training abroad by way of their placement in some of the well-known European and American centres of excellence. Locations where those young people would receive training were marked out in accordance with the specific nature of expertise required in Pakistan. There was the expectation that first generation of about 500 adequately qualified scientists would roll out to take up jobs awaiting them in the departments of nuclear energy, agriculture, electronics, medicine and chemical engineering in a matter of three to five years. There was considerable success within the given framework of time. 'We have succeeded in training, in the last three years, something like 500 men at the PhD level. Now that's a tremendous number for a country like ours'. Abdus Salam stated in 1964.[2]

Although the numbers were still strikingly insufficient, at least the journey seemed to have begun in the appropriate direction. At the same time, there was hope that the precedence could kindle interest among the youth to pursue careers in science and research. Under this plan, which Abdus Salam termed as a 'massive shock training program' the number of scientists and engineers, qualifying abroad as well as locally, was expected to hit the 7000 per year mark

---

[1] Abdul Ghani (1981): p. 65-66
[2] Ideals and Realities (1984): p.6

before the end of the decade. A good deal of support to the program was provided by inspiring academics like Professor Rafi Mohammed (1903–1988), a highly qualified Experimental Physicist who had studied at the Cavendish Laboratory in Cambridge under Ernest Rutherford before heading the Department Physics in Lahore's Government College.[1]

Abdus Salam used to reminisce how astoundingly the time lost in not having had enough science in the recent past in Pakistan was plugged in promptly. He paid tribute to those young physicists, mathematicians, health scientists and biologists, both men and women, who were despatched abroad to study in schools of research in the United States and the United Kingdom and then return home to serve Pakistan.[2]

Due to financial constraints, there was the expectation that youth placed abroad would complete their doctoral studies in two years; whereas, the hosting institutions took a different view. Occasionally, stressed out Pakistani students approached Abdus Salam and hoped that he might find them a reprieve through his influence. As a teacher and research supervisor himself, he was aware of the fact that successful completion of doctoral degrees required three years the least. He could see that only the 'very exceptional' might finish their work in two years. In January 1962, he took the matter up with the Ministry of Education. 'The study leave rules in this matter are completely antiquated and the sooner they are revised the better it will be for the scholars who have been sent under them. I think it is a matter of principle and I would like to address the Ministry of Finance, if they are the final authority in this subject. I would appreciate if you could let me know whom I should address. If it is not possible to revise these rules, my suggestion would be that it would be better not to send any scholars rather than to send them under the impression that they will complete their work in two years'. He wrote to the Secretary of the Pakistan Council of Scientific and Industrial Research (PCSIR) on 15 January 1962.

When he was awarded the Atoms for Peace Foundation award, he donated the accompanying sum of money to set up a scholarship trust for Pakistani students.

In his forty years of academic life, Abdus Salam would not miss the opportunity to write reference letters for Pakistani students. He would do so even when the candidate was not directly known to him. For example, there was the

---

[1] Feroz Khan (2013): pp. 26-27

[2] The Nation, Lahore (Pakistan), 21 August 1992, Friday Review, p. 8

reference letter he wrote to Leonard Katz, the President of American Astro Dynamics Corporation, about a Pakistani botanist. 'I am in no way connected with his research work and therefore cannot give my first-hand judgment about it', he started and then went on to introduce the candidate as a former student of Professor Sultan Ahmad (1910–1995) who happened to be 'one of the very few people' respected in Lahore for their 'painstaking' research in plant sciences.

Somewhat amazingly, the list of infrastructural disabilities and financial constraints weighing upon the training program was topped up by the bizarre belief held by Mohammed Sharif, the Secretary Education. Mohammed Sharif suffered from an intriguing political phobia of the American Central Intelligence Agency (CIA). He suspected that Pakistani students sent to the United States for higher studies were most likely to become intelligence agents. Why, where, when and how he picked up the eccentricity was not known to either Ishrat Usmani or Abdus Salam. Due to his trepidation, the Secretary Education preferred Europe over the United States. As a consequence of his obsession, students required to be placed somewhere in the United States found it harder to get their cases processed in time. Pakistan, according to Abdus Salam, ended up paying a price for the 'strange idea' professed by its top education officer. Not only the opportunity to gain expertise had been lost at a time when the country was in dire need of qualified people, the Indian scientists and professionals triumphed in sweeping the American job market. Those Indian students earned foreign exchange remittances for home, encouraged others to follow the example, held influential positions in the United States; and finally, many of them returned to serve science and research in India.

'Thousands of Indian students went to study in the United States. They manned almost every research institution of repute, surpassing the Japanese presence. On the average, in a department of ten students, no less than five would be from India compared to two or three from Japan. Sharif, on the other hand, blocked the way for Pakistani students. I don't know why and how did he form this opinion but he remained firmly tied to it up until his last day in office'. Abdus Salam remembered.[1]

In fact, Mohammed Sharif went too far. While attending a conference under the United Nations Committee on Education and Science (UNESCO), he warned India about the frightful consequences of sending students over to the United States. Abdus Salam remembered the occasion with a bit of embarrassment as

---

[1] Interviews 1984: Folder VI, pp. 15-17

Indira Gandhi, the future Prime Minister of India, then serving as a junior minister of her country, happened to be leading the Indian delegation. Mohammed Sharif's presumption was incomprehensible to Abdus Salam but then it was not feasible to confront or bypass Mohammed Sharif due to his influence; he had been a teacher of Ayub Khan.

At a time when the Atomic Energy Commission struggled to secure financial support for its growth, the uncanny obsession Mohammed Sharif held about the American intelligence network made only a part of the overall bureaucratic wrestling. At times, Ishrat Usmani himself appeared to be a part of the puzzle for he was a misfit in the bureaucracy. Every now and then, his candour, sharp tongue and biting wits would land him in politically incorrect and explosive situations. Both his equals and bosses found reason to frown upon him. Nearly always he ended up heightening the level of ongoing tensions. As much as Abdus Salam did not wish to get sucked into bureaucratic bickering, he felt obliged to step forward and defend Ishrat Usmani by approaching the President.

'Sharif is trying his level best to keep the National Science Council under the Ministry of Education, but I don't think he would succeed'. Ishrat Usmani informed Abdus Salam in a letter from Karachi on 15 September 1961. Few days later, he poured his anger out over Saeed Hassan, another of the powerful deputies of Ayub Khan. 'By the way, you will not be surprised when I say that Saeed Hassan is carrying on a whispering and vicious campaign against the whole atomic energy programme, particularly because it is headed by me. Not that I care very much, but I thought you should know about it'. He added. On another occasion, he urged Abdus Salam to stop behaving like a nice guy. 'To a very large extent the responsibility for the mess, if I may say so, rests on your timidity and failure to advise the President firmly'. He wrote to Abdus Salam on 31 October 1961.

By the end of 1961, plans were ready to build the first modern complex of laboratories for Pakistan Institute of Nuclear Sciences at Nilore near Islamabad. Edward Stone, the famous American architect was invited to prepare the architectural blueprint. Just when the construction activity started, Islamabad was shaken by two earthquakes within a month. Nazir Ahmad, the former chairman of the Atomic Energy Commission, wrote a letter to the Karachi-based daily newspaper *Dawn* demanding a review of the location for laboratories. His letter triggered panic and there was the apprehension that a tremor of relatively severe intensity might blow up the atomic reactor leading to widespread contamination in the neighbourhood. As fear campaign picked up momentum, the Chairman of the Capital Development Authority, in Islamabad, asked Ishrat Usmani to provide an assurance for safety. On his part, Ishrat Usmani suspected the whole affair as 'some underground conspiracy' aimed at subverting the atomic energy programme. He despatched a portfolio of related documentation to Abdus Salam urging him 'to discuss the issue with the President and see that categorical statement to this effect is issued at the highest level'. But then, for some reason, the uproar fizzled out on its own, the building work started on the site, and Abdus Salam was saved from the test of advocacy.

Next, Ishrat Usmani was castigated for being extravagant in selecting the lucrative design, as if he was about to build something like the Taj Mahal. He was accused of wasting public funds on 'domes and arches reminiscent of the Moguls era'. His opponents believed he should have gone straight for just a functional building and saved chunks of money for research programmes. As criticism mounted, the objection went to the powerful Inter-Services Bureau presided over by Ayub Khan himself. According to Abdus Salam, the President took a lighter view of the whole affair. Tell me, gentlemen, do we not wish our women folk to be well-groomed and look adorable instead of expecting them to be merely functional? Ayub Khan is reported to have remarked in a rather sexist tone that would surely have been bombed upon as an act of political incorrectness a few years later. Ishrat Usmani was let off the hook.[1]

VII

Indeed, in the end, it was the vibrant working alliance between Abdus Salam and Ishrat Usmani that enabled Pakistan to build up a steady and profitable nuclear establishment within a matter of few years. However, the cardinal question that remains to be addressed is where exactly did the two stand in relation to Pakistan's desire to manufacture nuclear weapons. What sort of place could be assigned to the two in the short history and map of nuclear Pakistan?

Of course, it did not take Ishrat Usmani more than three years in bringing the Atomic Energy Commission to confidently preside over a federation of highly talented manpower and gorgeous laboratories, with an enviable thrust to get into business. He muddled through bureaucratic impediments, survived hostile

---

[1] *Dawn*, Karachi [Circa Aug-Sep 1992]

criticism and yet equipped the country with a comprehensive package of nuclear sciences, electronics and radiobiology; with hundreds of scientists involved in a range of research projects. Apart from building the Pakistan Institute of Nuclear Science and Technology, he supervised the construction of eight research and training centres in radioisotopes, medicine and agriculture. Within a matter of few years, his institute in Nilore cemented together sturdy research groups in superconductivity, lasers and solid-state nuclear track detection. Pakistan found itself on the road to self-sufficiency in the production of nuclear fuel. When supplies disrupted from Canada, the needs of nuclear power plant in Karachi were met locally by facilities at Nilore. Some of the best libraries and databases in nuclear sciences were available at the institute, enabling its research reactor school to become a Centre for Nuclear Studies offering degree programmes.

'I only wished you were there personally to watch the very colourful ceremony in the cool October evening of Lahore. The President, of course, was tremendously impressed and remained in the laboratories for about an hour and was deeply interested in the variety of applications of atomic energy to some of our problems. He was pleasantly surprised to see our team of young men staffing the laboratories. I told him that modern science was a young men's job and the older people should be screened if Pakistan's science is to progress. He just nodded his head in agreement'. Ishrat Usmani wrote to Abdus Salam, on 31 October 1961, when the nuclear research centre in health sector was inaugurated in Lahore by Ayub Khan. Abdus Salam had been unable to make it to the occasion due to his academic commitments in London.

As for the cardinal question relating to the shared contribution of Ishrat Usmani and Abdus Salam in making Pakistan a nuclear power, any truthful answer remains embedded in historical pressures and caution surrounding the duo. While it is simply impossible to overlook the effort the two of them had put in towards raising the institutional establishment, a sharpened view of their ambition beyond the achievement of required expertise might come with declassification of state records, if any ever kept, in Pakistan.

Like the case with birth of Pakistan itself, the early years of the Atomic Energy Commission were marred with major security demands and challenges overtaking South Asia. In October 1962, India suffered a military humiliation at the hands of China. Two years later, China carried out its first nuclear test providing India the reason to do the same. Then, in September 1965, India and Pakistan warred over Kashmir. In other words, the very childhood of Pakistan's nuclear industry was overshadowed with demands of national defence and security. As a result, the debate over acquisition of capability to make weapons had begun almost at the very beginning of nuclear energy programs, and by 1965 it was raging between two camps of government. Zulfiqar Bhutto, the young and hawkish Foreign Minister, advocated to go nuclear without wasting time; the other side led by Finance Minister Mohammad Shoaib doubted the cost effectiveness of such a large-scale enterprise. Both sides agreed on the long-term value of gaining national autonomy in nuclear capability, only the consensus lacked on when and how. Caught between the two groups, Abdus Salam and Ishrat Usmani seemed to side with Zulfiqar Bhutto.[1]

Where did Ayub Khan stand on the nuclear issue? When Abdus Salam was quizzed about it, he considered it 'a very difficult question'. He did not wish to go public over it.[2] Ayub Khan, according to Abdus Salam, preferred caution and patience even when it was not easy for him to ignore the emerging balance of power in South Asia. As China moved closer to becoming a nuclear power, India stepped up its efforts towards enrichment of uranium and began winning greater expressions of support from the western block. There was no way the military-dominated state in Pakistan could stay aloof from such a volatile state of vulnerability. Pakistan had grown out of the political psyche of Liaquat Ali Khan who was prepared to disband the army in exchange for a security assurance from the United States. Ayub Khan had been a resolute believer of reliance upon the western block but he could just not discount the preferential treatment India had begun receiving after its thrashing by China. He valued the reality of nuclear technology but held the rather wishful belief that the stage to make weapons had yet to arrive.

About the end of 1960, a rather unusual proposal relating to the possibility of nuclear cooperation between Pakistan and the Federal Republic of Germany was presented to Ayub Khan. This proposal was based on an assumption that the Federal Republic of Germany might wish to cooperate with Pakistan in order to carry out a nuclear test at some remote geographical site. Pakistan was understood to have offered Federal Republic of Germany the facility to explode an experimental nuclear device somewhere in Baluchistan. According to Abdus Salam, this offer was made during the course of Ayub Khan's visit to Federal Republic of Germany in the summer of 1961. Both Abdus Salam and Ishrat

---

[1] Feroz Khan (2013): pp. 60-64
[2] Interviews 1984: Folder VII, p. 77

Usmani received the signal from Ayub Khan to accompany the presidential entourage. In return for the proposal advanced by Pakistan, the Federal Republic of Germany was expected to share necessary logistical requirements like training of personnel and ground facilities to carry out the experiment.[1]

Pakistan, in this way, dreamed of claiming the nuclear lead over India. In all probability, however, the whole affair might have been a case of misjudged perception or day-dreaming. Someone in the Government of Pakistan was somehow inclined to pick up the peculiar notion that Chancellor Konrad Adenauer (1875–1967), living in rebounded rivalries of post war Europe, nurtured nuclear ambition. In view of his survival out of an assassination attempt, masterminded by Menachem Begin (1913–1992), Konrad Adenauer must have been assessed an ally by default. But then, of course, the German grandee, concluding his final term in office, declined to oblige.

However, a consortium of four German firms, previously acting as consultants to the Atomic Energy Commission of Pakistan, did offer assistance in the setting up chemical laboratories at the Institute of Nuclear Science and Technology. Professor Siegfried Balke (1902–1984), the German Minister for Atomic Energy Affairs, hinted that Pakistan stood fairly good chances of qualifying for a soft term loan to benefit from the offer. Upon returning home, Ishrat Usmani followed-up with the German offer in a confidential memorandum to Musarrat Zuberi, the Secretary to the Ministry of Fuel, Power and Natural Resources. He viewed it as an opportunity to reprocess 'uranium fuel elements and separation of plutonium, together with a radioactive waste treatment facility'. He expected German scientists to visit Pakistan to offer assistance in research projects related to 'nuclear chemical processes of great importance and consequence'. Due to the special nature of the project, Ishrat Usmani urged Musarrat Zuberi to bypass the Development Working Party of the Planning Commission and approach the Federal Minister of Finance directly. 'You may also consider the desirability of making simultaneous approach through the German Ambassador here. In this connection, it may kindly be noted that the funds will not come out of the German loan, but will be provided from out of an ad hoc technical aid which Germany will give to a friendly country. There is no special fund of this nature in Germany and the requests from friendly countries, as I understand the position, are considered purely on the basis of merits and

---

[1] Based on notes taken during the course of 1984 interviews with Abduls Salam when he went off-the-record

need for technical assistance'. Ishrat Usmani added in the memorandum, dated 4 September 1961.

Even though Pakistan was not successful in bringing the Federal Republic of Germany around to an uncanny partnership for the explosion of nuclear device, the desire and intent to fabricate fuel did not fizzle out. For quite a while, Abdus Salam and Ishrat Usmani continued to advocate the view that any prolonged delay towards fuel fabrication was bound to cost Pakistan far more than India. Apart from the indexation of expenditures involved in the procurement of highly sophisticated equipment and technology, they feared the international opinion might as well take an unfavourable turn. But despite the strong urge to achieve self-sufficiency in fuel recycling, there was the lack of courage to come out in the open. In the first place, the inhibition was rooted in those bilateral agreements Pakistan and the United States had signed in the late 1950s 'for cooperation in civilian and peaceful uses of atomic energy'.[1] Any leakage of information, the duo feared, could derail the ongoing program for training of personnel. Under the spirit of its Atoms for Peace initiative, the United States Government funded the training of foreign students; and nobody in Pakistan wished to jeopardise the opportunity. Hence the caution to continue doing business as usual, from the training of personnel to making the choice in relation to a reactor for power generation.

'Conditions in West Pakistan are similar both in respect of the power potential as well as availability of natural fissile materials to those prevailing in western parts of India. For these and other reasons our programme has to follow the Indian pattern, except of course that the scale may be different'. Abdus Salam wrote to Ishrat Usmani, on 14 March 1962, voting in favour of a natural uranium graphite Calder Hall type of reactor. In view of the power shortage already facing Karachi, he believed 'a modest reactor producing 80 MW Electrical' should be sufficient for the time being.

As for the hold-up on uranium-plutonium reprocessing and enrichment, there was not the slightest doubt that nuclear power generation and the urgency to evolve an indigenous facility for production of weapon-grade fuel went side by side. In fact, a direct reference to the strategic linkage was avoided as a matter of tactical rather than an ideological necessity. Afterwards, Ishrat Usmani used to refer to his contribution as the setting up of a razor factory in Pakistan. It was for the consumers, he would remark, to decide whether they wished to shave off

---

[1] Feroz Khan (2013): p. 29

their beards or slaughter each other with the product.[1] Very few people in Pakistan realised that Ishrat Usmani had begun dreaming about indigenous fabrication of fuel soon after his induction as Chairman of the Atomic Energy Commission. 'I, as you know, rely on my transparent sincerity, patriotism and enthusiasm to do something genuinely solid for the country'. He had written to Abdus Salam in a confidential letter, dated 30 November 1961.

When the Indian intentions towards reprocessing of uranium were well known, Ayub Khan directed the Atomic Energy Commission to prepare a feasibility study for Pakistan to consider catching up with India. Ishrat Usmani prepared the case taking into account the full range of pros and cons. Ayub Khan's financial advisers knocked the plan down for its pronounced lack of cost effectiveness and economic viability.[2]

On 29 January 1967, the Rawalpindi-based Urdu-language daily newspaper *Kohistan* quoted Abdus Salam as predicting that India was about to explode a nuclear device. This newspaper had an influential market in northern Punjab, the home of Pakistan army. In his own way, Abdus Salam aimed at urging the government to consider the deterrence.[3]

Going off-the-record, Abdus Salam explained that Pakistan's dependence on western assistance inhibited Ayub Khan. Whereas, both Abdus Salam and Ishrat Usmani feared the abortion of an opportunity if action was not take in time. It was necessary, therefore, to make the move before the expenses on equipment or the stringency of international safeguards made the realisation of the dream impossible. This urgency, he stated, compelled the two of them to keep advocating the case for setting up the plant for uranium reprocessing. Like India, he added, once the capability to fabricate the right grade and quantity of nuclear fuel had been quietly achieved, the question of exploding a device could be settled in terms of an engineering expedition and political decision making.

'Around 1965 we begged Ayub Khan to give us a sum of 13 million rupees to complete the uranium separation project within two to three years'. Abdus Salam confided. 'At that time it was much easier to obtain the technology from France. If we had the money then, Pakistan would be fairly closer to making the bomb any time after 1968. But the President was not convinced, he feared the

---

[1] Daily *Jang*, Rawalpindi, 2 March 1988
[2] Ashok Kapur (1987): p. 81
[3] Daily *Kohistan* had a strong right-wing conservative leaning, but the newspaper lost its competitive edge before finally disappearing from the market in the 1970s.

diversion of money into a nuclear venture would portray a poor image of the economic performance of his government and the donors might blame Pakistan for wasting the aid. We went as far as having a high-powered cabinet committee to discuss the proposal for reprocessing plant. Apart from me, others in the committee included arch bureaucrats such as Mohammed Yusuf and Muzaffar Ahmad. Mohammed Yusuf was the Secretary for Foreign Affairs. He opposed the proposal. In one of the meetings, he chided me for my keenness on such a lucrative idea. You don't even live in Pakistan. Your home is England. What do you care about this country? He mocked. I vividly remember losing my cool, wishing to wring his neck. If some other members of the committee had not jumped in, I would have slapped him on the face, the least'. Abdus Salam recollected the episode.

Abdus Salam went on to reveal that after the German rebuke of 1961, Pakistan endeavoured to convince the Peoples Republic of China on similar lines. According to him, it happened in 1965, but the Chinese response was not any different from that of the Federal Republic of Germany. 'In the end, a few years later, not only costs shot up, France gave in to the United States' pressure and had cold feet over an agreed deal for the supply of re-processing plant'. He remarked.

In the end, Pakistan felt compelled to commence its nuclear weapons program only when India staged the Pokhran show in May 1974. Historically, the credit of being the most consistent advocates, throughout the 1960s, for Pakistan to acquire nuclear capability and leave behind a solid foundation for this purpose, cannot be denied to Ishrat Usmani and Abdus Salam. But the two avoided public posturing and rhetoric for fear of Pakistan's powerful sponsors in the west.

Chapter Seven
My Centre

One of Abdus Salam's major achievements, next to his landmark contribution in Theoretical Physics for which he won the Nobel Prize, was the creation of the International Centre for Theoretical Physics in Trieste, Italy. He is reported to have picked up the idea to hunt for the centre at the Rochester Conference in 1960. Historically, it was a time when the majority among physicists looked forward to the dawn of sophisticated accelerators to explore a much deeper understanding of sub-nuclear matter. Because it was always a challenge to raise colossal sums of money to accomplish such a state-of-the-art technology, the proposal to set up an international institution for theoretical physics sounded rather uncomplicated. As a theoretical physicist himself, Abdus Salam was aware of the logistical modesty of his tribe, that is, the ability of theoreticians to perform without costly equipment and laboratories.[1]

Once he began hammering the idea, there was more food for thought. In a global environment blended with the odd mix of dread and hope attached to the value of nuclear energy, his best bet was to get the United Nations engaged. He tabled the proposal, in September 1960, for a *school* of theoretical physics before the International Atomic Energy Agency.[2] After the proposal had been put together the agency membership of Pakistan served as the fast diplomatic channel to launch the idea. Apparently, the robust political animal in Abdus Salam took the plea that such a school was likely to facilitate the much-needed interaction between physicists belonging to the two super-power blocks. 'It need not be costly, it would not involve investment in expensive equipment that would be essential for a centre for experimental physics'. He argued.

---

[1] Ideals and Realities (1984): p. 192
[2] Abdul Ghani (1982): pp. 73-75

Afterwards, however, as months passed by and the support for the proposal picked up momentum, he added other compelling reasons in support of his case. For example, he raised alarm about the isolation of physicists in less developed countries. When the agency agreed to study the proposal, he began working on statutory layout and financial commitments required to realise the dream.

Meanwhile William Sterling Cole (1904–1987), the American Congressman who had presided over the agency since its inception in 1957, cleared the deck for Sigvard Eklund (1911–2000), the Swedish physicist determined to promote professional rather than bureaucratic style of leadership. Sigvard Eklund constituted a panel of prominent physicists to report on the feasibility of the centre proposed by Abdus Salam. Generally the response was favourable with some opposition. Henry Smyth (1898–1986), the American physicist who represented the United States, declined to entertain the idea on grounds that developing world did not produce scientists at a scale to be served with an international centre. Falling in line, there was the Australian ambassador who confused the whole idea with outright racism. He opposed the motion on grounds that Theoretical Physics was the 'Rolls Royce' of sciences and its promotion in economies driven by bullock-carts did not make much sense.[1]

Mindful of the fact that fielding questions generated by the superiority cum racist complex could sidetrack the proposal, Abdus Salam steered clear of the trap and, instead, touched upon a highly sensitive security chord. 'We dare not forget that there are still uncharted areas in theoretical plasma physics which are vital to the tapping of fusion power. We dare not forget that in spite of all our advances in nuclear physics, we still do not know the theoretical expression for the law of force between two nucleons'. Those areas, he reminded, posed direct and immediate concern to the mandate of the International Atomic Energy Agency. He assured that the proposed centre would serve as the clearing house for new ideas from theoretical physicists all over the world.[2]

As for housing the proposed centre, India qualified as one of the ideal places. In fact, India enjoyed a much wider range of diplomatic relations across ideological barriers of the time; its community of scientists and educational infrastructure checkmated many other locations including Abdus Salam's homeland, Pakistan. Homi Bhabha, a theoretical physicist himself, was expected to jump and grab the initiative. He was steeped in an arrogance of his own kind

---

[1] Jagjit Singh (1992): p. 70
[2] Ideals and Realities (1984): pp. 186,189-190

and did not seem to have taken the emergence of the International Atomic Energy Agency very kindly. He believed that India was mature enough to make and manage its future in atomic energy. From the very beginning, he despised the idea of flocking his country into the preferential drill of international safeguards. He did not have patience for any paternal tutoring and tutelage from either the United Nations or the western powers. Seldom did he travel to attend the meetings of the agency. Instead, he would nominate someone relatively junior to represent India. How could he entertain an agency proposal forwarded by Pakistan?

First, Homi Bhabha convened a meeting of the International Union of Pure and Applied Physics, in Bombay, to get the proposed centre brushed aside as unwise. Next, he travelled to Vienna to attend the meeting of the Board of Governors of the International Atomic Energy Agency. To his misfortune, the Board on that occasion was presided over by Ishrat Usmani, the Pakistani representative. Also, Abdus Salam had come a long way from his years of wilderness in Lahore. As Chief Scientific Advisor to the Government of Pakistan, he could not be distracted anymore by the glitter of Homi Bhabha's class, art, wealth and powerful connections. While speaking at the Board meeting, Homi Bhabha delivered his tirade of opposition by quoting the opinion he had mustered at the International Union of Pure and Applied Physics in their meeting in Bombay. Soon as Homi Bhabha concluded his arguments, the Italian delegate at the agency got up to move a technical objection. Did the agency formally authorise the Indian delegate to seek an opinion off the International Union of Pure and Applied Physics? Everyone looked towards the Director General, who denied the existence of any authorisation to that effect. In the absence of an official authorisation, the Italian representative demanded that any references made to the International Union of Pure and Applied Physics should be expunged from the proceedings of the Board.

Once the case prepared by Homi Bhabha imploded and he was driven into unsheltered territory, Abdus Salam took charge from the Italian delegate. 'May I ask Dr Bhabha as to when did he write his last research paper? And, may I ask him how many physicists below the age of 40 he has conversed with during the last ten years?' This amounted to shooting point blank, hitting the soft underbelly, below the belt. Homi Bhabha did not have much to offer in reply, he kept silent.

At the dinner reception later in the evening, Abdus Salam was amused to find the majority of Board members gathered around Homi Bhabha. It might have been an expression of politeness or an attempt at nursing the injured ego. Abdus Salam felt the pinch. He went to make peace with his Indian adversary, and offered to support the proposal for seating the centre in Bombay provided the idea was acceptable to the Government of India and supported by the majority of delegates at the International Atomic Energy Agency. Homi Bhabha played the master stroke in response to Abdus Salam's gesture of peace. He expressed his readiness to have the centre housed in Bombay provided Abdus Salam moved there to manage it. Abdus Salam considered it a logistical impossibility, and the proposal to house the proposed centre in Bombay faded out as quickly as it had popped up. Later, as the centre began working in Italy, Abdus Salam urged Homi Bhabha to send over physicists from India. Not only Homi Bhabha ignored the offer, he signalled his junior staff officers to respond and tell Abdus Salam that India had 'every conceivable facility' for the intellectual development of its theoretical physicists.

It took a while to get the centre approved, established, up and running. During the course of struggle for the centre, Abdus Salam used to carry a basketful of grapes on his desk to gain energy at meetings in Vienna. 'I seldom smoke, but I must have smoked fifty cigarettes along with eating a kilogram of grapes'. His hard work paid off when the resolution moved by Pakistan won 35 votes against 18 abstentions. Next, the question before the Board of Governors was to agree upon the location of the proposed centre.[1]

Every now and then someone from the shrinking community of science promoters back home in Pakistan laments about the manner in which Abdus Salam was snubbed when he pushed for the proposed centre to be housed in Pakistan. Did Abdus Salam really wish to have the centre in Pakistan? In all probability he was not in a position to raise the stakes on Pakistan due to a number of compelling reasons. He did check the proposal out with Ayub Khan by proposing Abbotabad as the possible home for the entre. Given the persecution of summer heat on southern plains of Pakistan, Abbotabad presented an ideal location. Here, next to the cantonment town in the scenic foothills of sub-Himalayan northwest, the mighty Indus turned left to flow in the direction of Arabian Sea. Abbotabad was also the home district of Ayub Khan, which

---

[1] Interviews 1984: VII, pp. 41 and 213

meant the President, might take a favourable view of the idea.[1] Incidentally, Abdus Salam was saved from the test by a financial adviser of Ayub Khan who, after going through the proposal, commented that the Professor wanted to build a five-star hotel devoted to scientists from all over the world.

Very few people in Pakistan know about the forthright advice Abdus Salam had received on this account from his good old friend Ishrat Usmani. Down-to-earth, Ishrat Usmani urged Abdus Salam to steer clear of the ambition to have the proposed centre housed in Pakistan. Pakistan, Ishrat Usmani suspected, suffered from a range of self-inflicted disabilities in offering world class hospitality.

'As to the merits of the proposal to locate the centre in Pakistan, my personal feelings are mixed because I don't think that men of international calibre would be prepared to come to Pakistan to spend long periods of time in the puritan atmosphere of Abbotabad. Unless, therefore, you have someone who can go along with you to staff the institute established in Pakistan, I have my serious doubts about its future. Further, we will have complications because of our government's attitude towards Israel, India and China'. Ishrat Usmani wrote to Abdus Salam on 23 October 1962.

Given the fact that international centres of scholarship in the world were gravitated in Europe and the United States, he pressed Abdus Salam to look straight and lobby with influential physicists like Victor Weisskopf and Robert Oppenheimer. Effectively, he urged Abdus Salam to quell the impression that the proposed centre might end up as some sort of an intellectual ghetto of physicists from the developing world. Not many people in Pakistan could offer such a forthright piece of advice to pull Abdus Salam out of his flight of imagination, if there was any, in relation to house the centre in Pakistan.

As prospects to realise the centre brightened up, a small number of countries signalled their readiness to offer hospitality to the centre. In the process, Turkey, Denmark, Austria and Italy expressed interest. In the end, the most generous offer came from Italy, largely due to the persistence of Paulo Budinich (1916–2013). Born and educated in Trieste, Paulo Budinich had worked assiduously to win the centre for Trieste right from the day the proposal for the centre had been first tabled at the International Atomic Energy Agency. Over the years, he

---

[1] In May 2011, the United States military commandos had apprehended and killed Osama Bin Laden, the leader of militant Al-Qaeda movement, in his hideout in Abbotabad.

became a lifelong friend of Abdus Salam, a companion in the class of Ishrat Usmani. For nearly two decades, Paolo Budinich served the centre as its Associate Director with Abdus Salam. 'It was a difficult battle, but a good one', he remarked in his autobiography *L'arcipelago delle meravigile* (The Archipelago of Wonders), published in Rome in 2001.

Taking up the position of Director at the institute amounted to a sharp turn in the life of Abdus Salam. Winning the centre with the support of diplomatic logistics provided by Pakistan, he gained a high-profile position in the international science establishment under the United Nations for three decades. Trieste added up as another regular station on his travel itinerary of high flying. After Jhang, Multan, Lahore, Cambridge, London, Karachi and Islamabad; he was set to gain a good taste of Trieste. His time was torn between two continents and three countries. Flights and connections, pick and drop at airports, immigration controls and custom checks, jetlag and variable time zones, occasional delays and cancellations tended to merge into what already was a tightly packed schedule of Physics, teaching, research, consultancy and family; all of this got topped up with the centre where a great deal of his attention was consumed in administrative work. He began suffering from 'constant bouts of fever' and stress. He was putting up in a 'poorly ventilated room' in Trieste. One of the local physicians diagnosed throat infection as the cause of temperature and advised Abdus Salam to undergo tonsillectomy.[1]

Regularly shuttling between England and Italy, putting long hours into work, he found hardly enough time to prepare food. Still, he did not compromise on his love of homemade Pakistani dishes. He found the way out by bringing frozen packets of cooked food from London until his stomach ached. His doctor in Trieste suspected appendicitis and advised him to return to London for surgery. In a compassionate letter of support, his brother, Abdul Hameed, cheered him up by stating that the stint in hospital equalled a well-earned break to rest.[2]

II

An increasing number of physicists began visiting Trieste under various associate-ship schemes, federation agreements, conferences, seminars, workshops and courses offered by the centre. Within a year of its foundation,

---

[1] Jagjit Singh (1992): pp. 72-73
[2] Abdul Hameed (circa 2000): p. 148

Robert Oppenheimer audited the centre as the focus of 'most fruitful and serious collaboration between experts from the United States and those from the Soviet Union'. He acknowledged the contribution the centre was able to make in bringing physicists closer. 'Without the Centre in Trieste it seems to me doubtful that this collaboration would have been initiated or continued'. He remarked.[1]

With the easing of ideological tension between the eastern and western blocks of power, Abdus Salam began expanding the scope of centre's activities beyond Theoretical Physics. But combining research and administration did not make an easy ride, especially when he found himself caught in battles to raise funds for the centre.[2] On such occasions, he would unleash his talent of oratory performance by citing fables from the medieval history of Europe and Central Asia. One of his favourite tales was related to Michael Scott (d circa 1235), the young scholar who was known to have travelled all the way from Scotland to Toledo, during the reign of King Frederick II. Michael Scott worked with scholars busy translating back the works of Aristotle then available in Arabic. His proficiency in Arabic language made him a valuable asset. It was a time when great physicians like the Danish Henrik Harpestraeng (1164–1244), wanted to profit from the treatises of Muslim clinicians.[3] Other contemporary scholars in Toledo included pioneers like Robert Anglieus who was the first translator of Koran. In fact, King Frederic II of Sicily was so friendly toward Muslims that a section of the faithful among Christians suspected him of conversion to Islam. Due to his religious eccentricity and the liberty he took with Vatican, the king was excommunicated twice.[4]

Next, Abdus Salam would cite the example of Saifuddin Salman, the young astronomer from the present-day Kandahar in Afghanistan, who had left home to work at an observatory in Samarkand.[5] According to Abdus Salam, scholars in the class of Michael Scott and Saifuddin Salman presented the 'most memorable international assays in scientific collaboration'. Those seekers of scholarship, stranded in remote regions of the world, unrecognised by any flourishing educational institution of the day, were determined to triumph over

---

[1] Ideals and Realities (1984): p. 198
[2] Ideals and Realities (1984): p. 205-206
[3] The Legacy of Islam, edited by Sir Thomas Arnold and Alfred Guillaume, Oxford University Press, 1931, p. 28
[4] Edward Burman: The Templers - Knights of God, Great Britain, 1986, pp. 125-126
[5] Ideals and Realities (1984): p. 85

prevailing obstacles. They were caught in the battle to bridge the economic and intellectual disparities of their time.[1]

Occasionally, the centre undertook exercises in public relations. With his experience of promoting the Department of Physics in Imperial College, Abdus Salam did not lack the knack for publicity. In 1968, the centre hosted series of evening lectures on the versatility of lives in physics. Giants like Werner Heisenberg (1901–1976), Paul Dirac (1902–9184), Rudolf Peierls (1907–1995), Hans Bethe (1907–2005), Eugene Wigner (1902–1995), Pascual Jordan (1902–1980), Oskar Klein (1894–1977) and Evgeny Mikhailovich Lifshitz (1915–1985) were invited to recount their lives and times in physics.

As a part of his publicity campaign to win grants for the centre, Abdus Salam launched the Third World Academy of Sciences. Next, in a bid to raise the profile of the centre among oil rich countries, he founded the Arab Friendship Society. In 1988, the centre hosted a conference to remember the Black American physicist, Edward Bouchet (1852–1918). Speaking on the occasion, Abdus Salam pressed for the need to promote interaction between Black American and African physicists. After the collapse of the Soviet Union, the centre organised a conference to discuss fresh opportunities of cooperation with East European countries.

Originally created for a probationary term of four years, the centre was able to survive with financial grants from the United Nations Educational and Scientific Committee, Ford Foundation, the Swedish International Development Agency (CIDA) and, above all, the Government of Italy.

For three decades in a row, Abdus Salam presided over the centre as its founding Director. He seemed to have developed a personal attachment with the place. Rather fondly he would refer to the place as 'my centre'.[2] He considered the centre as one of 'his most prized accomplishments' next only to the sharing of Nobel Prize for Physics in 1979.[3] In his lighter moments, on the other end, he recalled the effort as some kind of a venture in disbelief. 'I was naive then, I wouldn't dare do it today. People took it half-jokingly and many delegates abstained on the vote when it was approved for a preliminary study. I found out that the idea interested the poor countries. What I wanted to do was to give the poor a place of their own where they would not have to beg anybody. Why

---

[1] Ideals and Realities (1984): pp. 321-322
[2] Ideals and Realities (1984): p. 163
[3] Al-Nahl (Fall 1997): p. 126

shouldn't a bright youngster in Pakistan have the right to receive the same stimulating atmosphere as an Englishman or an American, provided they deserve it?' He asked during the course of an interview with one of his later day profile writers.[1]

When Abdus Salam's health nose-dived in 1994, he was obliged to relinquish charge as the Director of the centre. He was re-associated as the President of the centre. On the first anniversary of his death, in November 1997, the centre was officially renamed as the Abdus Salam International Centre for Theoretical Physics. 'Ask your friends in the Municipality of Trieste to dedicate to us two tomb-stones here in the Park of Miramare where we can rest at the end of our lives'. Abdus Salam is reported to have prompted his friend Paulo Budinich.[2]

---

[1] Ideals and Realities (1984): p. 212
[2] *Al-Nahl* (Fall 1997): p. 125

Chapter Eight
Demolition of Sanity

On a contemporary scale of capitalistic growth and financial achievement, Pakistan was well on the way to growing up as an Asian tiger when tables of regional security balance were turned upside down in South Asia. At an altitude of 14000 feet up in the Himalayan snow lands, in October 1962, the Chinese border force trounced the Indian troops, occupied large tract of territory and then returned to its preferred position. India had been punished and taught a lesson for messing up with boundary line, China declared. Although the whole episode was over within a matter of days, it blasted the overblown balloon of national and international pretensions of non-alignment Jawaharlal Nehru (1889–1964), the Prime Minister of India, had stuffed around his much-pampered image of neutrality with relish and indulgence. At the same time, Pakistan's one-sided love affair with the west crashed face down. India, in spite of its much-touted non-aligned socialistic idealism, turned out to be the darling of western block overnight as Pakistan was dumped without even the need to talk. In fact, there was suggestion that Pakistan should line-up behind India.

Historically, the border dispute between India and China dated back to the arbitrarily drawn McMahon Line enforced by British colonial authorities. Not in a mood to take dictation from abroad, the Chinese did not wish anyone to mess up in a part of the world where international trade had flourished along the ancient silk route over many centuries. After British withdrawal in 1947, the Indian signals of friendship lost meaning for China when Dalai Lama, the spiritual leader of Tibet, found political asylum in New Delhi. As such, the Indian notion that McMahon Line constituted an agreed border was not acceptable to China. Meanwhile, Pakistan maintained a close watch on the deterioration of ties between its two neighbours, and there was a good deal of relief in Islamabad to witness the size of Chinese claim over territories India perceived to own under custom and convention. From Pakistani viewpoint, the border dispute between

China and India added a new dimension to the Kashmir dispute. Ayub Khan asked his aides to explore the possibility of approaching China with a proposal for border demarcation with Pakistan. In the beginning, China played cool due to Pakistan's pride in being the frontline state in jihad against communism. During the course of his visit to the United States, Ayub Khan went public in support of China's entry into the United Nations, a logical proposition then blocked by Washington. Subsequently, the Chinese ambassador in Pakistan looked forward to calling upon the President with diplomatic keenness. Within a short span of time, in this way, Pakistan moved closer to China without raising much of an alarm in western capitals.

To his credit, Ayub Khan did attempt at taking Jawaharlal Nehru into confidence over the Pakistani perception of border demarcation in the northwest. He even handed over to the Indian Prime Minister the map prepared by Pakistani experts. Due to its traditional arrogance towards Pakistan, the gesture of goodwill was altogether ignored by India. After the Indian army was thoroughly thrashed and China declared ceasefire unilaterally, the western bloc judged India as an innocent victim of communist aggression. All varieties of support, from moral to diplomatic and economic to military, began pouring upon New Delhi; and the United States urged Pakistan to offer all the necessary support to prop India up against the communist China. Once again, Ayub Khan displayed statesmanship. Instead of taking advantage by occupying few strategic locations in Kashmir, he went as far as making the offer of a joint defence pact with New Delhi. Once again, his gesture was turned down by an overtly pampered Jawaharlal Nehru.

Nobody fights your fights, Ayub Khan observed in his pleadingly titled political autobiography 'Friends Not Masters'. Pakistan, he argued, had joined the capitalist alliance on equal grounds. 'It was this fear of communism that had impelled the Christian world to help the Muslim world, for the first time in history. The Muslim world occupied an area which was vital strategically and economically and that was the reason why the United States and other western countries thought it worth their while to befriend Muslims. The Muslim world itself was at that time emerging from the domination of western powers. It needed material assistance and also time and the technical know-how to develop its human and material resources. There was no reason why we should not have taken the advantage of the opportunity. For us, our own needs for development were paramount and that was the reason we joined the Pacts'.[1] He explained, once again in the shadow of thesis propounded by Olaf Caroe.

Under immense pressure from its western allies, Pakistan enhanced the level of communication with India and several sessions of diplomatic consultation were convened to resolve the dispute over Kashmir. There was no progress apparently due to the strategic advantage India enjoyed in the size and depth of its economic and military potential. Jawaharlal Nehru had been a champion of socialist idealism, national self-sufficiency and non-alignment; but he was unwell and ageing, the military debacle with China shook him to the core. It was time for India to tap the torrent of fresh possibilities. Pakistan had been ditched by its affluent and powerful friends in the west and there was hardly the reason to expect an early settlement on Kashmir. Ayub Khan found it hard to hide his disappointment with Pakistan's western allies, especially their unwillingness to influence India. His Foreign Minister, Zulfiqar Bhutto, brought him around to appreciate the futility of diplomatic course. Why would India oblige an abandoned Pakistan? A restless cluster of policy planners began pushing for the urgency to forget diplomacy and instead straighten matters out in the battlefield.

In April 1965, there was the military clash in the Rann of Kutch swamps on the coast of Arabian Sea. A swift diplomatic intervention initiated by Harold Wilson, the British Prime Minister, enforced ceasefire and Pakistan gained some five hundred square miles of territory. Ayub Khan and his advisers weighed the experience as a test war, they picked up the impression that Indian army was not impenetrable. Keeping with the show staged by China, back in October 1962, there was the belief that some lightening military action could bear similar fruit in Kashmir.

Into its late teens, Pakistan army was commanded by the final generation of officers commissioned under the British. Some of them were generals in the traditional sense, that is, they drank whisky in the officers' mess all night and yet woke up fresh and fighting fit next morning to report on duty. One of them, General Akhtar Malik (1914–1969), masterminded the scheme to inject some 5000 army commandos into the Indian side of Kashmir valley. Under the plan, codenamed Operation Gibraltar, those commandos were supposed to work with local pockets of Muslim militants, and set off mass uprising to topple the New Delhi-sponsored state government. An immediate justification for civic unrest was supplied by the rather mysteriously coincidental vanishing of a much-

---

[1] Mohammad Ayub Khan (1967): 1967, p. 154

revered relic of Prophet Mohammad from the 17th century Hazratbal Shrine in Srinagar. Once furious mobs of rioters took to streets and went on rampage in the valley, Pakistan army thought the time had come to strike the decisive blow. But the expectation of a widespread rebellion in the valley did not materialise as had been calculated, and there was alarm about the safety and sustenance of infiltrated commandos. Suffering from a fit of nervousness about the vulnerability of his soldiers as much as the impending wrath of his sponsors in the west, Ayub Khan changed the command in Kashmir at a crucial point in the operation. Recalled, General Akhtar Malik returned to the General Headquarter in Rawalpindi where he spent the night at officers' mess, drinking heavily and weeping bitterly, with a loaded pistol on the table!

India was not expected to sit idle, the temptation to teach Pakistan a lesson resulted into an all-out war between the two countries. Early in the morning on 6 September 1965, the Indian army gave Pakistanis the much-feared surprise by crossing the international border and got fairly close to the international airport in Lahore. Such forceful was the Indian thrust that Americans begged New Delhi for a temporary cessation of hostilities to enable the airlifting of their staff from Lahore. But before the Indians could dig in and consolidate their gains, Pakistanis recovered from the shock and fought back to survive through the test for another seventeen days when ceasefire, called by the United Nations Security Council, ended the war in a stalemate.

Staged against eleven years of political volatility, the military coup by Ayub Khan had been accommodated as a pathway to patrician model of governance. In a way, he had met considerable success in regulating the management of national wealth in fewer hands guarded by businessmen, bureaucrats, military officers and their powerful sponsors abroad. There was no compulsion upon him to expand opportunities in health, education, employment and empowerment of masses. He was not supposed to encourage democratic culture and accountability as rather superficially perceived in the west. Pakistan was not ready yet for any western model of democracy in which few centrist parties offered identical manifestoes to guard big business and corporate arms of the modern state. In fact, experimenting with democracy in Pakistan amounted to playing with fire. Devoid of settled party political tradition and favourably instructive media channels, the electorate of illiterate millions could fall for either mullahs or communists causing endless and rebellious peril to the cosiness of status quo.

War shook Pakistan to the core of stability often credited to Ayub Khan, the orderliness headed for a crash. Cracks began appearing in the regime, his young and energetic Foreign Minister, Zulfiqar Bhutto, who had been tirelessly championing the military dictator as the chief architect of modern Pakistan, turned against the boss. Ayub Khan was accused of betrayal and sell out. By this time the first generation of Pakistani youth, born and bred upon one-sided tales of partition horrors, was ready to take to streets. Those party-political organisations, from left to right, the military regime had coerced into silence on charges of extremism, regained voice. By the end of 1968, country went into the top gear of protest. People demanded that Ayub Khan should quit and the political package he had tailored be unstitched. Every now and then police clashed with protesters; violence crept into agitation. For 132 days between November 1968 and March 1969, the agitation went on without betraying the slightest signs of compromise.

Ayub Khan struggled to find breathing space. He convened a round table conference with his opponents, pleaded with angry mobs, made every effort to calm down the agitation and, finally, promised to stay out of the next election. His announcement of abdication resulted in panic among few supporters he had been left with. He felt heartbroken and dejected. On a wet spring evening in Rawalpindi, about the end March 1969, he resigned from office and handed the state over to his hand-picked Commander-in-Chief, General Yahya Khan, the officer who had been assigned the passive task of wrapping up Operation Gibraltar in Kashmir. Once again, the constitution was abrogated to pave way for proclamation of another martial law. Ironically, it was the same constitution that Abdus Salam and Ishrat Usmani had celebrated for Ayub Khan by firing the first successful rocket off the coast of Karachi back in June 1962.

Within days of taking over from his boss, Yahya Khan announced his plans to hold general elections on the basis of direct adult franchise. Pakistan went into a sharp upsurge of political activity and ideological polarisation. For the first time, the conformist mould of right-wing politics was shattered apart and there was an explosion of popular sentiment calling for socialistic equality and regional autonomy. Left wing intellectuals and party-political organisations took the centre stage, their calls for revolution alarmed the establishment. On the other hand, the turn of events gave fresh lease of life to religious parties and groups, especially those maintaining a tactical low-profile since the brisk military clamp down upon the anti-Ahmadiyah agitation in 1953. Suddenly, the religious right found a convenient role in the forefront of emerging scenario; the faithful were set to wage jihad against 'godless communists'.

Among other consequences of war was the blow served upon the nascent nuclear program of Pakistan. One of the vocal supporters of the program, Zulfiqar Bhutto had been sacked. Although Ishrat Usmani and Abdus Salam had never been able to make an ideal team with Zulfiqar Bhutto, their emphasis upon achieving the capability seemed to drift away. Even though Ishrat Usmani and Abdus Salam were shy of Zulfiqar Bhutto's ostentation and lack of discretion, the two worried about the escalation of costs as much as the stiffness of safeguards relating to acquisition of nuclear technology. As such, the case for swift acquisition of reprocessing capability was placed on temporary hold. Some historians of the country's nuclear program tend to agree with the proposition that an aversion of war with India might have benefitted Pakistan's desire to pursue nuclear capability.

II

An attempt at weighing the position Abdus Salam took on Pakistan-India ties indicates an irregular bearing between involvement and objectivity. In the first place, he belonged to the generation of people living in the dark shadows of bloodshed and bitterness accompanying the creation of Pakistan. He was in England when Punjab was hurriedly hacked by the British but the memory of tragic events born out of partition constituted a national trauma, especially among migrant communities. He did not live in quarantine and was not expected to cast off the national agony caused by mayhem, murder, rape and mass exodus. Many among the educated lot of people in Pakistan suspected the British to have left behind in the subcontinent a tall order of unfinished agenda, from an uneven policy towards accession of princely states to the unfair disbursement of inherited assets. There was the widespread belief that Pakistan had been a victim of British favouritism towards India. Even when his scientific objectivity arbitrated him to take a detached view, Abdus Salam took into account the levels of mainstream sensitivity. He appreciated popular opinion and took politically safe positions in both England and Pakistan in compliance with the stringency of political correctness at both ends.

Early in 1964, India played host to the twelfth session of Pugwash Conference in Udaipur. Named after a small village in the Nova Scotia state of

Canada, the conference embodied intellectual resistance to proliferation of nuclear weapons. Abdus Salam was invited to participate. Udaipur, the Venice of the East, known for its lakes, palaces and dreamy mansions was a medieval town in Rajasthan, the abode of the Rajput. Apart from its ideological flavour, the conference offered him the opportunity to be in the picturesque homeland of his long-distance ancestors.

As China was on the verge of carrying out its first nuclear test, the Udaipur session attached special significance to pre-empting the same in South Asia. A considerable amount of moral pressure was exerted upon both Homi Bhabha and Abdus Salam to lobby with their respective leadership in New Delhi and Islamabad in order to keep India and Pakistan from falling to the temptation. In other words, Abdus Salam was assigned the mission to convince Ayub Khan; whereas Homi Bhabha would approach Jawaharlal Nehru. Abdus Salam's youthful excitement was evident from the fact that he boarded the next available flight to Pakistan by standing in the cockpit all the way from New Delhi to Lahore because a seat could not be made available to him at the last minute. Because he did not have any prior appointment with the President, his friend Qudratullah Shahab got him through the protocol barrier. Ayub Khan listened to the Pugwash proposal with his usual patience and then told Abdus Salam that even if Pakistan agreed it would not make much difference because India was not likely to concur. Let us call the Indian bluff, Abdus Salam pressed. Ayub Khan expressed his readiness to meet Jawaharlal Nehru. Excited, Abdus Salam rushed back to India. But just as Ayub Khan had anticipated the thrill fizzled out. Jawaharlal Nehru declined to oblige.[1]

While still in India, Abdus Salam was encouraged to seek an interview with Jawaharlal Nehru. He was pursued by Hamayun Kabir, the federal cabinet minister for Education. Abdus Salam might have availed the opportunity of meeting someone who had played a prominent role in the struggle for freedom. He was deeply impressed by Jawaharlal Nehru's socialistic idealism. But he got alerted when Hamayun Kabir mentioned about an offer in the making. A senior position at the National Physical Laboratories had fallen vacant and the Indian Prime Minister, according to Hamayun Kabir, wished Abdus Salam to consider filling the vacancy. Unprepared and somewhat taken aback, Abdus Salam did not wish to be rude. He was the Science Adviser to the Government of Pakistan

---

[1]Jagjit Singh (1992): p. 34

and expected Hamayun Kabir to be mindful of his status especially in view of the peculiarities of India-Pakistan ties.

Professor Hamayun Kabir (1906–1969) was educated at Calcutta. He had been the Chairman of India's University Grants Commission before serving as the cabinet minister for education (1957–65). More of an intellectual in his political role, he belonged to the fast-diminishing creed of Muslim scholars who believed Indian nationalism provided sufficient basis for the followers of different religions and creeds to live under a joint statehood in the subcontinent. Still, Abdus Salam was at a loss in making sense out of the offer made by Hamayun Kabir. As such, he did not consider it wise to meet the Indian Prime Minister prior to getting necessary clearance from the Government of Pakistan. 'I feel much honoured to have this offer from you. But before I accept it, I must ask for the permission of my government. The job you intend to give me entails a tremendous amount of responsibility, and I should take my government into confidence'. He told Hamayun Kabir who appreciated the position taken by Abdus Salam.

On his next visit home, Abdus Salam briefed Ayub Khan about the episode and asked the President for an opinion. How do *you* feel about it? Ayub Khan is reported to have returned the question. Abdus Salam's answer was simple. He was not an Experimental Physicist and hence not interested in accepting the offer. But he asked Ayub Khan if there was any political reason for him to accept the offer from a Pakistani viewpoint. He expressed his readiness to take the job if it entailed any political advantage to Pakistan. Ayub Khan replied in negative. According to Abdus Salam the whole affair ended there and then, never to be followed up or mentioned ever again.[1]

Few months after the Pugwash Conference in Udaipur, Jawaharlal Nehru died. As the only son of his rich and anglophile father, Jawaharlal Nehru was schooled in Harrow; he studied Natural Sciences in Trinity College Cambridge and Law at London's Inner Temple. A high-profile public life was charted out for him as soon as he returned home. Soon he won fame for his secular stance in communally tattered India. He was praised for his scholarly idealism, socialist equality and non-alignment towards international power blocks. Adopted as the General President of Indian Science Congress, attending annual sessions of the group regularly, he attached great value to science as the shortest pathway to pull India out of starvation, poverty, ignorance, superstition and filth.

---

[1] Interviews 1984: Folder VII, p. 12

'What has been this quest of man, and whither does he journey? For thousands of years men have tried to answer these questions. Religion and philosophy and science have all considered them, and given many answers. I shall not trouble you with these answers, for the sufficient reason that I do not know most of them. But, in the main, religion has attempted to give a complete and dogmatic answer, and has often cared little for the mind, but has sought to enforce obedience to its decisions in various ways. Science gives a doubting and hesitating reply, for it is in the nature of science not to dogmatise, but to experiment and reason and rely on the mind of man. I need hardly tell you that my preferences are all for science and the methods of science'. Jawaharlal Nehru had once written to his daughter, Indira Gandhi, from jail where he served a number of terms on charges of political activism.[1]

Although Jawaharlal Nehru loved to be greeted as one of the charismatic giants of independence movement and a statesman of outstanding stature, he was unable to bring about any peaceful accord between India and Pakistan. Under the spell of egocentricity, he deferred settlement of differences between the two countries, especially the dispute over Kashmir, on one pretext or another, and passed the bitterness over to next generation of politicians. Instead of secular goodwill and enlightenment, he left behind a muddle of mistrust giving birth to wars, nuclear bombs and religious bigotry of the worst kind. His failure in displaying generosity towards Pakistan resembled the rich pampered child fixated with some of his toys. With his claims upon idealism for science, socialistic equality, scholarship and humanism it might have been easier for him to leave behind a legacy of peace and accommodation rather than arrogance and supremacy in the subcontinent. After all the people of Pakistan belonged to the same ethnic stock as their Indian neighbours, they qualified for compassion. Was he not aware that the livelihood of millions of farmers in north-western districts of the subcontinent depended on shared rivers originating in Kashmir? All of this remains a big sad question.

History did serve him the choice to be either a statesman or a politician. In collaboration with Mohandas Gandhi (1869–1948) and Vallabhbhai Patel (1875–1950), he blasted the prospects of a confederated subcontinent to avoid partition, bloodshed, rape and exodus. Field Marshal Archibald Wavell (1883–1950), the second-last British Viceroy, is credited for promoting the Cabinet

---

[1] Nehru, Jawaharlal: Glimpses of World History, Penguin Books, New Delhi, 2004, p. 175

Mission Plan in a last bid to secure geopolitical integrity of India in some way. Mohammed Ali Jinnah, breathlessly targeted for flouting the unity of *Mother India* by demanding Pakistan, accepted the proposal for a confederation whereas the pompous trio knocked it down. Scholarly historians, from Abul Kalam Azad (1888–1958) to Jaswant Singh (1938–2020), even though conservative, have born witness to the irony. Jawaharlal Nehru outlived Mohandas Gandhi and Vallabhbhai Patel by many years, but he departed without expressing any hint of remorse or responsibility for the hatred his generation of political leadership was leaving behind. He had the opportunity to behave either like an older brother or big brother to Pakistan. Sadly, he fell for the lesser.

Understandably, the childish ambition of Pugwash Conference, attended by top physicists like Niels Bohr, failed to raise any hopes of non-proliferation in South Asia. In line with the culture of other international non-government organisations, there were enough funds and hope to reconvene the next session at some other station in the world. Before bidding them farewell, Homi Bhabha took the participants for a visit to the ancient complex of Ajanta and Ellora caves. China went ahead with its nuclear program; India and Pakistan took few years in doing the same.

About the end of August 1965, Abdus Salam visited home to attend a specially called conference of Pakistani scientists. This conference, convened in Saidu Sharif, the capital city of Swat region bordering Afghanistan, was the first of its kind under the recently established Scientific and Technological Division reporting directly to the President. In spite of military tension mounting on the border with India, Ayub Khan arrived to attend the conference. Abdus Salam reiterated the need to liberate research from the executive control. Listing areas of national life where scientific investigation could be 'expected to make an early impact', he placed Defence Science at the top of his list; above industrial, agricultural, public health sectors and the universities. Due to its geographical remoteness, Saidu Sharif was selected as the seat of meeting to give the President a break from his omnipresent regiment of secretaries in order to win him over to the small-scale fuel processing program under the Atomic Energy Commission.[1]

According to Abdus Salam's biographer, Abdul Ghani, who attended the conference himself, the atmosphere at Saidu Sharif Conference was drenched with alarm bells of an impending war. Abdus Salam was visibly 'troubled and

---

[1] Interviews 1984: Off the record

saddened' over the imminent clash with India, he feared 'nothing meaningful' could come out of an 'ill-thought out' war other than the slaughtering of youth.[1]

Apparently, the scheme to gain presidential approval for processing of nuclear fuel and the view about futility of war did not sound complimentary to preference for peace. Yet the duality constituted a part of the need for Pakistan to start the journey for achievement of nuclear deterrence before it was too late. Both Abdus Salam and Ishrat Usmani understood it more than others in the government.

After the Saidu Sharif Conference, Abdus Salam returned to London only to receive the news about eruption of an all-out war in the subcontinent. He wanted to rush back home but the Government of Pakistan directed him to proceed to Washington immediately and lobby with his contacts like Jerome Wiesner to find a 'favourable settlement' to end the war. In recognition of his contribution towards world peace Jerome Wiesner had recently been decorated with the Star of Pakistan award. It remains only a matter of speculation as to how much of Abdus Salam's lobbying contributed towards the United Nations sponsored ceasefire agreed between India and Pakistan within a matter of days.

One afternoon, few weeks after the war and his visit to Washington, Abdus Salam watched Patrick Blackett approaching him. 'Now that you have failed to do any damage to India, is it not time to consider living in peace with your neighbour?' Patrick Blackett is reported to have asked.

'But we haven't lost the war', Abdus Salam hastened to cut through the sentence because he did not wish to hear the word defeat. Like the lot of staunchly patriotic Pakistanis, he was not prepared to entertain the notion of Pakistan being trounced by India, anywhere from a cricket test match to military combat. Apparently, Patrick Blackett appreciated the state of mind, he might have been just winding Abdus Salam up to a predictable reaction. In fact, Patrick Blackett was required to appreciate that Pakistani fixation with India manifested the desire to be treated with equality, not as a satellite of India.

Along with a hefty toll on national economy, the war turned out to be a wakeup call for Pakistan. Supplies were blocked due to Indian naval siege around Karachi port. Consumerism propped up by measured doses of American aid was questioned. Year after year, tones of surplus wheat grain from the United States got dumped in Pakistan under Public Law 480 program, and proceeds from its sale were shared between the two governments. Getting up from the deep

---

[1] Abdul Ghani (1982): pp. 75-76

slumber of dependence, the country expected its small community of scientists to step forward and offer assistance in tackling foreign reliance. 'Ah! We have arrived, at last we are there!' Abdus Salam remembered the famous Pakistani chemist, Salimuzzaman Siddiqui (1897–1994), making the statement in a voice choked with excitement and emotion. Salimuzzaman Siddiqui was elected a Fellow of the British Royal Society in 1961 at the proposal of Abdus Salam.

Pakistan's road to self-reliance was long and arduous, there were ups and downs. Abdus Salam recalled that post-war enthusiasm 'fizzled out in a matter of few months and our senior bureaucrats returned to their old habit of dependence on imports from abroad. As the war ended and naval blockade upon awaiting shipments was lifted, the overblown spirit of patriotism flattened out'. Not only the annual expenditure on defence and debt servicing shot up, beyond any democratic accountability, the bureaucracy simply did not have any faith in the need for science. When a whole lot of merchandise could be easily purchased in the international market, the top bureaucrats believed, there was hardly the need to consider the proposal for manufacturing locally. In fact, some of them actually feared self-sufficiency. For example, Mohammad Shoaib, the Secretary for Finance, used to state the government would fall if Pakistan achieved self-sufficiency in wheat production.

Then, as opposed to the industry for production and fabrication there was the predilection in favour of commerce and trade. Abdus Salam suspected that the attitude reflected a religious peculiarity of Muslims. He feared an uproar of the faithful and preferred caution towards touching upon such cultural sensitivities. Privately, however, he detested the clerical emphasis on commerce as a profession of the Prophet. Such a kink, he feared, provided reason to discount manufacturing. He expressed amazement over the volumes of oral tradition attributed to Prophet Mohammed in support of commerce and trade without ever making any meaningful reference to the equally important need for emphasis upon production and manufacturing.[1] As such, the crux of so-called intellectual activity among the elitist factions of Muslim intelligentsia was focused largely upon literature and theology. Because acquisition of knowledge in natural sciences required excellence in mathematics, the very desire to do science was inhibited by setting it aside as primarily a business of Hindus and Jews.

In the end, for Abdus Salam, the conflict between India and Pakistan had two faces. When it settled down to a perception of injustices committed to Pakistan,

---

[1] Interviews 1984: VII, p. 27

he adored the patriotic face. Otherwise, he tended to take a historical view. If French and German people could conquer their bitterness, dating back in a way to medieval times, what kept India and Pakistan from doing the same? He would ask.

III

When Abdus Salam likened the imminent war between Pakistan and India to an ill-thought-out merciless cull of the youth, he seemed to have overlooked the list of patriotic claims his Ahmadiyah community had been fond of making every now and then. For example, how could he shut his eyes upon the fact that General Akhtar Malik, who led Pakistan's military commando operation in Kashmir, was the scion of a devout Ahmadiyah household in northern Punjab. Left on his own though, General Akhtar Malik was only a proud professional soldier who cared the least about communal and party-political associations. In fact, he was known to have snubbed the Ahmadiyah caliph when the latter invited him to attend Friday afternoon congregational in the party's *Noor* mosque in Rawalpindi. 'I would rather do it, if compelled, in the company of those who die at my signal in the battlefield'. He is reported to have stated in response. His keenness on religion, especially an outward expression of indulgence, was minimal. On the other hand, the Ahmadiyah party publicists owned him enthusiastically due to his charismatic high profile in the army. He was promoted to be the one who came close to cutting India out of Kashmir in the *Akhnur* sector of the war in 1965. Then the wishful among the Ahmadiyah grumbled ceaselessly, when his command was terminated to please the United States.

Likewise was the case with Zafarullah Khan, never an end to the one-way repetition of diplomatic services he rendered to Pakistan and the Muslim world. Any civilized explanation behind his marked boycott of the funeral service of Mohammed Ali Jinnah, the father of the nation, was never offered.

Since 1953, after the efficient stemming of violent mass agitation by army troops in Lahore, the Ahmadiyah community lived under a self-imposed sense of security. Many in the enlightened liberal intelligentsia of Pakistan held the view that the role of religion in public affairs had been defined for a long time to come. Whereas, in actual fact, the silence of religious groups was only a tactical and temporary withdrawal. Needless to state that army had fixed a law and order situation, whereas the deep-rooted sectarian malaise remained unaddressed. In other words, the mission of sorting the Ahmadiyah schism out stayed on top of the agenda of fundamentalist clerics; they only waited for an opportune moment to strike back and guard the purity of Islamic doctrines from contamination. Their strategy was inadvertently supported by the inseparability of religion and state in Pakistan. If the clerics took the puritanical position, the mainstream of politicians valued the massive utility of religious card to silence the opposition, especially those propagating socialism and regional autonomy. Religion was a quickly available weapon against godless communists, secessionists and the recalcitrant posing threat to the evolving order of establishment. Major General Shahid Hamid, the chief of Inter-Services Intelligence Department, had already begun scaring western diplomats with the increased levels of communist threat and the need for a favourable line up of religious parties.[1]

Any indication of the religious zealots returning to national stage was not a good omen for the Ahmadiyah. In the fall of Ayub Khan, therefore, the schismatic sect faced an awfully disturbing mix of political choices.

On 10 March 1955, an assassination attempt was made on the life of the Ahmadiyah caliph, Bashiruddin Ahmad. He suffered a severe neck injury, survived the attack but did not regain full health. As the caliph, he held the office for life, it was not thinkable to replace him. His lingering sickness deprived his followers of a full-time spiritual guide. His sons, from about half-a-dozen wives, got sucked into the war of succession.

Bashiruddin Ahmad died in 1965. Although unwell and bedridden in the final years of his life, he left behind a tightly knit, efficiently organised, evangelically motivated and disproportionately loud tiny fraternity of the faithful. Way back in 1914, he had taken charge from Hakim Nooruddin, the first caliph of the group, a much smaller membership facing internal strife. At the time of his death, the numerical strength of the Ahmadiyah approached the one million mark. While the community itself appeared to be shy about its size, wishing to claim a much-exaggerated figure, the numerical strength of the Ahmadiyah qualified them as a sizeable religious minority caught in the hundred times bigger, predominantly Sunni, population of Pakistan.

Internally, the unity of the Ahmadiyah was powered by the cult-like spiritual authority of the caliph who demanded unquestionable devotion of his followers. As an embodiment of infallible sainthood, Bashiruddin Ahmad preferred to be

---

[1] Major General Shahid Hamid was the maternal uncle of famous writer Salman Rushdie

worshiped rather than merely obeyed. Titled as the *Commander of the Faithful* and the *Promised Reformer*, he believed his family to be out of the ordinary and expected the brood of Ghulam Ahmad to be received with exceptional fidelity. His children and close relations were mentioned as members of *the Khandan* or The Family; the wife of Ghulam Ahmed, the founder of the community, as the *Mother of the Faithful*. There was spiritual apartheid between the ordinary Ahmadiyah and the family of the caliph and it went as far as the exclusive demarcation in the cemetery in Rabwah, the party headquarter where only the certified faithful were buried.[1]

Even though the faithful contributed a considerable component of their hard-earned income in raising funds for party causes, they were not entitled to ask for any audit and accountability of their donation. Instead, during the course of party meetings members took oath of absolute loyalty to the caliph, pledging an all-out comprehensive readiness to sacrifice whatever they owned, from their lives to ownership, in response to his summon. As one of the stringent requirements under party discipline, the Ahmadiyah had been debarred from participating in prayer services with mainstream Muslims; they were not supposed to marry outside the community. Those found guilty of trespass were boycotted and expelled from the party, they were shamed and named, with their offences made public, in party meetings. If the British colonial authorities did not care about it, the Muslim mainstream in Pakistan was at a loss in accommodating the segregation. It was hard for the average to appreciate as to why a certain group, otherwise calling itself as the most genuine face of Islam, behaved like the Brahmin.

Due to their thin presence in the mainstream electorate, the Ahmadiyah did not have any meaningful representation in the Parliament. In fact, the numerical limitation made it rather impossible for the community even to dream about securing an elected office through direct contest. On the other hand, the party had succeeded in putting on a sizeable presence in the civilian bureaucracy and armed forces. Chiefly, it was due to the alertness toward education as the pathway to employment. For example, Muzaffar Ahmad, a nephew of Bashiruddin Ahmad, made it to the top in government bureaucracy. Then there were few army officers who went into commanding ranks. But then, despite the

---

[1] In a way, the concept of an exclusive cemetery was reminiscent of the medieval age practice under which Vatican issued certificates ensuring European royalty and aristocracy an entry into heaven.

clerical noise and fuss about those officers holding the so-called key positions, the incumbent were far from tilting the balance of power.

Bashiruddin Ahmad had not received any formal education beyond the local high school in Qadian, but he valued the force of organised religion. He was largely self-educated in areas of his interest like, for example, the working of modern political and religious organisations. One of his major achievements was the creation of a subservient tribe of salaried functionaries to meet the needs of Ahmadiyah headquarter in Qadian and party missions abroad. This party establishment presided over departments like finance, foreign affairs, judiciary, police and propaganda. A cursory view of the Ahmadiyah organisation resembled the state of a state within the state.

Nasir Ahmad (1909–1982) succeeded his father in the Ahmadiyah caliphate, it was a time when Pakistan struggled to cope up with the consequences of its reckless war with India. Ayub Khan confronted collapse. Nasir Ahmad was a *Hafiz*, that is, the one who memorised the full Arabic text of the Koran by heart. He had graduated from Lahore's Government College and then went to study at Balliol College in Oxford University, England. While serving as Principal of the prestigious postgraduate college in the Ahmadiyah headquarter, Rabwah, he had been a member of the Senate in Punjab University. In his personality, he offered a fair mix of classical and modern experience.

For many decades, the Ahmadiyah participation in national politics was identified with their whole-hearted support for the established order and compliance to the government of the day. From their alignment with the ruling Unionist Party, before the partition of Punjab, the Ahmadiyah had switched over, without any qualms, their loyalty to a spate of governments formed by Muslim League in Pakistan. Now Ayub Khan's vulnerability and imminent ouster from power seemed to have lifted the floodgate of religious, leftist and regional hopefuls.

Zulfiqar Bhutto, the mutinous Foreign Minister Ayub Khan, postured to take a hard line on Kashmir. At the United Nations, he defended Pakistan's Kashmir case with his arsenal of rhetorical fireworks and aimed at winning over those back home who suspected Ayub Khan for the vague outcome of war with India. Keeping a close watch on power reshuffle looming upon Islamabad, Nasir Ahmad despatched his younger brother, Tahir Ahmad, to call upon Zulfiqar Bhutto. Manifest in the Ahmadiyah keenness on Zulfiqar Bhutto, as the heir to Ayub Khan, was also a censure of the manner in which General Akhtar Malik had been recalled from the Kashmir front at a crucial point in the uprising. Tahir Ahmed congratulated Zulfiqar Bhutto and praised him for his bold stand on Kashmir. Fearing the intelligence watch upon his activities, Zulfiqar Bhutto hurried Tahir Ahmad out of his office as if the place was bugged.[1]

At that time, the political climate in Islamabad was not sufficiently clear to predict the future shape of events beyond the impending collapse of regime headed by Ayub Khan. Fashionable and ambitious, Zulfiqar Bhutto cherished the idea of being an heir to Ayub Khan, but he dreamed to claim the top job by staging an in-house change through ruling party caucus. Ayub Khan proved resilient, he hung on to power, denied any change of the party-political kind and handed the charge over to his heir within the army. Zulfiqar Bhutto was compelled to come out in the open.

General Yahya Khan, the new martial law administrator, announced plans to convene general elections about the end of 1970. It did not take long for the Ahmadiyah to break out of their isolation by declaring support for the Peoples Party headed by Zulfiqar Bhutto. According to some insiders, the decision to take the plunge in popular politics was prompted by Fareed Ahmad, the middle son of Nasir Ahmad. Fareed Ahmad was enrolled in Lahore's King Edward Medical College, his admission in the highly regarded school of medicine had been secured on Governor's quota by his influential uncle, Muzaffar Ahmad, the top-ranking bureaucrat. Fareed Ahmad lived like a pampered prince loitering about in local restaurants, cafes, clubs and bars; more or less everywhere other than the medical college. Somehow, he found his way into the social circle of Zulfiqar Bhutto who had recently been expelled from the government. After securing a considerable amount of media attention over his huffing and puffing on Kashmir, and public sympathy after he had been sacked, Zulfiqar Bhutto had gained a good deal of confidence. Ayub Khan's vulnerability had boosted the morale of left-wing forces and the air in the country was thick with socialist revolutionary jargon. Many left-wing intellectuals and groups offered him support in launching a political party of his own. It was around this time when Fareed Ahmad convinced his father, Nasir Ahmad, to put up a bet on Zulfiqar Bhutto.

Nasir Ahmad made up his mind on three arbitrarily drawn assumptions. In the first place, he believed that despite his radical bluster Zulfiqar Bhutto was at

---

[1] Iain Adamson; A Man of God: The Life of His Holiness Khalifatul Masih IV, George Shepherd Publishers, Bristol, Great Britain, 1991, pp. 91-92

best a liberal democrat who would steer clear of taking sides in religious controversies. Secondly, it was considered worthwhile to make inroads before the Peoples Party, launched by Zulfiqar Bhutto, went radical. An influential niche in the left-leaning party was deemed as a strategic advantage in the interest of establishment; infiltration in time meant the radicals could be neutralised from within. Thirdly, the Ahmadiyah feared that they had very little choice other than siding with the Peoples Party. After their 1952–53 experience with Mumtaz Daultana, they were not prepared to have all their eggs in one basket, that is, the centrist Muslim League party.

During the course of a follow-up meeting, Tahir Ahmad convinced Zulfiqar Bhutto that winning popular vote in the largely illiterate electorate of Pakistan with slogans like scientific socialism was not an easy task. He proposed the adoption of favourable jargon like the one preferred by his older brother. In a media interview, Nasir Ahmad, had postulated that the Islamic concept of equality and egalitarianism did not require Muslims to pursue alien creeds like socialism. Hence the need to draw upon more appealing terms like *Musawat-i-Mohammadi* or Mohammadan Equality, even the expression *Islamic Socialism* could serve the purpose. Not a communist by any definition, Zulfiqar Bhutto, valued the advice, he encouraged the Ahmadiyah to play a role in moderating the radical element of his party.

Tahir Ahmad then went as far as screening the list of party candidates for general election. Many 'communists' queuing up to win party nomination were dropped out in the light of his advice. In his authorised biography, published in England in 1991, Tahir Ahmad claimed credit for saving Pakistan from a communist takeover. He argued that left-wing targeted at riding the wave of Zulfiqar Bhutto's charismatic appeal to secure greater presence and then strike to gain full control at an appropriate moment in time. 'They had ensured that over 70 per cent of the candidates to the National Assembly were communists or fellow travellers'. He recalled.[1]

There was nothing extraordinary about taking part in a national event like general election, still the Ahmadiyah alliance with Zulfiqar Bhutto resulted in ruffling the feathers of their opponents among religious parties. Submerged in their intrinsic state of self-absorption, the Ahmadiyah overlooked the consequences of their move in a larger social context. Playing role in national politics meant higher public profile entailing rise and fall of fortunes; it offered

---

[1] Iain Adamson (1991): pp. 93-94

the opportunity to make friends as much as the risk of creating enemies. Instead of preparing themselves for a variety of interaction with other players, the Ahmadiyah tended to take a clandestine view of their political venture. They might have availed the opportunity to open dialogue with some of their old rivals, but then the self-styled arrogance prevailed to try only the time-tested backdoor hypocritical entry into the power scene.

Another religious organisation tightly disciplined like the Ahmadiyah was the *Jamaat Islami* headed by Abul Aa'la Maudoodi (1903–1979), a scholar very highly regarded among the educated professionals belonging to Wahabi mainstream. Like the founders of Islamic Brotherhood in Egypt, Abul Aa'la Maudoodi considered secularism as an obstacle to the rejuvenation of fundamental religious spirit and militancy among Muslims. This view found currency in the Cold War era as a highly favourable asset to fight the godless communists and pro-Soviet regimes in the Middle East. On the scale of its public acceptability, the *Jamaat Islami* enjoyed strategic advantage over the Ahmadiyah. In spite of being equally exclusive in its organisational strictness and selection of membership, the *Jamaat Islami* was not considered a pariah in the mainstream. Its youth wing won student union elections in colleges and universities all over the country at a time when the Ahmadiyah were held hostage to their self-inflicted isolation. While the Ahmadiyah remained egotistical and friendless, the Jamaat *Islami* brandished its influence among leaders in business, professions, government and the armed forces; boldly championing Muslim causes every now and then.

As election campaign picked up momentum, the right wing felt nervous about the rising typhoon of socialist popularity. Some of the religious parties did not mind striking suitable alliances. In this climate of concern and anxiety, the *Jamaat-i-Islami* made the bold move by delivering a signal of amity to the Ahmadiyah to join hands against the secular combination of communist intellectuals, socialist trade unions and secessionist regional parties. There was the increasing urgency to save the traditional establishment from a rout.

Abul Aa'la Maudoodi perceived the theatre of ideological war stretched far beyond sectarian wrangling in Pakistan and he felt the urgent need to strengthen the conservative alliance. Holding an olive branch, one of his sons arrived in the Ahmadiyah headquarter Rabwah. Although very little is known about his mission, and both sides have avoided to acknowledge much about the visit, the purpose possibly was to sound out the prospects of electoral cooperation.

Apparently, the *Jamaat Islami* rated the Ahmadiyah as a foe much smaller than the assortment of communists, socialists, secular liberals and atheists.

Instead of availing the rare advantage to break out of their isolation, the Ahmadiyah perceived the overture as an act in opportunism, bound to trigger scandal and disgrace. No dialogue, the Ahmadiyah believed, could hold value as long as those ecclesiastical proclamations, delivered by Wahabi clergymen, calling for the death of the apostate, were not withdrawn. Until the list of Ahmadiyah pre-conditions was met, the exercise of any cooperation amounted to hypocrisy, outright. They forgot the historical reality that a number of Muslim sects have lived together despite the prevalence of ecclesiastical bombardment among them in the past. Although the two sides could not agree upon any electoral cooperation, yet by playing host to the emissary of Jamaat-i-Islami, the Ahmadiyah had come fairly close to setting up channels of communications with one of their arch rivals in the religious arena of Pakistan. Had the chance worked, and the Ahmadiyah weighed their options more tactfully, a window might have been secured to explore some level of communication with the mainstream. Unable to benefit from the fortuitous possibility, the Ahmadiyah had none clue about the doom awaiting Pakistan within a matter of months.

IV

For the first time in its short history, Pakistan had its first ever general election called on the basis of direct and universal adult franchise. Under the fresh constitutional arrangement the country was going to have a Westminster style parliamentary form of government. An overwhelming majority of observers approved the conduct of election as fair and impartial. Paradoxically, however, the outcome of election turned out to be a referendum on the partition of Pakistan. In what was then East Pakistan, the Awami League party headed by firebrand Mujeeb Rahman (1920–1975), demanding freedom from the Punjab-dominated power clique, won an absolute majority taking all but one of the allocated seats. On the other hand, in western districts, Zulfiqar Bhutto's Peoples Party emerged as only the leading block devoid of moral authority to form government. Because the army did not have much faith in Mujeeb Rahman, the transfer of power was delayed. Zulfiqar Bhutto found encouragement to reject the majority won by the Awami League party as only a regional show of strength. He wanted a share in the future government to ensure the unity of Pakistan.

Courtesy the British, the geographical boundaries of Pakistan were drawn with a strikingly disruptive peculiarity in their makeup. Originally, the state of Pakistan comprised of two lumps of land, north of the subcontinent, detached by thousand miles of hostile Indian territory. Only the genius of British legal mind could elucidate the rationale behind giving birth to such a uniquely crippled country. This moth-eaten state of Pakistan, as Mohammed Ali Jinnah once named it, reflected the insensitivity and tactlessness that was rather ruthlessly displayed by the British at the time of their withdrawal from the subcontinent. Such matchless geographical peculiarity turned out to be the blueprint for disaster in waiting; an economically choked state of Pakistan was not expected to bear the strain of expenditure on communication, travel and defence to ensure political integrity of its geographically torn apart wings for very long. Regional leadership of the two wings suspected one another from the very beginning. Mohammed Ali Jinnah, the father of Pakistan, himself shocked the people of East Pakistan by telling them that their national language would be Urdu, not Bengali. For its utility as *lingua franca*, Urdu was just a popular version of Hindi, the language of Bollywood understood from Central Asia to the Bay of Bengal and beyond. But the people of East Pakistan did not wish to take dictation from anyone in their home affairs.

Over the next few years, the Bengali-speaking citizens of Pakistan considered themselves to be unequal stakeholder in the state business. Their suspicion was sharpened with the progression of bureaucratic-military axis rooted in Punjab and the Urdu-speaking migrant community from the United Provinces of India. Equally, some of the senior bureaucrats posted in East Pakistan despised Bengalis as lazy social outcasts inclined to Hindu more than Muslim identity. As expected, the attitude gave quick currency to wild tales of discrimination in the former East Pakistan. For example, the Chief Secretary, Aziz Ahmad, who had been dispatched from West Pakistan to preside over the Civil Secretariat in Dhaka, was blamed for behaving like an unrelenting Brahmin. He was stamped with the graceless notoriety of washing his hands after an unavoidable handshake with a Bengali subordinate.

Historically, the Punjabi perception of Bengal was rooted in the age-old racist mindset encouraged by the British. Those living in the northwest prided in their Afghan ancestry and looked down upon the inhabitants of northeast as a race of 'short, dark, devious, timid and treacherous people' capable of achieving anything other than great careers in government and the armed forces. Whereas, on the average, the people of East Pakistan were better educated with rich cultural and artistic tradition. To them, there was hardly the need to feel frightened from those 'tall, fair and forthright' Punjabis who had been conveniently siding with every foreign invader. By the close of 1960s, the people of East Pakistan made 54 percent of the population in Pakistan, yet they received only one-third of the share from national income. Only 13 percent of public servants in the federal government belonged to East Pakistan. In the armed forces, the Bengali representation was still in a single digit. Where was the income earned from export of jute, produced in East Pakistan, being spent? They asked and then pointed toward the vulnerability of East Pakistan during the war with India in 1965.

Mujibur Rahman demanded an urgent overhaul of the system to ensure equal opportunities and treatment in Pakistan. In his package of proposals, known as the *Six Point Formula—Our Right to Live,* he urged the federation to quit from all responsibilities other than foreign affairs and defence. Hurriedly, the state-controlled media charged Mujibur Rahman of sedition, scheming to break-up Pakistan with Indian intelligence support. He was jailed on charges of plotting against the integrity of Pakistan. When the government headed by Ayub Khan crumbled, Mujibur Rahman was released and sedition charges against him were withdrawn.

If the army was expecting a muddled outcome of general election then all hopes of the ruling clique came crashing down. East Pakistan had spoken with one voice. Yahya Khan was supposed to invite Mujibur Rahman and ask him, with due dignity and grace, to form the government and lead the country into democratic age. Instead, the military regime fell to the temptation of striking a mutually favourable bargain, some give and take to protect its corporate interests. Pakistan, at that time, happened to be in the midst of brokering a diplomatic communication between the United States and the Peoples Republic of China. Yahya Khan and his colleagues were imbued with self-styled importance. Even though Mujibur Rahman held pragmatic view of India and wanted to diffuse military tension in South Asia, it was never going to be easy for him to upset the existing balance of Pakistan's ties with China and the United States only to appease a regional player like India.

Yahya Khan invited Mujibur Rahman to visit Islamabad to set out details for transfer of power but the Awami League leader demanded a date for the inaugural session of the National Assembly. He proposed the assembly to meet in Dhaka rather than somewhere in West Pakistan. Next, he made it clear that any future constitution of Pakistan was bound to be designed in line with his *Six Point Formula*. Time, he stated, had arrived for constitutional measures to safeguard the interests of people in East Pakistan. Those in positions of authority in West Pakistan were not used to such candour. Still, Yahya Khan went to Dhaka for a meeting with the Awami League leader. He referred to Mujibur Rahman as the future prime minister of Pakistan. Mujibur Rahman expressed a readiness to work with Yahya Khan. In actual fact, the two sides marked time to watch who blinked first.

At this point, Zulfiqar Bhutto jumped in and claimed that his Peoples Party had won enough seats in West Pakistan to qualify as an unavoidable stakeholder in any future government. He was only throwing a spanner in the works on behalf of the army. He sounded like a candid politician, someone who could 'change continually, test things, attack from every side so as to single out his opponent's weak point and strike at it'. He hated to stick to any 'basic concept' and believed in contradiction as 'the prime virtue of the intelligent man and the astute politician'.[1] In actual fact, he confronted a huge dilemma. Going by the book, he was condemned to be a leader of the opposition at best. Once in opposition, there was no guarantee that feudal lords of Punjab and Sind, the Ahmadiyah had so proudly shortlisted for him to eliminate communists, would not negotiate crossing the floor within a matter of few months. He turned reckless and did not see any harm in playing the foul. His obsession with power had reached a stage where some political observers feared he might suffer a psychotic episode. To his opponents, the position adopted by Zulfiqar Bhutto risked the very federal integrity of Pakistan. Whereas, he claimed himself to be the architect of Ayub Khan's downfall, hence his demand for reward. His political voraciousness provided the military junta with a convenient reason to delay transfer of power for the sake of national accord.

Mujibur Rahman warned that a democratic parliamentary system could not afford two majority parties, side by side. Against tension escalating between the two political parties, Yahya Khan aimed at securing the corporate interests of military. He pretended to be playing the role of a neutral mediator. When the date for inaugural session of the National Assembly was announced, Zulfiqar

---

[1] Richard Sisson and Leo E. Rose: War and Secession: Pakistan, India and the Creation of Bangladesh, University of California Press, Berkeley and Los Angeles, California, 1990, pp. 59-60.

Bhutto refused to report for the session by demanding a prior assurance for his party's share in power. Yahya Khan postponed the schedule without consulting Mujibur Rahman, the leader of the majority party. Rioting erupted in East Pakistan. Scores of people were killed in clashes between security forces and militant workers of the Awami League party. Early in March 1971, Mujibur Rahman addressed a mammoth rally in the heart of Dhaka city. Short of handing down the death sentence upon the wavering federation of Pakistan, he urged his followers to resist the armed forces through civil disobedience. He proclaimed that time had arrived for the people to shed blood for independence.

With civil disobedience picking up momentum, the army troops confronted an open rebellion. An all-out war erupted between the local population and the troops dispatched from West Pakistan.

V

At one point during the course of their talks, Mujibur Rahman declined to go any further with Yahya Khan. He took the plea that the conference room in Dhaka Government House was bugged. At a short notice, it was not possible to find a viable venue, safe from security point of view. Yahya Khan signalled to move a couple chairs into one of the restrooms. Amused, he must have been, Mujibur Rahman agreed. A small desk was set up for a one-to-one discussion between the two most powerful men in the country. Somewhat satirically, the encounter led to resumption of formal negotiations to achieve consensus over the constitutional future of Pakistan and procedural details relating to transfer of power.

Marathon rounds of talks were convened for another ten days. Mujibur Rahman remained sceptical until one day when Yahya Khan summoned his *de facto* prime minister, Muzaffar Ahmad, from Islamabad. Perhaps now he wants to do business, was the feeling among Awami League leadership. Such was the image of professional competence wielded by Muzaffar Ahmad.

An old hand from the bygone British raj, Muzaffar Ahmad (1913–2002) had graduated from Lahore's Government College before moving to England to enter the coveted Indian Civil Service as probation officer in Oxford. He became a member of the District Administration upon returning home and opted for Pakistan to rise higher. He served as Federal Secretary under Ayub Khan in the departments of commerce and finance. Yahya Khan inherited Muzaffar Ahmad as the Deputy Chairman of the Planning Commission and gave him additional responsibilities in economic affairs. By virtue of his experience in finance, Muzaffar Ahmad gained greater political influence. He was the grandson of Ghulam Ahmad, the founder of the Ahmadiyah, and as such a nephew of Bashiruddin Ahmad and a cousin of Nasir Ahmad. Due to his high-profile in the government, he was targeted by those who considered it as some sort of a backroom conspiracy hatched by the schismatic Ahmadiyah. In September 1971, an assassination attempt was made on his life. Although his high-profile position in the government seemed to strengthen the Ahmadiyah political clout, he was not a fan of Zulfiqar Bhutto like his cousin Nasir Ahmad. In fact, he considered Zulfiqar Bhutto a political opportunist and undependable ally.

Upon arriving in Dhaka, Muzaffar Ahmad met with Awami League leaders and members of the government team. He analysed the implications of *Six Point Formula* and the government perception of it with the impartiality and detachment of a cold-blooded bureaucrat. It was the first dispassionate evaluation of complexities involved in implementing the plan as advocated by the Awami League party. Muzaffar Ahmad explained that delegation of trade and foreign assistance to the units of federation was often hard for external stakeholders to assimilate. He argued that such arrangement contradicted the very spirit of regional autonomy as demanded by the Awami League. If implemented in its letter and spirit, he told his audience, the *Six Point Formula* was most likely to restrict the ability of provincial governments to achieve 'equitable distribution of foreign exchange earnings and foreign aid and the ability to seek imported goods at the most favourable terms available'. Presenting his analysis 'ably and creatively' he reminded the Awami League leadership that conducting economic business with external partners was invariably 'a political process involving sovereign states and international lending agencies'. He warned that if the terms of donors 'were not coordinated' at the recipient end 'it would be impossible for any Pakistani province to bargain effectively'.[1] He underlined the need for political agreement as a precondition to 'working out some version' of provincial autonomy under the *Six Point Formula*.[2]

---

[1] Richard Sisson and Leo Rose (1990): p. 124

[2] Bangladesh: The Birth of a Nation (A handbook of background information and documentary sources), compiled by Marta Nicholas and Philip Oldenberg, Madras (India), 1972, p.81

Still, the effort to arrive at an agreement did not bear fruit. On 23 March 1971, the Awami League observed the Pakistan Day with desecration of national flag and by burning portraits of Mohammed Ali Jinnah. Everyday unrest began turning into armed militancy. Meanwhile, army reinforcements began arriving from the western wing, and Bengali officers were relieved from positions of command and control. Two of Yahya Khan's military governors resigned under mounting political pressure. General Tikka Khan (1915–2002), a military commander known for his professional brutality, was moved to East Pakistan in a bid to quell armed insurgency and save the terminally sick federation of Pakistan. He was a graduate of the Dehradun Military Academy under the Royal British Army, and had made it to media headlines in Pakistan for his gallant leadership in wars with India, first in the Rann of Kutch and then in Sialkot in 1965. He prided in his image of a stout soldier. On 7 March 1971, he arrived in Dhaka with a clear mind to secure territory rather than its inhabitants.

On the gloomy evening of 24 March 1971, Yahya Khan returned to Rawalpindi. At Dhaka airport, he took the ceremonial salute of senior army officer lined up to bid him farewell. Sort the bastards out! He is reported to have ordered Tikka Khan before boarding the last presidential flight out of Dhaka.

Within a matter of hours, the military launched its 'Operation Searchlight' and went into top gear of action by midnight. Mujibur Rahman was arrested and air-lifted to a prison in the western wing. A round the clock curfew was imposed, political activity banned and the popular media gagged. For once, the martial law shot itself out with the professional authenticity of a patriotic army. As the blanket of darkness fell upon cities and towns of East Pakistan, one of the most thickly populated regions in the world, millions of tragic tales were conceived. For decades, people remembered the night as *Kal Ratri*, that is, the night of dreadful darkness. 'A siren sounded in a looping, circular wail. Fiery sparks illuminated the horizon; a deep sound like faraway thunder reverberated through the air; then came smoke, and a small hush, as though it was over. But it wasn't. Seconds later it started all over again'.[1] A rebellious army officer proclaimed independent Bangladesh on one of the radio stations. It was the beginning of a final act soaked in desperation; savagery of murder, rape, destruction and devastation; the lush green landscape of eastern Bengal was painted with crimson strokes of human blood, mostly innocent. According to independent estimates, some half a million people were churned into the patriotic killings machines of

---

[1] Tahmina Anam: A Golden Age, John Murray (Publishers), London, 2007, p. 56

Pakistan army. How many got raped and maimed remains a matter of generally spineless imagination.

Tikka Khan was assisted by Major General Farman Ali, the General Officer Commanding of Dhaka Garrison. Born in Rajasthan and proud of his Rajput ancestry, Farman Ali (1922–2004), pretended to know East Pakistan and its people better than a whole lot of his colleagues. He had served in East Pakistan for many years. Tall, lean and sun burnt, he conversed in Bengali language. Behind his elegantly decorated military uniform, he concealed a cunning and ruthless character. He pioneered building up strategic linkage between the armed forces and Wahabi militants. He had achieved the mission by pitching the vulnerable *Bihari* migrant community of against their Bengali neighbours. At his behest, the armed gangs of insecure Bihari youth, charged with Wahabi vigour of jihad, set themselves upon the 'misguided' Bengali secessionist who wanted to destroy the holy land of Pakistan only to please the infidel Hindu.

By August 1971, Tikka Khan was well on the way to gaining control in urban areas. He was called back to signal the readiness of military junta for resumption of talks with the Awami League. At that time, a huge mass of displaced population, mostly members of the Hindu community, had been driven across into India. In October 1971, the number of refugees pouring into India touched the eight million mark making it increasingly difficult for Prime Minister Indira Gandhi to pretend aloofness. Also, there was the question as to why should India walk away from such a cost-effective humiliation of Pakistan. After experiencing wars with Pakistan and China, the Indian defence machine had matured a good deal. Indira Gandhi and her advisers maintained a close watch of the suicidal course Pakistan had embarked itself upon. There was no reason for India to act in rush, a decisively fatal blow upon the old foe could be best served when Pakistan had suffered massive internal bleeding. India began training militants and provided them with logistical facilities to attack Pakistani troops.

In the first week of December 1971, India and Pakistan were sucked into another round of all-out war. On this occasion though the bone of contention was East Pakistan, not Kashmir. General Jagjit Singh Arora (1916–2005), the Jhelum born chief of India's Eastern Command had the plan and the guts ready for a grand slam upon his Pakistani opponents. Once the signal was given, he took only twelve days to reach Dhaka. In a rare display of swiftness, he crossed broad rivers and marshlands. He gave Pakistan army the surprise Alexander the Great had given his ancestors by crossing overnight the swollen river at Jhelum some twenty-three centuries ago.

Battling the all-out rebellion of ordinary citizens was not known to Pakistani soldiers; the butchery of frail, helpless and unarmed people required some nerve. Trapped in alien marshlands, Pakistani soldiers discovered the jungle closed upon them like a tomb.[1] One last hope to save the Muslim army, Ayub Khan had proudly commanded in two hundred years of modern history in the subcontinent, from a total humiliation and rout rested upon the ceasefire call issued by the United Nations Security Council. Zulfiqar Bhutto grasped the initiative, he headed the Pakistani delegation, he would not miss the opportunity for his theatrical performance. Tearing up the copy of the Polish resolution calling for ceasefire, he stormed out of the session. Effectively, his action formalised the end of moth-eaten Pakistan the British had left behind. Hardly any possibility was left for the United Nations to save it.[2]

Few hours later, General Amir Abdullah, nicknamed as Tiger Niazi, who had replaced Tikka Khan as the General Officer Commanding in East Pakistan, plucked the insignia of rank off his uniform and presented it to General Jagjit Singh Arora. As the jubilant sea of humanity witnessed the ceremony of surrender, Amir Abdullah offered his army pistol to the Indian commander. General Jagjit Singh Arora quietly watched his Pakistani counterpart, a fellow Punjabi, signing the Instrument of Surrender. More than thrilled, the chief of India's Eastern Command looked composed and philosophical, perhaps a bit melancholy because the taming of the so-called tiger was not a spectacle of amusement. Over ninety thousand troops of Pakistan army were taken prisoner; they were at the mercy of their sworn enemy. Above all, on that winter afternoon in Dhaka, the Two Nation Theory constituting the ideological foundation of Pakistan, was buried to the utter disbelief of its bigoted adherents.

VI

Amazingly, Abdus Salam maintained an extremely low profile in relation to Pakistan's catastrophic military adventure prior to the emergence of Bangladesh. In fact, when the political ownership of Pakistan passed from one military

---

[1] Salman Rushdie: Midnight's Children, Jonathan Cape, London, 1981, p. 349
[2] Richard Sisson and Leo Rose (1990): p. 220

dictator on to the next, Abdus Salam did not seem to encounter any difficulty whatsoever in being a part of the acceded baggage. He went along with the change rather expediently, ready to serve the next military ruler. He did not care to distance himself from the regime when the popular mandate as expressed in the outcome of general election was flouted with military action and genocide in East Pakistan. Physicists, as natural philosophers, are known to have adopted bold positions on political and ideological issues especially when democracy and human rights were threatened. Abdus Salam just kept quiet as if nothing had happened and business was usual; it is hard to dig out if he ever expressed any notion of resentment privately somewhere. Of course, there seems none on public record of his displeasure over what went down in history as a matter of national shame for Pakistan. Had he been looking for reasons to bail himself out of a catastrophically mismanaged Pakistan, where nobody cared for his advice, an opportunity was lost.

Like Abdus Salam, his spiritual leader, Nasir Ahmad, maintained a tactful silence over the whole affair. Zulfiqar Bhutto had played an embarrassingly blatant foul with the Awami League, it might have served as a wakeup call for the Ahmadiyah. Instead of taking an ethical position in defence of democracy and human rights, the party failed to distance itself from Zulfiqar Bhutto. Instead the Ahmadiyah buried their head in the quick sands of a sinister power game staying openly faithful to Zulfiqar Bhutto. It might have been safer for the Ahmadiyah to watch the right rather than the left within the Peoples Party. Ditching the left led Pakistan into a lengthy lingering love affair with intolerance and religious bigotry.

Abdus Salam's association with the military regime of Yahya Khan gets glum in view of an observation made by his brother Abdul Hameed. According Abdul Hameed, there was occasion when Abdus Salam was purposely kept from an appointment with Yahya Khan, and the denial of access was triggered by an import scam. A senior Pakistani bureaucrat visiting Italy took Abdus Salam into confidence about the massive swindle of public funds. It worried the culprits when Abdus Salam reacted rather sharply by expressing his intention to take the matter up straight with the President. Soon the guilty party found protection with Lieutenant General Ghulam Mohammad Peerzada, the Chief of Staff to Yahya Khan. Ghulam Mohammad Peerzada made sure that Abdus Salam did not see the President without his clearance; he justified his action on security grounds. Abdus Salam was tagged as a security risk. In a strongly-worded note, Ghulam

Mohammad Peerzada urged Abdus Salam to better steer clear of the whole affair. Abdus Salam responded in the matching tone.[1] It is not known how far the matter went and what resolved it between the two sides because Abdus Salam's contact with Yahya Khan resumed. But this little-known episode raises serious questions about Abdus Salam's conduct. If he felt prompted to take the cudgels up with the government in a case of departmental corruption, what kept him from speaking up or walking away on the massacre and rape of innocent millions in East Pakistan?

While Pakistan hobbled through conflicts, crises and wars; Abdus Salam settled into a stable routine of his life divided between work and two wives. His more regular presence in London, Oxford and Trieste was sprinkled with international science meetings and conferences all over the world. When required, he reported to attend meetings at the Atomic Energy Commission in Pakistan.

After wedding Louise Johnson, he looked forward to be in Oxford and be in the company of the one he loved so much. Life with Louise Johnson echoed spontaneity; her presence symbolised a delightful blend of science and romance. Actually, his communal, cultural and religious setting was overdue for a bit of weeding out for the love affair to blossom.

As full-time Director at the International Centre for Theoretical Physics in Trieste he had condensed his academic presence in Imperial College. He did not wish to give up on London, a station of tremendous excitement for professional, logistical and intellectual pursuits. A continued attachment with Imperial College secured his presence on the forefront of academia. Then, London always had a great deal of amusing charm and excitement to offer. He remembered how one day the Military Attaché of Israel's Embassy in London, Yuval Ne'eman (1925–2006), marched into his room at Imperial College in full army uniform and demanded enrolment in the doctoral program in Theoretical Physics. Abdus Salam checked the academic credentials of this unscheduled visitor and found him fit. Only, you will have to go through the formalities of enrolment, Abdus Salam advised Yuval Ne'eman, adding that the military uniform was not compulsory.

Back in Pakistan, while addressing the National Science Council in Islamabad in September 1970, he expressed grief over the state of less than a dozen under-resourced and over controlled universities, catering for a population

---

[1] Abdul Hameed (circa 2000): p. 128

approaching the 150 million mark, with emphasis on social rather than natural sciences. After more than a century of its existence, the University of Punjab, in Lahore, he reminded had yet to produce a doctoral scholar in mathematics. He urged the private sector to share the burden of scientific investigation. Nuclear energy, he felt, was the only sector where success had been achieved in some measure due largely to the responsiveness on the part of the government. Pakistan, he warned, was drifting away from the world of ideas, literature and equipment; had been unable to host international science conferences due to its diplomatic preferences. Pakistani scientists, he lamented, were discouraged to travel abroad because of rigid bureaucratic controls and tedious procedures for security clearance.

'If there is one reform which I consider absolutely basic to the entire future of scientific research in Pakistan, it is the massive provision for research and its separate funding in the universities. Without this reform, Pakistani science can have no strength, no backbone, and no real future'. He cautioned. 'Research does not thrive in an atmosphere where the command structure, career opportunities, and procedures for acquiring needed equipment and facilities are those of a government executive department'. He urged the government to start diverting one percent of the Gross National Product towards scientific effort. Otherwise, he warned Pakistan stood no chances of transforming itself into a technologically modern country.[1]

It was a time when the country had gone into the top gear of election campaign and the Awami League advocated greater provincial autonomy for East Pakistan. Typically, Abdus Salam proposed to safeguard Pakistan's 'territorial integrity' by designing a coherent science policy to build up an educated and highly skilled manpower. As if only he knew how excellence in science might prevent the impending breakup of the Islamic Republic, he pressed for the need to develop both 'adaptive' and 'innovative' models of research planning in every sector of national life, from irrigation, fertilisers, flood control, dam building, soil improvement, cash crops, livestock and food to exploration and extraction of minerals, power generation, transport, telecommunications, medicine, pharmaceuticals and tropical diseases.

---

[1] Abdus Salam: Towards a Scientific Research and Development Policy for Pakistan, National Science Council, Karachi, December 1970.

Historically, as it turned out afterwards, this was his final piece of advice to the Government of Pakistan. He continued campaigning for scientific causes with unassailable eagerness though any signs of victory were not in sight.

At one point, Yahya Khan decided to update the National Education Policy. With a revamp in the order of priorities, the government pledged to universalise primary education and divert 60 per cent of school leaving students into scientific, technical and vocational programs by 1980. In the higher education sector, universities were granted greater professional freedom.[1] Abdus Salam participated in the process as if the new military regime had come to stay in power for a decade and not disappear after holding the election.

Muzaffar Ahmad, the finance and economic mandarin who had been bold enough to explain the impossibility of *Six-point Program* before the Awami League leadership in Dhaka, was known to Abdus Salam. During the course of a visit to London, he invited Abdus Salam to identify areas where the government could invest money. Never short of ideas even when funds were not forthcoming, Abdus Salam proposed the creation of Pakistan Science Foundation. Muzaffar Ahmad agreed to allocate a sum of ten million rupees. 'He had come to see me, the National Science Foundation was created in this house in Putney. He used to stay with me. It was on my suggestion that he sanctioned the grant. That's a good idea, he had remarked'. Abdus Salam remembered with pride.[2]

But then he overlooked the state of executive culture in Pakistan. Getting a grant of ten million rupees just like that, without the slightest hassle of preparing any formal case for it to carry submissions and summaries through government and parliamentary committees constituted a major procedural question in itself. Few months later, when the government headed by Yahya Khan collapsed, the grant was slashed to half by the next administration.

On 25 March 1969, the day when Ayub Khan relinquished power to clear the deck for next round of martial law in the country, Abdus Salam's ageing father, Mohammed Hussein, suffered a severe heart attack. He was flown from Multan to Karachi for treatment at a more advanced medical centre. Abdus Salam received the news in New York. Reflecting about those fatalistic remarks his father had been making recently about the end of a journey in the mortal world, he made frantic efforts to call his brother. But there was no luck in getting

---

[1] Contemporary Pakistan: Politics, Economy and Society, Edited by Manzooruddin Ahmed, Karachi, 1982, p. 254
[2] Interviews 1984: Folder VII, pp. 65-66

through the obsolete telephone exchange in Karachi. He even used his influence to call via special circuit available to the White House in Washington. Panicked and nervous, he boarded the first available flight to Pakistan. At Karachi airport, he found his younger brother, Abdul Hameed, helping a semi-unconscious Mohammed Hussein to get into the ambulance.

In between fits of weakness and delirium, the moment when Mohammed Hussein saw Abdus Salam, he kissed the hand of his prodigal son. Three days later, there was another heart attack and Mohammed Hussein passed away early in the morning. His body was airlifted to Punjab the same day for burial at the Ahmadiyah headquarter in Rabwah. It was late in the night when the coffin arrived in Rabwah, yet the Ahmadiyah caliph, Nasir Ahmad, arrived to lead the funeral service. Mohammed Hussein rested in peace for his dream of fathering an extraordinary son, envisioned in a mud-painted mosque outside the ancient town of Jang, on a sizzling hot June afternoon some 44 years ago, had come true.

After the burial of his father, Abdus Salam returned to London, he seemed to suffer from depression, began spending time in his room, grieving in isolation. Although he had sufficient time to prepare himself for the death of his father, it was hard to accept the breach when it approached. He reminisced about sacrifices his father had made in educating the children. He thought of the man who had stayed away from small comforts of everyday life only to ensure the best for his children.

While he grieved, his first wife, Amtul Hafeez got worried. She made a telephone call to Zafarullah Khan to come over and intervene. In those days, Zafarullah Khan resided in a guest room of the Ahmadiyah Mission. Zafarullah Khan signalled the Imam of the Ahmadiyah Mosque, Bashir Rafiq, to accompany him. Do you know that excessive mourning of the dead amounted to apostasy? Zafarullah Khan told Abdus Salam somewhat bluntly. According to the Imam, Abdus Salam just broke down; he wept until a good deal of the compressed emotional burden was offloaded.[1]

Earlier in his life, despite the upbringing in an intensely religious environment, where everyday life was frequently punctuated with references to the Koran and Islamic tradition, Abdus Salam did not happen to turn out overtly devout. Invariably, he credited Mohammed Hussein's rich thrust of prayers as the foundation of his academic success, including the winning of Nobel Prize.[2]

---

[1] *Khalid* (December 1997): p. 163
[2] Interviews 1984: Folder I, p. 39

In a way, therefore, the rush of professional and personal circumstances did appear to overtake the life of Abdus Salam at a time when the political leadership of Pakistan set the country upon a course of national suicide. Still, the search for any justification behind his loyalty with military regimes, along with his pin drop silence over military action in East Pakistan, remains hard to comprehend.

Commenting upon his years of association with Government of Pakistan, Abdus Salam described the journey starting with innocence and hope (1954–1964) driven to frustration and despair (1964–1974). He held a high regard for the scholarly disposition of Prime Minister Chaudhri Mohamed Ali who was stabbed in back by his own ruling party before being able to bring about any consequential change in the quality of Pakistani politics.

At a personal level, Abdus Salam did evolve fondness for the professional spontaneity displayed by Ayub Khan. He went as far as describing Ayub Khan as the architect of science in Pakistan. At the Pakistan Association for Advancement of Science, in 1962, he likened Ayub Khan's support for Pakistani science with the founding of the Royal Society by King Charles II of England and Napoleon's keenness upon the French Academy of Sciences. He expected Ayub Khan to clean up the political mess and start afresh. But this observation, made earlier in the 1960s, began giving way to anguish and gloom when the momentum of appetite for science was lost. Still, he felt, it was a fruitful time in some way as the recommendations of the National Science Commission were adopted to a great extent.

Even if Abdus Salam seemed to have hung on, more out of personal loyalty and regard rather than professional logic, he admitted the battle for science was never easy to win in Pakistan. In the beginning, he must have been attracted by the political glitter and glamour associated with working for the most powerful man in the country. He could approach the President anytime but, in the end, there was no way to score victory over the bureaucracy encasing the president. 'Every time I went to him with a case for an institution, he would advise me to go and convince his aides and those bastards were never convinced. Mohammad Shoaib, Shaikh Yusuf and Ghulam Ishaq Khan; they were all there, never ready to put a penny in science. They were just not convinced about the value attached to science. They did not see any reason to do so. We, therefore, lacked the real institutions. Science was not permitted to play a role in nation-building'. He recalled.[1]

---

[1] Interviews 1984: VII, pp. 23-24

According to Abdus Salam, even when Ayub Khan recognised the need for scientific culture in the country, his approach lacked consistency. Often, he behaved like a consumer with his fascination confined to the end product alone. Instead of understanding the significance of scientific knowledge behind industrial and technological processes, he believed the shortest route to social and industrial development passed through technical and vocational institutions.

'Because I had the privilege to talk freely, he used to listen even when we disagreed. Within few years of his departure from the political scene, people remembered him for a golden era in Pakistan, and it was so in a way'. Abdus Salam felt.[1]

Outside the circle of his secretaries, Abdus Salam considered Ayub Khan to be a fairly tolerant man. In his earlier days in power, Ayub Khan accepted a dinner invitation from Ahmad Dawood, a Karachi-based business tycoon. Abdus Salam considered it amounting to an elopement staged by the rich who exploited common man. 'I went to him and protested, he listened patiently. In fact, on another occasion he referred to this aspect of his personality, which enabled him to control his emotions and temper, as a blessing of God'.[2]

On the whole, Abdus Salam felt affection for Ayub Khan. 'I witnessed him meeting some of the top world leaders of his time. He had grown in stature'. He remembered Ayub Khan as a great man with big heart. 'I accompanied him on three different occasions outside the country, when he went to meet the American, European and Chinese leaders. I watched him very closely. He looked like a giant among men. I remember some of the German officials telling us that our president resembled Marshall Hindenburg'.

Ayub Khan died in April 1974. From the peace and quiet of his home on a hill next to government blocks in Islamabad, he must have watched the tumult unfolding in Pakistan with pain. Abdus Salam never felt at ease with the manner in which Ayub Khan had been ousted from power. He suspected that a part of the American money earned from wheat sale, provided to Pakistan under Public Law 480, was pumped back into subverting the government of Ayub Khan.[3] On a personal level the friendship between Abdus Salam and Ayub Khan survived the test of power politics. After the end of his government, Ayub Khan travelled to the United States on a private visit. On the way he stopped briefly in London

---

[1] Interviews 1984: VII, pp. 93-96
[2] Interviews 1984: Folder VI, pp. 94-96
[3] Interviews 1984: VII, p. 29

to see his doctors. Abdus Salam was one of those who made it to the airport to receive him. 'I called on him whenever and wherever it was possible'. Abdus Salam remarked, adding that he would do so despite the advice to the contrary from those who preferred to stay on the winning side.

In the order of their sincerity to promote science, Abdus Salam would just strike his experience with Yahya Khan out of the list. 'I think if we take the results of their contribution into consideration, as the criteria to pass judgment on their performance in science sector, the government headed by Yahya Khan hardly stands the test. We should forget about him straightaway for his was a time when nothing had been considered in any serious way'. He stated.[1]

Offering advice to Yahya Khan proved much harder than it had been in case with Ayub Khan. Mainly, of course, it was due to the irreversible mess the new chief had created for himself in East Pakistan. Yahya Khan simply did not have time for science. 'Everything went moribund in those days. Yahya Khan did not want any advice, would not encourage anyone to do so. It did not really matter if I called on the President or avoided altogether to meet him. None of the voices of scientists were ever heard during his time'. Abdus Salam recollected later. Occasionally, when Abdus Salam went to meet him, Yahya Khan listened with his mind caught somewhere else.

'Professor, you must write all these important points about science on a card for me. I'll hide the card up my uniform sleeve as a weapon to convince my corps commanders in our next meeting'. Yahya Khan used to tell Abdus Salam.[2] In his final days in power, Yahya Khan was so heavily stressed out by the failure in East Pakistan that he would rarely be sober.

This was in striking contrast to what Abdus Salam had experienced during the course of his official visit to China as a part of the entourage of Ayub Khan in 1965. He was amazed to observe the difference of attitude towards scientific scholarship between the leadership of two sides. He was pleasantly surprised upon receiving the invitation of an exclusive lunch with the Chinese Prime Minister, Zhou En-Lai (1898–1976). When the presidential party toured through Hangzhou, a popular location known for its scenic beauty, mild climate and cultural heritage in the Yangtze delta near Shanghai, Abdus Salam was escorted for an audience with Zhou En-Lai. In his conversation with the Chinese Prime Minister, the role of interpreter was played by the Vice Rector of Beijing

---

[1] Interviews 1984: VII, p. 74
[2] Interviews 1984: FVI, pp. 87-88

University. 'We began talking about ways to promote and popularise physics in China. At one point I felt we were getting entangled into finer details that might be unnecessary for a meeting at the level of the Prime Minister. For example, there were minor questions about personnel placements. When I expressed my amazement over the Prime Minister spending so much time on the subject and his keenness on trivialities, he remarked it was his responsibility'. Abdus Salam remembered the occasion. He was fascinated to observe how Zhou En-Lai realised the importance of physics despite his own lack of background in science.[1]

VII

By the time Yahya Khan woke up to the reality facing him in East Pakistan, he began receiving advice from Richard Nixon (1913–1994), the President of the United States. Powerless in holding on to East Pakistan, he was urged to 'concentrate his forces in the defence of West Pakistan'. It was a plan to retreat for the purpose of which he received assurance of 'complete support' by the American President. 'On December 17 the explosive situation on the western front was also resolved when Pakistan accepted the Indian offer of a cease-fire there. By using diplomatic signals and behind-the-scenes pressures we had been able to save West Pakistan from the imminent threat of Indian aggression and domination'. Observed Richard Nixon adding that 'The Indo-Pakistan war involved stakes much higher than the future of Pakistan—and that was high enough. It involved the principle of whether big nations supported by the Soviet Union would be permitted to dismember their smaller neighbours. Once the principle was allowed, the world would have become more unsafe'.[2]

At some point in his youth Zulfiqar Bhutto had aspired to become a film star in Bombay's Bollywood. Instead, he found the opportunity to sharpen his theatrical skills on political stage. One great opening had come his way in December 1971, when he represented Pakistan at the United Nations. After tearing apart the draft of peace resolution proposed by Poland, he stormed out of the Security Council session, dashed out of New York to seek audience with

---

[1] Interviews 1984: VII, pp. 24-26

[2] Richard Nixon: The Memoirs of Richard Nixon, Grosset $ Dunlop, USA 1978, pp. 528, 530

Richard Nixon at a yacht off the coast of Florida. After the brief interview with the American President, he went to Tehran to meet the Iranian Emperor, Reza Pahlavi (1919–1980) and then deflected to Europe. Fearing his past, he did not wish to return home without the blessings of the mighty and powerful. In what was left of Pakistan, a stunned nation looked towards him for some sort of consolation and hope. He was lucky to have survived the risk of a backlash from the younger military officers who had already taken the General Officer Commanding at Kharian cantonment, some 150 kilometres south of Islamabad, as a hostage in exchange for their demand to reshuffle the top brass.

As Yahya Khan bowed out, serving the purpose of a convenient scapegoat, Air Marshal Rahim Khan, the Chief of Air Staff, flew to Rome to escort Zulfiqar Bhutto back home as an expedient replacement in the new order. Ahead of the Christmas break in 1971, Zulfiqar Bhutto was installed into power with the twin responsibility as the President as well as the Chief Martial Law Administrator. It was an extraordinary example in transfer of power, performed with an exceptional spin in constitutional legality since the dubiousness of Constituent Assembly the British had left behind in 1947. Shrugging off the shame of disintegration, the one-armed Pakistan moved on as if the collapse of federation had been nothing more than a violent and messy divorce. Upon the ashes of a stunning surrender and humiliation in Dhaka, Zulfiqar Bhutto took the presidential salute of an amputated state. He vowed to build a 'New Pakistan' to restore the confidence of people and their national pride.

Like before, Abdus Salam received the signal to continue as Science Advisor to the Government of Pakistan. He accepted the offer without hesitation or caution. Not only he was agreeing to serve the third martial law administrator in row, there was a history of ties between him and Zulfiqar Bhutto. Contrary to Ayub Khan's patience and composure, Zulfiqar Bhutto was the pampered scion of a wealthy feudal house in Sind, with a born to rule mentality and known for the volatility and vindictiveness of his moods. As a part of the government under Ayub Khan, both Abdus Salam and Ishrat Usmani had known Zulfiqar Bhutto for several years. In view of their peculiar mix of accords and dissimilarities, the triangle of working relationship comprising Abdus Salam, Ishrat Usmani and Zulfiqar Bhutto had been far from ideal. Unlike Ayub Khan, who did not mind delegation of power onto adjoining tiers of executive, Zulfiqar Bhutto centralised authority to wield direct control in crucial areas like the nuclear establishment.

Zulfiqar Bhutto had found his place in the government when he was 30. He was mocked for his flamboyance as well as the Oxford background because the majority of ageing secretaries in the government of Ayub Khan happened to have graduated from Cambridge. Matters turned ugly as Zulfiqar Bhutto picked up one row after another with Ishrat Usmani. Often, he was very keen on promoting private contractors, suppliers and construction firms of his own choice. Ishrat Usmani disapproved the practice, he preferred a formal invitation of tenders. In another way, the rift between Ishrat Usmani and Zulfiqar Bhutto reflected the Migrant-Sindhi ethnic divide simmering in Karachi since the creation of Pakistan. Very often, Abdus Salam found himself caught in the crossfire and would end up taking sides with Ishrat Usmani.

Zulfiqar Bhutto was not comfortable with Abdus Salam's express ability to approach Ayub Khan. He could see how the Science Adviser protected the Chairman of the Atomic Energy Commission. Without having anything directly to do with bureaucratic business, Abdus Salam often got sucked into rivalries and tensions surrounding Ishrat Usmani.

There was one occasion when Abdus Salam found himself in a direct clash with Zulfiqar Bhutto. It happened in 1965, during the course of an official visit to China. Zulfiqar Bhutto led Pakistani delegation as the Minister for Foreign Affairs. Ayub Khan briefed the members of the delegation with an explicit advice to avoid touching upon a particular aspect of Pakistan's nuclear policy. Due to the sensitive nature of the subject, the President desired to take it up with the Chinese leadership by himself and that too at an appropriate moment. Once in Beijing, Abdus Salam was shocked to hear Zulfiqar Bhutto making a statement on the forbidden matter. In fact, he felt Zulfiqar Bhutto had gone too far, opening the possibility of misinterpretation. Upon returning home, Abdus Salam deemed it necessary to brief the President about the affair so that damage control measures were in place without delay. In a rare fit of rage, Ayub Khan summoned Zulfiqar Bhutto for an explanation. Although Abdus Salam had acted in honesty, he provoked the feudal vindictiveness of Zulfiqar Bhutto.

Later, in the summer of 1968, Abdus Salam went to attend a Science Conference in Dhaka. He ran into Zulfiqar Bhutto who had been expelled from the government. After the exchange of pleasantries, just when the two were about to go their ways, Abdus Salam proposed a more formal get together to catch up. 'You have time these days' was how Abdus Salam shot the joke out of his

Punjabi stock. Actually, he had trampled upon a highly sensitive chord of Zulfiqar Bhutto's political ego.

What do you mean? Zulfiqar Bhutto asked. He was visibly irritated and had not taken the remark in any lighter vein. To him, Abdus Salam was being sarcastic about his political redundancy. He walked away, angry, and had nothing to do with Abdus Salam until the score could be settled; the opportunity for which arrived sooner than expected.

Chapter Nine
Excommunication

Like the majority among Pakistani intelligentsia, stunned and spellbound in the wake of military capitulation in Dhaka, Abdus Salam yearned to move on as if the verdict on disfigured geography of his country was not a big deal, only there was the dire need now for a redefinition of national identity. Gloom and demoralisation demanded soul searching; while intellectuals, academics, religious scholars, politicians and sensitive citizens endeavoured to find answers; everyone wanted to understand what exactly went wrong where. How and why religion, the foundation of Pakistani state, failed to bridge the craters of ethnicity dividing Muslims of South Asia? What traded the Islamic fraternity and brotherhood with the brutality of a ruthless military action? Was the two-nation theory, securing for Muslims an irrevocable identity in the subcontinent, a sham?

In the absence of quick and suitable answers, especially in matters risking faith, the generally agreed upon course led to a national hush up. After a while, people came to terms with the shock as if 1971 simply did not exist in the passage of time. Zulfiqar Bhutto was granted an opportunity of a lifetime to change the course of history and liberate Pakistan from the repressive burden of its recent past. From time to time, the left wing bombarded on the coalition of feudal lords, big business, military generals, bureaucrats and clerics for every afflictions facing the country. Those with religious bent of mind viewed the shame of military defeat as the punishment to sinful and secular rulers of Pakistan. As always, the clerics began touting the implementation of Islamic Shariah laws; they insisted upon the absolute eradication of secular, socialist and western influences to achieve the goal of Islamic fraternity. Just as Winston Churchill prescribed more democracy to cure political ailment, the clerics in Pakistan pressed for greater dosages of religion to fix economic, social and political malaise threatening the Islamic Republic.

Immediate attention was required to soothe the youth nourished upon hatred of India and a self-proclaimed invincibility of Pakistan. In the deluge of national castigation, Abdus Salam received invitation to attend the Annual Convocation Ceremony in Government College Jhang. He accepted the invitation for it offered him the opportunity to speak about the calamity befalling upon the original state of Pakistan. Although his speech at the ceremony went relatively un-noticed, it remains one of the finest lectures ever heard in the emotional turbulence overwhelming Pakistan. Making just over five thousand words, the speech adds up to an inspirational mix of nostalgia and calculated idealism.[1]

'Accomplishment of Pakistan after two hundred years of slavery was not a small miracle. It was a divine opportunity God almighty, the Cherisher, endowed upon us, granting us the choice of making or breaking our destiny. We failed in cementing ourselves into the union of brotherhood and mutual regard. Our inadequacy made us unworthy and the Holy Creator recanted the blessing'. With such carefully chosen words rooted in his deeply religious state of mind, Abdus Salam grieved the break-up of Pakistan before a spellbound audience at the college where he had been a student himself some thirty years ago. He spoke in plain Urdu, adorned with characteristic inflection of southern Punjab. His deep husky voice sounded melancholy as if he shared a personal loss with family members.

He reminisced about his own time spent at the college and the local community of Jhang which in those days comprised of Muslims, Hindus and Sikhs; living together in peace and harmony. He remembered how the cultural versatility of academic staff laid the foundation of his later day achievements in life. 'I was admitted into the college in 1938, at the age of twelve. In those days it was only an Intermediate College, offering two years of instruction to those who had graduated through university matriculation stage. An overwhelming majority of students making it to the Intermediate level belonged to Hindu and Sikh communities. I consider myself exceptionally fortunate to have been placed under the care of very able and kind teachers'. He then went on to remember some of his old teachers from the Hindu and Sikh communities by name with subjects they used to teach. Reflecting upon the communal polarisation of undivided Punjab, he praised the scholarly preference of his Hindu and Sikh teachers assigned to teach mathematics and natural sciences as against the

---

[1] Many years later, a slightly edited version of the speech was printed by Muslim University in Aligarh, India.

traditional popularity of social sciences and linguistics among their Muslim counterparts. 'I am not making it up for the sake of the occasion; it remains a plain truth to me that the foundation of my later day achievements was actually laid here in this college. Nothing stops pupils, instructed with the attention and affection of their teachers, in gaining limitless heights'. He maintained.

He then turned toward the linkage between intellectual backwardness and social under-development that was keeping Pakistan from prosperity and peace. One of the major causes of national predicament confronting the country, he reminded his audience, could be traced straight back to the widespread neglect of education. Due to a general disregard of education, he stated, the pace of economic development suffered fatal blows upon the desire for nation building.

'We do not have any over-arching definition for nationhood because the concept varies with changing circumstances and experiences in the lives of countries and people at particular occasions in their historical development, yet there are many examples where the educational factor seems to determine the fate of national stability'. He postulated. 'You may take the case of America, where we find English, Irish, German, Italian, Swedish and French tribes of people living together in unity and harmony. They are the same people who rendered expensive sacrifices in the two world wars, back in Europe only recently, to uphold their separate national identities. Before adopting the United States as their new home, they spoke different languages and practiced un-identical religious beliefs. As far as profession and performance of religion is concerned, they continue to enjoy freedom, yet the educational machine of their new homeland has amalgamated them into one nation. Today, they are proud citizens of their present country, looking toward a successful future. None of them seems to be living the past, anymore. Indeed, the educational institutions and corporate media in the United States have played a vital role in achieving this miracle in national cohesion'. He construed.

'At this point in time, Pakistan comprises of four provinces. We are followers of Islam, ever ready to sacrifice our lives for the sake of our holy prophet'. He continued. 'We are bound together by bonds of common language and ethnicity. In a cultural perspective, the western Pakistan is one of the most strikingly homogenous regions in the world. Believe me, the gulf between England and Scotland is much greater compared to national contiguity in our situation. We find that physical and social collectiveness among Punjab, Sind, Baluchistan and the North Western Frontier Province is no less than anywhere else in the world.

Like the miracle of national integration pulled out in the United States, we should build up our educational system and evolve syllabi to promote ownership of each other. I would like to share with you a personal wish today. I aspire for the day when we evolve a new form of Urdu language, a grand meeting place of our national tongues and dialects, enriched by regional traditions of Sindhi, Baluchi, Pashto, Punjabi, Seraiki, and so on. I draw pride in being a part of the effort my respectable teacher, Sher Afzal Jaffrey, had initiated here in this college some twenty-five years ago, to blend Urdu with the Punjabi dialect of Jhang. I dream of a day when every student of this institution will be able to appreciate the lyrical works of great Sufi saints from all over Pakistan, just as we draw pride in the epic of Heer'. He touched upon the local chord.

Only three days before the Convocation Ceremony at Government College in Jhang, the epic tale of Heer Ranjha was staged at a theatre in Karachi by the veteran film actor Zia Mohiyuddin. Among dignitaries attending the show was Zulfiqar Bhutto, then President and Chief Martial Law Administrator of Pakistan. Overwhelmed by the invincibility of Heer, the heroin of the epic tale, Zulfiqar Bhutto danced on the stage and then declared that Heer belonged to the whole of Indus valley, not just to one district, province or ethnic group alone.

'In Pakistan, the average per capita income is fifty times less than that in the United States. In England, people earn twenty-times more than we do. Apart from the United States and Britain, we lag behind countries as diverse as Japan, Turkey, Iraq, Algeria, Egypt, Syria and Ghana. Why are we so miserably poor? For a while, in order to draw quick solace, we may attribute the causes of our poverty to colonial yoke or to the western affluence triggered by European discovery of America. But the question remains as to why on earth we were subjected to slavery so conveniently? Then, if the Europeans excelled in shipping, and we did not, was it their fault?' He invited the audience to ponder over the question and then reminded them that more than a military defeat, the collapse of Muslim power in Bengal, way back in 1757, was actually an admission of the technological superiority displayed by the Europeans. It was a lack of desire on the part of Muslim rulers to prop up an urge for scientific discovery that had paved the way for capitulation of Bengal. He pressed ahead telling his audience about Zaheeruddin Babur, the founder of Mogul Empire in India, who had employed Roman artillery practices in the famous battleground of Panipat. But the technological innovation was not followed up. 'Alas, the descendants of Babur paid no attention to developing the nascent art in warfare.

Muslim sultans and kings did not care to set up a single laboratory to carry out research in the development of ordnance. Even when social endowments constituted an integral part of religious activity in medieval Constantinople, where hospitals and schools were attached to an imperial network of mosques, the Turkish invaders remained disinclined towards introducing similar standards of scholarship in India. Instead of leaving behind a tradition for building research schools and laboratories, Muslim royalty preferred to be remembered by its rich legacy of tombs and sepulchres'. He went on.

He told his audience that Lord almighty had opened up the world of opportunity to Europeans only because they accepted challenges in pursuit of scholarship. 'The unflinching resolution of the west to discover new continents across vast and restless oceans, a prize for the determination to subordinate the fierce elements of nature, tornados and typhoons; was duly rewarded'. He made here a brief mention of the spirit behind the Industrial Revolution and the age of discovery and invention in Europe and the United States before citing more recent examples from Japan and the Peoples Republic of China.

First, he narrated the tale of Admiral Matthew Perry (1794–1858), the American naval commander who is credited with breaking the isolation of Japan in 1852. Abdus Salam told his audience how, for nearly two centuries before the arrival of the small American fleet, the Shogun rulers of Japan had discouraged their countrymen from having anything to do with the world abroad. Living in fear, the Japanese royalty believed that a tightly closed door was the best course to keep foreign military, economic and cultural invasion at a safe distance. As such, Japan lagged so far behind in metallurgical skills that even the casting of a plain horse-shoe was not known in the country.

One day, the great-story teller in Abdus Salam informed his spellbound audience, a horse was found missing from the floating stable of Admiral Matthew Perry. But soon afterwards the horse reappeared, rather mysteriously. Upon investigation, it turned out that the abduction had been master-minded by the Japanese only because they wanted to study and make a blueprint of the horse-shoe which from their point of view was a very useful invention. This attempt at stealing the patent, Abdus Salam dramatized, could be viewed as the turning point in the industrial fortunes of Japan. One century later, when transistor was developed in the United States, the Japanese engineers decoded the secret to usher an unstoppable revolution in the world of electronics. 'Today, the race for excellence in educational merit has reached a stage where the

Japanese children matriculating in mathematics, physics and chemistry are as good as the best elsewhere in the world'. Abdus Salam concluded the tale by paying tribute to the urge for knowledge in a country where isolation had been the state policy.

From Japan, he switched on to the Peoples Republic of China. Recently, he had been to China and was amazed to find middle school students, aged about twelve, enrolled to receive instruction in a full range of compulsory disciplines including mathematics, physics, chemistry and biology with emphasis on agriculture. Other than natural sciences they studied history, geography, performing arts and at least two foreign languages. At the same time, they were supposed to be in workshops to improve their understanding of the homeland.

'During my college days, we grew up with a widely-held impression that Muslims lacked the aptitude for learning mathematics'. Abdus Salam remembered. 'Now we are told that the majority of literate people in Pakistan are not inclined towards natural sciences. In China, however, the question is not about personal penchant, students are required to take both arts and sciences simultaneously. Inferring that a regimentation of this kind might pull down standards of academic performance, I attended classroom teaching in both mathematics and physics. There was no limit to my astonishment when I found fourteen-year-old Chinese students learning Order of Infinities. We offer such courses to our Bachelors level students. China, I must tell you, is determined to go through the industrial drill. Starting their present journey in national development two years after our independence, they have nearly mastered the art of electronics. In last twenty-five years, their steel production capacity has increased by 500 times of the original output. Now they are entering into fabrication of sophisticated machine tools'. He stated.

He summed up the address by urging younger Pakistanis to draw inspiration from the success stories of Europe, America, Japan and China; and battle against backwardness and disunity. Let there be no justification, he appealed passionately, to stay ignorant and continue living in abject poverty and pessimism.

Every scientist was an artist by birth, the Principal of the College had remarked while introducing Abdus Salam. Taking queue, Abdus Salam encouraged his audience to read the jargon both ways, to track down a scientist in every artist.

II

Making the atom bomb for Pakistan was a top priority for Zulfiqar Bhutto. His fancy with nuclear Pakistan dated back to years when the department dealing with nuclear energy constituted a part of his portfolio in the federal government under Ayub Khan. 'If Pakistan restricts or suspends her nuclear programme, it would not only enable India to blackmail Pakistan with her nuclear technology, but would impose crippling limitation on the development of Pakistan's science and technology'. He had written in 1967. Keeping pace with India, he advocated, was imperative even if the people of Pakistan were compelled to eat grass in order to save money to manufacture the bomb. Although his call to go nuclear sounded like a ploy in gaining quick popularity among masses, the fact remained that he happened to be the only prominent Pakistani leader who participated in the debate rather consistently. His ambition to manufacture nuclear warfare, in the immediate aftermath of a devastating military surrender and humiliation in Dhaka, sounded comically absurd. Perhaps, he considered the need to master nuclear capability had multiplied manifold in order to fix the disturbed balance of power in South Asia. At a time when Pakistan had been bullied by India and deserted by its powerful allies, he might have weighed, a gate-crash into the exclusive nuclear club as one of the best routes to reclaim respectability.

Within days of returning to power, in the wake of armistice in Dhaka, he convened a meeting of the leading nuclear scientists and engineers to discuss the bomb plan. By this time, as a result of the massive effort put in by Ishrat Usmani and Abdus Salam, a sizeable community of nuclear scientists and reactor engineers had grown up in Pakistan. In fact, a few restless heads among them believed they were under-utilised. Some of them wanted to drill their expertise in things more exciting like, for example, development of nuclear weapons.

Initially, Zulfiqar Bhutto's meeting with nuclear experts was scheduled to take place in Baluchistan, the vast expanse of barren hills and sand dunes west of Indus.[1] For logistical reasons, possibly to save the participants from the freezing fierceness of Siberian winds, the venue shifted to Multan where it was convened on the extensive lawns of a baronial mansion called the White House, owned by a local feudal lord. Zulfiqar Bhutto addressed the hastily gathered group of physicists and engineers, out in the open, under the mild winter sky of

---

[1] Here in Baluchistan, in 1998, Pakistan had carried out its first round of nuclear show.

southern Punjab, without any security checks and clearance. Unlike a highly guarded top-secret engagement, as the situation demanded, the whole affair presented the look of a public rally where anybody from anywhere, including media, enjoyed the freedom to walk in and walk out at their convenience. Against this untailored atmosphere, Zulfiqar Bhutto sounded his audience about starting the journey toward atom bomb. He told them to deliver and not worry about money.

How long would it take us to manufacture the bomb? Zulfiqar Bhutto asked the spellbound mix of his audience facing him. Someone younger got overexcited to promise an ambitious timeframe of two years. Zulfiqar Bhutto listened with amusement more than reassurance. For Abdus Salam and Ishrat Usmani, it was a novel experience, the two could not believe the bomb was being discussed out in the open. Abdus Salam had already spotted two foreign journalists sitting in the rear. He exchanged interrogative looks with Ishrat Usmani. Has the President gone nuts? Is he serious? Does he know the gravity of the subject involved? Who advised him to talk about the nuclear bomb in an unguarded gathering like this? Abdus Salam reminisced.

Much has been sensationalised about the meeting in Multan portraying the whole affair as a stage show more than a formal meeting to start planning for the bomb.[1] But to people who believed in miracles, the crisp late January morning in Multan made their day as Pakistan was going to have the bomb within a matters of few years. At the same time, Zulfiqar Bhutto won the credit for being honest and forthright. Actually, he seemed to have achieved more than a mere declaration of intent. On the stage, he sat flanked by Abdus Salam and Ishrat Usmani. He reminded the audience about his recent encounter in Dhaka with Abdus Salam. If the Professor thought I was over and done with, here I stand before you as the Chief Martial Law Administrator and President of Pakistan. He yelled at Abdus Salam. Next, he fired Ishrat Usmani by replacing him with Munir Khan, a Government College contemporary of Abdus Salam. Up until recently, Munir Khan had been serving as reactor engineer at the International Atomic Energy Agency in Vienna. Abdus Salam was signalled to continue as

---

[1] Written by Steve Weismann and Herbert Krosney, The Islamic Bomb (Times Books, New York, 1981) carries a thrilling and dramatic account of the January 1972 meeting in Multan.

Science Adviser without forgetting as to who called the shots in Pakistan. It was typical of his vindictiveness, Abdus Salam remarked afterward.[1]

Ishrat Usmani had been watching political situation unfolding in the country and he wished to bail himself out in time and find work somewhere in the United Nations. Inside the government, his position on the nuclear option was well known. Pakistan, he felt, had a crop of capable physicists to isolate and pile up weapon grade fuel; whereas, the making of atom bomb required massive metallurgical support. 'We have trained people in making the razor, it's for them now to decide whether they wish to use the technology for surgical purposes or shaving their beards or carrying out of carnage'. He used to say in his lighter moments.[2]

On the other hand, Zulfiqar Bhutto held the view that questions relating to metallurgical infrastructure were subordinate to the making of a political decision. It was not for Ishrat Usmani to worry about the size of infrastructural needs, he maintained. In fact, Zulfiqar Bhutto suspected that even when Ishrat Usmani and Abdus Salam agreed to have nuclear deterrence against India, the two feared the west and were prone to having cold feet.

Temporarily, Ishrat Usmani was kicked upwards as Federal Secretary to the recently created Ministry for Science and Technology. Then, a few months later, he was charged with involvement in espionage against the Peoples Republic of China. It was found that Pakistan International Airlines flights had been equipped with electronic devices to gather data about traces of nuclear activity in Chinese airspace. Somehow, the surveillance operation was traced back to the technical expertise solely available to Pakistan Atomic Energy Commission.[3] Ishrat Usmani managed to pull through the investigation and left the country to briefly serve as Energy Adviser at the United Nations Secretariat in New York.

As for Abdus Salam, he felt deeply saddened by the turn of events. He was prepared to pardon Zulfiqar Bhutto for any personal vindictiveness but the public debate to manufacture atom bomb stood beyond his comprehension. Asking a troupe of scientists, hurriedly gathered out in the lawn, to raise their hands over whether the country should make nuclear weapons or not, was hard for him to digest. Addicted to conducting sensitive official business with utmost care and confidentiality, he was overtaken by a state of disbelief and doubt. He castigated

---

[1] Interviews 1984: Folder VII, pp. 69-74
[2] *Daily Jang*, Rawalpindi, 2 March 1988
[3] *The Pakistan Times*, Rawalpindi, 21 January 1973

Zulfiqar Bhutto for being so flamboyant in blowing the cover off a state secret. From Abdus Salam's point of view, it was just not wise to go public until the country made it safely close to achieving the capability. 'It was so harmful to raise pretensions about our nuclear planning, so terrifying.' He remarked.[1]

Still, for the time being, Abdus Salam stayed where he was in his ceremonial role as Science Adviser to the Government of Pakistan. Even if Zulfiqar Bhutto nurtured the desire to fix Abdus Salam up for an implied cheekiness in Dhaka, there was no urgency to get rid of him. While appointing Ishrat Usmani as an heir to Nazir Ahmad at the Atomic Energy Commission, Ayub Khan had sought Abdus Salam's advice. Zulfiqar Bhutto had gone on to dump Ishrat Usmani and nominated Munir Khan without caring to consult Abdus Salam. Curiously, Abdus Salam pretended as if business had been usual. He seemed happy to work with both Zulfiqar Bhutto and Munir Khan just as he had served Ayub Khan and Yahya Khan.

Way back in 1958, the train journey to Multan had provided Abdus Salam and Ishrat Usmani the occasion to found a friendship strong enough to show Pakistan the route to nuclear capability. Nearly fourteen years and three martial law administrators down the political history of Pakistan the two were back in Multan, going their different ways. Somehow, Abdus Salam did not appear to mind the bomb. He went on to provide assistance to the Directorate of Technical Development, a select group of military personnel, scientists and engineers. His involvement with the group continued as far as March 1974. He retained his membership of the Atomic Energy Commission and continued to serve as adviser to the Government of Pakistan as if nothing had changed. Whatever his ideological preference, if any, in relation to nuclear proliferation, he maintained a tight lid, a sort of tactical silence, over his role in Pakistan's journey to manufacture nuclear weapons.

Working under Ayub Khan had been Abdus Salam's first high-level encounter with the government. He witnessed how financial and political considerations weighed upon the processes of policy and decision making. At the same time he became aware of protocols, policies, procedures, professional ethics, vested interest, competitive lobbying, intriguing, cronyism, backstabbing, corruption, and what not. He could see from the closest possible range the courage with which some people stood for principles and merit, and how

---

[1] Interviews 1984: Folder VII, p. 82

brazenly some others went about grinding their axes. It was an education of a very different kind; a direct instruction off the real world of power.

Looking back, the memory of those battles Abdus Salam and Ishrat Usmani fought, winning some and suffering defeat in others, constituted the sweet-sour candy of nostalgia. How the two of them had started from a scratch making sure that the upcoming nuclear establishment of Pakistan survived the tests of policy and budgetary approvals to grow up and build institutions and schools of scientists. In the process, the working relationship between Ishrat Usmani and Abdus Salam evolved into a close personal friendship.

In some ways Ishrat Usmani had been the opposite of Abdus Salam. He had deserted physics for a career in public service, experienced the pangs of partition when his family was divided between India and Pakistan. His mother passed away in India just when he arrived in Pakistan. As the kingpin in nuclear planning and development, Ishrat Usmani acted independently, called the shots, and was not under any obligation to oblige anyone. But he held tremendous regard for Abdus Salam. 'Most of the scientific effort in Pakistan is in a large measure due to Salam's imagination and the weight of his personality. Salam is a symbol of pride and prestige of our nation in the world of science'. Ishrat Usmani once told the science columnist Nigel Calder.[1]

If and when required, Ishrat Usmani went as far as playing a role in making sure that a sibling of Abdus Salam found a good job. He was the referee for Abdus Salam's brother Abdul Hameed, an engineering graduate, who sought employment with the British manufacturing company Lever Brothers. Ishrat Usmani knew Richard Howe, the manager of company's operations in Pakistan and an erstwhile colleague in the Indian Civil Service. 'I would do for him (Abdul Hameed) what I would for my own younger brother.' He had written to Abdus Salam in November 1961.

At times, Ishrat Usmani could read the mind of Abdus Salam, especially after the haste accompanying the 1957 Nobel Prize for Physics. On such occasions, he would urge Abdus Salam to return home, setup a school of research and become the Hideki Yukawa (1907–1981) of Pakistan. 'Nobody looks to you sitting in London as a real crusader for the science of Pakistan. If you start your *Ashram* with a number of disciples, as Yukawa has done in Japan, I am certain the world will acknowledge your greatness earlier and you would be picked up as one from an under-developed country for a Nobel Prize. I don't now believe

---

[1] Ideals and Realities (1984): p. 21-22

that the country would deny you the facilities of international travel or that you would not have a team of good young physicists around you'. He once advised Abdus Salam under a spell of enthusiasm but then corrected himself without much delay.

Despite his outspokenness, Ishrat Usmani survived in the job for well over a decade. He left the Government of Pakistan in 1972 to work as Energy Adviser to the United Nations on solar radiation. Between 1978 and 1985, he joined the International Atomic Energy Agency in Vienna. He was invited by the last monarch of Iran, Reza Pahlavi, to offer advice towards the establishment of nuclear power plant in the country but then Islamic Revolution changed the picture. In 1991, Ishrat Usmani returned home where death overtook him without much of a warning a year later.

Of all the friends Abdus Salam had in Pakistan, Ishrat Usmani was his closest and most trusted. In a memorial essay Abdus Salam remembered the times when he and Ishrat Usmani had fought together to snatch from the untutored rulers of Pakistan a fair share for science. 'I have felt no greater friendship than his', he remarked. 'Since Usmani was not an easy person to deal with and not much of a diplomat so far as his own interests were concerned, he was getting into trouble all the time with the Ministries. My major task and my humble service to him were to rescue him from time to time from the joint wrath of the President and his Ministers'. Abdus Salam added. He credited Ishrat Usmani for the training abroad of some 500 scientists and the foundation of the Institute of Nuclear Science and Technology, the installation of a nuclear power plant at Karachi, and the Space and Upper Atmosphere Research Committee.[1]

He remembered sitting with Ishrat Usmani for hours on discussing finer details of future plans before the Atomic Energy Commission. 'Even as Chairman of the Atomic Energy Commission, he did not preside over meetings in my presence and always invited me to do so. He respected scholarship and held on to the view that the Commission was to be run by scientists rather than the bureaucrats. We devised the policy for training of manpower, travelled all over Europe and the United States to place our youth in relevant institutions so that they may be given assignments upon completion of their studies'.[2]

How far did Abdus Salam's own stature among international atomic circles contribute toward the growth of nuclear program in Pakistan? He was asked.

---

[1] The Nation (Lahore) Friday Review, 21 August 1992
[2] Interviews 1984: VI, p. 58

First of all, he did not wish to be quoted on this question. Secondly, he desired to convert the question into more of an academic statement by pulling out of it the sting of nuclear component. 'I think the fact that one is a good scientist means that you are listened to, when you ask something for Pakistan you are taken seriously. For example, in the admission of our boys, as I told you, to get trained manpower for the Atomic Energy Commission, which exists at the present time in Pakistan, I think it was extremely helpful to be a good scientist. People respected you and took you seriously. That's a very important plus. So in that sense Pakistan's good name is well predicated by a good scientist. No question about it. This is true of all fields. One's eminence is always helpful'. He replied.[1] Munir Khan, the new chairman of the Atomic Energy Commission, was fully well aware of the professional weight of Abdus Salam.

Munir Khan (1926–1999) had graduated from the Government College in Lahore where he had been a contemporary of Abdus Salam. He went on to obtain a Masters in Electrical Engineering and then received training in reactor technology at the Argonne National Laboratory, in Illinois. He had served the International Atomic Energy Agency in Vienna since 1958 and participated in numerous conferences, meetings, seminars and workshops dealing with nuclear reactors, heavy water, gas cooling systems and the utilisation of fissile materials. In this way, he was aptly qualified and experienced to do the job Zulfiqar Bhutto had assigned him. His rich knowledge of western culture and business practices made him an exceptional asset for Pakistan at a time when the country sought technology to manufacture nuclear weapons. His brother Khursheed Khan, who served as the Minister for Law under Ayub Khan, had introduced him to Zulfiqar Bhutto. It is believed that Zulfiqar Bhutto had prepared Munir Khan to win Ayub Khan in favour of the urgent need for nuclear capability, but there was no luck. Our day will come, Zulfiqar Bhutto had told Munir Khan.[2] On the promised day, in January 1972, Zulfiqar Bhutto kept his word and signalled Munir Khan to replace Ishrat Usmani as the Chairman of the Atomic Energy Commission with explicit assignment to manufacture nuclear weapons.

Having known one another from their college days, Munir Khan and Abdus Salam interacted regularly at the headquarter of International Atomic Energy Agency in Vienna. Abdus Salam's great friend Ishrat Usmani had very little patience with Munir Khan. Still, a chart of Abdus Salam's professional

---

[1] Interviews 1984: Folder VII, p 80
[2] *The Nation*, Lahore, Web Edition, 22 April 2006 (essay written by M.A. Chaudhri)

acquaintances and personal friendships, drawn up in Pakistan, showed that Munir Khan did not stand far behind Ishrat Usmani. In fact, Abdus Salam's agreement to stay on as Member of the Atomic Energy Commission is attributed to Munir Khan. In spite of his own knowledge and bureaucratic experience in technological aspects of the assignment given to him, Munir Khan needed someone as prestigious as Abdus Salam at the Atomic Energy Commission.

One of Abdus Salam's favourite students, Mohammed Riazuddin, was given the extraordinary assignment to design theoretical framework for a 'fission explosive device'. Mohammed Riazuddin travelled to the United States to consult Manhattan Project archives in the United States Congress Library and National Information Centre in Maryland. He was also appointed as a Member Technical of the Atomic Energy Commission. He compared his contribution to the nuclear program of Pakistan equal to that of a tailor who, acting under professional obligation, advised clients about the dimension or texture of the fabric from which they intended to have their garments cut out and stitched.[1]

There is indication of Abdus Salam's involvement with the nuclear program as far as the end of March 1974 when he accompanied Munir Khan for a meeting with Major General Qamar Mirza, the Director General of the Wah Ordinance Factories near Islamabad. Also present in the meeting were Mohammed Riazuddin and another prominent physicist, Hafeez Qureshi. It was an important meeting with one-point agenda, that is, the setting up of a facility to test the implosion of a fission device. As a matter of fact, it was the beginning of the countdown for Pakistan to go nuclear.

Along with his association with the bomb project between January 1972 and March 1974, Abdus Salam is also reported to have participated in the preparation of an ambitious scheme to establish Islamic Science Foundation. Somewhat ironically, the proposal failed to get through due to lack of financial commitment by the Islamic Summit Conference, in Lahore, in February 1974.

III

Keeping his promise to raise the phoenix of new Pakistan, out of the ashes of military humiliation in Dhaka, Zulfiqar Bhutto moved at a steady pace. He signed the Simla Peace Accord with India, brought more than ninety thousand

---

[1] Shahidur Rehman: Long Road to Chaghi, Islamabad, 1999

Pakistani prisoners of war home, got back a good amount of the lost territory, pulled out of one-way treaties with the western capitalist alliances, gave the country a parliamentary democratic constitution; nationalised big industries, banks, insurance houses and educational institutions; introduced land reforms, sacked hundreds of corrupt bureaucrats; and the list of such feats went on, all done half-way into his first term in power.

He found himself in a world full of unforeseen opportunities. Arabs received another defeat at the hand of Israel in 1973. King Faisal Bin Abdul Aziz (1906–1975) declared an embargo upon oil supplies to flaunt the financial and political leverage Saudi Arabia wielded over global economy. As oil revenues shot up, there was an unprecedented explosion of commercial activity and employment opportunities in Muslim countries exporting petroleum. This boom offered Pakistan a tremendous opening to explore fresh venues of business and diplomacy. Zulfiqar Bhutto began tapping financial possibilities in Saudi Arabia, Iran, Persian Gulf and North Africa. Energetic and youthful, educated and articulate, diplomatic and ambitious; he embarked upon seizing the opportunity to claim a prominent position of leadership. He lived in times when the United States moved closer to conclude an arms control agreement with the Soviet Union, the Peoples Republic of China prepared to occupy its membership of the United Nations Security Council, the war in Vietnam headed to a painful conclusion, ancient monarchies crumbled in Afghanistan and Iran, and Indira Gandhi soiled the democratic facade of India with her rule of emergency.

Grasping the initiative, Zulfiqar Bhutto offered to host a summit conference of Muslim leadership and discuss challenges facing the followers of Islam. An impressive number of rulers from thirty-eight Muslim countries, other than the exception of Reza Shah Pahlavi, the Emperor of Iran, accepted his invitation and turned up to attend the meeting in Lahore in February 1974. In the face of its huge Muslim population, India was not invited for the summit. In fact, the snub to India went deeper when, in return for Pakistan's recognition of Bangladesh, Mujibur Rahman made a dramatic last-minute dash to Lahore. It was a breath-taking religious spectacle for the faithful in Pakistan to witness the Muslim leadership offering prayers together in the 17th century Imperial Mosque of Lahore.

Zulfiqar Bhutto addressed the colourful assembly of Muslim monarchs, presidents and prime ministers from all over the world. He shared with them his youthful dream, he had as a student in the United States, about an Islamic confederation to unite against the merciless exploitation of colonial powers. 'Unfortunately, because of our feebleness, our economic resources are being most unscrupulously exploited by outsiders. An Islamic confederation, even at its weakest, will take charge of the wealth of its people and place it in the hands of its own people'. He recalled the speech he made, back in 1948, at the University of Southern California.

'There have been periods in my life, like all of us; I have been assailed by doubts whether this vision of mine would be fulfilled. Today, despite all the difficulties in our path, I bow my head in gratitude to Allah for making me witness to a scene which should dispel those doubts'. He confessed before his stately audience. He turned toward the integrity of Palestine, Arab wars with Israel and the economic turmoil caused by the boycott of petroleum supplies by taking a functional approach. 'The war of last October has, however, precipitated a chain of events and created an environment in which the developing countries can at last hope to secure the establishment of a more equitable economic order. Some far-reaching possibilities have been opened by the demonstrated ability of the oil-producing countries to concert their policies and determine the price of their resources. This may well be a watershed in history. It may well presage the end of a deranged world order'. He hoped ambitiously.[1]

Both conservative Saudi Arabia and socialist Libya sounded keen on raising their stake in Pakistan. King Faisal of Saudi Arabia, a deeply religious man with staunchly Wahabi bent of mind, nurtured an inborn suspicion of the west. He was deeply moved by the Pakistani initiative. Muammar Al-Gaddafi of Libya felt so carried away by the diplomatic charm of Zulfiqar Bhutto that he expressed his readiness to supply Pakistan oil at production cost.

In his role as the custodian of holiest Muslim shrines, King Faisal Bin Abdul Aziz was aware of the emotional appeal he commanded in Pakistan. He was ideally placed to trade commerce and spirituality hand in hand. After testing the effectiveness of oil as a weapon, he aimed at using it for a cause. To the Sunni Muslims, making almost 80 per cent of the world of Islam, he was a *de facto* caliph.

Even though the embargo on oil supplies was not eternal and had to end after a while, the tide of expectations among the brotherhood of Islam took time to subside. In Pakistan, the first casualty of Islamic summit conference was the

---

[1] Zulfiqar Ali Bhutto: Thoughts on Some Aspects of Islam, Lahore, 1976, pp. 25-26, 32, 46-47

socialist influence in politics. Nearly all of the political appeal the left wing had succeeded in building up during the mass agitation against Ayub Khan and through the course of general election was washed down the drain. Populism became the housemaid of the conservative and religious right. Numerous non-governmental organisations, funded by the affluent in Saudi Arabia, appeared on the scene. Operating under the garb of Islamic philanthropy, those clusters were taken for granted to achieve pious religious goals, from seminaries and orphanages to bands of militants. Protected from audit and transparency, the gush of money began making its way into the revival of jihad industry. Soon the Central Intelligence Agency (CIA) of the United States and the Inter-Services Intelligence Directorate of the Pakistan's armed forces would join hands and lift the spillway to offload piety upon the godless Red Army trapped in Afghanistan.

At the same time, Pakistan witnessed a radical restructuring of its social and economic life. Millions of skilled, semiskilled and unskilled workers were exported to oil rich Muslim countries where they earned dollars to prop up foreign exchange reserves back home. Their income made its way into unplanned and shabby residential colonies, without town planning checks and services, outside every urban centre; injecting unbearable mess and chaos into local hygiene and human traffic. Those unable to make it abroad found their way into nationalised industries and companies through party political leverage more than competence and merit. Private investors deserted the scene giving way to managers free of obligation to deliver. No matter what model of social mobility and financial discipline or accountability the colonial masters had left behind, the new Pakistan of Zulfiqar Bhutto offered a short route to every possibility. Devoid of civic discipline, clean air and water, sewers and orderly streets, schools and parks, traffic regulation and medical facilities, human dignity and care; Pakistan presented the scene of a colossal unending slum.

Student unions associated with right wing parties controlled the day-to-day running of colleges and universities. In a meeting with Syed Abul Aa'la Maudoodi, the Amir of the Jamaat-i-Islami, Zulfiqar Bhutto declared that his love of socialism was confined only to the requirements of street agitation against Ayub Khan.[1] He assured the clerics that Islam was going to stay as the state religion of Pakistan. He promised them legislation in accordance with Islamic injunctions. Public offices like the President and the Prime Minister were

---

[1] Stanley Wolpert; Zulfi Bhutto of Pakistan: His Life and Times, Oxford University Press, 1993, p. 206.

apportioned to Muslims exclusively. He agreed to update the penal code with Shariah laws and include a clause in the Constitution to 'preserve and strengthen' special ties with Muslim countries. In a country where Muslims constituted almost 98 percent of the population, some of those measures betrayed a bizarre mix of political hypocrisy and apartheid against non-Muslim minorities.

Getting elected on a socialist manifesto, the ruling People Party shifted its ideological axis from left to right. In an interview with famous profile-writer Oriana Fallaci (1929–2006), in April 1972, Zulfiqar Bhutto damned the politician who remained static and immobile, failing to swing between left and right, or lacked contradictions and doubts as personal assets to deceive the enemy. In fact, he had begun making the move from 'scientific socialism' to 'scientific opportunism'; and his betrayal resulted in the defeat of secular preferences. Within a matter of three years, the founding members and scholarly ideologues Jalaluddin Abdur Rahim, Mobashar Hassan, Khursheed Mir and Meraj Mohammed Khan had been purged or side-lined without much of a hiccup.

Although the Ahmadiyah caliph, Tahir Ahmad, took nearly fifteen years to claim the credit for ditching communists, it was Zulfiqar Bhutto who had actually marvelled the feat. Let alone communists, he went on fixing up all those, including the Ahmadiyah, who posed challenge to his authority. As such, therefore, the rift between him and the Ahmadiyah arrived much faster than expected. Just like the *Prince* of Niccolo Machiavelli (1469–1527), he had a plan shaping up in his mind. He was aware of the volatile vulnerability as well as the self-inflicted sociological disability of the Ahmadiyah schism. Only he had to mark time to offload the liability in return for a profitable deal. Time was approaching for him to benefit from detachment just as he had managed to profit from the detested minority. His ruling party was, after all, not a political asylum. How long could he afford to shelter a frivolously overbearing pariah? He was confident about his ability to dispose the Ahmadiyah off anytime as the schism itself thrived living in world of its own, without bothering to build up friendship, partnership, association or an alliance.

In the early days of government headed by Zulfiqar Bhutto, a conga line of public servants rushed to Rabwah, the Ahmadiyah headquarter, to pick up a positive reference. Some of them asked for transfers to lucrative positions, others sought promotion, then there were those who sought protection to cover up their corrupt conduct; also those who suspected themselves to be under some sort of adverse political cloud. Less out of courtesy and more for the temptation to cultivate ties in the bureaucracy, Tahir Ahmad advocated their causes before political authorities. In a media interview, Mustafa Khar, who was Zulfiqar Bhutto's chief henchman in Punjab, revealed how every now and then Tahir Ahmad approached him with elaborate lists of public servants seeking favours out of turn.

Zulfiqar Bhutto went on to demonstrate his authority by naming the veteran politician Mumtaz Daultana as Pakistan's ambassador to the United Kingdom. Earlier in 1952–53, Mumtaz Daultana, as the Chief Minister of Punjab, had played a key role in nourishing the anti-Ahmadiyah mass agitation. His electoral elimination in December 1970, had been a cause for celebration for the Ahmadiyah as if an overdue score had been settled or another prophecy of Ghulam Ahmad come true. His appointment in London amounted to an outright snub to the Ahmadiyah, and probably this is what Zulfiqar Bhutto had actually desired.

When Zulfiqar Bhutto unfolded his program for nationalisation and land reforms, the Ahmadiyah received another jolt. They lost some 20,000 acres of prime agricultural land privately owned in Sind by their caliph and his close relatives. Also swept away in the nationalisation campaign were a couple of highly regarded educational colleges the community owned in Rabwah. No compensation, whatsoever, was offered in return.

Nasir Ahmad, the Ahmadiyah caliph, aspired to set up a summer camp in Abbotabad, near the Pakistan Military Academy training commissioned officers. Previously, his father had gone on public record to convert the strategic province of Baluchistan en masse over to the Ahmadiyah faith. Later, the community had purchased a considerable rural property in the Salt Range, near the scenic *Kalar Kahar* Lake, the military recruitment ground east of Indus valley.[1] Now Nasir Ahmad, in expressing his keenness on Abbotabad, appeared to have gone many steps ahead, from an ordinary recruiting ground to the home of commissioned officers' military academy. All watchful eyes among the intelligence and the clerics were raised in a unison. Instead of playing safe, Nasir Ahmad assured his followers that opposition to the community was blunting out.

In April 1973, the response to his overture came when the Legislative Assembly of Azad Kashmir adopted a unanimous resolution to excommunicate

---

[1] Travelling in his day, Zaheeruddin Babur, founder of Mogul dynasty, had named this part of the world as a Kashmir in miniature.

the Ahmadiyah from the pale of Islam. At the same time, the members of the Ahmadiyah community residing in Azad Kashmir were directed to get registered accordingly so that their presence in public sector employment could be trimmed in proportion to their minority status as non-Muslims. Meanwhile, the President of Azad Kashmir, Abdul Qayyum, launched a tirade to 'clean-up his government' from the 'treacherous' influence of the Ahmadiyah.

Hardly anyone in Islamabad was oblivious of the fact that the State Government of Azad Kashmir owed its financial lifeline to Pakistan. All political, economic, financial and diplomatic affairs of the hypothetical set up of 'free' territory' were managed by a low-key Deputy Secretary of the Government of Pakistan. There was hardly any doubt as to who pulled the strings in Azad Kashmir. Abdul Qayyum (1924–2015) was a former employee of the British army. Prone to political metamorphism espoused by Zulfiqar Bhutto, he switched sides with ease. When the Ahmadiyah were in favour with the rulers of Pakistan, Abdul Qayyum did not mind visiting Rabwah. In 1973, he cultivated close links with the World Islamic League, an organisation funded by Saudi Arabia.

Intriguingly, the Government of Pakistan maintained tactical silence over the show of bigotry in Azad Kashmir. In fact, the excommunication was met with approval on grounds of 'democratic principles'. After all, the ecclesiastical proclamation reflected the collective will of the electorate. Ironically, the Ahmadiyah caliph continued to live in a secluded world of his own creation; missing the opportunity to conduct a pre-emptive audit of ties with Zulfiqar Bhutto.

Early in 1974, when the groundwork for convention of Islamic summit conference was well underway, the Ahmadiyah found themselves grounded by the government. According to Tahir Ahmad, the army had been directed to make sure that none of the officers on duty call for conference should have any association with the Ahmadiyah community.[1] Even the upmarket *Shezan* chain of restaurants, owned by a prominent member of Ahmadiyah party, was declined the catering contract to supply food for state guests. At the same time, the government did not care to check lobbyists who approached conference delegates and briefed them about the 'schismatic and divisive' beliefs of the Ahmadiyah.

---

[1] Adamson Iain (1991): p. 95

To the Ahmadiyah, who believed they represented the most genuine face of Islam, this double-edged discrimination amounted to an unceremonious expulsion from the political arena. As such, at a time when Pakistan hosted the Islamic summit conference, the Ahmadiyah stood thoroughly abandoned, seeking solace in a variety of conspiracy theories. One of such theories was woven around the suspicion that King Faisal Bin Abdul Aziz of Saudi Arabia desired to become a caliph of the Muslim world. According to the plot, as perceived and lavishly painted by the Ahmadiyah, Zulfiqar Bhutto found Pakistan 'too small a stage for him' and he wanted to play a much bigger role. He did not have much of a chance to excel in the so-called Third World where India occupied the centre-stage, hence the need for him to explore prominence in the Muslim world. In the given scheme of things, his best bet rested upon playing the second fiddle to King Faisal Bin Abdul Aziz. Going far off the mark, the whole business of Islamic summit conference was viewed as a scheme to redeem the caliphate in Saudi Arabia.

King Faisal Bin Abdul Aziz belonged to the fundamentalist Wahabi sect among Sunni Muslims. He was not expected to demonstrate even the slightest patience with a schism like the Ahmadiyah. As the birthplace of Islam and the home of holy shrines, Saudi Arabian rulers occupied the centre-stage of Muslim world, and they would continue doing so. With oil wealth and western political support added to it, a Saudi Arabian monarch was already a *de facto* caliph to the Sunni followers of Islam.

In his official biography, published in England in 1991, Tahir Ahmad went on to extrapolate, rather narcissistically, that 'we had to be extinguished' to clear the way for installation of King Faisal Bin Abdul Aziz as the caliph. Tahir Ahmad went as far as adding the name of Idi Amin (1925–2003), 'the half-mad dictator of Uganda', as one of proponents of the new caliphate.[1] Whether a largely disowned caliphate based in Rabwah posed any serious challenge to the power and influence of King Faisal Bin Abdul Aziz, is a question the answer to which needs to be searched within the Ahmadiyah fetish of self-importance.

Few weeks after the summit conference in Lahore, the Muslim World League convened its annual session in Mecca. One of its unanimously adopted resolutions demanded the excommunication of the Ahmadiyah. Some 140 delegations, representing Muslim organisations from all over the world, consented with unanimity that beliefs held and propagated by the Ahmadiyah

---

[1] Adamson Iain (1991): pp. 97-99

amounted to subversion and deceit among the followers of Islam. One of the 'eminent deviations' attributed to the Ahmadiyah was their abolition of the concept of jihad. Muslim leadership was urged to maintain a 'vigilant eye' on the activities of this schismatic community by keeping its followers away from holding any positions of public responsibility. Apart from demanding the excommunication of the Ahmadiyah, the Muslim World League encouraged a social, cultural and economic boycott of this cunning community by keeping its members from visiting the holy lands.

Much sooner than expected, the anti-Ahmadiyah fraternity scored its first big victory in Pakistan. Air Marshall Zafar Chaudhry (1926–2019), a devout member of the Ahmadiyah community, who was appointed as the Chief of Air Staff in April 1972, was sacked half way into his term in the prestigious office. His opponents accused him for carrying out a ceremonial fly past over the annual congregation in Rabwah. Of course, more professional sources pointed towards his disapproval of Zulfiqar Bhutto's intervention in air force discipline relating to the conduct of some middle-ranking military officers.[1] He was a friend of Abdus Salam and the only among few senior military officers with candid Ahmadiyah connection who ever made it to the top in Pakistan. Whatever the truth behind his departure from the professional scene, Zulfiqar Bhutto won a greater amount of confidence with clerics.

IV

Solemn and sombre, meek and modest, devout and dutiful was the portrayal of the front row as Muslim rulers from different parts and ethnic stocks, some in their national attires, others wearing three-piece suits and neckties, still others in full military uniform; lined up for prayer in Lahore. On television and newspapers, public was used to seeing those faces in government meetings, international conferences, state ceremonies and rallies. But witnessing them together, shoulder to shoulder, in dozens, behind one *Imam* presented the spectacle the Imperial Mosque itself had not experienced in over three hundred years of its history. Was it a dream? Some kind of a reality show? People asked one another. Zulfiqar Bhutto was over the moon, he became the first politician to have snatched the religious card from clerics.

---

[1] Kunwar Idris, Dawn, Karachi, 8 July 2007

Sadly, the euphoria of delight was blown up by Indira Gandhi. Pakistan was shaken to another round of harsh reality. India turned the tables on Pakistan by exploding its nuclear device only fifty miles off the international border in Rajasthan. Zulfiqar Bhutto suffered from a fit of rage because he happened to have received the news via British Broadcasting Corporation. He was expecting a telephone call from Munir Khan, the Chairman of the Atomic Energy Commission. He addressed a hurriedly convened media conference in Lahore. 'I give a solemn pledge to all our countrymen that we will never let Pakistan be a victim of nuclear blackmail'. He declared.

On the fateful day, Abdus Salam took the first flight to Pakistan. He arrived in Lahore the day after the news conference and met Zulfiqar Bhutto in the Government House. 'I knew it. I knew they were going to do it. India had the mind made up. Didn't I say so? Did I not?' Zulfiqar Bhutto shouted as soon as he saw Abdus Salam. Even if Abdus Salam took the responsibility for misreading the Indian intention, the bomb had been exploded. India was a nuclear power. In fact, many well informed people had fairly good knowledge about the nuclear potential of India. Since 1964, when the Peoples Republic of China exploded its first atomic device, India had exercised restraint and the world got used to living with the expectation that despite achieving the required level of competence the idealism of Jawaharlal Nehru would keep New Delhi from falling to the trap of temptation. Abdus Salam shared this wishful view. Essentially, the failure to raise the alarm in time was the failure of Pakistan's intelligence agencies and diplomatic channels.

'India's atomic explosion was a very strange thing. For so many years they had the capability but they resisted. Nehru kept up his peaceful stance. So for Mrs Gandhi to have sanctioned that was a very strange thing'. Abdus Salam recalled. 'I don't remember if I have told you about it that during the course of my interview with her she said she was the person who kept her generals from attacking Pakistan. She said her generals wanted to move in but she refused it'.[1]

In May 1974, everyone expected Munir Khan to somehow pull out the miracle. Whereas Zulfiqar Bhutto feared public resentment, he could not afford to fritter away gains his government had made. Pakistan should gain parity as quickly as possible, he yearned and prayed. Abdus Salam did not have any quick and easy solution to offer.

---

[1] Interviews 1984: Folder VII, pp.82-83

Of all the people, the answer to Zulfiqar Bhutto's yearning came from Nasir Ahmad, the Ahmadiyah caliph. As if the Ahmadiyah caliph had been utterly forgetful about the scale of snubs despatched in his direction by the Peoples Party, Nasir Ahmad provided Zulfiqar Bhutto a most astounding exit out of dark memory cast by the nuclear show of India.

Around the time when India flexed its nuclear muscle in Rajasthan, a group of few dozen medical students boarded the north-bound Chenab Express train from Multan, they were set upon a summer excursion somewhere in the cool of a sub-Himalayan station beyond Islamabad. There was nothing special about the trip as thousands of people did the same to escape the persecution of summer in the south. Mostly student unions supported group activity to benefit from the offers of discounted fares from railway department.

When the train carrying medical students from Multan arrived in Rabwah, the Ahmadiyah headquarter, its journey was delayed for some technical reason. It was early evening, the end of another hot day without monsoons in sight. Some of the students disembarked on the deserted and dusty platform, hoping to get some fresh air. They had a whole night of journey ahead. What was this godforsaken place? Someone asked, and then there was the rush of excitement upon finding out that they were in Rabwah, the heart of Ahmadiyah exclusiveness, the so-called heaven of the community, where burqa-clad alluring nymphs abounded in a manmade paradise. They had grown up listening to the tales of distant mysteries about the Ahmadiyah cult. Some of them taunted loudly, others delivered a naughty tease in the direction of some *burqa*-clad women passing by the station. Soon as the train whistled to resume its journey, the noisy excursionists boarded back and, much to the relief of the Station Master, the service pulled out without any mishap.

For the size of its suburban business, the railway station in Rabwah was a meagre hut with minimal staff catering for the needs of nearly a dozen services in both directions every day. With its desolate appearance, the station was more of an asylum for the occasional tobacco addict because smoking in public was discouraged by the private police of the Ahmadiyah caliph. On the average, the passenger load in Rabwah was nominal, peaking only at the time of few seasonal congregations of the Ahmadiyah.

For some reason, the spontaneous show of rowdiness was perceived as a planned affront by the youth wing of the Jamaat-i-Islami. Since the electoral victory of Zulfiqar Bhutto's Peoples Party, the Ahmadiyah leadership deemed themselves as kingmakers. How dare those miserable mischief hunters of Jamaat-i-Islami we have so effectively drubbed in the general election only recently challenge us here at our own wicket? Fuming with frustration, the Ahmadiyah caliph is reported to have lost his cool. Instead of disregarding the episode, he made the telephone call to Zulfiqar Bhutto. Not even the elders of the Jamaat-i-Islami would have condoned bad behaviour of this kind. It was all the more important for the Ahmadiyah to play cool and safe at a time when Zulfiqar Bhutto had been delivering signals of betrayal one after another. When Nasir Ahmad asked the Prime Minister as to why a loyal ally like the Ahmadiyah was being bullied by the sworn enemies of the government? Zulfiqar Bhutto was believed to have proposed to 'fix up the bastards when they return'. It was as if the moment had arrived for the Ahmadiyah to fall in the trap.

After spending a pleasant break in the cool and light air up north, when the excursionists boarded the Karachi-bound Chenab Express at Rawalpindi railway station for their return journey home, they did not have the slightest notion of what awaited them at Rabwah railway station. Tired out of hiking on the steep mountain trails, they slept through the night as the train whistled past small towns and villages on Pothohar Plateau, crossing *Jhelum* to run along *Chenab*, steaming past the battleground of Chaillianwali and the ancient town of Bhera. None of them noted the strong-arm batch of Ahmadiyah youth boarding the train at Sargodha, little over an hour's journey to Rabwah.

Later in the morning, on 29 May 1974, when the 12 Down Chenab Express pulled into Rabwah railway station, the members of the Ahmadiyah youth force had already taken strategic positions at the platform. They looked forward to greeting the train with an unusual rush of adrenaline. Without wasting time, the engine was disengaged from the body of carriages, and then the tourists were dragged out of their carriage and given thorough physical thrashing. No sharp weapons were used, only hockey sticks and batons served the purpose on where and when required basis. Caught totally unprepared, the excursionists gave in without much of a resistance. Punches, blows, thumps, slaps and jabs pounded like a flash flood of fists and kicks; leaving the sympathisers of the Jamaat-i-Islami with black eyes, ruptures, bruises and humiliation within a matter of few minutes. Such was the fury of the operation payback that some members of the Ahmadiyah youth, who had boarded the train at Sargodha to act as markers were caught in the action to receive a fair share of the high-speed battering. Measured in swiftness, the operation graphed as a military performance of some well-trained commandos deployed to punish but not annihilate the band of rouges. When the train was permitted to leave, the total count of people receiving injuries did not cross the manageable figure of thirty. Rubbing salt on the wounds, some of the injured were provided first aid.

A landslide of misfortune overtook the Ahmadiyah within ten minutes of the train's departure from Rabwah. Crossing the *Chenab*, the train arrived in the historical town of Chiniot where an arch enemy of the Ahmadiyah, Manzoor Ahmad, presided over a seminary almost solely devoted to ridiculing the caliphate of Rabwah. There was hardly a need for the victims of violence to narrate their tales of suffering. Manzoor Ahmad pulled the pin on minefield and almost instantly the vast coterie of anti-Ahmadiyah clergymen went into a state of frenzy. They had waited for this moment since the proclamation of martial law in Lahore in March 1953. Hotlines were established through telephone exchanges linking the main centres of clerical stronghold.

By the afternoon, mosques from Peshawar and Quetta down to Lahore and Karachi began broadcasting highly spiced versions of the episode at Rabwah railway station. With powerful sound amplifiers installed on minarets of their mosques, the clerics began broadcasting gory details of Ahmadiyah assault upon a vulnerable group of Muslim youth. In some instances, the members of general public were invited to visit mosques to witness for themselves the mutilated organs of innocent victims. It was widely rumoured that the tongues of Muslim youth had been severed by the heartless enemy of Islam camped in Rabwah.

At a time when Zulfiqar Bhutto sought diversion from the detonation of Indian nuclear device, he found gods reaching out to offer him pillars of support. Providentially for him, the opportunity to bag double gain arrived just when he was looking for an excuse to offload the Ahmadiyah baggage bothering his government.

Next morning, every national newspaper, including the state owned, reported the incident prominently, with screaming headlines. In universities and colleges, all over the country, furious gangs broke into classrooms, libraries, laboratories and hostels; pulled out the identifiable members of the Ahmadiyah for trouncing, then looted and burnt out their belongings. Because the planners in Rabwah had not cared to consider the consequences of their operation payback fully well, the ordinary Ahmadiyah in other cities and towns were caught totally unprepared. For many years, the Jamaat-i-Islami had worked hard to achieve a broader alliance of Sunni clerics, the violence at Rabwah railway station provided the right reason to throttle-up agitation and cement unity in the Wahabi fundamentalist ranks. Time had arrived for the final round of mass agitation to close the Ahmadiyah shop. A succession of public meetings, protest marches, rallies and courting of arrests; with mosques serving as impenetrable fortification, returned Pakistan to the days of 1952–53.

Nasir Ahmad, who up until recently preferred receiving members of the parliament and senior bureaucrats at his residence in Rabwah, had to rush and seek bail before arrest at the Punjab High Court in Lahore. Logistically, the clerics commanded an advantage from the very outset; whereas the Ahmadiyah stood discredited, guilty of aggression and not the meek victims anymore as was the case in 1952–53. Once again, there was the demand for Ahmadiyah excommunication. Yet again, the clerics demanded the exclusion of the Ahmadiyah from key positions in the Government of Pakistan. They called for separate electorates for non-Muslim minorities. Finally, there was plea to abolish the private Ahmadiyah estate in Rabwah. Compared to its forerunner of 1952–53, when the tussle between Lahore and Karachi centres of power seemed to pollute the religious vigour of the *Ahrar*, the anti-Ahmadiyah mass agitation in the summer of 1974 was spontaneous, direct and single-minded.

As agitation picked up momentum, the clerics issued the *fatwa* calling for a social boycott, isolation and blockade of the Ahmadiyah. Consequently, food and medical supplies to the stranded and besieged households were suspended. Thousands of pickets were set up in cities and towns to enforce sanctions. According to one report, approximately 42 people died in violence erupting in the first week of June 1974. About two-third of the casualties belonged to the Ahmadiyah side. Unlike 1952–53, when the British trained police force struggled to maintain some semblance of law and order, the situation in the summer of 1974 was different. On this occasion police avoided any pretensions to neutrality and actually provided protective cover to rioters; the detachment was justified under the garb of religious sensitivities of the majority. As a consequence of this policy, the number of Ahmadiyah casualties climbed up steadily; and mobs felt free to trespass properties, businesses, farms, mosques, even graves of the dead buried in common cemeteries.

Zulfiqar Bhutto was fully aware of the vulnerability surrounding the Ahmadiyah, he placed the responsibility of provocation upon the local leadership in Rabwah. Pakistan was far from matching the Indian show of nuclear superiority. To him, the outbreak of anti-Ahmadiyah sentiment was a blessing in disguise. Comparing the eruption of sectarian volcano with that of a prairie fire, he argued that the controversy regarding the Ahmadiyah was an ideological phenomenon that had been haunting the Muslims of South Asia for nearly ninety years. He proposed to resolve the dispute in a democratic manner, by asking the parliament to judge upon the questionable nature of religious beliefs held by the Ahmadiyah in order to settle the issue once and for all.

V

About the end of June 1974, the Ahmadiyah caliph, Nasir Ahmad, was invited to explain his party's position on a whole range of fundamental Islamic doctrines before the National Assembly of Pakistan.

Some of the close advisers of Nasir Ahmad did not wish him to be questioned by a worldly parliament. Only God was the judge in matters of faith, they held the ancient view. Zulfiqar Bhutto made it clear that only the leader of the community will be acceptable. Nasir Ahmad presented a portfolio comprising of over 200 pages upon which he was subjected to cross-examination for nearly two weeks. He dealt with popular misgivings about the Ahmadiyah, the definition of a Muslim and legal implications of imposing religious beliefs upon others.

In view of the religious sensitivity, the proceedings of the house were conducted in camera. No access was given to public or media. But the proceedings were recorded and transcribed as matter of historical record. Other than few spur-of-the-moment questions, the greater part of interrogation was conducted formally, through the Attorney General with sufficient time permitted to the Ahmadiyah side for preparation of their response. On 7 September 1974, the National Assembly adopted the bill to excommunicate the Ahmadiyah from the pale of Islam. Zulfiqar Bhutto termed it as the most difficult decision ever made in Pakistan. Before arriving at the judgement, he stated, the ruling party had taken a whole range of political, economic and security considerations into account. It was not beyond human ingenuity, he remarked, to devise methods to defer important decisions. But postponement of a decision, according to him, might have dangerously affected the Islamic rationale behind the very creation of Pakistan. Some of his close aides urged him to cash upon the moment and call early election.[1]

Next day, the Karachi-based English-language newspaper *Dawn*, otherwise known for its secular and liberal policy, commented that the Ahmadiyah controversy had posed a threat to public peace and tranquillity. Getting it out of the way 'in conformity with the sentiments and aspirations of the people of Pakistan' had made history. Arriving at a decision through parliamentary process, the newspaper applauded 'augurs well for the growth of democracy in the country' because constitutionality was, after all, the 'breath of life in a democracy'. 'Prime Minister Zulfiqar Ali Bhutto deserves our praise and gratitude for first facing the issue boldly and then submitting it to the country's supreme sovereign body', the newspaper went on.

Pakistan's Minister for Law, Abdul Hafeez, the young man Zafarullah Khan had referred to Abdus Salam for guidance in finding a suitable university place in England, defended the excommunication on grounds of parliamentary supremacy. In his defence, he cited a 1919 act of the Punjab Legislative Assembly that had grouped the followers of Sikh religion as a community separate from the Hindu majority.

In a media interview, the Speaker of the National Assembly, Farooq Ali, confirmed that, while excommunicating the Ahmadiyah, the parliamentarians had acted in accordance with 'their faith and conscience'. As a direct consequence of excommunication, the Ahmadiyah were converted into second-class citizens overnight; their professional prestige, pride and loyalties stood compromised as they were outcast officially.

On his part, the Ahmadiyah caliph, Nasir Ahmad, had failed in winning a single member of the National Assembly over to share his view. On the contrary, some of the parliamentarians were disappointed by his ineptitude in building any bridges of enlightenment. On the contrary, the Ahmadiyah took a deeper plunge into introversion, blaming only their opponents. Instead of checking the likelihood of fault lines with the cult-like repressive apparatus of their own organisation, the faithful traced every word and action of the caliph to the will of God; awaiting some celestial 'fire and brimstone' punishing the enemy camp.

Zulfiqar Bhutto made an attempt to console the Ahmadiyah by justifying their excommunication on grounds that it was, in fact, meant to save them from

---

[1] Rafi Raza: Zulfikar Ali Bhutto and Pakistan 1967-1977, Oxford University Press, Karachi, 1997, pp. 309-310

an impending bloodshed. He argued that his government had actually served as a shock-absorber. He even delivered mixed signals to keep the Ahmadiyah guessing about a possible reversal of the excommunication. He invited Nasir Ahmad to have tea with him in Rawalpindi. He must have been pleasantly surprised when the Ahmadiyah caliph accepted the invitation.

On the lush green sprawling lawn of the Government House, as the two faced each other, Zulfiqar Bhutto reiterated his preference for the safety of the Ahmadiyah. He added that his government simply had to find a way to dampen the agitation and save the Ahmadiyah from total annihilation. He attempted to appease his guest by using the term 'excommunication' only as a matter of nomenclature to satisfy the clerics. In reality, he assured, the Ahmadiyah were free to enjoy the same civic rights as anyone else in the country. His immediate objective, he remarked, was to grab the initiative from the Wahabi fundamentalists.

When tea was served, Zulfiqar Bhutto poured a cup and offered it to Nasir Ahmad who declined to accept the gesture point blank. He had come to the party, Nasir Ahmad asserted, in veneration of the office, the Prime Minister of Pakistan. 'But to accept hospitality in your home when you have done so much against our community is quite different. So please excuse me, I cannot take this cup of tea'. Zulfiqar Bhutto quietly placed the cup back on the table.[1]

Only Nasir Ahmad knew the secret behind this extraordinary display of his eccentric logic. Did he travel all the way from Rabwah to Rawalpindi only to decline, in the full presence of other guests, the cup of tea specially poured for him by the Prime Minister of Pakistan himself? Was he not aware of the vindictive nature of the feudal lord in Zulfiqar Bhutto? Regardless of the purpose behind such an openly rude snub, the exploit was a reminder of Zafarullah Khan who, in September 1948, had arrived on the scene in Karachi only to display his *non-attendance* of the funeral service for Mohammed Ali Jinnah. For a moment, on that afternoon in Rawalpindi, Zulfiqar Bhutto might have experienced a good deal of liberation from the guilt, if he ever had any, for taking the course to excommunication.

Obviously, the Ahmadiyah high-profile in national politics did not turn out as rosy as Nasir Ahmad might have envisioned while raising his stakes on Zulfiqar Bhutto. Still, it was not imaginable for the faithful, contributing a considerable percentage of their hard-earned income for a spate of party causes,

---

[1] Adamson Iain (1991): p. 109

to ask questions let alone demand an audit of the whole affair. In fact, the cult-like set up within the Ahmadiyah bore close resemblance with the communal hold of medieval church. Like the absoluteness of papal authority, the Ahmadiyah caliph embodied an infallible and divinely guided envoy of God, above and beyond the requirement for accountability. It was simply inconceivable, therefore, to ever imagine questioning the conduct of Nasir Ahmad over his escapade with Zulfiqar Bhutto.

By taking the parliamentary route to excommunication, Zulfiqar Bhutto had played his cards exquisitely. Even when the parliament had not been elected to pass an ecclesiastical judgment, the exercise offered an enormous opportunity for improved understanding between the warring sides. Had Zulfiqar Bhutto opted to settle the matter with referendum, he was bound to walkover without the hassle of interrogation on National Assembly floor. Once before the National Assembly, Nasir Ahmad had the rare opportunity to deliver signals of peace at least toward some shape of mutual coexistence. People do not go for alteration in matters of religious belief but they do gather the need to give and take in a sociological framework. Fifty years down the lanes of time, it remains only a matter of speculation as to how far the verdict of National Assembly might have been softened if Nasir Ahmad had aimed at opening the channels of dialogue. But he did not seem to think about the middle ground. In the first place, he did not prefigure excommunication, no way. As a result of the Ahmadiyah psyche, typical of religious narcissism, when the axe fell it came down really hard.

After the detonation of Indian nuclear bomb in May 1974, Abdus Salam did not go to see the Prime Minister. From Europe, however, he wrote one letter after another to the Government of Pakistan, protesting over the state-sponsored discrimination of the Ahmadiyah. 'Whatever may be merits of the law under which you are functioning, and the law stinks, the rigorous imprisonment makes me simply mad with you and with the whole legal procedure in Pakistan at the present time'. Abdus Salam wrote to the judge who sentenced an Ahmadiyah cleric to two years of rigorous imprisonment.[1]

Like the Ahmadiyah caliphate, Abdus Salam seemed to have disregarded Zulfiqar Bhutto's flirtation with the Wahabi lobby, the verdict of Azad Kashmir Assembly, the expressly intimidating resolution adopted by the Muslim World League and, finally, the termination of Air Marshal Zafar Chaudhry from the Pakistan Air Force command. But he did not expect a nationwide agitation at

---

[1] Jagjit Singh (1992): p. 98

such a short notice. An all-out mass movement within a matter of days, he suspected, was not possible without government sponsorship.

He was surprised to observe how Zulfiqar Bhutto had avoided thwarting the agitation at any stage. To him, it was a bleak reminder of the anarchy and mob rule he had witnessed in Lahore in 1952–53. When the anti-Ahmadiyah agitation picked up momentum, Abdus Salam discovered how the real Pakistan felt like. He was shocked to fathom some of his close friends, otherwise highly educated and tolerant. In Lahore, he received a telephone call from Mohammed Sharif, the former Secretary of Education. Mohammed Sharif proposed that the two of them should go out for lunch.

As the two sat in the air-conditioned cool of *Shezan* restaurant, watching commercial life on The Mall, Abdus Salam prompted the old man to comment on the anti-Ahmadiyah agitation. As if Mohammed Sharif had come well prepared to face the question, he put the figure of those dying in riots at 39 in his home district of Gujranwala. Only nine of the victims, he added, belonged to the Ahmadiyah community. Do you consider it a fair balance? Mohammed Sharif asked a spellbound Abdus Salam. Mohammed Sharif did not stop there, his next question was even more difficult to tackle. Tell me how your community would have behaved if they were in power? He asked Abdus Salam who did not know what to say.

He could see the brutal divide hidden underneath the tolerant facade of urban intellectual life. He had never thought about it before. As a religious man on the edge, with the veneer of a sufferer himself since 1953, how far could he go in working out what or how the other side thought and perceived? Here, on this account, he was required to explore whether all religions were equal or some more equal than others? Could the islands of so-called truth ever make a single land mass of the righteous? Did he ever bother to appreciate the self-styled arrogance of his Ahmadiyah fraternity constituted a part of the problem?

VI

Two days after excommunication, Abdus Salam resigned from his position as Science Adviser to the Government of Pakistan. In a liberal sense of the arrangement, he had played this role since 1955 adding an element of regularity with the rise of Ayub Khan. Left on his own, he might have taken a while to think about separation but the hurry in forcing him to act was triggered by

Zafarullah Khan. Abdus Salam was in Trieste when the National Assembly of Pakistan passed the judgement. It is important here to note that Abdus Salam had resigned to express his disagreement with the Ahmadiyah excommunication, not because of the Pakistani ambition to manufacture atom bomb. In fact, he desired to hold on to his membership of the Atomic Energy Commission but had to give in to the pressure exerted upon him by Zafarullah Khan.

With bitterness piling up in the midst of street agitation and harassment of his religious community, Abdus Salam had watched the course of events unfolding in Pakistan from a distance. He switched between hope and disbelief, reflecting about his students back home. His train of thought would take him back to 1953 when the tide of sectarian violence had subsided, after all. He thought about fruitful times spent in the company of Ishrat Usmani and the friendly disposition of Ayub Khan.

How could a parliament judge upon matters of religious belief? For many people, the concept of *Takfeer* among Muslims resembled the practice of excommunication among Christians and *Cherem* of Jews; but it remained, in the end, an outdated tribal age instrument to enforce discipline. It was hard to appreciate how such a whip of theology could actually replace the common law in modern societies known for their religious, ethnic and cultural diversity. Seemingly, Abdus Salam's hope that sanity might prevail was rooted in the very unworkable nature of excommunication as an administrative tool in modern world.

When the news arrived from Pakistan, Abdus Salam sat in his room at the International Centre for Theoretical Physics in Trieste. Munir Khan, the Chairman of the Atomic Energy Commission, had arrived from Pakistan somewhat unexpectedly and kept Abdus Salam company. Although the outcome of the parliamentary process was not totally unexpected, still the pain of disbelief took its toll.

Munir Khan had a bit of hunch about the course of events in Pakistan, and he could imagine the state of mind overtaking Abdus Salam. At a time when the race to manufacture nuclear weapons had picked up momentum in South Asia, he believed it was important for a great physicist, like Abdus Salam, to retain association with Pakistan. Munir Khan's unscheduled dash to Trieste, in this way, might have been aimed at standing beside Abdus Salam and offer him support to absorb the shock as big as excommunication. It remains a matter of guess if Munir Khan had acted with the blessings of Zulfiqar Bhutto.

In his letter of resignation, addressed to Zulfiqar Bhutto and dated 10 September 1974, Abdus Salam termed the excommunication as 'contradictory to the spirit of Islam'. Faith to him, he stated, constituted a transaction between man and his Creator. Islam, he went on, did not licence the Government of Pakistan to set one segment of Muslims upon another. Referring to the verdict delivered by the Parliament, he declined to 'accept such a decision in any way, whatsoever'. He pronounced that 'the only honourable' venue available to him in the given circumstances was to detach himself from the government responsible for making 'an amazing order' such as the excommunication.[1]

'I must say I was flabbergasted, astonished, very surprised. Although the course of events indicated clearly what the outcome was going to be a couple of days ahead of the actual announcement, still I felt astounded'. He remembered the day. 'Now it is such a long time, and my relationship with the Government of Pakistan is history though I continue to feel strongly attached to the place. It was unbelievable. I used to write my impressions in a diary in those days. I don't remember where those notes were kept, here in London or somewhere at Trieste. Sometimes, I wish to read those diaries to revisit my state of mind in those days'.[2]

He had hoped against all odds for sanity to prevail in the end, as it had been the case in 1953. It was hard for him to believe that a petty scuffle at Rabwah Railway Station, howsoever thoughtless and ill-conceived, could trigger *his* excommunication from the pale of Islam. In August 1947, he had experienced the overnight change in his nationality and citizenship; sleeping as an Indian and waking up as a Pakistani, without ever actually exercising the right to make the choice. Now he stood expelled from Islam, a faith his family and forefathers had adhered to for nearly a millennium.

His defiance made it hard for him to offer Zulfiqar Bhutto any allowance. He wanted to take time and play cool before making up his mind, and not act in a temperamental swing of mood. But when the time had arrived to make the choice, Abdus Salam betrayed mood swings, he undulated between rage and serenity. Munir Khan pleaded with him to retain at least his membership of the Atomic Energy Commission. Abdus Salam tended to agree with Munir Khan.

No final decision had yet been made when Abdus Salam's Secretary put through to him a telephone call from London. On the other end of the line was Zafarullah Khan. Have you tendered your resignation? Zafarullah Khan asked at

---

[1] Abdul Ghani (1982): p. 87
[2] Interviews 1984: Folder VII, p.100

the very outset. Abdus Salam had grown up revering Zafarullah Khan as a prominent elder of the Ahmadiyah community, and as a distinguished statesman and jurist of international stature. Since the freezing wet day of their first encounter 28 years ago, at Liverpool Docks in northern England, Zafarullah Khan had also been a father-figure to him.

No, not yet, Sir. Abdus Salam mumbled.

You must, then; better do it right now. Zafarullah Khan snapped back.

In defence of his reluctance, Abdus Salam explained the plea taken by Munir Khan. Zafarullah Khan was not impressed at all. He asked Abdus Salam to pass the telephone receiver over to Munir Khan.

After listening to what the Chairman of the Atomic Energy Commission had to say, Zafarullah Khan ruled that the excommunication was a very grave matter, with consequences far beyond people could imagine at the moment. Abdus Salam, he directed, must quit before being shown the way out by those who had unleashed the dastardly chain of events. Abdus Salam drafted his letter of resignation and got it reviewed by Zafarullah Khan who recommended some minor changes. According to close family sources, Abdus Salam accepted those changes but he sounded resolute in keeping a certain sentence in the text. But once again, Zafarullah Khan prevailed and the edited letter was despatched to the Government of Pakistan.[1]

Over the years, Abdus Salam settled that his reaction was neither planned nor sudden. 'I had not planned anything. In fact, I was a bit reluctant because I thought this would not serve any purpose. I did not wish to dissociate myself from the Atomic Energy Commission. Zafarullah Khan forced me to do so. Munir Khan had come from Pakistan, perhaps he knew what was coming up and the effect it would leave upon me. He advocated in favour of my presence in the commission. But then Zafarullah Khan ordered me to resign, which I obeyed. His argument was that I might be asked by the Prime Minister or the Chairman of the commission to stay on, but eventually I would be humiliated and thrown out. I think he was right and a better reader of Zulfiqar Bhutto's character. In the end, I think Zafarullah Khan was right.'[2]

Zafarullah Khan was vindicated, much before anyone else could have imagined. By electing to excommunicate the Ahmadiyah, Zulfiqar Bhutto had unleashed upon Pakistan a monstrosity of formidable proportions, including the

---

[1] Abdul Hameed (circa 2000): p. 408
[2] Interviews 1984: Folder VII, pp.102-103

rot leading to his own destruction. It became much easier in Pakistan to find a convenient scapegoat in the Ahmadiyah. For example, there was tussle for power between two factions of the ruling party. One factions master-minded a show of anti-Ahmadiyah rioting in Sargodha.

On 5 October 1974, that is, within barely a month of the excommunication, the Ahmadiyah were accused of abducting a trade union leader. There was rioting in the town, more than forty residential properties and businesses owned by the Ahmadiyah were set ablaze within hours. Once again, the police avoided to intervene. Hafiz Masood Ahmed, the General Practitioner, who had despatched strong-worded cables to the Home Department in 1952–53, lost his practice and residence to ashes in one day, all that had been made in 25 years was gone in a few hours. Fasting, as it was the month of Ramazan, he and close members of his family were saved by the last-minute intervention of a courageous neighbour.

Even though the excommunication was a dire business with horrendous and far-reaching consequences as alarmed by Zafarullah Khan, it remained so largely from the Ahmadiyah view point. Actually a strong clue as to how the other side viewed the sectarian warfare had already been provided to Abdus Salam by one of his erstwhile peers, Mohammed Sharif. Perhaps he required a bit of detachment to accommodate the logic others applied on their part. After all, it was religion and not Theoretical Physics.

VII

Out of state courtesy, Abdus Salam visited Rawalpindi to pay a formal farewell call on the Prime Minister. When the date, toward the end of September, was agreed between the two sides, Zulfiqar Bhutto invited him to come over to the Prime Minister's Secretariat straight from Islamabad international airport. Abdus Salam had last met with Zulfiqar Bhutto in Lahore in May 1974, that is, in the immediate aftermath of nuclear explosion by India. He was not seen even at the meeting of the powerful Defence Committee of the Cabinet, convened on 15 June 1974, when the formal decision 'to develop a nuclear deterrent capability' was made.[1]

---

[1] Feroz Hassan Khan (2013): pp. 121-123

Autumn was setting in when Abdus Salam arrived for the farewell call. About a hundred miles from the border to Afghanistan, Rawalpindi was a chaotic jumble of dirty, dusty, stinking, over-crowded and under-developed suburbs. Earlier in the 20th century, Sir Alexander Cunningham (1814–1993), an engineer in the Royal Indian Army, who acquired interest in studying local history and archaeology, had uncovered in Rawalpindi cantonment the ruins of *Gajnipur*, an ancient town known to be founded by the Bhatti Rajput clan of rulers to whom the family of Abdus Salam claimed its lineage. As a military township, Rawalpindi gained formal recognition after the annexation of Punjab in 1848, in the Big Game playing out between the British and the Russian empires. Over time, Rawalpindi became the winter headquarters of the Royal British Army's Northern Command. Here, in Rawalpindi cantonment, the Colonial Government is reported to have carried out 'experiments' for testing the effects of poison gas on native troops.

In Pakistan, Rawalpindi earned the notoriety as the killer of prime ministers; two were gunned down and the third hanged to death at sites only walking distance off the place where Abdus Salam had arrived for his appointment with Zulfiqar Bhutto. Originally a spread-out private estate over the acreage, surrounded by manicured lawns and native flora, the Prime Minister House stood adjacent to the General Headquarter of Pakistan Army. In the event of a military coup, an army general could just walk out on the street and shout orders to arrest the sitting prime minister.

On that lightly warm and mildly humid afternoon, Abdus Salam did not have any formal agenda for his meeting with Zulfiqar Bhutto. He had known Zulfiqar Bhutto since 1958 when the two got inducted into the military government headed by Ayub Khan. Over the years, their working relationship had been far from ideal, visibly rough at times; but the two had blunted each other out in the interest of working together for Pakistan.

While sitting in the lobby with people waiting for their turn to be called in by the Prime Minister, Abdus Salam saw the familiar face of an old acquaintance Khuda Bakhsh, a landowner from Punjab who championed modernisation of agricultural practices. With his characteristic politeness, Khuda Bakhsh approached Abdus Salam and the two began talking. After a while, Khuda Bakhsh expressed sorrow over the plight and suffering of the Ahmadiyah. But then in the same breath he remarked that power politics was a heartless business.

How? Abdus Salam asked him.

'From a position of strength you would not have treated us any differently'. Khuda Bakhsh replied. Abdus Salam thought of his encounter in Lahore with Mohammed Sharif only a few weeks ago. Once again, he failed to make out why educated people in Pakistan felt in this way. Before the two could discuss any further, an officer arrived to escort Abdus Salam in the direction of Prime Minister's suite.

Zulfiqar Bhutto got up from his chair and stepped forward to greet Abdus Salam, and before even the warm shaking of hands he exclaimed: What is this? Why have you resigned? It was an affectionate disapproval of Abdus Salam's decision to quit. Zulfiqar Bhutto wanted Abdus Salam to keep up the association, especially his membership of the Atomic Energy Commission. In fact, he went as far as asking Abdus Salam to give more time to the nuclear program.

Abdus Salam explained that the excommunication of the community to which he subscribed devoutly had come to him as a unilateral divorce. He found it difficult to continue serving the country where his religion was defined by others.

'Give me time. I will change it. Believe me!' Zulfiqar Bhutto attempted to pour out words of consolation, adding that his own secular disposition was well known all over the world. Going as far as excommunication was never his personal choice, he added. He argued that his government was obliged to take the bitter pill only to avert a large-scale massacre of the Ahmadiyah. Had he not acted with tact and calculated appeasement, he claimed, the ferocious Wahabi fanatics were bent upon a jihad against the apostate by way of violent cleansing. He regretted the whole affair, sounded remorseful. He even resorted to using the term 'sorry' to cheer up Abdus Salam.

According to Khalid Hassan, then serving as Press Secretary to the Prime Minister, Zulfiqar Bhutto listened to Abdus Salam and stated that the excommunication was a political expediency and it could be retracted anytime in future.

They started talking about the nuclear program. Zulfiqar Bhutto expressed his displeasure over the slow pace of progress. He did not sound much pleased with Munir Khan. What was the hold up? He suddenly asked Abdus Salam.

'Well, you gave him the assignment. You better ask him'. Abdus Salam replied without referring to Munir Khan by name. Zulfiqar Bhutto repeated his assertion that Abdus Salam should consider taking a more direct part in the nuclear program.

'Right! Let us strike a bargain and settle terms. I am prepared to work for you and get the bomb ready within five years. But you have to undo the out casting of the Ahmadiyah'. He offered the deal. It remains a mystery if he had come prepared for it or acted spontaneously.

Done! Zulfiqar Bhutto shot back.

All right, Zulfi! Abdus Salam addressed the Prime Minister informally by first name. 'I believe you, but write down what you have told me on a plain piece of paper and it will remain between the two of us, forever and always'.

Politicians, replied Zulfiqar Bhutto, do not pledge in writing. 'I can't do that, I am a politician'. He stated.[1]

Notwithstanding what the state records may or may not reveal in the future, it remains a big question as to what exactly had prompted Abdus Salam to offer collaboration in the bomb project. If he had ever looked for an excuse to bail himself out of Pakistan's pursuit of nuclear weapons, the discriminatory treatment meted out to the Ahmadiyah was an ideal opportunity to walk away. On the contrary, he went the other way round by expressing his readiness to take charge of the bomb project in return for the retraction of excommunication.

Obviously, he had not come all the way from Europe to call the prime minister's bluff. Could the excommunication and the nuclear bomb be bracketed together? Did Abdus Salam make the offer on his own or he was doing it formally at the behest of the Ahmadiyah? What was the guarantee that Zulfiqar Bhutto would stay in power after the completion of his current term? What would be the value of a written assurance if the government changed? Finally, how could Abdus Salam promise a nuclear bomb within five years? Was he not aware of the feeble state of technological infrastructure in the country.

When time for the meeting was up, Abdus Salam asked the prime minister's permission to leave. Zulfiqar Bhutto urged him to continue offering necessary advice to the Government of Pakistan promising that such a counsel, even when informally made, would be welcome in matters related to science, higher education and technology. Abdus Salam promised to oblige in every possible way, and the two parted. Sadly it turned out to be their last encounter. Three years later, Zulfiqar Bhutto lost power in a military coup; he was then condemned to death on charges of his involvement in a murder case. In April 1979, he was hanged to death in an old jail few hundred yards from the mansion where Abdus Salam had come to pay him the farewell call.

---

[1] Khalid Hassan, Daily Times, Lahore (Pakistan), November 2006

'Our meeting lasted well over an hour. I remember one of the secretaries began hovering around to remind the Prime Minister of his next appointment. But the Prime Minister signalled this officer to leave. That was our last meeting. I never saw him again'. Abdus Salam recalled ten years later, he suspected Zulfiqar Bhutto fluctuated between acting and repentance. 'He was very contrite for this whole business. At the same time, he appeared to be doing a marvellous piece of acting. That's the only thing I can say. Very contrite and deeply sorry. In fact, he kept repeating the word sorry'.

Upon coming out of the Prime Minister's suite, Abdus Salam found Masood Mahmood, the Director General of the much-dreaded Federal Security Force entrusted to crush internal opposition, waiting for him. May I have a word with you? Masood Mahmood whispered into his ear.

Having known Masood Mahmood since 1945, from the Government College days in Lahore, Abdus Salam did not mind catching up with an old mate. After leaving the college, Masood Mahmood took commission in the police force. He was known for his bureaucratic experience, cultured disposition and attentive listening ability. He had met Zulfiqar Bhutto at a police club in 1958 where the two sipped dry Martini and became friends almost instantly.[1] While attending a career development course in London in 1956, Masood Mahmood had briefly shared accommodation with Abdus Salam and his brother Abdul Hameed.

Masood Mahmood escorted Abdus Salam to his posh office, where many telephone sets were neatly lined up on one side of the spacious desk. 'We must talk about this Ahmadiyah business. Tell me exactly what do you want and I shall see if there is a way to convince the Prime Minister'. He told Abdus Salam at the very outset. Amused to receive such an outlandish offer, Abdus Salam told Masood Mahmood that his reaction to the excommunication was not a secret, his resignation from the advisory role was self-explanatory.

As the two talked, one of the telephone sets began ringing. From the body language and respectful tone of Masood Mahmood it was not difficult for Abdus Salam to make out that the Prime Minister himself might be on the other end. When the call was over, Masood Mahmood asked Abdus Salam to wait for a few minutes as he had been summoned by the boss. Abdus Salam did not mind waiting but he was taken aback when Masood Mahmood signalled a security officer to guard the room during his absence. Few minutes later, when Masood Mahmood returned, the sentry disappeared respectfully.

---

[1] Stanley Wolpert (1993): p. 223

What was this drama of keeping a watch on me? Abdus Salam asked him.

'Well, you see, we have highly classified and sensitive documents in this room. You are not with the government anymore. Our role, in public service, is to go by the wind. I suppose you appreciate the need for caution'. Masood Mahmood replied as a matter of the fact. With a loathsome crunch sinking down his gullet, Abdus Salam delivered a four-letter Punjabi invective in the direction of Masood Mahmood, who only smiled back. 'I thought he was acting on his own, out of friendship with me. But then I am sitting there and a security guard is taking care of his documents. I was amazed that he should mistrust even me'. Abdus Salam reminisced over the baffling episode.

On that afternoon, the full scope of the seasoned advice offered by Zafarullah Khan dawned upon Abdus Salam. His desire to retain some semblance of connection with the Government of Pakistan, for the sake of science and education, was meaningless. He was an outsider, bound to be marginalised, ending up like a miserable hypocrite. Due to his association with an outcast religious minority, he was a suspect and a threat to national security.

From Rawalpindi, Abdus Salam travelled straight to Rabwah to seek an audience with Nasir Ahmad. He narrated the details of his encounter with Zulfiqar Bhutto, especially about the offer of cooperation in the bomb project in return for an annulment of excommunication. He informed Nasir Ahmad that Zulfiqar Bhutto was not prepared to go beyond a verbal assurance. Nasir Ahmad listened to Abdus Salam with a priestly poise, delivered a melancholy smile and then remarked that the unwillingness on the part of Zulfiqar Bhutto in tendering any written guarantee was possibly the only moment of truth in the whole encounter.[1] But why did Abdus Salam rush from Rawalpindi to Rabwah? Had he acted as an undercover emissary of the Ahmadiyah?

This last meeting Abdus Salam had with Zulfiqar Bhutto provides a clue into the partition of his life, a three-way segregation into Physics, Pakistan and the Ahmadiyah. Only he held the key to ensuring a balance. He deemed that a good deal of personal and private information, relating to his involvements outside Physics, should stay close to his heart. He was, of course, fully entitled to privacy, especially in relation to his religious belief and family life. His public profile demanded a good deal of openness.

---

[1] Interviews 1984: Folder VII, p. 97

VIII

Not enthusiastic to share information apart from Physics, Abdus Salam agreed one day to field a few direct questions about the Ahmadiyah and Pakistan lumps of his life. He appreciated the need to talk rather than leaving the scene open to speculation.[1]

In their spontaneously made comments, both Mohammad Sharif and Khuda Bakhsh had reflected upon the fact that a loathing of the Ahmadiyah was not confined to clerics and illiterate masses in Pakistan, at the same time it was not a one-way sentiment. By virtue of their better education and disproportionately large presence in employment, the tightly-knit mafia-like exclusiveness of Ahmadiyah community provoked the liberal and the bigoted alike. Some people went as far as sniffing evil behind the Ahmadiyah network of missions abroad, in countries like India and Israel.

On his part, Abdus Salam held the view that it was not easy for a socially compact and disciplined party like the Ahmadiyah to escape sceptic attention. But then he hinted that dispelling of misleading image required to be dealt at a different level, the least of all by him.

He was invited to comment on the chances of survival for a schismatic introvert minority like the Ahmadiyah in the Muslim world. Instead of getting entangled into the minefield of root causes, Abdus Salam agreed that there had been a failure on the part of the Ahmadiyah in creating pockets of influence especially in Pakistan. But he did not wish to get any further than making this brief statement of observation. 'I cannot answer this question. I think you are asking the wrong man. I am just one of the practicing members of the community who holds no office and has never held one. I meet the caliph and he gives me time, very kindly. I became a prominent member of the Ahmadiyah community because of a choice made by Ayub Khan who invited me to advise the government on scientific matters. Apart from that there is nothing special about it'. He stated by insisting that any channels of political consultation between him and the Ahmadiyah leadership simply did not exist.

He then went on to compare himself with Zafarullah Khan by citing the difference between the two of them. Zafarullah Khan held high-profile public offices in India, Pakistan and abroad without the slightest inhibition to

---

[1] Interviews 1984: VII/123-124

proselytise the message of the Ahmadiyah. 'I don't get involved into such business. Whenever there is a need, I speak for all Muslims instead of limiting myself to the advocacy of one or another group. My speeches, statements and writings are all very clear on this subject. I don't know what needs to be done to dispel an impression contrary to what actually is the case'. He stressed.

Something kept him from opening up beyond a certain point and, in spite of his razor-sharp scientific mind, he would just not go near touching upon the relationship between self-proclaimed righteousness and sociological effects of this attitude. On one hand, the Ahmadiyah claimed themselves to be the most genuine face of Islam, proposed a radical agenda of doctrinal reform and then, on the other end, the community cut itself from a whole heap of social transaction with the mainstream. They would not share the slightest of religious experience with their Muslim neighbours, no sharing of religious rites, practices and customs, none attendance of funeral services outside the community, no intermarriage whatsoever. How could such an outright rejection of the mainstream fit into the minds of ordinary people? On top of the awkward boycott of a community surrounding them, the Ahmadiyah had an eye on a disproportionately larger chunk of employment in public and private sectors in government and business. Effectively, in a way, the Ahmadiyah had excommunicated the mainstream much before the tide took a more natural course. But Abdus Salam would just not look beyond the ethical aspects of religious divide, especially where his community claimed the benefit of victimhood.

How come the Ahmadiyah bashing was such a handy tool to ignite political agitation in Pakistan? After all, few other sects among Muslims hold sets of belief far off the mainstream. What turned people, both educated as well as illiterate, so easily against the Ahmadiyah? Abdus Salam thought that it was like nicknaming the animosity. Just as the term 'Paki' mustered racist sentiment among sections of community in England, he argued. He listed the Ahmadiyah definition of jihad as a possible cause of mutual suspicion dating back to the British colonial era. Personally, with passage of time, he began taking a softer view of the excommunication and felt there was nothing new about the phenomenon. Historically, in organised religion, it had happened in the past and could be repeated again. He was worried only about the partisanship of the state. It was the loss of neutrality by the Government of Pakistan, according to him, which made excommunication of the Ahmadiyah so unique.

'Excommunication has been a universal practice among religions and sects, but the state to come into this business is rather unique. As a result of the government partisanship, we cannot perform the pilgrimage to Mecca. We are not allowed to recite the call to prayers. These are disabilities far above the curtailment of freedom to practice, preach or proselytise. This is why we want the excommunication to be folded back by the government. We want the state to undo it. Don't you think so? It is a disability caused by the state, from where should come the remedy'. He pressed.

Did he believe that a reversal could be possible in the near future? He appreciated that it was easier said than done proposition, yet the prospects of correcting a wrong depended upon the strength of leadership taking up such a challenge. Equally important, he remarked, was the public revulsion towards such an injustice. He did not wish to gamble on a timeframe. But he strongly felt that the Parliament of Pakistan was not competent to define the religious belief of a community. More than indulging into a medieval pastime, and causing a whole range of civic disabilities upon the Ahmadiyah, the action had contaminated the constitutional progress of Pakistan. Actions motivated by bigotry and injustice have never brought respectability to a nation or country in the long run, he remarked. Sooner or later, he hoped, a generation of educated Pakistanis might have to remove this curse from the Constitution. Pakistan, he feared, might not go very far with a constitutional licence for discrimination. He cited an oral tradition attributed to the prophet of Islam. A contaminated reservoir of drinking water could not be purified by drainage alone; if the putrid carcass of a dead dog was the cause of infection it had to be removed before anything else. He insisted.

Avoiding to take a position on the plight of the Ahmadiyah, Abdus Salam found refuge in the mystical course. He referred to Koranic tale of Abraha, the Christian commander who intended to overrun Mecca in the 6th century. After building a grand church in Yemen, according to Muslim historians, Abraha desired to deflect the pilgrims away from the ancient shrine of *Ka'aba*. When the town was under siege, Abdul Muttalib, the grandfather of Prophet Muhammad, is reported to have approached Abraha and asked for the return of his cattle captured by invaders. *Ka'aba* was the sanctuary and it would be defended by God, Abdul Muttalib warned Abraha. Within a matter of days the expedition failed and the army of Abraha was destroyed by an epidemic caused by birds.[1]

Allegorically, in this way, Abdus Salam aimed at conveying the message that the future of the Ahmadiyah, as the party of God, was secure with God. He was overwhelmed by the manner in which the Ahmadiyah had stood firmly united in the face of persecution in Pakistan. He credited Nasir Ahmad for leading the faithful through testing times with wisdom and patience. He seemed to have completely overlooked the fact that it was Nasir Ahmad who, in the first place, was responsible for exposing the Ahmadiyah to such a hazardous level of vulnerability.

Did the Ahmadiyah caliph seek his opinion before striking an electoral alliance with Zulfiqar Bhutto? It was a proposition, Abdus Salam rejected outright claiming that he had nothing to do, whatsoever, with the conduct of Ahmadiyah public affairs. 'I am nowhere in these decisions. People always think of me in the same breath as Zafarullah Khan or Muzaffar Ahmad. I am never consulted by the Ahmadiyah caliph. Not even today'. He stated. At the same time, however, he seemed aware of the fact that both Zafarullah Khan and Muzaffar Ahmad had expressed their aversion to the idea of backing Zulfiqar Bhutto. 'Everyone felt like encouraging Zulfiqar Bhutto as a very progressive politician. In the beginning, when he nursed what then was a battered and bruised Pakistani nation, I felt the Ahmadiyah support paid off. At that time, he acted like a superb organiser. Afterwards, he got detracted and started playing a different game'. Abdus Salam remarked.

He did not wish to speculate over the possible link between the nuclear show of India and the sudden outbreak of anti-Ahmadiyah rioting in Pakistan. Any logic relating to a startlingly close affinity, in terms of timing if not anything else, between the two episodes, he felt, should be studied by the Ahmadiyah side.

On personal level, in end, excommunication did take a toll on Abdus Salam. He began experiencing deeper indulgence into spirituality. He even started sporting a beard. No law, he stated, could keep him from observing the faith of his choice. In a way, he began digging deeper to express his defiance.

---

[1] F.E. Peters: Muhammad and the Origins of Islam, State University of New York Press, 1994, p.86

IX

In March 1977, Zulfiqar Bhutto confronted a mass agitation bigger than the one encountered by his former boss Ayub Khan. People marched on the streets and demanded an end to his rule. More than 200 lives were lost in the campaign. Zulfiqar Bhutto shot every weapon from his political armoury to appease the opposition; none worked. He faced an opposition dominated by religious parties refusing to give him any allowance for signing the peace accord with India, repatriating 93000 prisoners of war, reclaiming over 5000 square miles of territory lost in the war, nationalising industries and financial corporations to create employment for millions, introducing land reforms, sacking corrupt public servants, distancing from international treaties with the west, convening the Islamic Summit Conference and, above all, excommunicating the Ahmadiyah. He closed nightclubs, bars and casinos; prohibited alcohol, switched Sunday with Friday as the weekly day off; then promised to replace civil and criminal codes of procedures, introduced by the British, with Islamic laws. Aiming to get his sins pardoned, he donated solid gold cast entrance to one of the Sufi shrines in Sind. He urged the Kingdom of Saudi Arabia to appreciate his role in 'the very existence of Islam in South Asia'.[1]

Early in the morning, on 4 July 1977, General Ziaul Haq, the man Zulfiqar Bhutto had handpicked by superseding seven seniors generals to lead the army, staged the military coup.

Since making his debut on the national scene in 1958, Zulfiqar Bhutto had washed hands with almost all of his salient benefactors. From Iskander Mirza and Ayub Khan to Yahya Khan, from Left wing intellectuals and activists to the Ahmadiyah community; he had betrayed all those propping him up. His public career covered all the classical ingredients of a sensational political drama; from betrayal and deceit to greed, revenge and an eccentric mix of tragedy and humour. His turn to face the music had arrived. He was jailed to face trial on a nearly forgotten murder indictment. Rather effortlessly, Masood Mahmood, the Director General of the Federal Security Force, who had explained upon Abdus Salam the virtue of loyalty among public servants, turned himself in as an approver against the doomed prime minister. Within a matter of few months, the judges condemned Zulfiqar Bhutto to death.

---

[1] Stanley Wolpert (1993): pp. 288-289

Zafarullah Khan happened to be visiting Lahore when the Supreme Court of Pakistan heard Zulfiqar Bhutto's appeal against death sentence. Mushtaq Hussein, the Chief Justice of Punjab High Court, where the death sentence had been initially handed down, asked Zafarullah Khan to guess as to which way the Supreme Court might go. Like any other senior judge in his situation, Mushtaq Hussein felt nervous about the appeal pending before the Supreme Court. Without the slightest hesitation, Zafarullah Khan comforted Mushtaq Hussein to rest assured as the fate of Zulfiqar Bhutto had been sealed in a 'much higher' court. Approaching 87, Zafarullah Khan was not supposed to be diplomatic, he had an unflinching faith in the imminent doom of Zulfiqar Bhutto.[1]

In the first week of April 1979, Zulfiqar Bhutto was hanged in Rawalpindi District Jail. While walking out of the Prime Minister's Secretariat in Rawalpindi, less than five years ago, Abdus Salam had never imagined that the final act of Zulfiqar Bhutto's life was destined to be staged at the gallows next door. He also remembered the humiliating police watch Masood Mahmood had instituted upon him.

General Ziaul Haq and the clerics supporting his military regime believed that the fall and punishment of former prime minister betrayed all the hallmarks of Islamic justice and accountability. On the other end, the Ahmadiyah did not waste time in bragging and blustering about the coming true of a prophecy made by the founder of the community. Zulfiqar Bhutto had made history by excommunicating the Ahmadiyah; he deserved due attention. Rejoicing the elimination of an opponent betrayed an old-fashioned pagan psyche.

On the day Zulfiqar Bhutto was hanged in Rawalpindi, Zafarullah Khan who, in September 1974, had urged Abdus Salam to distance from the Government of Pakistan as hurriedly as possible, delivered a short sermon in London, at the Ahmadiyah Mission House in Putney. Reminder of the Biblical disposition, he spoke about the concept of divine justice, extolling the doom of those who mistreated the righteous. Among his audience sat a spellbound Abdus Salam. Listening to Zafarullah Khan was a unique experience for Abdus Salam. He had been saddened by the cruel treatment meted out to the deposed prime minister[2] but then the speech delivered by Zafarullah Khan seemed to have opened another vista for Abdus Salam to find perspective.

---

[1] Weekly *Atish Fishan*, Lahore, May 1981
[2] Interviews 1984: Folder VII, p. 98

'Zafarullah Khan delivered one of the best speeches from his brilliantly rich stock of oration on the subject'. Abdus Salam recalled. Like many others in the Ahmadiyah community, he believed that judges and generals in Pakistan were only instrumental in implementing what had been foretold. But just when the Ahmadiyah mission in London decided to publish Zafarullah Khan's sermon for the benefit of a wider audience, Nasir Ahmad curbed the move. Abdus Salam did not understand the last-minute censor. 'I have always felt very strongly about it, we should have gone ahead with publication of Zafarullah Khan's speech. Perhaps, the idea behind restraint was to maintain a regard for the grieving family'. He believed.[1]

Once again, Abdus Salam overlooked the fact that it was Nasir Ahmad who, in the first instance, had deposited the fate of his flock to the political antics of Zulfiqar Bhutto. Equally important for Abdus Salam was the need to ask if Nasir Ahmad had any clue to those prophesies of Ghulam Ahmad when he picked up Zulfiqar Bhutto as the heir to Ayub Khan?

Both Abdus Salam and Zulfiqar Bhutto belonged to the same age-group but in terms of their social background and career pathways the two fell worlds apart. Still the two evolved a working relationship, with its ups and downs, as part of the government under Ayub Khan. 'I knew him quite well. We were together in Ayub Khan's team since he was the Minister for Petroleum and Natural Resources. He was much younger and rather gaudy because of which some people did not take him very seriously. Because he had been to Oxford, those in the government who prided upon their Cambridge connection acted with a sort of snobbery'.[2] Abdus Salam recalled the Ayub Khan era with a tinge of nostalgic fondness. He appreciated how, in the final years of Ayub Khan, when political scenario begun changing, Zulfiqar Bhutto grabbed the initiative to reform his image. From a minister under military regime, he graduated himself into a bold campaigner of social equality and democracy. Against the block of feudal politicians, he sounded strikingly fresh and full of hope and promise.

In some ways, Zulfiqar Bhutto posed an enigma to Abdus Salam. 'He was very progressive and one felt like encouraging him. In the beginning, for a year or so, he nursed a wounded nation, signed a peace accord with Indira Gandhi and brought Pakistani prisoners of war back from India, and so on'. Abdus Salam credited Zulfiqar Bhutto with praise where he felt it was genuinely due. He

---

[1] Interviews 1984: Folder VII, pp. 98-99
[2] Interviews 1984: Folder VII, pp. 67-69, 73

believed there was ground to be positive especially after the lifting of martial law and promulgation of the Constitution. Even when the move to nationalise leading industries and financial institutions sounded drastic, Abdus Salam felt, the government had been able to create jobs, fund education and establish new universities.

There was considerable justification, Abdus Salam argued, behind the Ahmadiyah logic to support Zulfiqar Bhutto. He remembered discussing new projects with Zulfiqar Bhutto. 'We talked about various projects in the fields of electronics and petroleum development. He even set up the Electronic Commission and a separate ministry for petroleum exploration in line with my advice. Our petroleum expert Shahzad Sadiq was inducted into the government at my recommendation. Bhutto would listen in the beginning and was quite receptive with good instincts. But then gradually he turned more and more divorced from realities. I don't know what happened to him'. Abdus Salam remarked. He would just not see any reason to forgive Zulfiqar Bhutto for polluting the secular spirit of legislative culture. It was perplexing for Abdus Salam to adore anymore the man who gave Pakistan another chance in democracy and then hastened to set up a minefield in the works.

All hopes for the meaningful change were destroyed, according to Abdus Salam, when Zulfiqar Bhutto resorted to ruthless opportunism and the selfishness to stay in power at any cost. Democracy and religious fanaticism could not go hand in hand. He held Zulfiqar Bhutto responsible for destroying 'all hopes of democracy for ever' by driving Pakistan to the old wickedness of religious excommunication. He was displeased with the noise Zulfiqar Bhutto had made in Multan to gear up the nuclear program for it alerted the world needlessly. At the same time, he credited Zulfiqar Bhutto for taking a bold and dignified position when India blew up any hopes of non-proliferation in South Asia.

Once again, what Abdus Salam seemed to overlook was the quantity of upheaval overtaking the neighbourhood of Pakistan during the closing years of government headed by Zulfiqar Bhutto. An Islamic Revolution approached Iran, the monarchy collapsed clearing the way for a communist takeover in Afghanistan. Indira Gandhi experimented with emergency rule in India, the so-called largest democracy where an obnoxious caste system had been rather jealously guarded by prophets of peace like Mohandas Gandhi. For practical purposes, the secular facade of India singed with the rising temperature of Hindu fundamentalism. Of course, the Ahmadiyah faced persecution but it was more of a side effect in view of their peculiar placement in Pakistani situation. On the whole, the size of Ahmadiyah plight came nowhere near the historical records of crimes and wrongs committed on grounds of religion, race and skin colour. Jews in Europe, blacks in Africa and America, Palestinians in the Middle East; victims of colonial advance and wars in Australia, Vietnam, Iraq and Afghanistan; sadly the list is condemned to remain incomplete, always.

With the passage of time, as the noose of legislation tightened, everyday life did become challenging for the Ahmadiyah but there had been support upcoming from abroad.

In fact, Abdus Salam appeared to confront a predicament of his own. Way back in 1968, when he had won the Atoms for Peace prize, his father was delighted to find the symbolic significance of his name, *the Servant of Peace*. 'I know your heart is on the other prize. God willing you will get that one day'. He wrote to Abdus Salam.[1] Mohammed Hussein did not have the slightest clue that his son was already on the verge of qualifying for the 'other prize'. In fact, Abdus Salam had completed a crucial segment of his work relating to unification of forces, in Quantum Field Theory while his father still lived. He had been working on 'the idea of uniting weak interactions with electromagnetism'.[2] He was not put off even when the deceptive delay in integration of nuclear interactions began casting shadows of doubt on the very future of Quantum Field Theory. All of it happened just before the death of his father.

Still, there was no news about the 'other prize'. On the contrary, he confronted the dilemma of his disrupted ties with Pakistan. He struggled to come to terms with his expulsion from the pale of Islam; the Government of Pakistan had banned him from visiting the nuclear laboratories. Some hecklers in the country went as far as calling him a detestable foreign spy reporting to the American Central Intelligence Agency and 'his masters' in India.[3] When he proposed the need for intellectual cooperation with the west, columnists in Pakistan asked how could Muslims cooperate with those squandering their natural resources? How could the west permit Muslims to achieve capability in

---

[1] The Herald, Karachi (Pakistan), 01 August 1984, p. 114
[2] Ideals and Realities, edited by Hassan, Z. and Lai, C.H., World Scientific, Singapore, 1984, p. 331.
[3] Malik, Zahid: Abdul Qadeer Khan (Urdu), Hurmat Publications, Islamabad, 1989, pp. 22-23, 164

nuclear technology? What benefit the world of Islam could draw from Abdus Salam's research in the unified field theory in physics?[1]

Out of nowhere, one day, Abdus Salam found the press-clipping of an interview Masood Mahmood, the Director General of Zulfiqar Bhutto's Federal Security Force, had given to a weekly journal in Lahore.

In his interview, Masood Mahmood had claimed that Zulfiqar Bhutto was reluctant about the excommunication of the Ahmadiyah and intended to somehow reverse the parliamentary ruling soon after winning the second term in office. In the meanwhile, Masood Mahmood went on, the former prime minister struggled to find ways to appease the Ahmadiyah. As such, Zulfiqar Bhutto was reported to have directed Masood Mahmood to meet with Abdus Salam and convey an accordingly favourable message. Masood Mahmood stated that he received a blunt snub from Abdus Salam. 'Personally, my loyalty with Pakistan stands strong as ever before'. Abdus Salam was quoted to have told Masood Mahmood. 'But those who mistreated my community, I beseech their annihilation and destruction'. According the Masood Mahmood, this response of Abdus Salam was duly conveyed to Zulfiqar Bhutto.[2]

When a copy of this press article arrived on Abdus Salam's desk, he was overwhelmed with an enormous sense of vindication. By that time though he had forgotten about the exact exchange of words between him and Masood Mahmood; he did remember, however, the vulnerability of the Ahmadiyah in the summer of 1974. His memory did not fail him about the selective silence maintained by the Government of Pakistan. He also remembered his own humiliation by being subjected to police watch by someone no less than an old college-mate. He read through the press clipping, over and over again, unsure of words attributed to him. Even if he did not wish the outcome as harsh as it turned out for Zulfiqar Bhutto in less than five years, the whole story fitted well into Zafarullah Khan's thesis of divine retribution.

He folded the copy of that press clipping neatly and placed it in his vault. This was going to stay there the rest of his life, as an amulet and a talisman for better days ahead.

---

[1] Daily *Jang*, Friday Magazine, Rawalpindi, 29 April 1983
[2] *Badban*, Lahore, 18 May 1979, P. 35

Chapter Ten
Talisman Works

Early in October 1974 came the telephone call Abdus Salam had waited for years. He happened to be in London on that day.

First there was an alert from the office of Sigvard Eklund (1911–2000), the Swedish nuclear physicist, who served as the Director General of the International Atomic Energy Agency in Vienna. In a world preceding the dawn of digital revolution, Sigvard Eklund intended Abdus Salam to stay close to the telephone set. Both men had known each other from their atoms for peace conferencing days in the 1950s.

Shortly afterwards came the telephone call from Stockholm formally advising Abdus Salam that he had been selected to share the 1979 Nobel Prize for Physics along with two American physicists, Steven Weinberg (1933–2021) and Sheldon Glashow (1932-). Facing the news media in Imperial College, soon afterwards, Abdus Salam stated that he was not taken aback by the award from Stockholm. He had been waiting for the call for quite a while. Possibly, he alluded to the memory of his close brush with the prize earlier in 1957.

Historically, the prize shared by Abdus Salam added another chapter to the success stories in human urge to understand the natural phenomenon. Isaac Newton (1643–1727) had perceived the conformity between motion and gravity. James Clark Maxwell (1831–1879) found the link between electricity and magnetism. Albert Einstein (1879–1955) discovered relativity between space, time and gravitation. Presently, for their independently carried out work, Abdus Salam, Sheldon Glashow and Steven Weinberg found the tie between electromagnetic and weak nuclear forces.[1] How theoretical physicists could look into laws of nature, prior even to any experimental evidence, was a riddle latent

---

[1] Experimental confirmation of this work has led to winning of Nobel Prizes in 1977 and 1984.

in mathematical language and logarithm. A considerably adequate answer to this question has been provided by Robert Crease and Charles Mann, both physicists themselves, in their adorably titled study, *The Second Creation*, a breath-taking account of revolution makers in the 20th century physics.

Winning Nobel Prize in one of the listed disciplines of knowledge is considered to be the pinnacle of professional acknowledgment. Somewhat ironically, in his own lifetime, the founder of the prize, Alfred Nobel (1833–1896), the chemical engineer of Swedish origin, had been nicknamed as the Merchant of Death. He had some 355 patents, including dynamite, credited to his vast business empire. Prizes in physics, chemistry, physiology-medicine, literature and peace have been awarded since the beginning of the 20th century; with economics added to the list in 1969. On the average, the final list of winners is made after a tedious and highly classified process of nominations and selection largely carried out in Sweden. Only the peace prize is granted by the Norwegian Nobel Committee.

Under the statutes, candidates in Physics, Chemistry and Physiology-Medicine are queued up to pass-through a rigorous drill of selection process. It stands in sharp contrast to peace prizes awarded by the Norwegian Committee where, every now and then, political selection seems to overshadow the fitness of winners.

Unaware himself, Abdus Salam was recommended for the prize by his Cambridge University teacher, peer and one of the greatest among 20th century physicists, Paul Dirac. After taking the call from Stockholm, Abdus Salam rushed to the local Ahmadiyah Mosque in Southfields, London, to offer a prayer of thanksgiving. According to his brother and biographer, Abdul Hameed, he perceived a 'sign' in the very role played by Paul Dirac, an atheist. For him, it amounted to a grand piece of divine intervention bringing into play the services of a disbeliever to benefit a believer. This remark of Abdus Salam, made in an extraordinary state of mind, betrayed the standard psyche of the devout among believers. Richard Dawkins (1941-) has dealt with the subject ably.[1] Whatever the merit of such an insensitive logic on the part of Abdus Salam, the question remained how far a deeply religious person would go, as far as Paul Dirac did in favour of those he considered best on strict professional merit, in promoting an atheist? In the first place, there was hardly the need to have been carried away by such an uncalled-for analogy; the fact that Abdus Salam went straight to the

---

[1] Richard Dawkins: The God Delusion, Transworld Publishers, 2006, pp. 20-27, 211

mosque after receiving the long-awaited news was self-explanatory and sufficient in itself. But then it turned out to be an occasion of spontaneity reflecting religious bias constituting his personality.

What is the practical significance of his work? Someone asked Abdus Salam. He did not have any quick answer other than explaining how the unification of electricity and magnetism had cleared the way for Industrial Revolution leading to modern technological era. Scientific scholarship goes on unfolding the hidden layers of reality. Some three hundred years ago, Isaac Newton proved that terrestrial gravity, the force behind the falling of an apple on the ground, and celestial gravity the force due to which Earth rotated around sun, were interlinked. It was not possible at that time to predict that this linkage would open the gates to launching of satellites and extraordinary advances in space technology one day. In a similar vein Michael Faraday and Andre Ampere unified the forces of electricity and magnetism showing James Clerk Maxwell the way to discover the concept of radiation. Earlier in the 20th century, when physicists started penetrating into the realm of subatomic particles, nobody went as far as predicting the cultivation of nuclear energy. On his part, Abdus Salam hoped the contribution made by him and his colleagues, in linking the electromagnetic and weak forces, might facilitate an improved understanding of amino-acids, the basic biochemical units to explore the origin of life elsewhere in the universe.

First shot of celebration in his honour was fired by Altaf Gauhar (1923–2000), a college mate of Abdus Salam who joined the public service and retired as the Information Secretary of Ayub Khan. After that the floodgate was lifted upon a torrent of congratulatory messages. One of the messages came from the family of Zulfiqar Bhutto jointly signed by his widow Nusrat and daughter Benazir, both temporarily stationed in London. Six months had passed since the execution of Zulfiqar Bhutto while his family and party struggled to come to terms with their political fate as Pakistan was far from any semblance of democratic order. Abdus Salam reacted rather sharply. 'I am glad to have your message,' he shot back, adding it was the leader of your party who deprived me of equality in my homeland. I hope, he added, 'a future government will repeal the law that has turned people like me into exiles, without a place in their own country'. Afterwards, of course, he acknowledged the harshness of his tone.[1]

---

[1] Interviews 1984: Folder VII, p. 104

Benazir Bhutto would not forget the snub, she declined to receive him when he visited Islamabad during her first term as the prime minister of Pakistan.

Then there was a message from Nasir Ahmad, the Ahmadiyah caliph, who extolled Abdus Salam as the *first* among Muslims and Pakistanis to have won an honour such as the Nobel Prize.[1] Apparently, it was an expression of defiance and a refusal to go along with the verdict of excommunication handed down by the parliament of Pakistan.

Back home, the Government of Pakistan was taken by surprise, unsure whether to own or disown Abdus Salam. As such, the Ahmadiyah Mission in London picked up the impression that Prime Minister Indira Gandhi had taken lead in congratulating Abdus Salam. She was reported to have invited him to visit India. During the tense interval, as he awaited call from home, Britain offered him citizenship.[2] But then, in the end, President Ziaul Haq dispelled all notions of evasion soon after receiving a message from Pakistani ambassador based in London. In fact, Ziaul Haq handled the decoration of Abdus Salam with grace and political precision. His government celebrated the prize and accorded Abdus Salam the due recognition for raising the intellectual profile of Pakistan. For a while, any consideration pertaining to the prohibitive cost of Abdus Salam's Ahmadiyah baggage was set aside.

First, Ziaul Haq cabled Abdus Salam with an ornately worded message of congratulation for bringing the honour to Pakistan. Next, he made a telephone call to Abdus Salam's residence in London where Amtul Hafeez took the call and advised the President that her husband was currently in Trieste. Once the connection was established, the General congratulated Abdus Salam for making Pakistan proud by winning the prize. He invited him and Amtul Hafeez to visit Pakistan officially. It is not known if the President of Pakistan had much knowledge about Abdus Salam's second wife, Professor Louise Johnson.

Whatever the merit of speculation relating to hesitation in Pakistan, Abdus Salam was not expected to think twice in making his choice. Invitation or none, he was going to visit home before any other place within a week of picking up the prize. On 10 December 1979, he turned up in Stockholm in the company of his two wives, several children and a selection of close relatives and friends. He walked upon the royal stage by setting aside the European code of dress formally observed on such occasions. Instead, he wore an elegant Pakistani attire, that is,

---

[1] Abdul Hameed (circa 2000): p. 183
[2] The Nation, Lahore, 26 May 1993, p.6

the long black *Sherwani* coat, a white baggy trousers, stoutly starched turban and the pair of handmade *Khussa* shoes; all reminiscent of the Muslim nobility in northern India. In all probability, the robust political animal residing in his makeup, aimed at pleasing the constituency back home. At the same time, his exotic get-up received a much greater share of publicity in Stockholm.

In his brief remarks, made at the Nobel Banquet, he stated that physics was a shared heritage of the mankind. Next, he quoted the Koranic verse just as he had done earlier in his Inaugural address at the Imperial College some 22 years ago. While telecasting the ceremony alive, the state-owned media of Pakistan censored the component of his Koranic recitation because he was not a Muslim. But even if he was not, there was no legal compulsion debarring him from reciting verses from a holy book. What remains a bigger question is if, while doing so, he had the requisite approval from fellow physicists, Sheldon Glashow and Steven Weinberg on whose behalf he spoke.

He travelled to Pakistan where a state itinerary of his engagements, stretching over nine days, awaited him to attend receptions, lunches and dinners hosted to honour him in Islamabad, Peshawar, Lahore, Jhang, Multan and Karachi. He was treated as an official guest travelling on a special helicopter to places where ordinary flights were not available. Amtul Hafeez accompanied him to Pakistan but, as a requirement in *purdah*, she did not turn up in public and mixed gatherings. How was the participation of Louise Johnson held in abeyance remains another mystery. Pakistan, after all, did not have any cultural problem with bigamy. Going out of the way, Ziaul Haq invited Abdus Salam's siblings to attend all state functions hosted by the government. He went to government houses and universities, gave interviews to leading newspapers and the state television and radio broadcasting corporations. Apart from the trivial noise made by a fraction of the right-wing youth, the strategy worked well and the suspicion that Pakistan intended to disown him was dismantled.

In Karachi, the financial hub of Pakistan, he addressed meetings organised by the chamber of commerce and industry, two universities and the local Press Club where he was enrolled as a life-member. On the Pakistan International Airlines flight from Karachi to Multan, the captain announced Abdus Salam's presence aboard and congratulated him for winning the prize; the broadcast must have been a pleasant surprise to Abdus Salam. He tendered autographs to some of the fellow passengers; unable to grab a piece of paper, one of them asked him to do the favour on a hundred-rupee currency note.[1]

At a special convocation convened at the Parliament House in Islamabad, the President of Pakistan conferred the Doctor of Science degree upon Abdus Salam. At a ceremony convened in the President House, the President decorated Abdus Salam with *Nishan-i-Imtiaz* or the Hallmark of Eminence, the highest civil award in Pakistan. When guests had tea, Abdus Salam introduced his brothers to the President. At the state dinner the same evening, the President announced that a replica of the Nobel Prize won by Abdus Salam will be provided to fifteen universities of Pakistan. As a gesture of benevolence, the President lifted the embargo Zulfiqar Bhutto had imposed upon scientists travelling abroad. Ziaul Haq proclaimed the government desire to convert Abdus Salam's family home in Jhang into a national monument. Apparently, Abdus Salam had already given his consent for this purpose though one of his brothers did not wish to give away the family home off the cuff.[2]

His visits to universities in Islamabad and Lahore were steamed up with noise of opposition from the right-wing Wahabi youth of *Jamaat-i-Islami* party. He was not able to visit the university in Islamabad because of a hostage alert. In Lahore, the *Jamaat-i-Islami* youth hurled pieces of broken furniture and rotten old shoes upon him.[3] But he managed to speak urging his audience to strive hard and gain knowledge especially to liberate themselves from the state of inferiority. He expressed his desire to steer clear of everyday political preferences.

Still, there were occasions when Abdus Salam appeared to overstep the lines of Pakistani sensitivity but the General played cool and graciously declined to get drawn in because the government wanted to applaud Abdus Salam, not his Ahmadiyah party.

How long will the Ahmadiyah face religious persecution in Pakistan? Abdus Salam had asked Ziaul Haq when the two met in Rawalpindi in December 1979. Ziaul Haq was known for his cool composure, pleasant disposition and noble manners. He deflected the question by stating that if Abdus Salam was referring to the excommunication, it constituted a judgment handed down by the

---

[1] Abdul Hameed (circa 2000): p. 192
[2] Interviews 1984: Folder I, pp. 2-3, 17
[3] *Aajkal* (a weekly magazine), 7-13 September 1993, p.18

Parliament of Pakistan. Only the Parliament was authorised to change it, the General remarked.

Speechless, Abdus Salam then requested the General to publish the transcript of National Assembly proceedings relating to the cross-examination of Nasir Ahmad. Abdus Salam added that he was making the demand on behalf of the Ahmadiyah caliph. Ziaul Haq replied that publicising those records amounted to lifting the lid on communal hostilities, all over again. Still, he promised, to declassify the documentation as soon as the government felt it was safe to do so.[1]

Was Abdus Salam really supposed to get involved into such sectarian business? Especially at a time when he was on a state visit to celebrate his Nobel Prize in Physics? What was the need for him to play partisan in a shady zone of religious controversy? If the government was not bothered about the vulnerability of his Ahmadiyah connection, he might as well have steered clear of the clutter by leaving it to be handled by those who were actually responsible for piling it up over the decades. After all, he was a scientist, not a religious scholar or a political power broker. If there was an underlined purpose, it remains obscure, out of public sight, because he did not feel the need to offer any explanation. His entitlement to profess the Ahmadiyah faith was an ethical prerogative of personal nature, whereas playing the role of an emissary due to his high public profile constituted political activity.

On 18 December 1979, the proceedings of Convocation Ceremony, convened in the Parliament House of Islamabad to confer Doctor of Science degree on Abdus Salam, were briefly suspended to enable participants who wished to go for late afternoon *Asar* prayer. Ziaul Haq asked Abdus Salam if he would wish to accompany him for the ritual or be on his own. Abdus Salam snubbed the President by stating that he would be doing so separately.[2] Such inflexibility affirmed the obstinacy bluntly displayed by Zafarullah Khan at the funeral service of Mohammed Ali Jinnah, in Karachi, way back in September 1948. In this way, another opportunity in hinting at the desire to prefer accord over malice and to erase in some way the bitter memory of conflict-ridden divisiveness was aborted.

Throughout the course of Abdus Salam's commemorative journey across Pakistan, his Ahmadiyah party did not consider the option to celebrate the prize together with the mainstream, at a national level in some way. On the contrary,

---

[1] Interviews 1984: Folder VII, pp. 109-111, 118-120

[2] Abdul Hameed (circa 2000): p. 197

his arrival in Rabwah to avail an audience with the caliph and then speak before the annual Ahmadiyah congregation remained a strictly local partisan affair.

II

Somehow the plain talking and good mannerism of Ziaul Haq gave Abdus Salam the impression that he might be invited to play a role in the science establishment of Pakistan as had been the case under Ayub Khan. But any hope he nurtured was frustrated by an earth-shaking revolution in the neighbourhood of Pakistan. Almost simultaneously, the pro-western monarchy in Iran was pulled down by an elderly Shia cleric stationed in France, and then a communist take-over of Afghanistan brought the Soviet Red Army to Khyber Pass. Overnight, the semi-rogue state of Pakistan, bent upon manufacturing nuclear weapons, became a darling frontline state to launch jihad against the Soviet Union.

Historically, about the end of 19th century, when England suspected Russia of plotting to gain naval presence in the warm waters of Indian Ocean, the British military garrison besieged in Kabul was massacred. Out of sheer frustration, Alfred Lyall (1835–1911), a senior member of the colonial government, wished for the day when Russians would get themselves trapped in Afghanistan. He described the Afghans as 'treacherous barbarians with whom it was an unfortunate necessity to have any dealings at all'.[1]

Rudyard Kipling (1865–1936) went a step forward, he portrayed Afghan people as the pinnacle of selfish violence. 'To the Afghan, neither life, property, law, nor kingship are sacred when his own lusts prompt him to rebel. He is a thief by instinct, a murderer by heredity and training, and frankly and bestially immoral by all three. Nonetheless he has his own crooked notions of honour, and his character is fascinating to study. On occasions he will fight without reason given till he is hacked in pieces; on other occasions he will refuse to show fight till he is driven into a corner. Herein he is as unaccountable as the grey wolf, who is his blood-brother'. Measured Rudyard Kipling adding that the only

---

[1] Alfred Lyall: The Rise and Expansion of the British Dominion in India, John Murray, London, 1893, p. 236

weapon Afghans understand was 'the fear of death, which among some Orientals is the beginning of wisdom'.[1]

In December 1979, that is, one hundred years later, the somewhat perverse craving of Alfred Lyall was granted when the Red Army moved into Afghanistan. Overnight, the regional scene altered in Southwest Asia, and Afghans were metamorphosed into a loveable assortment of Mujahideen, fondly called the 'Muj' among western diplomats, for they were delighted to serve as human shield against the fire power of the Red Army of a godless Soviet Union.

All of this happened within weeks of the Nobel Prize shared by Abdus Salam. Pakistan was plunged neck-deep into a covert war propped up by hard cash from Saudi Arabia and military logistics off the western alliance headed by the United States. Everything turned upside down. Nobody in Pakistan really had time for anything other than jihad for it provided dollars in this world and *hoors* in the next. Abdus Salam and his ideas to foster science lost touch with political realities of a different kind. In fact, time had arrived to guard those *Wells of Power* the state of Pakistan had been set up to defend.

To the ordinary lot of faithful, Islam enshrined the final and complete code for everyday life, offering key to any amount and variety of questions, from past to present and future. Consequently, a convenient concept of Islamic Science was given birth and it gained considerable currency. With funds made available from Saudi Arabia, a series of so-called Islamic Science conferences were convened in Islamabad. One of those conferences was inaugurated by Ziaul Haq himself. Panel discussion was held on Things Known Only to God, and papers read out on the occasions offered an unlimited range of elucidation from the verses of Koran. Some of the participants went too far. One speaker expressed alarm that heathens intended to use empty copper shells to infiltrate into the paradise. Another, a Pakistani, came out with a formula to compute the level of hypocrisy among human beings. Yet another, worked out Prophet Mohammed's flight to Heavens within the framework of Albert Einstein's Theory of Relativity. As if Muslim countries had run short of eggheads, a German delegate presented his mathematical equation relating to the Angle of God. Then there was a senior employee of the Atomic Energy Commission postulating upon the Universal Transition of Ghosts on Electromagnetic Scale on the Day of Judgment.[2]

---

[1] Rudyard Kipling: Life's Handicap, Macmillan and Co., 1891, p. 256
[2] The Herald (a monthly magazine), Karachi, January 1988, p.102-106

In 1987, Mohammed Muttalib, an academic based in Cairo rejected the concept of gravity by proposing that mountains having roots deeper in the earth controlled the rotation of the globe. Sheikh Abdul Aziz (1910–1999), the Grand Mufti and Head of the Council of Senior Scholars in Saudi Arabia, insisted that the earth was flat and stationary; effectively taking a position the Catholic Church was caught into 350 years ago.

It happened at a time when the total number of science graduates in Muslim countries stood at 45000 mark compared to 36000 scientists in the tiny state of Israel alone. On the average, in 1988, Pakistan produced fourteen doctoral scholars a year compared to 3000 in India and 5000 in Britain for the same timeframe. In their numerical strength, Pakistani scientists engaged in research and development were one tenth of their counterpart in Israel, a country with twenty times smaller size of population.[1]

Rather gloomily, the question being raised in Pakistan was if the country really needed doctoral scholars in advanced disciplines of science? In the summer of 1986, during the course of a job interview at one of the reputed universities in Islamabad, a female candidate contesting for the position of Assistant Professor in Molecular Genetics was asked to speak out the names of Prophet Mohammed's wives. For a moment, the candidate, Dr Khalida Sultana, suspected there had been an administrative mix up and went on to explain that her area of expertise had nothing directly to do with early Islamic history. She might have been referred to another selection panel due to some administrative mix-up, she suspected. She was reminded that all selection panels, for science or else, were required to have a cleric aboard to verify the Islamic competence and credentials of candidates. Amazed, Dr Khalida Sultana declined to field the question; it was totally inappropriate from her professional point of view. Someone on the selection panel invited her to speak out a few names if not all. 'Sure, I can give you a few names from memory. But I shall not because there is a principle involved here'. She replied. Why was she sent abroad to study Molecular Genetics in the first place? She pondered for months on before making up her mind to apply for migration to Australia.

Ziaul Haq did pay tribute to Abdus Salam but that was the best he could do. Any rehabilitation of the Nobel Prize winner was not forthcoming, it just could not happen. Upon his occasional journey home, Abdus Salam did receive the due share of deference but nobody among the powerful and influential had time to

---

[1] Dawn, Karachi, 14 October 1988, Friday Magazine, p. ii

consider proposals he made. In fact, nobody had time to consider the worth of Abdus Salam's recipes for progress and technology. Why would, in the first place, people listen to someone who had no faith in militant jihad? As a Nobel Laureate and renowned scientist he was welcome to deliver speeches anytime anywhere, including the elitist National Defence College and Pakistan Ordinance Factories, but when it settled down to some degree of practical involvement, his Ahmadiyah stereotype provided sufficient reason for casting him out. In 1982, Abdus Salam is reported to have offered Ziaul Haq his services for the country, the General promised to return with a project in one year but then there was no news.

Whatever little contact existed between the two it came to a halt in 1985, after the promulgation of anti-Ahmadiyah Prohibition Ordinance. In order to appease clerics, patronising jihad in Afghanistan, Ziaul Haq barred the Ahmadiyah from profession and observance of Islamic faith and rituals; the Presidential Ordinance amended the Penal Code suitably. For example, offering of prayer in the Islamic way became an offence for the Ahmadiyah. Because the new legislation did not prescribe an alternate or acceptable mode of worship, and unless some new method for this purpose was agreed upon, the Ahmadiyah faced the deadly choice to either defy God or the law of the land. When Abdus Salam quoted from the Koran, he was annoying the Muslim mainstream as well as violating the law. By the end of 1984, he sounded exceedingly bitter and jittery; as if the talisman he had carried in vault worked only in the direction of Nobel Prize. In a fit of resentment, he ridiculed the Objectives Resolution, adopted by the Constituent Assembly of Pakistan in 1949. He suspected that the resolution amounted to the appointment God as the Viceroy of Pakistan. He proclaimed his homeland as the most intolerant society on earth. How could a bunch of clerics keep him from obeying the Koran? How come a small minority like the Ahmadiyah posed any serious threat to the majority of Muslims? He asked Ziaul Haq. Once again, the General was unflustered. He argued that those who attached wrong motives with words of holy book were bound to irritate the mainstream.

Actually, it was Abdus Salam, and not Ziaul Haq, who seemed to have lost touch with reality. He was required to study the theological history of Pakistan rather closely. His favourite role-model, Zafarullah Khan, would never miss the opportunity in pleading the merger of religion and politics.

Frustrated, Abdus Salam tended to prefer the facade of Indian secularism over that of outright religious bigotry in Pakistan. Can they make me the

President of Pakistan for cosmetic purpose? He asked out of bitterness. Once again, he sounded unaware of what awaited India in a matter of few years. On his part, Ziaul Haq responded only to the geopolitical compulsions surrounding his government. He did not wish to recall Abdus Salam back into the inner sanctum of Pakistan's top management overseeing the manufacture of nuclear weapons. At the same time, he did not have any problem with Abdus Salam's close friendship with Munir Khan, the Chairman of Atomic Energy Commission.

Had Abdus Salam struck a judicious balance between his Ahmadiyah faith and the religious preferences of Sunni-Wahabi mainstream in Pakistan, he was likely to win a much greater amount of support. He did his best to secure the image of a science campaigner but the exertion was flawed with his excessive advocacy of Ahmadiyah causes. He was marginalised, condemned to loneliness in the final years of his life.

Ziaul Haq presided over a Pakistan propped up by hard cash from Saudi Arabia and military logistics from the United States at a time when the Red Army was trapped in Afghanistan. Jihad against godless communism offered lucrative employment in dollars. With world attention focused upon the show down with the Soviet Union, Pakistan advanced to conclude its nuclear weapons program. A remarkable success was achieved on both fronts. But then, apparently out of nowhere in August 1988, Ziaul Haq perished in a mysterious air crash south of Multan. His departure in such violent manner was a cause of celebration for the Ahmadiyah. Like Zulfiqar Bhutto, he was assessed to be the prey of a prophecy foretold in the *Mubahila* challenge issued to him by Tahir Ahmad. Whatever the merit of Ahmadiyah merriment, the Pakistan Ziaul Haq left behind presented a ghastly example in religious narrow-mindedness much sharper than the one fashioned by Zulfiqar Bhutto. All hopes of the reedy secular liberal ideologues, looking forward to the dawn of enlightenment, were dashed as the state continued its march into intolerance and obscurantism.

Once the Soviet Union, posing threat to *Wells of Power*, was perceived to have been sorted out, mauled and battered; the United States and its western allies pulled out of the region rather thoughtlessly leaving Afghanistan on its own to fix the aftermath of jihad. This shrug of arrogance was a typical reminder of the manner in which the British had deserted the Indian subcontinent in the wake of World War II. Overnight, the Americans appeared to behave as if none tidying up whatsoever was essential. All suppliers, contractors and experts zipped up their bags and departed.

Pakistan, dumped yet again, confronted the consequences of a bloody war of attrition and the power vacuum next door. On an ethical scale, Afghanistan was no less than the post-war Europe in need of a Marshall Plan (1948) for recovery and rehabilitation. Did the tribal leadership of the Mujahideen fare intellectually better compared to post-Nazi Germans? How was the financial infrastructure, public and civic services, education, health and safety of women going to work? Like the childhood of Pakistan, the quick and easy answer came in the single stroke of Shariah and Koranic Law. If the Mujahideen could defeat the Red Army, they were capable of pulling out other miracles.

How the mighty empire of Soviet Union was actually defeated? More than anything else, the Mujahideen and their sponsors in Pakistan army believed, the war in Afghanistan had been fought and won with Muslim blood; there was the feeling that the United States and its western allies were blatantly opportunistic in the end. Once the Red Army was defeated in Afghanistan, there was perhaps the expectation to set the Mujahideen upon China. Not only the desire turned out to be gravely wishful, the west landed itself into the trap that had been originally cast for the Russians. It took the United States and its allies two decades and over four trillion dollars before pulling themselves out of their post September 2001 involvement in Afghanistan.

III

Many great scientists tend to slow down after winning the prize, others scale down the size of their work to take superannuation. Abdus Salam was in no mood to do any of the two. Ideally, he might have considered purchasing a farm house outside Oxford for retirement into a relaxed lifestyle around reading and walking. It was never a big deal for him to find ideal privacy with his children, grandchildren, siblings, nephews, nieces and close friends; at his convenience and pleasure. He had waited for the prize for more than two decades and had been obsessed with getting it. His father had been tirelessly praying for him to win it, the Ahmadiyah elders assuring him with their prophetic visions, and what not. Finally, when the prize arrived, it was viewed to have been earned on professional merit as well as the unseen forces of spirituality. He had all the justification to retire in comfort.

Instead, he fixed an ambitious gaze upon high-profile international roles like the leadership of the United Nations Educational, Scientific and Cultural

Organisation (UNESCO). Election for the position of UNESCO Director General was scheduled in 1987. His visits home picked up momentum to secure sponsorship from Pakistan, the slayer of the Soviet Union.

Some experts held the view that as an Asian candidate, along with his powerful academic credentials, he stood fairly good chances of winning the chair. One influential newspaper in Pakistan paid him the tribute of being an embodiment of the organisation in his own right.[1] Because the United States and some of its allies had pulled out of UNESCO, Abdus Salam was expected to restore the standing of the organisation. Also there was the hope that China and India might not object to his candidacy. But the Government of Pakistan had other ideas. Abdus Salam's candidacy was pre-empted by the promotion of Foreign Minister Yaqub Khan (1920–2016) for the job. Undoubtedly, Yaqub Khan commanded the image of a principled man. Having come from the old royal family of Bhopal in Central India, he was a brilliant linguist who was famed to have read the original unabridged Russian-language version of Leo Tolstoy's *War and Peace*. As commander of Pakistan army in the former East Wing he had declined to order military action against unarmed civilians. After leaving the army, he had served ambassadorial positions in Washington, Moscow and Paris. He had been the longest serving foreign minister of Pakistan. But even though he made an extraordinary candidate, his chances of winning fell short of Abdus Salam. Failing to win the nomination, Abdus Salam pulled out of the race.[2] According to one source, the decision to withdraw was influenced by his failing health.[3]

A Pakistani newspaper speculated that Abdus Salam was prepared to revoke his Pakistani citizenship in return for the sake of nomination from a group of other countries including Britain. He filed a libel case against the paper which ended up apologising publicly beside 'contributing' a symbolic sum of £500 to the Amnesty International in the process of settlement.[4]

In the meantime, Abdus Salam kept himself occupied with some of his favourite pastime. For example, he proposed the setting up of a Third World Academy Sciences. Scientists from Asia, Africa and Latin America met in Rome

---

[1] The Frontier Post, Peshawar, 2 September 1987, p.4

[2] In 1981, he made it to the agency in some little way by getting elected as Chairman of the agency's Panel on Science, Technology and Society.

[3] *Al Nahl* (Fall 1997): p. 148 [re. Michael Duff]

[4] The Herald, Karachi, September 1987, p.61-62

to draft a charter for the academy, and soon the idea was supported by the United Nations and it was formally launched by Secretary General Javier Perez de Cuellar (1920–2020) in July 1985. Abdus Salam visited China twice, in 1987 and 1988, to preside over the general sessions of the academy which awarded 1000 grants for research besides sponsoring 400 fellowships within the developing countries by 1994.[1]

In 1988, he went on to set up a Third World Network of Scientific Organisations to coordinate efforts aimed at gaining a greater share of resource allocation for science and technology, and to build up a data base of notable institutions operating in the developing countries. In 1990, he proposed the creation of a Commission on Science and Technology for Sustainable Development in the South. Carried away by the popularity of international women movement, and still going strong with his fondness for creating institutions, he went on to create the Third World Organisation for Women in Science by enlisting the support of 1200 women scientists from developing countries. Next, he urged the rich countries to spend money on development projects in the Third World rather than offering tax cuts to the affluent.[2]

At the end of the day, however, the message he received from Pakistan was loud and clear and Abdus Salam had to give up on the dream to stage any befitting comeback. His last public appearance in Pakistan was in Lahore where, in February 1988, he came to deliver the Faiz Memorial Lecture on Science and the Universe. Faiz Ahmed Faiz (1911–1984), a winner of the Lenin Prize and an erstwhile member of the Communist Party of Pakistan, was widely known for his revolutionary verses. Abdus Salam repeated his call for adoption of scientific attitude as a matter of lifestyle. Had there been no contact between nuclear and electromagnetic forces, he reflected, there might be no hydrogen, no water, no life as it appeared on the earth. He pleaded that the only route to altering the lot of people in Pakistan passed through science and technology. He reminded his audience that at least twelve percent of the Koranic message called for acquisition of knowledge. Keeping with the spirit of Koran, he asked the government to spend a matching twelve percent of national income on research and development. He remembered his science teacher in Jhang who had once told the class that electricity was available in Lahore and nuclear energy in Europe. 'Call me heretical or what you will, my objective is to build a future for

---

[1] The News, Rawalpindi, 4 October 1994, p.6

[2] The Nation, Lahore, 4 March 1988, Friday Magazine, p.2-3

our children. For heaven's sake, put me to work as you would a non-Muslim mason in the construction of a mosque'. He stated by alluding to an earlier plea of the 19th century Muslim reformist Syed Ahmed Khan.[1]

But as he went public in expressing his desire to return home, a newspaper commented, rather sarcastically, that no one had ever stopped him from doing so. He was reminded that his dissociation with Pakistan reflected his defiance to the popular verdict against the Ahmadiyah. As such, the newspaper wanted him to make up his mind first; whether he intended to comply with the religion of Mohammed or with that of Ghulam Ahmed? He was not indispensable anymore, the paper taunted with an obvious reference to Pakistan's success in going nuclear.[2]

About the same time, the Chief Minister of Punjab spoke of great people produced by Lahore's Government College. Rather remarkably, Abdus Salam missed out on the list.[3] He did not exist for the Chief Minister just as *Heer*, the greatest heroin of folklore in Punjab, was not mentioned among the names of prominent historical figures Abdul Hameed had catalogued to the credit of Jhang.

Ageing, he wanted to return home; his heart pounded at the thought. But it looked like as if he would never be able to do so. Abdus Salam lamented in May 1989. What had he valued most in life? Someone asked him. First there was science, and then the desire to get Pakistan and Muslims lined up for the same. He replied as his health showed signs of weakness. He held on to himself with the support of a walking stick. From Ayub Khan to Ziaul Haq, he observed, the leadership of Pakistan cheated him by only talking rather than acting.[4]

IV

About the end of May 1993, Abdus Salam suffered a fall in Oxford sparking off rumours about his health. His family confirmed that he had not been keeping well and that the process of his recovery had been slow. Another report, a few days later, suggested that he was hospitalised in Italy due to a stroke. He was suspected to be suffering from the rare Steel Richardson Syndrome or

---

[1] Daily *Jang*, Lahore, 28 February 1988, p.1
[2] Daily New-i-Waqt, Rawalpindi, 25 May 1989, Editorial note.
[3] The News, Rawalpindi, 29 January 1996, p.6
[4] The Nation, Lahore, 26 May 1989, Friday Magazine, p.2-3

Progressive Supranuclear Palsy, a neurological condition giving only a few years to the life to its victims. About 400 people were estimated to be suffering from this condition in England by the close of 20th century. Abdus Salam's son, Ahmed Salam, explained that his father was mentally alert but physically restricted.[1] In March 1996, Abdus Salam himself confirmed that he suffered from a 'disease which essentially leaves the brain functioning perfectly but slowly destroys the body's physical responses'.[2] An information relating to the deterioration of his health trickled in Pakistan through 'Letters to the Editor' in local newspapers. One of the papers carried a picture of his meeting with Prime Minister Nawaz Sharif who then happened to be visiting England. Abdus Salam sat on the wheel-chair and his face appeared to have been overtaken by age at a much faster speed. It is hard to guess why did he continue calling on those who only listened him rather than acting on his advice.

Prime Minister Benazir Bhutto, as she played the game of musical chairs with Nawaz Sharif, wrote to Abdus Salam expressing concern over his disposition. 'This country owes a permanent debt of gratitude for the many services' rendered by him and the great honour he had brought to Pakistan. 'It will be a pleasure, as indeed, a source of satisfaction, for the people and the Government of Pakistan to be of any service to you'. She wrote in July 1994.[3] Her letter was released to the media. According to another report, the prime minister approved the proposal for Government of Pakistan to bear the expenses of Abdus Salam's treatment by a board of medical experts in London.[4] But then fearing the clerics, in 1995, her government declined to name after him a centre proposed for Physics.[5] Personally, she would never forget how sharply he had reacted to her message of congratulation in 1979.

Reacting rather brusquely, Abdus Salam rejected Benazir Bhutto's contention about the expenses of his treatment. His wife, Louise Johnson, was quoted as saying that in fact he had been disturbed by such reports in the media. He did not wish to utilise 'valuable resources' of Pakistan to be spent on his treatment. Only a miracle could bring him relief, his wife remarked. Abdus Salam went on to state that God almighty had granted him sufficient resources

---

[1] Daily *Jang*, Rawalpindi, 8 October 1995, p.8

[2] Dawn, Karachi, 14 March 1996, p.3

[3] The Pakistan Times, Islamabad, 7 July 1994, p.3

[4] Daily Pakistan, Islamabad, 9 August 1994, p.12

[5] The News, Rawalpindi, 29 January 1996, p.6

to ensure very best medical care. He proposed that 'any resources ear-marked for his treatment should instead be directed toward an educational or research project in Pakistan'.[1]

Gul Gee, a prominent painter of Pakistan, travelled to London to draw seven sketches of Abdus Salam. He described his model as 'the grandeur of tall columns in a ruin' and a site where the artist could see both life and death at the same time.[2]

As if the countdown to the hour of departure had begun. In September 1993, Abdus Salam took retirement, simultaneously from the International Centre for Theoretical Physics in Trieste and Imperial College in London. His last major appointment with his circle of family and close friends happened in the winter of 1994, in London, at the wedding reception of his elder son, Ahmed Salam. He held the hand of an old friend, Zafar Chaudhry, and remembered in a muffled voice the bygone days the two had spent together in Lahore's Government College some fifty years ago.[3]

Most of the time from 1995 onwards, Abdus Salam lived in increased isolation, listening to the sound track of Koranic recitation.[4] Back in Pakistan, his birthday was celebrated by physicists who wished him well by way of formal gatherings as well as through Letters to the Editor columns in local newspapers. There was the proposal to release a commemorative postal stamp to mark the occasion but the wish was granted many years after his death. As always, those celebrations were haunted by the anti-Ahmadiyah groups who would not give up on condemning his 'blasphemous belief'. One of the detractors vowed that Abdus Salam was not welcome in Pakistan due to his 'passive role' in the development of country's nuclear program.[5]

On 21 November 1996, Abdus Salam died in Oxford, England. His mortal remains, as he had wished, were flown to Pakistan for burial in Rabwah, not very far from the sun burnt country town, Jhang, where his father had envisioned him coming some seventy years ago.

---

[1] Dawn, Karachi, 22 September 1994, p.10
[2] The News, Rawalpindi, 5 October 1994, p.2
[3] The Friday Times, Lahore, 3 July 1996
[4] The Muslim, Islamabad, 18 January 1996, p.6
[5] The Frontier Post, Peshawar, 15 February 1996, p.7

Chapter Eleven
Pastime Jumble

In 1975, a Swedish newspaper referred to Abdus Salam as the modern-day version of Albert Einstein.[1] On his part, Abdus Salam was very fond of Paul Dirac among his peers in Physics, from Werner Heisenberg and Wolfgang Pauli to Nicholas Kemmer, Freeman Dyson and Hans Bethe. He tended to place Paul Dirac above Albert Einstein and wished the former had continued working on for a while more instead of taking early retirement.

Between the two, both Abdus Salam and Paul Dirac bore striking similarities as well as pronounced variance. Rising from a relatively modest origin, the two had made it to the top en route Mathematics; both held multi-lingual proficiency. Paul Dirac had an unassuming personality; he loathed worldly riches like money, power and fame. Abdus Salam donated the money accompanying the awards won by him over to study grants and educational causes. Paul Dirac was not keen on fame; he was known to have nearly declined the Nobel Prize but then came around fearing greater fuss of publicity associated with a refusal. This was where the two began to diverge. Paul Dirac was an established sceptic as opposed to Abdus Salam's religious zeal. When Paul Dirac aspired to steer clear of fame and power, Abdus Salam had developed an obsession with winning the Nobel Prize, especially after his close brush with it in 1957.

In his academic journey from Jhang to Cambridge, Abdus Salam had witnessed the favourable linkage between merit and political clout; it was not easy for him to pass over the pragmatic value attached to centres of power. On a number of occasions in his life, when suitable pathways unbolted before him, he traced the blessing back to the prayers of his parents and elders. This grand fusion of merit, luck and faith was a hallmark of his life offering valuable insight into his occupation with Theoretical Physics, Pakistan and the Ahmadiyah.

---

[1] Trieste Tribute (1997): p. 41

For over forty years, the best part of Abdus Salam's time was consumed in teaching, research, reading, writing, seminars, tutorials, administration, meetings, conferences and travelling for work. He had hardly much space left for affairs and events other than physics. Still, Pakistan remained a matter of political affection for him. In a way, both his career in physics and the recently born state of Pakistan fell in the same age group.

His fondness of Pakistan was destined to crash-land in let-down and disappointment. It is worthwhile to note that in the earlier stages of his life, Abdus Salam did not betray any extraordinary signs of religiosity. He had been a believer of the moderate kind who would not go as far as holding an office in the Ahmadiyah party organisation. Given his lifestyle fused into demands of work in London and Trieste, involving a great deal of boarding and disembarking flights from one location to next and back, it was not possible for him to turn up in the mosque five times a day. Perhaps the closest he came was in Cambridge where he led the Friday afternoon congregational of Muslim Student Federation.[1] He also had a *mussal'ah* designated for this purpose in Trieste.

But then he began changing after the death of his father in 1969. 'I was as far as possible regular in prayers since childhood but reciting of Koran and prayers became important and meaningful part of my life in the real sense rather late, probably after my father's death. During his life one might be doing it as a responsibility laid out by him but after his death it became my personal responsibility. Now I read the Koran to understand it. This year I have so far finished it twice'. He stated in 1984.[2]

Historically, the birth of a political animal in the personality of Abdus Salam could be traced back to his arrival in Government College. Lahore exposed him to a world far ahead of his youthful experiences gathered in Jhang and Multan. Landing in Lahore at the age of 14, he found himself more than one hundred miles away from the razor-sharp gaze of his father. Suddenly, He was on his own. In the beginning, he was known as a shy country lad hardly noticed beyond classroom, library and hostel. It was hard to approach him because of the flabby padlock dangling on the door of his hostel room. Hardly any of the residents knew that it was actually an arrangement he had made with a college employee

---

[1] Princess Dina Bint Abdul Hameed (1929- 2019), the Queen of Jordan, as mentioned earlier, was one of the devotees in the congregation.

[2] Interviews 1984: Folder I, p. 39

to keep himself locked in and study for hours on without interruption and disturbance.

It did not take long for this rigorous drill of seclusion to blow up, his academic fame and toppling of existing records shoved him to the forefront academic popularity. In a couple of years, he discovered that his ease with Mathematics gave him the edge over others. His invincibility in holding the lead gave him confidence.[1] He joined the Boat Club for rowing at *Ravi*, became a member of the debating society, played chess in the Common Room, occasionally went out to watch a movie; and there was even a bit of infatuation with the cute daughter of the College Principal. He served as the editor of both English and Urdu language editions of the college magazine *Ravi*, and then he went on to win the students union leadership. It was not an ordinary feat to ride the crest of electoral popularity at a time when social scene in Punjab raged with communal tension among Hindu, Muslim and Sikh communities.

Out of his brief stint with student politics, Abdus Salam did not forget two occasions, both off 1946. First, when students demanded postponement of annual examinations; he regretted later because it amounted to corrupting the academic calendar. Next, it was a moment of honour when, as a member of the students' delegation in Lahore, he went to call on Mohammed Ali Jinnah. Abdus Salam stated he felt carried away by the demand for Pakistan.[2]

When independence came, he was in England sharing only from a distance the tragic tales of mass exodus, murder, rape and mayhem triggered by the tactless act of partition. He heard tales of political mismanagement accompanying the creation of a truncated moth-eaten Pakistan. His dedication to Pakistan was reinforced in the wake of unfinished political agenda the British were perceived to have left behind in the subcontinent rather mischievously, from the hastily drawing of international boundary line to a complete mess over distribution of assets and the accession of princely states.

In 1955, the invitation to attend the United Nations sponsored Atoms for Peace Conference, provided Abdus Salam his first big opportunity to appear on the national scene. Chaudhri Mohamed Ali was the first among Pakistani leaders who encouraged Abdus Salam to step forward and participate in the commencement of country's journey into nuclear age.

---

[1] Trieste Tribute (1997): p. 48
[2] Interviews 1984: Folder IV, pp. 52-53

Chaudhri Mohamed Ali had held masters in Chemistry, and he had taught the subject at a college in Lahore. His son, Javed Akhtar, who studied in Lahore's Government College in 1952, used to receive coaching from Abdus Salam. But the excitement triggered by the Atoms for Peace conference fizzled out soon when Chaudhri Mohamed Ali was stabbed in the back by his own ruling party colleagues. On his part, Abdus Salam hung on for a while. He hoped to strike a suitable employment deal with the Atomic Energy Commission of Pakistan provided freedom was granted to him to travel abroad for research. He did not wish to be caught in bureaucratic battles of the kind experienced with Sirajuddin Ahmed. Nothing happened until he found the Chair in London.

On a private visit to London in the summer of 1957, the proprietor of the *Pakistan Times*, Mohammed Iftikharuddin, was overwhelmed to witness Abdus Salam serving the Chair of Mathematics in Imperial College. Upon returning home, he directed the newspaper to run a detailed supplement on Abdus Salam's academic victory in England. In other words, the ground for his reclamation back home was well prepared by the time General Ayub Khan staged the military coup. Almost instantly after taking over, Ayub Khan invited Abdus Salam to start offering technical advice to the military government. Although more formal arrangements were made later, the choice made by Ayub Khan marked the commencement of Abdus Salam's unbroken service as science adviser to two-and-a-half martial law administrators for 14 years in a row.

In his advisory role, he reported to the head of the government. He was not accorded the status of a minister and, strangely enough, none bureaucratic paraphernalia whatsoever supported him. No office space, staff, stationery and equipment was allocated to him. He was not granted any budget or cost centre, not even a position description outlining expectations attached to his role. In other words, the term Science Adviser was purely a nominal and ceremonial title.[1] Such a wobbly arrangement, in the end, suited seasoned bureaucrats surrounding Ayub Khan for they always had one or another excuse to ignore, bypass and find flaws in the advice Abdus Salam would offer. According to one federal secretary, Abdus Salam's employment and residence abroad, coupled with lack of any structure or audit of his role so close to the President, posed a national security risk.[2]

---

[1] Interviews 1984: FVI, pp. 81-86 and FVII, pp. 64-69
[2] Interviews 1984 (Off the Record): FVII, p. 77

At the very outset of his role as adviser, Abdus Salam proposed the name of Ishrat Usmani as the Chairman of Atomic Energy Commission to replace the incumbent, Nazir Ahmad, who was about to retire. Ayub Khan agreed and, at the same time, asked Abdus Salam to become a member of the commission, a position the latter held up until his dissociation from the Government of Pakistan in September 1974. In fact, this was the only regular position Abdus Salam held to claim travel and accommodation expenses along with an official record of his professional input.

Apparently, the advice Abdus Salam offered Ayub Khan was more or less random, haphazard, intermittent and patchy; depending largely upon the shape of a suitable break. Generally, Abdus Salam was free to float proposals he deemed valuable. It was, for example, his idea to explore feasibility for addressing the curse of soil salinity eating vast tracts of agricultural land in western Pakistan. But no practicable solution was found despite field studies and ambitious proposals forwarded by American experts. On another occasion, Abdus Salam convinced Ayub Khan to take lead over India by launching a small rocket, once again, with technical assistance from the United States. In order to purchase necessary equipment and meet other expenses, Abdus Salam was appointed as the co-chairman of the Space and Upper Atmosphere Research Commission, with Ishrat Usmani. In between, Abdus Salam attempted at winning Ayub Khan over to launch electronic technology in Pakistan before it was too late. Often, he was quite keen to promote the case for reactor technology and Uranium enrichment *before* the inevitable sanctions.

Since Abdus Salam was perceived to enjoy direct access to Ayub Khan, many science organisations in Pakistan looked toward him for grants. As such, he was invited every now and then to preside over science related functions and meetings. He utilised such occasions to call for popularisation of science and research as the shortest route to economic development and national affluence.

In March 1969, Ayub Khan resigned to clear the deck for General Yahya Khan who simply inherited Abdus Salam as a baggage of the previous regime. Very soon, Yahya Khan got trapped in a hideous military operation in the eastern wing of Pakistan. There was not much for Abdus Salam to deliver other than turning up to attend the meetings of the Atomic Energy Commission. Still, he managed to get a hefty grant of ten million rupees in favour of the National Science Foundation from Muzaffar Ahmad, a prominent member of the Ahmadiyah community who served as the *de facto* prime minister of Yahya

Khan. On a subsequent visit to Pakistan, Abdus Salam forwarded yet another of his proposals for research and development. He blended the scheme with national security challenges threatening Pakistan.

By the end of 1972 Pakistan was squarely shamed and humiliated in its war against the coalition of Indian armed forces and freedom fighters demanding the creation of Bangladesh. Yahya Khan was ditched to pave the way for Zulfiqar Bhutto, the first ever martial law administrator Pakistan had without a rank and stars. Abdus Salam did not mind being conveniently passed on to the third martial law administrator in a row. He continued playing the open-ended role despite his knowledge of the temper characterising Zulfiqar Bhutto. Abdus Salam hung on even when Zulfiqar Bhutto expected him to work closely with Munir Khan to make the nuclear bomb for Pakistan. In bid to demonstrate as to who was calling the shots, Zulfiqar Bhutto slashed the grant Abdus Salam had won for National Science Foundation from Muzaffar Ahmad. As if nothing had changed and business was usual, Abdus Salam did not express any signs of discord, he just continued to hold on to the ambiguous position. In this way, Abdus Salam served the martial law and semi-martial law regimes headed by Ayub Khan, Yahya Khan and Zulfiqar Bhutto for fourteen years. He was with them without any remuneration, office space, support staff, budgetary allocations and departmental accountability. A fleeting audit of this formless and imprecise working bond earned him a mixed bag of profit and loss.

His advice to get Ishrat Usmani appointed as the Chairman of Pakistan Atomic Energy Commission proved successful beyond expectations. Both Ishrat Usmani and Abdus Salam supervised the upbringing of a 'critical mass' of professionally dedicated community of scientists in Pakistan. It was the foundation laid out by the two of them upon which the 'truncated and moth-eaten state of Pakistan' was able to gain nuclear parity with India.

Next to the nuclear achievement, Abdus Salam also gets credit for the space rocket Pakistan fired ahead of India, in June 1962; the day Ayub Khan lifted martial law to wear the civilian garb. Like the nuclear capability, it was more of a defence project serving the purpose of useful radar during the 1965 war with India.[1] Similarly, Abdus Salam attempted at bringing Ayub Khan around to setting up an electronic industry. He is understood to have argued that a sound base of expertise in electronics ensured entry into the missile age.

---

[1] Interviews 1984: Folder VI, pp. 70-81

His attitude to paint proposals with demands of national security reflected the militaristic compulsions of the state in Pakistan. He was obliged to lubricate his proposals with political requirements of the day. For example, his temptation to find a solution of salinity amounted to unfolding a business opportunity before the Americans. No homework was done over costs involved; Pakistan just could not afford the recipe. Consequently, the ambitious scheme flopped without bearing any fruit. Often he was perceived to skirt the bureaucratic ring around the President and make the debut from above. Naturally, the senior bureaucrats resisted him. Having lived and worked in the west, he should have been cautious about risks involved in bypassing the standard protocols and procedures surrounding the President.

There were occasions when Abdus Salam was caught off the guard. He asked Ayub Khan to appoint the former prime minister, Chaudhri Mohamed Ali, as the chairman of the Science Commission without checking the proposal with the latter. Ayub Khan agreed but Chaudhri Mohamed Ali declined to play the second fiddle with the army. Likewise was the case with those ten million rupees, Muzaffar Ahmad had allocated for National Science Foundation. Had the sanction been formally routed through departmental policies and procedures, it should not have been easy for Zulfiqar Bhutto to axe it.

Serving suitable military regimes was not a big deal during the Cold War. Abdus Salam might have escaped the undesirable tag if he had bailed himself out in time. But he continued to uphold the role even when General Yahya Khan unleashed a merciless military operation in the eastern wing of Pakistan. He did not speak up, betray any visible signs of protest by distancing him from the regime responsible for the ruthless killing and maiming of unarmed citizens demanding the creation of a free Bangladesh. His colleagues in the west would not have buried their heads in sand on such a revolting occasion.

In fact, his failure to dissociate himself from the criminal conduct of Pakistan's armed forces stationed in the erstwhile East Pakistan was strikingly pronounced only three years later. In 1974, he was infuriated at the treatment of his Ahmadiyah community in Pakistan. First, he dispatched strong notes of protest and then snapped his ties with the Government of Pakistan without losing much time. He did not bother to take into account the fact that the excommunication of the Ahmadiyah had been delivered by an elected parliament. Had he taken the military junta of Yahya Khan to task for the massacre in East Pakistan, his protest over the plight of the Ahmadiyah was bound to carry a good deal of value. In this way, the silence on one and the zealous rejection of the other illustrated a glaring example in selective objectivity.

For some reason Abdus Salam continued to serve Zulfiqar Bhutto who had gone public, as early as January 1972, in his desire to make the nuclear bomb and by mocking at Abdus Salam. It remains unclear as to where exactly did Abdus Salam stand on the principle of non-proliferation, especially in a context of regional power balance in South Asia. He began raising the alarm about India's ambition to gain nuclear hegemony much before Zulfiqar Bhutto's well-known catchphrase of eating the grass to make the bomb. It was way back in 1956 when the Rawalpindi-based Urdu-language newspaper, *Kohistan,* quoted Abdus Salam urging Pakistan to be watchful about India's nuclear ambition.

Occasionally, Abdus Salam would express his displeasure that governments in Pakistan did not care much about his advice. Why did he serve them, one after another? His dithering relationship with the Government of Pakistan was blown up only after the fate of the Ahmadiyah was sealed through an act of the parliament. Is it possible to assume then that business for him might have been as usual if the excommunication of the Ahmadiyah had not happened?

II

In the beginning, Abdus Salam's ownership of Pakistan was driven by the desire to serve and payback in return for those scholarship grants and sabbaticals he had received from his poverty-stricken homeland. At the same time, he ended up winning the International Centre for Theoretical Physics from the diplomatic forum and logistical support provided by Pakistan. Presiding over the centre, a 'clearing house' of ideas shared by younger physicists from all over the world, he enjoyed a high-ranking influential role for three decades.

Ideologically, Abdus Salam held the view that science and research paved the pathway to prosperity. Due to his own financial circumstances, it was not easy for him to campaign by himself alone. He availed the opportunity when it formally came his way riding on the crest of military coup staged by Ayub Khan. His full-time work in London did not permit him to go beyond a certain level of presence in Pakistan. Other than his membership of the Atomic Energy Commission, for which he was duly qualified as a world class physicist, his role as presidential adviser remained undefined, unbinding and sporadic; marked with bureaucratic bickering most of the time.

It was never difficult for him to get rid of the role but he hung on to it in the ugly face of military action in eastern Pakistan, and more so even when Zulfiqar Bhutto stood up to make the bomb. Having lost the opportunity twice to quit, Abdus Salam did not waste time to break out in 1974 when the Parliament of Pakistan expelled his Ahmadiyah community from the pale of Islam. Almost instantly, he dissociated himself from the Government of Pakistan. In a tersely worded letter to Zulfiqar Bhutto, he quit both his advisory role as well as the membership of the Atomic Energy Commission. In other words, in a Muslim country with population then exceeding the 100 million mark, Abdus Salam came out openly in support of a schismatic minority comprising of some 300,000 members at best.[1] His isolation was further highlighted ten years later when, according to an influential newspaper, the figure of the Ahmadiyah membership got reduced to 150,000 and he was perceived to be siding with the 0.1% of the population.[2] Even though he stood up for a principle, his isolation was strikingly gigantic in view of the democratic value attached to numbers. Then, rather curiously, he did not mind working for military regimes, including the one committing crimes against humanity, and the other declaring to manufacture the atom bomb; but any popular incursion of his religious belief was not acceptable to him.

Ditching the Government of Pakistan for the sake of his religious belief manifested the inauguration of a new stage in the life of Abdus Salam. He would bravely face the consequences of it the rest of his life. Ironically, the government handing down the judgment of excommunication had been elected to power by the all-out support of the Ahmadiyah.

One of the reasons behind Abdus Salam's devotion to the Ahmadiyah was exactly the same as the one he professed in support of his affection for Pakistan. As a student, he had benefitted from scholarship grants provided by the Ahmadiyah. Given the financial resources of his parents, he attached great value to those grants.[3] His father comforted him to fill the gap somehow if those grants

---

[1] Spencer Lavan (1974): p. 1
[2] Daily Jang, Lahore, 12 July 1984, p.4
[3] Mohammed Hussein (1974): p. 44

were not forthcoming. 'I don't think he could have. How could I ever get education in Lahore but for those scholarship grants'? He acknowledged.[1]

He was, in this way, indebted to both the Ahmadiyah as well as Pakistan for supporting his education in a time of dire need. Apparently, the course of events unfolding in the Pakistan of 1974 stunned him. Left on his own, he did not mind quitting partially while retaining membership of the Atomic Energy Commission. Finally, he caved in to cast off both under the pressure exerted by Zafarullah Khan and felt relieved soon afterwards.[2]

Such a profound display of loyalty with the Ahmadiyah, a highly organised and tightly knit cult-like religious fraternity, reveals one of the rare aspects of Abdus Salam's life outside Physics. Logically, the deep attachment with the Ahmadiyah could be traced back to his upbringing. But how the robust stock of his devotion was preserved over the years and decades, throughout the expedition of discovery in Theoretical Physics, constitutes an amazing mystery of its own class about him.

In June 1980, the Ahmadiyah community newspaper *Al-Fazal* carried his picture with Caliph Nasir Ahmad; it was captioned as 'Slave and Master'.[3] Striking a chord of political ethos prevalent in ancient Egypt or the North Korea of 20th century, the Ahmadiyah party organ simply desired to remind the faithful that their spiritual leader was supreme, infallible, almighty and an omnipresent divinity answerable only to God. If the divinely-guided caliph, a male and holding office for life, ever made a mistake it would be fixed by God Himself.[4] It is not known how Abdus Salam justified such infinity outside his life in Theoretical Physics.

Walking away from Pakistan for the sake of an archaic mode of devotion did not bring an end to the bitterness Abdus Salam had experienced over excommunication. His abhorrence of the ugly manner in which religious freedom had been blown up in Pakistan held tremendous value. But how could a mass of over ten million people, generally illiterate and bigoted, be expected to understand the need for religious tolerance without setting an educated example?

---

[1] Interviews 1984: Folder II, p. 19
[2] Interviews 1984: Folder VII, pp. 101-103
[3] *Al-Fazal*, Rabwah, 29 June 1980
[4] Iain Adamson (1991): pp.276-277 (Also see Nicholas Evans (2020): p 83

Then, within weeks of the separation, he attempted at striking a bizarre deal with Zulfiqar Bhutto. He expressed his readiness to cooperate in bomb making in exchange for the annulment of Ahmadiyah excommunication. In fact, he went as far as swearing a timeframe to achieve the bomb. Once again, it is not known if he was acting on his own or gambling on behalf of Nasir Ahmad. Whatever the case, Abdus Salam failed to strike the deal. His frustration multiplied. On a subsequent visit to Rabwah, about the end of 1974, he had an emotionally charged argument with caliph's brother Tahir Ahmad. He questioned Tahir Ahmad over the Ahmadiyah support for Zulfiqar Bhutto.[1]

In those days, Abdus Salam's political mentor, Zafarullah Khan, was quoted as stating that the fate of Zulfiqar Bhutto had been sealed by God. Abdus Salam felt mystified when, in a quick succession, Zulfiqar Bhutto was toppled in the military coup and then hanged on charges of murder. He was among the faithful who stumbled upon a prophecy of Ghulam Ahmad, the founder of the Ahmadiyah. According to that prophecy, the desolate doom of Zulfiqar Bhutto had been fore-written. In his vault, Abdus Salam kept the press-clipping of the interview his old classmate Masood Mahmood, the security chief of Zulfiqar Bhutto, had given to a newspaper. Masood Mahmood claimed that Abdus Salam had wished the wrath of God to erase those who had been cruel to the Ahmadiyah. Although Abdus Salam did not remember the narrative in exact detail, he housed the item in the inner pocket of his overcoat, next to his heart, as some kind of a talisman, just as villagers did in his home town Jhang. He was overwhelmed when Zulfiqar Bhutto was ousted from power and then hanged.

Within hours of Zulfiqar Bhutto's execution in Rawalpindi, Zafarullah Khan addressed a gathering of the faithful in London's Ahmadiyah mosque. He prided upon the inevitability of divine retribution. Abdus Salam prized the speech as one of the best pieces of oration he had ever listened to but he was put off when its publication was suppressed by Nasir Ahmad. Whereas, Abdus Salam felt there was no harm in going ahead with the publication. 'I always felt very sorry about this, it should have been published.' He remembered.[2]

Upon winning the Nobel Prize five years later, Abdus Salam found among messages of congratulation one from Benazir Bhutto. He thanked her adding, rather sharply, that the responsibility of his exile from home rested with her

---

[1] Abdul Hameed (circa 2000): pp. 364-365
[2] Interviews 1984: Folder VII, pp. 98-99

father, Zulfiqar Bhutto.[1] Ten years later, when Benazir Bhutto returned to power in Pakistan, she would not forget it. She declined to meet Abdus Salam but did send him a bouquet of flowers when he was unwell.[2]

In 1979, Abdus Salam visited Pakistan to celebrate the winning of his Nobel Prize at state level. For some reason, he landed himself in a discussion with General Ziaul Haq over the Ahmadiyah predicament in Pakistan. Ideally, as a national celebrity he should have steered clear of any divisive issues. He was visiting home as a world acclaimed scientist, not as a religious scholar to advocate the Ahmadiyah cause. Still, he asked Ziaul Haq about the future of excommunication. Only the parliament could repeal the legislation, Ziaul Haq replied. Abdus Salam then requested the president to permit the publication of National Assembly record of summer1974. Ziaul Haq sounded agreeable with a proviso of suitable political environment; he would do so only after making sure that sectarian sentiment was not inflamed all over again.[3]

After that Abdus Salam found himself caught into another argument with Ziaul Haq over the theological terminology relating to the *Finality of Prophethood*. Various translations of the Koran were brought in from the President House library in support of different views. Why did Abdus Salam permit himself to get trapped into something like that, in the first place, especially when it was not his area of expertise? He was calling on the president as a Nobel Laureate of Pakistan, not a clergyman holding the Ahmadiyah torch of clerical illumination.

Just in case the purpose of his debate with Ziaul Haq was meant to at least start talking with the military regime, the effort crashed down rather rapidly. At the Parliament House in Islamabad, all of a sudden, Ziaul Haq invited Abdus Salam to participate in the early afternoon prayer service. Abdus Salam declined to oblige the President.[4] In doing so, he repeated the performance of Zafarullah Khan who had declined to join in the funeral service of Mohammed Ali Jinnah. Be it mourning or celebration, the Ahmadiyah boycott stood resolutely stubborn. Although it amounted to a snub, Ziaul Haq played cool for his stars were on the rise with Soviet troops only days away from landing themselves into the Afghanistan trap.

---

[1] Interviews 1984: Folder VII, p. 104
[2] Al Nahl (Fall 1997): p. 152
[3] Interviews 1984: Folder VII, pp. 110, 118-120.
[4] Abdul Hameed (circa 2000): pp. 197, 365-366

With the passage of time, Abdus Salam's Ahmadiyah connection got intensified. Soon after winning the Nobel Prize, he granted a detailed interview to one of the senior journalists of Pakistan. At one point during the course of this interview, he was questioned about the presence of an Ahmadiyah mission in Israel. Abdus Salam landed straight into the trap by offering a justification for it. Actually, he was not required to go near the subject. His defensive position amounted to clouding his status of a national hero. He was being interviewed as a Pakistani, not a member of the Ahmadiyah party, who had won the Nobel Prize in Physics. He might have easily brushed the question aside by advising the journalist to contact those who were better qualified to field the question, that is, the Ahmadiyah.

Next, travelling in Africa, he is reported to have presented the specially arranged Ahmadiyah editions of the Koran to one or another head of the state.[1] Even though he was not a religious preacher himself, Abdus Salam maintained that the Ahmadiyah presented the most genuine face of Islam. In saying so, he replicated Zafarullah Khan. To Abdus Salam, the Ahmadiyah was a community of mystics, the injured party, putting up with religious persecution in Pakistan with dignity and courage.[2] It is hard to imagine if he had surveyed the Ahmadiyah victimhood in a broader historical context of crimes humans had committed against humanity.

On its own, the Ahmadiyah case against injustice stood upon political selectivity. Could there be a way to ignore the pain and suffering inflicted upon Africans, Jews, Palestinians and others targeted by crimes of apartheid and discrimination? What about those churned in revolutions, wars, the bombing of Hiroshima, Nagasaki, Vietnam, the Middle East and Afghanistan? How about those caught in the partition of Punjab, genocide in Rwanda and the Balkans? Where should the victims of opium wars against China stand? What about Chernobyl, Union Carbide, natural calamities and epidemics? As a matter of fact, the political referencing in human rights provided only cursory relief. Today, the Ahmadiyah and, unwittingly, other religious minorities like Christians, in Pakistan, confront the Blasphemy Law. Fewer people, on the contrary, seem well-informed about the role the Ahmadiyah caliph had played in the delivery of this peculiar piece of legislation.[3]

---

[1] *Khalid* (December 1997): p. 102

[2] *Al-Fazal*, Rabwah, 13 November 1979.

[3] Zafarullah Khan (1981): p. 360

Like his preference for victimhood, Abdus Salam did not seem to take a sociological view of the Ahmadiyah quandary in Pakistan. He tended only to take the party line and appeared to ignore the part the Ahmadiyah had played in their isolation from the mainstream. For many decades, the Ahmadiyah had found refuge in a self-imposed policy of social seclusion and exclusiveness. In all probability the sheltering was meant to protect their members from unwanted sway of religious syncretism and solidify the unshakable belief in being the only legitimate party of God ordained to defend, rejuvenate and spread Islam. But then rooted in fear and insecurity, the isolation was fed with one-dimensional arrogance of the righteous and it went too far like the apartheid and exclusivity of an obnoxious caste system. There was a universal embargo upon closer interaction outside the community; the Ahmadiyah were barred from having any religious, cultural and social contact abroad, especially with members of the Muslim mainstream. An absolute prohibition kept the community from participation in religious rites, ceremonies and prayers; from birth onwards to wedding and death, with relatives and friends belonging to other sects and communities.

An optimist did live in Abdus Salam. He hoped that a future government in Pakistan might undo the grave injustice committed against his community. He believed the distaste of persecution could give birth to the desire for settlement one day. He did not place a timeframe on it and suspected the exile of the Ahmadiyah could continue another century or so. He was not sure how the vulnerable members of the community would cope after their caliph had abandoned them in Pakistan.

Because of the widespread perception that Abdus Salam preferred his Ahmadiyah party over the national interest of Pakistan and that he suffered from a condition of divided loyalty, the gutter press in the country did not take long in caricaturing him as a foreign agent. He was suspected to have been commissioned to sabotage the nuclear program of Pakistan by Indians, Israelis and Americans. As an easy target of the sludge, he was viewed to be roaming around all over Pakistan without any security check. His name was censored from lists of credit and acclaim. Some people believed he and Ishrat Usmani had provided the American Central Intelligence Agency a blueprint of Pakistan's nuclear plans.[1] Others thought he had been awarded the Nobel Prize as a part of some Jewish conspiracy.[2]

In the end, although Abdus Salam's tilt in favour of the Ahmadiyah was obvious in the wake of excommunication, he did not give up his Pakistani citizenship even when there was the temptation to do so.

At the time of their departure from the subcontinent in 1947, the British left behind a Pakistan truncated by around one thousand miles of hostile territory. In 1972, the eastern wing of Pakistan won freedom to become Bangladesh and the new country was recognised by Britain, the creator of the original mess. Frustrated and shamed, Pakistan walked out of the British Commonwealth but then ended up embracing Bangladesh by itself for the sake of Islamic brotherhood. It did not take Pakistan long to re-join the British Commonwealth. Meanwhile a considerable number of Pakistani expatriates working and living in Britain were caught in the frivolous flourish, they did not know what privileges they might gain or lose in the process until the day was saved for them by the option of a dual citizenship.

Prominent among the affected lot of those Pakistani expatriates was Abdus Salam who had to travel all over the place for work. His friends and colleagues advised him to queue up for dual Pakistani-British citizenship. For all practical purposes, England had been his home since 1954. As a better informed elder in the Ahmadiyah community, Zafarullah Khan favoured the dual citizenship but he encouraged people to decide in the light of their individual circumstances. Abdus Salam declined the option of dual citizenship and held on to Pakistan. Reportedly, he wished the imminent prize to be associated only with Pakistan, the modest spring of his scholarship grants and sabbaticals. Often, he brushed the subject aside by stating 'don't go into those silly questions' but then acknowledged the underlined proposition. 'You don't budget such things but one obviously depends on God'. He once remarked.[3] His mind was already made up about the manner in which he would turn up to receive the prize in Stockholm. He had the formal attire of his father in mind.

---

[1] The Pakistan Times, Islamabad, 7 July 1989, p.1 (Friday magazine)
[2] Zahid Malik (1989): p. 164 [In fact, the attitude was not limited to Pakistan. Few years later, the British physicist, Normal Dombey, argued that Abdus Salam had plagiarized data and did not deserve a share in the 1979 Nobel Prize for Physics.
[3] Interviews 1984: Folder VII, pp. 61-63

In 1988, the British Government offered Abdus Salam honorary knighthood in recognition of his contribution to education. Being a citizen of Pakistan, he sought clearance from his government but the request was lost somewhere in red-tape. After waiting for many months, Abdus Salam declined the honour. At that point, the Pakistani High Commissioner in London intervened by bringing the matter to the notice of Ziaul Haq. In an instant telephone call to Abdus Salam, the President offered to write directly to the British Government. Consequently, the honour was affirmed. But even though he became a Knight of the British Empire, Abdus Salam was not entitled to wear the prefix *Sir* due to his lack of British citizenship.[1]

Afzal Hussain, who served two terms as the Vice Chancellor of Punjab University and also as Chairman of the Public Service Commission in the early day Pakistan, had been an ardent promoter of Abdus Salam. He was prominent among the lot of public servants playing an extraordinary role to get Abdus Salam proficiently through the labyrinth of bureaucratic network of approvals and set him upon the journey to Theoretical Physics. Way back in 1951, upon receiving the news of Abdus Salam's high-speed performance in Cambridge, Afzal Hussain corresponded with Mohammed Hussein. He was aware how keen Mohammed Hussein had been for his son to adopt a career in public service. But the amazing manner in which Abdus Salam won the right to do Physics; it was time for Afzal Hussain, himself a Cambridge graduate in Botany, to step in and act prophetically. 'People in the class of Abdus Salam did not belong to any particular community or country'. He wrote to Mohammed Hussein, adding that extraordinary youth like Abdus Salam were bound to secure a 'place is among the most brilliant in the world and, therefore, they belong to the entire humanity'. In all probability, Afzal Hussain wanted to make sure that Abdus Salam did not land himself in a bureaucratic drab and inhibit his intellectual growth.[2]

This observation about Abdus Salam's universality was clouded, if not compromised exactly, in the wake of his championship of the Ahmadiyah, a schismatic cult-like religious minority devoid of any electoral value in Pakistan. By plain inference, in the light of Afzal Hussain's opinion, if Abdus Salam could steer clear of the synthetic grandeur attached to public service in 1949, he might as well have repeated the feat twenty-five years later in 1974 by steering clear of the sectarian warfare in Pakistan.

---

[1] Abdul Hameed (circa 2000): pp. 378-379
[2] Afzal Husain's letter quoted in Abdul Hameed (circa 2000): pp. 72-73

III

Pakistan, the Ahmadiyah and, finally, Abdus Salam's family fitted somewhere in the midst of a deep occupation with Physics. He made sure that there was time for those dear to him both in the immediate and the extended circles of family. His two wives and six children made the immediate family with extension covering the parents and siblings. There would be occasions when close friends, colleagues and students looked like the family. According to his older son, Ahmad Salam, someone had once asked Abdus Salam how many children he had. A few thousand, Abdus Salam is reported to have replied. Those children were his students, the majority of them brilliant and, at the same time, in dire need of attention and logistical support.[1]

Amtul Hafeez (1924–2007) and Abdus Salam were married in 1949. In an interview soon after the death of her husband, Amtul Hafeez was invited to reminisce about their social life. There was hardly time for anything other than work for him, she replied. He would leave for work at eight in the morning, return in the evening, lie down after dinner to wake up early sometimes around midnight to read and write. 'He used to write on whatever was handy like, for example, napkin or newspaper. I avoided to take his time for the value he attached to it'. She recalled. He would ask children about their school, study and homework, and this perhaps was the closest to recurring interaction he had with them in a regular way. 'His own lifestyle was plain and simple yet he did not mind putting up with the burden of extended family. He was always there to meet the needs of his siblings, from their education to wedding'. She added.

After 1957, when the family moved from Cambridge to London, the pressure of work picked up momentum for Abdus Salam. There was no respite once he won the chair as founding Director of the International Centre for Theoretical Physics in Trieste. Due to his keenness on academic linkage with Imperial College, he shuttled between England and Italy for work, travelled to attend conferences and meetings in between, including those of the Atomic Energy Commission in Pakistan. Often, Amtul Hafeez drove him to or back from the airport as an integral part of the routine with him, she recalled. She remembered how one evening he went out of their Putney house in response to the call bell, and then returned the next moment. Someone was asking for the landlady, he

---

[1] Trieste Tribute (1997): p. 129

told his wife. It turned out to be a child from next door who had not seen Abdus Salam before and thought he was a lodger.[1]

Two years senior in age, Amtul Hafeez was a first cousin of Abdus Salam. She was the daughter of his uncle, Ghulam Hussein, who had passed the ownership of his land to Abdus Salam's father, Mohammed Hussein, in 1946. It was the change of title that had cleared the way for Abdus Salam to apply for a scholarship grant under the Peasant Welfare Fund and be able to study in Cambridge. Amtul Hafeez came to England in 1954, without any substantial amount of social exposure. It did not take her long to brave through loneliness, cold, rain, blizzards, looking alike streets and faces, alien language and culture; all far removed from what she had known in Punjab. She held the fort at home, learned fast to cope up with the work routine marked by the absence of her husband even when he was not travelling. Effectively, she ended up playing the role of a single mother to four children growing up fast.

Once in London, Amtul Hafeez got involved in the activities of the Ahmadiyah Women association, *Lajna Ima'ullah* or the Handmaids of Allah. She became the president of the organisation and served the office for 28 years. She got up to carve a social life of her own in a foreign land, without compromising on religious and cultural values of her upbringing; it was not an ordinary feat.

Her three daughters sat through the rare interview she gave about the end of 1996. Aziza, the oldest, remembered with relish those Saturday shopping excursions when the family would sit around a Fish & Chips meal together. Aziza recalled how firmly her father resisted the idea of having a television in the house; he abhorred the box as a sheer wastage of time. A reprieve was granted only during the India-Pakistan war by hiring a television set for few weeks. Asifa recalled the loving manner in which their father used to make telephone call from work or airport to make peace after getting worked up over something when he left home.

Back in the 1960s, Abdus Salam came fairly close to what would be chastised as political radicalism in the Margaret Thatcher-Ronald Regan era twenty years later. In Pakistan, 'his revolutionary ideas and emotions' focusing upon the gulf between the rich and the poor 'looked dangerous for the established order of society' and the need was felt to harness and tame him.[2] In London, sometimes,

---

[1] *Khalid* (December 1997): pp. 65-66
[2] Abdul Ghani (1982): p. 70

he participated in the left-wing inspired anti-war rallies. He socialised with the rebellious British philosopher, Bertrand Russell. Many of his colleagues, including Patrick Blackett, sympathised with the post-war left-of-the-centre Labour Party. On one such occasion, the youthful Abdus Salam, much different from what he turned out to be in the closing decades of his life, happened to meet Louise Johnson (1940–2012), a Physics undergraduate in University College London. It was an encounter typical of love at first sight bringing the two together for the rest of their lives.

Compared to the role of a housewife, for which Amtul Hafeez had been ideally cut and fated, Louise Johnson intended to excel in the academia. She was destined to stamp her mark upon Molecular Biology and Biophysics. An outstanding scientist in her own right, she headed to play a vital role in amino acid crystallography and made it to the top. Soon she would hold the David Phillips Chair as Professor of Molecular Biophysics for seventeen years, from 1990 to 2007, before being appointed as Professor Emeritus in Oxford University.

At a private gathering of close friends, in 1968, Abdus Salam and Louise Johnson went through the *Nikah* or Islamic wedding ceremony. Abdus Salam's old-time friend Paul Matthews played the role of single witness. Islam allowed its followers to marry the People of the Book, that is, Christians and Jews. He would be in a jam if it was Urmila because Hindus did not qualify as the People of the Book. A more formal version of the ritual was observed in 1973 and, once again, it remained a strictly private affair.

It is not known as to where exactly did the two services take place. Likewise, there is no clue if, when and how did Abdus Salam share the news of *Nikah* with his parents, Zafarullah Khan or the sitting Ahmadiyah caliph. Culturally, he was bound to bring elders in the information loop. Questions, mostly academic, have been raised about the union. Who and how many among family and friends attended which of the two functions? What was the point, in the first place, to go through the exercise twice? How did the two get away with the British common law prohibiting bigamy? Even if Islamic *Shariah* permitted Abdus Salam to practice limited polygamy, he was required still to seek written permission from his first wife, Amtul Hafeez, before marrying again in her life. Much to the chagrin of clerics in Pakistan, a package of family laws to this effect had been introduced by Abdus Salam's boss Ayub Khan.

When Abdus Salam first met Louise Johnson, she was just ten years older to his eldest daughter, Aziza Rahman. Measured against his own age, in this way, Amtul Hafeez was two years older and Louise Johnson 14 years younger to him. Hardly anyone would go as far as assuming that their wedding did not lift any eyebrows among family and friends. Remarkably, however, the news of the marriage was never formally broken to public. More so, the manifest commotion triggered by the event was efficiently pushed under the carpet of family privacy. Most certainly, some families are more adept at guarding their pride, even when hurt, than others. Patently, the impulse to put up a brave face of accord and understanding prevailed. Any tension and bitterness, a spontaneous outburst in such instances, had been kept well under control.

Essentially, an anxiety over the nuptials of Abdus Salam and Louise Johnson posed a problem to people suffering from the disability to see anything independent of their religious and cultural constipation. But then the matter would be far more simple and straightforward if Abdus Salam had opted to address the needless suspicion head on especially for the benefit of some of his brilliant Pakistani students. Out of ignorance caused by Abdus Salam's brand of privacy, one of his leading enthusiasts in Lahore, Professor Anis Alam, thought Professor Louise Johnson taught Mathematics in Oxford University.[1]

Michael Duff, the prominent physicist serving as Emeritus Professor of Theoretical Physics in London's Imperial College, once mentioned the ethical dilemma confronted by a student of Abdus Salam. This student suffered from suspicion that a fraction of his research results sounded risky. Abdus Salam, according to Michael Duff, is reported to have shot back, 'when all else fails, you can always tell the truth'.[2] But this loveable piece of lighter logic in everyday human relations was not stretched as far as those sectors of his life where Abdus Salam preferred to hold the lid rather tightly.

Over the years, Professor Louise Johnson and Abdus Salam had two children, a son Omar Salam (b. 1974) and a daughter Saeeda Hajira (b. 1982). On a scale of nostalgia, the combination of lovely names given to Saeeda Hajira can be traced back to the memory of Abdus Salam's step-mother Saeeda and real mother Hajira.

---

[1] The Nation, Lahore, 29 November 1996 (Quoted in Al-Nida: January - June 1997, p. 61)

[2] *Al Nahl* (Fall 1997): p. 148 [A Tribute to Abdus Salam by Michael Duff]

As an expedition in good luck, the two wives of Abdus Salam stood by him and held the domestic front, especially Louise Johnson, on top of her own workload at Oxford University. Both found it hard to keep up with his lifestyle revolving around work.[1] While travelling to pick up the Nobel Prize, Abdus Salam took an entourage of some 20 people, including his two wives, their children, relatives and family friends; all the way to Stockholm. During the course of the ceremony, the two sets of family were seated apart.

At the time of his death, Abdus Salam was in Oxford, living at the residence of Professor Louise Johnson. Upon receiving the news of his death, Amtul Hafeez, Ahmad Salam and Abdul Rashid drove straight to Oxford to transport his mortal remains to London for a funeral at Ahmadiyah mosque.

Occasionally, Professor Louise Johnson and her two children missed out their rightful mention relating to extended family business. In spite of being a scientist of exceptional category, Professor Louise Johnson went virtually unnoticed in the annals of family as well as the Ahmadiyah community. Amtul Hafeez did receive mention decorated with the title *Bhabhi*, that is, the sister-in-law in the 475-page Urdu-language biography Abdul Hameed wrote in praise of his brother Abdus Salam. Professor Louise Johnson could make it to the story just once, and there again with a passing reference as 'his second wife'.[2] On another occasion, the Ahmadiyah party organ *Al-Fazal* referred to her as 'the Italian wife' of Abdus Salam with the name of their daughter, Saeeda Hajira, incorrectly reported.[3] Likewise, Aziza Rahman failed to mention her step-siblings on at least two occasions while she wrote about her father.[4]

On the contrary, her step-brother, Umar Salam, did not slip-up on this account. 'On behalf of all my family, both here and in Pakistan' was how he graciously stated while remembering his father at the 1997 memorial meeting in Trieste. 'I would like to express our deepest gratitude for honouring my father [for] it was through his faith in his goals, his religion, and the people he had around him that he was able to turn his ideals into realities'. He granted.[5]

Similarly, Ahmad Salam sounded far more inclusive compared to his older sister. In his message to the memorial meeting, he recalled how visitors and

---

[1] *Khalid* (December 1997): pp. 65, 73
[2] Abdul Hameed (circa 2000): pp. 189, 190, 191, 396 and 473
[3] *Al-Nida* (1997), p. 70
[4] *Al-Nahl* (1997), pp. 50, 119
[5] Trieste Tribute (1997): p. 125

guests were 'amazed at the library in our bathrooms, in London, Oxford and Trieste with books and magazines ranging from Huxley, Waugh to Wodehouse and Shaw to *New Scientist, Physics Today* and *The Economist*'. He then mentioned about visits to bookshops with Umar Salam in the company of their father.[1]

At his Putney residence in London, Abdus Salam cherished to invite friends and students. As a tribute to the cooking expertise of Amtul Hafeez, he used to call his house 'the best restaurant in the city'. His guests, according to Aziza Rahman, 'included ministers, diplomats and foreign dignitaries, professors and quite often his students'.[2] Zafarullah Khan was the star guest at breakfast on Sundays. Both Zafarullah Khan and Abdus Salam commanded a fine taste in classical Persian poetry; the two remembered by heart dozens of mystical verses articulated by Hafiz Shirazi (1315–1390) and Jalaluddin Rumi (1207–1273). With a razor-sharp memory of political events and issues, stitched into half-a-century of his high-profile public career, Zafarullah Khan made a captivating story-teller.

Apart from those Sunday brunches, the Putney residence of Abdus Salam offered hospitality, sometimes for days on, to the members of the extended family and those among his close friends and former college-mates who held senior executive positions in the Government of Pakistan and happened to be visiting London.

Occasionally, Abdus Salam's friendship with the high and mighty paid well in favour of the scientific community. In 1970–71, he won a considerable amount of money from Muzaffar Ahmad for Pakistan Science Foundation. In 1987, his friend Giulio Andrioitti (1919–2013), went on to double the grant for the Trieste centre, from five to ten million dollars.[3]

Having experienced discrimination from the very outset of his debut on the forefront of Theoretical Physics, when he was nominated for a Fellowship at Princeton, Abdus Salam developed the approach to nip the evil of prejudice in the bud. He did not waste a moment in walking up to Victor Weisskopf who had, in all honesty hopefully, failed to give him the credit due for the breakthrough in parity violation. He would fasten the loose ends, straightaway. According to Ghulam Murtaza, the Professor of Physics in Islamabad University, Abdus

---

[1] Trieste Tribute (1997): pp. 130, 132
[2] *Al Nahl* (Fall 1997): pp. 50-54
[3] Trieste Tribute (1997): p. 23

Salam was well aware of the selective memory among human beings and he confronted the attitude in times of need.[1] During the course of a talk in Princeton, Eugene Wigner wanted to ask Abdus Salam a question. Abdus Salam is reported to have shot back with a remark that he wouldn't care much as long as the physics of his contention was in order.[2]

Despite being praiseworthy in combating racial bigotry, Abdus Salam tended to play safe in a few areas where his opinion carried tremendous intellectual weight. For example, he was aware of diplomatic impediments Pakistan faced in hosting international science conferences. He could see how Pakistan pushed itself into isolation by non-recognition of Israel and hostility towards India and the Communist Block. But he preferred to maintain a tactical silence just as had been the case with his apathy towards the merciless military action in the eastern wing of Pakistan. When quizzed about recognition of Israel, he agreed to take the question up on its political merit and, once again, without coming out in the open. This proviso to lie low contrasted him from many of his western colleagues who spoke out their mind on matters of principle without fear, favour, inhibition or restraint. Given the balance of power, or terror, in the Middle East of the 1980s, it was a territory of sharp internal divisions within the Palestinian Liberation Organisation, Jordan, Syria and Saudi Arabia. He preferred not to go near it.

In 1986, Japan expressed its inability to play the host for Rochester Conference. Abdus Salam wanted Munir Ahmed Khan to explore if Pakistan could grab the opportunity, but it was not possible due to diplomatic disability of the Islamic Republic. Abdus Salam believed if some other countries like India, Russia and China, have faced similar choices and worked their way out with innovation and went on holding one international meeting after another, giving their scientists the much-needed exposure; Pakistan could act tactfully. Although his response on the subject made perfect sense yet he cut it out from the 1984 interview transcripts stating, 'I was too accommodating, I should not have been'.[3]

Likewise, he would hold back in certain other areas of public interest. For example, despite his anxiety over the state of intellectual decline among Muslim, he avoided to be direct. Instead, he preferred to side-track by quoting Koranic

---

[1] *Khalid* (December 1997): p. 94
[2] Trieste Tribute (1997): p. 44
[3] Interviews 1984: Folder VI, pp. 35-37; Folder VII, pp. 47-59

verses on the value attached to scholarship. He preferred to find a way around crucial areas like the status and treatment of women in Muslim communities. Rarely did he speak his mind over issues like controversies over the sighting of moon, a marker in Islamic calendar. In fact, his friend Ishrat Usmani was brave enough in discarding altogether the universal value Muslims attached to the lunar calendar.[1]

Back in the 1980s when communism was one of the chief political ideologies, he deflected questions relating to idealistic goals like equality, fraternity and justice thrown up originally by the French Revolution. Like Winston Churchill, he praised democracy as the best available system. On that account, he had been lucky to have passed away before witnessing the siege of modern state in the west by submission to wealth and control of the fewer and fewer. He lived on the threshold of an era when world capitulated to multinationals, weapon manufacturers, media moguls and storytellers.

Another area in which Abdus Salam maintained ambiguity was the weapon-oriented nuclear program of Pakistan. Even when the right-wing in Pakistan suspected him of disloyalty, he did not cross over to the champions of non-proliferation. All he could make was only a plain academic statement. Nuclear weapons amounted to madness, he was reported to have stated in India in 1981. He avoided repeating the same in Pakistan for fear of public outrage. His voice must have amounted to historical guidance after the prize.

Actually, Pakistan's restless relationship with India was another subject on which Abdus Salam exercised a good deal of restraint. His caution made considerable sense in the historical context, especially circumstances surrounding the creation of Pakistan, from the pangs of indecently cut out boundaries, communal rioting, murder, rape, mass exodus, and the unfinished agenda over accession of princely states. He felt himself a part of the national memory haunted by what had been perceived as grave injustice.

While in Pakistan, Abdus Salam's association with nationalistic military regimes held him firmly in line with the official view of India, that is, a hostile neighbour. Over the years, his choices were defined by the bitterness caused between the two countries by wars and lack of political settlement over disputes. He did not seem to approve war with India[2] but then he dared not come out in

---

[1] Dawn, Karachi, 2 March 1981.
[2] Abdul Ghani (1982): p. 75

open for his belief. He adhered to his preference of strategic silence over the ruthless military action in the eastern wing.

In October 1979, when the Nobel Prize for Physics was announced, Abdus Salam was reported to have received the invitation to visit India from Indira Gandhi before even the telephone call made to him by Ziaul Haq. Abdus Salam did visit India but only after a comprehensive state tour of Pakistan.

He enjoyed the Indian hospitality thoroughly and was overwhelmed with the spontaneity of affection at both formal and informal levels; all the way from touring through universities and science organisations to meeting with Indira Gandhi. He met some of his old teachers and member of the Jhang fraternity in New Delhi. Prior to his meeting with Indira Gandhi, the Pakistani ambassador alerted him that she was not much of a talker and as such he might be required to speak most of the time. Abdus Salam arrived for the meeting a little earlier but she received him instantly. He noted that she lived in modest house and the room in which the two were scheduled to sit was yet to be formally tidied up. Like a 'flustered housewife' she was annoyed over the shabbiness of her staff. After the usual exchange of pleasantries, Abdus Salam advised her about the 'great desire' he had observed among people in both India as well as Pakistan 'to come together' and move on from what had happened in the past in order to 'make a new beginning'.

Here, Abdus Salam cited his opinion about the historical enmity between France and Germany. He credited Charles de Gaulle (1890–1970) and Konrad Adenauer (1876–1967) for bringing the two sides closer. He then remarked that circumstances were other way round in the subcontinent where people wanted peace but the political leadership had other ideas. Indira Gandhi did not agree with the oversimplification proposed by Abdus Salam. She alluded to her own contribution to peace, from keeping her generals on the leash in 1971 to prompting Zulfiqar Bhutto to make up his mind. Do you want to play for the moment or forever, she was reported to have asked Zulfiqar Bhutto. At that point, Abdus Salam sided with Zulfiqar Bhutto. As the vanquished party in Simla, it was not possible for Zulfiqar Bhutto to seek permanent solutions, he stated. Indira Gandhi then filled Abdus Salam in with her experience of interaction with Pakistani, Russian and American leaders.

Russians, Abdus Salam postulated, were always expanding under the guise of their defence. They took Tashkent in defence of Moscow, Kabul to protect

Tashkent; may go for Islamabad to guard Kabul. What if they eye upon Delhi to defend Islamabad? He quizzed her.

'You may be right up to Islamabad', she replied, 'but not Delhi, never. The whole Afghan business has happened with the connivance of Americans and has nothing to do with Russian expansion'. She concluded. Abdus Salam remembered how their discussion continued for about forty minutes. 'It was quite clear that she had other people to see. She wouldn't ask me to leave'. Abdus Salam's intention to discuss academic issues was buried under regional politics. 'After the meeting, I went straight to our ambassador and briefed him about the encounter. 'So you made her speak', the ambassador remarked. He must have reported it all to Islamabad, Abdus Salam thought.

Next day, upon arriving in Hyderabad, he wrote her a letter expressing his concern over the dismal state of Muslims in science. He counselled her to make sure that universities in India did not leave science at the mercy of institutes. He also apologised for failing to offer condolence over the death of her son Sanjay Gandhi.

He received her hand-written reply within a few days. She agreed that Muslim penchant for literature, art and sports distracted the community from thinking about science. Also, she agreed with Abdus Salam's concern about race between universities and institutes; and promised to address those challenges.

Did Indira Gandhi ever happen to touch upon the Ahmadiyah plight in Pakistan? Abdus Salam was asked. No, not a thing, he replied.[1] In 1974, when the anti-Ahmadiyah mass movement raged in Pakistan, someone from the Indian High Commission in London approached Abdus Salam and offered diplomatic protection, if required. Abdus Salam snubbed the emissary.[2]

In Pakistan, Abdus Salam was aware how the place was condemned to consume the best part of its national effort on defence spending, debt servicing and fighting unwinnable wars in between. Any hope to find funds for social development, education and health was mere idealism. Hardly anyone in the intelligentsia had the guts or courage to propose reform in the existing order of order of priorities. With his prestigious academic occupation in Europe, along with the amount of respect and regard commanded by him among Pakistani intelligentsia, Abdus Salam might have taken a chance to stand up boldly and

---

[1] Interviews 1984: Folder III, pp. 51-60
[2] Interviews 1974: Folder III, pp. 58-60

demand reordering of national priorities. Instead, he appeared to comply with the system propping up the military state in Pakistan.

He began taking somewhat of a firm a position only when his Ahmadiyah community was expelled from the pale of Islam. There again, as if the door had not been finally slammed, he made an attempt, after winning the Nobel Prize, to establish some level of communication with the military regime of Ziaul Haq.

IV

In Trieste, the first death anniversary of Abdus Salam was celebrated by renaming after him the International Centre for Theoretical Physics he had presided over for three decades since its establishment in 1964. His two sons, a nephew along with many colleagues and students were invited to participate in the memorial ceremony.

If ever there had been a way for Abdus Salam to be a part of the occasion as an observer, he would be delighted as well as amused. People who had been enriched with the experience of being his colleagues found him nearly as tough as hinted by his two wives. One of his colleagues, Luciano Bertocchi, remembered Abdus Salam as someone who wanted to do much at once. 'In physics as well as in managing and creating new things, he always preferred to do 100 things, 10 of which were wrong, 80 right but normal, and 10 excellent; rather than carefully analysing a new idea before trying, and in this way avoiding failures by doing only 10 things, 9 of which were right and normal, and only one excellent'. Luciano Bertocchi added how Abdus Salam trusted him. 'This is what I want: find the way'. Not that he expected people to play havoc with rules; it was just his way 'to find within the existing and applicable rules the way of realising what he had in mind'.[1]

Another colleague, Andre-Marie Hemende, recalled the eagerness of Abdus Salam. 'He was at times very impatient and each time he had been somewhat rude to me, he would send me a note of apologies accompanied by a small present. I must also mention that I have always been impressed by his multi-tasking capacity: he could switch from one subject to the other with the velocity of lightening'.[2]

---

[1] Trieste Tribute (1997): pp. 6-7
[2] Trieste Tribute (1997): p. 24

Robert Delbourgo (b. 1940), a physicist, defined Abdus Salam as someone who 'would not tolerate pedantry; he was scathing of persons who did not measure up to his high standards'. Such people equalled as 'tom-tits' or 'broken-reeds' to Abdus Salam. On weekends in Trieste, Abdus Salam cherished going out to get his grilled fish meal. 'Being impatient to get back to work, he had a mischievous way of gaining immediate attention from the waiters'. Robert Delbourgo added.[1]

Gordon Feldman (b. 1928), the physicist who served Johns Hopkins University, reminisced about the cheerful younger days of travelling with Abdus Salam to attend a conference in Trieste back in the early 1960s. 'We had a hilarious train ride from London to Trieste in which he (Abdus Salam) presented himself as an Eastern potentate and I was his white factotum (always walking at least three paces behind him). I don't think we were very successful in the pretence. Travelling 3rd class could not have helped the image'.[2]

Gerhard Mack (b. 1940), the physicist who served the University of Hamburg, remembered the tender side of Abdus Salam. Gerhard Mack had to rush home to Germany due an accident with his father. While Abdus Salam was always in the midst of struggle to meet financial ends to run the centre in Trieste, he approved the return journey for Gerhard Mack to travel straightaway.[3]

Nigel Calder (1931–2014), the British science writer, explained the nature of anger Abdus Salam felt. 'I often saw him angry. I don't mean in a petty sense of getting cross with somebody who had annoyed him. I mean a sort of cosmic anger. He was, for example, deeply proud of medieval Islamic science, but angry about the way it had declined, and about how difficult it was to revive. He had a special anger for world poverty. He would put down a newspaper and almost shout at me about the wickedness of the terms of trade that were turning adversely against the Third World, and were thereby wiping out everything that was being given by way of aid and technical assistance'. Abdus Salam, according to Nigel Calder, knew how the scientific and industrial revolution in the 18th century Europe had divided the globe into rich and poor species of human race.[4]

One of the best contribution at the Trieste memorial meeting came from Ahmad Salam, the older son of Abdus Salam. It was a graceful account and an

---

[1] Trieste Tribute (1997): p. 34, 36
[2] Trieste Tribute (1997): p. 39
[3] Trieste Tribute (1997): P. 44
[4] Trieste Tribute (1997): p. 98

impressive glimpse into the little-known personal side of Abdus Salam. Steering clear of adjectives and superlatives, Ahmad Salam shared a fond picture of his father torn between his children and work.

When in London, Abdus Salam made sure that the family had at least one dinner together 'where he would go around the table and ask what we were studying at school, how we were doing and whether we had any problems he could help us with'. Ahmad Salam remembered. Because Abdus Salam went to bed early, the policy at home was not to take any telephone calls during the dinner or when he had retired to bed. 'People who did so were asked to call back. This was a golden rule. Father would sleep very well indeed; I was often amazed at his ability to close his eyes and sleep, wherever he may be without exceptions, in a car, on a plane or wherever he had a few minutes to close his eyes'.

After a lunch in Buckingham Palace once, Ahmad Salam recounted, his father returned to ask for the napkin that had been assigned to his seat; he happened to have written some notes on the napkin.

According to Ahmad Salam, his father used to breakfast with sausages, eggs or smoked haddock; but then moved on to fish fingers and muesli. Chocolates, mango pickle and Pakistani sweets were among his favourite. He justified his sweet tooth as the source of energy. 'He would travel with large amounts of sweets, biscuits and nuts in his bag' and the stock had to be kept up regularly.

Shopping was not a forte of Abdus Salam because he considered it wastage of time. But 'he loved a bargain'. Ahmad Salam remembered how his father picked up 15 shirts in New York only because he was tempted by the deal. Abdus Salam did not mind going to annual sales though he was not fussed about clothing. He began having his suites tailored at Gieves and Hawks in Seville Row, London, due to the stability of their fashion which saved him time. 'Appearance was very important to father and he took great pride later on ensuring he was well turned out'.

Buying books remained a lifelong hobby of Abdus Salam. He knew his favourite spots of old and new books of all kinds from Multan to Lahore, Cambridge, London and elsewhere. In the collection Abdus Salam left behind, Ahmad Salam found books like '*Teach Yourself Russian, Teach Yourself Air Navigation, Teach Yourself Ballroom Dancing*' though the last item might have been an error. Ahmad Salam added and then mentioned a number of dictionaries that remained unused.

Before he got busier, Abdus Salam was fond of opera; his favourite being *Gilbert and Sullivan*. Over the years he had a collection of classical music, like Mozart, along with Koranic recitations. Ahmad Salam recollected his father's 'total love of all things Islamic'. For example, Abdus Salam had been thrilled to 'see the Whirling Dervishes' when they visited London. Ahmad Salam accompanied his father. 'I of course did not realise the significance of this sight, but Father was absolutely enchanted and loved the evening. He loved Islamic art and poetry'. Ahmad Salam recalled.

'During the last years of his life, when the illness was getting worse and becoming more and more crippling, right to the very end, he never ever cursed his misfortune or complained'. Ahmad Salam complimented the patience and courage with which Abdus Salam travelled through the test of his health. 'He suffered very quietly; having been a man of great independence to suddenly become totally dependent on people, and to have to need people for doing the everyday things we all take for granted, must have been very hard for him. He only ever allowed a very few people to see him at his most vulnerable. He accepted that the illness was entirely Allah's will and therefore it was to be accepted with complete serenity. He was never angry or bitter about his illness. He had tremendous courage and strength. Even when he was in such obvious discomfort and pain, he never once voiced his anger or frustration'.[1]

Some of Abdus Salam's colleagues and students wrote about him in *Al Nahl*, a publication of the Ahmadiyah community in the United States.

Tahira Arshad from the University of Tennessee recalled that during the course of a visit to Trieste Abdus Salam had once wished her to help his son Umar Salam with the reading of the *Koran*. When she expressed her readiness to oblige, Abdus Salam conditioned the arrangement with remuneration. Tahira Arshad also remembered that some of the fellows visited the centre with their families but found it hard to afford the exorbitant fees they had to pay for the education of their children at the local International School. Abdus Salam was requested to intervene in the matter to explore if the school could offer some concession. He won those parents a 'special rebate' and then approved the balance to be paid by the centre. She also recalled about a fellow visiting from Zambia whose wife was expecting with a history of miscarriages. Once again,

---

[1] Trieste Tribute (1997): p. 127-133

Abdus Salam reached out to help the couple by extending the term of contract for this fellow under a different cost centre.[1]

In an interview, the Pakistan physicist, Faheem Hussain, stated that Abdus Salam had some 'quite big' failures taking him to 'the edge'. While making the comment, Faheem Hussain possibly had Abdus Salam's enthusiasm in the area of superstrings in mind.[2]

Early in 1997, a memorial essay featured Abdus Salam's 'deceptively soft, husky voice' as a mask hiding his 'iron will and ruthless ambition'. He could unleash argument 'as an intellectual weapon to pry upon a difficult problem or seek new ideas'.[3]

Jogesh Pati, the physicist who served the University of Maryland and had closely collaborated with Abdus Salam for many years remembered occasions of their disagreement. 'My dear sir, what do you want? Blood?' Abdus Salam would say in a state of excitement. 'No. Professor Salam, I would like something better'. Jogesh Pati remembered responding back, of course, both taking the disagreement in good spirit.[4]

Fewer scientists, according to Seif Randjbar-Daemi, were aware of the vocabulary Abdus Salam had introduced to Physics. He cited expressions like electroweak theory, Astro-particle physics and supersymmetry.[5]

V

Could science prove the existence of God? A local journalist asked Abdus Salam in Rabwah where he had been invited to celebrate the prize by addressing a session of the annual *jalsa* festival of the Ahmadiyah. Without taking a pause, Abdus Salam shot back with a plain no adding that the proposition did not work because God was bigger than science.[6] He was aware how people expected great physicists to be better informed in tackling questions tormenting human mind for centuries. He might have taken the academic approach by stating that the two

---

[1] *Al Nahl* (Fall 1997): p, 71
[2] *Al Nahl* (Fall 1997): p. 127
[3] *Al Nahl* (Fall 1997): p. 145 (Off CERN Courier, January-February 1997)
[4] *Al Nahl* (Fall 1997): p. 155 (off Nature, Vol. 384, 12 December 1996, p. 520)
[5] *Al Nahl* (Fall 1997): p. 165
[6] Abdul Hameed (circa 2000): p. 300

belonged to separate spheres of human perception and needed to be approached accordingly. But he preferred to pursue the devout view.

In a bid to understand the God of Abdus Salam, it is worthwhile to appreciate the scope of the abstraction. Any scientific and philosophical exploration relating to the central deity precludes the range of communal ownerships celebrated as Brahma, Yahweh, Trinity, Allah and others denominations. In a way, the personal icons of Hindu, Jewish, Christian, Muslim and other communities are swept into one central idiom behind the original act of creation. Historically, the image of God was modernised by the 17th century Dutch philosopher Baruch Spinoza (1632–1673). He detached the function of God from presiding and judging over everyday lives of human beings to that of an equivalent of the natural phenomenon. Among physicists, Albert Einstein gets the credit for injecting a certain amount of bloom into the sketch proposed by Baruch Spinoza. Albert Einstein raised the question if God had any choice other than creation.[1] Stephen Hawking (1942–2018) used to equate God with the mind of nature. On the other end, the American theologian Paul Tillich (1886–1965) proposed that only physicists, among scientists, could speak about God 'without embarrassment'. Abdus Salam could easily top the list on this scale.

Both Sheldon Glashow (b. 1932) and Steven Weinberg (1933–2021), who shared the 1979 Nobel Prize of Physics with Abdus Salam, were known to have confirmed their intellectual adherence to atheism. Sheldon Glashow described himself as a practicing atheist. Steven Weinberg went a step ahead; he proposed to keep the laws of nature from God and the historical freight of religious terminology. Steven Weinberg did not wish the two to be confused with one another, even metaphorically. He stated that religion amounted to an insult upon human dignity.

With Abdus Salam in the trio of winners, in this way, the Nobel Prize for Physics, in 1979, typified the extent to which human mind could reach regardless of its cultural setting and upbringing. Although Sheldon Glashow and Steven Weinberg had known each other from their Bronx High School days in New York, the two shared the Jewish immigrant affinity, and had their academic journeys crisscrossed in the United States and Europe; the two qualified for the prize independent of each other. Abdus Salam, on the other hand, had taken the rather rutted and accidental course to study and make it to the top in Physics; his destiny did not shape up predictably as might have been the case if he was born

---

[1] Walter Isaacson (2007): pp. 384-393

and drilled through the industrial environment of Europe or the United States. He struck out rather prominently also for his hefty religious baggage far above the nominal ownership of an average believer in the west.

At the end of the day, Abdus Salam did not qualify as a believer of the western kind. In spite of living the best part of his time in the company of minds who treaded in the finest zones of natural phenomenon, he preferred a formal compliance of religion. His association with the Ahmadiyah as well as Pakistan attained peculiarity for it amounted to involvement with organised religion, patriotism and power politics; a territory alien to the ordinary mainstream believer in the secular west. Although his God was a historical extension of the Lord of Old Testament, Abdus Salam owned and displayed his belief publicly, without the least embarrassment on Paul Tillich scale. From his Inaugural Lecture in Imperial College in 1957 to the Nobel Banquet in Sweden in 1979, he went on quoting Koranic verses on creation. Physicists, according to him, experienced the wonder and excitement associated with intellectual discovery; the deeper they search the greater their sense of amazement.[1]

In fact, he went farther by resting his faith in an experimental evidence of proton decay. He quoted another Koranic verse in support of his contention. 'All that is there will pass away; and there will remain *only* the Person of thy Lord, Master of Glory and Honour'.[2] Abdus Salam believed in *Allah* the creator, originator, first and last, ever living, omniscient, all-seeing, watchful, provider, preserver, sustainer, dominating, merciful, forgiving, raiser of the dead, avenger and pardoner, knower of hidden and giver and taker of life; to name a few off the ninety-nine titles attributed to the Lord of Islam. All of his six younger brothers were named within the same lyrical format; starting with the prefix of Abdul, each name concluded with an attribute of *Allah* as the surname. In this way, just as Abdus Salam meant the Servant of Peace; the names of his brothers, in order of seniority, would the patterned as the servants the all hearing (Abdus Samee), the praiseworthy (Abdul Hameed), the illustrious and magnificent (Abdul Majid), the capable and powerful (Abdul Qadir), the guide and infallible (Abdul Rasheed), and the giver of gifts (Abdul Wahab).

---

[1] Ideals and Realities (1984): pp. 116-117
[2] The Koran 55:27-28. Also see *Khalid*, December 1997

Next, Abdus Salam bowed to the Ahmadiyah caliph who, for all practical purposes, was accepted as the true and infallible personification of God.[1]

Despite his rich experience of public affairs, Zafarullah Khan, the political mentor of Abdus Salam, advocated the interminable marriage between spiritual and temporal spheres of life. But Abdus Salam, at one point in his life, after the rise of religious militancy among Muslims, came around to prefer secular polity. He ridiculed the Objectives Resolution of 1951 adopted by the Constituent Assembly of Pakistan.[2] Had he made the bold attempt at tackling the Pakistani obsession with religion in time, his advocacy might have made some difference or at least placed him on historical record for stating the fact.

Although Abdus Salam placed God above science, his atheist colleagues like Sheldon Glashow and Steven Weinberg did not see any reason to treat him unequally in any way. A believer making it to the top with two atheists tempted Abdus Salam's brother, Abdul Hameed, to detect some kind of a godly sign behind the prize. Surely, this was not the way great scientists felt for they had their eyes on the big game in science, not petty catch in everyday belief. At their level of professional exchange and socialisation, the sharpness of humour had its own class close to the one displayed from time to time by Wolfgang Pauli.

Steven Weinberg remembered Abdus Salam as a 'very devout Muslim' who wanted to promote science in the Gulf states. But the task turned tough because the ruling class worried that science was 'corrosive to religious belief'. Steven Weinberg loved the corrosive part of Abdus Salam's observation. 'Damn it, I think they were right; it is corrosive of religious belief, and it's a good thing too'. He remarked.

In his message of condolence, Sheldon Glashow remembered Abdus Salam as a 'beloved friend and gentle soul'. He rated Abdus Salam as 'one of the most delightful characters in the world of physics'.[3] On the scale of temperament whipping up ideas for research and investigation, Abdus Salam and Sheldon Glashow resembled each other more than their relatively poised partner, Steven Weinberg. Here, Sheldon Glashow avoided to mention how he had dragged Abdus Salam into the shady quarter of a town in Turkey where the two had been on a teaching assignment. Typical of an American youth, Sheldon Glashow

---

[1] Nicholas Evans: Far From the Caliph's Gaze, Cornell University Press, Ithaca and London, 2020, pp. 80-83, 85

[2] Interviews 1984: Folder V, pp. 9-22

[3] *Al-Nahl* (Fall 1997): p. 161

looked for hashish. Although Abdus Salam disapproved, yet he did not seem to mind accompanying his colleague.[1]

VI

While a toddler, Abdus Salam was one day carried to participate in the health contest of infants in Jhang. He won the first prize for being the chubbiest.[2]

Over the years, he grew up in the country air and was nourished chiefly on bread, butter, milk, curries and seasonal fruit. In those days, *ghee* or clarified butter was not dreaded and its utility in healthy cooking took lead upon lighter vegetable oils. Abdus Salam started the day with a *paratha* breakfast of layered *chapatti* fried in *ghee*, he would have mutton and vegetable curry, his mother was adept at making, during the day. He is known to have loved his food including the potato-mutton curry frequently served in Government College dining hall.[3] At Cambridge, it took him a while to acclimatise with the radical change of cuisine. At Imperial College in London, he did not mind the English refectory food.[4] While going to a restaurant in Trieste, he would order his favourite dish of *ossobuco*.[5] His fondness of desserts and sweets, especially Pakistani, was well known in the family. He loved fried fish sold in the old city of Lahore.

Even though Abdus Salam did not have much of an inclination upon constitutionals like walking or jogging, he was not overweight. His sturdy physique saved him from picking up any adverse health condition associated with dietary indulgence. From taking a little while before starting to talk as an infant, and having few minor mishaps and occasional bouts of sickness here and there, he remained in good shape and commanded an impressive stature with a height around 5.8 and handsome presence. In other words, his Rajput warrior genes sustained the highly demanding lifestyle he had tightly woven around work from the very outset. As such, he was able to serve Physics, Pakistan, the Ahmadiyah and a large extended family that included his parents, siblings, two

---

[1] Robert Crease and Charles Mann (1986): p. 230
[2] Interviews 1984: p. 29
[3] *Al-Nahl* (Fall 1997): p. 36
[4] Trieste Tribute (1997): p. 33
[5] Trieste Tribute (1997): p. 57 [prepared with beef shin, ossobuco contains a good amount of bone marrow]

wives, six children, guests and friends. He spent the best part of his income, including the cash component accompanying awards and prizes, since 1958, on instituting scholarship grants and foundations in support of talented youth worldwide.[1]

Against such a pristine health card, the affliction that overtook him from nowhere was appallingly tragic as much as unkind and hurtful. Among the diversity of loveable features attributed to the personality of Abdus Salam, his unadulterated laughter was one for sure. John Ziman (1925–2005), who served Bristol University as Professor Emeritus, called that laughter 'a part of Physics'.[2] Michael Duff (b. 1949), who served the Abdus Salam Chair in Imperial College, used to say the laughter reminded him of the barking sea-lion.[3] Mournfully, the terminal sickness took most away, including that resonating laughter. Abdus Salam was unable to communicate during the last three years of his life.

In the final stages of his sickness, he was confined to wheelchair and bed. By then, a number of his contemporaries and those dear to him were already gone; they included Wolfgang Pauli, Bashiruddin Ahmad, Robert Oppenheimer, Mohammed Hussein, Afzal Hussain, Ayub Khan, Patrick Blackett, Oskar Klein, Werner Heisenberg, Hajira Hussein, Paul Dirac, Evgeny Lifshitz, Hideki Yukawa, Chaudhri Mohamed Ali, Samuel Goudsmit, Nasir Ahmad, Zafarullah Khan, Paul Matthews, Richard Feynman, Ishrat Usmani, Julian Schwinger, Rudolf Pierels, and the list was building up fast.

Any retrospective speculation over the idea that Abdus Salam should have taken early retirement, lived a relaxed life in a farm house near Oxford or Cambridge, enjoyed walks, read and wrote; it all sounds like a melancholy yearning. Such was the momentum of his life that he did not imagine to stop working. When the affliction struck, it had been a surprise of gruesome proportions; he must have taken a bit of time in coming to terms with it. Likewise must have been the case with his family especially when he got stranded, on his own, in Trieste. Witnessing his condition, a couple of his younger colleagues from Pakistan raised questions if the Ahmadiyah community had a system in place to arrange some kind of nursing for him.

---

[1] Mohammad and Hajira Hussain Foundation set up with Nobel Prize money to grant scholarships to deserving students. [*Al Nahl* Fall 1997: p. 53]
[2] Trieste Tribute (1997): p. 55
[3] *Al Nahl* (Fall 1997): p. 148

What exactly kept Abdus Salam from returning to Pakistan by himself? Like Zafarullah Khan, he could have divided his time between Pakistan and England and tested if the arrangement worked. If he did not wish to retire in the tranquil beauty of rural England, his hometown Jhang might have been an option. He could be a hermit in Pakistan as Ishrat Usmani had once suggested him in 1962. Did someone stop him in Pakistan? Why did he condition his return with a signal from the Government of Pakistan? His fans, thousands in the country, held the view that he was set to bag another Nobel Prizes.[1] They would have loved to find him in their midst.

How much Abdus Salam longed to return home was evident in the Faiz Memorial Lecture he delivered in Lahore prior to falling sick. He related to the tale of a Christian clock-maker in the medieval Emirate of Bukhara. This clock-maker was permitted to enter the mosque only when the clock, installed upon a minaret, needed repair or servicing. If the people of Pakistan did not like his association with the Ahmadiyah, Abdus Salam remarked, he could be permitted to play the role of that clock-maker to promote scientific scholarship in the country.

He might as well have cited another example by referring to the oldest mosque in Kuala Lumpur, the Sultan Abdul Samad Jamek Mosque, built in 1909, and designed by the English architect, Arthur Hubback (1871–1948).

Next, there was something rather unthinkable. Earlier in the 6th century, a Syrian craftsman, Pachomius, was employed to refurbish *Ka'aba*. Upon completing the work assigned to him, Pachomius left behind a set of fresco-statues on the roof of the sacred dwelling. His engraving depicted the images of Abraham, Mary and Child Jesus. Later, when *Ka'aba* was reclaimed by Muslims in 630, the prophet is reported to have permitted to retain the icons of Mary and Jesus. But he ordered to destroy the one of Abraham as it resembled *Hubal*, a pre-Islamic idol. It is believed that the two acceptable relics were lost when the shrine caught fire, some five hundred years down the passage of time, in 12th century.[2]

Even though Abdus Salam, on his part, did not mind playing the role of either the Syrian craftsman, Christian clock-maker or the English architect; he was perceived to have bungled the prospect up himself with his unmanageable tilt in favour of the Ahmadiyah. Many in Pakistan hold the view that despite the ample

---

[1] The News, Rawalpindi, 26 January 1996, p.6
[2] F. E. Peters (1994): p. 49

support and opportunity granted to him up until 1974, he made the choice of rejecting the popular, and much awaited, verdict of history upon his Ahmadiyah community.

While the mortal remains of Abdus Salam awaited burial under a star-studded early winter sky above Rabwah and the uneven tracts of *Chenab* country all the way to Jhang, a multitude of faithful arrived to participate in his funeral. 'He belongs to them, not to us, anymore'. Umar Salam consoled his mother.[1]

Abdus Salam was once asked how exciting it had been for him to dwell upon the forefront of 20th century Physics for over four decades. He replied that pursuit of excellence depended upon one's flexibility of mind and ability to learn. In his case, he added, the success was made easy by the grace of God and the prayers of his parents. His earthly remains found a permanent abode near the graves of Hajira and Mohammed Hussein.

---

[1] *Khalid* (December 1997): p. 74

Bibliography

- Aftab. A. (2005) Personal Profiles (Urdu), Islamabad.
- *Al Nahl* (Fall 1997) A publication of the Ahmadiyah community in the United States.
- Ali, C. M. (1967) *The Emergence of Pakistan*, New York & London: Columbia University Press.
- Anam, T. (2007) *A Golden Age*, London: John Murray (Publishers).
- Bangladesh: The Birth of a Nation (A handbook of background information and documentary sources), compiled by Marta Nicholas and Philip Oldenberg, Madras (India).
- Bhutto, Z. A. (1976) *Thoughts on Some Aspects of Islam*, Lahore.
- Binder, L. (1961) *Religion and Politics in Pakistan*, USA: University of California Press, Berkeley and Los Angeles.
- Burman, E. (1986) *The Templers - Knights of God*, Great Britain.
- Callard, K. (1958) *Pakistan: A Political Study*, London: George Allen & Unwin Ltd.
- Caroe, O. (1951) *Wells of Power*, London: Macmillan.
- Chopra, G. L.(2nd ed.) (1960) *The Punjab as a sovereign state (1799–1839)*, Hoshiarpur (India).
- Choudhury, G. W. (1988) *Pakistan Transition from Military to Civilian Rule*, Essex (England): Scorpion Publishing Ltd.
- Collins, L. and Lapierre, D. (1975) *Freedom at Midnight*, New York.
- Connel, J. (1959) *Auchinleck*, Cassel, London.
- (1947) 'Constituent Assembly of Pakistan: Debates', 1, 2.
- Manzooruddin, A. (ed.) (1982) *Contemporary Pakistan: Politics, Economy and Society*, Karachi, 1982.
- Dawkins, R. (2006) *The God Delusion*, Transworld Publishers.
- Jones, D. E. and Jones, R. W. (1982) *Education Policy Development in Pakistan: Quest for a National Program*. [Essay contributed to

'Contemporary Pakistan: Politics, Economy and Society; edited by Manzooruddin Ahmed, Karachi, 1982, p. 253]

- Sir Durand, M. (1913) *Life of the Rt. Hon Sir Alfred C Lyall*, Edinburgh & London.
- Major Edwardes, H. B. (1964) *A Year on the Punjab Frontier in 1848-49*, II, reprinted in Lahore.
- Fraser, G. (2008) *Cosmic Anger*, Oxford University Press.
- Freeland, A. (1968) *Islam and Pakistan*, Ithaca, New York: Cornell University Press.
- Friedmann, Y. (1989) *Prophecy Continuous - Aspects of the Ahmadi Religious Thought and Its Medieval Background*, Oxford University Press.
- (1884) *Gazetteer of the Jhang District 1883-84*, compiled and published under the authority of Punjab Government, Lahore.
- Ghalib (1972) (Edited by Ralph Russell) *The Poet and His Age*, London.
- Ghani, A. (1982) *Abdus Salam - A Nobel Laureate from a Muslim Country - A Biographical Sketch*, Karachi.
- Hodson, H.V. (1985) *The Great Divide*, Oxford (U.K.): Oxford University Press.
- Holger K. (1998) *Jesus Lived in India*, Berlin.
- Iain, A. (1991) *A Man of God: The Astonishing Story of His Holiness Khalifatul Masih IV*, 9, Maggs House, Bristol Great Britain: George Shepherd Publishers.
- Hassan, Z. and Lai, C. H. (ed.) (1984) *Ideals and Realities: Selected Essays of Abdus Salam*, Singapore.
- Interviews 1984: Transcription of 1984 voice recording in VIII handwritten folders, include comments and note by Abdus Salam.
- Jalal, A. (1990) *The State of Marshal Rule - The origins of Pakistan's political economy and defence*, Cambridge, England: Cambridge University Press.
- Johnson, P. (1996) *Intellectuals*, London: Orion Books Ltd.
- Kac, M. (1987) *Enigmas of Science*, University of California Press.
- Kapur, A. (1987) *Pakistan's Nuclear Development*, New York: Croom Helm.
- Khan M. A. (1967) *(President of Pakistan): Friends Not Masters (A Political Autobiography)*, 130, London: Oxford University Press.

- Khan, F. H. (2013) *Eating Grass - The Making of the Pakistani Bomb*, India: Cambridge University Press.
- Kipling, R. (1891) *Life's Handicap*, Macmillan and Co.
- Latif, S. M. (1965) *The Early History of Multan*, Calcutta, 1891 (reprinted in Lahore).
- Lavan, S. (1974) *The Ahmadiyah Movement - A History and Perspective*, Delhi.
- Life of Abdus Salam (an Urdu-language biography compiled by his brother Abdul Hameed), Lahore, circa 2000.
- Lyall, A. (1893) *The Rise and Expansion of the British Dominion in India*, London: John Murray.
- Malik, Z. (1989) *Abdul Qadeer Khan (Urdu)*, Islamabad: Hurmat Publications.
- Mohammed Hussein (Urdu-language autobiography edited by Mohammed Ismail), Lahore, 1974.
- Mohammed Z. K. (1971) *Tahdees-i-Ne'maat (an autobiography)*, Lahore: Packages Ltd.
- Monthly *Khalid*, Rabwah, December 1997.
- Moore, L. T. (1962) *Isaac Newton: A Biography*, New York: Dover Publications Inc.
- Nehru, J. (2004) *Glimpses of World History*, New Delhi: Penguin Books.
- Nevile, P. (1997) *Lahore - A Sentimental Journey*, India: HarperCollins.
- Nicholas E. (2020) *Far From the Caliph's Gaze*, Ithaca and London: Cornell University Press.
- Nixon, R. (1978) *The Memoirs of Richard Nixon*, USA: Grosset & Dunlop.
- Simpson, P. (1974) *Imperial Mendicancy and Resource Diplomacy* (thesis submitted in partial fulfilment of an Honours Degree in Arts), Sydney, Australia: The University of New South Wales.
- Peters, F.E. (1994) *Muhammad and the Origins of Islam*, 86, State University of New York Press.
- Powick, F. M. and Emden, A. B. (ed.) (1936) *Rashdall's Medieval Universities*, II, Oxford.
- Raza, R. (1997) *Zulfikar Ali Bhutto and Pakistan 1967–1977*, Karachi: Oxford University Press.

- Rehman, S. (1999) *Long Road to Chaghi*, Islamabad.
- (1954) *Report of the Court of Inquiry: Punjab Disturbances*, Lahore.
- Crease, R. and Mann, C. (1986) *The Second Creation - Makers of the Revolution in 20th Century Physics*, New York: Macmillan Publishing Company.
- Rushdie, S. (1981) *Midnight's Children*, London: Jonathan Cape.
- Select Documents on Partition of Punjab, Edited by Dr Kirpal Singh, Delhi, 1991
- Gibb, AAR., Kramers, J. H. and Leiden (ed.) (1953) *Shorter Encyclopaedia of Islam: Edited on behalf of the Royal Netherlands Academy*, 312-3.
- Singh, J. (1992) *Abdus Salam - A Biography*, New Delhi: Penguin India.
- Singh, J. (2009) *Jinnah - India-Partition-Independence*, New Delhi.
- Sisson, R. and Rose, L. E. (1990) *War and Secession: Pakistan, India and the Creation of Bangladesh*, Los Angeles, California: University of California Press.
- Sir Temple, R. (1881) *India in the 1880*, London, 1881 (Second Edition).
- Sir Thomas, A. and Guillaume, A. (ed.) (1931) *The Legacy of Islam*, Oxford University Press.
- Hamende, A. M (ed.) (1999) *Tribute to Abdus Salam*, Trieste, Italy, 1999.
- Virk, Z. (1996) *Ramooz-i-Fitrat*, Kingston (Canada).
- Wolpert, S. (1993) *Zulfi Bhutto of Pakistan: His Life and Times*, Oxford University Press.
- Woolf, V. (2004) *To the Light House*, London: Vintage Books.

Index

1953 Martial Law in Lahore 398

Abdus Salam, 24, 25, 35, 477
Ahmad Salam, 165, 458
469, 470
Ahmad, Major Mahmud 212
Ahmad, Muzaffar 322
347, 349, 356
Ahmad, Nazir 279, 280
289, 382
Ahmadiyah 9, 20, 34
56, 73, 390, 392, 394
398, 400, 407, 415, 418
423, 443, 453, 456, 471
Ahmadiyah mission house 135
Ahmadiyah Mission
House london 125, 419
Ahmed, Aftab 107, 110
Ahmed, Bashiruddin 53
54, 211, 215, 346, 347
Ahmed, Ghulam 49, 50
52, 54, 211, 214
Ahmed, Nasir 348
Ahmed, Riaz 280, 281
Ahmed, Sirajuddin 109, 110
191, 195, 203, 204, 227, 312
Ahmed, Tahir 348, 350
391, 435, 452

Ahrar 214, 216, 218, 221, 399

Air Marshal Zafar
Chaudhry 403
Akhtar, Javaid 276, 295
Ali, Chaudhri Mohamed 276
282, 288, 295, 444, 448, 477
Amir Chang 64, 65
Ashraf, Inam 18
Aslam, Mohammed 194
201, 222, 286
Athenaeum Club, London 250
atoms for peace 424
Atoms for Peace 16, 58
274, 276, 286, 321, 445
Awan, Shaukat 106, 112
Azad Kashmir
Legislative Assembly 391
Aziz, King Abdul 38

Bambah, Ram Prakash 150
162, 166
Bethe, Hans 249, 250, 331, 442
Bhabha, Homi 166, 198
199, 200, 201, 202, 273, 274
Bhatti Rajput 26, 36, 409
Bhutto, Benazir 23, 427
440, 453

Bhutto, Zulfiqar 12, 21, 112
  318, 335, 350, 376, 392, 435
Bodhraj 64
Budinich, Paulo 328, 332

Cambridge 10, 30, 95, 105
  109, 116, 118, 119, 128, 132
  142, 161, 340, 457, 476
Campion Road, Putney 259
Caroe, Olaf 114, 184
  271, 286
Cavendish Laboratory 148
  149, 154, 155, 165, 235, 248
Central Model School 77
  78, 98
Chowla, Sri 103
Cockcroft, John 234, 235
  274, 301

Department of Education,
Punjab 153
Devons, Samuel 165, 166
Dhaka Science
Conference 1961 295
Dickenson, Eric 118
Dirac, Paul 144, 145
  182, 202, 243, 425
Dyson, Freeman 169
  170, 179, 288

Eddington, Arthur 252
Einstein, Albert 24, 145
  173, 175, 181, 239, 252
Eklund, Sigvard 288
excommunication 12, 210
  393, 406, 410, 417, 450, 456

F. O. Franconia 122
Fellowship at St John's 154
fellowship of Royal
Society 258
Flowers, Brian 249, 253
Freud, Sigmund 9, 130

Government College 77, 78
  90, 110, 192, 222
  294, 374, 439, 445

Hafeez, Amtul 39, 142
  163, 237, 259, 267, 427
Hajira 56, 461, 477, 479
Hajira, Saeeda 267, 461
Hameed, Abdul 35, 158
  238, 254, 329
Haq, Ziaul 23, 112
  419, 428, 429, 430
Hashmi, Bilal 160
HCM Inquiry 199
Heer 10, 34, 35, 376
Heisenberg, Werner 166
  167, 477
Hoyle, Fred 146, 147
  230, 242, 256, 257
Hu, Ning 175
Hussein, Afzal 477
Hussein, Ghulam 37, 38, 42
Hussein, Mohammed 84
  93, 96, 116, 118, 121, 141

Iftikharuddin,
Mohammed 287, 445
Ikramullah, Mohammed 242
  251, 281

Imperial College	10, 58
	243, 252, 256, 264, 291
	362, 458, 474, 477
Indian Civil Service	28
	58, 67, 77, 94, 116, 283, 383
Institute of Advanced Study, Princeton	171
International Centre for Theoretical Physics, Trieste	261
International Union of Students	135
invitation from Moscow	234
	235, 236
Jatki	19, 36
Jewish conspiracy	456
Jewish Conspiracy	12
Jhang	9, 26, 27
	28, 31, 32, 40, 74, 105, 264, 466
jihad	13, 54, 87, 214
	236, 334, 410, 431
Jihad	435
jihad in Afghanistan	434
Johnson,	265
Johnson, Louise	440, 462
Kabir, Hamayun	339, 340
Karachi	107, 152, 157
	159, 209, 216, 343, 367
	384, 402, 428
Kemmer, Nichola	180
Kemmer, Nicholas	167
	288, 442
Khaliq, Ghulam	119, 153
Khalistan Riddle	1, 19
Khan, Ayub	284, 289

	290, 292, 293, 303, 306, 322
	340, 366, 367, 418, 446, 449
Khan, Liaquat Ali	213, 319
Khan, Munir	77, 380
	395, 407, 435
Khan, Tikka	358, 359, 360
Khan, Yahya	447
Khan, Zafarullah	56, 124
	177, 216, 274, 407, 420
	430, 452, 463
Khiva Gate Primary School	62
King Faisal Bin Abdul Aziz	387, 388, 393
Kipling, Rudyard	106
Kirana Hills	27, 29
Lahore	32, 39, 56, 60
	72, 100, 124, 161, 194
	220, 279, 398, 429
Lal Nath Temple	28, 36
Lawrence of Arabia	262
Linstead, Reginald	252
	253, 254
Mahmood, Masood	112
	412, 413, 419, 423, 452
Malang	30, 34
Malik, Akhtar	335, 336, 345
Matthews, Paul	168
	169, 176, 477
Minai, Saeed	123
Mir, Mohammed	274, 280
Mudie, Francis	161
Multan	43, 84, 85, 86
	88, 91, 129, 163, 164, 194
	221, 291, 379, 382, 396, 428

National Science Foundation	364, 446 447, 448	Qadian	39, 50, 55 70, 117, 215, 348
Neem extract	72	Qureshi, Waheed	104
new house	42, 43, 64	Rabwah Rail Station	397, 398
Nobel Prize	9, 11, 19 65, 173, 230, 241, 268 383, 432, 454, 466, 473	Radcliffe, Cyril	138
		Rahman, Aziza	263, 463
		Rahman, Fazal	69, 124
nuclear program of Pakistan	338	Rahman, Mujibur	354
		Ramanujan, Srinivasa	108
		Rawalpindi	220, 307 308, 402, 408, 409, 413
Objectives Resolution	188 189, 434, 475	renormalisation	168 176, 177, 201, 202
Offer of Chair from Imperial College	281	Revelle, Roger	304
old house	42	Riazuddin, Mohammed	386
Oppenheimer, Robert	166 167, 172, 175, 288, 330	Rochester Conference	232 243, 244, 324
ownership of Pakistan	360, 449	Russell, Bertrand	265 302, 303
Pakistan Atomic Energy Commission	291 381, 447	Salam, Abdus	16, 473
		Salam, Omar	461
Pakistan Science Commission	290, 295	Santokdas	26, 57
		Security risk in Pakistan	445
Pauli, Wolfgang	180 181, 477	Servepalli Radhakrishnan	253
		Seville Row, London	470
Peasant Welfare Scheme	117 119, 142, 150, 163	Shah Jewna	29, 34, 48
		Shahi, Agha	301, 302, 308
Prince Phillip, Duke of Edinburgh	289	Sharif, Mohammed	203 225, 312, 404
Princess Dina Bint Abdul Hameed	134	Shoaib, Mohammed	290 344, 366
Public Law 480	343, 367	Sial	28, 31, 33, 34
Pugwash Conference in Udaipur	338, 340	Simla, the summer capital	91
		Simla, the Summer Capital	119

Six Point Formula	354	Theoretical Physics	10, 13
	355, 357		146, 153, 180, 230, 251
Sondhi, Gurudat	108, 195		264, 362, 449, 461
Sondhi, Urmila	109, 204	Tiger Niazi	360
space research committee	305	Tiwana, Khizer Hayat	117
St John's College	119		
	130, 154, 161	unification of forces	233, 422
St John's College	120	University of Punjab	10
	199, 231		37, 78, 183, 192, 276, 363
Steel Richardson		Usmani, Ishrat	290, 291, 305
Syndrome	439		
Stockdale, Peter	19	Varma, Inder	111
Stokes Lecturer	166		
	224, 231	Webb, James	304, 305
Sultana, Khalida	433	Whitehead, Alfred	250, 253
Surrender in Dhaka	370	Wiesner, Jerome	304
		Wilkinson, Denys	149
Ta'azia floats	91	Wordie, James	134
Tata Institute of Fundamental			
Research	198, 200	Yuval Ne'eman	362
Temple, George	252		
Thacker, Maneklal	302	*Zamzama*	99
theoretical physics	287, 324	Zhou En-Lai	368